Frommer's®

Belgium, Holland & Luxembourg

10th Edition

by George McDonald

Here's what the critics say about Frommer's:

"Amazingly easy to use. Very portable, very complete."
—*Booklist*

"Detailed, accurate, and easy-to-read information for all price ranges."
—*Glamour Magazine*

"Hotel information is close to encyclopedic."
—*Des Moines Sunday Register*

"Frommer's Guides have a way of giving you a real feel for a place."
—*Knight Ridder Newspapers*

Wiley Publishing, Inc.

About the Author

George McDonald has lived and worked in both Amsterdam and Brussels, as deputy editor of the in-flight magazine for KLM and as editor-in-chief of the in-flight magazine for Sabena. Now a freelance journalist and travel writer, he has written extensively on both the Netherlands and Belgium for magazines and for travel books. In addition to *Frommer's Belgium, Holland & Luxembourg*, he is the author of *Frommer's Amsterdam* and a coauthor of *Frommer's Europe*.

Published by:

Wiley Publishing, Inc.

111 River St.
Hoboken, NJ 07030-5774

ISBN: 978-0-470-06859-5

Editors: Jennifer Anmuth & Jamie Ehrlich
Production Editor: Michael Brumitt
Cartographer: Anton Crane
Photo Editor: Richard Fox
Anniversary Logo Design: Richard Pacifico
Production by Wiley Indianapolis Composition Services

Front cover photo: Belfry Tower in Bruges, Belgium
Back cover photo: Restaurants and cafes at dusk on Butcher Street in Brussels, Belgium

For information on our other products and services or to obtain technical support, please contact our Customer Care Department within the U.S. at 800/762-2974, outside the U.S. at 317/572-3993 or fax 317/572-4002.

Wiley also publishes its books in a variety of electronic formats. Some content that appears in print may not be available in electronic formats.

Manufactured in the United States of America

5   4   3   2   1

Contents

9 Liège, the Meuse River & Hainaut   187

10 The Ardennes   215

11 Planning Your Trip to Holland   230

12 Amsterdam   245

13 Haarlem & Noord-Holland   305

List of Maps

An Invitation to the Reader

In researching this book, we discovered many wonderful places—hotels, restaurants, shops, and more. We're sure you'll find others. Please tell us about them, so we can share the information with your fellow travelers in upcoming editions. If you were disappointed with a recommendation, we'd love to know that, too. Please write to:

Frommer's Belgium, Holland & Luxembourg, 10th Edition
Wiley Publishing, Inc. • 111 River St. • Hoboken, NJ 07030-5774

An Additional Note

Please be advised that travel information is subject to change at any time—and this is especially true of prices. We therefore suggest that you write or call ahead for confirmation when making your travel plans. The authors, editors, and publisher cannot be held responsible for the experiences of readers while traveling. Your safety is important to us, however, so we encourage you to stay alert and be aware of your surroundings. Keep a close eye on cameras, purses, and wallets, all favorite targets of thieves and pickpockets.

Other Great Guides for Your Trip:

Frommer's Amsterdam

Frommer's Amsterdam Day by Day

*Frommer's Brussels & Bruges
with Ghent & Antwerp*

Frommer's Europe

Frommer's Gay & Lesbian Europe

Europe For Dummies

Frommer's Star Ratings, Icons & Abbreviations

Every hotel, restaurant, and attraction listing in this guide has been ranked for quality, value, service, amenities, and special features using a **star-rating system.** In country, state, and regional guides, we also rate towns and regions to help you narrow down your choices and budget your time accordingly. Hotels and restaurants are rated on a scale of zero (recommended) to three stars (exceptional). Attractions, shopping, nightlife, towns, and regions are rated according to the following scale: zero stars (recommended), one star (highly recommended), two stars (very highly recommended), and three stars (must-see).

In addition to the star-rating system, we also use **seven feature icons** that point you to the great deals, in-the-know advice, and unique experiences that separate travelers from tourists. Throughout the book, look for:

Finds	Special finds—those places only insiders know about
Fun Fact	Fun facts—details that make travelers more informed and their trips more fun
Kids	Best bets for kids and advice for the whole family
Moments	Special moments—those experiences that memories are made of
Overrated	Places or experiences not worth your time or money
Tips	Insider tips—great ways to save time and money
Value	Great values—where to get the best deals

The following **abbreviations** are used for credit cards:

AE	American Express	DISC	Discover	V	Visa
DC	Diners Club	MC	MasterCard		

Frommers.com

Visit our website at **www.frommers.com** for additional travel information on more than 3,500 destinations. We update the site regularly, to give you instant access to the most current trip-planning information available. At Frommers.com, you'll find scoops on the best airfares, lodging rates, and car rental bargains. You can even book your travel online through our reliable travel booking partners. Other popular features include:

- Online updates of our most popular guidebooks
- Vacation sweepstakes and contest giveaways
- Newsletters highlighting the hottest travel trends
- Online travel message boards with featured travel discussions

What's New in Belgium, Holland & Luxembourg

Unfortunately, U.S. visitors to Amsterdam, Brussels, Bruges, and other Benelux cities continue to experience pocketbook pain. At this writing (late 2006), a dollar buys approximately 0.80€—down from a high of 1.20€ earlier this century! The Canadian, British, Australian, and New Zealand currencies haven't gone down as drastically, but citizens of these countries certainly don't have the luck of the eurozone Irish, who walk the Benelux streets with even more spring than usual in their steps. The good news is that there are plenty of bargains if you shop around.

Many hotel, restaurant, store, museum, attraction, and entertainment prices haven't gone up by much, if at all, in the past 2 years, and some have even come down (though higher oil prices are having an impact on transportation costs).

VISITOR INFORMATION Bruges's tourist information office has moved from its former palatial premises in the 18th-century Landhuis van het Brugse Vrije on the Burg to the ultra-modern setting of the city's new Concertgebouw concert hall. It's now known as **In&Uit Brugge,** Concertgebouw, 't Zand 34, 8000 Brugge (© **050/44-46-46;** fax 050/44-46-45; www.brugge.be).

GETTING THERE Transeuropa Ferries (© **01843/595522** in the U.K.; www.transeuropaferries.com) recently introduced car-ferry service between the English Channel port of Ramsgate and Ostend, Belgium. This is the only such service from southern England to Belgium, though ferries sail from both Hull in northeast England and Rosyth (Edinburgh) in Scotland to Zeebrugge. Unlike these two routes, the Ramsgate-Ostend service transports only cars, other private vehicles, and commercial trucks, along with their drivers and passengers. No foot passengers are accepted. See chapter 2 for more details.

GETTING AROUND Construction of the underground stations and tunnels for Amsterdam's Noord-Zuid (North-South) Metro line, slated to be completed in 2011, continues. The line will run from Amsterdam-Noord, under Het IJ waterway to Centraal Station, and from there to Station Zuid/World Trade Center on the city's southern ring-road expressway. A new fast-tram line, no. 26, goes east from Centraal Station to the artificial islands of the new IJburg residential projects along the IJsselmeer's southern shore. The tram stops at the new Muziekgebouw aan 't IJ concert hall, the cruise-ship Passenger Terminal Amsterdam, and other new waterfront facilities. Centraal Station will for some years be a confusing construction site. A Metro station, the hub of the Noord-Zuid line, is being dug out and fitted out at the front; a new main entrance to the rail station, and improved passenger facilities inside, are being created; and the waterfront zone at the rear is being revamped. Harbor ferries now operate from the new

Waterplein-West dock behind Centraal Station. See chapter 12 for more details about all of these changes.

By the end of 2008, all public transportation in the Netherlands should be using the new *OV-chipkaart.* This chip-enabled smart card is loaded with a pre-selected number of euros that are then reduced automatically by electronic readers as you ride. During a transition period, both the new card and the old tickets will be accepted. See chapter 12 for more details.

Only two Benelux cities still have electric trolley buses: Ghent and Arnhem. Ghent's single trolley-bus line, no. 3, suspended for several years for refurbishment, was reintroduced in 2005. Arnhem has reorganized its trolley-bus service into four lines (nos. 1, 3, 5, and 7) and confirmed its continuation until at least 2015. See chapters 7 and 16 for more details.

WHERE TO STAY   Ostend's famously plush **Oostendse Compagnie Hotel,** housed in the waterfront former Royal Villa, has closed. The hotel's equally renowned **Au Vigneron** restaurant is reportedly looking for suitable new premises and may reappear.

WHERE TO DINE   British celeb chef Jamie Oliver has brought his Fifteen restaurant concept from London to Amsterdam by opening a branch there. Try out his fun cooking at **Fifteen Amsterdam,** Pakhuis Amsterdam, Jollemanhof 9 (© **0900/343-8336;** www.fifteen.nl), in the harbor redevelopment zone east of Centraal Station.

An old city favorite has been brought back from suspended animation. **Pier 10,** De Ruyterkade, Steiger 10 (© **020/427-2310;** www.pier10.nl), was disassembled while construction work was being done on its pier behind Centraal Station, but it has now been reassembled. See chapter 12 for more details about both of these restaurants.

On closings, city foodies got a shock in 2006 when French-born ace chef Jean-Christophe Royer sold up his canal-side, Michelin star restaurant **Christophe,** where he had been making magic for 20 years, and moved on to new challenges outside Holland.

WHAT TO SEE & DO   Ghent's **Museum voor Schone Kunsten (Fine Arts Museum),** Citadelpark (© **09/222-17-03;** www.mskgent.be), remains closed for renovations at the time of writing. It's slated to reopen in 2007. See chapter 7 for more details.

In Antwerp, a futuristic aquarium, **Aquatopia,** Koningin Astridplein 7 (© **03/205-07-40;** www.aquatopia.be), containing exotic fish, has opened in the Astrid Park Plaza Hotel opposite Centraal Station. See chapter 7 for more details.

Mons's **Musée des Beaux-Arts (Fine Arts Museum),** rue Neuve 8 (© **065/40-53-06**), which closed for several years during renovations, is due to reopen in 2007. See chapter 9 for more details.

In Amsterdam, the old harbor along Het IJ waterfront west, east, and north of Centraal Station is a giant redevelopment zone. This is a new kind of Amsterdam—modern, bright, shiny, and on an untypically Dutch gargantuan scale. It remains to be seen how all this sits with the city's erstwhile homey, grungy, and seedy rep. In the meantime, a tour of these areas affords an idea of where Amsterdam—for good or ill—is headed.

The city's (and the nation's) premier cultural treasure house, the 1885-vintage **Rijksmuseum,** Jan Luijkenstraat 1B (© **020/647-7047;** www.rijksmuseum.nl), is nearing the end of its 5-year mission to renovate and rebuild for a new era. Important paintings by the 17th-century Dutch Masters, among them Rembrandt's *The Night Watch,* and other highlights from its vast inventory, are exhibited under the title *De Meesterwerken* (The Masterpieces) in the Philips Wing. An information bureau in the museum gardens affords an insight into how the radically spruced-up institution will look when it reopens in 2008.

Another stellar museum with regular premises undergoing R & R is the modern-art **Stedelijk Museum CS,** Oosterdokskade 5 (© **020/573-2911;** www.stedelijk.nl), which has set up shop temporarily in the old TPG Post building just east of Centraal Station (and temporarily added that "CS" tag to denote the change). Its projected date of return to its usual stamping ground at Paulus Potterstraat 13, just off Museumplein, has been kicked back to 2008. Over the next few years, **Hermitage Amsterdam,** Nieuwe Herengracht 14 (© **020/530-8751;** www.hermitage.nl), a satellite of the world-famous State Hermitage in St. Petersburg, Russia, should fully occupy its premises in the neoclassical Amstelhof building on the Amstel River. See chapter 12 for more details about all of these places.

The Hague's **Galerij Prins Willem V,** Buitenhof 35 (© **070/302-3435;** www.gemeentemuseum.nl), has closed until 2008 because of construction work going

on around it. Some of the Rembrandts and works by other Dutch Old Masters have been reinstalled in other galleries around town. See chapter 14.

In Gouda, the antique pipe and *plateel* (Gouda pottery) collections from the Museum De Moriaan, which closed in 2006, are now displayed in the town's **Museum Het Catharina Gasthuis,** Achter de Kerk 14 (© **0182/588-440**). See chapter 14.

SHOPPING   Amsterdam's renowned **American Book Center** has moved to a new home at Spui 12 (© **020/625-5537;** www.abc.nl). See p. 296.

AFTER DARK   An ocean of glass and steel constructed on uncompromisingly modern lines, the **Muziekgebouw aan 't IJ,** Piet Heinkade 1 (© **020/788-2000;** www.muziekgebouw.nl)—Amsterdam's new concert hall for modern, jazz, and experimental music—has opened for business on the IJ waterfront east of Centraal Station. Occupying a kind of annex to this mega-building is the jazz club **Bimhuis,** Piet Heinkade 3 (© **020/788-2188;** www.bimhuis.nl). See chapter 12 for more details.

1

The Best of Belgium, Holland & Luxembourg

Although they're small, each of these three countries contains a diversity of culture, language, and tradition that defies easy definition. Belgium is fractured along the age-old European great divide between the Germanic north and the Latin south. This division is expressed in the constant regional bickering between Dutch-speaking Flanders and French-speaking Wallonia that threatens to split the country entirely.

Holland (the Netherlands) has its great divide, too, along the "three great rivers"—the Maas, the Waal, and the Rhine. The northerners are straitlaced and Calvinist and (to hear the southerners say it) only know what to do with a glass of beer because they've been shown by the exuberant, Catholic southerners. Then there's the matter of nations within the nation. Friesland, Zeeland, and Limburg have their notions of separateness and their own languages to back them up.

As for Luxembourg, you'd think a country so small that—even on a big map—its name can't fit within its borders would be simpler. Not a bit. Luxembourgers are such a mixed bag that they're still trying to sort out the mess left behind when the Germanic tribes overran the Roman Empire's Rhine defenses in A.D. 406.

Diversity is the greatest asset of the Benelux countries. The visitor from afar may be more impressed by their shared characteristics, which include a determined grasp on the good life, than by the differences that separate them.

1 The Best Travel Experiences

- **Seeing the Grand-Place for the First Time** (Belgium): There's nothing quite like strolling onto the Grand-Place. You'll never forget your first look at this timelessly perfect cobbled square, surrounded by gabled guild houses and the Gothic tracery of the Hôtel de Ville (Town Hall) and Maison du Roi (King's House). See chapter 5.

- **Admiring Art Nouveau** (Belgium): Brussels considers itself the world capital of Art Nouveau, and local architect Victor Horta (1861–1947) was its foremost exponent. You can view the master's colorful, sinuous style at his former home, now the Horta Museum, and in buildings around town. See chapter 5.

- **Traveling Through Time in Bruges** (Belgium): Without a doubt, Bruges is one of Europe's most handsome small cities. Its almost perfectly preserved center sometimes seems like a film set or museum. Its historical buildings run the gamut of architectural styles from medieval times to the 19th century. The picturesque canals are the icing on Bruges's cake. See chapter 6.

- **Riding the Kusttram (Coast Tram)** (Belgium): Onboard the modern Kusttram, the 2-hour ride along the

The Benelux Countries

Belgian coast, from De Panne on the French border to Knokke-Heist near the Dutch border, still seems like an old-fashioned adventure. Along the way, you can stop at inviting resorts, beaches, horseback-riding trails—whatever takes your fancy. See chapter 8.

- **Touring the Ardennes** (Belgium and Luxembourg): The Ardennes, which covers the eastern third of Belgium, beyond the Meuse River and on into Luxembourg, is unlike any other Benelux landscape. Steep river valleys and thickly forested slopes set it apart. This region of castles, stone-built villages, and farms has resort towns like Spa and Bouillon; unequaled cuisine created from fresh produce and game; winter skiing; nature and fresh air in abundance; and towns like Bastogne and Ettelbruck that recall the sacrifice American soldiers made for victory in the Battle of the Bulge. See chapters 10 and 19.

- **Skating on the Canals** (Holland): When the thermometer drops low enough for long enough, the Dutch canals freeze over, creating picturesque highways of ice through the cities and countryside. At such times, the Dutch take to their skates. Joining them could be the highlight of your trip. See p. 295.

- **Relaxing in a Brown Cafe** (Holland): Spend a leisurely evening in a brown cafe, the traditional Amsterdam watering hole. See chapter 12.

- **Following the Tulip Trail** (Holland): The place to see the celebrated Dutch tulips in their full glory is Keukenhof Gardens at Lisse, where vast numbers of tulips and other flowers create dazzling patches of color in the spring. Combine your visit with a trip through the bulb fields between Leiden and Haarlem. See chapter 13.

- **Checking Out the Windmills at Zaanse Schans** (Holland): In flat Holland, wind is ever present, so it's not surprising that the Dutch have used windmills to assist with their hard labor, from draining polders to sawing wood. At one time, the Zaan district, northwest of Amsterdam, had almost 500 windmills. Of the 12 that survive, five have been reconstructed at Zaanse Schans, together with other historical buildings reminiscent of the area's past. See chapter 13.

- **Celebrating Carnival in Maastricht** (Holland): The country never seems so divided by the great rivers as it does during Carnival season. Southerners declare that their celebrations are superior, and if you ever run into a southern Carnival parade, you'll have to admit they know how to party. In Maastricht, the festivities are especially boisterous— people parade through the streets in an endless procession of outrageous outfits and boundless energy. See p. 440.

- **Driving the Wine Trail** (Luxembourg): Follow the Route du Vin along the banks of the Moselle River from Echternach to Mondorf-les-Bains. Here, the low hills of Luxembourg are covered with vineyards. Several wineries open their doors to visitors, offer guided tours, explain how their wine is produced, and treat you to a little of what they have stored in their barrels. See chapter 19.

2 The Best Castles & Stately Homes

- **Beersel** (near Brussels, Belgium): This 13th-century castle, 8km (5 miles) south of Brussels, is a castle just like Disney makes them, with turrets, towers, a drawbridge, a moat, and the spirits of all those who have, willingly or unwillingly, resided within its walls. It looks like the ideal place for pulling up the drawbridge and settling in for a siege—if only the owners had had the foresight to amply stock the rustic Auberge Kasteel Beersel restaurant inside. See p. 114.

- **Het Gravensteen** (Ghent, Belgium): Even 900 years after it was constructed, the castle of the Counts of Flanders in Ghent can still summon up a feeling of dread as you peruse its gray stone walls. It's a grim reminder that castles were not all for chivalrous knights and beautiful princesses. This one was intended as much to subdue the independent-minded citizens of Ghent as to protect the city from foreign marauders. Inside are the tools of the autocrat's profession: torture instruments that show that what the Middle Ages lacked in humanity they made up for in invention. See p. 143.

- **Bouillon** (near Dinant in the Ardennes, Belgium): This was the seat of the valiant but hard-handed and ruthless Godfrey of Bouillon, who led the First Crusade in 1096. His castle still stands today, atop a steep bluff overlooking the town, the bridge over the Semois River, and the road to Paris. You can tour its walls, chambers, and dungeons. See p. 215.

- **Menkemaborg** (Uithuizen, in Groningen province, Holland): A *borg* is the Groningen version of a stately home, developed from an earlier, defensive structure. Once home to Groningen landed gentry, Menkemaborg is a fine example of the style. Rebuilt in the 1700s, it was owned by the same family until the beginning of the 20th century. Nowadays it's a museum, with period furnishings re-creating a vivid picture of the life and times of a wealthy provincial squire. See p. 384.

- **Het Loo Palace** (near Apeldoorn, Holland): William III, who became king of England, had a royal hunting lodge built here in the forests surrounding Apeldoorn. Subsequent members of the House of Orange made alterations to the palace, especially during the 19th century. Restoration has revealed much of the original decoration, and what couldn't be saved has been redesigned according to the original plans. The gardens have been restored to their original 17th-century splendor. See p. 401.

- **Ammersoyen Castle** (near 's-Hertogenbosch, Holland): This magnificent example of a moated fortress, with sturdy towers at each corner, dates from the second half of the 13th century. Ammersoyen's history was turbulent—it burned down in 1590 and was left in ruins for half a century before being rebuilt. See p. 432.

3 The Best Museums

- **Musées Royaux des Beaux-Arts** (Brussels, Belgium): Paintings by many of the finest Belgian artists are assembled in this twin museum's neoclassical Museum of Historical Art. An entire section is devoted to Brueghel, and there are works by Rubens, van Dyck, Hieronymus Bosch, and many others. Go underground to the Modern Art Museum for works by Magritte, Delvaux, Ensor, Rops, Alechinsky, and others. See p. 96.

- **Koninklijk Museum voor Schone Kunsten Antwerpen** (Royal Fine Arts Museum; Antwerp, Belgium): If you want to see the Flemish Masters in all their glory, head to Antwerp, where the Fine Arts Museum has the world's best collection of their works, including the largest group of Rubens masterpieces in existence. See p. 154.

- **Rijksmuseum** (State Museum; Amsterdam, Holland): The Rijksmuseum houses some of the Netherlands's most important works of art: Rembrandt's world-famous *The Night Watch,* four of Vermeer's miniatures, and numerous works by Frans Hals. All in all, this is one of the most impressive collections of Old Masters in the world. Unfortunately, until mid-2008 you'll be able to view a lot fewer than previously, since most of the museum is closed for refurbishment. But in the sole wing that remains open, the Rijksmuseum has assembled *The Masterpieces,* highlights from its collection of 17th-century Dutch Golden Age collections. See p. 282.

- **Van Gogh Museum** (Amsterdam, Holland): An extensive collection of van Gogh's work is here: 200 paintings and 500 drawings, ranging from the famous *Sunflowers* to earless self-portraits. The permanent collection includes important works by van Gogh's 19th-century contemporaries, and frequent temporary or visiting exhibits concentrate on the same period. See p. 283.
- **Mauritshuis** (The Hague, Holland): An intimate museum set in the 17th-century palace of a Dutch count, it contains a small but impressive collection of Golden Age art treasures. See p. 332.
- **Museum Boijmans Van Beuningen** (Rotterdam, Holland): This eclectic museum features a range of art forms, from visual to applied arts, covering a period of over 7 centuries. Here you see paintings by the likes of Brueghel and van Eyck, and surrealists like Magritte and Dalí. See p. 347.
- **Museum Het Catharijneconvent** (St. Catherine's Convent; Utrecht, Holland): Housed in a former convent, the museum provides a picture of Holland's Christian heritage. The collections of medieval art and illuminated manuscripts are impressive. See p. 395.
- **National Museum of Military History** (Museum of the Battle of the Bulge; Diekirch, Luxembourg): There's something special about this tribute to the heroes of the Battle of the Bulge (1944–45), something gritty and immediate that sets it apart from other war museums. Its centerpiece is a series of dioramas that give you an eerie sense of being there in the battle, in the snow, with danger all around. See p. 469.

4 The Best Cathedrals & Churches

- **Onze-Lieve-Vrouwekerk** (Church of Our Lady; Bruges, Belgium): The soaring 122m (396-ft.) spire of this church can be seen from a wide area around Bruges. The church holds a marble *Madonna and Child* by Michelangelo, a painting by Anthony van Dyck, and the 15th-century bronze tomb sculptures of Charles the Bold and Mary of Burgundy. See p. 132.
- **Onze-Lieve-Vrouwekathedraal** (Cathedral of Our Lady; Antwerp, Belgium): You can't miss this towering example of the Flemish Gothic style if you visit Antwerp or even pass close to the city. Its 123m (400-ft.) spire dominates the area. This is the biggest church in the Benelux countries, with seven naves and 125 pillars. But oversize statistics are not Our Lady's only attraction—no fewer than three Rubens masterpieces are inside, along with paintings by other prominent artists. See p. 154.
- **Cathédrale Notre-Dame** (Cathedral of Our Lady; Tournai, Belgium): With a harmonious blending of the Romanesque and Gothic styles, this cathedral has five towers, magnificent stained-glass windows, and paintings by Rubens and Jordaens. Equally

- **Domkerk** (Utrecht, Holland): This magnificent cathedral was begun in the 13th century. Its 111m (365-ft.) tower, which dominates old Utrecht's skyline, offers a great view of the city. See p. 394.
- **Sint-Servaasbasiliek** (Basilica of St. Servatius; Maastricht, Holland): One of the oldest churches in Holland, this basilica was built over the grave of St. Servatius, the first bishop of Holland. Over the centuries, people have honored St. Servatius with gifts, and now the Treasury holds a collection of incredible richness and beauty. Most impressive are the reliquaries of St. Thomas and of St. Servatius, created by Maastricht master goldsmiths in the 12th century. See p. 438.
- **Notre-Dame Cathedral** (Luxembourg City): The cathedral was built late for the Gothic style—in the early 17th century—but is nevertheless a great Gothic monument, albeit one clearly influenced by Renaissance ideals. The Octave of Our Lady of Luxembourg takes place here every year before the statue of the Virgin, which is said to have miraculous powers. See p. 460.

- interesting are the opulent objects in the Treasury, especially a gold-and-silver reliquary, The Shrine of Our Lady, dating from 1205. See p. 212.
- **Westerkerk** (West Church; Amsterdam, Holland): The Westerkerk's 85m (277-ft.) tower, the Westertoren, is the tallest in Amsterdam, providing a spectacular view of the city. Anne Frank could hear every note of the carillon's dulcet tones while in hiding from the Nazis in her nearby house. See p. 289.
- **Sint-Bavokerk** (St. Bavo's Church; Haarlem, Holland): The moment you enter Haarlem's main square, this church is revealed in all its splendor. Completed after an unusually short construction period, it has a rare unity of structure and proportion. Regular concerts are given here on the famous organ built by Christian Müller in 1738. The young Mozart once played on this instrument. See p. 306.
- **Sint-Janskerk** (St. John's Church; Gouda, Holland): At 122m (400 ft.), this is the longest church in Holland, and it has magnificent stained-glass windows. See p. 358.

5 The Best Offbeat Trips

- **Walking on the Wadden Sea** (Holland): At low tide, the Wadden Sea, between the northern coast and the Wadden Islands, virtually disappears, and if you're up for a walk in the mud, you can join a Wadden Walking *(Wadlopen)* trip and plow your way over land to one of the islands. If you're lucky, you might encounter seals gallivanting in pools left by the retreating tide or sunbathing on the flats. See p. 379.
- **Riding White Bikes in Hoge Veluwe National Park** (Holland): It was tried once in Amsterdam—providing free white bikes for everyone to use—but the bikes mysteriously disappeared and turned up in private hands with fresh coats of paint. The scheme has worked much better in this beautiful national park (which apparently doesn't shelter as many bike thieves). Just head to Hoge Veluwe's parking lot, pick up a bike, and explore the traffic-free scenery. See p. 402.

6 The Best Outdoor Activities

- **Hiking Across the Hautes Fagnes** (Belgium): Wooden walkways stretch like the Yellow Brick Road across the high, bleak moorland plateau of Hautes Fagnes Nature Reserve in eastern Belgium, between Eupen and Malmédy. On these walkways, you can explore the remnants of an ancient morasslike landscape that has claimed lives in bad weather through the centuries and into recent times. It is a beautiful, wild place and satisfying to cross at any time of year. A fine summer's day may be best, but venturing onto the moor, adequately clothed, in the middle of a snowbound winter night also has its attractions. See chapter 10.

- **Sand-Yachting at De Panne** (Belgium): Conditions on the beach at De Panne are ideal for this exciting, unusual sport. See chapter 8.

- **Skiing the Ardennes** (Belgium and Luxembourg): Some years it snows and some years it doesn't. But when it does snow enough, the Ardennes is a very pleasant place to ski. You'll find a dozen or so downhill centers, but most skiing in the Ardennes is cross-country. A particularly good location is Hautes Fagnes Nature Reserve between Eupen and Malmédy, but you can ski only on the designated trails because this is a protected landscape. See chapters 10 and 19.

- **Biking in Holland:** To fully engage in the Dutch experience, you positively have to board a bicycle and head out into the wide green yonder. The tourism authorities have marked out many cycling tour routes and have published descriptive booklets and maps to go along with them, available from VVV offices. Many rail stations around the country have bikes for rent.

- **Canoeing in the Biesbosch** (Holland): This unique natural park of marshland, meadows, and willow woods was formed during the St. Elizabeth floods of 1421, when 16 villages were submerged and polderland became an inland sea. There are several possibilities for exploring the Biesbosch, including tour boat, but paddling your own canoe is the best way to get close to nature. See chapter 17.

7 The Best Romantic Getaways

- **Château Vacations** (Wallonia, Belgium): The French-speaking region of Belgium is noted for its beautiful châteaux, dating from the 17th, 18th, and 19th centuries, set in the countryside amid ornamental gardens and often surrounded by moats. Nowadays, some of these venerable, stately homes have been transformed into hotels or restaurants, offering guests luxurious living and fine dining. A weekend in one of these châteaux is surely among the most romantic getaways imaginable. For more information, contact the **Wallonia-Brussels Tourist Office** (© 02/504-0200). See chapter 9.

- **Kasteel Wittem** (Wittem, Holland; © 043/450-1208): This romantically idyllic 12th-century castle is also a hotel. It's the perfect place to stay after exploring the south of Holland's Limburg province. In the summer, you can dine or have breakfast on a magnificent terrace overlooking the garden and moat. See p. 443.

8 The Best Deluxe Hotels

- **Métrople** (Brussels, Belgium; ✆ **02/ 217-23-00**): This century-old hotel in the heart of Brussels maintains the Belle Epoque splendor of its first days and combines it with modern furnishings and service. Its **L'Alban Chambon** restaurant is one of Brussels's best. See p. 78.

- **Le Méridien Hotel des Indes** (The Hague, Holland; ✆ **070/361-2345**): Within this opulent hotel, you can lean over the balustrade on the first-floor landing to watch the cream of The Hague's society having tea in the lounge, the lights of chandeliers reflecting in the polished marble pillars. The rooms are equally grand and comfortable. See p. 336.

- **Hotel Lauswolt** (Beetsterzwaag, near Leeuwarden, Holland; ✆ **0512/381-245**): This 19th-century country house has been converted into a luxury hotel equipped with the latest amenities and leisure facilities. Some 2,700 acres of forest and heather offer ample opportunity for walking or horseback riding. You can play golf or tennis, and there are two swimming pools. All this activity will surely stir your appetite—luckily, the cuisine is of the same high standard as the other comforts in the hotel. See p. 368.

- **De Campveerse Toren** (Veere, Holland; ✆ **0118/501-291**): This ancient inn guards the harbor of Veere. With the Veerse Meer (Lake Veere) lapping at the walls below your room, you overlook the length of the lake to the harbor where pleasure boats are moored. Little is as calming to the spirit as a walk through the old streets of Veere at dusk. Later, back in your room at the inn for the night, you'll be gently lulled to sleep by the murmuring waters of the lake. See p. 426.

- **Grand Hôtel Cravat** (Luxembourg City; ✆ **22-19-75**): The Grand Hôtel Cravat has been a Luxembourg institution for nearly a century. And for fine dining nearby, you won't need to look much farther than its own Le Normandy. See p. 463.

9 The Best Moderately Priced Hotels

- **Comfort Art Hotel Siru** (Brussels, Belgium; ✆ **02/203-35-80**): An art-aficionado owner had the innovative idea of inviting Belgium's top artists to decorate a room with a painting, sculpture, or installation on the theme of travel. Many of them took up the challenge, with the result that each room is a miniature single-exhibit art gallery. The art is, obviously, contemporary, so the response from guests can vary. Some regulars ask for a different room each time so that after a hundred visits they'll have toured the full "gallery"; some always ask for the same room; others, shaken by an unsettling image, ask for a room change in the middle of the night. See p. 81.

- **Welcome** (Brussels, Belgium; ✆ **02/ 219-95-46**): This is the best little hotel in Brussels, a small place with a big welcome, and the standard of the rooms is high. Try to get owner Michel to tell you about the hotel's history, preferably over a glass or two of Kwak beer—but be careful: It's a long story and Kwak is strong beer. See p. 79.

- **Egmond** (Bruges, Belgium; ✆ **050/ 34-14-45**): You can think of the Egmond as your own country mansion, for not much more than a hundred bucks a room. There's just one problem with this image: The Egmond is not actually in the country. In compensation, it has its own grounds and gardens, and stands next to the Minnewater (Lover's Lake). See p. 122.

- **Ambassade** (Amsterdam, Holland; ℂ 020/555-0222): This hotel occupies 10 neighboring canal houses on the "Golden Bend"—for centuries the city's most fashionable address. Here, you really feel that you're in the home of a rich 17th-century merchant. Most of the individually styled and spacious rooms have large windows overlooking the canal, as does the split-level chandeliered breakfast room. If you need some modern—in fact, New Age—relaxation, you can take to the flotation tanks or relax into a deep massage at the hotel's Koan Float center. See p. 258.

- **Seven Bridges** (Amsterdam, Holland; ℂ 020/623-1329): At some hotels, the owners aren't just running a business—they're doing what they love. The Seven Bridges is that kind of place. Pierre Keulers and Günter

Glaner have found both their hobby and their profession in this fine hotel in Amsterdam. It's no exaggeration to say that all the furniture, fixtures, and fittings have been selected with loving care, and guests receive the same conscientious attention. See p. 260.

- **Best Western Hotel du Casque** (Maastricht, Holland; ℂ 043/321-4343): The Hotel du Casque overlooks the Vrijthof, which basks in its reputation as the liveliest square in the liveliest city in the country. Despite its prestigious address, this hotel is as moderately priced as you'll find in Maastricht. See p. 440.

- **Hôtel du Parc** (Clervaux, Luxembourg; ℂ 92-06-50): The northern Luxembourg town of Clervaux is one of the most dramatic in the Ardennes; it's situated in a plunging valley, watched over by a castle on the mountain heights. The Grand Hôtel du Parc offers old-fashioned charm with all the benefits of modern facilities, including a sauna and solarium, at a downright affordable price. See p. 471.

10 The Best Restaurants

- **Comme Chez Soi** (Brussels, Belgium; ℂ 02/512-29-21): If Michelin were to introduce a four-star category, Comme Chez Soi would undoubtedly be one of the first to collect the extra star. The irony about this culinary holy of holies is its name: "Just Like Home"—maybe this is standard fare at owner and master chef Pierre Wynants's place. A hallowed silence descends on diners as they sample their first mouthful of his French specialties with added Belgian zest. This being Belgium, the silence doesn't last long, but the taste and the memory linger. See p. 83.

- **In 't Spinnekopke** (Brussels, Belgium; ℂ 02/511-86-95): For a different

kind of Brussels eating experience, try this down-home restaurant dating from 1762. Here, traditional Belgian dishes are given the care and attention expected of more refined—though not necessarily more tasty—cuisine. See p. 88.

- **Le Sanglier des Ardennes** (Durbuy, Belgium; ℂ 086/21-32-62): This restaurant, in a hotel in one of the prettiest of Ardennes villages, has the rustic looks and ideal location to go along with its fine country food. Walking in the surrounding wooded hills is the perfect preparation for lunch or dinner here. See p. 222.

- **La Rive** (in the Amstel Intercontinental Hotel, Amsterdam, Holland;

© 020/520-3264): La Rive has a special table where you can watch how the chefs actually do the business. While dining, you can enjoy the view through tall French windows to the broad Amstel River. The service and wine cellar are in the finest modern French traditions. See p. 278.

- **Le Restaurant** (in the Hotel des Indes, The Hague, Holland; © 070/ 361-2345): The Hague's nickname "Dowager of the Dutch East Indies" could well apply to the elegant Hotel Des Indes. The food it serves is refined and delicious, combining European and colonial flavors. See p. 337.

- **De Echoput** (Apeldoorn, Holland; © 055/519-1463): Game features prominently on the menu at this restaurant, set amid the forests near Apeldoorn, on the edge of the Royal Wood. During the hunting season, you can try wild boar, venison, and any kind of fowl—always succulent and prepared with flair. In spring and summer, the menu's just as delectable,

and in fair weather you can dine on the terrace in the fresh forest air. See p. 402.

- **Château Neercanne** (Maastricht, Holland; © 043/325-1359): "To live like a god in France" goes the Dutch proverb expressing the pinnacle of earthly pleasure. You might imagine yourself to be both a god and in France if you dine at this château, which was designed following French models. What's more, in true French culinary style, the food here is seductively elegant and the wine cellar is unique and impressive—the wines are kept under perfect conditions in the marlstone caves behind the château. See p. 442.

- **Le Bouquet Garni/Salon Saint-Michel** (Luxembourg City; © 26-20-06-20): The Saint-Michel occupies a little side street in the Old Town, but lights up the entire city with classic French cuisine that makes no concessions where quality is concerned. See p. 464.

11 The Best Cafes & Bars

- **Le Falstaff** (Brussels, Belgium; © 02/ 511-87-89): Le Falstaff deserves the highest accolades for its eclectic, accomplished mix of Art Nouveau and Art Deco, and its extensive drink list. This is self-satisfied, bourgeois Brussels at its best. See p. 111.

- **In Den Engel** (Antwerp, Belgium; © 03/233-12-52): There are cafes in Antwerp with a lot more action, but for a genuine Antwerp bar it's hard to beat De Engel. A location on a corner of the Grote Markt adds to the attraction. To experience De Engel's crowning glory, order a glass of Antwerp's own, lovingly poured De Koninck beer—a golden-brown liquid in a glass called a *bolleke* (little ball) that glows like amber in the sunlight

streaming through De Engel's windows. See p. 162.

- **'t Dreupelkot** (Ghent, Belgium; © 09/224-21-20): Ghent has no shortage of fine cafes, and you can just about guarantee that any one you enter will provide pleasant memories. 't Dreupelkot adds a particularly warm glow of appreciation, but you should know that its stock in trade is *jenever,* one of the most potent alcoholic liquids known to humankind. Actually, some of 't Dreupelkot's 100 varieties are fairly mild, while others have been flavored with herbs and spices. The atmosphere in the cafe is great—it's filled with cultured *jenever* buffs, not drunks. See p. 150.

- **Cafe 't Smalle** (Amsterdam, Holland; 𝒞 **020/623-9617**): This cozy, crowded brown cafe on Amsterdam's Egelantiersgracht is usually thick with cigar smoke, *jenever* vapor, and lively conversation. You can escape the crush on the splendid canal-side terrace, a perfect place to watch cyclists and cars rushing past while you rest your legs on the terrace railing. See p. 303.

- **In den Ouden Vogelstruys** (Maastricht, Holland; 𝒞 **043/321-4888**): This friendly, popular Maastricht watering hole was already well-trodden territory when it came under artillery fire in some war or another in 1653, and took a hit from a cannonball that remains lodged in one of its walls. The place attracts a broad—in some individual cases very broad—cross section of Maastricht society. See p. 443.

12 The Best Shopping

- **Antiques** (Brussels, Belgium): You'll need luck to score a bargain at the weekend antiques market on place du Grand Sablon—the dealers are well aware of the precise worth of each item in their stock and are calmly determined to get it. But it's still fun to wander the market, browsing and haggling, and who knows? You just might stumble on that hard-to-find affordable treasure. See chapter 5.

- **Diamonds** (Antwerp, Belgium): One thing is for sure, you'll be spoiled for choice in Antwerp's Diamond Quarter, which does six times as much diamond business as Amsterdam. Much of the trade here is carried on by the city's Orthodox Jewish community, whose conservative ways and traditional black clothing make a striking contrast to the glitter of their stock in trade. See chapter 7.

- **Lace** (Belgium): There are two kinds of Belgian lace: exquisitely handmade pieces, and machine-made stuff. Machine-made lace is not necessarily bad, but this is the form used to mass-produce pieces of indifferent quality to meet the demand for souvenirs. The highest-quality lace is handmade. Brussels, Bruges, and Ghent are the main, though not the only, points of sale. See chapters 5, 6, and 7.

- **Chocolates** (Belgium): The Swiss might want to argue the point, but the truth is that Belgian handmade chocolates, filled with various fresh-cream flavors, are the best in the universe. You can't go wrong if you buy chocolates made by Wittamer, Nihoul, Leonidas, and Neuhaus, available in specialist stores all over Belgium (and in Holland and Luxembourg, too). See chapter 5.

- **Delftware** (Holland): Originally, the pottery made in the factories at Delft was white, imitating tin-glazed products from Italy and Spain. But during the 16th century, blue Chinese porcelain was imported to Holland, and this was soon recognized to be of superior quality. So the Delftware factories started using a white tin glaze to cover the red clay and decorating the pottery in blue. This Delft Blue became famous the world over, along with Makkumware, which is pottery produced in the Dutch town of Makkum. Delftware and Makkumware are for sale in specialized stores all over the country, but it's far more interesting to go to one of the workshops in the towns themselves and see how it's made. Little has changed over the centuries, and all the decorating is still done by hand. See chapters 14 and 15.

- **Flower Bulbs** (Holland): You'll have no problem buying bulbs for home. You might not know what kind to buy, though; it's difficult to choose from the incredible variety of shapes and colors offered in Holland. Some bulbs flower early in January; others wait until the warmer months of May or June. Knowing this, you can choose bulbs with different flowering times, so you can enjoy their blooming over a long period in spring. Check before buying, however, as not all bulbs are certified for entry into the United States. Packages must have a numbered phytosanitary certificate attached to the label, allowing you to import the bulbs. In Amsterdam, you can't do better than buy them from the Floating Flower market on the Singel canal. See chapter 12.

- **Wine** (Luxembourg): Holland's tiny output notwithstanding, Luxembourg is the only real wine producer in the Benelux countries. The vintage in question is the highly regarded Moselle wine, perhaps not as well known outside the Grand Duchy and its immediate neighbors as German and French wines, but fine stock nonetheless. See chapter 19.

2

Planning Your Trip to Belgium, Holland & Luxembourg

Before any trip, most of us like to do a bit of advanced planning. When should I go? What's this trip going to cost? Will there be a holiday when I visit? We'll answer these and other questions for you in this chapter. For more specific information on each country included in this book, see chapters 4, 11, and 18.

1 The Countries in Brief

Taken together, the Benelux nations of Belgium, Holland (the Netherlands), and Luxembourg form a small area—not much greater than that of West Virginia. But arguably, no other comparably sized place in Europe compresses so many points of interest. Topping the list are artistic masterpieces, cultural events, and substantial reminders of a long and colorful history. Space remains for scenery that, while mostly lacking in drama, can still be lyrically beautiful. There are also the more mundane (but agreeable) advantages of convenience, economy, and friendly populations, not to mention a host of other travel delights—the exquisite food and drink of Brussels, the exuberant sociability of Amsterdam, and Luxembourg's sidewalk cafes.

BELGIUM For a graphic image of Belgium's two ethnic regions, Dutch-speaking *Vlaanderen* (Flanders) and French-speaking *Wallonie* (Wallonia), draw an imaginary east-west line across the country just south of Brussels. North of the line is Flanders, where you find the medieval cities of Bruges, Ghent, and Antwerp, and Belgium's North Sea coastline. South of the line is Wallonia. The art

cities of Tournai and Mons, and the scenic resort towns of the Meuse River valley and the Ardennes, are the attractions of this region. Then there's Brussels, the capital, roughly in the geographic middle, and going off on a trajectory of its own as the "capital of Europe."

HOLLAND The Netherlands is a *WYSIWYG* kind of country: What you see is what you get. There are no dramatic canyons or towering peaks. The nation's highest point wouldn't top the roof of a New York City skyscraper, and its average altitude is just 11m (37 ft.) above sea level. This makes for few panoramic vantage points; you can't see most of its canals and lakes until you're about to fall into them. Does this mean the views are boring? The answer is a flat "No." As the famous 17th-century Dutch landscape painters showed the world, vistas in Holland are among the most aesthetic anywhere: wide-angle views of green pastures and floating clouds, with tiny houses, church spires, and grazing cattle silhouetted against the horizon.

LUXEMBOURG At first sight, Luxembourg—a county-size nation with a population barely bigger than a small- to medium-size city—might appear to have an obvious provincial aspect. But size isn't everything, and in this case at least, small really is beautiful. Luxembourg packs into its handful of square miles a fascinating little capital city and an enviable roster of cultural diversity and scenic splendor.

2 Visitor Information

The official tourist agency for each country maintains overseas branches that provide excellent in-depth information on a vast array of subjects, including special interests. Overseas addresses for all three countries are provided below (national and local tourist office addresses are listed in the appropriate chapters).

BELGIUM

U.S. **Belgian Tourist Office,** 220 E. 42nd St., Suite 3402, New York, NY 10017 (℃ **212/758-8130;** fax 212/355-7675; www.visitbelgium.com).

CANADA   Residents of Canada should call ℃ **514/457-2888** to be switched through to the **Belgian Tourist Office** in New York.

For information concerning Brussels and French-speaking Wallonia (not Flanders), francophone Canadians should contact the **Office de Promotion du Tourisme Wallonie-Bruxelles,** 43 rue de Buade, Bureau 525, Quebec Ville, Quebec, G1R 4A2 (℃ **418/692-4939;** fax 418/692-4974; www.belgique-tourisme. qc.ca).

U.K. & IRELAND   Brussels and French-speaking Wallonia (and its German-speaking district): **Belgian Tourist Office Brussels-Wallonia,** 217 Marsh Wall, London E14 9FJ (tourist inquiries ℃ **0906/302-0245,** official business ℃ 020/7531-0390, brochure line ℃ 0800/ 954-5245; fax 020/7531-0393; www. belgiumtheplaceto.be).

Brussels and Dutch-speaking Flanders: **Tourism Flanders and Brussels,** 1A Cavendish Sq., London W1G 0LD (℃ **020/7307-7738,** brochure line ℃ 0800/954-5245; fax 020/7307-7731; www.visitflanders.co.uk).

Destination Belgium, Holland & Luxembourg: Pre-Departure Checklist

- If you purchased traveler's checks, have you recorded the check numbers, and stored the documentation separately from the checks?
- Do you have a safe, accessible place to store money?
- Did you bring ID cards that can entitle you to discounts, such as AAA and AARP cards, student IDs, and so forth?
- Did you pack your camera and an extra set of camera batteries, and purchase enough film or memory disks for your digital camera? All of these items are easily available in the Benelux countries—but they might cost more than at home.
- Have you booked your tickets yet for classical music at the Concertgebouw, and for opera and dance at the Muziektheater (see "The Performing Arts," in chapter 12)?
- Did you pack an umbrella? You'll likely need it.

HOLLAND

U.S. Netherlands Board of Tourism & Conventions, 355 Lexington Ave., 19th Floor, New York, NY 10017 (© **212/370-7360;** fax 212/370-9507; www.holland.com).

CANADA Netherlands Board of Tourism & Conventions, 14 Glenmount Court, Whitby, Ontario, L1N 5M8 (© **905/666-5960;** fax 905/666-5391; www.holland.com).

U.K. & IRELAND (Mail inquiries only): **Netherlands Board of Tourism & Conventions,** P.O. Box 30783, London WC2B 6DH (© **020/7539-7950,** premium-rate brochure order line © 09068/717777; fax 020/7539-7953; www.holland.com).

LUXEMBOURG

U.S. & CANADA Luxembourg National Tourist Office, 17 Beekman Place, New York, NY 10022 (© **212/935-8888;** fax 212/935-5896; www.visitluxembourg.com).

U.K. & IRELAND Luxembourg Tourist Office, 122 Regent St., London W1B 5SA (© **020/7434-2800;** fax 020/7734-1205; www.luxembourg.co.uk).

3 Entry Requirements & Customs

ENTRY REQUIREMENTS
PASSPORTS

Citizens of the United States, Canada, the United Kingdom, Ireland, Australia, and New Zealand need only a valid passport for a visit of less than 3 months to Belgium, Holland, and Luxembourg. If you're a citizen of another country, be sure to check the travel regulations before you leave.

See the box "How to Get a Passport," below—the websites listed provide downloadable passport applications and the current fees for processing passport applications.

VISAS

Citizens of the United States, Canada, the United Kingdom, Ireland, Australia, and New Zealand need only a valid passport for a visit to a Benelux country of less than 3 months. If you're a citizen of another country, be sure to check the travel regulations before you leave. You can get these in English from the website of the Ministry of Foreign Affairs in The Hague: **www.minbuza.nl**.

MEDICAL REQUIREMENTS

For information on medical requirements and recommendations, see "Health & Safety," p. 24.

CUSTOMS

Duty-free shopping has been abolished in all European Union countries, so standard allowances do not apply to goods bought in one EU country and brought into another. In this case, there are no import limitations for most goods for personal use, but the following guideline limits may apply (above these limits you could be asked to prove the goods are for personal use): 3,200 cigarettes, 400 cigarillos, 200 cigars, and 3 kilograms of tobacco; 10 liters of liquor, 20 liters of aperitifs (port and so on), 90 liters of wine (of which 60 liters may be sparkling wine), and 110 liters of beer.

WHAT YOU CAN BRING INTO BELGIUM, HOLLAND & LUXEMBOURG

Travelers 17 and older residing in a country outside the EU can bring in, free of duty, 200 cigarettes, 100 cigarillos, 50 cigars, or 250 grams of tobacco; 1 liter of liquor or 2 liters of wine; and 50 milliliters of perfume. Import of most other goods is unlimited, so long as import duty is paid—the duty must not exceed a value of 100€ (Belgium); 250€ (The Netherlands); or 180€ (Luxembourg).

How to Get a Passport

Allow plenty of time before your trip to apply for a passport; processing normally takes 3 weeks but can take longer during busy periods (especially spring). And keep in mind that if you need a passport in a hurry, you'll pay a higher processing fee.

For Residents of Australia: You can pick up an application from your local post office or any branch of Passports Australia, but you must schedule an interview at the passport office to present your application materials. Call the **Australian Passport Information Service** at © **131-232,** or visit the government website at www.passports.gov.au.

For Residents of Canada: Passport applications are available at travel agencies throughout Canada or from the central **Passport Office,** Department of Foreign Affairs and International Trade, Ottawa, ON K1A 0G3 (© **800/567-6868;** www.ppt.gc.ca).

For Residents of Ireland: You can apply for a 10-year passport at the **Passport Office,** Setanta Centre, Molesworth Street, Dublin 2 (© **01/671-1633;** www.irlgov.ie/iveagh). Those under age 18 and over 65 must apply for a 3-year passport. You can also apply at 1A South Mall, Cork (© **021/272-525)** or at most main post offices.

For Residents of New Zealand: You can pick up a passport application at any New Zealand Passports Office or download it from their website. Contact the **Passports Office** at © **0800/225-050** in New Zealand or 04/474-8100, or log on to www.passports.govt.nz.

For Residents of the United Kingdom: To pick up an application for a standard 10-year passport (5-year passport for children under 16), visit your nearest passport office, major post office, or travel agency; or contact the **United Kingdom Passport Service** at © **0870/521-0410** or search its website at www.ukpa.gov.uk.

For Residents of the United States: Whether you're applying in person or by mail, you can download passport applications from the U.S. State Department website at **http://travel.state.gov**. To find your regional passport office, either check the U.S. State Department website or call the **National Passport Information Center** toll-free number (© **877/487-2778)** for automated information.

Forbidden products include firearms, counterfeit goods, banned narcotic substances, and protected animals and plants and products made from these.

For more information, contact:

Belgian Customs (© **02/753-48-50,** 32-2/753-48-50 from outside Belgium).

Netherlands Customs (© **0800/0143,** 31-20/586-751 from outside the Netherlands; www.douane.nl).

Luxembourg Customs (© **352/290-19-11,** 352/290-19-11 from outside Luxembourg; www.etat.lu/DO).

WHAT YOU CAN TAKE HOME FROM BELGIUM, HOLLAND & LUXEMBOURG
U.S. Citizens
For specifics on what you can bring back and the corresponding fees, download the

invaluable free pamphlet *Know Before You Go* online at **www.cbp.gov**. (Click on "Travel," and then click on "Know Before You Go! Online Brochure.") Or contact the **U.S. Customs & Border Protection (CBP),** 1300 Pennsylvania Ave. NW, Washington, DC 20229 (✆ **877/287-8667**) and request the pamphlet.

Canadian Citizens

For a clear summary of Canadian rules, write for the booklet *I Declare,* issued by the **Canada Border Services Agency** (✆ **800/461-9999** in Canada, or 204/983-3500; **www.cbsa-asfc.gc.ca**).

U.K. Citizens

For information, contact **HM Customs & Excise** at ✆ **0845/010-9000** (from outside the U.K., 020/8929-0152), or consult their website at **www.hmce.gov.uk**.

Australian Citizens

A helpful brochure available from Australian consulates or Customs offices is *Know Before You Go.* For more information, call the **Australian Customs Service** at ✆ **1300/363-263,** or log on to **www.customs.gov.au**.

New Zealand Citizens

Most questions are answered in a free pamphlet available at New Zealand consulates and Customs offices: *New Zealand Customs Guide for Travellers, Notice no. 4.* For more information, contact **New Zealand Customs,** The Customhouse, 17–21 Whitmore St., Box 2218, Wellington (✆ **04/473-6099** or 0800/428-786; **www.customs.govt.nz**).

4 Money

Admittedly, the three Benelux countries are by no means inexpensive. Clearly, whether you agree with this statement will depend on how much you can bring to bear—or bear to bring—in the way of financial resources. If you're used to the prices in New York and London, those in Amsterdam, Brussels, and Luxembourg City likely won't seem too out of whack. But opportunities for scoring genuine bargains run a thin gamut from few-and-far-between to nonexistent. In your favor is that the natives themselves display a reluctance to part unnecessarily with a euro. A sound rule of thumb is that if you lodge, dine, and entertain yourself in the same places where "ordinary" locals do, you can limit the financial damage.

CURRENCY

The **euro** (€) is the currency in Belgium, Holland, and Luxembourg. There are 100 euro cents to each euro. Eight euro **coins** are in circulation: 0.01€, 0.02€, 0.05€, 0.10€, 0.20€, 0.50€ (1, 2, 5, 10, 20, and 50 euro cents, respectively), 1€, and 2€. The seven euro **notes** are: 5€, 10€, 20€, 50€, 100€, 200€, and 500€—the last two notes listed won't be of much practical use unless you're into money-laundering or some other nefarious activity.

CURRENCY EXCHANGE

The currency-exchange offices at the main rail stations in Brussels, Amsterdam, and Luxembourg City offer fair

---

Price Conversions

The price conversions in this book are based on an exchange rate of 1€ = US$1.25, and 1€ = £0.70. Bear in mind that exchange rates fluctuate daily. For up-to-the-minute currency conversions, go to **www.xe.com/ucc**.

The Euro, the U.S. Dollar & the British Pound

Euro €	US$	UK£	Euro €	US$	UK£
1	1.25	0.69	10	12.50	6.90
2	2.50	1.38	20	25.00	13.80
3	3.75	2.07	30	37.50	20.70
4	5.00	2.76	40	50.00	27.60
5	6.25	3.45	50	62.50	34.50
6	7.50	4.14	75	93.75	51.70
7	8.75	4.83	100	125.00	68.95
8	10.00	5.52	125	156.25	86.20
9	11.25	6.21	150	187.50	103.45

rates for cash and traveler's checks, as do banks, offices of **Travelex** in Belgium and Luxembourg; **GWK Travelex** in Holland; and VVV tourist information offices in Holland. Exchange rates at currency-exchange offices at each country's national airport are lousy. Other currency-exchange offices throughout the Benelux countries, which are open regular hours plus evenings and weekends, may charge a low commission, or none at all, but give a low rate of exchange. Hotels should be avoided as a currency-exchange resource unless there's no alternative.

The Travelex and GWK Travelex offices can arrange money transfers through **Western Union.**

ATMs

The easiest and best way to get cash away from home is from an ATM (automated teller machine), sometimes referred to as a "cash machine," or a "cashpoint." The **Cirrus** (© **800/424-7787;** www.mastercard.com) and **PLUS** (© **800/843-7587;** www.visa.com) networks span the globe; look at the back of your bank card to see which network you're on, and then call or check online for ATM locations at your destination. Be sure you know your personal identification number (PIN) and

daily withdrawal limit before you depart. *Note:* Remember that many banks impose a fee every time you use a card at another bank's ATM, and that fee can be higher for international transactions (up to $5 or more) than for domestic ones (where they're rarely more than $2). In addition, the bank from which you withdraw cash may charge its own fee. For international withdrawal fees, ask your bank.

If you have a 5- or 6-digit PIN, be sure to obtain a 4-digit number from your bank to use in the Benelux. Some cards with 5- or 6-digit PINs might work, but it depends on what bank you use. The best advice is to get a 4-digit number from your bank.

ATMs are widespread in Benelux cities and towns, and you can even find them in some villages. They accept bank cards and credit cards linked to the Cirrus and PLUS networks. Use the ATMs at Brussels, Amsterdam, and Luxembourg City airports to avoid the bad deals from the airport's currency-exchange offices.

CREDIT CARDS

Credit cards are another safe way to carry money. They also provide a convenient record of all your expenses, and they generally offer relatively good exchange rates.

Tips Easy Money

You'll avoid lines at airport ATMs by exchanging at least some money—just enough to cover airport incidentals and transportation to your hotel—before you leave home.

When you change money, ask for some small bills or loose change. Petty cash will come in handy for tipping and public transportation. Consider keeping the change separate from your larger bills, so that it's readily accessible and you'll be less of a target for theft.

You can withdraw cash advances from your credit cards at banks or ATMs, provided you know your PIN. Keep in mind that you'll pay interest from the moment of your withdrawal, even if you pay your monthly bills on time. Also, note that many banks now assess a 1%-to-3% "transaction fee" on **all** charges you incur abroad (whether you're using the local currency or your native currency).

Visa and **MasterCard** (also known as **EuroCard** in Europe) are the most widely used cards in the Benelux lands. **American Express** is often accepted, mostly in the middle- and upper-bracket category. **Diners Club** is not as commonly accepted as American Express. Credit cards are not as commonly accepted as they are in the United States and Britain. Many restaurants and stores, and some hotels, don't accept them at all, and others add a 5% charge for card payment. They are almost universally accepted by gas stations, and for travel by plane, train, and even taxi (not all taxis). The smaller the business, the less likely it is to accept credit cards.

TRAVELER'S CHECKS

These days, traveler's checks are less necessary because the Benelux countries have plenty of 24-hour ATMs. However, you will be charged an ATM withdrawal fee if the bank is not your own, so if you're going to withdraw money every day, you might be better off with traveler's checks, which will be replaced if lost or stolen.

You can get traveler's checks at almost any bank, and from **American Express, Thomas Cook, Visa,** and **MasterCard.**

Euro **traveler's checks** are accepted at locations where dollar and pound traveler's checks may not be, but you'll have to convert any unused ones or keep them for a future trip to a euro-zone country.

You can buy traveler's checks at most banks. They are offered in denominations of $20, $50, $100, $500, and sometimes $1,000. Generally, you'll pay a service charge ranging from 1% to 4%.

The most popular traveler's checks are offered by **American Express** (© **800/ 807-6233,** or 800/221-7282 for card holders—this number accepts collect calls, offers service in several foreign languages, and exempts Amex gold and platinum cardholders from the 1% fee); **Visa** (© **800/732-1322**—AAA members can obtain Visa checks at a $9.95 fee for sums up to $1,500 at most AAA offices or by calling © **866/339-3378**); and **MasterCard** (© **800/223-9920**).

American Express, Thomas Cook, Visa, and **MasterCard** offer **foreign currency traveler's checks,** which are useful if you're traveling to one country, or to the euro zone; they're accepted at locations where dollar checks may not be.

If you carry traveler's checks, keep a record of their serial numbers separate from your checks in the event that they are stolen or lost. You'll get a refund faster if you know the numbers.

5 Travel Insurance

The cost of travel insurance varies widely, depending on the cost and length of your trip, your age and health, and the type of trip you're taking, but expect to pay between 5% and 8% of the vacation itself. You can get estimates from various providers through **InsureMyTrip.com**. Enter your trip cost and dates, your age, and other information for prices from more than a dozen companies.

TRIP-CANCELLATION INSURANCE

Trip-cancellation insurance will help you retrieve your money if you have to back out of a trip or depart early, or if your travel supplier goes bankrupt. Permissible reasons for trip cancellation can range from sickness to natural disasters to the State Department declaring a destination unsafe for travel.

For more information, contact one of the following recommended insurers: **Access America** (✆ 866/807-3982; www.accessamerica.com); **Travel Guard International** (✆ 800/826-4919; www.travelguard.com); **Travel Insured International** (✆ 800/243-3174; www.travelinsured.com); or **Travelex Insurance Services** (✆ 888/457-4602; www.travelexinsurance.com).

MEDICAL INSURANCE

For travel overseas, most U.S. health plans (including Medicare and Medicaid) don't provide coverage, and the ones that do often require you to pay for services upfront and reimburse you only after you return home. As a safety net, you may want to buy travel medical insurance.

Whether your plan does or doesn't cover overseas treatment, be advised that hospitals in Belgium and Holland do not make you pay your bills upfront, but send the bill either to your insurance company directly or to you at home; in some circumstances, you might be asked for a down payment. Hospitals in Luxembourg require payment as soon as treatments are completed; should this be a problem, they might be willing to accept payment later. In all three countries, the process will be smoother if you can show the hospital that you have current and recognized medical insurance coverage.

If you require additional medical insurance, try **MEDEX Assistance** (✆ 410/453-6300; www.medexassist.com) or **Travel Assistance International** (✆ 800/821-2828; www.travelassistance.com; for general information on services, call the company's Worldwide Assistance Services, Inc., at ✆ 800/777-8710).

LOST-LUGGAGE INSURANCE

On flights within the United States, checked baggage is covered up to $2,500 per ticketed passenger. On international flights (including U.S. portions of international trips), baggage coverage is limited

---

Travel in the Age of Bankruptcy

Airlines go bankrupt, so protect yourself by **buying your tickets with a credit card.** The Fair Credit Billing Act guarantees that you can get your money back from the credit card company if a travel supplier goes under (and if you request the refund within 60 days of the bankruptcy). **Travel insurance** can also help, but make sure it covers against "carrier default" for your specific travel provider. And be aware that if a U.S. airline goes bust midtrip, a 2001 federal law requires other carriers to take you to your destination (albeit on a space-available basis) for a fee of no more than $25, provided you rebook within 60 days of the cancellation.

to approximately $9.07 per pound, up to approximately $635 per checked bag. If you plan to check items more valuable than what's covered by the standard liability, see if your homeowner's policy covers your valuables, get baggage insurance as part of your comprehensive travel-insurance package, or buy Travel Guard's "BagTrak" product.

If your luggage is lost, immediately file a lost-luggage claim at the airport, detailing the luggage contents. Most airlines require that you report delayed, damaged, or lost baggage within 4 hours of arrival. The airlines are required to deliver luggage, once found, directly to your house or destination free of charge.

6 Health & Safety

STAYING HEALTHY

There are no particular health concerns in the Benelux—if you don't count the "risk" in Amsterdam and other Dutch towns of occasionally breathing in a whiff of someone else's legally tolerated hashish smoke (and of course they'd likely argue that it's perfectly healthy). You will encounter few other health problems when traveling. The tap water is safe to drink, the milk is pasteurized, and healthcare is excellent.

No health and vaccination certificates are required. You don't need any shots before your trip, but if you suffer from a chronic illness, consult your doctor before your departure. Pack **prescription medications** in your carry-on luggage, and carry them in their original containers, with pharmacy labels—otherwise they won't make it through airport security. (Also, in light of recent events, travelers might want to visit **www.tsa.com** for up-to-date regulations on what is and isn't permissible to pack in carry-on baggage.) Carry the generic name of prescription medicines, in case a local pharmacist is unfamiliar with the brand name. Don't forget an extra pair of contact lenses or prescription eyeglasses.

Contact the **International Association for Medical Assistance to Travelers (IAMAT;** ✆ **716/754-4883** or, in Canada, 416/652-0137; www.iamat.org) for tips on travel and health concerns in the countries you're visiting, and for lists of local, English-speaking doctors.

WHAT TO DO IF YOU GET SICK IN BELGIUM, HOLLAND, OR LUXEMBOURG

If a medical emergency arises, your hotel staff can usually put you in touch with a reliable doctor. Most hospitals have walk-in clinics for emergency cases that are not life-threatening; you may not get immediate attention, but you won't pay the high price of an emergency room visit. Embassies in Brussels and The Hague can provide a list of area doctors who speak English (meaning just about any doctor). Hospitals, embassies, and emergency numbers are listed in this book under "Fast Facts" in the various country planning and capital city chapters.

The state-owned healthcare systems in the Benelux lands are among the world's best, even if they have begun to show signs of the strain of universal healthcare for all. It's easy to get over-the-counter medicines for minor ailments, and both local brands and generic equivalents of most common prescription drugs are available. Many doctors speak English (though the words they use might be a little disturbing, like the doctor who told me he knew what "disease" I had when I reported a minor ailment).

STAYING SAFE

In Holland, be wary of pickpockets on trams, buses, and Metro trains; in rail and Metro stations; on busy shopping streets and in busy stores; and even in your hotel lobby. The rest of the Netherlands is not

Avoiding "Economy-Class Syndrome"

Deep vein thrombosis, or as it's known in the world of flying, "economy-class syndrome," is a blood clot that develops in a deep vein. It's a potentially deadly condition that can be caused by sitting in cramped conditions—such as an airplane cabin—for too long. During a flight (especially a long-haul flight), get up, walk around, and stretch your legs every 60 to 90 minutes to keep your blood flowing. Other preventative measures include frequent flexing of the legs while sitting, drinking lots of water, and avoiding alcohol and sleeping pills. If you have a history of deep vein thrombosis, heart disease, or another condition that puts you at high risk, some experts recommend wearing compression stockings or taking anticoagulants when you fly; always ask your physician about the best course for you. Symptoms of deep vein thrombosis include leg pain or swelling, or even shortness of breath.

as bad in this respect as the capital, though Rotterdam and The Hague are not so far behind.

Belgium is generally safe—even the big cities are low-crime areas. However, like many countries, Belgium has experienced a creeping spread of drug-related crime. In Brussels, the Métro has been plagued by muggers, and though increased police presence and video surveillance have brought this under control, it's still better not to venture alone into deserted Métro access corridors after dark; when other people are around, it's generally safe.

Both Holland and Belgium are showing an increase in votes for right-wing political parties that are ideologically opposed, to one degree or another, to immigration, or even to the continued presence of immigrant communities. Rising levels of some crimes—muggings, break-ins, pickpocketing, bag snatching, and auto theft—attributed to legal and illegal immigrants and to ethnic minorities, appear to be fueling this trend. Indigenous Dutch and Belgian criminals are quite capable of generating trouble of their own, of course, as demonstrated by the violent hooligans associated with some Dutch soccer clubs, and by homicidal pedophilia cases in Belgium during the '90s.

Both Brussels and Antwerp have well-defined red light zones, in which more than a little caution is in order. Don't confuse these places with the Red Light District up the road in Amsterdam, which is a pretty big tourist attraction in its own right, and mostly safe for casual visitors. Brussels's red light zone in particular is a down-and-dirty, creepy, low-life zone, and though Antwerp's is not quite so bad it's still not really a place to go for sightseeing. Bruges and Ghent have only minimal facilities of this kind, so this is not a factor there.

And then there's Luxembourg. In the unlikely event that you become a victim of any kind of crime in the squeaky-clean Grand Duchy, watch out—you'll likely be stuffed and placed in a museum for the astonishment of future generations.

DEALING WITH DISCRIMINATION

U.S. visitors might—and I emphasize *might*—encounter some hostility, due primarily to current (late 2006) circumstances in Iraq and the Israeli/Palestinian conflict. Among other local pet beefs could be the U.S.'s refusal to sign up for both the Kyoto Protocol on global warming and the International Criminal Court in The Hague; and its "support" for gene-modified ("Frankenstein") foods and the death penalty. (Some Europeans aren't all that keen on apple pie either.)

Healthy Travels to You

The following government websites offer up-to-date health-related travel advice.

- **Australia:** www.dfat.gov.au/travel
- **Canada:** www.hc-sc.gc.ca/index_e.html
- **U.K.:** www.dh.gov.uk/PolicyAndGuidance/HealthAdviceForTravellers/fs/en
- **U.S.:** www.cdc.gov/travel

Some native Belgians and some of the country's significant Muslim population might want to take issue with you on one or more of these topics, in ways ranging from open discussion, to surly service, to the cold shoulder, or even to verbal aggression. I know of no cases of physical aggression and would guess that it's vanishing or nonexistent.

Flemish Belgians are showing an increasing propensity to vote for the extreme right-wing (some commentators say neo-fascist) nationalist Vlaams Belang (Flemish Interest) political party, which is opposed to allowing more economic migrants and political refugees into Belgium, and to the continued presence of ethnic minorities who don't accept "European values." They get 25% of the vote across the region and more than a third in Antwerp. Rising levels of some crimes—muggings, break-ins, pickpocketing, bag snatching, and auto theft—attributed to immigrants, legal and illegal, and ethnic minorities, appear to be fueling this trend. This attitude could easily translate into discrimination against non-white visitors—but note that the overwhelming majority of Belgians would be appalled by this.

Antwerp has both an Orthodox Jewish minority and a significant minority of North African (Arab) origin. Tensions caused by the Israeli/Palestinian conflict have led to a spate of anti-Semitic attacks. Jewish visitors who dress in a way that clearly identifies them as Jewish should be aware of this, even though the chances of being a victim of such an attack are very small. In neighborhoods with a big proportion of North African immigrants, radical Arab youths have staged vigilante patrols, but these are directed more at imaginary enemies, and at occasional real ones in the shape of right-wing, white racist thugs, than against members of the Jewish community (who in any case have other things to do with their time than wander around these neighborhoods).

Note: Listing some of the possible dangers together like this can give a false impression of the threat from crime or discrimination in the Benelux lands. None of these dangers is statistically significant, and by no stretch of the imagination can any Benelux city be described as dangerous. The overwhelming probability is that you will not notice any of these problems, far less encounter one of them. But it can't hurt to be aware of them.

7 Specialized Travel Resources

TRAVELERS WITH DISABILITIES

Most disabilities shouldn't stop anyone from traveling. There are more options and resources out there than ever before.

Many hotels and restaurants now provide easy access for people with disabilities, and some display the international wheelchair symbol in their brochures and advertising. It's always a good idea to call ahead to find out what the situation is before you book. Both Brussels National Airport and Amsterdam Airport Schiphol have services to help travelers with disabilities through the airport. There's also comprehensive assistance for travelers with disabilities throughout the railway systems of all three countries. Inquire also at the national tourist board offices in each country for specific details on the available resources.

Not all trams in Brussels, Antwerp, Amsterdam, The Hague, Rotterdam, and other cities are easily accessible for travelers in wheelchairs, but the new trams being introduced on some routes have low central doors that are accessible. The Metro system is fully accessible, but that's not as good as it sounds, because few Metro stations are near places where visitors want to go. Taxis are also difficult, but new minivan taxis are an improvement. There's comprehensive assistance for travelers on **Netherlands Railways** (✆ 030/235-5555) trains and in stations. If you give them a day's notice of your journey by visiting a station or calling ahead, they can arrange for assistance along the way.

Two good sources of information in the Netherlands are **NIZQ** (✆ 030/230-6603) and **ANWB Disabled Department** (✆ 070/314-1420). In Luxembourg, contact **Info Handicap,** rue de Contern 20, 5955 Itzig (✆ 352/366-466; fax 352/360-885).

Many travel agencies offer customized tours and itineraries for travelers with disabilities. Among them are **Flying Wheels Travel** (✆ 507/451-5005; www.flying wheelstravel.com); **Access-Able Travel Source** (✆ 303/232-2979; www.access-able.com); and **Accessible Journeys** (✆ 800/846-4537 or 610/521-0339; www.disabilitytravel.com). **Avis Rent a Car** has an "Avis Access" program that offers such services as a dedicated 24-hour toll-free number (✆ 888/879-4273) for customers with special travel needs; special car features such as swivel seats, spinner knobs, and hand controls; and accessible bus service.

Organizations that offer assistance to travelers with disabilities include **Moss-Rehab** (www.mossresourcenet.org); the **American Foundation for the Blind (AFB;** ✆ 800/232-5463; www.afb.org); and **SATH** (Society for Accessible Travel & Hospitality; ✆ 212/447-7284; www.sath.org). **AirAmbulanceCard.com** is now partnered with SATH and allows you to preselect top-notch hospitals in case of an emergency.

Also check out the quarterly magazine *Emerging Horizons* (www.emerging horizons.com), and *Open World* magazine, published by SATH.

The Royal Association for Disability and Rehabilitation (RADAR), Unit 12, City Forum, 250 City Rd., London EC1V 8AF (✆ 020/7250-3222; minicom 020/7250-4119; www.radar.org.uk), publishes three holiday "fact packs" for £2 each or £5 for all three. The first one provides general information, including planning and booking a holiday, insurance, and finances; the second outlines transportation available when going abroad and equipment for rent; the third covers specialized accommodations.

GAY & LESBIAN TRAVELERS

In Amsterdam, you can get information, or just meet people, by visiting **COC,** Rozenstraat 14 (✆ 020/626-3087; www.cocamsterdam.nl), the Amsterdam branch of the Dutch lesbian and gay organization. On the premises are a daytime cafe serving coffee and quiche, a meeting space for special-interest groups, weekend discos (mainly men Fri, women Sat), and a special ethnic evening called Strange Fruit on Sunday. The **Gay and Lesbian Switchboard** (✆ 020/623-6565; www.switchboard.nl), open daily from 10am to 10pm, can provide you with all kinds of information and advice.

You shouldn't have much trouble finding information about gay and lesbian bars and clubs because they're well publicized.

Also see "Gay & Lesbian Bars" under "The Bar & Cafe Scene," in chapter 12. The free biweekly listings magazine *Shark* is a great source of cultural information, in particular for the offbeat and alternative scenes, and comes with a centerfold pullout, titled *Queer Fish,* which has excellent lesbian and gay listings. *Gay News Amsterdam* and *Gay & Night,* competing monthly magazines in both Dutch and English, are available free in gay establishments around the city.

In Belgium, contact the gay and lesbian community centers **Tels Quels,** rue du Marché-au-Charbon 81 (© **02/512-45-87;** Métro: Bourse), open Saturday to Thursday from 5pm to 2am, and Friday from 8am to 4am; and **Maison Arc-en-Ciel,** av. Winston Churchill 175 (© **02/347-67-56;** tram: 23 or 90). For Flanders, try the **Federatie Werkgroepen Homoseksualiteit,** Vlaanderenstraat 22 (© **09/238-26-26**), in Ghent.

In Luxembourg, the gay men's organization is **Rosa Letzebuerg,** bd. Patton 94, 2316 Luxembourg-Ville (© **021-412-812;** www.gay.lu).

The International Gay and Lesbian Travel Association (IGLTA; © **800/448-8550** or 954/776-2626; www.iglta.org) is the trade association for the gay and lesbian travel industry, and offers an online directory of gay- and lesbian-friendly travel businesses; go to their website and click on "Members."

Many agencies offer tours and travel itineraries specifically for gay and lesbian travelers. Among them are **Above and Beyond Tours** (© **800/397-2681;** www. abovebeyondtours.com); **Now, Voyager** (© **800/255-6951;** www.nowvoyager. com); and **Olivia Cruises & Resorts** (© **800/631-6277;** www.olivia.com).

Gay.com Travel (© **800/929-2268** or 415/644-8044; www.gay.com/travel or www.outandabout.com) is an excellent online successor to the popular *Out & About* print magazine. It provides regularly updated information about gay-owned, gay-oriented, and gay-friendly lodging, dining, sightseeing, nightlife, and shopping establishments in every important destination worldwide.

The following travel guides are available at many bookstores, or you can order them from any online bookseller: *Frommer's Gay & Lesbian Europe* (www.frommers. com), an excellent travel resource to the top European cities and resorts; *Spartacus International Gay Guide* (Bruno Gmünder Verlag; www.spartacusworld. com/gayguide) and *Odysseus: The International Gay Travel Planner* (Odysseus Enterprises Ltd.); and the *Damron* guides (www.damron.com), with separate, annual books for gay men and lesbians.

SENIOR TRAVEL

Mention the fact that you're a senior when you make your travel reservations. Some sightseeing attractions may offer senior discounts, but only to local residents when they produce an appropriate ID. Be sure to ask when you buy your ticket.

Members of **AARP** (formerly known as the American Association of Retired Persons), 601 E St. NW, Washington, DC 20049 (© **888/687-2277;** www. aarp.org), get discounts on hotels, airfares, and car rentals. AARP offers members a wide range of benefits, including *AARP: The Magazine* and a monthly newsletter. Anyone over 50 can join.

Many reliable agencies and organizations target the 50-plus market. **Elderhostel** (© **877/426-8056;** www.elder hostel.org) arranges study programs for those aged 55 and over. **ElderTreks** (© **800/741-7956;** www.eldertreks.com) offers small-group tours to off-the-beaten-path or adventure-travel locations, restricted to travelers 50 and older. **INTRAV** (© **800/456-8100;** www. intrav.com) is a high-end tour operator that caters to the mature, discerning traveler (not specifically seniors), with trips around the world that include guided safaris, polar expeditions, private-jet adventures, and small-boat cruises down jungle rivers.

Recommended publications offering travel resources and discounts for seniors include: the quarterly magazine *Travel 50 & Beyond* (www.travel50andbeyond. com); *Travel Unlimited: Uncommon Adventures for the Mature Traveler* (Avalon); *101 Tips for Mature Travelers,* available from Grand Circle Travel (© **800/221-2610** or 617/350-7500; www.gct.com); and *Unbelievably Good Deals and Great Adventures That You Absolutely Can't Get Unless You're Over 50* (McGraw-Hill), by Joann Rattner Heilman.

FAMILY TRAVEL

To locate accommodations, restaurants, and attractions that are particularly kid-friendly, refer to the "Kids" icon throughout this guide.

As for keeping the children amused, what child wouldn't be happy exploring the castles that are scattered across the Benelux landscapes? Give your youngsters a head start with a short rundown on the people who constructed these fascinating structures and what happened within their walls, and you'll soon find their imaginations running wild. In the cities, small towns, and villages, the colorful pageantry of past centuries as depicted in numerous festivals will surely delight the younger set. In Holland, watch faces light up at the Lilliputian "Holland in a Nutshell" miniatures at Madurodam. In Belgium, Brussels's *Manneken-Pis* statue, a famous national monument of a little boy urinating, is usually a winner. And look for wildlife centers in all three countries. Virtually every sightseeing attraction admits children at half price, and many offer family-ticket discounts.

Arrange ahead of time for such necessities as a crib, bottle warmer, and car seat (small children are not allowed to ride in the front seat). For information on babysitters, see "Fast Facts: Brussels," in chapter 5; and "Fast Facts: Amsterdam," in chapter 12.

Familyhostel (© **800/733-9753;** www. learn.unh.edu/forms/FHregisterform. html) takes the whole family, including kids ages 8 to 15, on moderately priced U.S. and international learning vacations. Lectures, field trips, and sightseeing are guided by a team of academics.

Recommended family travel websites include **Family Travel Forum** (www. familytravelforum.com), **Family Travel Network** (www.familytravelnetwork. com), **Traveling Internationally with Your Kids** (www.travelwithyourkids. com), and **Family Travel Files** (www.the familytravelfiles.com).

WOMEN TRAVELERS

Check out the award-winning website **Journeywoman** (www.journeywoman. com), a "real life" women's travel-information network where you can sign up for a free e-mail newsletter and get advice on everything from etiquette and dress to safety; or the travel guide *Safety and Security for Women Who Travel* by Sheila Swan and Peter Laufer (Travelers' Tales, Inc.), offering common-sense tips on safe travel.

In Amsterdam, it's safe for groups of women to go around in the city's famed (or notorious) Red Light District—always supposing they can stomach seeing other women serving purely as sex objects—but a young woman on her own, particularly after dark, could be subject to at least verbal harassment, and misrepresentation as a "working girl."

Public transportation is usually busy even late at night, so you generally won't have to worry about being alone in a bus, tram, or Metro train. If you feel nervous, sit close to the driver whenever possible.

Holland has long enjoyed a relaxed attitude to exposing nontrivial amounts of the undraped female form—a recent government DVD, part of a now-mandatory "education" for would-be migrants, portrays going topless at the beach as an integral part of Dutch culture. Far fewer women are actually going without at the beach or in the park these days, and those who do are less likely to be younger women and teens. Catholic Belgium and Luxembourg always were less relaxed about this, and remain so.

STUDENT TRAVEL

If you're traveling internationally, you'd be wise to arm yourself with an **International Student Identity Card (ISIC)**, which offers substantial savings on rail passes, plane tickets, and entrance fees. It also provides you with basic health and life insurance and a 24-hour help line. The card is available from **STA Travel** (© 800/781-4040 in North America; www.sta.com or www.statravel.com; or www.statravel.co.uk in the U.K.), the biggest student travel agency in the world. If you're no longer a student but are still under 26, you can get an **International Youth Travel Card (IYTC)** from STA, which entitles you to some discounts (but not on museum admissions). **Travel CUTS** (© 800/667-2887 or 416/614-2887; www.travelcuts.com) offers similar services for both Canadians and U.S. residents. Irish students may prefer to turn to **USIT** (© 01/602-1600; www.usitnow.ie), an Ireland-based specialist in student, youth, and independent travel.

SINGLE TRAVELERS

On package vacations, single travelers are often hit with a "single supplement" to the base price. To avoid it, you can agree to room with other single travelers or find a compatible roommate before you go, from one of the many roommate-locator agencies.

Travel Buddies Singles Travel Club (© 800/998-9099; www.travelbuddies worldwide.com), based in Canada, runs small, intimate, single-friendly group trips and will match you with a roommate free of charge. **TravelChums** (© 212/787-2621; www.travelchums.com) is an Internet-only travel-companion matching service with elements of an online personals-type site, hosted by the respected New York–based Shaw Guides travel service. For more information, check out Eleanor Berman's latest edition of *Traveling Solo: Advice and Ideas for More Than 250 Great Vacations* (Globe Pequot), a guide with advice on traveling alone, either solo or as part of a group tour.

8 Planning Your Trip Online

SURFING FOR AIRFARES

The most popular online travel agencies are **Travelocity** (www.travelocity.com, or www.travelocity.co.uk); **Expedia** (www.expedia.com, www.expedia.co.uk, or www.expedia.ca); and **Orbitz** (www.orbitz.com).

In addition, most airlines now offer online-only fares that even their phone agents know nothing about. For the websites of airlines that fly to and from your destination, go to "Getting There," p. 33.

Other helpful websites for booking airline tickets online include:

- www.biddingfortravel.com
- www.cheapflights.com
- www.hotwire.com
- www.kayak.com
- www.lastminutetravel.com
- www.opodo.co.uk
- www.priceline.com
- www.sidestep.com
- www.site59.com
- www.smartertravel.com

Frommers.com: The Complete Travel Resource

For an excellent travel-planning resource, we highly recommend **Frommers. com** (www.frommers.com), voted Best Travel Site by *PC Magazine*. We're a little biased, of course, but we guarantee that you'll find the travel tips, reviews, monthly vacation giveaways, bookstore, and online-booking capabilities to be thoroughly indispensable. Special features include our popular **Destinations** section, where you can access expert travel tips, hotel and dining recommendations, and advice on the sights in more than 3,500 destinations around the globe; the **Frommers.com Newsletter,** with the latest deals, travel trends, and money-saving secrets; and our **Travel Talk** area featuring **Message Boards,** where Frommer's readers post queries and share advice, and where our authors sometimes show up to answer questions. Once you finish your research, the **Book a Trip** area can lead you to Frommer's preferred online partners' websites, where you can book your vacation at affordable prices.

SURFING FOR HOTELS

In addition to **Travelocity, Expedia, Orbitz, Priceline,** and **Hotwire** (see above), the following websites will help you with booking hotel rooms online:

- www.hotels.com
- www.quickbook.com
- www.travelaxe.net
- www.travelweb.com
- www.tripadvisor.com

It's a good idea to **get a confirmation number** and **make a printout** of any online booking transaction.

SURFING FOR RENTAL CARS

For booking rental cars online, the best deals are usually found at rental-car company websites, although all the major online travel agencies also offer rental-car reservations services. Priceline and Hotwire work well for rental cars, too; the only "mystery" is which major rental company you get, and for most travelers the difference between Hertz, Avis, and Budget is negligible.

9 The 21st-Century Traveler

INTERNET ACCESS AWAY FROM HOME
WITHOUT YOUR OWN COMPUTER

To find cybercafes in Benelux towns and cities, check **www.cybercaptive.com** and **www.cybercafe.com**.

Aside from formal cybercafes, most **youth hostels** and **public libraries** have Internet access. Avoid **hotel business centers** unless you're willing to pay exorbitant rates.

Brussels National and Amsterdam Schiphol airports have **Internet kiosks** scattered throughout their gates. These give you basic online access for a per-minute fee that's usually higher than cybercafe prices.

WITH YOUR OWN COMPUTER

More and more hotels, cafes, and retailers are signing on as Wi-Fi (wireless fidelity) "hotspots." Mac owners have their own networking technology: Apple AirPort.

To locate hotspots that provide **free wireless networks** in cities around the world, go to **www.personaltelco.net/index.cgi/WirelessCommunities**.

For dial-up access, most business-class hotels throughout the world offer data-ports for laptop modems, and many hotels in Europe now offer free high-speed Internet access. In addition, major Internet Service Providers (ISPs) have **local access numbers** around the world, allowing you to go online by placing a local call. The **iPass** network also has dial-up numbers around the world. You'll have to sign up with an iPass provider, who will then tell you how to set up your computer for your destination(s). For a list of iPass providers, go to www.ipass.com and click on "Individuals Buy Now." One solid provider is **i2roam** (www.i2roam.com; ⓒ **866/811-6209** or 920/235-0475).

Wherever you go, bring a **connection kit** of the right power and phone adapters,

Online Traveler's Toolbox

Veteran travelers usually carry some essential items to make their trips easier. Following is a selection of handy online tools to bookmark and use.

- **Airplane Food** (www.airlinemeals.net)
- **Airplane Seating** (www.seatguru.com and www.airlinequality.com)
- **Foreign Languages for Travelers** (www.travlang.com)
- **Maps** (www.mapquest.com)
- **Time and Date** (www.timeanddate.com)
- **Universal Currency Converter** (www.xe.com/ucc)
- **Visa ATM Locator** (www.visa.com), **MasterCard ATM Locator** (www.mastercard.com)
- **Weather** (www.intellicast.com and www.weather.com)
- **Belgium Tourist Information** (www.visitbelgium.com, www.opt.be, www.wallonie-tourisme.be, www.toervl.be, www.brusselsinternational.be, and www.visitflanders.com)
- **Independent Belgian Travel Information** (www.trabel.com and www.xpats.com)
- **Hotels in Belgium** (www.hotels-belgium.com)
- **Dining Out in Belgium** (www.resto.be)
- **Holland Tourist Information** (www.visitholland.com and www.visitamsterdam.nl)
- **Hip Places to See and Be Seen in Amsterdam** (www.amsterdamhotspots.nl)
- **Virtual Tour of Amsterdam** (www.channels.nl)
- **Museums in Holland** (www.hollandmuseums.nl)
- **Reserve an Amsterdam Hotel Online** (www.go-amsterdam.org)
- **Eating Out in Holland** (www.specialbite.nl)
- **Luxembourg Tourist Information** (www.luxembourg-ville.lu)
- **Luxembourg Cultural and Tourist Agenda** (www.agendalux.lu)
- **Luxembourg Hotels** (www.hotels.lu)
- **Luxembourg Restaurants** (www.resto.lu)

a spare phone cord, and a spare Ethernet network cable—or find out whether your hotel supplies them to guests.

CELLPHONE USE

The three letters that define much of the world's wireless capabilities are GSM (Global System for Mobiles), a big, seamless network that makes for easy cross-border cellphone use throughout Europe and dozens of other countries worldwide. If your cellphone is on a GSM system, and you have a world-capable multiband phone such as many Sony Ericsson, Motorola, or Samsung models, you can make and receive calls across civilized areas around much of the globe. Just call your wireless operator and ask for "international roaming" to be activated on your account. Unfortunately, per-minute charges can be high—usually $1 to $1.50 in western Europe.

For many, **renting** a phone is a good idea. (Even worldphone owners will have to rent new phones if they're traveling to non-GSM regions, such as Japan or Korea.) While you can rent a phone from any number of overseas sites, including kiosks at airports and at car-rental agencies, we suggest renting by phone before you leave home. North Americans can rent one before leaving the country from **InTouch USA** (© 800/872-7626; www.intouchglobal.com) or **RoadPost** (© 888/290-1606 or 905/272-5665; www.roadpost.com). InTouch will also, for free, advise you on whether your existing phone will work overseas; simply call © **703/222-7161** between 9am and 4pm EST, or go to **http://intouchglobal.com/travel.htm**.

Buying a phone can be economically attractive, as many nations have cheap prepaid phone systems. Once you arrive at your destination, stop by a local cellphone shop and get the cheapest package; you'll probably pay less than $100 for a phone and a starter calling card. Local calls may be as low as 10¢ per minute, and in many countries incoming calls are free.

10 Getting There

BY PLANE
FLYING TO BELGIUM

Brussels National Airport, at Zaventem, 11km (7 miles) northeast of the center city, is Belgium's only significant international airport. It has direct rail connection to Brussels and from there to Bruges, Ghent, Antwerp, and other Belgian cities; to Amsterdam, Rotterdam, and The Hague; and to Luxembourg City. See "Orientation," in chapter 5.

FROM THE U.S. & CANADA Carriers with flights to Brussels from cities that include Atlanta, Boston, Chicago, New York, and Toronto are **Air Canada** (© **888/247-2262;** www.aircanada.ca); **American Airlines** (© **800/433-7300;** www.aa.com); **Delta** (© **800/221-1212;** www.delta.com); and **United Airlines** (© **800/538-2929;** www.united.com).

FROM THE U.K. British Airways (© 0870/850-9850; www.britishairways.com); **SN Brussels Airlines** (© 020/7559-9787; www.flysn.com); **Virgin Express** (© 0870/730-1134; www.virgin-express.com); and **bmi** (© **0870/607-0555;** www.flybmi.com) fly to Brussels from cities that include Edinburgh, Belfast, Birmingham, Bristol, Glasgow, Leeds/Bradford, London, Manchester, and Sheffield. **Ryanair** (© **0871/246-0000;** www.ryanair.com) flies from London and Glasgow to Charleroi.

FROM IRELAND Aer Lingus (© **0818/365000;** www.aerlingus.com) and **SN Brussels Airlines** (in Britain © 020/7559-9787; www.flysn.com) fly from Dublin to Brussels. **Ryanair** (© **01/609-7881;** www.ryanair.com) flies from Dublin to Charleroi.

FROM AUSTRALIA   KLM (© 1300/ 392192; www.klm.com) and **Qantas** (© 131313; www.qantas.com.au) fly from Sydney to Amsterdam, where you can transfer for Brussels.

FROM NEW ZEALAND   Air New Zealand (© 0800/737000; www.airnew zealand.com) flies from Auckland to London, where you can transfer for Brussels.

FLYING TO THE NETHERLANDS

Amsterdam Airport Schiphol, 13km (8 miles) southwest of the center city, has quick, direct rail links to Amsterdam's center city; to Rotterdam, The Hague, Utrecht, and other Dutch cities; and to Antwerp and Brussels. See "Orientation," in chapter 12.

In 2004, the Netherlands flag carrier KLM Royal Dutch Airlines merged with Air France, in what was widely interpreted as a takeover of the Dutch airline by the French one. It remains to be seen what effect control by the lumbering, state-controlled French giant will have on the services of a formerly lean and efficient (but small for a would-be global player) KLM.

FROM THE U.S. & CANADA   Carriers with frequent flights to Amsterdam from cities that include Atlanta, Boston, Chicago, Detroit, Houston, Los Angeles, Minneapolis/St. Paul, Memphis, Montreal, Newark, New York, San Francisco, Seattle, Toronto, Vancouver, and Washington, D.C., are **Air Canada** (© 888/ 247-2262; www.aircanada.ca); **Continental Airlines** (© 800/231-0856; www.continental.com); **Delta** (© 800/ 221-1212; www.delta.com); **KLM Royal Dutch Airlines** (© 800/225-2525; www.klm.com); **Northwest Airlines** (© 800/225-2525; www.nwa.com); and **United Airlines** (© 800/538-2929; www.united.com).

FROM THE U.K.   British Airways (© 0870/850-9850; www.britishairways.

com), **BMi** (© 0870/607-0555; www. flybmi.com), **easyJet** (© 0905/560- 7777; www.easyjet.com), and **KLM Royal Dutch Airlines** (© 0870/507- 4074; www.klm.nl) and its subsidiaries KLM Cityhopper and KLM UK, fly to Amsterdam from cities that include Aberdeen, Belfast, Birmingham, Bristol, Cardiff, Edinburgh, Glasgow, Leeds/ Bradford, Liverpool, London, Manchester, Newcastle, Norwich, and Teesside; KLM Cityhopper flies also from London to Rotterdam; and KLM Exel flies from London to Eindhoven and Maastricht.

FROM IRELAND   Aer Lingus (© 0818/365000; www.aerlingus.com) flies daily from Dublin to Amsterdam.

FROM AUSTRALIA   KLM (© 1300/ 392192; www.klm.com) and **Qantas** (© 131313; www.qantas.com.au) fly from Sydney to Amsterdam.

FROM NEW ZEALAND   Air New Zealand (© 0800/737000; www.air newzealand.com) flies from Auckland to London, where you can transfer for Amsterdam.

FLYING TO LUXEMBOURG

Luxembourg Airport is 6km (4 miles) northeast of Luxembourg City. See "Getting Around," in chapter 18.

FROM NORTH AMERICA   You can fly to Brussels and Amsterdam (see "Flying to Belgium" and "Flying to the Netherlands," above), and transfer for Luxembourg City.

FROM THE U.K.   British Airways (© 0845/773-3377; www.britishairways. com) flies from London to Luxembourg City. **Luxair** (© 01293/596663; www. luxair.lu) flies from London and Manchester to Luxembourg City.

FROM IRELAND   Aer Lingus (© 0818/365000; www.aerlingus.com) and **Luxair** (© 44-1293/596663 in Britain; www.luxair.lu) fly from Dublin to Luxembourg City.

Tips   Getting Through the Airport

- Arrive at the airport 1 hour before a domestic flight and 2 hours before an international flight; if you show up late, tell an airline employee and he or she will probably whisk you to the front of the line.
- Beat the ticket-counter lines by using airport electronic kiosks or even online check-in from your home computer, from where you can print out boarding passes in advance. Curbside check-in is also a good way to avoid lines.
- Bring a current, government-issued photo ID such as a driver's license or passport. Children under 18 do not need government-issued photo IDs for flights within the U.S., but they do for international flights to most countries.
- Speed up security by removing your jacket and shoes before you're screened. In addition, remove metal objects such as big belt buckles. If you've got metallic body parts, a note from your doctor can prevent a long chat with the security screeners.
- Use a TSA-approved lock for your checked luggage. Look for Travel Sentry certified locks at luggage or travel shops and Brookstone stores (or online at www.brookstone.com).
- Visit **www.tsa.com** for up-to-date regulations on what is and isn't permissible to pack in carry-on baggage.

FROM AUSTRALIA KLM (℗ 1300/ 392192; www.klm.com) and **Qantas** (℗ 131313; www.qantas.com.au) fly from Sydney to Amsterdam, where you can transfer for Luxembourg City.

FROM NEW ZEALAND Air New Zealand (℗ 0800/737000; www.airnewzealand.com) flies from Auckland to London, where you can transfer for Luxembourg City.

FLYING FOR LESS: TIPS FOR GETTING THE BEST AIRFARE

- Passengers who can book their tickets either **long in advance** or **at the last minute,** or who **fly midweek** or **at less-trafficked hours,** may pay a fraction of the full fare. If your schedule is flexible, say so, and ask if you can secure a cheaper fare by changing your flight plans.

- Search the **Internet** for cheap fares (see "Planning Your Trip Online," earlier in this chapter").
- Keep an eye on local newspapers for **promotional specials** or **fare wars,** when airlines lower prices on their most popular routes. You rarely see fare wars offered for peak travel times, but if you can travel in the off-months, you may snag a bargain.
- Try to book a ticket in its **country of origin.** If you're planning a one-way flight from Johannesburg to Bombay, a South Africa–based travel agent will probably have the lowest fares. For multi-leg trips, book in the country of the first leg; for example, book New York–London–Amsterdam–Rome–New York in the U.S.
- **Consolidators,** also known as bucket shops, are great sources for international tickets, although they usually

can't beat Internet fares within North America. Start by looking in Sunday newspaper travel sections; U.S. travelers should focus on the *New York Times, Los Angeles Times,* and *Miami Herald.* U.K. travelers should search in the *Independent, The Guardian,* or *The Observer.* For less-developed destinations, small travel agents who cater to immigrant communities in large cities often have the best deals. ***Beware:*** Bucket shop tickets are usually nonrefundable or rigged with stiff cancellation penalties, often as high as 50% to 75% of the ticket price, and some put you on charter airlines, which may leave at inconvenient times and experience delays. Several reliable consolidators are worldwide and available online. **STA Travel** has been the world's lead consolidator for students since purchasing Council Travel, but their fares are competitive for travelers of all ages. **ELTExpress** (or **Flights.com**; © **800/TRAV-800**; www.eltexpress. com) has excellent fares worldwide, particularly to Europe. They also have "local" websites in 12 countries. **FlyCheap** (© **800/FLY-CHEAP**; www.1800flycheap.com), owned by package-vacation megalith MyTravel, has especially good fares to sunny destinations. **Air Tickets Direct** (© **800/778-3447**; www.airtickets direct.com) is based in Montreal and leverages the currently weak Canadian dollar for low fares; they also book trips to places that U.S. travel agents won't touch, such as Cuba.

- Join **frequent-flier clubs.** Frequent-flier membership doesn't cost a cent, but it does entitle you to better seats, faster response to phone inquiries, and prompter service if your luggage is stolen or your flight is canceled or delayed, or if you want to change your seat. And you don't have to fly to earn

points; **frequent-flier credit cards** can earn you thousands of miles for doing your everyday shopping. With more than 70 mileage awards programs on the market, consumers have never had more options. Investigate the program details of your favorite airlines before you sink points into any one. Consider which airlines have hubs in the airport nearest you, and, of those carriers, which have the most advantageous alliances, given your most common routes. To play the frequent-flier game to your best advantage, consult Randy Petersen's **Inside Flyer** (www.insideflyer.com). Petersen and friends review all the programs in detail and post regular updates on changes in policies and trends.

LONG-HAUL FLIGHTS: HOW TO STAY COMFORTABLE

- Your choice of airline and airplane will definitely affect your legroom. Find more details about U.S. airlines at **www.seatguru.com**. For international airlines, the research firm Skytrax has posted a list of average seat pitches at **www.airlinequality.com**.
- Emergency-exit seats and bulkhead seats typically have the most legroom. Emergency-exit seats are usually left unassigned until the day of a flight (to ensure that able-bodied persons fill the seats); it's worth getting to the ticket counter early to snag one of these spots for a long flight. Many passengers find that bulkhead seating (the row facing the wall at the front of the cabin) offers more legroom, but keep in mind that bulkheads are where airlines often put baby bassinets, so you may be sitting next to an infant.
- To have two seats for yourself in a three-seat row, try for an aisle seat in a center section toward the back of coach. If you're traveling with a

companion, book an aisle and a window seat. Middle seats are usually booked last, so chances are good you'll end up with three seats to yourselves.

- Ask about entertainment options. Many airlines offer seatback video systems where you get to choose your movies or play video games—but only on some of their planes. (Boeing 777s are your best bet.)
- To sleep, avoid the last row of any section or the row in front of an emergency exit, as these seats are the least likely to recline. Avoid seats near highly trafficked toilet areas. Avoid seats in the back of many jets—these can be narrower than those in the rest of coach. You also may want to reserve a window seat so you can rest your head and avoid being bumped in the aisle.
- Get up, walk around, and stretch every 60 to 90 minutes to keep your blood flowing. See the box "Avoiding 'Economy-Class Syndrome,'" under "Health & Safety," p. 24.

- Drink water before, during, and after your flight to combat the lack of humidity in airplane cabins. Avoid alcohol, which will dehydrate you.
- If you're flying with kids, don't forget to carry on toys, books, pacifiers, and chewing gum to help them relieve ear pressure buildup during ascent and descent.

GETTING THERE BY BOAT

TO BELGIUM P&O Ferries (© 08705/980333 Britain, 02/710-64-44 Belgium; www.poferries.com) has daily car ferry service between Hull in northeast England and Zeebrugge. The overnight trip time is 12½ hours.

Superfast Ferries (© 0870/234-0870 Britain, 050/25-22-92 Belgium; www.superfast.com) has daily car ferry service between Rosyth, across the Forth River from Edinburgh, Scotland, to Zeebrugge. The overnight trip time is 17½ hours.

At Zeebrugge a bus shuttles between the harbor and the rail station, and there's hourly train service from there to Brussels, via Bruges and Ghent.

Tips Coping with Jet Lag

Jet lag is a pitfall of traveling across time zones. If you're flying north-south and you feel sluggish when you touch down, your symptoms will be the result of dehydration and the general stress of air travel. When you travel east-west or vice versa, however, your body becomes thoroughly confused about what time it is, and everything from your digestive system to your brain is knocked for a loop. Traveling east, say from Chicago to Paris, is more difficult on your internal clock than traveling west, say from London to Hawaii, because most peoples' bodies are more inclined to stay up late than fall asleep early.

Here are some tips for combating jet lag:

- **Reset your watch** to your destination time before you board the plane.
- **Drink lots of water** before, during, and after your flight. Avoid alcohol.
- **Exercise and sleep well** for a few days before your trip.
- If you have trouble sleeping on planes, **fly eastward on morning flights.**
- **Daylight** is the key to resetting your body clock. At the website for **Outside In** (www.bodyclock.com), you can get a customized plan of when to seek and avoid light.

Transeuropa Ferries (© **01843/ 595522** in Britain, 059/34-02-60 in Belgium; www.transeuropaferries.com), has three car-ferry sailings daily, from Ramsgate in southern England to Ostend; the trip time is 4 hours. This service transports only cars and other vehicles along with their drivers and passengers; foot passengers aren't accepted.

TO THE NETHERLANDS Stena Line (© **08705/707070** Britain, 0900/ 8123 Holland; www.stenaline.com) has twice-daily fast car-ferry service, and overnight and daytime "superferry" service, between Harwich in southeast England and Hoek van Holland (Hook of Holland) near Rotterdam. The fast-ferry trip time is 3 hours and 40 minutes, and the "superferry" trip time is 6 hours and 15 minutes. Frequent trains depart from Hoek van Holland to Amsterdam.

P&O Ferries (© **08705/980333** Britain, 020/210-3333 Holland; www. poferries.com) has daily car ferry service between Hull in northeast England and Rotterdam (Europoort). The overnight trip time is 10 hours.

DFDS Seaways (© **0870/252-0524** Britain, 0255/546-666 Holland; www.dfds seaways.co.uk) has daily car ferry service between Newcastle in northeast England and IJmuiden on the North Sea coast west of Amsterdam. The overnight trip time is 15 hours. From IJmuiden, you can go by train to Amsterdam Centraal Station.

GETTING THERE BY TRAIN

Rail service to the Benelux countries from major European cities is frequent, fast, and generally inexpensive compared to air travel.

TO BELGIUM Britain is connected to the Continent (or as the Brits might say, the Continent is connected to Britain) through the Channel Tunnel. On the **Eurostar** high-speed train, with a top speed of 300kmph (186 mph), travel

times between London Waterloo station and Brussels Midi station are 2 hours and 40 minutes. Departures are approximately every 2 hours. For Eurostar reservations, call © **08705/186186** in Britain; 02/ 528-28-28 in Belgium. Or book online at **www.eurostar.com**. Tickets also are available from main rail stations and travel agents.

The **Thalys** high-speed train, with a top speed of 300kmph (186 mph), that connects Paris, Brussels, Amsterdam, and Cologne, has cut travel times from Paris-Nord station to Brussels Midi station to 1 hour and 25 minutes. Departures are approximately every hour. For Thalys information and reservations in France, call © **3635;** in Belgium, © **020/528- 28-28;** in Germany, © **11861;** and in Holland, © **0900/9296.** Or book online at **www.thalys.com**. Tickets also are available from main rail stations and travel agents.

Further high-speed train connections are the TGV, which arrives in Brussels from France (excluding Paris), and the ICE trains that speed in from Frankfurt, Germany.

TO THE NETHERLANDS On the **Thalys** high-speed train, travel times from Paris-Nord station to Amsterdam Centraal Station (via Brussels, Antwerp, Rotterdam, The Hague, and Schiphol Airport) are 4 hours and 10 minutes, and from Brussels Midi station they are 2 hours and 15 minutes. Departures are approximately every hour. For Thalys reservations in Holland, call © **0900/ 9296.** Or book online at **www.thalys. com**. Tickets also are available from main rail stations and travel agents.

TO LUXEMBOURG Direct, though relatively slow, international trains connect Luxembourg with Brussels, Amsterdam, Paris, and Cologne. None of the high-speed international trains—Eurostar, Thalys, TGV—serve Luxembourg City.

GETTING THERE BY BUS

Eurolines has the most comprehensive bus network in Europe. For reservations, call ℭ **08705/143219** in Britain; ℭ **02/274-13-50** in Belgium; or ℭ **020/560-8788** in the Netherlands. Or book online at **www.eurolines.com**.

TO BELGIUM Eurolines has bus service (through the Channel Tunnel) between London Victoria bus station and Brussels's Gare du Nord bus station, with up to four departures daily. Travel time is 8 hours.

TO THE NETHERLANDS Eurolines has bus service between London and Amsterdam, with four departures daily. Travel time is 12 hours.

TO LUXEMBOURG Luxembourg City can be reached by **Eurolines** bus from London, with two departures a day, and from Amsterdam, both via Brussels. Travel time is 13 hours from London and 7 hours from Amsterdam.

GETTING THERE BY CAR

The Benelux countries are crisscrossed by a dense network of major highways connecting them with other European countries. Distances are relatively short. Road conditions are excellent throughout all three Benelux countries, service stations are plentiful, and highways have good signs. Traffic congestion in both Brussels and Amsterdam, however, can cause monumental tie-ups—in these two cities, it's best to park your car at your hotel garage and use local transportation or walk (the best way, incidentally, to see either city).

VIA THE CHANNEL TUNNEL FROM BRITAIN The fast and efficient **Eurotunnel** (ℭ **08705/353535** in Britain; www.eurotunnel.com) auto-transporter trains transport your car through the Channel Tunnel from Folkestone, England, to Calais, France (a 35-min. trip). Departures are every 15 minutes at peak times, every 30 minutes at times of average demand, and every hour at night.

11 Packages for the Independent Traveler

Package tours offer a way to buy the airfare, accommodations, and other elements of your trip (such as car rentals, airport transfers, and sometimes even activities) at the same time and often at discounted prices.

 Ask Before You Go

Before you invest in a package deal or an escorted tour:

- Always ask about the **cancellation policy.** Can you get your money back? Is a deposit required?
- Ask about the **accommodations choices and prices** for each. Then look up the hotels' reviews in a Frommer's guide and check their rates online for your specific dates of travel. Also find out what types of rooms are offered.
- Request a complete **schedule.** (Escorted tours only)
- Ask about the **size** and demographics of the group. (Escorted tours only)
- Discuss what is included in the **price,** such as transportation, meals, tips, airport transfers, and so on. (Escorted tours only)
- Finally, look for **hidden expenses.** Ask whether airport departure fees and taxes, for example, are included in the total cost—they rarely are.

One good source of package deals is the airlines themselves. Most major airlines offer air/land packages, including **American Airlines Vacations** (© 800/321-2121; www.aavacations.com), **Delta Vacations** (© 800/221-6666; www.deltavacations.com), **Continental Airlines Vacations** (© 800/301-3800; www.covacations.com), and **United Vacations** (© 888/854-3899; www.unitedvacations.com). Several big **online travel agencies**—Expedia, Travelocity, Orbitz, Site59, and Lastminute.com—also do a brisk business in packages.

In addition, travel packages are listed in the travel section of your local Sunday newspaper. Or check ads in the national travel magazines such as *Arthur Frommer's Budget Travel Magazine, Travel + Leisure, National Geographic Traveler,* and *Condé Nast Traveler.*

12 Escorted General-Interest Tours

Escorted tours are structured group tours with a group leader. The price usually includes everything from airfare to hotels, meals, tours, admission costs, and local transportation.

Despite the fact that escorted tours require big deposits and predetermine hotels, restaurants, and itineraries, many people derive security and peace of mind from the structure they offer. Escorted tours—whether they're navigated by bus, motorcoach, train, or boat—let travelers sit back and enjoy the trip without having to drive or worry about details. They take you to the maximum number of sights in the minimum amount of time with the least amount of hassle. They're particularly convenient for people with limited mobility and they can be a great way to make new friends.

On the downside, you'll have little opportunity for serendipitous interaction with locals. The tours can be jampacked with activities, leaving little room for individual sightseeing, whim, or adventure—plus they often focus on the heavily touristed sites, so you miss out on lesser-known gems.

13 Getting Around Belgium, Holland & Luxembourg

BY TRAIN

One of the best rail systems in the world operates in and between these small countries. There is virtually no spot so remote that it cannot easily be reached by trains that are fast, clean, and almost always on time. Furthermore, rail travel is a marvelous way to meet the locals, because the people of the Benelux countries spend as much time riding public transportation as they do behind the wheel of an automobile. Schedules are exact—if departure is set for 12:01pm, that means 12:01pm precisely, not 12:03pm—and station stops are sometimes as short as 3 or 4 minutes, which means you must be fleet of foot in getting on and off.

RAIL PASSES

An important consideration for anyone planning to travel a lot by train is an appropriate pass allowing reduced-rate travel. In addition to those referred to below, Belgium, the Netherlands, and Luxembourg have discount rail passes for travel within their own country's borders. In each country there are many lower-cost options, including cheaper weekend and day returns, reductions for multiple journeys, and reductions for more than one passenger (not all options are available in each country). You should always ask about lower-cost options before buying. You'll find more details in the planning chapters of each country.

EURAIL PASSES The **Eurailpass** (www.eurail.com) allows unlimited first-class travel throughout the rail systems of many European countries, including the Benelux countries, at a cost of $588 for 10 days and $762 for 15 days. The **Eurail Youth Pass** gives you the same deal at discount rates and in second class, and there are other variations. These passes should be purchased before you leave the United States (they're more expensive if you buy them in Europe) and are available from **Rail Europe** (✆ **800/438-7245;** www.raileurope.com) and from travel agents.

BENELUX PASS If all or most of your travel within Belgium, Holland, and Luxembourg will be by train—and provided you plan to travel by train *a lot*—a good investment may be the **Benelux Tourrail Pass,** available through **Rail Europe** (✆ **800/438-7245;** www.raileurope.com), and through travel agents. It gives you unlimited travel in all three countries on any 5 days in a 1-month period. The pass costs $228 for first class, $163 for second class. But if you're not traveling far, or often, don't bother with this pass. It's hard to make it pay off because most trips in these three countries are so short and relatively cheap. Even if you cram in Amsterdam, Haarlem, Leiden, Delft, The Hague, Antwerp, Bruges, Ghent, and Brussels, you'll still spend on point-to-point tickets significantly less than what you'd pay for a Benelux Tourrail Pass.

BY CAR

Drivers need only produce a valid driver's license from your home country. While getting around by train is relaxing and fast, and touring by bicycle is healthier and more human in pace, traveling by car still gives you the most freedom to ramble at your own speed, either on or off the beaten path. You'll find information on specific requirements, rules of the road, gasoline prices, maps, automobile clubs, and other driving assistance resources in the appropriate chapters for each country.

There is a major proviso to this, however. The Benelux countries have a high density of population in relation to their size, so roads are busy. In addition, many drivers in the region have high-density road aggression, so driving can degenerate into a struggle for survival. The major roads are often busiest precisely at the most popular vacation times, and accidents are not uncommon.

Virtually all major **car-rental** companies have offices in the three capital cities and some other large cities, though arranging a rental outside a metropolitan area can present problems. Names and locations of rental companies are listed in the appropriate chapters for each country.

BY BUS

Intercity bus service ranges from poor to nonexistent throughout the Benelux countries. This is not as bad as it sounds, because the rail network is among the best in the world, and fast, comfortable intercity trains do most of the work. If you really want to, you can travel intercity by bus, but the buses stop a lot en route, so trip times are long, and you often have to change at an intermediate town—for example, a trip from Brussels to Liège is two journeys: Brussels to Leuven and Leuven to Liège. Tourist offices and bus stations can furnish schedule and fare information.

The exception to the avoid-the-bus rule is in sparsely populated places where there is little or no rail service, such as Zeeland in Holland and the Ardennes in Belgium. In such areas there are more regional bus services, though the buses still may be few and far between. In general, unless you have a specific reason for wanting to go by bus, you'll always find it better to go by train.

All cities have excellent bus and/or tram (and in two cases, electric trolley bus) service. Some have metro (subway) service, which means you can easily leave your car at the hotel and avoid city driving woes.

BY PLANE

The Benelux cities are so close together that air travel is really not worth the added expense unless time is a vital factor (and even then you might still get to your destination quicker by train). Air service among the three countries is provided by **KLM Cityhopper, KLM Exel,** and **SN Brussels Airlines.** The KLM associates fly frequent scheduled services between Amsterdam, Rotterdam, Eindhoven, Maastricht, Groningen, and Enschede in Holland; to Brussels and Antwerp in Belgium; and to Luxembourg City. SN Brussels Airlines flies from Brussels to Amsterdam. For current schedules, fares, and reservations, contact **KLM** (© 020/ 474-7747; www.klm.com) in Holland; and **SN Brussels Airlines** (© 070/35-13-13; www.flysn.com) in Belgium. See "Getting There," earlier in this chapter, for other KLM, SN Brussels Airlines, and Luxair contact details.

BY BICYCLE

Belgium, Holland, and Luxembourg are all ideal biking countries. In Holland, especially, and in parts of Flanders, there are often special bicycle tracks in towns and cities, and well-signed long-distance routes. You can also take your bike on a train. Rental bikes are usually available at major rail stations and often at smaller ones, and some even allow you to pick up and return bikes at stations at either end of a particular route. All three national tourist boards can help you plan an itinerary best suited to your physical condition and time restraints. Holland's excellent *Cycling in Holland* publication is especially useful. Organized bicycle tours can be arranged through **International Bike Tours,** P.O. Box 754, Essex, CT 06426 (© **860/767-7005;** fax 860/ 767-3090); and **Cycletours,** Keizersgracht 181, 1016 DR Amsterdam (© **20/ 627-4098;** fax 20/627-9032).

BY HITCHHIKING

Hitchhiking is permitted (not encouraged) in Belgium and Luxembourg, though prohibited on highways (you can, however, stand on the approach road). It's officially forbidden in Holland, but many a blind eye is turned by officialdom to those standing in a safe spot to hitchhike.

14 Tips on Accommodations

Traditional European hotels tend to be simpler than American ones and emphasize cleanliness and friendliness over amenities. For example, even in the cheapest American chain motel, free cable is as standard as indoor plumbing. In Europe, few hotels below the moderate level have in-room TVs.

Unless otherwise noted, all hotel rooms in this book have private en-suite bathrooms. However, the standard European hotel bathroom might not look like what you're used to. For example, one European concept of a shower is a nozzle stuck in the bathroom wall and a drain in the floor. Shower curtains are optional. In some cramped private bathrooms, you have to relocate the toilet paper outside the bathroom before turning on the shower and drenching the whole room. Another interesting fixture is the "half tub," in which there's only room to sit, rather than lie down. Hot water may be available only once a day and not on demand—this is especially true with shared bathrooms. Heating water is costly, and many smaller hotels do so only once daily, in the morning.

Tips Dial E for Easy

For directions on how to call places in Belgium, Holland, and Luxembourg, see the "Telephones" listings in the "Fast Facts" sections of chapters 4, 11, and 18.

Belgium, the Netherlands, and Luxembourg established the Benelux Hotel Classification System back in 1978 and updated the standards in 1994. Each establishment that accepts guests must publicly display a sign indicating its classification (from "1" for those with minimum amenities to "5" for deluxe, full-service hotels). The national tourist boards do an excellent job of providing full accommodations listings and advance booking for visitors. The Belgian and the Netherlands tourist offices (see "Visitor Information," earlier in this chapter), and the **Netherlands Reservations Center (NRC),** Nieuwe Gouw 1, 1442 LE Purmerend, Netherlands (© **0299/689-144** or 0299/689-154; www.hotelres.nl), will reserve accommodations for you at no charge before you leave home. The Luxembourg Tourist Office can furnish a complete list of accommodations in the Grand Duchy.

In all three countries, you can choose among luxury hotels in city or rural locations; smaller urban hotels with moderate rates and somewhat limited facilities; and charming, family-run country inns. No matter what end of the price scale it's on, each lodging will be spotlessly clean and will feature a staff dedicated to personal attention and excellent service. The rates quoted include the service charge (usually 15%), tax and, in most cases, breakfast.

Be sure to inquire about discounts when you book your room. Many hotels have a variety of room rates. It's sometimes possible to pay less if you settle for a shower instead of full bathroom facilities. Also, weekend or midweek rates are often available.

3

Suggested Benelux Itineraries

The quintessential Benelux experience is a city one. Not many foreign visitors come for the Belgian beaches, even fewer for the Dutch mountains, and none at all for Luxembourg's vast empty spaces. On the other hand, Benelux cities—big and small—are among Europe's cultural and historical glories. This doesn't mean there are no places of scenic beauty; there are actually more than you might think.

Most important, bring as much time with you as you can afford. You might want to indulge yourself by stepping onboard an occasional slow train rather than always rushing to catch the high-speed Thalys or an InterCity Express; and you can drive on at least some country roads instead of zipping along on expressways. Even going by bike isn't out of the question.

Getting around Benelux is a snap, but deciding what to take in and what to leave out is difficult. Hopefully, these suggested itineraries will help you organize your time as you plan your own trip to Benelux.

1 Belgium & Holland in 1 Week

Few countries can boast of cities more justly celebrated than Amsterdam, Brussels, and Bruges. Not far behind are Ghent, Antwerp, The Hague, Maastricht, Delft, Leiden, and Luxembourg City, among others. Some of these stellar places can't fit on this itinerary. (Don't blame me: It was you who decided to come for only a week!) Travel between the cities listed here is easy—you can go by car or ride Belgium and Holland's excellent trains.

Day 1: Arrive in Amsterdam ★★★
Get in early and get going—time is of the essence! First up is a 1-hour **canal cruise** (p. 292). This is the Dutch capital's tourist-trap par excellence, but it is also *the very best* way to view much of this canal-threaded city in a reasonable time. Now choose *just one*—a tough decision that will depend on your own interests—from Amsterdam's three standout museums: the **Van Gogh Museum** (p. 283), the **Rijksmuseum** (p. 282), and the **Anne Frank House** (p. 279). A walk in the old hippie-paradise **Vondelpark** (p. 292) to clear your head can be followed by drinks at the **Café Américain** (p. 275) on Leidseplein. Dine in the evening at a traditional Dutch restaurant like **Haesje Claes** (p. 268) or an Indonesian one like **Tempo Doeloe** (p. 274).

Day 2: The Hague ★★
The Dutch seat of government is a 50-minute train ride from Amsterdam. Parliament is in the heart of town, in the **Binnenhof** and **Ridderzaal** (p. 332), and you can take a guided tour if you've planned ahead. Visit the **Koninklijk Kabinet van Schilderijen** (p. 334), in the **Mauritshuis** palace, for its superb

paintings by the Old Dutch and Flemish Masters. Then hop on a tram and take a short ride to the seacoast at **Scheveningen** (p. 340), where you can breathe in fresh sea air and have coffee at the splendid **Kurhaus Hotel** (p. 343) before taking the tram back to The Hague to catch a late-afternoon train to Brussels.

Day 3: Brussels 🎇🎇🎇

If you don't want to be packing and unpacking every day, lodge in Brussels and do Belgium's historic cities as easy day trips. In the "capital of Europe," start out at the **Grand-Place** (p. 90), taking time to absorb the magnificent old square's architectural details and animated spirit. A date with Rubens, Brueghel, Magritte, and other notable Belgian artists awaits you in the elegant **Musées Royaux des Beaux-Arts** (p. 96). Next, you might want to stroll amid Masonic symbols in the **Parc de Bruxelles** (p. 101), and view the **Palais Royal** (p. 96) and the **Palais de la Nation (Parliament;** p. 101), on opposite sides of the park. In the evening, dine at **'t Kelderke** (p. 85), a traditional Bruxellois restaurant on the Grand-Place.

Day 4: Bruges's Medieval Splendor 🎇🎇🎇

By train, Bruges is an hour from Brussels. Once you arrive, hire wheels at the rail station or at a store in town and you can easily tour the city by **bicycle** (p. 117). A must-do is a **canal cruise** (p. 135); this will mark you indelibly as a tourist, but what you lose in street cred you'll make up for by seeing a lot in a short time. Later, stroll around the connected medieval **Burg** (p. 127) and **Markt** (p. 126) central squares. On the Burg, visit the **Heilig-Bloedbasiliek** (p. 127) for a glimpse of a relic that's said to be drops of Christ's blood; on the Markt, climb the **Belfry** (p. 126) for splendid city views. Next, head to **Kantcentrum** (p. 131) and watch how Bruges's handmade lace is crafted.

Day 5: Ghent 🎇🎇

Just a half-hour train ride from Brussels, Ghent has a different, thoroughly Flemish, character. Scoot to the center of town by tram, and get your bearings by climbing the stairs or taking the elevator up above the city's rooftops to the 14th-century **Belfry's** (p. 143) viewing platform. Across elegant Sint-Baafsplein from the Belfry, **Sint-Baafskathedraal** (p. 144) holds one of the world's greatest medieval artworks: Jan van Eyck's altarpiece *The Adoration of the Mystic Lamb* (1432). From the cathedral, stroll to the medieval inner harbor along **Korenlei** and **Graslei** (p. 146), past the forbidding castle of the counts of Flanders, **Het Gravensteen** (p. 143), and then go through the restored medieval **Patershol** district (p. 147).

Day 6: Antwerp 🎇🎇

Forty minutes by train from Brussels, Antwerp is Belgium's second-largest city. Make the most of your time here by riding a tram to the center of town. Visit the **Grote Markt** (p. 155) to view its dramatic Brabo sculpture-fountain, and then stop for a *bolleke* (round glass) of Antwerp's De Koninck beer at the grand old tavern **In Den Engel** (p. 162) on the square. Antwerp means Rubens; to learn more about the artist, go to his former home, the **Rubenshuis** (p. 155), and view his paintings at the **Museum voor Schone Kunsten** (p. 145). Back at Antwerp Centraal Station, stroll around the city's celebrated (though not exactly handsome) **Diamond Quarter** (p. 158) before catching your train.

Day 7: Back to Amsterdam

If you have an early flight home from Amsterdam's **Schiphol Airport,** you'll be happy to know that InterCity trains to Amsterdam from Brussels and Antwerp stop at Schiphol. If you have time to kill in Amsterdam but don't want to stray too far from Centraal Station, take a

Suggested Benelux Itineraries

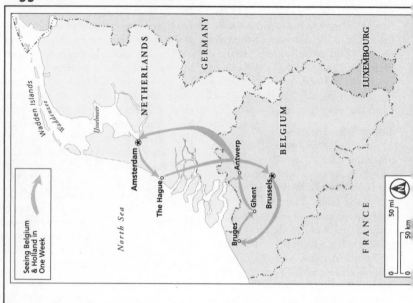

Seeing Belgium & Holland in One Week

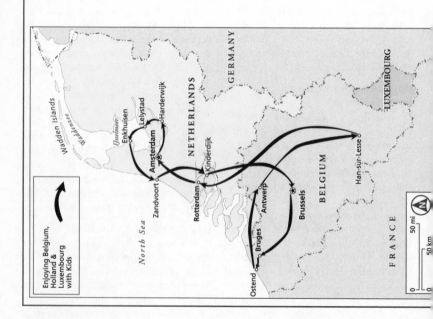

Enjoying Belgium, Holland & Luxembourg with Kids

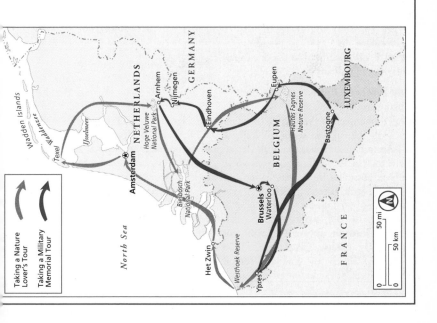

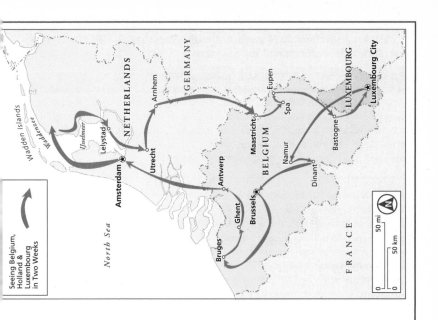

ride onboard one of the **harbor ferries** (p. 250) that depart from the Waterplein-West dock behind the station, for fine views of Amsterdam harbor. More time might permit you to visit historic **Haarlem** (p. 305).

2 Belgium, Holland & Luxembourg in 2 Weeks

If you have 2 weeks in the Benelux lands, you can breathe more easily. You can stroll where you might otherwise have needed to hop on a city tram or bus, and you'll have time to visit Luxembourg. Yes, there's a lot to be said for having 2 weeks. This itinerary is designed for you to travel by car, but you can do most of it by train and an occasional bus. You'll just have to modify some elements.

Day 1: Arrive in Amsterdam ✯✯✯

With 2 weeks, you can take your time—all the while looking cool and laid-back. But before you do the cool thing, I suggest you don a disguise and step onboard a touristy **canal-cruise boat** (p. 292). The view of Amsterdam is best from the water, and how else are you going to see it? Afterward, stroll along part of the 17th-century Golden Age *Grachtengordel* or **Canal Belt** (p. 248)—comprising the Herengracht, Keizersgracht, and Prinsengracht canals—starting out at the **Westerkerk** (p. 290) and going by way of **Leidseplein** (p. 248) to **Rembrandtplein.** For dinner, head to the fine canalside *eetcafé* **De Prins** (p. 275).

Day 2: More of Amsterdam's Best

This morning, you have to make a choice—between the **Van Gogh Museum** (p. 283), the **Rijksmuseum** (p. 282), or the **Anne Frank House** (p. 279). (If you want to visit Anne's home, try to go as early as possible.) In the afternoon, tour the **Red Light District** (p. 292) or, if that sounds like an indecent proposal, walk through the old working-class—now trendy—**Jordaan** district (p. 248). For dinner, try **Haesje Claes** (p. 268), a traditional Dutch restaurant, or **Tempo Doeloe** (p. 274) for Indonesian cuisine.

Day 3: The IJsselmeer ✯✯

Today, rent a car and go north out of Amsterdam along the western shore of the IJsselmeer (p. 311), a freshwater lake that was once a sea known as the Zuiderzee. Go through **Marken** (p. 313), **Monnickendam** (p. 313), **Volendam** (p. 312), **Edam** (p. 314), **Hoorn** (p. 315), **Enkhuizen** (p. 316), and **Medemblik** (p. 318). Cross over the **Afsluitdijk** (p. 319), the great barrier completed in 1932 that closed off the mouth of the Zuiderzee. Turn south along the eastern IJsselmeer shore, through **Makkum** (p. 370), **Hindeloopen** (p. 370), **Stavoren** (p. 372), and **Urk** (p. 416), before driving across the flat polders of **Flevoland** province (p. 392) back to Amsterdam.

Day 4: Driving to Arnhem

On the road again. Places worth taking in along the way include **Breukelen** (p. 398), the village from which Brooklyn, New York, takes its name (it even has a Breukelen Bridge!); the **Vinkeveense Plassen** lakes landscape; and **Utrecht** (p. 392) for a brief stroll through this historic ecclesiastical city's canal-threaded Old Town. **Arnhem** (p. 404) was the target of a gallant but doomed Allied airborne assault in World War II, and you can view its storied "bridge too far" across the Rhine. Visit the nearby **Hoge Veluwe National Park** (p. 402)—where you can get around by borrowing a free white bicycle—and its surprising **Kröller-Müller Museum** (p. 403), which contains 278 works by Vincent van Gogh.

Day 5: Drive to Maastricht

This morning, head south to **Nijmegen** (p. 407), once a Roman legionary fortress and later a favorite seat of the Frank king Charlemagne. When you hit the Maas River at inauspiciously named **Grave**, follow its course south. A brief side excursion through **Thorn** (p. 444), the comely "white village," can break up the journey on your way to **Maastricht** (p. 435). This most southerly Dutch city's squares and cobblestone streets are filled with southern charm, not to mention plenty of fine restaurants and cafes.

Day 6: Spa ᚴᚴ

Just over an hour's drive from Maastricht is Spa, Belgium's elegant "town of waters." When you arrive, you can tour the mineral springs in the forests around the town. Then follow an easy circuit from Spa through the northern **Ardennes** (p. 215). Along the way, you can stop in **Eupen** (p. 226), the "capital" of Belgium's small German-speaking community; the **Hautes Fagnes Nature Reserve** (p. 226), where you can take time out for a walk on this wind-swept high moorland; **Malmédy**; the attraction park at **Coo (Trois Ponts);** and **Stavelot.**

Day 7: Luxembourg City ᚴᚴ

Driving south through the Ardennes in Belgium and Luxembourg, by way of **Bastogne** (p. 218), today you'll make your way toward the capital of the Grand Duchy of Luxembourg. Stroll its streets and squares, with their affluent yet somewhat Ruritanian air. View the dramatic gorge that separates the Old Town from the New Town, and take in the **casemates** (p. 460), remnants of once powerful fortifications; the grand duke's seat in the **Palais Grand-Ducal** (p. 460); and the **Cathédrale de Notre-Dame** (p. 460).

Day 8: Namur ᚴᚴ

On day 8, take a 2-hour trip on the expressway from Luxembourg City to Namur on the Meuse River. For a more scenic route, go by way of the **Abbaye Notre-Dame d'Orval** (p. 218), which will add an hour or two to your drive. In Namur, visit the hilltop **Citadelle** (p. 199), and stroll through **Le Corbeil** (p. 198), the oldest part of town. A short, charming out-of-town excursion is along the Meuse to **Dinant** (p. 202), which you can combine with a visit to the **Jardins d'Annevoie** (p. 200). In the evening, try your luck at Namur's **Casino** (p. 200).

Day 9: Brussels ᚴᚴᚴ

Today, you'll scoot along the expressway to Belgium's capital. The magnificent **Grand-Place** (p. 90) is an ideal staring point for the drive. You might also want to fit in a "pilgrimage" to the nearby *Manneken-Pis* statue (p. 94). Following this, stop at the **Musées Royaux des Beaux-Arts** (p. 96) to view works by Rubens, Brueghel, Magritte, and other notable Belgian artists. Then stroll amid Masonic symbols in the **Parc de Bruxelles** (p. 101), stopping to see the **Palais Royal** (p. 96) and the **Palais de la Nation** (**Parliament**; p. 101)—on opposite sides of the park. In the evening, dine on the Grand-Place at **'t Kelderke** (p. 85), a traditional Bruxellois restaurant.

Day 10: More of Brussels's Best

After breakfast, go shopping (or window-shopping) at the 19th-century **Galeries Royales St-Hubert** (p. 105) and then make your way to the **Cathédrale des Sts-Michel-et-Gudule** (p. 98). Go up onto rue Royale and take a tram to **place du Grand Sablon** (p. 91) to browse its antiques stores (or, on weekends, the antiques market). When you're finished there, cross over rue de la Régence to tranquil **place du Petit Sablon** (p. 91) and enjoy a rest in its central garden. In the afternoon, take a trip to the **Atomium** and **Bruparck** (p. 71) complex on Brussels's northern edge; or to the **battlefield of Waterloo** (p. 113), just south of the city.

Day 11: Bruges ★★★

Not much more than an hour on the expressway (once you've broken free from Brussels's congested ring road), Bruges is the Benelux's prime medieval property. Do a **canal cruise** (p. 135) to give yourself an easy introduction to the city's layout and character. Afterward, you can stroll around the connected medieval **Burg** (p. 127) and **Markt** (p. 126) central squares. On the Burg, visit the **Heilig-Bloedbasiliek** (p. 127) for a glimpse of a relic that's said to be drops of Christ's blood; on the Markt, climb the **Belfry** (p. 126) for splendid city views. In the late afternoon, go to **Kantcentrum** (p. 131) and see how Bruges's handmade lace is crafted.

Day 12: More of Bruges's Best

This morning, try to visit the **Groeninge Museum** (p. 130) to view its fine collection of works by the Flemish Old Masters dubbed the "Flemish Primitives." Next, stroll through the courtyard of the 15th-century, Burgundian-era **Palace of the Lords of Gruuthuse** (p. 131). There's a museum inside if you want to check it out. On the way to the **Begijnhof** (p. 133), pop into **Onze-Lieve-Vrouwekerk** (p. 132) to see its *Madonna and Child* sculpture by Michelangelo. In the afternoon, if you have time, consider taking a side trip to the venerable nearby canal-side village of **Damme** (p. 138).

Day 13: Ghent ★★ & Antwerp ★★

These two Flemish cities are close to Bruges and close together (by road, Ghent is 53km/33 miles from Bruges; and Antwerp is 91km/56 miles from Bruges and 64km/40 miles from Ghent). When you arrive in Ghent, head to its central district and up to the top of the 14th-century **Belfry** (p. 143) for beautiful city views. In nearby **Sint-Baafs-kathedraal** (p. 144), you can lay eyes on a medieval masterpiece: Jan van Eyck's *The Adoration of the Mystic Lamb* (1432). From the cathedral, stroll to the medieval inner harbor along **Korenlei** and **Graslei** (p. 146). Next, it's onto Antwerp. Here you can visit the **Grote Markt** (p. 155) and view its dramatic Brabo sculpture-fountain. For an insight into the artist Rubens, visit his home, the **Rubenshuis** (p. 155).

Day 14: Back to Amsterdam

From Antwerp, Amsterdam's Schiphol Airport is a couple hours up the expressway. If you have time before your flight, consider spending it in one of the following places (all close to the airport). In spring, you can breathe the scent from millions of flowers at **Keukenhof Gardens** (p. 322) in Lisse; at other times of year, tour sites in **Leiden** (p. 359) associated with the Pilgrim Fathers. Should neither option appeal, perhaps you'd prefer a visit to the beach at **Zandvoort** (p. 309).

3 Belgium, Holland & Luxembourg for Families

The young folks'll be pleased to learn there's more to the Benelux lands than paintings by the Old Masters *(sigh!)*; Gothic architecture *(groan!)*; struggling with French, Dutch, and Lëtzebuergesch *(aak!)*; and eating mussels *(no way!)*. Actually, you don't need to worry too much about the lingo since most natives speak English. And there are hundreds of fun family-friendly things to see and do in these three countries—remember, Benelux burghers have kids too!

Day 1: Brussels ★★★

Whenever the kids step out of line in Brussels, uttering these magic words

should get their attention: "Maybe we should tour the European Union administrative buildings today." I'd wager that they (and you) would prefer the **Atomium** (p. 102). And while you're there, in the city's northern **Bruparck** district (p. 71), you can spend some time at the **Océade** water park (p. 71) and **Mini-Europe** (p. 103). Back in the center of town, treat the kids to an exposé of bold little *Manneken-Pis* (p. 94); grown-ups usually wonder what all the fuss is about, but kids love him. By the way: Going around the city by **tram** (p. 72) can't hurt.

Day 2: More of Brussels

Boys, especially, might want to take a look under the hood of **Autoworld** (p. 97) today. And is it being sexist to suggest that the girls might prefer costumes and lace at the **Musée du Costume et de la Dentelle** (p. 100)? Both genders will likely agree that the comic strips and characters at the **Centre Belge de la Bande-Dessinée** (p. 102) are pretty cool.

Day 3: Bruges 🎡🎡🎡

In this historic Flemish city, you can swerve past Old Masters, Gothic architecture, and mussel-slurping diners in one fast move. Achieve this satisfying feat by visiting the **Boudewijn Seapark** (p. 135) or the **Kinderboerderij Domein De Zeven Torentjes** (p. 135)—(or maybe both?). The open-top **canal-cruise boats** (p. 135) are another good bet. And it's safe to go around by rented **pedal-bike** (p. 117) in the center of town.

Day 4: The Belgian Coast

A day at the seacoast is a no-brainer for families, especially in summer—just imagine building sandcastles on the beach, swimming in the sea, and riding beach buggies and **sand-yachts** (p. 180). You can get around by **Coast Tram** (p. 166). At Ostend there's the **Noordzeeaquarium** (p. 173), and the museum ships *Mercator* (p. 172) and *Amandine* (p. 172). Up the coast at Knokke-Heist, allow some

time to check out the bird sanctuary **Natuurreservaat Het Zwin** (p. 176).

Day 5: Antwerp 🎡🎡

Begin day 5 in Antwerp, with a visit to Belgium's only traditional **zoo** (p. 157). Then, in the afternoon, you can cross over to **Aquatopia** (p. 157). For other options, consider a **cruise** (p. 158) downriver to the harbor, and/or a visit to the **National Maritime Museum** (p. 156).

Days 6 & 7: The Ardennes

From Antwerp, the drive here takes long enough that I'd suggest allocating 2 days for your family's visit to **Han-sur-Lesse** (p. 219). On the first day, drive to the village and visit the underground caverns of the **Grottes de Han** (p. 219); the next day, spend some time at the **Réserve d'Animaux Sauvages** (p. 220) before moving on.

Day 8: Rotterdam 🎡

Today, make your way to the **Euromast** (p. 347) for the greatest views of Rotterdam. Afterward, you'll probably need to choose between a **boat tour** (p. 349) of the city's vast harbor and a visit to the outstanding **Blijdorp Zoo** (p. 349), but if you have time for both, by all means fit them in.

Day 9: Amsterdam 🎡🎡🎡

Going around Amsterdam by **tram** (p. 249) is fun for the whole family. I'm not sure, though, about going by **bicycle** (p. 250). Parents might need to spend too much time watching out for the kids. I suppose it all depends on what age the children are. A **canalboat cruise** (p. 292) is a good idea. A visit to the **Anne Frank House** (p. 279) is interesting and thought-provoking for children about as old as Anne was when she hid from the Nazis here and wrote her famous diary. After this, try the **Artis Zoo** (p. 289), or—if you've had enough of zoos by now—the **Scheepvaartmuseum (Maritime Museum;** p. 286), where you can go onboard the *Amsterdam,* a full-size replica 18th-century ocean-going sailing ship.

Day 10: More of Amsterdam

Today, choose between a visit to **Madame Tussaud's** (p. 290) and the **NEMO Science Center** (p. 291)—either one is worthwhile, but both in a single day can be too much, unless it's raining. By way of variation, you could try **in-line skating** in Vondelpark (p. 294), ice skating at **Jaap Edenbaan** (p. 294), or bowling at **Knijn Bowling** (p. 294).

Day 11: Dolphins & Sailing Ships

From Amsterdam (your base), drive east today to **Harderwijk** (p. 401) and visit the outstanding **Dolfinarium** (p. 401). Cross over into Flevoland province and head to Lelystad. Here, at **Batavia Wharf** (p. 415), a full-size replica of a 17th-century sailing ship, the *Batavia,* is moored, and a man-of-war from the same century, *De Zeven Provinciën,* is being constructed.

Day 12: Enkhuizen ⟡

This town lies on the western shore of the IJsselmeer, a freshwater lake that until 1932 was a sea known as the Zuiderzee. Enkhuizen hosts the superb **Zuiderzeemuseum** (p. 317), which aims to recreate traditional life around the transformed sea. Between getting to and from Enkhuizen and visiting both sections of this large museum, you'll need most of a day to do it all justice.

Day 13: Zandvoort

Always supposing the weather is good, there's nothing your standard young Amsterdammer likes more than to take a train for the short ride to Amsterdam's favorite seacoast resort, **Zandvoort** (p. 309), on the North Sea.

Day 14: Back to Brussels

One way to break the monotony of a 3-hour drive back to Brussels is to stop off at the cluster of windmills at **Kinderdijk** (p. 353), close to Rotterdam.

4 A Nature Lover's Tour

The natural world exists in Benelux, and not only in the great landscape paintings by 17th-century Dutch Old Masters. This tour takes you to see some of the region's prettiest nature reserves, national parks, and scenic places.

Day 1: Arrive in Amsterdam

In your rented car from Schiphol Airport, swing nimbly past the city's Red Light District haunts and dope dens on the ring road expressway. Head north to **Den Helder** (p. 324), at the tip of the Noord-Holland peninsula. From the harbor, cross over on the ferry (with or without your car) to **Texel** (p. 326), the largest of Holland's string of Wadden Islands. From the **EcoMare** visitor center (p. 326), you can observe many species of birds at several reserves, which together cover a third of the island.

Day 2: Drive to Apeldoorn

Spend the morning on Texel before crossing over on the ferry back to Den Helder.

Drive to "Royal Apeldoorn," a good home base for visiting the Hoge Veluwe National Park tomorrow.

Day 3: Hoge Veluwe National Park ⟡⟡

Enjoy a full day at the **national park** (p. 402), which has a landscape consisting of heathland, sand drifts, and forest. The park's animal inhabitants include deer, wild boar, and mouflon. You can get around by borrowing one of the park's free white bicycles.

Day 4: Drive to Dordrecht

Dordrecht, a town close to Rotterdam. is the northern access point to the **Biesbosch National Park** (p. 430), a freshwater tidal zone of wetlands, marshes, and partly drowned islands in the estuary of the Maas and Waal rivers. Visit the northern sector today, from the **Biesboschcentrum Dordrecht** (p. 430).

Day 5: The Southern Biesbosch

On day 5, drive to the southern access point for the **Biesbosch National Park** (p. 430) at Drimmelen, and tour the southern sector from the **Biesbosch Bezoekerscentrum Drimmelen** (p. 430).

Day 6: Drive to Eupen

A small town that's the "capital" of Belgium's German-speaking East Cantons district, **Eupen** (p. 226) is a convenient base for getting out to the nearby **Hautes Fagnes Nature Reserve** (in German, the Höhes Venn; p. 226).

Day 7: The Hautes Fagnes 𝄞𝄞𝄞

Walk along the boardwalks and forest trails that snake through the **Hautes Fagnes** (p. 226). Stop by the **Botrange Visitor Center** (p. 226), and other access points at **Mont Rigi** and **Baraque Michel.** If there's time, check out another segment of the park on the Eupen-Monschau (Germany) road, **Haus Ternell.**

Day 8: Drive to De Panne 𝄞

At the opposite end of Belgium, right next to the French border, this North Sea coast resort is home to the dunes landscape of the **Westhoekreservaat (Westhoek Reserve)** (p. 180). Tour the reserve.

Day 9: Het Zwin Nature Reserve 𝄞

Today, drive to the northern end of the Belgian coast and visit **Het Zwin** (p. 176), a small but important breeding and feeding ground for seabirds and wetlands birds.

Day 10: Back to Amsterdam

Head north into Holland's Zeeland province, and cross over the Western Schelde estuary by the road tunnel. Continue to Rotterdam and the expressway north to Schiphol Airport.

5 A Military Buff's Tour of the Benelux

I call this a "military buff's tour," but it may be more appropriate to think of it as a military memorial tour. Belgium and Luxembourg have long histories as battlefields, usually in other countries' quarrels. Belgium was particularly badly handled in World War I, and Holland in World War II. Although this itinerary revolves around a grim subject, it also passes through scenic parts of all three countries. The tour is best done by car.

Day 1: Waterloo 𝄞

South of Brussels, the French emperor Napoleon Bonaparte met final defeat at the **Battle of Waterloo** (p. 113) in 1815. You can tour this largely preserved battlefield and visit the duke of Wellington's headquarters, now the **Musée Wellington** (p. 114).

Day 2: Drive to Ypres (Ieper)

A 2-hour drive from Brussels, bypassing Ghent and Kortrijk, brings you to the medieval cloth town of **Ypres** (p. 182), a crucible of fighting on the World War I

Western Front that claimed the lives of 500,000 soldiers—Allied and German. The now peaceful Flanders fields are sprinkled with military cemeteries and a few sections of trenches.

Day 3: Drive to Bastogne

Drive east past Tournai and Mons, to the Meuse River at **Namur** (p. 198). Continuing eastward into the rolling **Ardennes** hills (p. 215), you'll pass the scenes of many a hard-fought action from the Battle of the Bulge in the winter of 1944 and 1945, at places like Marche-en-Famenne,

Rochefort, and La Roche-en-Ardenne. None was harder than the struggle that surrounded U.S. troops waged to hold the strategic crossroads town of **Bastogne** (p. 218). Visit the star-shaped **Mardasson Memorial** (p. 219) outside of town.

Day 4: Drive to Eupen

Cross into Luxembourg today. Starting at **Echternach** (p. 472), follow the Our River upstream along the German border. This was a thinly manned but staunchly defended U.S. front line on December 16, 1944, when the surprise German offensive in the Ardennes erupted. Pass through **Vianden** (p. 471) and **Clervaux** (p. 470); then take the road the GI's dubbed the "Skyline Drive," to Sankt-Vith. From Losheim to Rocherath-Krinkelt, you'll cross the assault route taken by Hitler's SS *panzer* divisions. Foxholes once held by American troops still exist in the forests. The U.S. Fifth Corps headquarters was in **Eupen** (p. 226).

Day 5: Drive to Nijmegen

Take the expressway via Liège and Maastricht, for rapid deployment to **Eindhoven** (p. 433), the first scene of action in the Allied offensive into Nazi-occupied Holland in September 1944. Follow the bitterly contested "Hell's Highway" north through Veghel and Grave to **Nijmegen** (p. 407). The U.S. 82nd Airborne Division suffered heavy losses taking and holding the Groesbeek Heights east of town, the road bridges over the Maas River at Grave, and the Waal in Nijmegen.

Day 6: Arnhem ⚑

From Nijmegen, north to **Arnhem** (p. 404) is just 16km (10 miles)—a distance that proved fatal for the British 1st Airborne Division, which landed on heathland west of the city to take Arnhem's road bridge over the Rhine—the famous "bridge too far." The British held out for a week at **Oosterbeek** (p. 405), while Polish paratroops landed at **Driel** (p. 406).

Day 7: Return to Brussels

An expressway goes southwest from Arnhem to connect with the north-south expressway at Breda. From there, you can go south via Antwerp to Brussels.

4

Planning Your Trip to Belgium

Belgium is not a difficult country to come to grips with—thanks to its widespread use of English, relatively small size, and excellent tourist infrastructure—but a little forethought when planning your trip can still save you precious time and effort. This chapter gives you the practical information you need to plan your trip.

For information that covers the Benelux countries in general, see chapter 2.

1 The Regions in Brief

Modest little Belgium has never been known to boast of its charms, yet its variety of language, culture, history, and cuisine would do credit to a country many times its size. Belgium's diversity stems from its location at the cultural crossroads of Europe. The boundary between the Continent's Germanic north and Latin south cuts clear across the nation's middle, leaving Belgium divided into two major ethnic regions: Dutch-speaking Flanders and French-speaking Wallonia.

Although international attention is focused on Brussels as the "capital of Europe," there's another Belgium of Gothic cathedrals, medieval castles, cobblestone streets, and tranquil canals waiting in the wings. In a country the size of Maryland, the timeless beauty of Bruges and Ghent are accessible, even to the most hurried visitor, and to get away from it all, there's no better place than the unhurried Ardennes.

BRUSSELS In a sense, Brussels has a split personality. One is this brash new "capital of Europe," increasingly aware of its power and carrying a padded expense account in its elegant leather pocketbook. The other is the old Belgian city—once a seat of emperors, but lately more than a little provincial, tenaciously hanging onto its heritage against the wave of Euroconstruction that has swept over it.

These two cities intersect, of course, generally in a popular bar or restaurant, though they may sit together uneasily. Most foreigners who live here long enough, or who stay on an extended vacation, find they need to choose between the two. As an outsider, it's easy enough to live in the Eurocity. Getting below the surface to the real Brussels is more difficult, but worth the effort.

BRUGES From its 13th-century origins as a cloth-manufacturing town to its current incarnation as a tourism mecca, the main town of West Flanders province seems to have changed little. As in a fairy tale, swans glide down the winding canals, and the stone houses look as if they're made of gingerbread. Even though glass-fronted stores have taken over the ground floors of ancient buildings, and swans scatter before tour boats chugging along the canals, Bruges has made the transition from medieval to modern with remarkable grace. The town seems revitalized rather than crushed by the tremendous influx of tourists.

Belgium

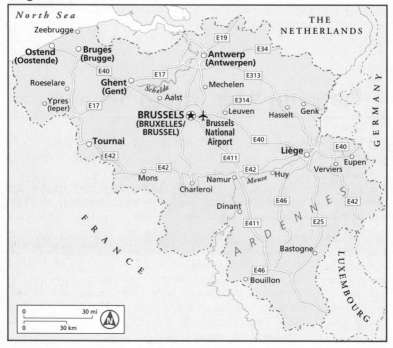

GHENT & ANTWERP The old town at the confluence of the Scheldt and Leie rivers has been spruced up, and **Ghent** has never looked so good. Although this former seat of the powerful counts of Flanders is larger and more citified than Bruges, it has enough cobblestone streets, meandering canals, and antique Flemish architecture to make it nearly as magical as its more famous sister.

Antwerp is a port city, with all the liveliness, sophistication, and occasional seediness you'd expect from the world's fifth-largest port. The city is the acknowledged "Diamond Center of the World," the leading market for cut diamonds and second only to London as an outlet for raw and industrial diamonds. It boasts a magnificent cathedral, a fine-arts museum full of Flemish masterpieces, a maze of medieval streets in the town center, and a vibrant cultural life.

THE BELGIAN COAST & YPRES At the center of the seacoast is **Ostend,** the "Queen of the Coast." It retains a little of the cachet and some of the ambience of its great days as a Victorian beach resort. It's complemented by more modern resorts such as **Knokke-Heist** and **De Panne.**

Having suffered through centuries of intermittent warfare and almost total destruction during World War I, **Ypres (Ieper)** has picked itself up in the years since, its indomitable spirit intact—a spirit that shines in the perseverance underlying its 20th-century rebuilding of 13th-century buildings.

LIEGE, THE MEUSE RIVER & HAINAUT The rugged Meuse River valley, the heartland of French-speaking Wallonia, is speckled with resort towns in which fine cuisine is a way of life. A visit to **Liège, Namur, Huy,** and **Dinant** after being to Brussels and the Flemish art cities of Bruges and Ghent adds another dimension to Belgium.

Tucked into an area south of Brussels that stretches to the French border, Hainaut, Belgium's "green province," can seem isolated from the mainstream of Belgian life, yet possesses prime assets in the historic towns of **Mons** and **Tournai.**

THE ARDENNES   Belgium's wildest, most heavily forested region is its least populated, part of the rugged Ardennes–Eifel Massif, which stretches across into Germany, Luxembourg, and France. French is the most common language, but in the northeast, in the area called the *Ostkantone* (East Cantons), you most often hear German spoken, a residue from the years before 1919 when this part of the Ardennes belonged to Germany.

2 Visitor Information

For contact details of the Belgian tourist offices in the United States, Britain, and other countries, see "Visitor Information," in chapter 2.

In Belgium, for Brussels and French-speaking Wallonia (and its mainly German-speaking Ostkantone district) contact **OPT,** rue St-Bernard 30, 1000 Bruxelles (② **070/221-021,** brochure line 02/ 509-24-00; fax 02/513/04-75; www. opt.be). This is an administrative office only, and is not open for personal visits.

For Brussels and Dutch-speaking Flanders, contact **Toerisme Vlaanderen,** rue du Marché aux Herbes/Grasmarkt 61–63, 1000 Bruxelles (② **02/504-03-90;** fax 02/504-04-75; www.visit flanders.com; Métro: Gare Centrale). The office is open for personal visits April to June and September to October, Monday to Friday from 9am to 6pm; July to August, Monday to Friday from 9am to 7pm, and Saturday to Sunday from 9am to 1pm and 2 to 7pm; and November to March, Monday to Friday from 9am to 6pm, Saturday from 9am to 1pm and 2 to 6pm, and Sunday from 9am to 1pm.

Tourist offices in French-speaking areas are generally called the *Office du Tourisme,* and in small places the *Syndicat d'Initiative.* In Dutch-speaking areas, it's *Toerisme Whatever,* such as Toerisme Brugge for Bruges, or *VVV* followed by the place name; in the German-speaking area, look for the *Verkehrsamt.*

The Euro

Belgium's currency is the euro (see "Currency," in chapter 2).

⌐*Tips* **Rooms with a View**

If you like the idea of staying on a working farm, in a château, in an old-fashioned country home, or even in an old school converted to character-filled lodging, Belgium has two organizations that can smooth your path to the front door. In Wallonia, contact **Gîtes de Wallonie,** av. Prince de Liège 1, 5100 Jambes-Namur (② **081/31-18-00;** fax 081/31-02-00; www.gitesdewallonie. net). For Flanders, it's the **Vlaamse Federatie voor Plattelandstoerisme,** Minderbroederstraat 8, 2000 Leuven (② **016/24-21-58;** fax 016/24-21-87; www. plattelandstoerisme.be).

3 When to Go

"In season" in Belgium means from mid-April to mid-October. The peak of the tourist season is July and August, when the weather is at its finest. You'll find Belgium every bit as attractive during other months. Not only are airlines, hotels, and restaurants cheaper and less crowded during this time (with more relaxed service, which means you get more personal attention), but some very appealing events are going on. For example, Brussels swings into its rich music season in April, and Tournai turns out for the colorful thousand-year-old Procession of the Plague the second Sunday in September.

CLIMATE

Belgium's climate is moderate, with few extremes in temperature either in summer or winter. It does rain a lot, though there are more showers than downpours. (It's a good idea to pack a raincoat.) Temperatures are lowest in December and January, when they average 42°F (6°C), and highest in July and August, when they average 73°F (23°C).

In the springtime, when the parks are coming up flowers, the first sidewalk tables put in a tentative appearance, but the weather can be variable. July and August are the best months for soaking up rays at a sidewalk cafe, dining at an outdoors restaurant in the evening, and swimming and sunbathing at the seacoast. September usually has a few weeks of fine late-summer weather, and there are even sunny spells in winter, when brilliant, crisp weather alternates with clouded skies.

In the hilly, forested Ardennes, autumn's falling leaves bring out visitors searching for the finest fall colors. It's not quite New England, but it's spectacular enough, and any shortcomings on the color spectrum are compensated for by the culinary feasts on the menus of the many great restaurants here during the hunting season for wild game.

Winters at the coast, moderated a touch by the North Sea, most often are rainy. Inland, it's a different story. Some years, though not very often, the temperature falls low enough for canals (in places like Bruges and Ghent) and lakes to freeze sufficiently and become playgrounds for ice skaters. In the hilly, forested Ardennes, snow brings out cross-country skiers, and even downhill skiers to the region's handful of ski lifts and short runs. Expect lots of gray skies in Brussels—Eurocrats from sunny Mediterranean lands confess to going stir-crazy for the sight of blue skies and sun during winter in the capital.

You're well advised to pack a fold-up umbrella at any time of year. Likewise, carry a raincoat (with a wool liner for winter). Second, pack a sweater or two (even in July) and be prepared to layer your clothing at any time of year. Don't worry: In the summer, you can leave some space for T-shirts, skimpy tops, and sneakers.

HOLIDAYS

National holidays are January 1 (New Year's Day); Easter Sunday and Monday; May 1 (Labor Day); Ascension Thursday; Pentecost Sunday and Monday; July 21 (Independence Day); August 15 (Assumption); November 1 (All Saints); November 11 (World War I Armistice Day); and December 25 (Christmas Day). In Flanders only, July 11 is Flemish Community Day, the anniversary of the Battle of the Golden Spurs in 1302. In Wallonia only, September 27 is French Community Day, recalling liberation from Dutch rule in 1830.

BELGIUM CALENDAR OF EVENTS

Belgium is big on festivals. You could arrive in a town or village to find that the populace has turned out, some of them in costume, to honor with all due solemnity (followed by some fun and games) the local cheese. The country has a lively and colorful Carnival tradition, which includes, in the otherwise unprepossessing town of Binche, one that's among the most spectacular in Europe.

The Festival of Flanders is a program of cultural events that runs at venues throughout Flanders from September to June. Contact **Festival van Vlaanderen** (✆ 012/23-57-19; www.festival.be).

The Festival of Wallonia is a program of classical music that runs at venues throughout Wallonia from September to June. Contact **Festival de Wallonie** (✆ 081/73-37-81; www.festival dewallonie.be).

For more information about what's on and where, visit **www.agenda.be**.

January

Festival of Fools, Ronse. *Zotte Maandag* (Crazy Monday) festivities, with masked characters called *Bommels,* actually take place on a Saturday. Contact **VVV Ronse** (✆ 055/23-28-16). Saturday after the Epiphany (Jan 6).

Snow and Ice Sculptures, Bruges. Cool works of art with a too-short shelf life can be viewed on Stationsplein in front of the rail station. Contact **In & Uit Brugge** (✆ 050/44-86-86; www.brugge.be). For 2 weeks from the end of December.

Antiques Fair, Tour & Taxis, av. du Port, Brussels. The top Belgian antiques dealers and selected dealers from abroad get together to show off their wares. **Contact Foire des Antiquaires de Belgique** (✆ 02/513-48-31; www.antiques-fair.be). Last 10 days of January.

February

Carnival, Eupen. Five days of pre-Lenten revelry in the capital town of Belgium's German-speaking district. Highlight is the *Rosenmontag* (Rose Monday) Procession. Contact **Verkehrsamt Eupen** (✆ 087/55-34-50; www.eastbelgium.com). Thursday to Shrove Tuesday (the day before Ash Wednesday).

Carnival, Malmédy. The pre-Lenten festival brings good-natured mayhem to the streets of this otherwise sober town. Sunday is the day of the big parade, when costumed characters called *Banes Courants* chase people through the streets and others called *Haguètes* snare passersby with long wooden pincers. Contact **Office du Tourisme de Malmédy** (✆ 080/33-02-50). Saturday to Shrove Tuesday.

Carnival, Aalst. Three days of pre-Lenten festivities, including the Giants' Parade with the horse Bayard, onion-throwing from the roofs of the Grote Markt, and the parade of *Vuil Jeannetten*—men dressed as women. Contact **VVV Aalst** (✆ 053/73-22-70). Sunday to Shrove Tuesday.

Carnival, Binche. One of Europe's most colorful street carnivals, led on Shrove Tuesday by the sumptuously costumed Gilles of Binche, modeled, or so it is believed, on Inca nobles. Contact **Office du Tourisme de Binche** (✆ 064/33-67-27). Sunday to Shrove Tuesday.

March

Bal du Rat Mort, Ostend. This outrageous fancy-dress event takes its grisly name from a chic Paris cafe. Proceeds go to charity. Contact **Toerisme Ostend** (✆ 059/70-11-99; www.toerisme-oostende.be). First Saturday in March.

Carnival, Stavelot. The *Blancs Moussis,* characters with long red noses and hooded white costumes, are the stars of the town's Laetere procession. Contact

Office du Tourisme de Stavelot (✆ **080/86-27-06**). Sunday (3 weeks before Easter).

Carnival, Fosses-la-Ville. Costumed characters called Chinels parade through the streets. Contact **Syndicat d'Initiative Fosses-la-Ville** (✆ **071/71-46-24;** www.fosses-la-ville.be). Saturday and Sunday (3 weeks before Easter).

Brussels International Festival of Fantasy Film, Passage 44 and Cinema Nova, Brussels. Screens science fiction and fantasy films. Contact **BIFFF** (✆ **02/204-00-13;** www.bifff.org). Mid-March.

April

Sablon Spring Baroque Music Festival, place du Grand Sablon, Brussels. Open-air concerts on the square. Contact **Brussels International Tourism** (✆ **02/513-89-40;** www.brussels international.be). April/May.

May Day's Eve Festival, Hasselt. Participants in the *Meieavondviering* plant a May Tree in the Grote Markt and burn dummies representing winter, while "witches" dance. Contact **VVV Hasselt** (✆ **011/23-95-40;** www.hasselt.be). April 30.

May

Queen Elisabeth Contest, Brussels. For promising young musicians, featuring a different instrument each year. Generally at Bozar (Palais des Beaux-Arts), and a few other venues. Contact **Concours Reine Elisabeth** (✆ **02/213-40-50;** www.concours-reine-elisabeth.be). First 4 weeks in May.

KunstenFESTIVALdesArts (KFDA), Brussels. Arts festival famed across the cultural universe for its irritatingly scrunched-up name, which means—brilliantly original, this—Arts Festival, in both Dutch and French. It spotlights stage events, putting an emphasis on opera, theater, and dance, but finds space for cinema, music concerts, and fine-arts exhibits. Various auditoriums and venues around town. Contact **KFDA** (✆ **02/219-07-07;** www.kfda.be). Three weeks in May.

Festival of the Cats, Ypres (Ieper). During the traditional *Kattestoet,* toy cats (it used to be live ones!) are thrown from the town hall belfry. Contact **Toerisme Ieper** (✆ **057/23-92-00;** www.ieper.be). Every third year on the second Sunday in May. May 13, 2007; May 11, 2008.

Procession of the Holy Blood, Bruges. The bishop of Bruges carries a relic of the Holy Blood through the streets, while costumed characters act out biblical scenes. Contact **In & Uit Brugge** (✆ **050/44-86-86;** www.brugge.be). Ascension Day (fifth Thurs after Easter).

Chariot of Gold Procession, Mons. Religious procession of guilds and the reliquary of St. Waudru, followed by a street performance, the *Lumeçon,* in which St. George slays the dragon. Contact **Office du Tourisme de Mons** (✆ **065/33-55-80;** www.mons.be). Holy Trinity Sunday (first Sun after Pentecost).

Brussels Jazz Marathon, Brussels. Enjoy a long weekend of jazz, all kinds, at a slew of concerts on the Grand-Place, place du Grand Sablon, and place Ste-Catherine; at other open-air venues around town; and in jazz clubs, cafes, and hotel bars. Contact **Jazztronaut** (✆ **0900/00-750** or 02/456-04-82; www.brusselsjazzmarathon.be). Third week in May.

June

Day of the Four Processions, Tournai. Features flower-decked floats, a military band, and the highlight, a procession of giants representing historical characters, including King Chílderic of the Franks and France's King Louis XIV. Contact **Office du Tourisme de Tournai** (✆ **069/22-20-45**; www. tournai.be). Second Sunday in June.

International Cartoon Festival, Knokke-Heist. Belgium is a big producer and consumer of cartoons and comic strips for both adults and children. Here it celebrates the national fascination with the "Ninth Art." Contact Cultuurcentrum Knokke-Heist (✆ **050/63-04-30;** www.cartoonfestival.be). Mid-June to early September.

Carillon Concerts at St. Rombout's Tower, Mechelen. Home to Belgium's Royal Carillon School, Mechelen is one of the world's centers of carillon music, in which a classically trained musician employs a keyboard to play music on clusters of bells hanging in belfries. Contact **VVV Mechelen** (✆ **015/29-76-55**). Saturday to Monday evenings, mid-June to August.

Couleur Café Festival, Brussels. Three days of Afro, Caribbean, and Latin music and dance, ably supported by heaps of soul food, at the Tour & Taxis cultural complex, in a former warehouse zone next to the Willebroeck Canal dock. Contact **Couleur Café** (www.couleurcafe.be). June 1 to July 31, 2007; June 1 to July 31, 2008.

July

Entertainment, Grand-Place, Brussels. Concerts, theater, dance, exhibits, and other forms of entertainment animate the Grand-Place. Contact **Brussels International Tourism** (✆ **02/ 513-89-40;** www.brusselsinternational tourism.be). Entire month.

Ommegang, Brussels. A dramatic annual historical pageant that dates from the 13th century and represents the city guilds, magistrats, and nobles

honoring the Virgin Mary. Participants wearing period costume from the time of the "joyous entry" of Emperor Charles V into Brussels in 1549, escorted by a mounted cavalcade and waving medieval banners, go in procession from place du Grand Sablon to the Grand-Place. Contact **Ommegang de Bruxelles** (www.ommegang.be). First Tuesday and Thursday in July.

Brosella Folk and Jazz Festival, Brussels. A small-scale specialized music fest that takes place over a weekend at the Théâtre de Verdure in Parc d'Osseghem. Contact **Les Amis de Brosella** (✆ **02/270-98-56;** www. brosella.be). Mid-July.

Belgian National Day, Brussels. Marked throughout Belgium but celebrated most in Brussels, with a military procession and music at the Royal Palace. Contact **Brussels International Tourism** (✆ **02/513-89-40;** www.brusselsinternationaltourism.be). July 21.

Gentse Feesten, Ghent. Free street entertainment of music, dance, theater, puppet shows, and general fun and games marks the annual Ghent Festivities. Contact **Dienst Feestelijkheeden** (✆ **09/269-46-00;** www.gentse feesten.be). July 14 to July 23, 2007; July 19 to July 28, 2008.

August

Visiting the Royal Palace, Brussels. Exceptionally, the Royal Palace on place des Palais is open to free guided tours. King Albert and Queen Paola won't be there! Contact **Palais Royal** (www.monarchie.be). Throughout August (dates vary year by year but generally include the last week or so of July and the first week or so of Sept).

Planting of the Meiboom (May Pole), Brussels. Despite the name, this does happen in August, on the Feast of

St. Lawrence, on the Grand-Place, and celebrates Brussels's victory over Leuven in 1213 (nowadays it's more a celebration of summer). Contact **Société Royale des Compagnons de Saint-Laurent** (© 02/217-39-43). August 9.

Tapis des Fleurs, Grand-Place, Brussels. The historic square is carpeted with two-thirds of a million begonias arranged in a kind of tapestry. Contact **Brussels International Tourism** (© 02/513-89-40; www.brussels internationaltourism.be). Mid-August in even-numbered years.

Marktrock Rock Festival, Leuven. Three days of rock and jazz on the square in front of the Stadhuis (Town Hall). Contact **Dienst Toerisme Leuven** (© 016/20-30-20; www. leuven.be) or visit www.marktrock.be. Mid-August.

Outre-Meuse Folklore Festival, Liège. Music, dance, and theater performances. Contact **Office du Tourisme de Liège** (© 04/221-92-21; www.liege.be). Mid-August.

September

Liberation Parade, Brussels. The *Manneken-Pis* statue is dressed in a Welsh Guard's uniform in honor of the city's liberation in 1944. Contact **Brussels International Tourism** (© 02/513-89-40; www.brusselsinternational tourism.be). September 3.

Procession of the Plague, Tournai. Commemorates the terrible epidemic of 1090. Contact **Office du Tourisme de Tournai** (© 069/22-20-45; www. tournai.be). Second or third Sunday in September.

Brussels Heritage Days. Taking a different theme each year, this program allows you to visit some of the finest buildings in town that are usually closed to visitors. Contact or visit

the **Centre d'Information,** Les Halles de St-Géry, place St-Géry (© **0800/ 40-400;** Métro: Bourse), open Monday to Saturday from 10am to 5pm. Third weekend of September.

October

Flanders International Film Festival, Ghent. Belgium's top international film festival, and an event that has grown in stature over the past 3 decades to become one of Europe's premier movie showcases. As many as 150 full-length movies and 100 shorts are screened each year. Contact **Internationaal Filmfestival van Vlaanderen-Gent** (© 09/242-80-60; www.filmfestival. be). During 11 days, midmonth.

December

Christmas Market, Brussels. Stands selling seasonal trinkets, traditional craft items, and food and drink are set up on place Ste-Catherine. Contact **Brussels International Tourism** (© 02/ 513-89-40; www.brusselsinternational tourism.be). Throughout the month, daily from 11am to 10pm.

Christmas Market, Bruges. Stands selling seasonal trinkets, craft items, and food and drink, alongside an ice-skating rink, are set up on the Markt. Throughout the month, daily from 11am to 10pm. A second market is on Simon Stevinplein, daily from 11am to 7pm. Contact **In & Uit Brugge** (© 050/44-86-86; www.brugge.be).

Christmas Market, Ghent. Stands selling seasonal trinkets, craft items, and food and drink are set up on Sint-Baafsplein. Contact **Dienst Toerisme Gent** (© 09/266-52-32; www.gent. be). Throughout the month, daily from 11am to 10pm.

Nativity Scene and Christmas Tree, Grand-Place, Brussels. The crib has real animals. Contact **Brussels International Tourism** (© 02/513-89-40;

www.brusselsinternationaltourism.be).
Throughout the month.

Winter Fun, Brussels. An ice-skating rink and a big wheel are set up on the Marché aux Poissons; on neighboring place Ste-Catherine there's a baroque carousel. Contact **Brussels International Tourism** (© **02/513-89-40;** www.brusselsinternational.be) or visit www.plaisirsdhiver.be. Throughout the month.

4 Getting Around

Belgium's compact size makes it easy on travelers. The roads are excellent (though often busy), and the comprehensive train and bus system is one of Europe's best.

BY TRAIN

All major tourist destinations in Belgium can be done easily in a day trip by train from Brussels, on the excellent railway network of the **Société Nationale des Chemins de Fer Belges/SNCB,** or **NMBS** in Dutch (© **02/528-28-28;** www.sncb.be). Antwerp is just 29 minutes away; Ghent, 32 minutes; Namur, 40 minutes; Bruges, 55 minutes; and Liège, 60 minutes. These times are by the fast Intercity (IC) trains; Inter-Regional (IR) trains are somewhat slower; Local (L) trains are the tortoises of the system, stopping at every station on the way.

If all or most of your travel will be by train, a good investment is a **Rail Pass,** good for 10 single journeys anywhere on the network, except stations at international borders, within a month of it being issued. It costs 68€ ($85).

Another option is the discounted **weekend return** ticket, valid from noon on Friday to noon on Monday; the more people you travel with, the greater the discount per ticket. Even if you make only 1 or 2 day trips by rail, be sure to inquire about **Minitrips**—1-day excursion tickets to major sightseeing destinations at discount prices.

Main rail stations, and some minor ones, have bicycles for rent. If you travel by train and would like to have a trusty steed awaiting you when you arrive, use the Belgian Railways *Train + Vélo/Trein + Fiets* (Train + Bicycle) formula to reserve a bike at the same time you buy your ticket.

BY BUS

Brussels, Bruges, Ghent, Antwerp, Liège, and all other important towns and cities, have good local bus service. Regional buses serve every area of the country, with fares and schedules available from bus or train stations, but they're slow, are often infrequent, and may require transfers at intermediate points for long-distance journeys.

Tips Life in the Slow Lane

A network of special walking, cycling, and horseback-riding routes in Wallonia provides a healthy alternative to touring by car, and links scenic parts of the region that are off the beaten track. RAVeL (Réseau Autonome des Voies Lentes/Independent Network of Slow Routes) gives new life to old ways by employing disused rail and tram routes, river and canal towpaths, and other minor paths, connected by purpose-built sections. Four main RAVeL routes and a web of secondary ones crisscross the region. Guide booklets with maps are available from tourist offices.

BY CAR

Driving conditions are excellent in Belgium, with lighted highways at night. Belgian drivers, though, are not as excellent. They're notoriously fast and aggressive and have clocked some of the worst road-accident statistics in Europe, so drive with care.

RENTALS   Rental cars are available from **Hertz** (℃ **800/654-3001** in the U.S.), bd. Maurice Lemonnier 8, Brussels (℃ **02/720-60-44**); **Avis** (℃ **800/331-2112** in the U.S.), rue de France 2, Brussels (℃ **02/527-17-05**); **Budget,** av. Louise 327B, Brussels (℃ **02/753-21-70**); **Europcar,** chaussée de Waterloo 538, Brussels (℃ **02/348-92-12**). All four companies have desks at Brussels National Airport. Expect to pay from 60€ ($75) a day, and 200€ ($250) a week, including insurance and other charges, and for unlimited mileage.

DRIVING RULES   To drive in Belgium, U.S. citizens need only a valid passport, a U.S. driver's license, and a valid auto registration. The minimum age for drivers is 18. On highways, speed limits are 70kmph (43 mph) minimum, 120kmph (74 mph) maximum; in all cities and urban areas, the maximum speed limit is 50kmph (31 mph). Lower limits might be posted. Seat belts must be worn in both the front seats and in the back. One important driving rule is the *priorité de droite* (priority from the right), which makes it perfectly legal most of the time to pull out from a side road to the right of the flow of traffic. That means, of course, that you must keep a sharp eye on the side roads to your right (see "Driven Crazy," below).

Driven Crazy

The behavior of many Belgian car drivers could easily be described as "hog-like," a moderate term employed because finding the pertinent adjective would tax even the considerable powers of the English language as an instrument of personal abuse.

Part of the blame attaches to the *priorité de droite* (priority from the right) traffic rule, whereby in some cases (not always), traffic from the right has the right of way. You won't believe how this plays at multiple-road intersections, particularly since many Belgians will give up their *priorité* under no known circumstances, cost what it might. Be ready to stop instantly at *all* such intersections. ***Note:*** Poles with orange diamond signs, which you see mostly on main roads, mean that priority lies with traffic already on the road, so you don't have to stop.

At rotaries, traffic entering the rotary has the right of way over traffic already on it, unless STOP lines on the road indicate otherwise. This system has caused so much mayhem it's being changed at some accident hot spots and obvious danger zones. Not everyone knows about the changes or acts according to them, so stay alert.

Hoglike driver behavior is extended to pedestrians. Don't expect cars to stop for you just because you're crossing at a black-and-white "pedestrian crossing." Only in recent years have drivers been obliged legally to stop at these, and many haven't received the message yet.

ROAD MAPS   Tourist offices provide excellent city, regional, and country maps. Michelin map nos. 213 and 214 cover the country; they are detailed and reliable, and are available from bookstores, news vendors, some supermarkets, and other outlets.

BREAKDOWNS/ASSISTANCE   Roadside telephones connect to emergency services, whose yellow "TS" (Touring Secours) cars patrol major highways to render emergency service at minimal cost. If you have car trouble, pull off the road and dial 𝄢 **070/34-47-77** at one of the phones; then wait for the TS. On other roads, call TS from the nearest telephone or your cellphone.

FAST FACTS: Belgium

Airport See "Getting Around," in chapter 5.

American Express See "Fast Facts: Brussels," in chapter 5.

Area Codes See "Telephones," below.

Business Hours Banks are usually open Monday to Friday from 9am to 1pm and 2 to 4:30pm, and some branches are open on Saturday morning. Stores generally are open from 10am to 6pm Monday to Saturday, and some are also open on Sunday. Most department stores have late hours on Friday, remaining open until 8 or 9pm.

Car Rentals See "Getting Around," above.

Climate See "When to Go," earlier in this chapter.

Currency See "Money," in chapter 2.

Driving Rules See "Getting Around," above.

Drugs Belgium has rigid prohibitions against the possession and use of controlled narcotic drugs, and a strict enforcement policy that virtually guarantees stiff fines and/or jail sentences for offenders. This can be especially important if you are traveling from neighboring Holland, where the rules are more tolerant and enforcement (for soft drugs) is generally lax.

Drugstores For such items as toothpaste, deodorant, and razor blades, go to a supermarket. See also "Pharmacies," below.

Electricity Belgium runs on 220 volts electricity. You need to take with you a small voltage transformer and a European-style adapter plug (available in drug and appliance stores and by mail order) that plugs into the round-holed European electrical outlet.

Embassies These are all in Brussels. **U.S.:** bd. du Régent 25–27 (𝄢 **02/508-21-11**; www.usembassy.be; Métro: Arts-Loi), open for visa applications Monday to Friday from 9am to noon, and for assistance to U.S. citizens from 1:30 to 4:30pm. **Canada:** av. de Tervuren 2 (𝄢 **02/741-06-11**; Métro: Merode), open Monday, Wednesday, and Friday from 9am to noon and 2 to 4pm, Tuesday and Thursday from 9am to noon. **U.K.:** rue Arlon 85 (𝄢 **02/287-62-11**; Métro: Maalbeek), open for visa applications Monday to Friday from 9:30am to noon, and for other matters from 9:30am to 12:30pm and 2:30 to 4:30pm. **Australia:** rue Guimard 6–8 (𝄢 **02/286-05-00**; Métro: Arts-Loi), open Monday to Friday from

9am to 12:30pm and 2 to 4pm. **New Zealand:** Square de Meeûs 1 (© **02/512-10-40;** Métro: Trone), open Monday to Friday from 9am to 1pm and 2 to 3:30pm. **Ireland:** rue Wiertz 50 (© **02/235-66-76;** Métro: Schuman), open Monday to Friday from 10am to 1pm.

Emergencies   For police assistance, call © **101.** For an ambulance or the fire department, call © **100.**

Holidays   See "When to Go," earlier in this chapter.

Language   Belgians speak either French or Dutch (or as you may hear it called, Flemish), and a tiny minority in the east is German-speaking. Many Belgians speak two or all three of the national tongues but, since language is a sensitive subject in the land, they might not be willing to prove this by actually doing so in practice. English is in effect the second language, and it is taught in the schools from the early grades, with the result that many Belgians speak fluently. You may speak English in Belgium almost as freely as you do at home, particularly to anyone in the business of providing tourist services, whether cabdriver, hotel receptionist, waitperson, or store assistant.

Mail   Postage for a postcard or letter to the U.S., Canada, Australia, New Zealand, and South Africa is 0.80€ ($1); to the U.K. and Ireland 0.75€ (95¢).

Pharmacies   For both prescription and nonprescription medicines, go to a pharmacy (*pharmacie* in French; *apotheek* in Dutch). Regular pharmacy hours are Monday to Saturday from 9am to 6pm (some close earlier on Sat). Each pharmacy posts a list of late-night and weekend pharmacies on the door; or contact © **0900/105-00;** www.apotheek.be.

Police   For emergency police assistance, call © **101.**

Post Office   Most post offices are open Monday to Friday from 9am to 5pm.

Restrooms   In primarily French-speaking Brussels and in Wallonia, these likely will display an "H" or *Hommes* for men, and an "F" or *Femmes* for women; in Dutch-speaking Flanders, it'll be an "H" or *Heren* for men, and a "D" or *Damen* for women (or there'll be a graphic that should leave no doubt either way). Be sure to pay the person who sits at the entrance to a *toilette*. He or she has a saucer where you put your money, usually around 0.50€ (65¢).

Safety   See "Health & Safety," in chapter 2.

Taxes   On top of a 16% service charge, there's a value-added tax (TVA/BTW) of 6% on hotel bills and 21.5% on restaurant bills. The higher rate is charged on purchased goods, too. If you spend over 125€ ($156) in some stores, and you are not a resident of the European Union, you can recover it by having the official receipt stamped by Belgian Customs on departure and returning the stamped receipt to the store. Your refund should arrive by check or be credited to your credit card within a few weeks. Not all stores participate in this scheme so it pays to ask first, particularly for major purchases.

Telephones   The country code for Belgium is **32.** When calling Belgium from abroad, you do not use the initial **0** in the area code. For example, if you're calling a Brussels number (area code **02**) from outside Belgium, you dial the international access code (which is **011** when calling from North America, and **00** from elsewhere in Europe) and then **32-2,** followed by the subscriber number.

You only dial the initial **0** of the area code if you're calling within Belgium (and this includes if you're calling another number in the same area-code zone). When you call someone in Belgium, you always need to use the area code even if you're calling from inside the same area. There are two main formats for Belgian phone numbers. In the main cities, a two-digit area code followed by a seven-digit number; and for other places, a three-digit area code followed by a six-digit number. For instance, Brussels's tourist information number is **02/513-89-40**; Ypres's is **057/23-92-00**.

For information in English, both domestic and international, dial ✆ **1405**.

To make international calls from Belgium, first dial **00** and then the country code. To call the United States or Canada, dial **00** (the international access code) + **1** (the country code) + the area code + the number. For example, if you want to call the British Embassy in Washington, D.C., dial 00-1-202-588-7800. Other country codes are: United Kingdom, **44**; Ireland, **353**; Australia, **61**; New Zealand, **64**. International calls, per minute, cost: **U.S., Canada, U.K., Ireland:** 0.35€ (45¢); **Australia, New Zealand:** 1€ ($1.25).

You can use most pay phones in booths all around town with a Belgacom *telecard* (phone card), selling for 5€ ($6.25), 10€ ($13), and 20€ ($25) from post offices, train ticket counters, and newsstands. Some pay phones take coins, of 0.10€, 0.20€, 0.50€, 1€, and 2€. Both local and long-distance calls from a pay phone are 0.30€ (40¢) a minute at peak time (Mon–Fri 8am–7pm) and the same amount for 2 minutes at other times. Calls dialed direct from hotel room phones are usually more than twice the standard rate.

To charge a call to your calling card, contact: **AT&T** (✆ 0800/100-10); **MCI** (✆ 0800/100-12); **Sprint** (✆ 0800/100-14); **Canada Direct** (✆ 0800/100-19); **British Telecom** (✆ 0800/100-24); **Telecom New Zealand** (✆ 0800/100-64).

Time Zone Belgium is on Western European Time (WET), which is Coordinated Universal Time (UTC) or Greenwich Mean Time (GMT) plus 1 hour. Clocks are advanced by 1 hour for Western European Summer Time (WEST) between the last Sunday in March and the last Sunday in October.

Tipping The prices on most restaurant menus already include a service charge of 16%, so it's unnecessary to tip. However, if the service is good, it's customary to show appreciation with a tip. It's enough to round up the bill to the nearest convenient amount, if you wish, rather than leave a full-fledged tip. Otherwise, 10% is adequate, and more than most Belgians would leave. Service charge is included in your hotel bill as well. Taxis include the tip in the meter reading. You can round up the fare if you like, but you need not add a tip unless you have received extra service like help with luggage. Here's a general guide to tipping for other services: Give 1€ ($1.25) to ushers in some theaters and cinemas, 20% of the bill to hairdressers (leave it with the cashier when you pay up), and 1€ to 2€ ($1.25–$2.50) per piece of luggage to porters.

Water The water from the faucet in Belgium is safe to drink. Many people drink bottled mineral water, though, generally Belgian brands like Spa and Bru.

Weather For local forecasts, go to **www.meteo.be**.

5

Brussels

Brussels (pop. 992,000)—the headquarters of the European Union—both symbolizes Europe's vision of unity and is a bastion of officialdom, a breeding ground for the regulations that govern and often exasperate the rest of the Continent.

The Bruxellois have mixed feelings about their city's transformation into a power center. At first, the waves of Eurocrats brought a new cosmopolitan air to a somewhat provincial city (though once the seat of emperors), but as old neighborhoods were leveled to make way for office towers, people wondered whether Brussels was losing its soul. After all, this city doesn't only mean politics and business. It inspired surrealism and Art Nouveau, worships comic strips, prides itself on handmade lace and chocolates, and serves each one of its craft beers in a unique glass.

Fortunately, not all of Brussels's individuality has been lost in this transition, and though the urban landscape has suffered from wanton development, the city's spirit survives in traditional cafes, bars, bistros, and restaurants. Whether elegantly Art Nouveau or eccentrically festooned with posters, curios, and knick-knacks, such centuries-old establishments provide a convivial ambience that is peculiarly Belgian.

1 Orientation

ARRIVING

BY PLANE

For details on air travel to Belgium, see chapter 2. The country's main international airport, **Brussels National Airport** (© **0900/70-000** in Belgium, or 02/753-77-53 from abroad; www.brusselsairport.be), served by most major European airlines and many other international carriers, is at Zaventem, 11km (7 miles) northeast of the center city. There's direct train service to Brussels's three main rail stations (Gare du Nord, Gare Centrale, and Gare du Midi) every 20 minutes daily from 5:30am to 11:30pm, for a one-way fare of 2.60€ ($3.25). The trip time to Gare Centrale is around 25 minutes. Most airport trains have wide corridors and extra space for baggage.

The **Airport Line bus,** no. 11 or 12, departs from the airport one to five times an hour to multiple stops in the city, and costs 3€ ($3.75). **De Lijn bus** BZ connects the airport hourly with Gare du Nord rail station, for the same fare.

Taxis that display an orange sticker depicting a white airplane offer reduced fares from the airport to the center city. Others charge about 32€ ($40), and some offer reduced rates for a reserved return journey (ask your driver for details). Go to the taxi stand and wait your turn. Be sure to use only licensed cabs.

Impressions
Brussels was a surprise. Not the city of Euro bureaucrats and dusty bourgeois burghers it is often said to be, it was far trendier than we expected, like the more laid-back quarters of Paris fifteen or twenty years ago, with lots of bars and crowds of young people eating outside. We wandered along narrow streets, tree-lined avenues and across pretty squares, soaking up the atmos-phere, listening to buskers and street performers, enjoying the sunshine and looking forward to dinner.
                    —Ewan McGregor and Charley Boorman, *Long Way Round* (2004)

BY TRAIN

High-speed Eurostar trains from London; Thalys from Paris, Amsterdam, and Cologne; TGV from France (not Paris); and ICE from Frankfurt zip into town from all points of the compass. The Brussels metropolitan area has three main rail stations: **Gare Centrale,** Carrefour de l'Europe; **Gare du Midi,** rue de France (the Eurostar, Thalys, TGV, and ICE terminal); and **Gare du Nord,** rue du Progrès. All three are served by Métro, tram, and bus lines, and have taxi ranks outside. For train informa-tion and reservations, call © **02/528-28-28,** or visit **www.sncb.be**.

Warning: Attracted by rich pickings from international travelers, bag-snatchers roam the environs of Gare du Midi, and pickpockets work the interior. Do not travel to or depart from the station on foot if you can avoid so doing—take a taxi or use public transportation; inside, keep a close eye on your possessions.

BY BUS

Eurolines (© **02/274-13-50;** www.eurolines.com) buses from London, Paris, Ams-terdam, and other cities arrive at the bus station below Gare du Nord rail station.

BY CAR

Major expressways to Brussels are E19 from Amsterdam and Paris, and E40 from Bruges and Cologne. If possible, avoid driving the "hell on wheels" R0 Brussels ring road. And once you're settled at a hotel, do yourself a favor: Leave the car at a park-ing garage.

VISITOR INFORMATION

The city tourist office, **Brussels International Tourism,** Hôtel de Ville, Grand-Place, 1000 Bruxelles (© **02/513-89-40;** fax 02/513-83-20; www.brusselsinternational.be; Métro: Gare Centrale), is on the ground floor of the Town Hall. Good information is available here, including a comprehensive visitors' booklet, *Brussels Guide & Map.* The office makes last-minute reservations for city hotels; organizes paid-for guided walk-ing tours in summer; and has well-trained, multilingual tour guides whom you can engage by the hour or the day. The office is open April to October, daily from 9am to 6pm; November to December, Monday to Saturday from 9am to 6pm, and Sunday from 10am to 2pm; and January to March, Monday to Saturday from 9am to 6pm.

There are now tourist information desks in the Arrivals hall at Brussels National Air-port and in the TGV/Thalys/Eurostar lounge at the city's Gare du Midi rail station.

For English-speaking visitors, the most useful publication is the weekly magazine *The Bulletin,* published on Thursdays and filled with local news, articles, shopping, and information on cultural events.

CITY LAYOUT

Brussels is divided into 19 *communes* (districts)—"Brussels" being both the name of the central commune and of the city as a whole (which comprises the Brussels Capital Region). The center city, once ringed by fortified ramparts, is now encircled by broad boulevards known collectively as the **Petite Ceinture.** Most of the city's premier sightseeing attractions are in this zone. Around 14% of the zone's total area of 160 sq. km (63 sq. miles) is occupied by parks, woods, and forest, making this one of Europe's greenest urban centers.

Brussels sits smack-dab on Europe's great Continental Divide, the often edgy interface between its Latin south and Germanic north. You'll hear both French and Dutch (along with a Babel of other tongues) spoken in its streets. The city is bilingual: *Bruxelles* in French and *Brussel* in Dutch, and street names and places are in both languages. Grand-Place is *Grote Markt* in Dutch; Gare Centrale is *Centraal Station;* Théâtre Royal de la Monnaie is *Koninklijke Munttheater.* **Note:** For convenience and to save space, I use only the French names in this chapter.

STREET MAPS   Go to Brussels International Tourism and pick up its *Brussels Guide & Map,* which has a fairly detailed street map of the inner city marked with principal tourist attractions. If you need a comprehensive street map, you can purchase the *Géocart Bruxelles et Périphérie* at most news vendors and bookstores.

NEIGHBORHOODS IN BRIEF

Brussels is flat in its center and western reaches, where the now-vanished Senne River once flowed. To the east, a range of low hills rises to the upper city, which is crowned by the Royal Palace and has some of the city's most affluent residential and prestigious business and shopping districts. The **Grand-Place** stands at the heart of Brussels and is both starting point and reference point for most visitors.

The Old Center comprises the **Grand-Place** and environs, place du Grand Sablon and place du Petit Sablon, and adjacent streets. Central Brussels includes the **Marché aux Poissons (Fish Market)** district and the **Haute Ville (Upper City),** east of and uphill from the Grand-Place, along rue Royale and rue de la Régence, and abutting the working-class Marolles district.

Just north of the center lies **Gare du Nord** and nearby place Rogier.

Beyond the center, things start to get hazier. On either side of **avenue Louise,** a chic boulevard south of the center city, are the classy districts of Ixelles and Uccle. They're both good areas for restaurants and shopping, and both border the wide green spaces of the Bois de la Cambre and the Forêt de Soignes.

East of the center city lies a part of Brussels whose denizens are regarded by many Bruxellois with the same suspicion they might apply to just-landed extraterrestrials. I refer, of course, to the **European Union district** around place Schuman, where the European

---

Damage Assessment

As Brussels's architectural heritage has taken a hit—by unscrupulous property developers, venal local officials, and the steamroller of Euroconstruction—the phenomenon has been dubbed *Bruxellisation:* the destruction of beautiful old buildings and their replacement by dreary office towers.

Commission, Parliament, and Council of Ministers buildings jostle for space in a warren of offices populated by civil servants, journalists, and lobbyists. (The area is home to a wealth of restaurants and cafes that cater to Euro-appetites.) A quaint old neighborhood was made to disappear to make way for these noble edifices.

In the north of the city (and something of a leap of the imagination) is the **Bruparck.** Inside this recreation complex is the Mini-Europe theme park; the 26-screen Kinepolis multiplex movie theater; a made-to-order village with stores, cafes, and restaurants; and the Océade water park. Beside it are the Atomium, Brussels Planetarium, Roi Baudouin soccer stadium, and Parc des Expositions convention center.

2 Getting Around

Brussels's center is small enough that walking is a viable option. There's no better way to explore the historical core than walking, especially around Grand-Place. You'll likely also enjoy strolling uptown around place du Grand Sablon. Traffic can be heavy and frantic, creating a tiring experience. The best solution, if you have several days, is to divide your time into walking tours. Otherwise, a combination of walking and using the excellent public transportation is best. In any case, beyond the center, using public transportation is a virtual necessity.

Be careful when crossing roads at the black-and-white pedestrian crossings with no signals. Astonishingly, pedestrians at these crossings were only recently given legal priority over cars! Drivers are not yet completely reconciled to the change. Watch out for cars turning (legally) right or left at traffic lights, even when the green "walking man" indicates you can cross.

BY PUBLIC TRANSPORTATION

Maps of the integrated transit network—Métro (subway), tram (streetcar), and bus—are available free from the city tourist office, from offices of the **STIB** public transportation company at Galérie de la Toison d'Or 15 (© **0900/10-310;** www.stib. irisnet.be; Métro: Louise), and from the Porte de Namur, Rogier, and Gare du Midi Métro stations. In addition, transit maps are posted at all Métro stations and on many bus and tram shelters. The full system operates from 6am to midnight, after which a limited night-bus system takes over. If possible, avoid the crush at morning and evening rush hours. Watch out for pickpockets, especially at busy times, and avoid walking alone in deserted access tunnels, particularly after dark—the risk of being mugged is small but not entirely absent.

FARE INFORMATION & DISCOUNT PASSES   Fares on the city's Métro trains, trams, and buses are 1.50€ ($1.90) for a single ride (known as *un direct*), and 6.70€ ($8.40) for a five-ride card. You can purchase both from the driver. A 10-ride card is available from Métro and rail stations for 11€ ($13), and a 1-day card valid on all urban services is available for 4€ ($5). There are several multiday options. Children under 12 ride free on the STIB transit network; they need to get a free pass called an *Abonnement J.* A maximum of four children under 6 can ride free per paying adult.

VALIDATION   You validate your card by inserting it into the orange electronic machines inside buses and trams and at the access to Métro platforms. Though the card must be revalidated each time you enter a new vehicle, you're allowed multiple transfers within a 1-hour period of the initial validation, so you can hop on and off Métros, trams, and buses during that time, and only one journey will be canceled by the electronic scanner. If more than one person is traveling on one card, the card must be validated each time for each traveler.

BY METRO   The Métro is quick and efficient, and covers many important center-city locations, and the suburbs, the Bruparck recreation zone, and the Heysel congress center. Stations are identified by signs with a white M on a blue background. A trip underground takes you into an art center—Métro stations are decorated with specially commissioned paintings by contemporary Belgian artists.

BY TRAM & BUS   An extensive network of tram lines provides the ideal way to get around the city. Both trams and urban buses are silver and bronze. Their stops are marked with red-and-white signs and often have a shelter. You stop a tram or bus by extending your arm as it approaches so the driver can see it; if you don't signal, the bus or tram might not stop.

Two bus companies provide service to points outside the city (and stop at some points within it): **TEC** (✆ 010/23-53-53; www.infotec.be), which provides orange buses covering French-speaking Wallonia, and **De Lijn** (✆ 070/22-02-00; www.de lijn.be), which has white buses covering Dutch-speaking Flanders.

BY TAXI

Taxi fares start at 2.40€ ($3) from 6am to 10pm, and at 4.40€ ($6) between 10pm and 6am, increasing by 1.25€ ($1.55) per kilometer inside the city (tariff 1) and 2.45€ ($3.10) per kilometer outside (tariff 2)—make sure the meter is set to the correct tariff. Tip and taxes are included on the meter price, and you need not add an extra tip unless there has been extra service, such as help with heavy luggage (though drivers won't refuse tips). All taxis are metered. They cannot be hailed on the street, but there are taxi stands on many principal streets, particularly in the center city, and at rail stations. To request a cab by phone, call **Taxis Bleus** (✆ 02/268-00-00), **Taxis Oranges** (✆ 02/349-43-43), or **Taxis Verts** (✆ 02/349-49-49).

Tips Ride the Rails

Though not as fast as the Métro, trams are generally faster than buses and are a great way to get around, not least because you can view the cityscape while you ride. Line nos. 92, 93, and 94 pass by key sights along rue Royale and rue de la Régence, and as far as avenue Louise.

The fare starts at 2.40€ ($3) from 6am to 10pm, and at 4.40€ ($6) between 10pm and 6am, increasing by 1.25€ ($1.55) per kilometer inside the city (tariff 1) and 2.45€ ($3.10) per kilometer outside (tariff 2)—make sure the meter is set to the correct tariff. You cannot hail them on the street, but there are stands at prominent locations around town. Call **Taxis Bleus** (© 02/268-00-00), **Taxis Oranges** (© 02/349-43-43), or **Taxis Verts** (© 02/349-49-49).

BY CAR

Driving in Brussels is akin to life during the Stone Age: nasty and brutish—though it's rarely short. Normally polite citizens of Brussels turn into red-eyed demons once they get behind the steering wheel. Driving is fast, except at rush hour, and always aggressive. At rush hour (which actually lasts about an hour to either side of 9am and 5pm), it is almost impossible to move on main roads inside the city and on the R0 outer ring road (beltway). Sunday and early morning are better, and evening is not too bad.

Park your car either at your hotel or in one of the many public parking garages—your hotel can furnish the address of the nearest one—and do not set foot in it again until you're ready to leave the city. Good public transportation and an occasional taxi ride will get you anywhere you want inexpensively and hassle-free.

If you must drive, watch out for the notorious *priorité de droite* (priority from the right) traffic system (see "Driven Crazy," in chapter 4).

RENTALS   See "Getting Around," in chapter 4.

FAST FACTS: Brussels

Airport   See "Orientation," earlier in this chapter.

American Express   The office at bd. du Souverain 100, 1000 Bruxelles (© 02/676-21-11; Métro: Horrmann-Debroux), is open Monday to Friday from 9:30am to 5:30pm. Call ahead before visiting, because it has limited services for visitors—it does not cash traveler's checks, for instance.

ATMs   You'll find many **ATMs** around town, identified by BANCONTACT and MISTER CASH signs. A convenient bank with an ATM is **CBC,** Grand-Place 5 (© 02/547-12-11; Métro: Gare Centrale), open Monday to Friday from 9am to 5pm.

Babysitters   Many hotels can provide reliable babysitting services. A student babysitting roster is maintained by U.L.B. Service, "Jobs," av. P. Héger 22, 1000 Bruxelles (© 02/650-21-71).

Business Hours   See "Fast Facts: Belgium," in chapter 4.

Car Rentals   See "Getting Around," in chapter 4.

Currency Exchange   **Travelex,** Grand-Place 4 (© 02/513-28-45; Métro: Gare Centrale), has fair rates. See "Money," in chapter 2.

Doctors & Dentists   For doctors, call **Médi Garde** (© 02/479-18-18) or SOS **Médecins** (© 02/513-02-02) and ask for an English-speaking doctor. For emergency dental care, call © 02/426-10-26.

Drugstores   See "Fast Facts: Belgium," in chapter 4. See also "Pharmacies," below.

Electricity   See "Fast Facts: Belgium," in chapter 4.

Embassies & Consulates See "Fast Facts: Belgium," in chapter 4.

Emergencies For police assistance, call ✆ **101**. For an ambulance or the fire department, call ✆ **100**.

Hospital **Cliniques Universitaires St-Luc,** av. Hippocrate 10 (✆ **02/764-11-11;** Métro: Alma), has an emergency department.

Internet Access A short walk uphill from the Grand-Place, **BXL Café-Bar,** place de la Vieille Halle aux Blés 46 (✆ **02/502-99-80;** Métro: Gare Centrale), is open Sunday to Thursday from noon to midnight, and Friday to Saturday from noon to 1am; access is 1.50€ ($1.90) an hour. This is a gay- and lesbian-friendly cafe.

Mail See "Fast Facts: Belgium," in chapter 4.

Pharmacies See "Fast Facts: Belgium," in chapter 4. A centrally located pharmacy is **Grande Pharmacie de Brouckère,** Passage du Nord 10–12 (✆ **02/218-05-07;** Métro: De Brouckère).

Police In an emergency, call ✆ **101**. In non-urgent situations, go to **Brussels Central Police Station,** rue du Marché au Charbon 30 (✆ **02/279-79-79;** Métro: Bourse), just off the Grand-Place. Many Brussels police officers have a poorly developed sense of public service, and a surly and unconcerned attitude to visitors' problems is not uncommon, even at this office where tourists in difficulty often end up. Many officers speak English.

Post Office Most post offices are open Monday to Friday from 9am to 5pm. The office at Centre Monnaie, place de la Monnaie (✆ **02/226-39-07;** Métro: De Brouckère), is open Monday to Friday from 9am to 6pm, and Saturday from 10am to 4pm. The office at Gare du Midi, av. Fonsny 1E/F (✆ **02/538-33-98;** Métro: Gare du Midi), is open 24 hours.

Restrooms See "Fast Facts: Belgium," in chapter 4. Should you have a toilet emergency in Brussels, the best place to find relief is the Hotel Métropole (see "Where to Stay," below).

Safety Brussels is generally safe, but there is a growing trend of pickpocketing, theft from and of cars, and muggings in places such as Métro station foot tunnels. Don't overestimate the risk, but take sensible precautions, particularly in obvious circumstances such as on crowded Métro trains and when withdrawing cash from an ATM at night.

Taxes See "Fast Facts: Belgium," in chapter 4.

Telephones See "Fast Facts: Belgium," in chapter 4. The area code for Brussels is **02**. You need to dial this area code both from inside Brussels and from elsewhere in Belgium (you always need to dial the area code in Belgium). When you're calling from outside Belgium, the area code for Brussels is **2**.

Tipping See "Fast Facts: Belgium," in chapter 4.

Transit Info For information regarding tram, bus, and Métro service, call ✆ **0900/10-310**.

Useful Phone Numbers The baggage office (✆ **02/753-68-20**) in the Arrivals hall of Brussels National Airport can help if you have lost luggage or other property aboard an aircraft or in the airport. The bigger rail stations have lost-property offices as well; call ✆ **02/555-25-25** if you lose something on a train.

Property lost on the Métro, tram, or bus may be recovered from STIB, av. de la Toison d'Or 15 (© **02/515-23-94**). If you lose something on the street, try the local police station; many Belgians are honest enough to hand in property they've found.

3 Where to Stay

The business of Brussels is business (and politics), a fact reflected in the cost and nature of available accommodations. Hotels in the upper price range, including deluxe hotels of just about every international chain, have a wealth of facilities for business travelers and efficient, though invariably impersonal, service. At every level, hotels fill up during the week and empty out on weekends and during July and August. In off-peak periods, rates can drop as much as 50% from those quoted below; be sure to ask for lower rates and confirm that you're quoted the correct rates, which include 6% value-added tax (TVA) and a 16% service charge.

Brussels International Tourism (see "Visitor Information," earlier in this chapter) makes reservations for the same day if you go to their offices in person and pay a small fee (which is deducted by the hotel from their room rate).

AROUND THE GRAND-PLACE
VERY EXPENSIVE

Amigo ✹✹   In Brussels slang, an "amigo" is a prison, and indeed a prison once stood here, in a highly convenient location (both then and now) across the street from the Town Hall. But any resemblance to the former accommodations is nominal. The Amigo has gone from being a worthy but somewhat dull hotel to one of the city's finest. Its Spanish Renaissance architecture, stately corridors, and flagstone lobby are right at home in this ancient neighborhood. Some of the previous incarnation's antiques, sculptures, wall tapestries, and wood accents have been retained, to good effect. The rooms are quite spacious and traditionally elegant, but with touches of modern Flemish design to brighten things up. Tintin motifs in the bathrooms add an element of whimsy. Ask for a room with a view of the Town Hall's fantastic Gothic spire.

Rue de l'Amigo 1–3 (off the Grand-Place), 1000 Bruxelles. © **02/547-47-47**. Fax 02/502-28-05. www.roccoforte hotels.com. 174 units. 195€–500€ ($244–$625) double; from 890€ ($1,113) suite. AE, DC, MC, V. Valet parking 20€ ($25). Métro: Bourse. **Amenities:** Restaurant (French/Belgian); bar; lounge; health club; concierge; 24-hr. business center; 24-hr. room service; babysitting; laundry service; same-day dry cleaning; nonsmoking rooms; executive rooms. *In room:* A/C, TV w/pay movies, fax, dataport, minibar, hair dryer, safe.

EXPENSIVE

Le Dixseptième ✹   This graceful, 17th-century house that was once the official residence of the Spanish ambassador stands close to the Grand-Place in a neighborhood of restored dwellings. Guest rooms, reached via a carved-wood stairway, have wood paneling and marble chimneys, and are as big as suites in many hotels; some have balconies. All are in 18th-century style and are named after Belgian painters from Brueghel to Magritte. Two beautiful lounges are decorated with carved-wood medallions and 18th-century paintings.

Rue de la Madeleine 25 (off place de l'Albertine), 1000 Bruxelles. © **02/517-17-17**. Fax 02/502-64-24. www.le dixseptieme.be. 24 units. 200€–270€ ($250–$338) double; 350€ ($438) suite. Rates include buffet breakfast. AE,

Where to Stay & Dine in Brussels

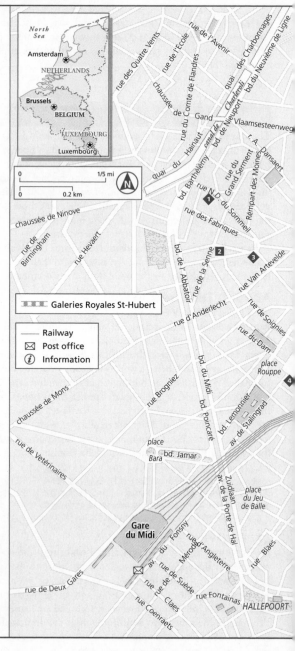

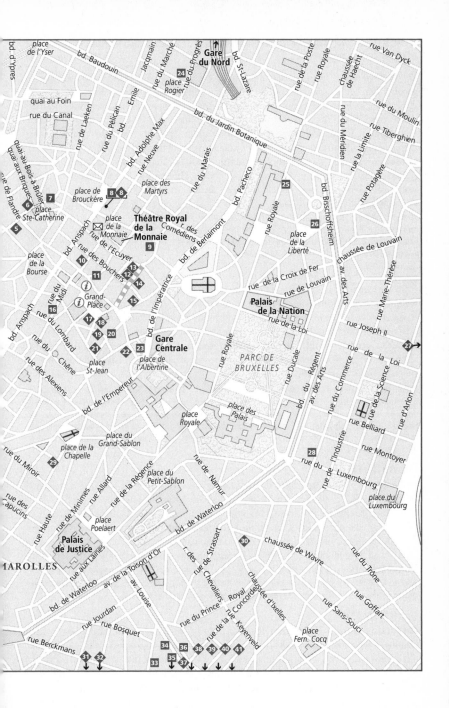

DC, MC, V. Limited street parking. Métro: Gare Centrale. **Amenities:** Lounge; laundry service; dry cleaning. *In room:* A/C, TV, minibar, hair dryer, safe.

Métropole ★★ Even if you're not staying here, the hotel is worth a visit on its own account. An ornate, marble-and-gilt interior distinguishes this late-19th-century hotel several blocks from the Grand-Place, intimating Victorian elegance without rejecting the convenience of modern amenities. Soaring ceilings, potted palms, and lavishly decorated public rooms add to the Belle Epoque allure. Spacious guest rooms have classic furnishings and some modern luxuries, including heated towel racks, hair dryers, and trouser presses. An elegant French restaurant, **L'Alban Chambon,** caters to the sophisticated diner, and the sumptuous Belle Epoque **Le 19ième Bar** and the associated sidewalk Café Métropole (see "Where to Dine," below) to the sophisticated cafe hound.

Place de Brouckère 31 (close to Centre Monnaie), 1000 Bruxelles. © **02/217-23-00.** Fax 02/218-02-20. www. metropolehotel.com. 305 units. 329€–429€ ($411–$536) double; from 650€ ($813) suite. Rates include buffet or continental breakfast. AE, DC, MC, V. Parking 15€ ($19). Métro: De Brouckère. **Amenities:** Restaurant (French); lounge; sidewalk cafe; health club and spa; concierge; 24-hr. room service; laundry service; dry cleaning. *In room:* TV w/pay movies, minibar, coffeemaker, hair dryer, safe.

Radisson SAS ★ Modern, yet in harmony with its neighborhood a few blocks from the Grand-Place, this highly regarded hotel incorporates part of the medieval city wall. The large rooms are decorated in a variety of styles, including Scandinavian, Asian, and Italian, and the Royal Club rooms are plushly upholstered. There's a huge atrium with cafe terraces and fountains; some rooms look out on this atrium rather than the outside world. The **Sea Grill** restaurant wins deserved plaudits for its seafood, and the **Bar Dessiné** (which has a roster of 200 Scotch malt whiskeys) has a Belgian comic strip theme.

Rue du Fossé aux Loups 47 (close to Galeries Royales St-Hubert). © **800/333-3333** in the U.S. and Canada, or 02/219-28-28. Fax 02/219-62-62. www.radissonsas.com. 281 units. 220€–405€ ($275–$506) double; 590€–890€ ($738–$1,113) suite. AE, DC, MC, V. Valet parking 25€ ($31). Métro: Gare Centrale. **Amenities:** 2 restaurants (seafood; Belgian/international); bar; lounge; health club; Jacuzzi; sauna; concierge; courtesy car; business center; 24-hr. room service; massage; babysitting; laundry service; dry cleaning; nonsmoking rooms. *In room:* A/C, TV w/pay movies, fax, dataport, minibar, coffeemaker, hair dryer, iron, safe.

MODERATE

Arlequin You can't get closer to the heart of the city than this, with the restaurant-lined rue des Bouchers right outside the hotel's back entrance. Then there's the fine view, from some rooms, of the Town Hall spire on the neighboring Grand-Place (which is spectacular when lit at night), and of the Old City's rooftops and narrow medieval streets from the top-floor breakfast room. The guest rooms themselves are not quite so spectacular, but all have modern, comfortable furnishings and most have plenty of natural light.

Rue de la Fourche 17–19 (off rue des Bouchers), 1000 Bruxelles. © **02/514-16-15.** Fax 02/514-22-02. www.arlequin.be. 92 units. 125€ ($156) double. Rates include buffet breakfast. AE, DC, MC, V. No parking. Métro: Bourse. **Amenities:** Limited room service; laundry service; dry cleaning. *In room:* TV w/pay movies, hair dryer.

INEXPENSIVE

Mozart Go up a flight from the busy, cheap-eats street level, and guess which famous composer's music wafts through the lobby? Salmon-colored walls, plants, and old paintings create a warm, intimate ambience that's carried into the rooms. Furnishings are in Louis XV style, and exposed beams lend each unit a rustic originality. Several are duplexes with a sitting room underneath the loft bedroom. Top-floor rooms have a great view.

Value Passport to Brussels

One of the best discounts is the **Brussels Card,** available from the Brussels Inter-national tourist office on the Grand-Place, and from hotels, museums, and offices of the STIB city transit authority, for 30€ ($38). Valid for 3 days, it allows free use of public transportation; free and discounted admission to around 30 of the city's museums and attractions; and discounts at some restaurants and other venues, and on some guided tours.

Rue du Marché aux Fromages 23 (close to Grand-Place), 1000 Bruxelles. © **02/502-66-61.** Fax 02/502-77-58. www.hotel-mozart.be. 47 units. 95€ ($119) double. AE, DC, MC, V. No parking. Métro: Gare Centrale. **Amenities:** Lounge; laundry service. *In room:* TV, hair dryer.

AROUND THE FISH MARKET
MODERATE
Welcome ✸✸   The name of this gem of a hotel, overlooking the Fish Market, couldn't be more accurate, thanks to the untiring efforts of the husband-and-wife pro-prietors, Michel and Sophie Smeesters. You can think of it as a country *auberge* (inn) right in the heart of town. Rooms are furnished and styled on individual, unrelated international and travel themes, such as Provence, Tibet, Egypt, Africa, Jules Verne, and Laura Ashley, all to a high standard. You'll find several good dining options on the Marché aux Poissons. There's a free airport shuttle to and from Brussels National Air-port. Reserve as far ahead of time as possible, for the Welcome's regular guests are fiercely loyal.

Quai au Bois-à-Brûler 23 (at the Marché aux Poissons), 1000 Bruxelles. © **02/219-95-46.** Fax 02/217-18-87. www. hotelwelcome.com. 15 units. 85€–120€ ($119–$163) double; 130€–180€ ($163–$225) suite. Rates include buffet breakfast. AE, DC, MC, V. Parking 10€ ($13). Métro: Ste-Catherine. **Amenities:** Lounge; Internet desk. *In room:* A/C (some rooms), TV, dataport, minibar, hair dryer, safe.

INEXPENSIVE
George V ✸   This agreeable little hotel is tucked away in a corner of the center city that looks more down-at-the-heels than it really is and is currently being reborn as a trendy shopping and eating area. The George, in a town house from 1859 within easy walking distance of the Grand-Place, provides a free shuttle bus to this square, the main museums, and Gare du Midi. The rooms are plain but clean and have new fur-nishings. However, some of the fittings—such as the carpets and curtains—are some-what worn and in need of replacement.

Rue 't Kint 23 (off place du Jardin aux Fleurs), 1000 Bruxelles. © **02/513-50-93.** Fax 02/513-44-93. www.george5. com. 16 units. 75€ ($93) double. Rates include continental breakfast. AE, MC, V. Parking 7€ ($9.40). Métro: Bourse. **Amenities:** Restaurant (Belgian); bar; 24-hr. room service. *In room:* TV.

THE UPPER CITY
EXPENSIVE
Astoria ✸   You're transported to a more elegant age the moment you walk into this hotel's Belle Epoque foyer, where the sumptuous surroundings feature Corinthian columns, antique furnishings, and textured marble. The Astoria dates from 1909, and its plush interior recalls the panache of that vanished heyday. Rooms, which are some-what smaller than those in other hotels of this category, are attractively and comfortably

furnished, though not extravagantly so, in a style that's in keeping with the character of the hotel. You can dine at the beautiful French restaurant **Le Palais Royal** and have a drink in the ornate **Pullman Bar,** which is based on the restaurant car of the legendary Orient Express train. Plus, Astoria's location is ideal for exploring both the old Brussels of the center city and the newer upper city.

Rue Royale 103 (close to Colonne du Congrès), 1000 Bruxelles. ℂ **800/SOFITEL** in the U.S. and Canada, or 02/227-05-05. Fax 02/217-11-50. www.sofitel.com. 118 units. 139€–350€ ($174–$438) double; from 480€ ($600) suite. Weekend double rates include buffet breakfast. AE, DC, MC, V. Parking 18€ ($23). Métro: Botanique. **Amenities:** Restaurant (French); lounge; health club and spa; concierge; 24-hr. room service; laundry service; dry cleaning. *In room:* A/C, TV w/pay movies, dataport, minibar, coffeemaker, hair dryer, safe.

AROUND AVENUE LOUISE
EXPENSIVE
Bristol Stéphanie Brussels ⭐⭐   Every feature of this sleek, Norwegian-owned hotel on one of the city's toniest shopping streets, from its lobby fittings to furnishings in the kitchenette suites, is streamlined, functional, and representative of the best in Nordic design. Some rooms have four-poster beds and "anti-allergy" hardwood floors; all are furnished to a high level of modern style and comfort (though the standard rooms could use a little more drawer space). The rooms are quite large, but if you need more space, it's worth the extra 40€ ($50) or so to upgrade to a far larger executive room. Try to get a room in the main building; the security in the back building is good, but nothing beats a 24-hour doorman. Restaurant **Le Chalet d'Odin** has a refined Continental menu, and the breakfast room serves a pretty reasonable American-style buffet breakfast.

Av. Louise 91–93, 1050 Bruxelles. ℂ **02/543-33-11.** Fax 02/538-03-07. www.bristol.be. 142 units. 365€–425€ ($456–$531) double; from 625€ ($781) suite. AE, DC, MC, V. Parking 20€ ($25). Métro: Louise. **Amenities:** Restaurant (Continental); lounge; bar; heated indoor pool; exercise room; Jacuzzi; sauna; concierge; business center; 24-hr. room service; babysitting; laundry service; dry cleaning; nonsmoking rooms; executive rooms. *In room:* A/C, TV w/pay movies, dataport, minibar, coffeemaker, hair dryer, iron, safe.

Stanhope Brussels ⭐   An old convent and some recently acquired neighboring properties in the upmarket shopping district around avenue Louise and Porte de Namur have been transformed into this graceful hotel. The ambience of the Stanhope combines that of a country retreat with a prime metropolitan location. All guest rooms are individually decorated in variations of Old English style. For all the hotel's English image, the in-house restaurant, **Brighton,** is French. But it's certainly tasteful.

Rue du Commerce 9 (off rue du Trône), 1000 Bruxelles. ℂ **02/506-91-11.** Fax 02/512-17-08. www.stanhope.be. 96 units. 120€–325€ ($150–$406) double; 625€ ($781) suite. AE, DC, MC, V. Valet parking 10€ ($13). Métro: Trône. **Amenities:** Restaurant (French); bar; tearoom; health club and spa; concierge; business center; 24-hr. room service; in-room massage; babysitting; laundry service; dry cleaning. *In room:* A/C, TV, dataport, minibar.

MODERATE
Agenda Louise ⭐   This fine, small, middle-of-the-road hotel affords a good balance of advantages for both leisure visitors who are looking for modern comforts without spending too much to get them, and for business visitors who don't have sheaves of locked-and-loaded plastic to get by on. The recently renovated, spiffily decorated rooms feature light-colored wood furniture and gold-and-orange curtains. They have enough room to swing a cat, so long as it's not an overly big one, and all include complete kitchens. The bathrooms have tiled walls and floors and just about break out of the shoehorned-in syndrome that afflicts many moderately priced city hotels. Ask for a room that overlooks the inner courtyard for the best view.

Rue de Florence 6–8 (off av. Louise), 1000 Bruxelles. © 02/539-00-31. Fax 02/539-00-63. www.hotel-agenda.com.
37 units. 116€ ($145) double. Rates include buffet breakfast. AE, DC, MC, V. Parking 6€ ($7.50). Métro: Louise. **Ameni-ties:** Lounge; same-day dry cleaning; nonsmoking rooms. *In room:* TV, dataport, minibar, coffeemaker, hair dryer.

Melia Avenue Louise Boutique Hotel ⚜   You'll find typically English country-house decor here, down to the fireplace in the lobby. The spacious, attractively fur-nished guest rooms all have private bathrooms, hair dryers, writing desks, and trouser presses. Some have kitchenettes. An English-style buffet breakfast is served in a pleas-ant and intimate breakfast room—so if you like your ham 'n' eggs done with a touch of class, this gem of a hotel could be the place for you.

Rue Blanche 4 (off av. Louise), 1050 Bruxelles. © 02/535-35-00. Fax 02/535-96-00. www.solmelia.com. 80 units.
130€–260€ ($163–$325) double; 360€ ($450) suite. Rates include buffet breakfast. AE, DC, MC, V. Limited street parking. Métro: Louise. **Amenities:** Bar; sauna. *In room:* TV, minibar.

INEXPENSIVE
De Boeck's *Kids*   In a well-maintained 19th-century town house, this graceful hotel has unusually spacious and quiet rooms. They don't quite measure up to the Victorian elegance of the public spaces but are adequately furnished, with comfortable modern beds, soft carpeting, and floral-patterned curtains. Some rooms, ideal for families and small groups, can be used as quads or even quints.

Rue Veydt 40 (off chaussée de Charleroi), 1050 Bruxelles. © 02/537-40-33. Fax 02/534-40-37. www.hotel-deboecks.be.
46 units. 62€–100€ ($78–$125) double. Rates include buffet breakfast. AE, DC, MC, V. Limited street parking. Métro: Louise. *In room:* TV, hair dryer.

AROUND GARE DU NORD
MODERATE
Comfort Art Hotel Siru ⚜   Yes, this area of town was formerly decrepit—it used to be a red-light district and still has some peep-show joints and offbeat appliance stores—but it has been going upmarket fast since a slew of fancy office blocks were constructed nearby. What sets the fascinating midsize Siru apart is that the owner per-suaded 130 Belgian artists, including some of the country's biggest names, to "deco-rate" each of the coolly modern, well-equipped rooms and the corridors with a work on travel. The Siru is best summed up as an art-gallery-cum-hotel in a redeveloped business district. Given the unpredictable nature of reactions to modern art, some clients apparently reserve the same room time after time; others ask for a room change in the middle of the night. It is not easily forgotten. The tony **Brasserie Saint-Ger-main** next door is the "unofficial" hotel restaurant.

Place Rogier 1 (opposite Gare du Nord), 1210 Bruxelles. © 800/228-3323 in the U.S. and Canada, or 02/203-35-80.
Fax 02/203-33-03. www.comforthotelsiru.com. 101 units. 85€–250€ ($106–$313) double. Rates include buffet breakfast. AE, DC, MC, V. Parking 15€ ($19). Métro: Rogier. **Amenities:** Restaurant (French/Belgian); babysitting; laundry service; same-day dry cleaning; nonsmoking rooms; executive rooms. *In room:* TV w/pay movies, dataport, minibar, hair dryer, safe.

INEXPENSIVE
Sabina   This small hostelry is like a private residence, presided over by hospitable owners. A grandfather clock in the reception area and polished wood along the restau-rant walls give it a warm, homey atmosphere. Rooms vary in size, but all are comfort-able and simply yet tastefully done in modern style with twin beds. Three rooms have kitchenettes.

Rue du Nord 78 (at place des Barricades), 1000 Bruxelles. © 02/218-26-37. Fax 02/219-32-39. www.hotelsabina.be.
24 units. 75€–105€ ($94–$131) double. Rates include buffet breakfast. AE, DC, MC, V. Limited street parking. Métro: Madou. *In room:* TV, hair dryer.

AIRPORT HOTELS
VERY EXPENSIVE
Sheraton Brussels Airport ★   You can't be more conveniently located to Brussels National Airport than here—without lodging on the runway. You'll find all the comfort you would expect of a top-flight Sheraton, including soundproof rooms with big, comfortable beds. The Concorde restaurant has a French slant complemented by international dishes.

Luchthaven Brussel Nationaal (facing Departures), 1930 Zaventem, Belgium. © **800/325-3535** in the U.S. and Canada, or 02/725-10-00. Fax 02/725-11-55. www.sheratonairport.be. 533 units. 275€–335€ ($344–$419) double; from 590€ ($738) suite. AE, DC, MC, V. Parking 12€ ($15). **Amenities:** Restaurant (French/international); bar; health club; sauna; concierge; 24-hr. room service; laundry service; dry cleaning; nonsmoking rooms; executive rooms. *In room:* A/C, TV w/pay movies, minibar, coffeemaker, hair dryer.

MODERATE
Express by Holiday Inn Brussels Airport   For a cheaper near-airport option than the Sheraton, try this efficient small place that's just a 5- to 10-minute shuttle ride away. Rooms often are steeply discounted, so always inquire. If you get the munchies, you can dine at its big brother Holiday Inn next door. There's free long-term parking and an airport shuttle.

Bierkenlaan 5, 1831 Dieghem (access road opposite NATO HQ). © **02/725-33-80.** Fax 02/725-38-10. www.ichotels group.com. 87 units. 50€–130€ ($188–$313) double. Rates include buffet or continental breakfast. AE, DC, MC, V. Parking 10€ ($13). **Amenities:** Bar. *In room:* TV.

4 Where to Dine

Food is a passion in Brussels, which boasts more Michelin-star restaurants per head than Paris. People here regard dining as a fine art and their favorite chef as a grand master. It's just about impossible to eat badly, no matter what your price range. The city has no fewer than 1,500 restaurants. You can spend as much as 200€ ($250) for a meal in one of the culinary giants or as little as 15€ ($19) for one prepared with maybe as much loving care in an informal place. Even if you're on a tight budget, you should try to set aside the money for at least one big splurge in a fine restaurant— nourishment for both the soul and the stomach.

The Brussels restaurant scene covers the entire city, but there are one or two culinary pockets you should know about. It has been said that you haven't truly visited this city unless you've dined at least once along **rue des Bouchers** or its offshoot, **Petite rue des Bouchers,** both of which are near the Grand-Place. Both streets are lined with an extraordinary array of ethnic eateries—most with a proudly proclaimed specialty, and all with modest prices (under 15€/$19)—and some great Belgian restaurants. Reservations are not usually necessary in these colorful, and often crowded, restaurants—if you cannot be seated at one, you simply stroll on to the next one.

Then there's the cluster of fine restaurants at the **Marché aux Poissons (Fish Market),** a short walk from the Grand-Place around place Ste-Catherine. This is where fishermen once unloaded their daily catches from a now-covered canal. Seafood, as you'd expect, is the specialty. A well-spent afternoon's occupation is to stroll through the area to examine the bills of fare exhibited in windows and make your reservation for the evening meal. Don't fret if the service is slow: People take their time dining out here.

AROUND THE GRAND-PLACE
VERY EXPENSIVE
Comme Chez Soi ⭐⭐⭐ CLASSIC FRENCH   A visit to the revered, Art Nouveau "Just Like Home" will surely be the culinary highlight of your trip to Brussels. Although the food is a long way from what most people eat at home, the welcome from master chef Pierre Wynants is warm, and his standards are high enough for the most rigorous taste buds. Ask for a table in the kitchen, where you can watch the master at work. Reserve as far ahead as possible. Getting a table at short notice is more likely at lunchtime, which is generally a shade less busy than the evenings. Diners are emerging with even more of a spring in their step than usual. Under the influence of associate chef Lionel Rigolet, the dishes are looking lighter—even the Burgundian Bruxellois are conforming to a faster, slimmer world.

Place Rouppe 23 (at av. de Stalingrad). ⓒ 02/512-29-21. www.commechezsoi.be. Reservations required. Main courses 34€–125€ ($39–$118); fixed-price menus 67€–168€ ($70–$155). AE, DC, MC, V. Tues–Sat noon–1:30pm and 7–9:30pm. Métro: Anneessens.

La Maison du Cygne ⭐ BELGIAN/FRENCH   This grande dame of Brussels's internationally recognized restaurants overlooks the Grand-Place from the former guild house of the Butchers Guild—where Karl Marx and Friedrich Engels cooked up *The Communist Manifesto* during a 3-year sojourn in Brussels. The service, though a tad stuffy, is as elegant as the polished walnut walls, bronze wall sconces, and green velvet. The menu has haute cuisine Belgian and French classics, such as *waterzooï de homard* (a souplike lobster stew), veal sautéed with fresh wild mushrooms, and *tournedos* (filet steak) with green peppercorns. There are fine chicken and fish dishes, and specialties such as *huîtres au champagne* (oysters in champagne) and *goujonette de sole mousseline* (sole mousse). Because of its location, the restaurant is usually crowded at lunchtime, but dinner reservations are likely to be available.

Grand-Place 9 (entrance at rue Charles Buls 2). ⓒ 02/511-82-44. www.lamaisonducygne.be. Reservations recommended. Main courses 30€–58€ ($38–$73); *menu du jour* 90€ ($113). AE, DC, MC, V. Mon–Fri noon–2:15pm and 7pm–midnight; Sat 7pm–midnight. Métro: Gare Centrale.

EXPENSIVE
Aux Armes de Bruxelles ⭐ TRADITIONAL BELGIAN   A Brussels institution since it opened in 1921, this family-owned establishment offers gracious, rather formal service, combined with a casual, relaxed ambience. It's an excellent place for your introduction to Belgian cooking, since it combines traditional cuisine with great quality, and offers just about every regional specialty you can think of, including mussels in every conceivable style. To save valuable eating time at busy lunchtimes, do as many regulars do and just order *un complet*—within minutes a pan of steamed mussels accompanied by french fries and a beer will land on your table. You can also sample anything from an excellent beef stewed in beer to a delicious *waterzooï* fish or chicken stew, to a steak with pepper-and-cream sauce, all at fair prices.

Rue des Bouchers 13 (off the Grand-Place). ⓒ 02/511-55-98. www.auxarmesdebruxelles.be. Main courses 14€–44€ ($18–$26); *menu du jour* 31€–46€ ($35–$54). AE, DC, MC, V. Tues–Sun noon–11:15pm. Métro: Gare Centrale.

De l'Ogenblik ⭐ FRENCH/BELGIAN   In the elegant surroundings of the Galeries Royales St-Hubert, you'll find a Parisian bistro-style setting restaurant that's popular with off-duty actors and audiences from the nearby Gallery theater, among others. It often gets busy, but the ambience in the split-level, wood-and-brass-outfitted dining room, with a sand-strewn floor, is convivial, though a little too tightly packed when it's full. Look for garlicky meat and seafood menu dishes, and expect to pay a smidgeon more for atmosphere than might be strictly justified by the results on your plate. If you like duck, try the *magret du canard mulard aux deux poivres, gratin dauphinois* (filet of duck with peppers and potatoes gratin). A good seafood choice is the *ragoût de coquilles St-Jacques et gambas, sauce diable* (scallop and prawn stew in a "devil"—spicy—sauce).

Galerie des Princes 1 (in the Galeries Royales St-Hubert). ℂ 02/511-61-51. www.ogenblik.be. Main courses 22€–29€ ($28–$35); *plat du jour* (lunch only) 11€ ($14). AE, DC, MC, V. Mon–Thurs noon–2:30pm and 7pm–midnight; Fri–Sat noon–2:30pm and 7pm–12:30am. Métro: Gare Centrale.

Le Scheltema BELGIAN   This is one of those solid restaurants in the Ilot Sacré district that keeps going day in, day out, year after year, serving up much the same fare but never forgetting that quality counts. Good service and fine atmosphere complement the seafood specialties at this brasserie-style restaurant, which is similar to others in the district but always goes the extra mile in class and taste. Pâté, *bisque d'homard* (lobster soup), *croquettes aux crevettes* (prawn croquettes), mussels (in season), and a wide range of fish and meat options all grace the excellent menu.

Rue des Dominicains 7 (off rue des Bouchers). ℂ 02/512-20-84. www.scheltema.be. Main courses 20€–52€ ($25–$65); seafood platter 68€ ($85). AE, DC, MC, V. Mon–Thurs noon–3pm and 6–11:30pm; Fri–Sat noon–3pm and 6pm–12:30am. Métro: Gare Centrale.

MODERATE
Brasserie de la Roue d'Or ✦ TRADITIONAL BELGIAN   With dark wood, mirrors, a high frescoed ceiling, Magritte images on the walls, and marble-topped tables, this welcoming Art Nouveau brasserie has a loyal local following. An extensive menu, ranging from grilled meats to a good selection of cooked salmon and other seafood, and old Belgian favorites like *stoemp* (mashed potatoes and carrots with sausage, a steak, or other meat), caters to just about any appetite. The beer, wine, and spirits list is equally long.

Rue des Chapeliers 26 (off the Grand-Place). ℂ 02/514-25-54. Main courses 13€–23€ ($16–$29); *menus du jour* 23€–28€ ($29–$35). AE, DC, MC, V. Daily noon–12:30am. Métro: Gare Centrale.

Le Marmiton BELGIAN/FRENCH   A welcoming environment, hearty servings, and commitment to satisfying customers are hallmarks of this cozy, two-floor restaurant. On a menu that emphasizes fish, the seafood cocktail starter is a heap of shellfish and crustaceans substantial enough to be a main course, and the sole is excellent. Meat dishes are available, too. The menu is complemented by an excellent wine list selected by Portuguese/Belgian owner and chef Antonio Beja da Silva, whose love of his own cooking shows in his waistline and in the attention he devotes to his customers.

Tips On Your Guard in the Ilot Sacré

A few restaurants (not reviewed here) in this colorful restaurant district just off the Grand-Place take advantage of tourists. If you decide to dine at a restaurant not reviewed here, and you don't want to get fleeced, be sure to ask the price of everything *before* you order it. Most visitors leave the Ilot Sacré with no serious complaint (other than an expanded waistline), but a little caution is in order.

Rue des Bouchers 43A (off Grand-Place). © **02/511-79-10**. www.lemarmiton.be. Main courses 12€–18€ ($15–$23); *menu du jour* 20€ ($25). AE, DC, MC, V. Daily noon–3pm and 6–11:30pm (12:30am weekends). Métro: Gare Centrale.

INEXPENSIVE

Cafe Métropole ✿ LIGHT FOOD   Many Brussels visitors never get beyond the pleasant heated-sidewalk section of this massive Victorian-style cafe. Inside, in the associated Le 19ième Bar, you find a casually elegant decor, highlighted by a marble fireplace, colorful wood puppets hanging from the high ceilings, and comfortable leather seating arranged in cozy groupings. The menu includes sandwiches, soups, quiches, and other light meals. The bar menu fills no fewer than six pages, including some rather exceptional specialties from the head barman.

In the Hôtel Métropole, place de Brouckère 31. © **02/217-23-00**. www.metropolehotel.com. Reservations not accepted. *Plat du jour* 9€ ($11); light meal 9€–13€ ($11–$16). AE, MC, V. Mon–Sat 11am–2am; Sun 3–11pm. Métro: De Brouckère.

Chez Léon SEAFOOD/BELGIAN   Think of it as the mussels from Brussels. This big, basic restaurant is the city's most single-minded purveyor of that marine delicacy. Léon has been flexing its mussels since 1893 and now has clones all over Belgium, among them one at the Bruparck amusements complex (see later in this chapter). The mollusks in question are top quality, at low prices, in a variety of styles, such as *moules marinières* (mussels boiled in vegetable stock) and *moules au vin blanc* (mussels in white-wine sauce). If you don't like mussels, there are plenty of other fishy delights—including eels in green sauce, cod, and bouillabaisse.

Rue des Bouchers 18 (off of Grand-Place). © **02/511-14-15**. www.chezleon.be. Main courses 9.40€–22€ ($12–$28); *menu Formule Léon* 14€ ($18). AE, DC, MC, V. Sun–Thurs 11:30am–11pm; Fri–Sat 11:30am–11:30pm. Métro: Gare Centrale.

L'Auberge des Chapeliers ✿ *Value* TRADITIONAL BELGIAN   In a 17th-century building that was once the headquarters of the hatmakers' guild, the Auberge des Chapeliers preserves its historic charm. Behind a beautiful brick facade, the first two floors are graced with timber beams and paneling and connected by a narrow timber staircase. Popular with locals who live and work in the area, and with tourists fortunate enough to find it, it can be crowded at the height of lunch hour, so it's a good idea to come just before noon or just after 2pm. The food is hearty Belgian fare, with an accent on mussels in season and dishes cooked in beer.

Rue des Chapeliers 1–3 (off Grand-Place). © **02/513-73-38**. Reservations recommended on weekends. Main courses 9.50€–18€ ($12–$23); set-price menus 15€–21€ ($19–$26). AE, DC, MC, V. Mon–Thurs noon–2pm and 6–11pm; Fri noon–2pm and 6pm–midnight; Sat noon–3pm and 6pm–midnight; Sun noon–3pm and 6–11pm. Métro: Gare Centrale.

Paradiso ITALIAN   This great little Italian restaurant is close enough to the Grand-Place to be convenient, but just far enough away to not be immediately obvious to the crowds. As such, it is one of Brussels's best-kept secrets. Owner/chef Santino Trovato has created a little gem, with pasta and pizza just like *Mamma* used to make and a list of fine Italian wines as long as your arm.

Rue Duquesnoy 34 (off place St-Jean). © **02/512-52-32**. Main courses 8.50€–14€ ($11–$18). No credit cards. Tues–Fri noon–3pm and 6:30pm–midnight; Sat–Sun 6:30pm–midnight. Métro: Gare Centrale.

't Kelderke ✿ TRADITIONAL BELGIAN   Despite being on the square that is the focus of tourism in Brussels, this is far from being a tourist trap. As many Bruxellois as tourists throng the long wood tables in a 17th-century, brick-arched cellar, and all are welcomed with time-honored respect, even if that should be perceived as being a little rough-and-ready. Memorable traditional Belgian fare, with little in the way of frills, is served up from an open kitchen. This is a great place to try local specialties such as *bloedpens* (blood sausage) *à la Bruxelloise, stoemp* (mashed potato and vegetable) with *boudin* (sausage), *carbonnades à la Flamande* (Flemish beef stew), *lapin à la gueuze* (rabbit in Brussels beer), and big steaming pans piled high with Zeeland mussels.

Grand-Place 15. (*C*) 02/513-73-44. Main courses 9.50€–19€ ($12–$24); *plat du jour* 8.50€ ($11). AE, DC, MC, V. Daily noon–2am. Métro: Gare Centrale.

AROUND AVENUE LOUISE
EXPENSIVE
La Quincaillerie ✦✦ MODERN FRENCH/SEAFOOD In the Ixelles district, where fine restaurants are as common as streetlights, this spot stands out, even though it may be a little too aware of its own modish good looks and a shade pricey. The setting is a traditional former hardware store from 1903, with a giant rail-station clock, wood paneling, and masses of drawers, designed by students of Art Nouveau master Victor Horta. It's busy enough to get the waitstaff harassed and absent-minded, yet they're always friendly. Seafood dishes dominate the menu. Specialties include *escalope du saumon rôti au gros sel* (salmon in roasted rock salt) and *canette laquée au miel et citron vert* (baby duck with a crust of honey and lime). You don't need to look much farther than a crisp Sancerre as the ideal wine accompaniment to most dishes.

Rue du Page 45 (at rue Américaine). (*C*) 02/533-98-33. www.quincaillerie.be. Main courses 15€–26€ ($19–$33); fixed-price menus 26€–30€ ($33–$38). AE, DC, MC, V. Mon–Fri noon–2:30pm and 7pm–midnight; Sat–Sun 7pm–midnight. Tram: 81, 82, 91, or 92 to chaussée de Charleroi.

La Table de l'Abbaye ✦ FRENCH If you're a French-cuisine enthusiast who likes things done just so and you're not too enamored of nouvelle cuisine, La Table de l'Abbaye is for you. The setting is a well-appointed town house near the tranquil grounds of the Abbaye (Abbey) de la Cambre. The food here is hard to beat and its prices are not excessive, considering the quality of the fare and its presentation. Look for many French favorites, all best accompanied with a fine wine—from France, of course. Lobster flexes its claws in several interesting ways on the menu here: in pancakes with caviar butter, in a mixed salad, and with a pepper-cream sauce. Lamb marinated in Bourgogne wine is another specialty. In a romantically atmospheric touch, candlelight provides the main illumination for the classic decor, enlivened by sculptures and paintings.

Rue de Belle-Vue 62 (off av. Louise). (*C*) 02/646-33-95. www.la-table-abbaye.be. Main courses 15€–25€ ($19–$31). AE, DC, MC, V. Daily noon–4:30pm and 7–11pm. Closed Dec 20–30. Tram: 94 (to top of av. Louise).

MODERATE
Au Vieux Bruxelles BELGIAN/SEAFOOD This convivial, brasserie-style restaurant from 1882 specializes in mussels, which it serves in a wide variety of ways. In Belgium, the personality of the humble but tasty mussel is a staple of conversation as much as of diet, and people assess the quality of each year's crop with the same critical eye that other countries reserve for fine wines. Au Vieux Bruxelles, a kind of temple to the Belgian obsession with mussels, serves the shellfish in 15 different ways, including raw (accompanied only by a light white-wine sauce), baked, fried, grilled,

and broiled, and in traditional dishes like *moules marinières* (boiled in water with vegetables) and *moules au vin* (boiled in wine). Should you not wish to work on the mussels, you can get great steaks like *steak au poivre flambé* (flamed pepper steak), *escargots* (snails), and crepes.

Rue St-Boniface 35 (close to Porte Namur). ✆ 02/503-31-11. www.auvieuxbruxelles.com. Reservations not accepted. Main courses 15€–21€ ($19–$26). AE, MC, V. Tues–Sun noon–2:30pm and 6:30–11pm. Métro: Porte de Namur.

L'Amadeus ♔ MODERN BELGIAN   The postmodern chic of this restaurant/ wine bar/oyster bar in a former sculptor's studio with garden-courtyard terrace makes a refreshing change from traditional Belgian style. Its candlelit interior is so dim you would think they're hiding something, but the cooking is nothing to be ashamed of. The menu includes such vegetarian treats as vegetarian lasagna, and ricotta and spinach tortellini; and for meat eaters, caramelized spareribs and several salmon dishes, all accompanied by delicious homemade nut bread. The Sunday brunch is an all-you-can-eat affair that includes smoked fish, cheese, eggs, bread, cereal, juice, and coffee.

Rue Veydt 13 (off chaussée de Charleroi). ✆ 02/538-34-27. Main courses 15€–23€ ($19–$29); *plat du jour* (Mon–Fri) 9.50€ ($12); Sun brunch 18€ ($23). AE, DC, MC, V. Tues–Fri and Sun noon–2:30pm and 7pm–1am; Mon and Sat 7pm–1am. Tram: 91 or 92.

Le Pain et le Vin MEDITERRANEAN   The owners of this restaurant were once steeped in the Michelin-star milieu but now have decided to jettison the rigorous requirements of that system and concentrate on having some good, clean, tasty fun instead. "Bread and Wine" fits the bill perfectly—and the bill won't be excessive either. The restaurant, in a converted house, looks out onto a garden. There's a terrace for alfresco dining in good weather. Whether the dish is chicken, fish, meat, or vegetables, the preparation concentrates on bringing out the natural taste, rather than smothering it with over-rich sauces. For interesting variations on common dishes, try the chicken ravioli with basil and Parmesan, or the lobster and shrimp lasagna with ginger sauce. Vegetarian dishes are available on request, and vegetable side dishes form a big part of the menu offerings.

Chaussée d'Alsemberg 812A. ✆ 02/332-37-74. www.painvin.be. Main courses 12€–16€ ($15–$20). AE, MC, V. Mon–Fri noon–2pm and 6–10pm; Sat 6–10pm. Tram: 55.

INEXPENSIVE

La Grande Porte TRADITIONAL BELGIAN   It's hard to think of a Brussels eatery that is more traditional Belgian than this archetypal place in the down-at-the-heels Marolles district. Dark wood furnishings, paper lanterns, marionettes hanging from the ceiling, old posters, and fashionably shabby walls, not to mention the whole place suffused with the sounds of canned French cabaret, combine to create a cozy, convivial dining space. The mostly regional main courses are served in bountiful portions. Sure to impart a warm glow of appreciation are hearty standards like the *carbonnades à la flamande* (beef braised in beer), *waterzooï à la Gantoise* (chicken stew), and *stoemp* (mashed potatoes and carrots) with sausage. But a touch of bistro-level sophistication in starters such as the chicory with smoked salmon and the warm goat's cheese salad lifts the menu out of the plain class. The late-night open hours are an added plus.

Rue Notre-Seigneur 9 (off rue Blaes). ✆ 02/512-89-98. Main courses 11€–14€ ($14–$18). V. Mon–Fri noon–3pm and 6pm–2am; Sat 6pm–2am. Bus: 20 or 48.

Shanti VEGETARIAN/SEAFOOD   An exotic look here is consistent with the restaurant's multicultural menus: Lots of greenery and flowers create a gardenlike feel, and crystal lamps, mirrors, and old paintings adorn the walls. Try "Neptune's pleasure," crab with avocado and seaweed, as a starter. For a main course, shrimp masala with mixed vegetables and coriander is excellent, as is eggplant with ricotta in a tomato-and-basil sauce.

Av. Adolphe Buyl 68. ✆ 02/649-40-96. Main courses 8€–13€ ($10–$16); fixed-price menus 22€–25€ ($28–$31). AE, DC, MC, V. Tues–Sat noon–2pm and 6:30–10pm. Tram: 92 or 93.

WEST OF THE BOURSE
EXPENSIVE
François ★★ SEAFOOD   A bright and cheerful ambience complements fine cuisine at this restaurant on the ground floor of a 19th-century *maison de maître* (townhouse) that has housed a fishmongers/traiteur since 1922, and the tradition is taken seriously. Tiled walls and dark wood tables grace a small dining room. *Superb* is the best word to describe seafood specialties, like the *sole ostendaise* (North Sea sole cooked in butter) and the *bouillabaisse* (fish soup), and their signature lobster dishes, mussels, and Zeeland oysters. The menu includes a few meat choices. The presentation is professional yet relaxed. In fine weather, you can dine on a great sidewalk terrace across the street on the old Fish Market square. If you're dining indoors, try to get one of the window tables that have a view on the square.

Quai aux Briques 2 (corner of place Ste-Catherine and Marché aux Poissons). ✆ 02/511-60-89. www.restaurant francois.be. Main courses 18€–58€ ($23–$73); fixed-price menu 25€–36€ ($31–$45). AE, DC, MC, V. Tues–Sat noon–2:30pm and 7–11:30pm. Métro: Ste-Catherine.

MODERATE
In 't Spinnekopke ★★ *Finds* TRADITIONAL BELGIAN   "In the Spider's Web" occupies a stagecoach inn from 1762, just far enough off the beaten track downtown to be frequented mainly by "those in the know." You dine in a tilting, tiled-floor building, at plain tables, and more likely than not squeezed into a tight space. This is one of Brussels's most traditional cafe/restaurants—so much so, in fact, that the menu lists its hardy standbys of regional Belgian cuisine in the old Bruxellois dialect. *Stoemp mi sossisse* is hotchpotch with sausage, and *toung ave mei* is sole. The bar stocks a vast selection of traditional beers.

Place du Jardin aux Fleurs 1 (off rue Van Artevelde). ✆ 02/511-86-95. www.spinnekopke.be. Main courses 11€–22€ ($14–$28); *plat du jour* 11€ ($14). AE, DC, MC, V. Mon–Fri noon–3pm and 6–11pm; Sat 6pm–midnight (bar Mon–Fri 11am–midnight; Sat 6pm–midnight). Métro: Bourse.

La Manufacture ★ FRENCH/INTERNATIONAL   Even in its former incarnation, this place was concerned with style—it used to be the factory of chic Belgian leather-goods maker Delvaux. Fully refurbished, with hardwood floors, leather banquettes, polished wood, and stone tables, all set amid iron pillars and exposed air ducts, it produces trendy world cuisine on a French foundation, for a mostly youthful public. You may find it a little disconcerting at first, being able to mix Asian menu dishes like dim sum and sushi with Moroccan couscous, Lyon sausage, sliced ostrich filets with mango and green pepper, and Belgian specialties like *waterzooï*, but you soon get the hang of it (the menu changes seasonally, so these particular dishes might not be available). Some evenings there's live piano music. On sunny days in summer, you can dine outdoors on a terrace shaded by giant bamboo plants.

Rue Notre-Dame du Sommeil 12–20 (off place du Jardin aux Fleurs). ✆ 02/502-25-25. www.manufacture.be. Main courses 12€–21€ ($15–$26); *menu du jour* (lunch only) 14€ ($18); fixed-price menus 30€–65€ ($38–$81). AE, DC, MC, V. Mon–Fri noon–2pm and 7–11pm; Sat 7pm–midnight. Métro: Bourse.

INEXPENSIVE
Le Paon Royal BELGIAN   One of my favorite small, family-owned restaurants, this typically Bruxellois treat is in a house dating from 1631 that has a rustic wood-and-exposed-brick interior and timber-beamed ceiling. You can have just a snack with one of the 65 brands of beer, six of them draft beers, behind the tiny bar (some of which are used in the cooking), or try the hearty *plat du jour,* invariably a traditional Belgian dish offered at lunchtime only. Specialties of the house are roast suckling pig in a mustard sauce, and cod filet in a *Hoegaarden* (Belgian white beer) sauce. In fine weather, chairs are generally set beneath a cluster of plane trees in a little park just across the street.

Rue du Vieux Marché aux Grains 6. ℰ **02/513-08-68.** www.paonroyal.com. Main courses 9.95€–18€ ($12–$23); *plat du jour* 9.90€ ($12). AE, DC, MC, V. Tues–Sat 11:30am–9:30pm. Métro: Ste-Catherine.

THE EUROPEAN DISTRICT
EXPENSIVE
Le Stévin BELGIAN/FRENCH   If you're experiencing an uncontrollable desire to rub shoulders with the European Union's politicos and bureaucrats—including an occasional commissioner or government minister from an EU member state—this tranquil town house is the place to go. True, that's not much of a recommendation, but fine food can make all the difference. Belgian specialties are prepared in a light, modern way that makes a pleasant change from the weightbound portions in traditional Belgian eateries. You can take a pre-meal drink at an Art Deco bar, and in fine weather dine alfresco in a garden at the back. The traditional wood-paneled setting features antique furnishings and old pictures of Brussels. Popular dishes here are sole, red mullet, and grilled or roast lamb. Wild mushrooms make a nice accompaniment for any of these meat and fish dishes.

Rue St-Quentin 29 (off Sq. Ambiorix). ℰ **02/230-98-47.** Main courses 18€–25€ ($23–$31); fixed-price lunch 20€–25€ ($25–$31). AE, DC, MC, V. Mon–Fri noon–2:30pm and 7–11:30pm. Métro: Schuman.

SOUTH BRUSSELS
VERY EXPENSIVE
Villa Lorraine ✦✦ TRADITIONAL FRENCH   You'll find one of the city's top kitchens in this renovated château on the fringes of the Bois de la Cambre park. The dining rooms are spacious, with wicker furnishings, flower arrangements, and a skylight. In good weather, enjoy drinks outside under the trees. Among the classic French offerings are saddle of lamb in a delicate red-wine-and-herb sauce, cold salmon in an herb sauce, partridge cooked with apples, and baked lobster with butter rose.

Chaussée de la Hulpe 28. ℰ **02/374-31-63.** www.villalorraine.be. Main courses 38€–95€ ($48–$119); *menu déjeuner* 55€ ($69); *menu du soir* 85€ ($106). AE, DC, MC, V. Mon–Sat noon–3:30pm and 7–9:30pm. Closed 3 weeks in July. Tram: 41.

INEXPENSIVE
Le Mâcon BELGIAN/SWISS   Tasty, uncomplicated Belgian fare, such as mussels *(moules)* and steak with french fries *(steak frites),* is this superior neighborhood cafe-restaurant's stock in trade. The extensive menu has slightly more exotic items—try the tournedos Rossini in port sauce, and skate *au beurre noir* (in black butter). Service is simple, and the cozy, wood-paneled dining area is a style-free zone (smoky, too), but there are a few tables with tablecloths, usually kept for regulars unless you ask for one. A Swiss menu, including fondue, is served every Thursday.

Rue Joseph Stallaert 87 (off av. Winston Churchill). ℰ **02/343-89-37.** Main courses 7.50€–20€ ($9.40–$25); fixed-price menus 9.50€–25€ ($12–$31); Swiss menu 22€ ($28). No credit cards. Daily noon–dawn. Tram: 23 or 90.

5 Seeing the Sights

Brussels has such a variety of things to see and do that it can sometimes be overwhelming. There are more than 75 museums dedicated to just about every special interest under the sun, in addition to impressive public buildings, leafy parks, and interesting squares. History is just around every corner. Fortunately, numerous sidewalk cafes offer respite for weary feet, and there's good public transportation to those attractions beyond walking distance of the compact, heart-shaped center city, which contains many of Brussels's most popular attractions.

THE CITY'S PRINCIPAL SQUARES

GRAND-PLACE ✿✿✿

Ornamental gables, medieval banners, gilded facades, sunlight flashing off gold-filigreed rooftop sculptures, a general impression of harmony and timelessness—there's a lot to take in all at once when you first enter the **Grand-Place** (Métro: Gare Centrale or Bourse). Once the pride of the Hapsburg Empire, the Grand-Place (*Grote Markt* in Dutch) has always been the heart of Brussels. Jean Cocteau called it "a splendid stage."

Its present composition dates mostly from the late 1690s, thanks to France's Louis XIV. In 1695, his army lined up its artillery on the heights of Anderlecht and blasted away at the medieval Grand-Place, using the Town Hall spire as a target marker. The French gunners destroyed the square, but ironically the Town Hall spire escaped undamaged. Other structures were not so fortunate, however, such as the wood-fronted buildings of the great trading and mercantile guilds.

But the Bruxellois weren't about to let a mere French king do away with their centuries-old corporate headquarters. The guildsmen had the place up and running again within 4 years, on the same grand scale as before but on more solid foundations. The result throws your sense of time out of joint, as the medieval atmosphere is conjured up mostly in the baroque style known as the Flemish Renaissance. The Town Hall, though badly damaged by Louis's guns, is the real thing, however, dating from the early 1400s.

Top honors go to the Gothic **Hôtel de Ville (Town Hall)** ✿✿ and the neo-Gothic **Maison du Roi (King's House)** ✿, which houses the **Musée de la Ville de Bruxelles (Museum of the City of Brussels;** see below).

You'll want to admire no. 9, the former headquarters of the guild of butchers—where Karl Marx created an ideology that would change the world when he wrote *The Communist Manifesto* there—and now a tony restaurant, **Le Cygne;** no. 10, **L'Arbre d'Or,** headquarters of the guild of brewers and location of the Brewing Museum; and nos. 13 to 19, an ensemble of seven mansions known as the **Maison des Ducs de Brabant,** adorned with busts of 19 dukes. Victor Hugo spent part of his time in exile at no. 26 **(The Pigeon),** firing off literary broadsides at Napoleon III until the City Fathers asked him to leave for fear the outraged French emperor would send an army to break his pen.

Tips Free Culture

Be sure to take advantage of the free admission some museums offer on the first Wednesday afternoon of every month.

Tips **Up Close & Personal**

In styles ranging from Gothic through Flemish Renaissance and baroque to neo-Gothic, the Grand-Place has a wealth of architectural and decorative elements. Bring a small pair of binoculars or even an opera glass with you so you won't miss even the tiniest details.

Don't miss the cafes lodged within the opulent wood-beamed interiors of old guild houses; their upper-floor windows overlooking the Grand-Place give some of the best views in Europe. And be sure to take in the *son-et-lumière* on summer evenings. This sound-and-light show, in which a series of colored lamps on the Hôtel de Ville (Town Hall) are switched on and off in sequence to appropriately grand music, is admittedly kind of kitsch. But who cares? It's magical.

PLACE DU GRAND SABLON ⊕

Though the traffic passing through it diminishes the experience, **Place du Grand Sablon** (tram: 92, 93, or 94) is filled with sidewalk cafes and lined with gabled mansions. Locals consider it a classier place to see and be seen than the Grand-Place. The Grand Sablon is antiques territory; many of its mansions house antiques stores or private art galleries with pricey merchandise on display. The dealerships have spread onto neighboring side streets as well. Saturday and Sunday mornings, an excellent antiques market sets up its stalls in front of **Notre-Dame du Sablon** (✆ **02/511-57-41**). This flamboyantly Gothic church, with no fewer than five naves, was paid for by the city's Guild of Crossbowmen in the 15th century. The statue of Minerva on the square dates from 1751. The church is open Monday to Friday from 9am to 5pm, and weekends from 10am to 6:30pm. Admission is free.

PLACE DU PETIT SABLON

Just across rue de la Régence is the Grand Sablon's little cousin, **place du Petit Sablon** (tram: 92, 93, or 94). An ornamental garden with a fountain and pool, it's a magical little retreat from the city bustle. The 48 bronze statuettes adorning the surrounding wrought-iron fence symbolize Brussels's medieval guilds. Two statues in the center commemorate the counts of Egmont and Hornes, who were beheaded in 1568 for protesting the cruelties of the Council of Blood, the enforcement arm of Spain's Holy Inquisition in the Low Countries.

PLACE ROYALE ⊕⊕

Brussels's royal square, **place Royale** (tram: 92, 93, or 94), is at the meeting point of rue de la Régence and rue Royale, two streets that hold many of the city's premier attractions. The 18th-century square, which was laid out in neoclassical style, is graced by an appropriately heroic **equestrian statue** of the leader of the First Crusade, Duke Godefroid de Bouillon. The inscription describes him as the "First King of Jerusalem," a title Godefroid himself refused, accepting instead that of "Protector of the Holy Places" (which amounted to the same thing). On the north face of the square is the **Eglise St-Jacques-sur-Coudenberg.** Archaeologists have excavated the foundations of the Royal Palace of Emperor Charles V on the square, and the site has been covered over again.

What to See & Do in Brussels

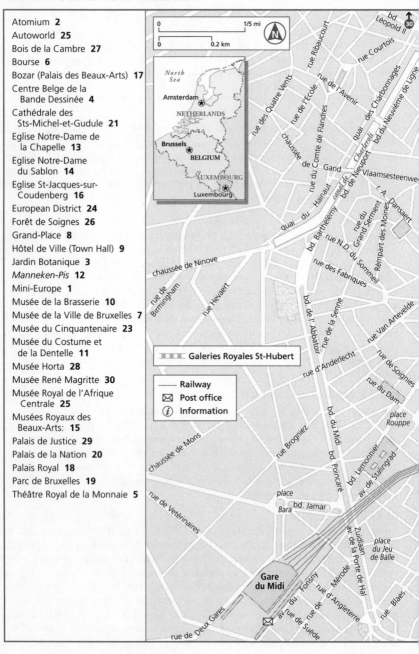

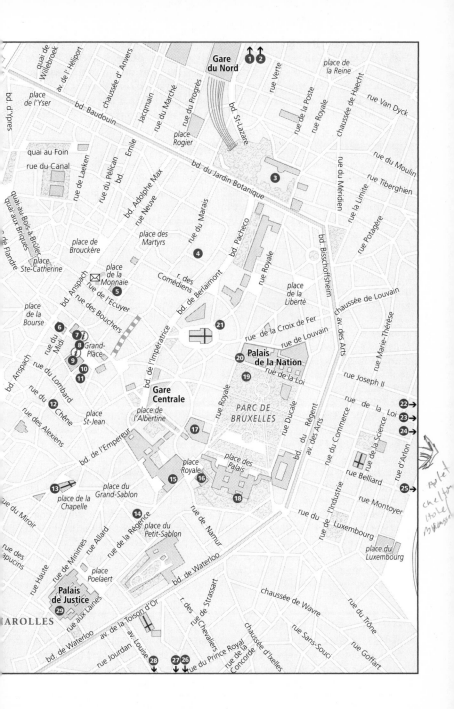

Gare
du Nord

place de
la Reine

rue Verte

rue Van Dyck

place
de l'Yser

bd. d'Ypres

quai de
Willebroek

av. de l' Héliport

chaussée d' Anvers

bd. Baudouin

Jacqmain

rue du Marché

rue du Progrès

bd. St-Lazare

rue de la Poste

rue Royale

chaussée de Haecht

quai au Foin

rue du Canal

rue de Laeken

rue du Pélican

bd.

Emile

place
Rogier

bd. du Jardin Botanique

rue du Moulin

rue Tiberghien

rue du Méridien

rue de la Limite

rue Potagère

quai au Bois-à-Brûler
quai aux Briques

de Flandre

place
Ste-Catherine

place de
Brouckère

place
de la
Monnaie

bd. Adolphe Max

rue Neuve

place des
Martyrs

rue du Marais

bd. Pacheco

rue Royale

bd. Bisschoffsheim

place
de la
Liberté

chaussée de Louvain

rue Marie-Thérèse

av. des Arts

place
de la
Bourse

bd. Anspach

rue de l'Ecuyer

r. des
Comédiens

rue des Bouchers

bd. de Berlaimont

rue de la Croix de Fer

rue de Louvain

rue Joseph II

6

7 *i*

8

Grand-
Place

9

10

11

rue du Midi

rue du Lombard

bd. Anspach

rue du Chêne

place
St-Jean

bd. de l'impératrice

21

Palais
de la Nation

20

19

rue de la Loi

12

des Alexiens

Gare
Centrale

place de
l'Albertine

rue Royale

PARC DE
BRUXELLES

bd. du Régent

av. des Arts

rue du Commerce

rue de la Loi

22 →
23 →
24 →

bd. de l'Empereur

17

rue Ducale

rue de la Science

rue d'Arlon

13

place de la
Chapelle

place du
Grand-Sablon

15

16

place
Royale

place des
Palais

18

rue Belliard

rue de l'Industrie

25 →

rue du Miroir

14

place du
Petit-Sablon

place du
Grand-Sablon

rue de la Régence

rue de Namur

rue Montoyer

rue du Luxembourg

place du
Luxembourg

des
apucins

rue Haute

rue de Minimes

rue Allard

place
Poelaert

bd. de Waterloo

chaussée de Wavre

rue du Trône

Palais
de Justice

29

MAROLLES

rue aux Laines

bd. de Waterloo

av. de la Toison d'Or

rue Jourdan

av. Louise

28

27 26

r. des Chevaliers

rue de Strassart

rue du Prince Royal
rue de la
Concorde

chaussée d'Ixelles

rue Sans-Souci

rue Goffart

93

PLACE DES MARTYRS

A few years ago, the once-elegant 18th-century **place des Martyrs** (Métro: Brouck-ère) in the lower city, near the Théâtre Royal de la Monnaie, was in a sorry state, lit-erally crumbling to the ground. It entombs the "500 Martyrs" of Belgium's 1830 War of Independence. It has been extensively restored, and though it lost some of its for-mer ragged charm in the process, the square is once again an important and attractive public place.

IMPORTANT BUILDINGS & MONUMENTS

The celebrated *Manneken-Pis* statue ✸, on the corner of rue du Chêne and rue de l'Etuve (Métro: Gare Centrale), 2 blocks from the Grand-Place, is Brussels's favorite little boy, gleefully doing what a little boy's gotta do. More often than not he's watched by a throng of admirers snapping pictures. Children especially seem to enjoy his bravura performance. This is not the original statue, which was prone to theft and anatomical maltreatment and was removed for safekeeping.

It's known that the boy's effigy has graced the city since at least the time of Philip the Good, who became count of Flanders in 1419. Among the speculations about the boy's origins are that he was the son of a Brussels nobleman who got lost and was found while answering nature's call; another is that he was a patriotic Belgian kid who sprinkled a hated Spanish sentry passing beneath his window. Perhaps the best theory is that he saved the Town Hall from a sputtering bomb by extinguishing it—like Gulliver—with the first thing handy.

Louis XV of France began the tradition of presenting colorful costumes to "Little Julian" to make amends for the French abduction of the statue in 1747. Since then the statue has acquired around 800 outfits, which are housed in the Musée de la Ville on the Grand-Place.

The ornately decorated **Bourse (Stock Exchange),** rue Henri Maus 2 (✆ 02/509-12-11; Métro: Bourse), at boulevard Anspach, a landmark of the French Second Empire architectural style, dates from 1873. It's a temple to the venerable religion of making money and is not open to casual visitors. Along its north facade, on rue de la Bourse, you can visit the interesting little **Bruxella 1238** museum (see below).

You may not want to spend too much time around the **Palais de Justice (Palace of Justice),** place Poelaert (✆ 02/508-65-78; Métro: Louise), adjacent to place Louise. This is, after all, where people who have run afoul of the law go directly to jail. Nonetheless, it's worth viewing architect Joseph Poelaert's extravagant (some would say megalomaniac) 19th-century neoclassical temple dedicated to the might and majesty of the law. The palace's domed magnificence stands on the old Galgenberg hill, once an open-air place of execution where criminals were hanged in public. It looms over the rebellious, working-class Marolles district, a none-too-subtle warning that its creators undoubtedly considered salutary. A modern elevator out on the

---

First Protestant Martyrs

In 1523, Hendrik Voes and Johann van den Esschen, two Augustinian monks from a cloister in Antwerp, were burned at the stake on the Grand-Place. The first martyrs for the Reformation, they were condemned by the Inquisition for following Martin Luther's precepts and refusing to recant.

> **Fun Fact** **The Lost River**
>
> Believe it or not, Brussels is constructed on a river called the Senne. In the 19th century, the City Fathers had it covered up, but you can still see traces of the missing river at courtyards off place St-Géry in the Lower Town.

palace's esplanade brings you down the steep hillside to the Marolles. You can visit the reception hall of the palace, which is open Monday to Friday from 9 to 11:30am and 1:30 to 3pm. Admission is free.

Not much has survived of the architecture of Burgundian-era Brussels; even the royal palace of the Burgundians and their Habsburg successors bit the dust due to fire. Part of the 15th- to 16th-century palace survives aboveground, 2 blocks east of Gare Centrale, in the red-brick **Hôtel Ravenstein,** rue Ravenstein 1–3 (Métro: Gare Centrale). Like the Hôtel de Ville, this is not a hotel at all. It houses a professional institute and the fancy French restaurant Le Relais des Caprices. But it does give you some idea of what Burgundian Brussels looked like—at least in those parts of the city occupied by the blue bloods.

The only surviving gateway from Brussels's once imposing 14th-century defensive walls is the squat and imposing **Porte de Hal,** at the junction of avenue de la Porte de Hal and chaussée de Waterloo (Métro: Porte de Hal).

THE TOP MUSEUMS & ATTRACTIONS

Hôtel de Ville (Town Hall) ★★   The facade of the dazzling Town Hall, from 1402, shows off Gothic intricacy at its best, complete with dozens of arched windows and sculptures—some of these, like the drunken monks, a sleeping Moor and his harem, and St. Michael slaying a female devil, displaying a sense of humor. A 66m (215-ft.) tower sprouts near the middle, yet it's not placed directly in the center. A colorful but untrue legend has it that when the architect realized his "error," he jumped from the summit of the tower.

You can visit the interior on 40-minute tours, which start in a roomful of paintings of the past foreign rulers of Brussels, who have included the Spanish, Austrians, French, and Dutch. In the spectacular Gothic Hall, open for visits when the city's aldermen are not in session—and surrounded by mirrors, presumably so each party can see what underhanded maneuvers the others are up to—you can see baroque decoration. In other chambers are 16th- to 18th-century tapestries. One of these depicts the Spanish duke of Alba, whose cruel features reflect the brutal oppression he and his Council of Blood imposed on the Low Countries; others show scenes from the life of Clovis, first king of the Franks.

Grand-Place. (C) 02/279-43-65. Admission (for guided tours only) 3€ ($3.75) adults; 2.50€ ($3.15) seniors, students; 2€ ($2.50) children 6–15, free for children under 6. Guided tours in English: Apr–Sept Tues–Wed 3:15pm, Sun 10:45am and 12:15pm; Oct–Mar Tues–Wed 3:15pm; tours at other times in French or Dutch. Closed Jan 1, May 1, Nov 1 and 11, Dec 25. Métro: Gare Centrale.

Musée de la Ville de Bruxelles (Museum of the City of Brussels) ★   This museum is in the neo-Gothic King's House (which, despite its name, has never housed a king). Exhibits inside document the history of Brussels. Among the most fascinating displays are old paintings and modern scale reconstructions of the historic center

open Sunday

city, particularly those depicting riverside activity along the now-vanished Senne. There are exhibits on traditional arts and crafts, such as tapestry and lace. The pride of the museum, however, is the more than 750 costumes donated to outfit Brussels's famous *Manneken-Pis* statue—including an Elvis outfit—each equipped with a strategically positioned orifice so that the little sculpture's normal function is not impaired.

Grand-Place 1. ✆ **02/279-43-50.** www.brucity.be. Admission 3€ ($3.75) adults, 2.50€ ($3.15) seniors/students, 1.50€ ($1.90) visitors with limited mobility/children 6–15, free for children under 6. Tues–Sun 10am–5pm. Closed Jan 1, May 1, Nov 1 and 11, Dec 25. Métro: Gare Centrale.

Musées Royaux des Beaux-Arts de Belgique (Belgian Royal Fine Arts Museums) 👁👁👁 In a vast museum of several buildings, this complex combines the **Musée d'Art Ancien** and the **Musée d'Art Moderne** under one roof (connected by a passage). The collection shows off works, most of them Belgian, from the 14th to the 20th centuries, starting in the historical section with Hans Memling's portraits from the late 15th century, which are marked by sharp lifelike details, works by Hieronymus Bosch, and Lucas Cranach's *Adam and Eve.* You should particularly seek out the subsequent rooms featuring Pieter Brueghel, including his *Adoration of the Magi* and *Fall of Icarus.* Don't miss his unusual *Fall of the Rebel Angels,* with grotesque faces and beasts. But don't fear—many of Brueghel's paintings, like those depicting Flemish village life, are of a less fiery nature. Later artists represented here include Rubens, van Dyck, Frans Hals, and Rembrandt.

Next door, in a circular building connected to the main entrance, the modern art section has an emphasis on underground works—if only because the museum's eight floors are all below ground level. The overwhelming collection includes works by van Gogh, Matisse, Dalí, Tanguy, Ernst, Chagall, and Miró, as well as local boys Magritte, Delvaux, De Braekeleer, and Permeke.

Place Royale 1–3. ✆ **02/508-32-11.** www.fine-arts-museum.be. Admission 5€ ($6.25) adults, 3.50€ ($4.40) students/seniors/visitors with disabilities, free for children under 12, free for everyone 1st Wed afternoon of the month (except during special exhibits). Tues–Sun 10am–5pm. Closed Jan 1, May 1, Nov 1 and 11, Dec 25. Métro: Parc.

Palais Royal (Royal Palace) 👁 The King's Palace, which overlooks the Parc de Bruxelles, was begun in 1820 and had a grandiose Louis XVI–style face-lift in 1904. The older side wings date from the 18th century and are flanked by two pavilions, one of which sheltered numerous notables during the 1800s. Today the palace is used for state receptions. It contains the offices of King Albert II, though he and Queen Paola do not live there—their *pied à terre* is the Royal Palace at Laeken. The national flag flies when the sovereign is in Belgium.

Place des Palais. ✆ **02/551-20-20.** www.monarchie.be. Free admission. From 3rd week of July to mid to late Sept (exact dates announced yearly). Tues–Sun 10:30am–4:30pm. Métro: Parc.

Impressions

The principal [fountain] whereof is the Mannicke Piss, being the figure of a brass boy erected upon a pedestal, the water issuing from his privy member (at a good distance) into a stone cistern.

—William Lord Fitzwilliam, *Touring the Low Countries: Accounts of British Travellers, 1660–1720,* Amsterdam University Press

A New Art

A new design style appeared toward the end of the 19th century and flourished for a few decades. It was called Art Nouveau in the United States and Britain. Art Nouveau's prime materials were glass and iron, which were crafted into decorative curved lines and floral and geometric motifs. Belgium produced one of the movement's greatest exponents: Victor Horta (1861–1947). His work can be seen in Brussels. The Tassel House (1893) and the Hôtel Solvay (1895) were forerunners of the ambitious Maison du Peuple (1896–99), with its concave, curved facades and location within an irregularly shaped square. His most prestigious building was the Innovation department store (1901), which was destroyed by fire.

PARC DU CINQUANTENAIRE ⊛

Designed to celebrate the half-centenary of Belgium's 1830 independence, the Cinquantenaire (Golden Jubilee) Park was a work in progress from the 1870s until well into the 20th century. Extensive gardens have at their heart a triumphal arch, the **Arc du Cinquantenaire,** topped by a bronze four-horse chariot sculpture, representing *Brabant Raising the National Flag,* and flanked by pavilions that house several fine museums.

Autoworld *Kids*   Even if you're not a car enthusiast, you'll find this display of 500 historic cars set in the hangarlike Palais Mondial fascinating. The collection starts with early motorized tricycles from 1899 and moves on to a 1911 Model T Ford, a 1924 Renault, a 1938 Cadillac that was the official White House car for FDR and Truman, a 1956 Cadillac used by Eisenhower and then by Kennedy during his June 1963 visit to Berlin, and more.

Parc du Cinquantenaire 11. ℂ 02/736-41-65. www.autoworld.be. Admission 6€ ($7.50) adults; 4.70€ ($4.65) students, seniors, and visitors with disabilities; 3€ ($3.75) children 6–13; free for children under 6. Apr–Sept Mon–Fri 9:30am–6pm, Sat–Sun 10am–6pm; Oct–Mar daily 10am–5pm. Closed Jan 1, Dec 25. Métro: Mérode.

Musée du Cinquantenaire ⊛   This vast museum shows off an eclectic collection of antiques, decorative arts (sculptures, tapestries, lace, porcelain, silver, furniture, toys, stained glass, jewels, folklore, and old vehicles including 18th-century coupes, sedan chairs, sleighs, and royal coaches), and archaeology. Some highlights are an Assyrian relief from the 9th century B.C., a Greek vase from the 6th century B.C., a tabletop model of imperial Rome in the 4th century A.D., the A.D. 1145 reliquary of Pope Alexander, some exceptional tapestries, and colossal statues from Easter Island.

Parc du Cinquantenaire 10. ℂ 02/741-72-11. www.kmkg-mrah.be. Admission 4€ ($5) adults, 2.50€ ($3.10) students and seniors, 1.50€ ($1.90) children 12–18, free for children under 12. Free admission every 1st Wed afternoon of the month (except during special exhibits). Tues–Fri 9:30am–5pm; Sat–Sun and holidays 10am–5pm. Closed Jan 1, May 1, Nov 1 and 11, Dec 25. Métro: Mérode.

Musée Royal de l'Armée et d'Histoire Militaire (Royal Museum of the Army and Military History) *Kids*   Because Belgium is not and never has been a great military power, this is one of Brussels's often forgotten museums. But its huge collection is one of the finest in Europe. It includes an extensive display of armor, uniforms, and weapons from various Belgian campaigns (like the Congo), a massive amount of World War I artillery, an aircraft hangar of 130 impressive planes (among them a Spitfire and

Moments **Drive-in Movie Palace**

In summer, the Arc du Cinquantenaire becomes the backdrop for the screen of a drive-in movie theater set around the fountain between the Porte de Ter-vuren and the Palais du Cinquantenaire.

---

a Hurricane that recall Belgian pilots' gallant service with the Royal Air Force during the Battle of Britain in 1940), and a World War II collection of Nazi flags that brings the Nürnberg rallies to mind. Anyone interested in military history shouldn't miss this superb though cluttered collection.

Parc du Cinquantenaire 3 (opposite Autoworld). ℭ 02/737-78-33. www.klm-mra.be. Free admission. Tues–Sun 9am–noon and 1–4:45pm. Closed Jan 1, May 1, Nov 1, Dec 25. Métro: Merode.

SIGHTS OF RELIGIOUS SIGNIFICANCE

Cathédrale des Sts-Michel-et-Gudule ✸✸   Victor Hugo considered this mag-nificent church, dedicated to the city's patron St. Michael and to St. Gudula, to be the "purest flowering of the Gothic style." Its choir is Belgium's earliest Gothic work. Begun in 1226, it was officially consecrated as a cathedral only in 1961. The 16th-century Habsburg Emperor Charles V donated the superb stained-glass windows. Apart from these, the spare interior decoration focuses attention on soaring columns and arches. The bright exterior stonework makes a fine sight. On Sunday at 10am the Eucharist is celebrated with a Gregorian choir. In July, August, and September, poly-phonic Masses are sung by local and international choirs at 10am. From August to October, chamber-music and organ concerts are occasionally performed on weekdays at 8pm. In spring and autumn at 12:30pm, Mass is sung accompanied by instrumen-tal soloists and readings by actors (in French).

In the crypt and an associated archaeological zone are foundations and other con-struction elements from an earlier church dating from the 11th century. The Trésor (Treasury) is also worth visiting, for its religious vessels in gold, silver, precious stones, and ecclesiastical vestments.

Parvis Ste-Gudule (off bd. de l'Impératrice 2 blocks west of Gare Centrale). ℭ 02/217-83-45. www.kathedraalst michiel.be. Cathedral, free admission; crypt, treasury, archaeological zone 2.50€ ($3.15). Mon–Fri 8am–6pm; Sat–Sun 8:30am–6pm. Métro: Gare Centrale.

Eglise Notre-Dame de la Chapelle (Our Lady of the Chapel)   This Romanesque-Gothic church is historically and architecturally interesting. François Anneessens (1660–1719), a Brussels hero who lost his head for campaigning for civil rights, is buried here. Anneessens was a champion of the freedom of the Belgian com-munes against the centralist rule of Belgium's Austrian masters. Condemned to death, he refused to plead for forgiveness, saying, "Never! I die innocent. May my death expi-ate my sins and be of service to my country." He was then beheaded on the Grand-Place. A statue of Anneessens stands on the square named after him—place Anneessens—in the center city, and you'll find a commemorative plaque dedicated to him in Notre-Dame's Chapel of the Holy Sacrament. Notre-Dame de la Chapelle is the burial site of Pieter Brueghel the Elder and his wife; their epitaph is in one of the chapels.

Place de la Chapelle. ℭ 02/512-21-40. Free admission. Tram: 92, 93, or 94.

Eglise Notre-Dame du Sablon (Church of Our Lady of the Sablon) ⚜ This flamboyant late-Gothic church, dating from around 1400 to about 1594, was paid for by the city's Guild of Crossbowmen, who called it optimistically Notre-Dame des Victoires (Our Lady of Victories), and it was their guild church. It is noted for its fourfold gallery with brightly colored stained-glass windows, illuminated from the inside at night, in striking contrast with the gray-white arches and walls. Worth seeing are the two baroque chapels decorated with funeral symbols in white marble. Inside is a celebrated statue of St. Hubert with an interesting history: It was actually stolen from Brussels and taken to Antwerp but was seized and returned to the Church in 1348, where it has remained ever since.

Rue Bodenbroek 6 (at place du Grand-Sablon). ℂ **02/511-57-41.** Free admission. Mon–Fri 9am–5pm; Sat–Sun 10am–6:30pm. Tram: 92, 93, or 94 to Petit-Sablon.

Eglise St-Nicolas (Church of St. Nicholas)   This delightful little church behind the Bourse is almost hidden by the fine old houses surrounding it, just as its 11th-century Romanesque lines are hidden by a 14th-century Gothic facade and the repairs made after the French bombardment of 1695. The church holds a small painting by Rubens, the *Virgin and Sleeping Child;* a bronze shrine dedicated to the Catholic Martyrs of Gorcum (Gorinchem), tortured and killed by Protestant Dutch rebels in 1572; and the *Vladimir Icon,* painted by an artist from Constantinople in 1131.

Rue au Beurre (facing the Bourse). ℂ **02/513-80-22.** Free admission. Mon–Fri 8am–6:30pm; Sat 9am–6pm; Sun and holidays 9am–7:30pm; closed to casual visitors during services. Métro: Bourse.

MORE MUSEUMS & ATTRACTIONS

The Brussels Bourse (Stock Exchange) stands on the grounds of a Franciscan convent, Les Récollets, which succumbed over the centuries to wars, fire, and religious conflict. Excavations begun in 1988 uncovered the convent's foundations and a bunch of medieval tombs. There's now a small underground museum, **Bruxella 1238,** rue de la Bourse (ℂ **02/279-43-50**), on the site. The most important tomb is that of the duke of Brabant, Jean I, who died in 1294. You can visit here only on guided tours that depart from the Musée de la Ville (see "Grand-Place," under "The City's Principal Squares," earlier in this chapter), Wednesday 10:15am (English), and 11:15am and 3pm (French). The tour costs 3€ ($3.75).

⸨ *Moments* Underground Art

Most of Brussels's Métro stations have been decorated with works of art—a painting, sculpture, mosaic, or installation—by leading Belgian modern artists. Taken together, they form an underground museum that you can tour for the price of a Métro ticket. Among interesting Métro stations are: **Bourse,** in the center city, which has a mural of old Brussels trams by the surrealist painter Paul Delvaux; **Stockel,** the eastern terminus of line 1B, where the walls are decorated with strips from the comic series *Tintin,* which was created by local hero Hergé; and **Horta,** south of Gare du Midi, which pays homage to Brussels's Art Nouveau architect Victor Horta, by way of elements from some of the buildings and interiors he designed.

Jardin Botanique   This graceful 19th-century glass-and-wrought-iron palace is no longer the Botanical Gardens of Brussels, but it merits a visit as a monument of 19th-century architecture. There's still a fine ornamental garden outside. Nowadays the Botanique functions as a cultural center in which theater, music and dance performances, and visiting art exhibitions are held.

Rue Royale 236. (℃ **02/226-12-11.** Free admission to gardens, main building; admission varies for cultural events. Métro: Botanique.

Musée de la Brasserie (Brewing Museum)   Operated by the Confederation of Belgian Breweries, the museum is housed in the Maison des Brasseurs, the home of the Brewers' Guild, the Knights of the Mash Staff. A permanent exhibition on modern high-tech brewing methods has joined an old one on traditional techniques. You'll find numerous paintings, stained-glass windows, and collections of pitchers, pint pots, and old china beer pumps. And you get a chance to sample some of your host's finished product.

Grand-Place 10. (℃ **02/511-49-87.** Admission 3€ ($3.75) adults. Apr–Nov daily 10am–5pm; Dec–Mar Sat–Sun noon–5pm. Métro: Gare Centrale.

Musée du Costume et de la Dentelle (Costume and Lace Museum)   The collections here include fine examples of historical Belgian lace styles from the once-renowned factories of Mechelen, Bruges, Antwerp, Binche, Turnhout, Poperinge, and Sint-Truiden. In addition, the museum houses displays of costumes, including an array of dresses from the 16th to the 19th centuries.

Rue de la Violette 12 (near Grand-Place). (℃ **02/213-44-50.** Admission 3€ ($3.75), 2€ ($2.50) children 6–16, free for children under 6. Mon–Tues and Thurs–Fri 10am–12:30pm and 1:30–5pm (until 4pm Oct–Mar); Sat–Sun 2–4:30pm. Closed Jan 1, May 1, Nov 1 and 11, Dec 25. Métro: Gare Centrale.

Musée Horta (Horta Museum) ✦   Art Nouveau might take its name from the gallery opened by art dealer Siegried Bing in Paris in 1895, but Brussels considers itself the capital of this medley of related art styles that burst across the Western world at the end of the 19th century and drew on exotic sources, including Celtic, Viking, Asian, and Islamic art. The city owes much of its rich Art Nouveau heritage to the inspired creative vision of Victor Horta, a resident architect who led the style's development. His home and an adjoining studio have been restored to their original condition and are now a museum. They showcase his use of flowing, sinuous shapes and colors in interior decoration and architecture.

Rue Américaine 25 (off chaussée de Charleroi). (℃ **02/543-04-90.** www.hortamuseum.be. Admission 7€ ($9) adults, 3.50€ ($4.40) seniors/students, 2.50€ ($3.15) children 5–18, free for children under 5. Tues–Sun 2–5:30pm. Closed holidays. Tram: 81, 82, 91, or 92.

Musée René Magritte   From 1930 to 1954, the great Belgian surrealist artist René Magritte lived and worked in an undistinguished town house in suburban Jette in northwest Brussels. Now restored, that 19-room house is a museum of the artist's life. You can visit most of the rooms, but can only view through glass the dining room-cum-studio where he painted many of his fantastical masterpieces while wearing a three-piece suit. You can even look through the famous window, with a view of nothing in particular, onto which Magritte projected images that would revolutionize art and the way we look at the world. Be warned, though, that there's little to see—*This is not a studio*, you might say—even though the museum's founders have been diligent in uncovering bits and pieces of the artist's banal private life. On the first and second

Moments A Stroll Through the Marolles

The scuzzy Marolles district, lying beneath the long shadow of the Palace of Justice, is a special place where the old Brussels dialect called _Brusseleir_ can still be heard. The generally poor community is under constant threat of encroachment and gentrification from neighboring, far wealthier areas—a process the Marolliens seem to want nothing to do with. Locals remain resolutely unimpressed by the burgeoning "Capital of Europe."

floors are a few original sketches; his easel and trademark bowler hat; a pipe; his passport; his checkbook and will; household objects; and letters and photographs illustrating his commercial work, negotiations with museums about exhibitions, and contacts with art dealers.

Rue Esseghem 135 (off bd. De Smet de Naeyer). ℂ **02/428-26-26.** www.magrittemuseum.be. Admission 7€ ($8.75) adults, 6€ ($7.50) for those under 23. Wed–Sun 10am–6pm. Closed Jan 1, Dec 25. Tram: 81 or 84 to Cimitière de Jette.

Musée Royal de l'Afrique Centrale/Koninklijk Museum voor Midden Afrika (Royal Museum of Central Africa) ★★   Originally founded to celebrate Belgium's colonial empire in the Belgian Congo (now the Democratic Republic of Congo), this museum has moved beyond imperialism to feature exhibits on ethnography and environment, mostly in Africa, but also in Asia and South America. The beautiful grounds of this impressive museum are as much a draw as the exhibits inside. The collection includes some excellent animal dioramas, African sculpture, and other artwork, and even some of the colonial-era guns and artillery pieces that no doubt helped make Belgium's claim to its African colonies more persuasive. A modern perspective is added by environmental displays that explain desertification, the loss of rainforests, and the destruction of habitats.

Leuvensesteenweg 13, Tervuren (a suburban Flemish _gemeente_ district just east of Brussels). ℂ **02/769-52-11.** www.africamuseum.be. Admission 4€ ($5) adults, 1.50€ ($1.90) children 13–18, free for children under 13. Tues–Fri 10am–5pm; Sat–Sun 10am–6pm. Closed Jan 1, May 1, Dec 25. Tram: 44 from Métro Montgomery station to Tervuren terminus.

Palais de la Nation (National Palace)   The Parliament building opposite the Parc de Bruxelles is quite an elegant place, if you ignore the politicians squabbling in the Chamber of Representatives and the Senate—bickering, after all, is part of the charm of democracy. The building dates from 1783 and was constructed originally to house the Sovereign Council of Brabant. You can enter only during sessions of either house.

Rue de la Loi 16. ℂ **02/519-81-36.** Free admission. Métro: Parc.

GREEN BRUSSELS

Brussels is a green city with a great extent of parks and gardens. Once a hunting preserve of the dukes of Brabant, the **Parc de Bruxelles (Brussels Park),** rue Royale (Métro: Parc), between Parliament and the Royal Palace, was laid out in the 18th century as a landscaped garden. In 1830, Belgian patriots fought Dutch regular troops here during the War of Independence. Later it was a fashionable place to stroll and to meet friends. Although not very big, the park manages to contain everything from carefully trimmed borders to rough patches of trees and bushes, and has fine views along its main paths, which together with the fountain form the outline of Masonic symbols. In 2001, the park was closed for refurbishment and restored as close as possible to its 18th-century look. Diseased chestnut trees have been cut down and lime trees replaced with sturdier specimens, statues have been restored and cleaned, and the 1840s bandstand by Jean-Pierre Cluysenaer has been refurbished so it now hosts regular summer concerts. The cleanup diminished the various unwholesome nighttime activities in the park.

The big public park called the **Bois de la Cambre** begins at the top of avenue Louise (tram: 92 or 93) in the southern section of Brussels. Its centerpiece is a small lake with an island in its center that can be reached by a neat little electrically operated pontoon. The park gets crowded on sunny weekends. A few busy roads with fast-moving traffic run through it, so be careful with children. The **Forêt de Soignes,** south of the Bois, is no longer a park with playing areas and regularly mown grass, but a forest that stretches almost to Waterloo. This is a great place to escape the maddening crowds and fuming traffic, particularly in the fall, when the colors are dazzling.

ESPECIALLY FOR KIDS

Atomium 🎡 *Kids*   There's nothing quite like this cluster of giant spheres representing the atomic structure of an iron crystal enlarged 165 billion times, rising 102m (335 ft.) like a giant plaything of the gods that's fallen to earth. The view from the viewing deck is marvelous, and you can even wander around inside the spheres. The model was constructed for the 1958 World's Fair. Whatever you think of its founding impulse, it's a fair bet that when you stand underneath this vast schematic you'll be suitably impressed. There may be something last-century about this paean of praise to the wonders of science and technology, but the Atomium has somehow moved beyond this, taking on a monumental life of its own. The view from the deck on the top sphere is marvelous, and you can even wander around inside the spheres.

Bd. du Centenaire, Heysel. (✆) 02/475-47-77. www.atomium.be. Admission 7€ ($8.75) adults, 4.50€ ($5.65) children 12–17, free for children under 12. Daily 10am–5:30pm. Métro: Heysel.

Centre Belge de la Bande-Dessinée (Belgian Center for Comic-Strip Art) 🎡🎡 *Kids* Grown-ups will love this place as much as kids do. Called the CéBéBéDé for short, the center, in a side street not far from the Gothic spires and baroque guild houses of the Grand-Place, is dedicated to comic strips and takes a lofty view of what it calls "the Ninth Art." As icing on the cake, it's in a restored Art Nouveau department store from 1903, the Magasins Waucquez designed by Victor Horta, which was slated for demolition before the center took it over. A model of the red-and-white checkered rocket in which Hergé's Tintin and Snowy flew to the Moon, long before Armstrong and Aldrin did it in mere fact, takes pride of place at the top of the elegant staircase. Beyond is a comic strip wonderland. All the big names appear in a library of 30,000 books and in permanent and special exhibitions, including Tintin, Asterix, Thorgal, Lucky Luke, the Smurfs, Charlie Brown, Andy Capp, Suske and Wiske—yes, even Superman, Batman, and the Green Lantern—along with many lesser heroes.

Moments Ferry Tale

Taking a ferryboat trip in the Bois de la Cambre is a literal moment. The ferry in question is a tiny, electrically operated pontoon that makes a 1-minute crossing to Robinson's Island in the lake at the heart of the park.

Rue des Sables 20 (off bd. de Berlaimont). ℂ 02/219-19-80. www.cbbd.be. Admission 7.50€ ($9.40) adults, 6€ ($7.50) students and seniors, 3€ ($3.75) children under 12. Tues–Sun 10am–6pm. Closed Jan 1, Dec 25. Métro: Gare Centrale.

Mini-Europe 🌟 *Kids*   Kids and adults alike will get a kick out of strolling around such highlights from member states of the European Union as London's Big Ben, Berlin's Brandenburg Gate, the Leaning Tower of Pisa, the Bull Ring in Seville (complete with simulated sounds of fans yelling ¡*Olé!*), and Montmartre in Paris, and more modern emblems of Continental achievement such as the Channel Tunnel and the Ariane rocket. Meanwhile, Mount Vesuvius erupts, gondolas float around the canals of Venice, and a Finnish girl dives into the icy waters of a northern lake. As the scale is 1:25, the kids will feel like giants.

Bruparck, Heysel. ℂ 02/478-05-50. www.minieurope.com. Admission 12€ ($15) adults, 8.80€ ($11) children under 13, free for children under 1.2m (4 ft.) accompanied by parents. Mid-Mar to June and Sept daily 9:30am–6pm; July–Aug daily 9:30am–8pm (mid-July to mid-Aug Fri–Sun 9:30am–12am); Oct–Dec and 1st week Jan daily 10am–6pm. Closed rest of Jan to mid-Mar. Métro: Heysel.

THE EUROPEAN DISTRICT

Home to the European Commission, European Parliament, Council of Ministers, and related institutions, Brussels has no less than 1.2 million sq. m (12.7 million sq. ft.) of office space packed with 20,000-plus Eurocrats to back up its "capital of Europe" tag. Entire neighborhoods full of character were swept away to make room for them.

To tour the heartland of European Union governance, take the Métro to Schuman station. If you wish to view that exotic species, the European civil servant, in its native habitat, you'll want to do this tour Monday to Friday. The district is dead during the weekend. You can grab a bite to eat in one of the fancy restaurants favored by the Euro-crowd or a drink in one of the Irish bars that speckle the district. When you're done, head for the Schuman or Maelbeek Métro stations for the fast-track back to civilization.

Your first sight is the X-shaped **Palais de Berlaymont (Berlaymont Palace),** the commission's former headquarters, at Rond-Point Schuman. Across rue de la Loi, the Council of Ministers headquarters, the **Consilium,** is instantly recognizable for its facade's lavish complement of rose-colored granite blocks. On its far side, a soothing stroll through little Parc Léopold brings you to the new, postmodern **European Parliament** and **International Conference Center,** an architectural odyssey in white marble and tinted glass. Take the passageway through the building's middle to place Léopold, an old square that looks lost and forlorn in comparison to its powerful new neighbors.

ORGANIZED TOURS

BY BUS   Bus tours, which last 3 hours and operate throughout the year, are available from **Brussels City Tours,** rue de la Colline 8 (ℂ **02/513-77-44;** www.brussels-city-tours.com; Métro: Gare Centrale). Each tour is 26€ ($33) for adults, 21€ ($26) for students and seniors, and 10€ ($13) for children. Reservations can be made through most hotels, and hotel pickup is often available.

From June 15 to September 15, **Le Bus Bavard,** rue des Thuyas 12 (ℂ **02/673-18-35;** www.busbavard.be), operates a daily 3-hour "chatterbus" tour at 10am from the Galeries Royales St-Hubert (Métro: Gare Centrale), a mall next to rue du Marché aux Herbes 90, a few steps off the Grand-Place. A walking tour covers the historic center, followed by a bus ride through areas the average visitor never sees. You hear about life in Brussels and get a real feel for the city. The price is 8€ ($10). You don't need a reservation for this fascinating experience—just be there by 10am.

ARAU, bd. Adolphe-Max 55 (🕾 **02/219-33-45;** www.arau.org; Métro: De Brouck-ère), organizes tours that help you discover not only Brussels's countless treasures but also problems the city faces. It runs 3-hour themed coach tours: "Grand-Place and Its Surroundings," "Brussels 1900—Art Nouveau," "Brussels 1930—Art Deco," "Surprising Parks and Squares," and "Alternative Brussels." Reserve ahead. Tours by bus are 15€ ($19), and 12€ ($15) for those under 26; tours by foot are 10€ ($13). They take place on Saturday mornings from March to November; private group tours can be arranged year-round.

6 Sports & Recreation

BOWLING   Leading bowling alleys are **Bowling Crosly,** quai du Foin 43 (🕾 **02/217-28-01**); and **Bowling Crosly,** bd. de l'Empereur 36 (🕾 **02/512-08-74**).

HORSEBACK RIDING   For information on riding stables, contact the **Fédération Royale Belge des Sports Equestres,** av. Houba de Strooper 156 (🕾 **02/478-50-56**).

ICE-SKATING   There's ice-skating from September to May at **Forest National,** av. du Globe 36 (call 🕾 **02/345-16-11** for hours and fees), reached by bus no. 48 or 54; and at **Poseidon,** av. des Vaillants 4, in Woluwe-St-Lambert (🕾 **02/762-16-33;** Métro: Tomberg).

SOCCER   The **Maison du Football,** av. Houba de Strooper 145 (🕾 **02/477-12-11**), can arrange tickets for international soccer matches if you phone Monday to Friday between 9am and 4:15pm. The local team is FC Anderlecht, which is always in contention for Belgian prizes and usually in the running for European honors as well. During Continental tournaments, some of the crack European soccer squads can often be seen in action in Brussels.

7 Shopping

Brussels is not the place to come looking for bargains. It's rather expensive on the whole, though no more so than neighboring big cities like Paris, Amsterdam, and Cologne. Still, there are reasonable prices to be found, and even bargains. A lot depends on where and when you shop. As a general rule, the upper city around avenue Louise and the Porte de Namur is more expensive than the lower city around rue Neuve and the city-center shopping galleries around La Monnaie and place de Brouckère. But this is not a fixed rule. For example, rue Haute, in the upper city, is generally inexpensive, while the Galeries Royales St-Hubert, in the lower city, is generally expensive.

Shopping hours are generally from 9 or 10am to 6pm Monday to Saturday. On Friday evening, many city-center stores, particularly department stores, stay open until 8 or 9pm. A useful source of shopping information is the weekly English-language magazine *The Bulletin,* which keeps tabs on the latest shopping ideas and trends, and reviews individual stores.

SHOPPING PROMENADES

Many of Brussels's most interesting stores are clustered along certain promenades or arcades. The **rue Neuve,** which starts at place de la Monnaie and extends north to place Rogier, is practically a pedestrian shopping mall; this busy and popular area is home to many boutiques and department stores, including City 2, a modern shopping complex. **Boulevard Anspach,** which runs from the Stock Exchange up to place de Brouckère,

Belgian Specialties: Chocolate & More

Belgians know a thing or two about chocolate. Just ask anyone who has ever bitten into one of those devilish little creations—handmade pralines, made and sold by Wittamer, Nihoul, Cornez, Neuhaus, Léonidas, and . . . well, it's a long list. So addictive are they that they really should be sold with a government health warning. You find some of the finest confections at **Chocolatier Mary** (see "Shopping A to Z," below).

Lace is another old favorite that's widely available in the city, particularly in and around the Grand-Place. Purchase from **Maison Antoine** or **Manufacture Belge de Dentelle** (see "Shopping A to Z," below).

For local beers like *gueuze, kriek,* and *faro*—among the 450 or so different Belgian beers—head for **A la Mort Subite** (see "Bars" under "Brussels After Dark," later in this chapter).

Other traditional products include *geneva* (gin), of which there are some 270 brands produced by 70 distilleries; crystal, particularly superb Val-Saint-Lambert crystal from Liège; ceramics; jewelry; hand-beaten copper or bronze; and even diamonds, though Brussels is nowhere near as sparkling in this respect as Antwerp.

Finally, sweet-toothed shoppers should try **Dandoy** (see "Shopping A to Z," below).

is home to a number of fashion boutiques, chocolate stores, and electronic-appliance stores. The **Anspach Center** (near place de la Monnaie) is a shopping mall.

One of Europe's oldest "malls," the glass-roofed **Galeries Royales St-Hubert,** is a light and airy arcade hosting boutiques and other upmarket stores, sidewalk cafes, a theater and a movie theater, and street musicians playing classical music. Constructed in Italian neo-Renaissance style and opened in 1847, architect Pierre Cluysenaer's gallery offers shopping with a touch of class and is well worth strolling through even if you have no intention of window-shopping. The elegant gallery has three connected wings—Galerie du Roi, Galerie de la Reine, and Galerie des Princes—and was the forerunner of other city arcades like the Burlington in London. It is just north of the Grand-Place, between rue du Marché aux Herbes and rue d'Arenberg, and is split by rue de Bouchers. There are entrances on all three of these streets.

Avenue Louise attracts those in search of world-renowned, high-quality goods from such stores as Cartier, Burberry's, Louis Vuitton, and Valentino.

The **Galerie Agora** (off the Grand-Place) offers a wide variety of modestly priced merchandise, including leather goods, clothing, souvenirs, records, and jewelry.

OUTDOOR MARKETS
At the **Vieux Marché** flea market on place du Jeu de Balle, a large square in the Marolles district, you can find some exceptional decorative items, many recycled from the homes of the "recently deceased," and unusual postcards, clothing, and household goods. So you should be able to snap up a bargain on everything from the weird to the wonderful. The market is held daily from 7am to 2pm.

Every weekend, the place du Grand Sablon hosts a fine **Antiques Market.** The salesmanship is low-key, the interest is pure, the prices are not unreasonable (don't expect bargains, though), and the quality of the merchandise—which includes silverware, pottery, paintings, and jewelry—is high. The market is open Saturday from 9am to 6pm and Sunday from 9am to 2pm.

May to October, Tuesday to Sunday, the Grand-Place hosts a **Flower Market** that's open from 8am to 6pm. Nearby, at the top end of rue du Marché aux Herbes, in a square called the place de l'Agora, there's a weekend **Crafts Market** here, with lots of fine specialized jewelry and other items, mostly inexpensive.

From mid-May to September, painters, sculptors, potters, photographers, and other artists sell their work—and some of them produce it, too—at the **Marché d'Art,** Parvis Saint-Pierre, Uccle. The market is on Sunday from 10am to 1pm.

Two weekends before Christmas is the occasion for the **European Union Christmas Market** on place Ste-Catherine. From Friday evening until Sunday evening, the square is a hub of activity, as each country of the EU sets out its stall with traditional foods and products. There's music, singing, and dancing, and the festive spirit is fueled by mulled wine and typical national drinks. The main problem is that at times the square gets so busy that it is almost impossible to move. Still, this is another colorful and memorable event.

SHOPPING A TO Z

Here's a short list of my personal recommendations, only a small sampling of Brussels's best shopping.

ART

Ma Maison de Papier 🎯   Owner Marie-Laurence Bernard is an enthusiast for vintage posters—she has written three books on the subject—that do more than hide a crack on your bathroom wall. You can purchase any kind of poster here, from a 1930s cigarette ad to a reproduction Toulouse-Lautrec, to original Art Nouveau and Art Deco works by Belgian, French, and other masters of the genre. Galerie de la Rue de Ruysbroeck 6, rue de Ruysbroeck (off place du Grand Sablon). ℂ 02/512-22-49. Tram: 92, 93, or 94 to Petit Sablon.

BOOKS

Waterstone's   It's not so easy to find a wide selection of English-language books in Brussels, but the major British bookstore chain does have a full-size branch here that sells magazines, newspapers, and books. The books, however, usually cost 30% to 60% more than in Britain. Bd. Adolphe Max 71. ℂ 02/219-27-08. Métro: Rogier.

Tips An Affordable Wine Source

If you're planning to purchase wine by the bottle, don't be fooled into the idea that you have to go to an expensive wine store to get something worthwhile. The midprice **Delhaize** supermarket chain has built up an enviable reputation and a loyal local following for the quality of its wine department. Delhaize's buyers look for good value in all price categories and have an adventurous streak that makes them look beyond the classic names. There are Delhaize supermarkets all over Brussels (and Belgium). Ask at your hotel desk for the nearest branch.

CHILDREN

Boutique de Tintin   Forget computer games and other electronic toys. If you need to buy a gift for the kids, take home some Tintin mementos from this excellent, if somewhat pricey, store. Rue de la Colline 13. ✆ 02/514-45-50. Métro: Gare Centrale.

EURO-STUFF

Eurotempo   One of the most surprising marketing phenomena of recent years has been the popularity of the European Union's symbol: a blue flag with a circle of 12 stars. At Eurotempo you can find this logo on an astonishing range of products: umbrellas, T-shirts, pens, golf balls, watches, hats, knives, towels—you name it. Where better to buy Euro stuff than in the capital of Europe? Rue du Marché aux Herbes 84. ✆ 02/502-37-47. Métro: Gare Centrale or Bourse.

FASHION & APPAREL

Delvaux   This local company makes and sells some of the best—and priciest— handbags and leather goods in Belgium. Galerie de la Reine 31. ✆ 02/512-71-98. Métro: Gare Centrale station or Bourse.

Ganterie Italienne   This is a glove store with Italian style, selling attractive handwear that keeps out the winter cold. It's open Monday to Saturday from 10am to 12:30pm and 1:30 to 6pm. Galerie de la Reine 3 (off the Grand-Place). ✆ 02/512-75-38. Métro: Gare Centrale or Bourse.

Olivier Strelli   This top-rated Belgian fashion designer is just one of several big names with boutiques in this area. His store is strong on elegant, ready-to-wear items. Av. Louise 72. ✆ 02/511-21-34. Métro: Louise.

FLOWERS

Les Fleurs Isabelle de Baecker ⌾   This superb flower store in a superb Art Nouveau location is just the place for that important bouquet. Rue Royale 13. ✆ 02/217-26-69. Métro: Botanique.

FOOD & WINES

Chocolatier Mary ⌾   Supplier of pralines to the Belgian royal court—which tells you right away that these are no plain chocolates—Mary's is a small store, but its wares look every bit as good as they taste. Rue Royal 73. ✆ 02/217-45-00. Métro: Parc.

Dandoy ⌾⌾   Dandoy is the place for sweet-toothed cookies-'n-cakes fans. Try the traditional Belgian house specialties: spicy *speculoos* cookies (made with brown sugar, cinnamon, ginger, and almonds, and baked in wood molds), and *pain à la grecque* (thin, spicy caramelized, sugary flaky pastries). Rue au Beurre 31. ✆ 02/511-03-26. Métro: Bourse.

De Boe ⌾   Don't miss this small store near the Fish Market. It has a superb selection of roasted and blended coffees and wines in all price categories, and an array of specialty crackers, nuts, spices, teas, and gourmet snacks, many of which are canned, making them suitable for transport home. Hours are Tuesday to Saturday from 9am to 1pm and 2 to 6pm. Rue de Flandre 36. ✆ 02/511-13-73. Métro: Ste-Catherine.

Neuhaus   This chocolatier sells some of the best of the dangerously delicious Belgian handmade chocolates. You can purchase gift pralines here. Galerie de la Reine 25–27. ✆ 02/502-59-14. Métro: Gare Centrale or Bourse.

Wittamer   Wittamer makes some of the best handmade pralines in the world. Their rolls, breads, pastries, and cakes have been winning fans here since 1910. Place du Grand Sablon 12. 🕾 **02/512-37-42.** Tram: 92 or 93.

LACE

Maison Antoine   This lace boutique is one of the best in Brussels and surely has the best location, a former guild house where Victor Hugo lived in 1852. The quality is superb, the service friendly, and the prices decent. Hours are daily from 10am to 7pm. Grand-Place 26. 🕾 **02/512-14-59.** Métro: Gare Centrale or Bourse.

Manufacture Belge de Dentelle   This is a good source for top-quality handmade Belgian lace. Galerie de la Reine 6–8. 🕾 **02/511-44-77.** Métro: Gare Centrale or Bourse.

MULTIMEDIA

FNAC   This good-value books, electronics, and photo chain has a branch in the City 2 multistory shopping mall off rue Neuve. It also sells concert tickets. City 2. 🕾 **02/209-22-11.** Métro: Rogier.

8 Brussels After Dark

Brussels is not known for its nightlife, but that's partly because it's overshadowed by the worldwide reputations of neighboring capitals like Paris and Amsterdam. Nightlife is actually alive and well in Brussels, and if the range is inevitably thinner than in bigger cities, the quality is not.

For current information on after-dark entertainment during your visit, consult the **Brussels International Tourism** office in the Town Hall, Grand-Place, Brussels (🕾 **02/513-89-40;** www.brusselsinternational.be); or purchase the weekly English-language magazine *The Bulletin,* which has an extensive "What's On" section.

THE PERFORMING ARTS

OPERA & BALLET   An opera house in the grand style, the **Théâtre Royal de la Monnaie** 🟊🟊, place de la Monnaie (🕾 **02/229-12-00;** www.lamonnaie.be; Métro: De Brouckère), is home to the Opéra Royal de la Monnaie, which has been called the best in the French-speaking world, and to the Orchestre Symphonique de la Monnaie. The resident modern dance company, Anne Teresa de Keersmaeker's group **Rosas** (🕾 **02/344-55-98;** www.rosas.be), is noted for its original moves. The box office is open Tuesday to Saturday from 11am to 6pm. Tickets run 10€ to 150€ ($13–$188); for those age under 28, they're 10€ ($13) and available 5 minutes before a show.

CLASSICAL MUSIC   Bozar, rue Ravenstein 23 (🕾 **02/507-82-00;** www.bozar.be; Métro: Gare Centrale)—formerly the Palais des Beaux-Arts—is home to Belgium's National Orchestra. The box office is open Monday to Saturday from 11am to 6pm, with tickets running 10€ to 75€ ($13–$94).

Tips   **Heritage Days**

On the third weekend in September, the annual Brussels Heritage Days program allows you to visit some of the finest buildings in town that are usually closed to visitors. Sixty or so sites are open. For more details, visit the Information Center, Halles St-Géry, Place St-Géry (🕾 0800/40-400; Métro: Bourse), open Monday to Saturday from 10am to 5pm (admission is free).

Concerts are performed at the **Cirque Royal,** rue de l'Enseignement 81 (✆ **02/ 218-20-15;** Métro: Parc), which was formerly a real circus but is now a venue for music, opera, and ballet. The box office is open Tuesday to Saturday from 11am to 6pm, with tickets for 10€ to 65€ ($13–$81).

Le Botanique, rue Royale 236 (✆ **02/218-37-32**), generally focuses on small-scale modern and avant-garde performances, not only of classical music but also of jazz and other forms.

THEATERS   Brussels theater is important among French-speaking countries, with more than 30 theaters presenting performances in French, Dutch, and (occasionally) English. Among the most important is the **Théâtre Royal du Parc,** rue de la Loi 3 (✆ **02/505-30-30;** www.theatreduparc.be; Métro: Parc), a magnificent edifice occupying a corner of the Brussels Park more or less opposite Parliament, where classic and contemporary drama and comedies are performed. Recently installed in its shiny new premises is the mainstream **Théâtre National de la Communauté National Wallonie Bruxelles,** bd. Emile Jacqmain 111–115 (✆ **02/203-41-55;** www.theatre national.be; Métro: De Brouckere), and the **Théâtre Royal des Galeries,** Galerie du Roi 32 (✆ **02/512-04-07;** Métro: Gare Centrale), is known for its wide variety of offerings, including drama, comedy, and musicals. Also important are the Art Deco–style **Théâtre du Résidence Palace,** rue de la Loi 155 (✆ **02/231-03-05;** Métro: Maelbeek) and **Le Botanique,** rue Royale 236 (✆ **02/218-37-32;** Métro: Botanique), which inclines toward the experimental in mostly French theater. Bringing theater to the city in Dutch, the **Koninklijke Vlaamse Schouwburg,** quai aux Pierres de Taille (✆ **02/210-11-00;** www.kvs.be; Métro: Yser), is located in new premises around the corner from their recently refurbished, neo-Renaissance–style building, dating from 1887, on rue de Laeken.

PUPPET THEATER
Théâtre Toone VII ✮   Look for the small wooden sign in the tiny alleyway—impasse Schuddeveld—to reach this theater, in an upstairs room in a bistro of the same name. It's the latest in the Toone line of puppet theaters, which dates back to the early 1800s—the title being passed from one puppet master to the next—and it may be the most popular theater in Brussels. At Toone, puppet master José Géal presents his adaptation of such classic tales as *The Three Musketeers, Faust,* and *Hamlet* in the Brussels dialect, Brussels Vloms, and in English, French, Dutch, and German. In any case, language should present no difficulties since it's easy to follow the action on stage. Impasse Schuddeveld 6, Petite rue des Bouchers 21. ✆ 02/513-54-86. www.toone.be. Ticket prices and performance times vary; check in advance. Métro: Gare Centrale.

JAZZ & BLUES CLUBS
Phil's Jazz Kitchen Café, rue Haute 189 (✆ **02/513-95-88**), a relaxed bar with good atmosphere, has jazz or other music most nights of the week, and a jam session on Wednesday. **L'Archiduc,** rue Antoine Dansaert 6 (✆ **02/512-06-52**), had the brilliant idea of putting on after-shopping jazz concerts on Saturday, beginning at 5pm, and then went one better by repeating the idea (minus the shopping) on Sunday. The **Marcus Mingus Jazz Spot,** Hotel Arlequin, rue de la Fourche 17–19 (✆ **02/514-16-15**), lights up jazz, Brazilian, Latin, blues, funk, or whatever, from Tuesday to Sunday at 10pm. For those who like their licks a little more restrained, there's a jazz brunch at the **Airport Sheraton Hotel,** facing the terminal building (✆ **02/725-10-00**), every Sunday from noon to 3pm. **Studio Athanor,** rue de la Fourche 17–19

Puppet Shows: A Belgian Passion

A special word is in order about a special sort of theater—that of the wooden marionettes that have entertained Belgians for centuries. In times past, puppet theaters numbered in the hundreds nationwide (Brussels alone had 15), and the plays were much like our modern-day soap operas. The story lines went on and on, sometimes for generations, and working-class audiences returned night after night to keep up with the *Dallas* of the times. Performances were based on folklore, legends, or political satire.

Specific marionette characters came to personify their home cities: A cheeky ragamuffin named Woltje (Little Walloon) was from Brussels; Antwerp had the cross-eyed, earthy, ne'er-do-well Schele; Pierke, from Ghent, was modeled on the traditional Italian clown; and Liège's Tchantchès stood only 16 inches high and always appeared with patched trousers, a tasseled floppy hat, and his constant companion, the sharp-tongued Nanesse (Agnes).

Today a few Belgian puppet theaters still survive and their popularity has increased in recent years after a decline following World War II, when bombing raids severely damaged many theaters and destroyed many marionettes.

(© 02/502-02-97; Métro: Gare Centrale), attracts top local performers and an occasional international name, Tuesday to Sunday at 10pm.

During the 3-day, mid-May Brussels **Jazz Marathon** (© 02/456-04-75), there are more than 125 concerts, covering all known jazz forms, at outdoor venues like the Grand-Place and Place du Grand Sablon, and at clubs, bars, and indoor cultural venues around town. Outdoor concerts are free; a pass for all indoor concerts is 14€ ($18), and 12€ ($15) if you reserve ahead of time.

DANCE CLUBS

Nothing in life changes quite so fast as the "in" discos. But there are a few that stand the test of time—and that of course makes them anathema to genuine disco hounds. Since the turnover rate is so high, be sure to check locally to see if the following are still in operation before setting out for a night of dancing. The most sophisticated dance club in Brussels is **Griffin's Club** in the Royal Windsor Hotel, rue Duquesnoy 5 (© 02/505-55-55), which is in full swing every night except Sunday. **Mirano Continental,** chaussée de Louvain 38 (© 02/227-39-70), is more of a dance hall than a disco, a classy place for those whose wildest years are a few years behind them but who still like to enjoy themselves. **Nostalgia Club,** rue de la Fourche 49 (© 02/513-3291), is similar, with hits from the '60s and '70s at the top of the bill.

Le Sparrow, rue Duquesnoy 18 (© 02/512-66-22), just off the Grand-Place, always seems on the verge of going out of style yet never quite gets there, even if it has lost the wild and wonderful cachet of its earlier days. A location just off the Grand-Place undoubtedly helps, as does its consistently up-to-date approach to the music. **Cartagena,** rue du Marché au Charbon 70 (© 02/502-59-08), is as hot as a night in, well, Cartagena, and dispenses drinks and music from all over Latin America. If only techno will do (along with a dab of house), **Le Fuse,** rue Blaes 208 (© 02/511-97-89), is the place—on the first Friday of every month it reinvents itself as the women-only **Pussy Lounge,** and every Sunday as the men-only **La Démence.**

BARS

Now you're talking. Bars are where Brussels lives. It's hard to be disappointed, whether you pop into a neighborhood watering hole where a *chope* or *pintje* (a glass of beer) will set you back a mere 2€ ($2.50), or whether you prefer to fork out several times as much in one of the trendier places.

Unique, to say the least, is a Brussels favorite, **A la Mort Subite,** rue Montagne aux Herbes Potagères 7 (ⓒ **02/513-13-18**), a bistro of rather special character whose name translates to "Sudden Death," which is the name of one of the beers you can purchase here. Don't worry. The name is just a name—it comes from a dice game regulars used to play. The decor consists of stained-glass motifs, old photographs, paintings, and prints on the walls; and plain wood chairs and tables on the floor. Specialties are traditional Brussels beers: *gueuze, lambic, faro,* and *kriek;* and abbey brews like Chimay, Maredsous, and Grimbergen.

In a quite different vein is **La Fleur en Papier Doré** ✸, rue des Alexiens 55 (ⓒ **02/511-16-59**), in a 16th-century house. From its beginnings in 1846, this bistro and pub has been a mecca for poets and writers. Even now, about once a month, young Brussels poets gather here informally for poetry readings—the dates vary, but you might inquire by phone or, better yet, drop by and ask in person. This is a wonderfully atmospheric old pub, much like a social club, where patrons gather for good conversation and welcome any and all newcomers. The place serves what is possibly the best onion soup in Brussels, a great late-night snack.

The following are only a few of the many Brussels pubs and bistros worthy of recommendation. **Au Bon Vieux Temps,** rue du Marché aux Herbes 12 (ⓒ **02/217-26-26**), hidden away at the end of a narrow alleyway, is a gloomily atmospheric old tavern that seems to hearken back to a bygone era. You should try the appropriately named Duvel (Devil) beer here—just go easy, that's all. **A l'Imaige Nostre-Dame,** impasse des Cadeaux (ⓒ **02/219-42-49**), off rue du Marché aux Herbes 6, is a good, quiet place to drink and read or reflect if you're alone, or to converse with a companion without having to compete with a blaring jukebox.

Le Cirio, rue de la Bourse 18 (ⓒ **02/512-13-95**), is across the road from the Stock Exchange, and indeed many of the bar's customers look like they've just made a killing on the stock market and have retired to a state of genteel splendor. And what better place to do it in? Le Cirio is a quiet, refined sort of place to sip your beer, in attractive surroundings that make the whole exercise seem worthwhile. **Toone VII,** impasse Schuddeveld 6, Petite rue des Bouchers 21 (ⓒ **02/513-54-86**), is the home of the puppet theater and an artistic hangout.

Art Nouveau design from 1904 by master Paul Hamesse (incorporating a plaster-covered interior wall that mimics a rock face) and an extensive range of Belgian beers are two good reasons to visit trendy bar-brasserie **De Ultieme Hallucinatie,** rue Royale 316 (ⓒ **02/217-06-14;** Métro: Botanique). You sit in little booths on 1930s railroad station benches designed by Henry Van de Velde or at a long bar. In summertime, you can tan while you quaff beer on a courtyard terrace at the back. Salads, snacks, and full meals are available in the brasserie.

Shock and horror reverberated through the city a few years back when **Le Falstaff,** rue Henri Maus 17–25 (ⓒ **02/511-87-89**), the legendary 1904 Art Nouveau tavern, enlivened with a dash of Art Deco and rococo, went bankrupt and closed. Reopened under new management, it has shed its former, notoriously vain waitstaff and slipped a few notches on the hip scale as a result. If such considerations don't worry you, there's still the same stunning decor, stained-glass scenes in the style of Pieter Brueghel the Elder depicting Shakespeare's Falstaff tales, and reasonably priced brasserie food.

Rick's, av. Louise 344 (© **02/640-03-05**), brings a touch of Humphrey Bogart and Ernest Hemingway, accompanied by American and Mexican food, to the stylish avenue Louise. The decor might give you the creeps at **Halloween,** rue des Grands-Carmes 10 (© **02/514-12-56**), where gargoyles, devils, and other assorted creatures from the darker recesses of the mind help create an unforgettable ambience. Fortunately, it's a pretty good bar. Something sad has happened to the painfully chic denizens of **L'Archiduc,** rue Antoine Dansaert 6 (© **02/512-06-52**)—they've loosened up a little. Not much, mind you—just enough so that you don't see a hundred lips curling with disdain when you enter wearing clothes that were de rigueur last week instead of today.

GAY & LESBIAN BARS

Rue des Riches-Claires and **rue du Marché au Charbon** host some gay and lesbian bars. **Macho 2,** 108 rue du Marché au Charbon (© **02/513-56-67;** Métro: Bourse), a block from rue des Riches-Claires, houses a gay men's sauna, pool, steam room, and cafe. It's open Monday to Thursday from noon to 2am, Friday and Saturday from noon to 4am, and Sunday from noon to midnight. Admission is 12€ ($15) or 8€ ($10) for men under 25 (Thurs 8€/$10 for everyone); students enter for 5€ ($6.25). **Le Fuse** and **Le Sparrow** (see above) have gay nights.

For more information, stop by the gay and lesbian community center, **Tels Quels,** rue du Marché au Charbon 81 (© **02/512-45-87;** Métro: Bourse), open Saturday to Thursday from 5pm to 2am and Friday from 5pm to 4am.

MOVIES

Since most movies in Brussels are shown in the original language, you'll always be able to find many English-language films in the theaters. Major cinemas in the center city, several of them multiplexes, are: **Actor's Studio,** Petite rue des Bouchers 16 (© **02/ 512-16-96**); **Arenberg/Galeries,** Galerie de la Reine 26 (© **02/512-80-63**); **Aventure,** Galerie du Centre, rue des Fripiers 17 (© **02/219-17-48**); **UGC Toison d'Or,** av. de la Toison d'Or 8 (© **0900/10-440**); and **UGC De Brouckère,** place De Brouckère 38 (© **0900/10-440**). **Kinepolis,** bd. du Centenaire 20 (© **0900/00-555**), is the best-equipped and the biggest, with 26 screens and an IMAX screen. Part of the Bruparck recreation complex beside the Atomium, Kinepolis is likely to have something for everyone. Most movies shown here are big releases, usually from Hollywood, which is no doubt the main reason why the place is so popular. **Nova,** rue d'Arenberg

---

(Tips **Belgian Brews Pack a Punch**

Brussels is known for its *lambic* beers, which use naturally occurring yeast for fermentation, are often flavored with fruit, and come in bottles with champagne-type corks. They're almost akin to sweet sparkling wine. *Gueuze,* a blend of young and aged lambic beers, is one of the least sweet. If you prefer something sweeter, try raspberry-flavored *framboise* or cherry-flavored *kriek.* *Faro* is a low-alcohol beer, sometimes sweetened or lightly spiced.

3 (℗ **02/511-24-77**), is an art-house cinema. The **Musée du Cinema,** rue Baron Horta 9 (℗ **02/507-83-70**), often features little-seen classic films from the past.

9 Side Trips from Brussels

The lovely Brabant countryside around Brussels offers scenic beauty and several sight-seeing attractions well worth the short trip.

WATERLOO
10km (6 miles) S of Brussels

The battle that ended Napoleon's empire was fought on rolling farmland near **Waterloo,** just south of Brussels. On June 18, 1815, 72,000 British, Dutch, Belgian, and German troops, aided before the day's end by around 40,000 Prussians, defeated the mighty Napoleon Bonaparte and his 76,000 French, leaving 40,000 dead and wounded on the field. Napoleon survived, but his attempt to rebuild his empire was crushed; he was exiled to the island of St. Helena, where he died 6 years later.

The battlefield remains much as it was on that fateful day. To visit, though, you don't go to the town of Waterloo, which is a pleasant suburb of Brussels—and the capital town of Brabant-Wallon (Walloon Brabant) province. The Battle of Waterloo wasn't actually fought there. A stretch of rolling farmland speckled with stoutly constructed manor-farmhouses several miles to the south got that "honor."

Before touring it, you should study a 360-degree **Panoramic Mural** featuring the massed French cavalry charge led by Marshal Ney and see a short audiovisual presentation of the battle, including scenes from Sergei Bondarchuk's epic movie *Waterloo,* at the **Centre du Visiteur (Visitor Center),** route du Lion 252–254, Braine l'Alleud (℗ **02/385-19-12**; www.waterloo1815.be). To survey the battlefield, climb the 226 steps to the top of the nearby **Butte du Lion (Lion Mound),** a conical hill surmounted by a bronze lion, behind the center—it takes an active imagination to fill the peaceful farmland with slashing cavalry charges, thundering artillery, and 200,000 colorfully uniformed, struggling soldiers. Across the road from the Visitor Center is the **Musée des Cires (Waxworks Museum),** where Napoleon, Wellington, Blücher, and other key participants appear as rather tatty wax figures.

You can draw rations from one of the cafes or restaurants, which have names like Le Hussard, Bivouac de l'Empereur, and Les Alliés. Souvenir stores sell everything from Napoleonic corkscrews to hand-painted model soldiers. Beside the crossroads at the Brussels–Charleroi road are monuments to the Belgians and Hanoverians; to Colonel Gordon, Wellington's aide; and to General Picton, shot down at the head of his division. A little way down the Brussels–Charleroi road is La Haie–Sainte, a farmhouse that played a crucial role in Napoleon's defeat by shielding Wellington's center from direct assault.

These four sites are open daily April to October from 9:30am to 6:30pm, and November to March from 10am to 5pm, closed January 1 and December 25. Admission to the Visitor Center is free. Admission to its audiovisual presentation and the four on-site attractions is 8.50€ ($11) for adults, 6.50€ ($8.10) for seniors and students, 5€ ($6.25) for children ages 7 to 17, and free for children under 7.

From Brussels, bus W departs twice hourly for Waterloo from Gare du Midi (Métro: Gare du Midi). The 18km (11-mile) ride takes 50 minutes and costs 3€ ($3.75). The bus stops at both the Wellington Museum in Waterloo itself and at the battlefield Visitor Center, south of the town. By car from Brussels, take the ring road (R0) to Exit 27 for Waterloo, and N5 south to the battlefield.

In Waterloo itself is the well-ordered **Musée Wellington (Wellington Museum),** chaussée de Bruxelles 147 (© **02/354-78-06**), in an old Brabant coaching inn that was the duke's headquarters. It was from here that Wellington sent his historic victory dispatch. The museum is open April to September, daily from 9:30am to 6:30pm; November to March, daily from 10:30am to 5pm. Admission, which includes an audio guide, except for children under 6, is 5€ ($6.25) for adults, 4€ ($5) for seniors and students, 2€ ($1.25) for children ages 6 to 12, and free for children under 6.

BEERSEL
9km (5½ miles) SW of Brussels

The only local example of a still-intact **fortified medieval castle** is at Beersel, a little off the Mons road (watch for the signpost). The three-towered, 13th-century castle is set in a wooded area and surrounded by a moat, which you cross via drawbridge. Pick up the excellent English-language guidebook at the entrance for a detailed history of the castle and its inhabitants, and then wander through its rooms for a trip back through time. End your visit with a stop at the magnificent mausoleum that holds the alabaster effigies of Henry II of Witthem and his wife, Jacqueline de Glimes, who lived here during the early 1400s.

Leafy pathways through the castle grounds make this a favorite rural retreat for Brussels residents, especially during the summer months. At the entrance to the park, you find **Auberge Kasteel Beersel,** Lotstraat 65, Beersel (© **02/377-10-47**), a charming rustic restaurant with a decor of dark wood, exposed brick, and accents of copper and brass. In good weather there's service on the shaded outdoor terrace. Light meals (omelets, salads, soups, and sandwiches) are available, and complete hot meals are offered for both lunch and dinner. Prices are moderate. If you don't want a meal, you're welcome to stop in for a draft of Belgian beer.

GAASBEEK
13km (8 miles) SW of Brussels

The ancestral **château of the counts of Egmont** is at Gaasbeek, beyond the village of Vlezenbeek. The furnishings of **Kasteel van Gaasbeek,** Kasteelstraat 40 (© **02/531-01-30;** www.kasteelvangaasbeek.be), are nothing less than magnificent, as is the castle itself. All the rooms are splendid, and far from presenting a dead "museum" appearance, they create the eerie impression that the counts and their families may come walking through the door any moment. Before each guided tour, a slide show will augment your appreciation of the countless works of art, silver items, religious objects, and priceless tapestries you see in the castle. The castle is open April to October, Tuesday to Sunday from 10am to 6pm; the park is open daily from 8am to 8pm (to 6pm Oct–Mar). Admission to the castle is 4.50€ ($5.65) for adults; 2.50€ ($3.15) for seniors, people with disabilities, students, and children ages 7 to 18; and free for children under 7. Admission to the park is free. To get there by car from Brussels, take the R0/E19 Brussels ring road west to Exit 15A, for Vlezenbeek, and continue through this village to the castle; by public transportation, take De Lijn bus no. 142 (Gaasbeek-Leerbeek) from Brussels's Gare du Midi/Zuidstation, and get out at the Kasteel van Gaasbeek stop.

Bruges

Graceful Bruges has drifted down the stream of time with all the self-possession of the swans that cruise its canals. To step into the old town is to be transported back to the Middle Ages, when Bruges (Brugge in Dutch) was among the wealthiest cities of Europe. Unlike so many European cities that have had their hearts torn out by war, Bruges has remained unravaged, its glorious monumental buildings intact. UNESCO has awarded the historical center World Cultural Heritage status.

The city (pop. 117,000, of whom 25,000 live in the old center) is the capital town of West-Vlaanderen (West Flanders) province, and the pride and joy of all Flanders.

Medieval Gothic architecture is the big deal here. Oh, there's a layer of Romanesque; a touch of Renaissance, baroque, and rococo; a dab of neoclassical and neo-Gothic; and a smidgeon of Art Nouveau and Art Deco. But Gothic is what Bruges does, in quantities that come near to numbing the senses—and likely would do so if it wasn't for the distraction of the city's contemporary animation.

In the 15th century, Bruges was a center for the Hanseatic League and has a rich heritage of civic buildings from the period: guildhalls, exchanges, warehouses, and the residences of wealthy merchants.

1 Orientation

ARRIVING
BY TRAIN

Trains arrive in Bruges every hour or so from Brussels, Antwerp, and Ghent, and from the ferry port of Zeebrugge and the North Sea resort of Ostend (Oostende). Journey time is 1 hour from Brussels and Antwerp, 30 minutes from Ghent, and 15 minutes from Ostend and Zeebrugge. Train information is available from Belgian Railways (© 02/528-2283-28; www.sncb.be).

From London, Eurostar high-speed trains to both Paris and Brussels stop at Lille in northern France, from where a train connects to Bruges; or take the Eurostar to Brussels and transfer there. From Paris, Thalys high-speed trains go via Brussels direct to Bruges; on the slower and cheaper International trains, you transfer in Brussels. From Amsterdam, you can go via Antwerp or Brussels, either on Thalys, or on International and Inter-City trains. From Cologne, Thalys trains stop in Brussels; International trains via Brussels to Ostend stop in Bruges.

Although the city is called Bruges in English and French, look out for its Flemish name, BRUGGE, written on the station name boards. The station is on Stationsplein, 1.6km (1 mile) south of the center of town, a 20-minute walk or a short taxi or bus ride—choose any bus labeled CENTRUM and get out at the Markt.

Impressions

The difference between Bruges and other cities is that in the latter, you look about for the picturesque, and don't find it easily, while in Bruges, assailed on every side by the picturesque, you look curiously for the unpicturesque, and don't find it easily.

—British novelist Arnold Bennett, *The Journals* (1896–1931)

BY BUS

Buses are less useful than trains for getting to Bruges, though there is frequent service from Zeebrugge, Ostend, and other Belgian seacoast resorts. The Bruges bus station adjoins the rail station. Schedule and fare information is available from **De Lijn** (*© **070/22-02-00**; www.delijn.be).

Eurolines (see "Getting There by Bus," in chapter 2) operates daily bus service from London, Amsterdam, Paris, Cologne, and other cities around the Continent, to Brussels or Bruges, or to both.

BY CAR

Bruges is 92km (57 miles) northwest of Brussels and 51km (32 miles) northwest of Ghent on A10/E40; 102km (63 miles) west of Antwerp on A14/E17 and A10/E40; 16km (10 miles) south of the ferry port of Zeebrugge on N31 and N371; and 30km (19 miles) southeast of Ostend on A10/E40. From Calais, France, and the Channel Tunnel, take E40 east.

VISITOR INFORMATION

Bruges's tourist information office is **In&Uit Brugge,** Concertgebouw, 't Zand 34, 8000 Brugge (*© **050/44-46-46;** fax 050/44-46-45; www.brugge.be), inside the city's Concert Hall, about midway between the rail station and the heart of town. The office is open daily from 10am to 6pm (Thurs to 8pm). This friendly, efficient office can make last-minute hotel reservations and provides brochures that outline walking, coach, canal, and horse-drawn carriage tours. It's a good place to find detailed information on many sightseeing attractions. Ask for the free annual *events@brugge* brochure and monthly *Exit* newsletter; both are excellent directories of current goings-on. In addition, there's a booth for tourist information and hotel reservations outside the rail station. Belgium's Brussels-based weekly magazine in English, *The Bulletin,* also covers Bruges, though not in as much depth as it does the capital.

CITY LAYOUT

Narrow streets fan out from the adjacent central squares, the Markt and the Burg, and a network of canals threads its way to every section of this small city. The center is almost encircled by a canal that opens at its southern end to become the Minnewater (Lake of Love), filled with swans and other water birds, and bordered by the Begijn-hof and a fine park. On the outer side of the Minnewater is the rail station.

2 Getting Around

The center of Bruges is compact and filled with pedestrians-only streets, which makes walking the best way to get around. Just be sure to wear comfortable shoes; those charming cobblestones can be hard on your feet.

BY BUS

Most city and regional buses, operated by **De Lijn** (© 070/22-02-00; www.delijn.be), depart from the bus station beside the rail station, or from a secondary station at 't Zand, and many buses stop in the center at the Markt. Schedules are prominently posted. A single-journey ticket for the city costs 1€ ($1.25) and is available in units of 1, 2, and 10 tickets. A *dagkaart* (day card), affording unlimited travel on all city buses, costs 5€ ($6.25) for 1 day and 15€ ($19) for 5 days when purchased before boarding; and 6€ ($7.50) and 18€ ($23), respectively, onboard the vehicle.

BY BICYCLE

Cycling is a terrific way to get around Bruges, or to get out of town to the nearby village of Damme (see later in this chapter) by way of scenic canal-side roads. Unlike most Belgian cities, Bruges has made cyclists privileged road users. They can travel in both directions on many of the narrow, one-way streets in the center city—but some streets are one-way only and you can be fined if you're caught riding against the traffic flow. Ride with caution, because the streets are filled with visitors, many of whom have no experience of bikes en masse and are liable to step in front of you without looking.

You can rent a pedal-bike from the rail station for 9€ ($11) per day; you get a discount on rentals of 3 days or more. In addition, many hotels rent bikes to guests, and there are at least a dozen rental stores around town. A good one is **De Ketting,** Gentpoortstraat 23 (© 050/34-41-96), for 6€ ($7.50) a day.

BY CAR

Don't drive. Leave your car at your hotel parking lot (if it has one), at one of six big, prominently labeled underground parking garages in the center (these get expensive for long stays), at one of four cheap park-and-ride lots beside the rail station, or at a free parking zone outside the center city. It's a short walk into the heart of the old city from any of the parking lots. Driving the narrow streets, many of them one-way, can be confusing. Parking rules are firmly enforced, and unlawfully parked cars will be ticketed, wheel-clamped, or towed.

BY TAXI

There are taxi stands at the Markt (© 050/33-44-44) and outside the rail station on Stationsplein (© 050/38-46-60).

FAST FACTS: Bruges

American Express There is no office in Bruges; the nearest one is in Brussels (see "Fast Facts: Brussels," in chapter 5).

Car Rental If you must rent a car, you'll find **Avis** at Koningin Astridlaan 97/7 (© 050/39-44-51), and **Hertz** at Baron Ruzettelaan 6 (© 050/37-72-34).

Currency Exchange The tourist office (see "Visitor Information," above) is a good place to change money and traveler's checks, as are banks. ATMs can be found on the Markt and at numerous other points in the center city.

Doctors For a doctor on night and weekend duty, call © 050/36-40-10.

Where to Stay & Dine in Bruges

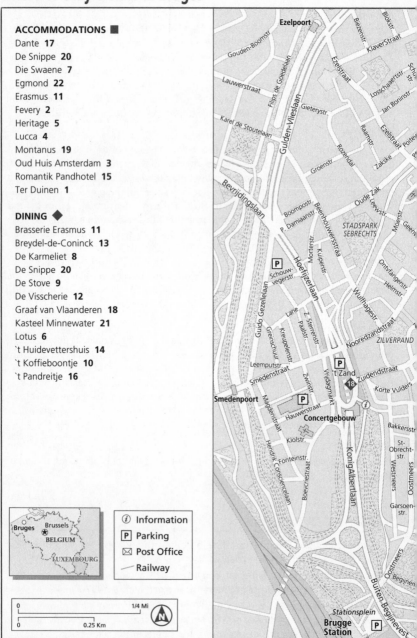

ⓘ Information
Ⓟ Parking
⊠ Post Office
— Railway

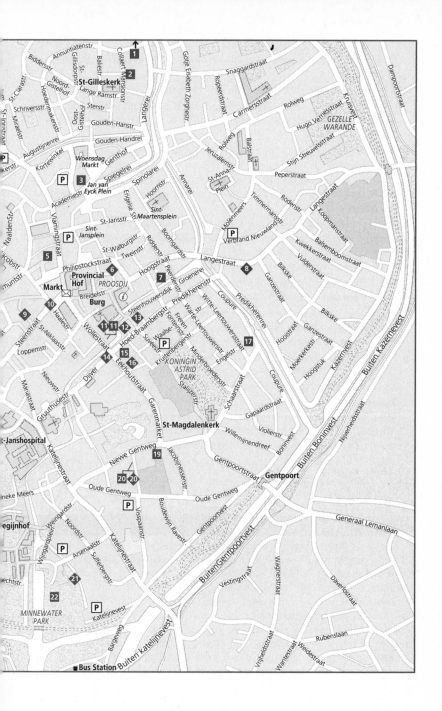

Emergencies For the police, dial ☏ **101;** for firefighters and ambulance, call ☏ **100.**

Hospital **Academisch Ziekenhuis Sint-Jan,** Riddershove 10 (☏ **050/45-21-11**).

Internet Access A centrally located Internet cafe is **The Coffee Link,** Mariastraat 38 (☏ **050/349973;** www.thecoffeelink.com), in the medieval Oud Sint-Jan Hospital complex.

Pharmacies A pharmacy is called an *apotheek* in Dutch. Regular pharmacy hours are Monday to Saturday 9am to 6pm (some close earlier on Sat). Try **Soetaart Apotheek,** Vlamingstraat 17 (☏ **050/33-25-95**), just north of the Markt. All pharmacies have details of the nearby all-night and Sunday pharmacies posted on the door.

Police (Politie) In an emergency, call ☏ **101.** In nonurgent situations, go to the **Central Police Station,** Hauwerstraat 7 (☏ **050/44-88-44**). Unlike in Brussels, the Bruges police are likely to be both professional and helpful to visitors with problems, and you're sure to be attended to by an officer who speaks English.

Post Office The main post office, Markt 5 (☏ **050/33-14-11**), is open Monday to Friday from 9am to 6pm, and Saturday from 9am to 3pm.

Restrooms The finest place to find relief in the center of Bruges is the **Crown Plaza Brugge Hotel,** on the Burg. There are tolerable public restrooms on the west side of the Minnewater lake, close to the Begijnhof.

Safety Bruges is safe and there are no areas you need be leery of going into. That said, since it's a big tourist center, it can't hurt to take routine precautions against pickpocketing and other types of theft.

Telephones The telephone area code for Bruges is **050.** You need to dial the **050** area code both from inside Bruges and from elsewhere in Belgium. Dial **50** (without the initial 0) if you are phoning Bruges from outside Belgium. For more details, see "Fast Facts: Belgium," in chapter 4.

Transit Info Information regarding the city bus service is available from **De Lijn** (☏ **070/22-02-00;** www.delijn.be).

3 Where to Stay

If a high-rise luxury hotel is your cup of tea, I'd suggest you stay in Brussels and commute to Bruges. But if you like the idea of small, atmospheric accommodations, perhaps on the banks of a picturesque canal, with modern (if not necessarily luxurious) facilities, opt for one of the places reviewed below.

Try to arrive with a reservation. Considering the four million visitors it welcomes in a year, Bruges is Belgium's premier tourist destination. Even though many visitors are day-trippers, it's essential to make your hotel reservations at least 2 weeks in advance if you plan to stay overnight. Having said that, if you do come into town without a place to stay, head immediately to the tourist office, which has a last-minute reservation service. Accommodations are more likely to be full on weekends.

Note that where hotels have no private parking, there's another option beyond the "limited street parking" that might be listed in the service information. Bruges's small center city holds six large public parking garages, all clearly marked on access roads. There will always be at least one within a short walk of your hotel.

EXPENSIVE

De Snippe ★★   Set in an early-18th-century building in the center of town, De Snippe offers luxurious and spacious rooms, all furnished with restrained elegance and some with fireplaces. Two rooms have Jacuzzis. All bathrooms have been fully renovated. The hotel has one of Bruges's leading restaurants (see "Where to Dine," below).

Nieuwe Gentweg 53, 8000 Brugge. ℂ **050/33-70-70.** Fax 050/33-76-62. www.desnippe.be. 9 units. 145€–195€ ($181–$244) double; 310€ ($388) suite. Rates include full breakfast. AE, DC, MC, V. Free parking. Bus: 1 or 11. **Amenities:** Restaurant (French); bar; concierge; limited room service; in-room massage; babysitting; laundry service; dry cleaning. *In room:* A/C, TV, minibar, hair dryer, iron, safe.

Die Swaene ★★★   This small hotel on the beautiful city-center Groenerei canal has rightly been called one of the most romantic in Europe, thanks in great part to the care lavished on it by the Hessels family. The comfortable rooms are elegantly and individually furnished, and the lounge, from 1779, was formerly the Guildhall of the Tailors. You might be expected to lodge in an annex, across the canal, where the rooms are luxurious enough but not so convenient—you have to recross the canal to take advantage of the main building's amenities, for instance. The in-house restaurant, best for its seafood and regional cuisine, has won favorable reviews from guests and critics.

Steenhouwersdijk 1 (across the canal from the Burg), 8000 Brugge. ℂ **050/34-27-98.** Fax 050/33-66-74. www.dieswaene-hotel.com. 32 units. 185€–295€ ($231–$361) double; 350€–460€ ($438–$575) suite. Rates include buffet breakfast. AE, DC, V. Parking 10€ ($13). Bus: 1 or 6. **Amenities:** Restaurant (seafood/Flemish); bar; lounge; heated indoor pool; exercise room; sauna; concierge; secretarial services; limited room service; babysitting; laundry service. *In room:* A/C (some rooms), TV, dataport, minibar, hair dryer.

Romantik Pandhotel ★★   Close to the Markt, this lovely 18th-century mansion surrounded by plane trees is an oasis of tranquillity. Although it provides modern conveniences, its exquisite, old-fashioned furnishings lend special grace to comfortable rooms. Guests praise Mrs. Chris Vanhaecke-Dewaele for her hospitality and attention to detail. You can use an Internet-connected computer in the lobby to send and receive e-mail.

Pandreitje 16, 8000 Brugge. ℂ **050/34-06-66.** Fax 050/34-05-56. www.pandhotel.com. 24 units. 150€–320€ ($188–$400) double. Rates include full breakfast. AE, DC, MC, V. Limited street parking. Bus: 1 or 6. **Amenities:** Bar; concierge; 24-hr. room service; in-room massage; babysitting; laundry service; dry cleaning; nonsmoking rooms. *In room:* A/C, TV, dataport, minibar, hair dryer, safe.

MODERATE

Dante   Taking its name from a reference to Bruges in the Florentine poet Dante Alighieri's *Divine Comedy*, this ultramodern brick hotel alongside a lovely canal artfully combines old Bruges style with modern amenities and fittings. Its spacious guest rooms are restfully decorated in warm colors like peach and are furnished with bamboo and rattan beds. The hotel is a short walk west from the city center, and most rooms have a view of the canal at Coupure. The vegetarian restaurant here, called Toermalijn, is highly regarded locally.

Coupure 29A, 8000 Brugge. ℂ **050/34-01-94.** Fax 050/34-35-39. www.hoteldante.be. 27 units. 155€–265€ ($194–$331) double. Rates include buffet breakfast. AE, DC, MC, V. Limited street parking. Bus: 6. **Amenities:** Restaurant (vegetarian); game room; limited room service; laundry service; same-day dry cleaning; nonsmoking rooms. *In room:* TV, minibar, hair dryer.

Egmond ✹✹   The Egmond has just eight rooms, in a rambling mansion next to the Minnewater Park, but the lucky few who stay here will find ample space, plenty of family ambience, abundant local color, and lots of peace and tranquillity. All rooms have recently been redecorated and are furnished in individual styles with views of the garden and the Minnewater Park. Every afternoon, free coffee and tea are served on the new garden terrace or in the lounge, which has an 18th-century fireplace. There's an "honesty bar," where you help yourself to a drink and leave payment. Some rooms have air-conditioning.

Minnewater 15 (at Minnewater Park), 8000 Brugge. ✆ 050/34-14-45. Fax 050/34-29-40. www.egmond.be. 8 units. 98€–120€ ($125–$150) double. Rates include buffet breakfast. No credit cards. Parking 10€ ($13); maximum 25€ ($31) per stay. Bus: 1 or 11. **Amenities:** Nonsmoking rooms. *In room:* TV, dataport, hair dryer, safe.

Erasmus ✹   This small, cozy hotel is set in a picturesque little square alongside a canal in the town center. The rooms were renovated in 2001, with new carpets and new bathroom fixtures and fittings. All rooms have attractive, modern furnishings, and some have air-conditioning.

Wollestraat 35 (near the Belfry), 8000 Brugge. ✆ **050/33-57-81.** Fax 050/33-47-27. www.hotelerasmus.com. 10 units. 80€–175€ ($100–$219) double. Rates include buffet breakfast. MC, V. No parking. Bus: 1 or 6. **Amenities:** Restaurant (Belgian); bar; limited room service; laundry service; nonsmoking rooms. *In room:* TV, dataport, minibar, coffeemaker, hair dryer.

Heritage ✹   The Heritage, a short walk from the Markt in a mansion dating from 1869, has a well-established reputation in Bruges. Its rooms are modern and not overly big, but they are warmly furnished and decorated, and are fitted with DVD players. The beds are comfortable, the staff friendly, and the ambience welcoming. The ornamental ceiling in the breakfast room is a reminder of the building's respectable origins.

Niklaas Desparsstraat 11, 8000 Brugge. ✆ **050/44-44-44.** Fax 050/44-44-40. www.hotel-heritage.com. 20 units. 135€–218€ ($169–$273) double; 310€–370€ ($388–$463) suite. Rates include buffet breakfast. AE, DC, MC, V. Valet parking 15€ ($19). **Amenities:** Bar; lounge; health club; bike rental; concierge; 24-hr. room service; laundry service; same-day dry cleaning; nonsmoking rooms. *In room:* A/C, TV, fax, dataport, minibar, hair dryer, iron, safe.

Montanus ✹   The former budget Hotel St. Christophe now has new ownership, a new name, and a new upmarket ethos. This three-story hotel offers a range of price options for comfortable accommodations. Some of the individually styled guest rooms overlook a big and lovely garden.

Nieuwe Gentweg 78, 8000 Brugge. ✆ 050/33-11-76. Fax 050/34-09-38. www.montanus.be. 24 units. 108€–220€ ($135–$275) double. Rates include continental breakfast. AE, DC, MC, V. Parking 15€ ($19). Bus: 1 or 11. **Amenities:** Bar. *In room:* TV, minibar, hair dryer, iron, safe.

Oud-Huis Amsterdam ✹✹   Philip and Caroline Traen have made a fine hotel out of these four canal-side buildings, parts of which date back to the 1300s. Rooms are large and sumptuously furnished. The colors and decorative accents hearken back to the building's origins, based on meticulous research and restoration. Some of the bathrooms feature whirlpool tubs. The elegant guest rooms in the front overlook the canal; those in back overlook the garden and picturesque rooftops. The entrance hall, the small salon off the reception area, and the popular bar called The Meeting all have a pleasant atmosphere. In the rear, there's a charming little courtyard with umbrella tables and a garden off to one side—the setting for Sunday concerts in June. The famed Traen hospitality makes a stay here in the town center very special. Around half of the guest rooms have air-conditioning.

Spiegelrei 3, 8000 Brugge. ☎ **050/34-18-10**. Fax 050/33-88-91. www.oha.be. 34 units. 140€–238€ ($175–$298) double; 388€ ($485) suite. AE, DC, MC, V. Parking 13€ ($16). Bus: 4 or 8. **Amenities:** Bar; limited room service; babysitting; laundry service; dry cleaning; nonsmoking rooms. *In room:* TV, dataport, hair dryer.

Ter Duinen ☆   Here's an ideal marriage of classical style and modern conveniences. Brightly decorated guest rooms are ample in size and have modern furnishings. Some rooms have wooden ceiling beams, and some have a great view overlooking the tranquil Langerei canal, just north of the town center and within easy walking distance. Proprietors Marc and Lieve Bossu-Van Den Heuvel take justified pride in their charming hotel and extend a friendly welcome to guests.

Langerei 52 (at Kleine Nieuwstraat), 8000 Brugge. ☎ **050/33-04-37**. Fax 050/34-42-16. www.terduinenhotel.be. 20 units. 98€–149€ ($123–$186) double. Rates include full breakfast. AE, DC, MC, V. Limited street parking. Bus: 4 or 8. **Amenities:** Lounge; limited room service; dry cleaning. *In room:* A/C, TV, hair dryer, safe.

INEXPENSIVE

Fevery ☆   Don't be put off by the name: It's the Fevery (*fay*-ver-ee), not Fevery as in "feverish." This recently renovated family hotel is on a side street in a quiet part of town, facing the Sint-Gilliskerk (St. Giles's Church), just north of the center city, a short and pleasant walk away. The modern and comfortably furnished guest rooms, enlarged through a rebuilding program that ended in 2002, are cheery and immaculate, with new bathrooms and monogrammed pressed sheets. One room is a quad. There's a downstairs lounge and breakfast room. The proprietor, Mr. Asselman, has a wealth of local information and clearly takes great pride in his establishment.

Collaert Mansionstraat 3 (off Langerei), 8000 Brugge. ☎ **050/33-12-69**. Fax 050/33-17-91. www.hotelfevery.be. 12 units. 60€–80€ ($75–$100) double. Rates include buffet breakfast. AE, MC, V. Free parking. Bus: 4 or 8. **Amenities:** Lounge; bike rental. *In room:* TV.

Lucca ☆ *Value*   Built in the 14th century by a wealthy merchant from Lucca, Italy, the high ceilings and wide halls of this mansion right in the heart of romantic Bruges convey a sense of luxury. The welcome is warm, and the guest rooms are in fair condition and sport pine furnishings. Rooms with bathrooms have TVs. Breakfast is served in a cozy medieval cellar decorated with antiques.

Naaldenstraat 30 (off Sint-Jakobsstraat), 8000 Brugge. ☎ **050/34-20-67**. Fax 050/33-34-64. www.hotellucca.be. 19 units, 14 with bathroom. 50€ ($63) double without bathroom; 65€–85€ ($81–$106) double with bathroom. Rates include buffet breakfast. AE, DC, MC, V. Limited street parking. *In room:* TV (some rooms).

4 Where to Dine

Bruges certainly has no shortage of restaurants. You'll practically trip over them in the center city. The restaurants featured below aim to make dining a memorable part of your Bruges experience.

VERY EXPENSIVE

De Karmeliet ☆☆ BELGIAN/FRENCH   In 1996, chef Geert Van Hecke became the first Flemish chef to be awarded three Michelin stars. He has described his award-winning menu as "international cuisine made with local products" that aims to combine French quality with Flemish quantity. The result is outstanding fine cuisine served in an elegant setting. Van Hecke will happily whip up something special from a pig's trotter and can do things with the humble potato that would turn heads in Idaho—his deceptively plain-sounding potato bouillon with shelled shrimps and cod is a long-standing favorite, and the somewhat disturbing-sounding *ratte* combines potatoes with cauliflower and caviar. You'll find the local Oud Brugge cheese both as an ingredient and on the cheese board, and some sauces are made using Belgian *jenever* (gin) and Belgian beers.

Langestraat 19 (off Hoogstraat). ℂ 050/33-82-59. www.dekarmeliet.be. Reservations required. Main courses 20€–35€ ($25–$44); fixed-price menus 65€–95€ ($81–$119). AE, DC, MC, V. Tues–Sat noon–2pm and 7–9:30pm; Sun 7–9:30pm (except June–Sept).

't Pandreitje ☆☆ FRENCH/BELGIAN   This restaurant sits in the shade of the medieval Market Hall's bell tower, just off the Rozenhoedkaai, one of the most beautiful canalsides in Bruges. The interior of this Renaissance-era private home has been turned into an elegant Louis XVI setting for a menu of classic dishes. The four-course a la carte meal is superb, and the menu of pre-selected choices is excellent. Try the sea bass served with fennel, parsley sauce, and sautéed potatoes, or the salad of Dublin Bay prawns with artichoke and a truffle vinaigrette.

Pandreitje 6 (off Rozenhoedkaai). ℂ **050/33-11-90.** www.pandreitje.be. Reservations required. Main courses 30€–40€ ($38–$50); lunch menu 40€ ($50); *gastronomische* menu 50€–80€ ($63–$100). AE, DC, MC, V. Mon–Tues and Thurs–Sat noon–2pm and 7–9:30pm.

EXPENSIVE

De Snippe ☆ NOUVELLE FRENCH   De Snippe enjoys a well-earned reputation as one of Bruges's finest restaurants. Its seafood dishes are particularly good. If you like crustaceans, try the delicious *pot au feu* (stockpot soup) of lobster with basil and a sesame crust.

In De Snippe Hotel, Nieuwe Gentweg 53. ℂ **050/33-70-70.** www.desnippe.be. Main courses 16€–35€ ($20–$44); fixed-price menus 71€ ($89). AE, DC, MC, V. Mon 7–10pm; Tues–Sat noon–2:30pm and 7–10pm.

De Visscherie ☆☆ SEAFOOD   This attractive restaurant faces the old Fish Market in the town center and, as you might expect, "fruits of the sea" take top billing on the menu. Freshness is guaranteed. Specialties include a delicious lobster stew, shellfish in many guises (try the spotted scallops with roe), and Channel sole.

Vismarkt 8. ℂ 050/33-02-12. www.visscherie.be. Main courses 32€–53€ ($40–$66). AE, DC, MC, V. Wed–Mon noon–2pm and 7–10pm.

't Huidevettershuis ☆☆ FLEMISH/SEAFOOD   This charmer, right on a canal in the town center, is in a stone building dating from 1630 with flowers blooming in diamond-paned windows. It used to be the Ambachtshuis der Huidevetters (Tanners' Guild House) and now houses a cozy, intimate room downstairs and a pleasant, larger one upstairs. Look for Flemish specialties such as the souplike *waterzooï* (with chicken), in addition to ham, rabbit, and herring dishes. A notable and, for Flanders, surprising, absentee from the menu is mussels, but the same people own the De Visscherie seafood restaurant (see above) and a restaurant specializing in mussels (De Mosselkelder, also on Huidenvettersplein), so maybe that explains it.

Huidenvettersplein 10–11. ℂ **050/33-95-06.** www.huidevettershuis.be. Main courses 22€–58€ ($28–$73). AE, DC, MC, V. Wed–Mon noon–2pm and 6–10pm.

MODERATE

Breydel-de-Coninck ☆ SEAFOOD   An aquarium of tropical fish at the entrance sets a marine mood in this seafood restaurant just off the Markt. Wood beam ceilings and plaid upholstery are cheerful, but the real attraction is the seafood. The specialties here are mussels, eels, and lobsters prepared with white wine, cream, or garlic sauces that enhance the flavor of the seafood without overwhelming it. Try a pail full of plain mussels, or go for something with a little more zest, like the *moules Provençal* (mussels in a light red sauce with mushrooms, peppers, and onions). And the homemade ice cream with caramel sauce is a good way to wind up.

Breidelstraat 24. © **050/33-27-46.** Main courses 9.90€–21€ ($12–$26); fixed-price meals 16€–36€ ($20–$45). AE, MC, V. Thurs–Tues noon–3pm and 6–9:30pm.

De Stove ✿✿ FLEMISH/SEAFOOD   This small, family-owned restaurant combines a rustic atmosphere with a more modern style than is the norm in Bruges. The seafood specialties are well worth a try, particularly the Flemish fish stew with *fruits de mer.*

Kleine Sint-Amandsstraat 4. © **050/33-78-35.** www.restaurantdestove.be. Reservations recommended on weekends. Main courses 16€–28€ ($21–$38); fixed-price menu 42€–57€ ($53–$71). AE, MC, V. Fri–Tues noon–1:45pm and 6:30–9:30pm.

Kasteel Minnewater ✿✿ *Value* BELGIAN/FRENCH   Old paintings on the walls, a marble fireplace, chandeliers, and fine table linen all complement this château-restaurant's superb location on the Minnewater (Lake of Love). It exudes an unstuffy charm that makes château dining not just something for lords and ladies, and though prices have been edging up, it still provides a good deal considering the setting. Specialties include a suite of unpretentious Flemish seafood dishes such as the *zeetong in boter gebakken en gebakken aardappelen* (sole baked in butter with baked potatoes) and, for a starter, the tasty *huisgemaakte garnaalkroketten met salade* (homemade shrimp croquettes with salad), made with the little gray North Sea shrimps. There's an excellent, Marseilles-influenced bouillabaisse, but using North Sea ingredients like cod, sole, shrimps, and shellfish. Carnivores can go for the *varkenhaasje Archiduc en gebakken aardappelen* (pork filet Archiduc with baked potatoes).

Minnewater 4 (at Minnewater Park). © **050/33-42-54.** Main courses 25€–45€ ($31–$56); Markt-menu 30€ ($37). V. Summer: daily 11am–11pm (food at lunch and dinner times only). Winter: Mon–Fri noon–2:30pm and 6:30–11pm, Sat–Sun 11am–11pm (food at lunch and dinner times only).

INEXPENSIVE

Brasserie Erasmus ✿ FLEMISH   Small but popular, this is a great stop after viewing the cathedral and nearby museums. It serves a large variety of Flemish dishes, all prepared with beer. If you need help making a selection, you can ask owner Tom for advice, or try these suggestions: The typically Flemish souplike stew dish *waterzooï* is very good here, and it's served with fish, as it's supposed to be, although they also make it with chicken instead, a style that has become the norm elsewhere. If that doesn't grab you, how about *lapin à la bière* (rabbit in a beer sauce)? About 150 different brands of beer are available (for drinking), 10 of them on tap.

In the Hotel Erasmus, Wollestraat 35. © **050/33-57-81.** www.hotelerasmus.com. Main courses 15€–25€ ($19–$31); fixed-price 20€–38€ ($25–$48). MC, V. Tues–Sun noon–4pm (summer also Mon) and 6–11pm.

Graaf van Vlaanderen STEAK/SALADS   This reasonably priced restaurant near the railroad station has an extensive menu and a decor that relies heavily on mirrors and plants. The fare is equally simple, featuring minute steak (steak so thin it cooks in 1 min.), spaghetti, salads, and *steak-frites* (steak and french fries).

't Zand 19 (in the Graaf van Vlaanderen hotel). © **050/33-31-50.** www.graafvanvlaanderen.be. Main courses 13€–19€ ($16–$24). AE, DC, MC, V. Fri–Wed 7:30am–10pm.

Lotus ✪ VEGETARIAN　Even non-vegetarians will likely enjoy the delicious lunch here. There are just two menu options—but at least you can choose from a small, medium, or large serving—each with a hearty assortment of imaginatively prepared vegetables, served in a tranquil but cheery Scandinavian-style dining room.

Wapenmakersstraat 5 (off the Burg). ✆ 050/33-10-78. Fixed-price lunch menus 9€–11€ ($11–$14). No credit cards. Mon–Sat 11:30am–2pm.

't Koffieboontje SEAFOOD/FLEMISH　The bright, modern interior here strikes a noticeably stylish contrast to the often-dark ambience of many Bruges restaurants. An extensive menu is equally cheery, featuring good, but not fancy, seafood specialties like lobster and salmon, and Belgian staples like mussels, steak, and sole.

Hallestraat 4. ✆ 050/33-80-27. Main courses 9.75€–17€ ($12–$21). AE, DC, MC, V. Daily noon–11pm.

5 Seeing the Sights

A leading contender for the title of Europe's most romantic small city, Bruges is really one big attraction—a fairy-tale mixture of gabled houses, meandering canals, magnificent squares, and narrow cobblestone streets. Perhaps the most astonishing thing is the consistently warm welcome its residents provide to the swarms of visitors. The basis for this is more than mere economics—those who live in Bruges love their city and appreciate that others want to experience it.

THE MARKT

Heraldic banners float from venerable facades on the Markt. This square, along with the Burg (see below), is the heart of Bruges and the focal point of your sightseeing. Most major points of interest in the city are little more than 5 or 10 minutes' walk away.

Belfort en Hallen (Belfry and Market Halls) ✪✪　The Belfry was, and is, the symbol of Bruges's civic pride. What poet Henry Wadsworth Longfellow in 1856 called "the beautiful, wild chimes" of its magnificent 47-bell carillon peal out over the city every quarter-hour, and several times a day in longer concerts during the summer. The tower stands 84m (272 ft.) high. Its lower section dates from around 1240, with the corner turrets added in the 14th century, and the upper, octagonal section in the 15th century. You can climb the 366 steep steps to the Belfry's summit for panoramic views of Bruges and the surrounding countryside all the way to the sea. Pause for breath at the second-floor Treasury, where the town seal and charters were kept behind multiple wrought-iron grilles. From the 13th to the 16th century, much of the city's commerce was conducted in the Hallen. They have recently been brought back into use, as an exhibition center operated by a consortium of local art dealers.

Markt. ✆ 050/44-87-11. Admission 5€ ($6.25) adults, 3€ ($3.75) seniors and those 13–26, free for children under 13. Tues–Sun 9:30am–5pm (open Easter Monday, Pentecost Monday). Closed Jan 1, Ascension Day afternoon, Dec 25.

OTHER SIGHTS AROUND THE MARKT

The **sculpture group** in the center of the Markt depicts a pair of Flemish heroes, butcher Jan Breydel and weaver Pieter de Coninck. The two led an uprising in 1302 against the wealthy merchants and nobles who dominated the guilds, and then went on to win an against-the-odds victory over French knights later that same year in the Battle of the Golden Spurs. The small, castlelike building called the **Craenenburg** (it's now a restaurant), at the corner of Sint-Amandsstraat, was used by a rebellious citizenry

---

(Fun Fact Swans Forever

In addition to locking up the heir to the Habsburg throne, Bruges's vexed 15th-century taxpayers removed the head of his counselor Pieter Lanchals, who had argued for the tax increase in the first place. Lanchals's family emblem was a swan, and for this crime Maximilian exacted a "penalty" from the citizens that has added a note of pure beauty to the city ever since: He obliged them to keep swans on the canals forever.

---

to imprison the Habsburg Crown Prince Maximilian of Austria in 1482 over a small matter of increased taxes. In revenge for that humiliation, Maximilian later hit Bruges in its pride by transferring his capital to Ghent, and in its pocketbook by transferring its trading rights to Antwerp. The large neo-Gothic **Provinciaal Hof (Provincial Palace)** dates from the 1800s and houses the government of the province of West Flanders.

THE BURG

The Burg, a public square just steps away from the Markt, holds an array of beautiful buildings, which together add up to a kind of trip through the history of European architecture. On this site, Baldwin Iron Arm, count of Flanders, once built a fortified castle (or "burg"), around which a village developed into Bruges.

Heilig-Bloedbasiliek (Basilica of the Holy Blood) ⟨★★⟩   A 12th-century Romanesque basilica with a Gothic upper floor, the church houses a venerated relic of Christ and is well worth a visit for the richness of its design and its other treasures. It is the repository of a fragment of cloth stained with what is said to be the blood of Christ, wiped from his body after the crucifixion by Joseph of Arimathea. Legend says the relic was brought to Bruges at the time of the Second Crusade by count of Flanders Diederik van de Elzas, who received it from the Patriarch of Jerusalem and donated it to the church in 1150. More likely, it arrived later from the Byzantine capital Constantinople, which in 1204 was sacked by the Crusader army of count of Flanders Baldwin IX.

The relic is embedded in a rock-crystal vial, which itself is held inside a small glass cylinder adorned at each end with a golden crown. Normally the relic is kept in a magnificent tabernacle on a side altar in the upstairs chapel, but it is brought out regularly so that the faithful can kiss it. In the Basilica Museum, a reliquary created in 1617 by Bruges goldsmith Jan Crabbe has a gem-encrusted hexagonal case to hold the relic, and at the top a golden statue of the Virgin. A second reliquary, dating from 1612, with a lid from 1716, is silver with a golden flower garland added in 1890. Every year, in the colorful Procession of the Holy Blood, on Ascension Day, the bishop of Bruges leads the relic through the streets, accompanied by costumed residents acting out biblical scenes.

Burg 10. ⟨℃⟩ **050/33-67-92.** www.holyblood.org. Basilica free admission. Museum 1.50€ ($1.90) adults, 0.50€ (65¢) children 5–18, free for children under 5. Apr–Sept daily 9:30–11:50am and 2–5:50pm (except Wed afternoon); Oct–Mar daily 10am–11:50 and 2–3:50pm (except Wed afternoon). Closed Jan 1, Nov 1, Dec 25.

Landhuis van het Brugse Vrije (Palace of the Liberty of Bruges) ⟨★⟩   Dating mostly from 1722 to 1727, when it replaced a 16th-century building as the seat of the Liberty of Bruges—the Liberty being the name of the district around Bruges in the

What to See & Do in Bruges

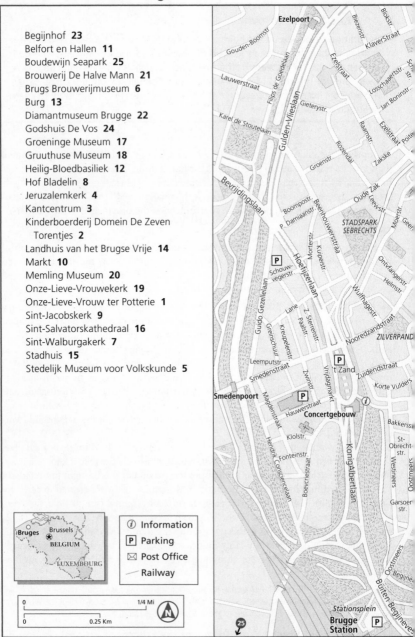

ⓘ Information
P Parking
⊠ Post Office
— Railway

0 ——————— 1/4 Mi
0 ——————— 0.25 Km

St-Gilleskerk

St-Magdalenkerk

Gentpoort

KONINGIN
ASTRID
PARK

GEZELLE
WARANDE

MINNEWATER
PARK

■ Bus Station

Middle Ages—the palace later became a courthouse and now houses the city council's administration. Inside, at no. 11A, is the **Renaissancezaal Brugse Vrije (Renaissance Hall of the Liberty of Bruges)** ✸✸, the Liberty's council chamber, which has been restored to its original 16th-century condition. The hall has a superb black marble fireplace decorated with an alabaster frieze and topped by an oak chimneypiece carved with statues of Emperor Charles V, who visited Bruges in 1515, and his grandparents: Emperor Maximilian of Austria, Duchess Mary of Burgundy, King Ferdinand II of Aragon, and Queen Isabella I of Castile.

Burg 11. ✆ 050/44-87-11. Admission: courtyard free; Renaissance Hall, 2.50€ ($3.15) adults, 1.50€ ($1.90) seniors/ages 13–26, free for children under 13. Tues–Sun 9:30am–5pm (open Easter Monday, Pentecost Monday). Closed Jan 1, Ascension Day afternoon, Dec 25.

Stadhuis (Town Hall) ✸   This Gothic structure was built in the late 1300s, making it the oldest Town Hall in Belgium. Don't miss the upstairs **Gotische Zaal (Gothic Room)** ✸✸ with its ornate decor and wall murals depicting highlights from Bruges's history. Most spectacular of all is the vaulted oak ceiling, dating from 1402, which features scenes from the New Testament. The statues in the niches on the Town Hall facade are 1980s replacements for the originals, which had been painted by Jan van Eyck and were destroyed by pro-French rebels in the 1790s.

Burg 12. ✆ 050/44-87-11. Admission 2.50€ ($3.15) adults, 1.50€ ($1.90) seniors/ages 13–26, free for children under 13. Tues–Sun 9:30am–5pm (open Easter Monday, Pentecost Monday). Closed Jan 1, Ascension Day afternoon, Dec 25.

OTHER SIGHTS AROUND THE BURG

The **Oude Civiele Griffie (Old Civic Registry),** built beside the Town Hall as the offices of the Town Clerk, has the oldest Renaissance facade in the city, dating from 1537, and now houses the city archives. Facing the Town Hall is the baroque **Proosdij (Provost's House),** dating from 1666, which used to be the residence of the bishop of Bruges and is now occupied by government offices of West Flanders province.

TOP MUSEUMS & ATTRACTIONS

Groeninge Museum ✸✸✸   The Groeninge ranks among Belgium's leading traditional museums of fine arts, with a collection that covers painting in the Low Countries from the 15th to the 20th centuries. The Gallery of Flemish Primitives holds some 30 works—many of which are far from primitive—by painters such as Jan van Eyck (there's a portrait of his wife, Margerita van Eyck), Rogier van der Weyden, Hieronymus Bosch *(The Last Judgment),* and Hans Memling. Works by Magritte and Delvaux also are on display. Among works by van Eyck that you can view in the museum are his beautiful altarpiece *The Madonna and Child with Canon Joris van der Paele* (1436), in which the Flemish cardinal is being presented to the Virgin Mary and the infant Jesus, and a portrait of his wife Margareta, created in 1439.

Fun Fact   **Size Isn't Everything**

Here's your chance to compare codpieces. Ahem, I mean, to admire the finely carved suits of armor of the statues of Emperor Charles V, Emperor Maximilian of Austria, and King Ferdinand II of Aragon on the chimneypiece in the Hall of the Liberty of Bruges. (I say Charles's is the biggest.)

Dijver 12. ☎ **050/44-87-11.** Admission (combined ticket with neighboring Arentshuis) 8€ ($10) adults, 6€ ($8) seniors and ages 13–26, free for children under 13. Tues–Sun 9:30am–5pm (open Easter Monday, Pentecost Monday). Closed Jan 1, Ascension Day afternoon, Dec 25.

Gruuthuse Museum 🎔

The Flemish nobleman and herb merchant Lodewijk Van Gruuthuse, who was a counselor to the dukes of Burgundy in the 1400s, lived in this ornate Gothic mansion. Among the 2,500 numbered antiquities in the house are paintings, sculptures, tapestries, lace, weapons, glassware, and richly carved furniture.

Dijver 17 (in a courtyard next to the Groeninge Museum). ☎ **050/44-87-11.** Admission 6€ ($7.50) adults, 4€ ($5) seniors/ages 13–26, free for children under 13. Tues–Sun 9:30am–5pm (open Easter Monday, Pentecost Monday). Closed Jan 1, Ascension Day afternoon, Dec 25.

Kantcentrum (Lace Center) 🎔🎔

A combination workshop, museum, and salesroom is where the ancient art of lacemaking is passed on to the next generation. You'll get a firsthand look at the artisans making many of the items for future sale in all those lace stores. When you purchase lace, ideally you should specify that you want handmade lace, which is more expensive and of higher quality than the machine-made stuff. The most famous laces to look for are *bloemenwerk, rozenkant,* and *toversesteek.* Your ticket is valid also in the neighboring Jeruzalemkerk (Jerusalem Church; see "More Churches," below).

Peperstraat 3A (at Jeruzalemstraat). ☎ **050/33-00-72.** www.kantcentrum.com. Admission 2.50€ ($3.15) adults, 2€ ($2.50) seniors and children 7–11, free for children under 7. Mon–Fri 10am–noon and 2–6pm; Sat 10am–noon and 2–5pm. Bus: 6 or 16 to Langestraat.

Memling Museum 🎔🎔

This museum is housed in the former Sint-Janshospitaal (Hospital of St. John), where the earliest wards date from the 13th century. To get a sense of the vastness of the wards when this was a functioning hospital, take a look at the old painting near the entrance that shows small, efficient bed units set into cubicles along the walls. The 17th-century apothecary in the cloisters near the entrance is furnished exactly as it was when this building's main function was to care for the sick. Nowadays visitors come to see the typical medieval hospital buildings filled with furniture and other objects that illustrate their history, and the magnificent collection of paintings by the German-born artist Hans Memling (ca. 1440–94), who moved to Bruges from Brussels in 1465 and became one of the city's most prominent residents. At this museum you find such Memling masterpieces as the three-paneled altarpiece of St. John the Baptist and St. John the Evangelist, which consists of the paintings *The Mystic Marriage of St. Catherine, Shrine of St Ursula,* and *Virgin with Child and Apple.*

Mariastraat 38. ☎ **050/44-87-11.** Admission 8€ ($10) adults, 5€ ($7.50) seniors/ages 13–26, free for children under 13. Tues–Sun 9:30am–5pm (open Easter Monday, Pentecost Monday). Closed Jan 1, Ascension Day afternoon, Dec 25.

Stedelijk Museum voor Volkskunde (Municipal Folklore Museum) 🎔

Housed in the low whitewashed houses of the former Shoemakers Guild Almshouse, the Folklore Museum aims to recreate life in Bruges in times gone by. Exhibits depict a primary school class, a cooper's and a milliner's workshop, a spice store and a candy store, and everyday household scenes. A new emphasis is on the history of the important regional textile industry. Most refreshing of all is an old inn, De Zwarte Kat (The Black Cat), which has real beer on tap. In summer, children and adults can play traditional games in the garden.

Balstraat 43 (at Rolweg). ☎ **050/44-87-64.** Admission 3€ ($3.75) adults, 2€ ($2.50) seniors/ages 13–26, free for children under 13. Tues–Sun 9:30am–5pm (open Easter Monday, Pentecost Monday). Closed Jan 1, Ascension Day afternoon, Dec 25. Bus: 6 to Kruispoort.

HISTORICAL CHURCHES

Onze-Lieve-Vrouwekerk (Church of Our Lady) 𝕲𝕲

It took 2 centuries (13th–15th) to build this church, whose soaring 119m (396-ft.) spire can be seen for miles around Bruges. Among the many art treasures here is a beautiful Carrara marble sculpture of the *Madonna and Child* 𝕲𝕲𝕲 by Michelangelo. This statue, made in 1504, was the only one of Michelangelo's works to leave Italy in his lifetime and is today one of the few that can be seen outside Italy. It was bought by a Bruges merchant, Jan van Mouskroen, and donated to the church in 1506. The church holds a painting of the *Crucifixion* by Anthony van Dyck, and the impressive side-by-side **bronze tomb sculptures** 𝕲 of the duke of Burgundy, Charles the Bold, who died in 1477, and his daughter, Mary of Burgundy, who died in 1482 at age 25, after falling from her horse. A windowpane under the tombs allows you to view the 13th- and 14th-century graves of priests.

Onze-Lieve-Vrouwekerkhof Zuid. 🕐 050/34-53-14. Admission: Church and Madonna and Child altar free; chapel of Charles and Mary and Museum 2.50€ ($3.15) adults, 1.50€ ($1.90) seniors/ages 13–26, free for children under 13. Mon–Fri 9–12:30pm and 1:30–5pm; Sat 9–12:30pm and 1:30–4pm; Sun 1:30–5pm.

Sint-Salvatorskathedraal (Holy Savior's Cathedral)

This mainly Gothic church with a 100m (325-ft.) belfry has been Bruges's cathedral since 1834 (its predecessor, Saint Donatian's on the Burg, was demolished by the French around 1800). The 15th-century wooden choir stalls flanking the altar bear a complete set of escutcheons of the Knights of the Golden Fleece, who held a chapter meeting here in 1478. The Cathedral Museum (Mon–Fri 2–5pm, Sun 3–5pm) houses the *Martyrdom of St. Hippolytus* by Dirk Bouts with a side panel by Hugo van der Goes, and the Cathedral Treasury of gold and silver religious vessels, reliquaries, and Episcopal vestments.

Sint-Salvatorskerkhof (off Steenstraat). 🕐 050/33-68-41. Admission: Cathedral free; Treasury 2.50€ ($3.15) adults, 1.50€ ($1.90) seniors/students, free for children under 13. Museum: Mon 2–5:45pm, Tues–Fri 8:30–11:45am and 2–5:45pm, Sat 8:30–11:45am and 2–3:30pm, Sun 9–10:15am and 2–5:45pm; closed to casual visitors during services. Treasury: Sun–Fri 2–5pm.

MORE CHURCHES

There's no shortage of notable churches in Bruges, but you probably don't want to spend *all* your time visiting them. Anyone with a particular interest in churches, however, should try to visit at least a few of these.

The magnificent **Sint-Walburgakerk (St. Walburga's Church)** 𝕲, in Sint-Maartensplein (1619–43), is one of the few baroque monuments in this Gothic-fixated city. It has a satisfying amount of marble and a notable altar, pulpit, and communion bench. Sint-Walburgakerk was the Jesuit church of Bruges until 1774.

The wealthy Adornes merchant family constructed the **Jeruzalemkerk (Jerusalem Church)** 𝕲, Peperstraat 3, beside the Lace Center (see above), between 1471 and 1483, along the lines of the Church of the Holy Sepulcher in Jerusalem. A replica of Christ's Tomb is in the crypt underneath the choir. The admission to the Lace Center (see "Top Museums & Attractions," above) allows you to visit this church as well.

Also owing much of its ornamentation to wealthy benefactors is **Sint-Jakobskerk (St. James's Church)** in Sint-Jakobsplein. This heavy-looking 15th-century Gothic construction has an intricately carved wooden pulpit, with figures at the base representing the continents.

Founded in 1276 as a hospice, **Onze-Lieve-Vrouw ter Potterie (Our Lady of the Pottery)**, Potterierei 78–79, is now a seniors' home. Part of it houses the **Potterie**

Museum (© **050/44-87-11**), which has a collection of tapestries, 15th- to 17th-century furniture, silverware, religious objects, books, and early Flemish paintings. The adjoining 14th-century church, with a fine baroque interior, was the Potters Guild chapel. The museum is open Tuesday to Sunday from 9:30am to 12:30pm and 1:30 to 5pm (open Easter Monday, Pentecost Monday; closed Jan 1, Ascension Day afternoon, Dec 25). Admission is 2.50€ ($3.15) for adults, 1.50€ ($1.90) for seniors and ages 13 to 26, and free for children under 13.

Tranquil Escapes

Through the centuries, since it was founded in 1245 by the Countess Margaret of Constantinople, the **Prinselijk Begijnhof ten Wijngaarde (Princely Beguinage of the Vineyard)** ✵✵✵, Wijngaardstraat (© **050/33-00-11**), at the Lake of Love, has been one of the most tranquil spots in Bruges, and so it remains today. *Begijns* were religious women, similar to nuns, who accepted vows of chastity and obedience, but drew the line at poverty, preferring to earn a living by looking after the sick and making lace. They provided an option for women to live without a husband and children, but without becoming a nun—there was little in the way of alternatives at the time.

The *begijns* are no more, but the Begijnhof is occupied by Benedictine nuns who try to keep the *begijns'* traditions alive. This beautiful little cluster of 17th-century whitewashed houses surrounding a lawn with poplar trees and flowers makes a marvelous escape from the hustle and bustle of the outside world. One of the houses, the **Begijnhuisje (Beguine's House)**, has been made over into a museum and can be visited, as can the convent church during a service. The Begijnhof courtyard is always open and admission is free. The Beguine's House is open from March to November, Monday to Saturday from 10am to noon and 1:45 to 5:30pm, Sunday from 10:45am to noon and 1:45 to 5:30pm; from December to February, Monday, Tuesday, and Friday from 11am to noon and 1:45 to 4:15pm, Wednesday and Thursday from 1:45 to 4:15pm, Saturday from 10am to noon and 1:45 to 5:30pm, Sunday from 10:45am to noon and 1:45 to 5:30pm. Admission is 2€ ($2.50) for adults, 1.50€ ($1.90) for seniors, and 1€ ($1.25) for students and children.

A fine example of the *godshuizen* (houses of God, or almshouses), built by the rich in Bruges from the 13th century onward as refuges for widows and the poor, is the **Godshuis de Vos (De Vos Almshouse),** from 1713, at the corner of Noordstraat and Wijngaardstraat, near the Begijnhof. The moneybags weren't being entirely altruistic, since the residents had to pray for their benefactors' souls twice a day in the chapel that was an integral part of an almshouse's facilities. The pretty courtyard garden here is surrounded by a chapel and eight original houses, now converted to six, which are owned by the city and occupied by seniors. Admission is not permitted, but you can view the complex from over a low wall out front.

OTHER SIGHTS OF INTEREST

Diamantmuseum Brugge (Bruges Diamond Museum)   Diamond polishing has been an important local industry for centuries, ever since Antwerp dealers, looking for cheaper skilled labor, brought the craft to Bruges. The technique of polishing diamonds using diamond powder on a rotating disk may have been invented by the Bruges goldsmith Lodewijk van Berquem around 1450. This museum focuses on the history of diamond polishing in Bruges, with demonstrations and displays of the equipment employed by the craftspeople.

Katelijnestraat 43B (at Oude Gentweg). ✆ 050/34-20-56. www.diamondmuseum.be. Admission: Museum 6€ ($7.50) adults, 3€ ($3.75) students/children; Diamond-polishing demonstration and museum 9€ ($11) adults, 6€ ($7.50) students/children. Daily 10:30am–5:30pm; diamond-polishing demonstration daily 12:15pm. Closed Jan 1, Dec 25.

Hof Bladelin (Bladelin House)   This 15th-century mansion, which is now a seniors' home, was built by Pieter Bladelin, treasurer to Duke Philip the Good. The Medici Bank of Florence took over in 1466 and gave the place an Italian look, particularly in the courtyard, which is thought to be the earliest example of the Renaissance style in the Low Countries. On the facade are medallions depicting Lorenzo de Medici and his wife Clarice Orsini.

Naaldenstraat 19. ✆ 050/33-64-34. Free admission; donation appreciated. Apr–Sept Mon–Sat 10am–noon and 2–5pm, Sun and holidays 10.30am–noon; Oct–Mar Mon–Sat 10am–noon and 2–4pm, Sun and holidays 10.30am–noon.

CITY GATES

The now-vanished city wall once boasted nine powerfully fortified gates dating from the 14th century. The four that survive are (clockwise from the rail station) the imposing **Smedenpoort; Ezelpoort,** which is famed for the many swans that grace the moat beside it; **Kruispoort,** which looks more like a castle with a drawbridge; and **Gentpoort,** now reduced in status to a traffic obstacle. Only one defensive tower remains, the **Poertoren,** which was used as a gunpowder store and overlooks the Lake of Love.

WINDMILLS

The park that marks the line of the city walls between Kruispoort and Dampoort in the northeast is occupied by a row of very photogenic windmills. They are (from south to north) the **Bonne Chière Mill,** built in 1888 at Olsene in East Flanders and moved here in 1911; **Sint-Janshuismolen,** built in 1770 and open free to the public from April to September, daily from 9:30am to 12:30pm and 1:30 to 5pm; **Nieuwe Papegaai Mill,** an oil mill rebuilt here in 1970; and **Coeleweymolen,** dating from 1765, rebuilt here in 1996 and open free to the public from June to September, daily from 9:30am to 12:30pm and 1:30 to 5pm.

BREWERY TOURS

Brugs Brouwerijmuseum (Bruges Brewery Museum)   Bruges's second major brewery has been operating in this area since 1587. The old malthouse, which holds the museum, dates from 1902 and still has its beer vats and other equipment in place. Exhibits here feature not only the museum's parent brewery, but also the other 31 breweries that were in operation in the city at the turn of the 20th century. From here it's just a quick shuffle to Langestraat 45 and the **brewery** itself, which can only be visited by guided tour. Here you can see such popular beers as Brugse Tarwebier, Brugse

---

Tips **Strolling the Back Streets**

You don't need to visit the top 10 highlights to enjoy Bruges. Shut your guide-book, put away the street map, and just wander, taking time out to make your own discoveries. Bruges's inhabitants live their everyday lives in absurdly beauti-ful surroundings and aren't always engaged in putting on a show for the tourists.

Tripel, and Abdij Steenbrugge being brought to life, and you get to taste some of the finished product. Tours are by prior arrangement only.

Verbrand Nieuwland 10 (at Langestraat). © 050/31-15-04. www.brugsbrouwerijmuseum.be. Admission 4€ ($5). May–Sept Wed–Sun 2–6pm.

Brouwerij De Halve Maan ⍟   The brewery here was mentioned in dispatches as early as 1546 and has been in use in "modern" times since 1856. Today, it produces the famous (in Belgium) Straffe Hendrik beer, a strapping blond brew that can be sampled in the brewery's own brasserie—it has a clean, heavenly taste.

Walplein 26. © 050/33-26-97. www.halvemaan.be. Admission 4€ ($5). Guided visits Apr–Sept daily on the hour 11am–4pm; Oct–Mar (except Jan) daily 11am–3pm. Closed Jan 1 and Mon–Fri; Dec Wed and 25, 26.

ESPECIALLY FOR KIDS

Boudewijn Seapark, A. De Baeckestraat 12 (© **050/40-84-08;** www.dolfinarium.be; bus no. 7 or 17), in the southern suburb of Sint-Michiels, is a big favorite with chil-dren, who for some reason seem to prefer its rides, paddleboats, dolphins, and sea lions to Bruges's many historical treasures. Strange but true! Admission is 20€ ($25) for adults, 16€ ($20) for seniors and visitors with reduced mobility, 17€ ($21) for children over 1m (39 in.) and up to age 12, and free for children under 1m (39 in.). The park is open June to August, daily from 10:30am to 5pm, and during Easter week and weekends in September from 11am to 5pm. The Dolfinarium is open intermit-tently at other times.

In the eastern suburbs, **Kinderboerderij Domein De Zeven Torentjes (Seven Towers Estate Children's Farm),** Canadaring 41, Assebroek (© **050/35-40-43;** bus no. 2), is a 14th-century manor farm that has been transformed into a children's farm, with pigs, hens, horses, and other animals. All the buildings—farmhouse, barns, coach house, bakery, and more—have been restored and a large playpark added. An on-site cafeteria has a kids-friendly menu. A 16th-century dovecote has niches for 650 doves. The farm is open Monday to Friday from 8:30am to 5:15pm, Saturday from 10am to 6pm, and Sunday from 1 to 6pm. Admission is free.

Both the theme park and the farm can be reached by bus from the rail station and from the Markt.

ORGANIZED TOURS & EXCURSIONS

A must for every visitor is a **boat cruise** ⍟⍟⍟ on the city canals. There are several departure points, all marked with an anchor icon on maps available at the tourist office. Those open-top canalboats can be scorching in hot weather and bracing in cold, but they're fun and they give you a uniquely satisfying view of the city. They operate March to November daily from 10am to 6pm, and December to February on week-ends, school vacations, and public holidays from 10am to 6pm (except if the canals are frozen!). A half-hour cruise is 5.70€ ($7) for adults, 2.80€ ($3.50) for children ages 4 to 11 accompanied by an adult, and free for children under 4. Wear something warm if the weather is cold or windy. There's even a sternwheeler that sails on the canal to the village of Damme (see below).

Another lovely way to tour Bruges is by **horse-drawn carriage.** From March to November, carriages are stationed on the Markt (on Wed on the Burg). A 30-minute ride is 30€ ($38), and 15€ ($19) for each extra 15 minutes.

Minivan tours by **Sightseeing Line** (✆ **050/35-50-24;** www.citytour.be) last 50 minutes and depart hourly every day from the Markt. The first tour departs at 10am; the last tour departs at 8pm July to September, at 7pm April to June, at 6pm October, at 5pm March, and at 4pm November to February. Fares are 12€ ($14) for adults, 6€ ($8) children ages 6 to 11, free for children under 6, and 30€ ($38) for a family of two adults and two children.

From March to October, you can get some exercise and at the same time visit little-known parts of Bruges, or head out of town to explore the nearby flat Flemish countryside and the village of Damme, on a bike tour, with commentary in English, led by **QuasiMundo Biketours Brugge** (✆ **050/33-07-75;** www.quasimundo.com). You can choose a city bike or mountain bike. Tours are 18€ ($23) for adults, 16€ ($20) for ages 8 to 26, and free for children under 8. Call ahead to make a reservation. The meeting and departure point is the Burg.

If you'd like a trained, knowledgeable guide to accompany you in Bruges, the tourist office can provide one for 50€ ($63) for the first 2 hours, and 25€ ($31) for each additional hour. Or in July and August, you can join a daily guided tour at 3pm that leaves from the tourist office; it costs 5€ ($6.25) for adults and is free for children under 14. For self-guided tours, audio guides with taped details in English are available from the tourist office for 8€ ($10) for one or two people.

Folklore Events in Bruges

One of the most popular and colorful folklore events in Belgium is Bruges's **Heilig-Bloedprocessie (Procession of the Holy Blood),** which dates back to at least 1291 and takes place every year on Ascension Day. During the procession, the bishop of Bruges proceeds through the city streets carrying the golden shrine containing the Relic of the Holy Blood (see "The Burg," earlier in this chapter). Residents wearing Burgundian-era and biblical costumes follow the relic, acting out biblical and historical scenes along the way.

Every 3 years, the canals of Bruges are the subject and location of a festival called the **Reiefeest.** This evening event is a combination of historical tableaux, dancing, open-air concerts, and lots of eating and drinking. It takes place on 6 non-consecutive days in August. The next Reiefeest is due in 2007.

The **Praalstoet van de Gouden Boom (Golden Tree Pageant)** recalls the great procession and tournament held on the Markt to celebrate the 1468 marriage of the duke of Burgundy, Charles the Bold, to Margaret of York. It takes place every 5 years in the last half of August, and the next one will be in 2007.

6 Shopping

No one comes here for stylish shopping—for that you need Brussels or Antwerp. What Bruges is famous for is **lace.** Most of it is machine-made, but there's still plenty of genuine, high-quality (if expensive) handmade lace to be found. The most famous lace styles are bloemenwerk, rozenkant, and toversesteek. Souvenirs of a more perishable nature include Oud-Brugge **cheese,** and local **beers** such as Straffe Hendrik, Brugse Tarwebier, and Brugse Tripel. The contents of a stone bottle of *jenever* (gin) and a box of handmade chocolate **pralines** should go down well.

Upmarket stores and boutiques can be found on the streets around the Markt and 't Zand, including Geldmuntstraat, Noordzandstraat, Steenstraat, Zuidzand- straat, and Vlamingstraat. There are souvenir, lace, and small specialty stores everywhere. Most stores are open Monday to Saturday from 9am to 6pm, with late- night shopping to 9pm on Friday. Many open on Sunday, especially in summer.

> **Impressions**
>
> *In Bruges old images are still para- mount, and an air of monastic life among the quiet goings-on of a thinly-peopled city is inexpressibly soothing; a pensive grace seems to be cast over all, even the very children.*
>
> —William Wordsworth, *Memorials of a Tour on the Continent* (1822)

Housed in a building dating from 1518, **Brugs Diamanthuis** ✪, Cordoeaniersstraat 5 (© 050/34-41-60), off Vlamingstraat, has a sparkling array of diamonds. The com- pany has a second store at the **Bruges** Diamond Museum (see above), Katelijnestraat 43 (© 050/33-64-33).

MARKETS

The **Antiques and Flea Market** on the Dijver is a fine show in a scenic location beside the canal. It runs from March to October, Saturday and Sunday from noon to 5pm. There are **general markets** on the Markt, every Wednesday from 7am to 1pm, and in 't Zand and nearby Beursplein every Saturday from 7am to 1pm. The **fish market** on the colonnaded Vismarkt dating from 1821 may be less important—although you can buy ready-to-eat prawns and raw herring here—but it's still interesting to see. It takes place Tuesday to Saturday from 8am to 1pm.

7 Bruges After Dark

For information on what to do after dark, pick up the free monthly brochure *Exit* and the free monthly newsletter *events@brugge* from the tourist office, hotels, and per- formance venues. The monthly newspaper *Brugge Cultuurmagazine,* free and avail- able at these locations, is in Dutch, but its performance dates and venue details are fairly easy to follow.

THE PERFORMING ARTS

The new, ultramodern **Concertgebouw,** 't Zand (© 070/22-33-02; www. concertgebouw.be), which opened in 2002, nicely in time for Bruges's reign as Euro- pean Capital of Culture, is the main venue for opera, classical music, theater, and dance—and is the home base of the **Symfonieorkest van Vlaanderen** (© 050/ 84-05-87)—all of which take place regularly throughout the year. This has left the **Koninklijke Stadsschouwburg (Royal Municipal Theater),** Vlamingstraat 29

(℃ **050/44-30-60**), from 1869, the former principal venue for these events in Bruges, to back up the new mother-ship by mounting smaller-scale performances. Note that theater at both venues is likely to be in Dutch or French, and rarely if ever in English. Another important venue is the **Joseph Ryelandtzaal,** Achiel Van Ackerplein (℃ **050/44-86-86**). Smaller-scale events, such as recitals, are often held at the **Prinsenhof,** Prinsenhof 8 (℃ **050/34-50-93**), which used to be the palace of the dukes of Burgundy, and at **Sint-Salvatorskathedraal, Sint-Jakobskerk,** and other churches.

Theater pieces—mostly in Dutch—are performed at theater **Het Net,** Sint-Jakobsstraat 36 (℃ **050/33-88-50**), which has a puppet theater, **Marionettentheater Brugge,** for what is a sophisticated, centuries-old art.

A different kind of theater is on the menu at **Brugge Anno 1468 (Bruges Year 1468),** Celebrations Entertainment, Vlamingstraat 86 (℃ **050/34-75-72;** www. celebrations-entertainment.be). In the atmospheric setting of the neo-Gothic former Heilige-Hartkerk (Sacred Heart Church), from 1885, which belonged to the Jesuit Order, actors recreate the wedding of the duke of Burgundy, Charles the Bold, to Margaret of York, while visitors pile into a medieval banquet. Performances are April to October, Thursday to Saturday from 7:30 to 10:30pm; November to March, Saturday from 7:30 to 10:30pm. Tickets are 57€ to 74€ ($71–$93) for adults, 50% of the adult price for children ages 11 to 14, 13€ ($16) for children ages 6 to 10, and free for children under 6.

LIVE-MUSIC CLUBS

The **Cactus Club,** Sint-Jakobsstraat 33 (℃ **050/33-20-14**), presents an eclectic concert schedule Friday and Saturday nights. Try **De Vuurmolen,** Kraanplein 5 (℃ **050/33-00-79**), for a raucous dancing-on-the-tables kind of night; it's open nightly 10pm until the wee hours. **Ma Rica Rokk** ✯, 't Zand 7–8 (℃ **050/33-83-58**), is another bar with dancing; it attracts a young, techno-oriented crowd nightly 7pm to 4am (9pm–6am weekends). A good gay-friendly place is the bar/disco **Ravel,** Karel de Stoutelaan 172 (℃ **050/31-52-74**), open Wednesday and Friday through Monday from 10pm. **Vino Vino,** Grauwwerkersstraat 15 (℃ **050/34-51-15**), somehow manages to successfully combine Spanish tapas and the blues. For jazz, from bebop to modern, you can't do better than **De Versteende Nacht** ✯, Langestraat 11 (℃ **050/34-32-93**).

BARS

't **Brugs Beertje** ✯, Kemelstraat 5 (℃ **050/33-96-16**), is a traditional cafe that serves more than 300 different kinds of beer. 't **Dreupelhuisje,** Kemelstraat 9 (℃ **050/34-24-21**), does something similar with *jenever,* stocking dozens of artisanal examples of this spirit. **Gran Kaffee De Passage,** Dweersstraat 26 (℃ **050/34-02-32**), is a quiet and elegant cafe that serves inexpensive meals.

8 A Side Trip to Damme ✯

This village, just 7km (4½ miles) from Bruges, was once the city's outer harbor, where seagoing ships loaded and unloaded their cargoes, until the Zwin inlet silted up in 1520. The marriage of Charles the Bold and Margaret of York was celebrated here in 1468—which indicates the importance of Damme at the time. Today, visitors come to see the picturesque Markt (which holds a statue of native Jacob van Maerlant, the "father of Flemish poetry") and the beautiful canal-side scenery en route from Bruges. It's easy to make a day trip to Damme; plan to have lunch there.

THE ESSENTIALS

GETTING THERE   Getting to Damme is half the delight. One of the nicest ways is to take the small sternwheeler *Lamme Goedzaak.* Departures are from the Noorweegse Kaai in the north of Bruges, five times daily from April to September. The delightful half-hour trip along the poplar-lined canal takes you past a landscape straight out of an old Flemish painting. Round-trip tickets are 6.70€ ($8.40) for adults, 5.70€ ($7.15) for seniors, 4.70€ ($5.90) for children ages 3 to 11, and free for children under 3. For schedules and other details, contact **Rederij Damme–Brugge** (🕿 09/233-84-69).

You can take one of the minibuses of the **Sightseeing Line** (🕿 050/35-50-24; www.citytour.be). The 2-hour tours run from April to September, at 2pm and 4pm from the Markt, returning from Damme on the sternwheeler *Lamme Goedzaak.* Round-trip tickets are 17€ ($21) for adults, 8.25€ ($10) for children ages 6 to 11, and free for children under 6.

Public transportation buses depart six times daily in July and August, and three times daily from September to June, Monday to Saturday, from the rail station and the Markt in Bruges to Damme Town Hall.

You can drive, bike, or even walk from Bruges to Damme, along the scenic canal-side road Daamse Vaart Zuid from Dampoort in Bruges.

VISITOR INFORMATION   **Toerisme Damme,** Jacob van Maerlantstraat 3, 8340 Damme (🕿 **050/28-86-10;** fax 050/37-00-21; www.vvvdamme.be), faces the Stadhuis (Town Hall) on the Markt.

SEEING THE SIGHTS

The Gothic **Town Hall (Stadhuis)** on the Markt dates from 1464 to 1468. On its facade are statues of Charles the Bold and Margaret of York, among other historical notables. In front of it stands a statue of the poet Jacob van Maerlant (1230–96), who wrote his most important works in Damme.

Across from the Town Hall, at Jacob van Maerlantstraat 3, is the 15th-century mansion called **De Groote Sterre.** This was the Spanish governor's residence in the 17th century and is now occupied by the Damme Tourist Office, the **Uilenspiegel Museum,** and the **Van Hinsberg Forge and Foundry Museum.** Tijl Uilenspiegel is a 14th-century German folk-tale character (Till Ulenspiegel) who came to Damme by a roundabout route and has been adopted by the village. The museums are open from May to September, Monday to Friday from 9am to noon and 2 to 6pm, Saturday and Sunday from 10am to noon and 2 to 6pm; October to April, Monday to Friday from 9am to noon and 2 to 5pm, Saturday and Sunday from 2 to 5pm. At Jacob van Maerlantstraat 13 is a 15th-century mansion, the **Saint-Jean d'Angély House** ⊀, where in 1468 Charles the Bold married Margaret of York.

In Kerkstraat, which runs south from the Markt, are the Gothic **St. John's Hospital (Sint-Janshospitaal)** at no. 33, a hospital for the poor, endowed in 1249 by Countess Margaret of Constantinople; and the **Church of Our Lady (Onze-Lieve-Vrouwekerk),** dating from around 1340.

Across the bridge over the Bruges-Sluis Canal, at Dammesteenweg 1, is the 18th-century whitewashed **De Christoffelhoeve (St. Christopher's Farm).** Note the ornamental gate and the monumental barn with its mansard roof. A little way to the west along the Daamse Vaart is the **Schellemolen,** a windmill built in 1867.

Beside the jetty where the *Lamme Goedzaak* ties up is a modern **sculpture group** featuring the legend of Tijl Uilenspiegel.

7

Ghent & Antwerp

Although Ghent and Antwerp can't match Bruges for sheer medieval good looks, many Belgians believe them to be the true heartland of Flemish culture. Both cities have a grittier, more lived-in feel when compared with Bruges's museum-piece air, and neither would yield a millimeter in any argument over relative historical importance, artistic heritage, and contemporary vibrancy.

1 Ghent ✶✶

48km (30 miles) NW of Brussels; 46km (28 miles) SE of Bruges

Ghent is often considered a poor relation of Bruges, with historical monuments and townscapes that aren't as distinguished as those in its sister city. Many people might suggest that you visit Ghent only if you have time after visiting Bruges. There is some validity in this recommendation—but not much. Life moves faster in Ghent (Gent in Dutch; Gand in French), an important inland port and industrial center, and it compensates for its less precious appearance with a vigorous social and cultural scene.

This magnificent old city, the capital town of Oost-Vlaanderen (East Flanders) province, at the confluence of the Leie and Schelde rivers, has always been a pivotal point for Flanders. Ghent was a seat of the counts of Flanders, who built a castle here in the 12th century, but local fortifications predate their reign, back to the 900s.

After a history of economic ups and downs, Ghent (pop. 220,000) has reemerged as a major industrial center. Its medieval treasures are preserved, not as dry, showcase relics, but as living parts of the city. And there are flowers everywhere, oases of color that remind you this is the heart of a prosperous horticultural region.

ESSENTIALS

GETTING THERE   Ghent is a 32-minute train ride from Brussels. The main rail station, **Gent Sint-Pieters station** (✆ 09/222-44-44), on Koningin Maria-Hendrikaplein, 1.5km (1 mile) south of the center city, dates from 1912 and has a very decent station restaurant. To get quickly and easily to the center, take tram no. 1 from the nearest platform under the bridge to your left as you exit the station, and get out at Korenmarkt. Unless you need to count every euro, don't walk to the center; it's a dull route. Save your energy for sightseeing in the oldest part of town.

The **bus station** (✆ 09/210-94-91) adjoins Sint-Pieters rail station. By **car,** take A10/E40 from both Brussels and Bruges, and A14/E17 from Antwerp.

VISITOR INFORMATION   To get information by mail, fax, or e-mail, contact Ghent's tourist office, **Dienst Toerisme Gent,** Predikherenlei 2, 9000 Gent (✆ 09/266-56-60;** fax 09/266-56-73; www.gent.be).

Ghent

PATERSHOL
Burgstraat
Groentenmarkt
Korenlei
Grasler
Hoogpoort
Belfortstraat
Kraanlei Oudburg
Lieve
Leie
Steendam
Nieuwport
Nieuw-Brug-Kaai
Baudelokaai Nieuw-Brug-kaai
Ham
Dampoortstraat
Schoolkaai
Sint-Baafsplein
Volderstraat
Lieven
Bauwensplein
Burg
Lippensplein
Kouter
Ketelvest
Savaanstraat
Brabantdam
President
Wilsonplein
Graf van
Vlaanderenplein
Bagattenstraat
Jozef Plateaustraat
St.-Pietersnieuwstraat
Opperschelde
Keizer-Karelstraat
Slachthuisstraat
Lousbergskaai
Visserij
Lange Violettenstraat
Tweebruggenstraat
Brusselsepoortstraat
Nederschelde
Recollettenlei
Veldstraat
Iepenstraat
Lindenlei
Nederkouter
Leie
van
Duyseplein
Burgemeester Charles
de Kerchovelaan
To Gent
Sint-Pieters
Train Station
CITADEL
PARK
St.-Amandstraat
Overpoortstraat
Kunstlaan
Sint-
Pietersplein
Muinkaai
MUINKPARK
Bernardstraat
Ter Platen
Hofstraat
Pres. Fr. D. Rooseveltlaan
KONING
ALBERTPARK
Frère Orbanlaan
Zuidstationlaan

0   1/5 mi
0   0.2 km

ATTRACTIONS ●
Belfort en Lakenhalle **17**
Bijlokemuseum **20**
Design museum Gent **3**
Graslei **12**
Het Gravensteen **4**
Huis van Alijn **5**
Korenlei **11**
Museum voor Schone
   Kunsten **21**
Sint-Baafskathedraal **18**
Sint-Niklaaskerk **14**
Stadhuis **16**
Vrijdagmarkt **8**

ACCOMMODATIONS ■
Adoma **22**
Eden **19**
Erasmus **10**
Gravensteen **2**
Sofitel Gent Belfort **15**

DINING ◆
Amadeus **6**
Brasserie Pakhuis **13**
Jan Breydel **1**
Keizershof **9**
't Buikske Vol **7**

Ghent ✲ Brussels
BELGIUM
LUXEMBOURG

Church †
Post office ⊠
Information ⓘ
Canal cruises ⛴

> **⟨Moments⟩ Silent Running**
>
> Ghent has Belgium's only remaining electric trolley-bus service (line 3). It hums quietly through the center of town on an east-west route and is useful for getting to some places of interest—but you might want to step aboard as much for the novelty value of the ride as for any other reason.

For personal visits, go to the helpful and efficient **Toerisme Gent Infokantoor (Ghent Tourist Information Office)** in the Raadskelder (Council Cellar) of the **Belfort (Belfry),** Botermarkt 17A (⟨ **09/266-52-32**). The office is open April to October, daily from 9:30am to 6:30pm; and November to March, daily from 9:30am to 4:30pm (closed Jan 1 and Dec 25). In addition to providing information, they can make last-minute hotel reservations.

GETTING AROUND   Ghent has an excellent **tram** and **bus** network, and a single **trolley-bus** line, no. 3, which reentered service in 2005 after being down for some years for technical reasons. All are operated by **De Lijn** (⟨ **070/22-02-00;** www. delijn.be). Many lines converge at Korenmarkt and Sint-Pieters rail station. All four of the city's tram lines (1, 4, 21, 22) converge on the station, and all four eventually reach the center. Walking is the best way to view the center and experience its combination of history and modernity at a human pace. Farther out, you're better off using public transportation, particularly the trams (and the electric trolley bus; see Moments box "Silent Running," below). A single fare is 1.50€ ($1.90); a *lijnkaart* (line card), purchased before boarding the vehicle, costs less. A *dagkaart* (day card) costs 5€ ($6.25) for 1 day, 15€ ($19) for 5 days when purchased before boarding, and 6€ ($7.50) and 18€ ($23), respectively, onboard the vehicle.

For taxis, call **V-Tax** (⟨ **09/222-22-22**).

SPECIAL EVENTS   During 10 days around July 21, plunge into the swirl of Belgium's greatest extended street party, the **Gentse Feesten** (**Ghent Festivities;** ⟨ **092/ 269-46-00**), a time of free music, from classical through Tin Pan Alley to alternative rock and the latest disco sounds, along with dance, street theater and performance art, puppet shows, a street fair, special museum exhibits, and generally riotous fun and games in the heart of town.

CITY LAYOUT

Korenmarkt lies at the center *(Centrum)* of the city. Most of the city's important sights—including the Town Hall, Saint Bavo's Cathedral, and the Belfry—lie within 1km (⅓ mile) of Korenmarkt. The **Leie River** winds through the center to connect with the Schelde River and a network of canals that lead to the busy port area. **Citadel Park,** location of the Fine Arts Museum, is near Sint-Pieters station. **Patershol** (the word for the cave—or hole—in which monks lived a hermit's existence), an ancient enclave not far from the Castle of the Counts, is now something of a gastronomic center sprinkled with restaurants in renovated old buildings.

SEEING THE SIGHTS

This is a city best seen by walking its streets, gazing at its gabled guild houses and private mansions, and stopping on one of its bridges to look down at the canal below. Ghent's historical monuments have not all been prettified. Some of them look downright gray and forbidding, which, oddly enough, gives them a more authentic feel. The Castle of the Counts of Flanders was *meant* to look gray and forbidding, since the citizens of Ghent were so often in revolt against its overlord.

THE TOP ATTRACTIONS

The "Three Towers of Ghent" that have become a signature image of the city are **St. Bavo's Cathedral, the Belfry,** and **St. Nicholas's Church.** They form a virtually straight line pointing toward St. Michael's Bridge.

Belfort en Lakenhalle (Belfry and Cloth Hall) 🕐🕐   Across the square from the cathedral, the Cloth Hall and Belfry tower above it form a glorious medieval ensemble. The Cloth Hall dates from 1425 and was the gathering place of wool and cloth merchants. The Belfry holds the great bells that have rung out Ghent's civic pride through the centuries, the most beloved being a 1315 giant bell known as Roeland, destroyed by Charles V in 1540 as punishment for Ghent's insubordination. No fewer than 28 of the 54 bells that now make up the huge carillon are from Roeland's remains. The massive Triomphante, cast in 1660 to replace the favorite, now rests in a small park at the foot of the Belfry, still bearing the crack it sustained in 1914.

A baroque extension from 1741 on Goudenleeuwplein was used until 1902 as a prison, dubbed *De Mammelokker* (The Suckler). The name comes from a relief above the doorway that depicts the

> **Impressions**
>
> *The Ley and the Scheld meeting in this vast Citty divide it into 26 Ilands which are united togethere by many bridges somewhat resembling Venice.*
>
> —English diarist John Evelyn (1641)

Roman legend of Cimon, starving to death in prison, being suckled by his daughter Pero. Appropriately, this newer section is now the office for the city's *Ombudsvrouw* (Ombudswoman).

Take the elevator to the Belfry's upper gallery, 66m (215 ft.) high, to see the bells and take in fantastic panoramic views of the city. A great iron chest was kept in the Belfry's *Secreet* to hold the all-important charters that spelled out privileges the guilds and the burghers of medieval Ghent wrested from the counts of Flanders.

Emile Braunplein. 📞 09/223-99-22. Admission 3€ ($3.75) adults, 2.50€ ($3.15) seniors and students, free for children under 13. Mid-Mar to mid-Nov daily 10am–12:30pm and 2–6pm; free guided tours of Belfry Easter vacations and May–Sept Tues–Sun 2:10, 3:10, and 4:10pm. Tram: 1 or 4 to Sint-Baafsplein.

Het Gravensteen (Castle of the Counts)   "Grim" is the word that springs to mind when you first see this fortress crouching like a gray stone lion. The Gravensteen was clearly designed by the counts of Flanders to send a "don't-even-think-about-it" message to rebellion-inclined Gentenaars. It's safe to say the castle's appearance helped instill the awe and fear needed to keep the populace in line. It was built by Count Philip of Alsace, count of Flanders, soon after he returned from the Crusades in 1180 with images of similar crusader castles in the Holy Land. If its walls (2m/6 ft. thick), battlements, and turrets failed to intimidate attackers, the count could always turn to a well-equipped torture chamber inside. You can view relics of the chamber—a small guillotine, spiked iron collars, branding irons, thumb screws, and a special kind of pitchfork designed to ensure that people being burned at the stake stayed in the flames—in a small museum in the castle. Climb up to the ramparts of the high central building, the donjon, which has great views of Ghent's rooftops and towers.

Value **Your Passport to Ghent**

One of the best discounts in town is the **Gent museumpas,** available from Toerisme Gent's Infokantoor at the Belfry (see "Visitor Information," above) for 13€ ($16). The pass affords admission for no additional cost to 15 museums and monuments.

Sint-Veerleplein. ✆ 09/225-93-06. www.gent.be/gravensteen. Admission 6€ ($7.50) adults, 1.20€ ($1.50) seniors and ages 13–25, free for children under 13. Apr–Sept daily 9am–6pm; Oct–Mar daily 9am–5pm. Closed Jan 1, Dec 24–25 and 31. Tram: 1 or 4 to Sint-Veerleplein.

Sint-Baafskathedraal (St. Bavo's Cathedral) ✿✿✿   Even if you see nothing else in Ghent, you shouldn't miss this massive cathedral. Don't be put off by its rather unimpressive exterior, an uncertain mixture of Romanesque, Gothic, and baroque architecture. The interior is filled with priceless paintings, sculptures, memorials, and carved tombs. St. Bavo's showpiece is the 24-panel altarpiece *The Adoration of the Mystic Lamb,* completed by Jan van Eyck in 1432. Van Eyck's luminous use of oils and naturalistic portrayal of nature and people represented a giant step away from the rigid style of Gothic religious art. But besides its importance in the history of art, the *Mystic Lamb* is simply spellbinding. The work was commissioned by a wealthy city alderman in 1420. Other art treasures in the cathedral include Rubens's restored *The Conversion of St. Bavo* (1623) in the Rubens Chapel on the semicircular ambulatory behind the high altar. About midway along the vaulted nave is a remarkable pulpit in white marble entwined with oak, reminiscent of Bernini.

Sint-Baafsplein. ✆ 09/269-20-45. Cathedral: Free admission. Apr–Oct Mon–Sat 8:30am–6pm, Sun 1–6pm; Nov–Mar Mon–Sat 8:30am–5pm, Sun 1–5pm. *Mystic Lamb* chapel and crypt: 3€ ($3.75) adults (includes audio guide in English), 1.50€ ($1.90) children 6–12, free for children under 6. Apr–Oct Mon–Sat 9:30am–5pm, Sun 1–5pm; Nov–Mar Mon–Sat 10:30am–4pm, Sun 1–4pm. Tram: 1 or 4 to Sint-Baafsplein.

MORE MUSEUMS & ATTRACTIONS

Bijlokemuseum   Weapons, uniforms, musical instruments, coins, clothing, glass objects, tapestries, and household items from daily life long ago are on view in a 14th-century former Cistercian convent (14th–17th c.), the Bijlokeabdij (Bijloke Abbey). Art from Ghent and Flanders is exhibited inside the House of the Abbess.

Godshuizenlaan 2 (south of the Coupure canal). ✆ 09/225-11-06. Admission 2.50€ ($3.15) adults, free for children under 12. Thurs 10am–1pm and 2–6pm; Sun 2–6pm. Closed Jan 1–2, Dec 25–26.

Design museum Gent ✿   Something of a split personality, this worthwhile museum is housed in the Hotel de Coninck (1755), an elegant baroque mansion with an ultra-modern extension at the rear. In the same spirit, its collection ranges through a series of period rooms furnished and decorated in 18th- and 19th-century style in the old place, and modern design in the new. Tapestries and a collection of Chinese porcelain are among the stellar items. Some of these belonged to France's King Louis XVIII, who passed a period of exile in Ghent in 1815 during Napoleon's brief return to power. The new wing is strong on Art Nouveau—from Belgian Masters of the genre such as Victor Horta, Henry van de Velde, and Paul Hankar, among others—and Art Deco design. You can see most everything here in about an hour.

Jan Breydelstraat 5 (off Korenlei). ✆ 09/267-99-99. http://design.museum.gent.be. Admission 2.50€ ($3.15) adults, 1.20€ ($1.50) students, free for children under 12. Tues–Sun 10am–6pm. Closed Jan 1, Dec 25–26 and 31.

Huis van Alijn (Alijn House) ☆ Ghent's fascinating folklore museum is in a *god-shuis* (almshouse) founded in the 1300s and rebuilt in the 1500s, which functioned as a children's home and hospital. Set around a grassy courtyard, it creates an oasis of tranquillity. Inside the cluster of folksily restored cottages are replicas of typical rooms in homes at the turn of the 20th century, and workshops where crafts and skills such as weaving, metalwork, and carpentry were practiced. You can visit the almshouse's late Gothic **Sint-Catharinakapel (St. Catherine's Chapel),** dating from 1540. A marionette theater troupe, **Poppenkast 't Spelleke van de Folklore** (✆ **09/269-23-67**), presents performances for children (in Dutch) on specified days of the week; call for current schedules. While the kids are being thus entertained, the adults can kick back over drinks at the museum's own traditional tavern, **'t Cafeetse.**

Kraanlei 65 (across the Leie River from Vrijdagmarkt). ✆ **09/269-23-50.** www.huisvanalijn.be. Admission: museum 3€ ($3.75) adults, 1.75€ ($2.20) seniors/students/children 6–18, free for children under 6; free for individual visitors Sun 10am–1pm; marionette theater 3€ ($3.75). Museum Tues–Sun 11am–5pm; marionette theater performances Sept–June Wed and Sat 2:30pm. Closed Jan 1, Dec 25. Tram: 1 or 4 to Sint-Veerleplein.

Museum voor Schone Kunsten (Fine Arts Museum) ☆☆ Ancient and modern art masterpieces are housed here. Highlights include works by Peter Paul Rubens, Anthony van Dyck, Hieronymus Bosch, and Théodore Géricault, along with such moderns as James Ensor, Theo van Rysselberghe, George Minne, and Constant Permeke. *Note:* The museum is closed for renovations until 2007; during the period of closure, exhibits from the collection will be mounted at nearby Leopold Barracks, Charles de Kerchovelaan 187A (✆ **09/240-07-00**), and other museums in Ghent.

Citadelpark (near the rail station). ✆ **09/222-17-03.** www.mskgent.be. Admission 2.50€ ($3.15) adults, 1.20€ ($1.50) seniors and those 12–25, free for children under 12; free admission Sun 10am–1pm. Tues–Sun 10am–6pm. Closed Jan 1–2, Dec 25–26. Tram: 1 to Kortrijksesteenweg.

Sint-Niklaaskerk (St Nicholas's Church) ☆ A mixture of surviving Romanesque elements and the Flemish architectural style known as Schelde Gothic, the impressive 13th- to 15th-century church was paid for by Ghent's wealthy medieval merchants and guilds. In recent years, it has undergone extensive renovation work that's still ongoing. The tower is one of the "three towers of Ghent"—in fact, it was the first of the three to grace the city skyline. A baroque high altar and other rich decorations embellish the interior; all of these date from after the Protestant *Beeldenstorm* (Iconoclastic Fury) of 1566, during which Catholic churches across the Low Countries were wrecked.

Korenmarkt (entrance on Cataloniëstraat). ✆ **09/225-37-00.** Free admission. Mon 2:30–5pm; Tues–Sun 10am–5pm. Tram: 1 or 4 to Korenmarkt.

MORE ATTRACTIONS

Ghent's large **Stadhuis (Town Hall)** ☆, Botermarkt/Hoogpoort (✆ **09/223-99-22**), turns a rather plain Renaissance profile to Botermarkt, and an almost garishly ornamented Gothic face to Hoogpoort. Its schizophrenic appearance probably came about because its construction, begun in 1518, was interrupted by Emperor Charles V, began again at the end of the century, was halted once more in the early 1600s, and wasn't completed until the 18th century. The changing public tastes and available moneys of those years are reflected in the building's styles. In its Pacificatiezaal (Pacification Room), the Pacification of Ghent was signed in 1567. This document declared to the world the repudiation by the Low Countries provinces of Spanish Habsburg rule and their intention to permit freedom of religion within their boundaries. The Town Hall can be visited on guided tours (May–Oct Mon–Thurs 3pm) that depart from the tourist office in the Belfry cellar.

Graslei 🌟🌟, a beautiful canal-side street, is home to a solid row of towering, gabled guild houses built between the 1200s and 1600s, when the neighboring waterway formed the city's harbor. To fully appreciate their majesty, walk across the bridge over the Leie to **Korenlei** on the opposite bank and view them as a whole; then return to stroll past each, and imagine the craftsmen, tradesmen, and merchants for whom these buildings were the very core of commercial and civil existence.

The building at no. 1 was the House of the Free Boatmen from the 1500s; no. 2, the Annex House of the Grain Measurers from the 1600s; no. 3, the House of the Receiver of the Staple (Customs) from the 1600s; no. 4, the Staple Warehouse from the 1200s; no. 5, the Main House of the Grain Measurers from the 1500s; no. 6, the House of the Free Masons from the 1500s; and no. 7, the House of the Boatmen. The dramas that unfolded within the walls of each are enough to fill a library of books based on Ghent's independence of spirit. This is an ideal spot for leisurely exploration and for snapping a picture that captures the essence of Ghent.

VRIJDAGMARKT 🌟🌟

Ghent's main square—huge, tree-shaded, ever bustling—is surrounded by old guild houses and mansions, most of which these days host restaurants and cafes that sprout sidewalk terraces when the sun shines. In addition, Vrijdagmarkt (Friday Market Sq., a fixture since the 13th c.) is the scene of lively street markets on Friday (7:30am–1pm) and on Saturday (11am–6pm), as well as the Sunday bird market (7am–1pm).

Throughout the city's long history, when trouble erupted in Ghent, as it so often did, Vrijdagmarkt was nearly always the rallying point, and up to 1863 it was a venue for public executions. There were jousting tournaments, parades, and other happy events. When the future Habsburg Emperor Charles V was born in Ghent during the bitterly cold winter of 1500, the square was flooded so that the populace could skate on the ice.

The bronze statue of **Jacob van Artevelde** (1863) is a tribute to a 14th-century rebel leader. Its base is adorned with the shields of 52 medieval guilds and four female figures representing the maids of Flanders, Ghent, Bruges, and Ypres (Ieper). Van Artevelde was assassinated amid scenes of factional violence that on "Evil Monday" in 1345 saw the Vrijdagmarkt heaped with corpses.

As you go around the square, you can't easily miss a curiously shaped, step-gabled building on its east side (nos. 33–36), incorporating a round tower. This is the 15th-century **Gildenhuis van de Huidevetters (Tanners' Guild House),** and the guild's talisman—a mermaid—forms the weathervane on top. A poetry society now occupies the building. The round tower, dubbed the **Toreken (Little Tower),** was once used by the city's cloth commission. They ordered that any bolt of cloth that didn't pass muster should be hung from a metal ring on the outside of the tower for all to see. What was once the commission's own premises, the **Lakenmetershuis (Cloth Measurers' House;** 1770), stands on the square's north side at no. 25.

On the west side is the remarkable **Ons Huis (Our House).** This approximately Art Nouveau confection, dating from 1902, was headquarters of the Ghent Socialist Workers Society *Vooruit* (Forward). Still spelled out (in Dutch) in large gold letters on the facade is Karl Marx's famous call to proletarian solidarity: WERKLIEDEN ALLER LANDEN VEREENIGT U (WORKERS OF THE WORLD UNITE). Ons Huis is now offices of a local welfare organization.

Among the most notable of Vrijdagmarkt's multifarious eateries and drinkeries are the restaurant **Keizershof** at no. 47 (see "Where to Dine," below) and, a few doors along, the cafe **Dulle Griet** at no. 50 (see "Ghent After Dark," below).

Off the west end of Vrijdagmarkt, a smaller square, **Groot Kanonplein,** is named after the large red cannon, *Dulle Griet* (Mad Meg), emplaced there. Measuring more than 5m (16 ft.) and weighing 16,400 kilograms (16 tons), it served in the 1400s during military operations of the Burgundian dukes, but cracked a century later while defending Protestant Ghent against a besieging Spanish Catholic army.

PATERSHOL ⍟

Few traditional sights clutter the small yet beguiling **Patershol** neighborhood that lies just west of the center, along the west bank of the Leie and north of the Lieve. But the area is charming and provides an authentic taste of Old Ghent; about 100 of its buildings are protected monuments.

The district's name comes from the monks of the Caermersklooster (Carmelite Monastery), founded in the 13th century and expanded over the centuries, that still stands (more or less), on Vrouwebroersstraat. The 16th- to 17th-century monastery church now houses the **Provinciaal Centrum voor Kunst en Cultuur (Provincial Art and Cultural Center).** Don't let that provincial tag put you off—it just means that the facility belongs to East Flanders province and is not necessarily a comment on the quality of the exhibits. The center is open Tuesday to Saturday from 10am to 5pm when an exhibit is taking place; admission is free.

Patershol's nest of narrow, pedestrianized streets and tightly packed small brick houses replaced the medieval tanners' quarter and was built in the 17th century for the city's weavers, craftsmen, and tradesmen. This modest nature remains even though renewal and gentrification was carried out in the 1980s.

A new generation of entrepreneurs has revitalized the old neighborhood (which had degenerated into a slum and red-light district), turning some of the little houses into trendy restaurants, bustling cafes, and offbeat stores. The number of these is regulated, so as not to destroy Patershol's residential character. Still, its "indigenous" residents are alive and well and show no sign of succumbing to the gentrification going on around them. In its long history, the Patershol has seen plenty of trends and fashions come and go, and it will still be there whether the trendy restaurants and boutiques prosper or not.

SIGHTSEEING TOURS

The tourist office can arrange qualified guides for private **walking tours** at a charge of 50€ ($63) for the first 2 hours (Mon–Fri) and 25€ ($31) for each additional hour. Ask them about organized group-walking tours sometimes conducted during summer months at a fee of 6€ ($7.50) for adults and free for children under 12 (admission to see *The Adoration of the Mystic Lamb* included).

A **cruise** ⍟ on the canals with **Rederij Dewaele** (ⓒ **09/223-88-53;** www.deboot jesvangent.be) is a good way to view the city's highlights. Tour boats sail from Graslei and Korenlei April to October, daily from 10am to 6pm, and November to March on weekends from 11am to 4pm. Cruises begin at 5€ ($6) for adults; 4.50€ ($6) for seniors, students, and those under 26; 2.50€ ($3.15) for children ages 3 to 12; and free for children under 3, for 40 minutes; longer tours are available.

From Easter to October, **horse-drawn carriages** (ⓒ **09/227-62-46**) depart from Sint-Baafsplein and Korenlei from 10am to 6pm for half-hour rides that cost 25€ ($31).

WHERE TO STAY
EXPENSIVE
Gravensteen ★★   The entrance to this lovely mansion—built in 1865 as the home of a Ghent textile baron—is through an old carriageway (made up of ornamented pillars and an impressive wall niche occupied by a marble statue), which sets the tone for what's inside. The elegant, high-ceilinged parlor is a sophisticated blend of pastels, gracious modern furnishings, and antiques, with a small bar tucked into one corner. The rooms are attractive and comfortably furnished. Those in front look out on the moated Gravensteen castle (see earlier), while those to the back have city views. There's a top-floor lookout, with windows offering magnificent views of the city. Afternoon tea is available. There's no dining room, but plenty of good restaurants are within easy walking distance. Some rooms have air-conditioning.

Jan Breydelstraat 35 (close to the Castle of the Counts), 9000 Gent. ✆ 09/225-11-50. Fax 09/225-18-50. www.gravensteen.be. 45 units. 115€–208€ ($144–$260) double. AE, DC, MC, V. Parking 8€ ($10). **Amenities:** Bar; laundry service. *In room:* A/C in some units, TV, minibar, hair dryer.

Sofitel Gent Belfort ★   If you like to experience historical towns while sleeping in modern and comfortable accommodations, the Sofitel might be the place for you. The chain's often bland style is mitigated here—it was designed to at least partly fit into its venerable surroundings, and it sits atop medieval cellars and foundations. Plus, it's set on an ideal location just across the road from Town Hall, within easy distance of the city's premier tourist attractions. Belgian specialties and international dishes are served in the Van Artevelde Brasserie, and outside on the patio in good weather; drinks are served in the cellar bar. At the end of 2004, a cluster of 45 new rooms opened.

Hoogpoort 63, 9000 Gent. ✆ 09/233-33-31. Fax 09/233-11-02. www.sofitel.com. 172 units. 245€–320€ ($306–$400) double; 415€ ($519) suite. AE, DC, MC, V. Parking 13€ ($16). **Amenities:** Restaurant (Belgian/international); bar; health club; concierge; 24-hr. room service; babysitting; laundry service; same-day dry cleaning; nonsmoking rooms; executive rooms. *In room:* A/C, TV, dataport, coffeemaker, minibar, hair dryer.

MODERATE TO INEXPENSIVE
Adoma   The facilities and atmosphere at this renovated hotel have taken a big leap forward, yet the rates remain reasonable. Rooms are spacious and brightly decorated, with modern furnishings. You'll find it to be a comfortable, if not luxurious, experience.

Sint-Denijslaan 19 (behind Sint-Pieters rail station), 9000 Gent. ✆ 09/222-65-50. Fax 09/245-09-37. www.hotel-adoma.be. 15 units. 60€–100€ ($75–$125) double. Rates include continental breakfast. MC, V. Free parking. *In room:* TV.

Eden ★ *(Value)*   The entrance to this personable small hotel is under an archway, and you climb a flight of stairs to reach the reception, where an elevator awaits you. Each of the decent-size guest rooms has a wall tapestry, adding an old-fashioned Flemish touch to rooms that otherwise have mostly functional furnishings, such as faux-leather armchairs. The rooms I most recently saw were painted in pastel tones and have new carpets and bedspreads. A toilet, sink, and shower are crammed into the smallest bathrooms; larger ones have a bathtub. The hotel stands on a busy street with easy access to the center of town and is close to shops, bars, and restaurants—and to Ghent's small red-light district, though you likely won't even be aware of this if you stick to the main drag. Rooms at the back are quieter.

Zuidstationstraat 24, 9000 Gent. ✆ 09/223-51-51. Fax 09/233-34-57. 28 units. 70€–95€ ($88–$119) double. Rates include buffet breakfast. MC, V. Free parking. *In room:* TV.

Erasmus ✹✹   Each room is different in this converted pair of 17th-century Flemish mansions, and all are plush, furnished with antiques and knickknacks. Rooms have high oak-beam ceilings, and bathrooms are modern. Some rooms have leaded-glass windows, some overlook a carefully manicured inner garden, and some have elaborate marble fireplaces. You can, if you so choose, hide yourself away in the attic den. Breakfast is served in an impressive room that would have pleased the counts of Flanders, as well as in the garden—weather permitting.

Poel 25 (off Sint-Michielsstraat), 9000 Gent. ✆ **09/224-21-95**. Fax 09/233-42-41. www.hotelerasmus.be. 11 units. 99€–130€ ($124–$163) double. Rates include buffet breakfast. AE, MC, V. Limited street parking. **Amenities:** Bar. *In room:* TV, coffeemaker, hair dryer.

WHERE TO DINE
EXPENSIVE
Jan Breydel ✹✹ SEAFOOD/FRENCH   High honors go to this exquisite restaurant on a quaint street near the Castle of the Counts. Its interior is a garden delight of greenery, white napery, and light woods. Proprietors Louis and Pat Hellebaut see to it that dishes issued from their kitchen are as light as the setting, with delicate sauces and seasonings enhancing fresh ingredients. Seafood and regional specialties like the traditional Ghent souplike fish stew *waterzooï* are all superb. In summertime you can dine on an outdoors terrace beside the confluence of the Leie River and the Lieve canal, and next to a pretty little garden called Appelbrug Parkje.

Jan Breydelstraat 10 (opposite Design museum Gent). ✆ **09/225-62-87**. www.janbreydel.com. Main courses 18€–32€ ($23–$40); fixed-price menus 31€–48€ ($39–$60). AE, DC, MC, V. Tues–Sat noon–2pm and 7–10pm; Mon 7–10pm.

MODERATE
Brasserie Pakhuis ✹✹ FLEMISH/CONTINENTAL   In a vast, beautifully restored 19th-century warehouse down a narrow lane, this see-and-be-seen hangout is replete with painted cast-iron pillars, green pipes and tubing, ceiling fans, track lighting, soaring wrought-iron balconies, oak and marble tables with specially designed table settings, and a granite mosaic floor. Although a bit too conscious of its own sense of style, Pakhuis (which means "warehouse" in Dutch) is stocked in matters of taste. The oyster and seafood platters are notable, and you won't go wrong with meat-based offerings like baked ham in a mustard sauce or Flemish favorites like *waterzooï* (chicken stew) and *garnaalkroketten* (shrimp croquettes). Outside of lunch and dinner times, you can join the local smart-set for afternoon tea or for a late-night drink at the curving oak-and-riveted-copper bar.

Schuurkenstraat 4 (off Veldstraat). ✆ **09/223-55-55**. www.pakhuis.be. Main courses 11€–20€ ($14–$25); fixed-price menus 23€–28€ ($29–$35). AE, DC, MC, V. Mon–Thurs 11:30am–1am; Fri–Sat 11:30am–2am (full meals at lunch and dinner only).

Keizershof ✹✹ BELGIAN/CONTINENTAL   Despite being modern in tone and, to an extent, in cuisine by offering plenty of salads and other light fare, Keizershof is too smart to let you miss out on traditional Belgian standbys like *Gentse stoverij* (Ghent stew) and *mosselen* (mussels). Convivial and trendy, this retiring yet far-from-shy place on the garish market square has an attractively informal ambience and a positive price/quality ratio. Behind its narrow, 17th-century baroque facade, even a capacity crowd of 150 diners can seem sparsely dispersed at the plain wood tables on multiple floors around a central stairwell. The decor beneath the timber ceiling beams is spare, tastefully tattered, and speckled with paintings by local artists. Service for office workers doing lunch is fast but not furious; in the evenings you're expected to linger. In summertime, you can dine alfresco in a courtyard at the back.

Vrijdagmarkt 47. 🕐 **09/223-44-46.** www.keizershof.net. Main courses 9€–17€ ($11–$21); fixed-price menus 14€–20€ ($18–$25). AE, MC, V. Tues–Sat noon–2:30pm and 6–11pm.

't Buikske Vol 🞰🞰 BELGIAN/FRENCH   Thanks to chef Peter Vyncke's insistence on the best ingredients, served in a cozy, intimate atmosphere, 't Buikske Vol is one of the city's gems. It isn't open much, but when it is, it's busy.

Kraanlei 17. 🕐 **09/225-18-80.** www.buikskevol.com. Reservations recommended on weekends. Main courses 14€–25€ ($18–$31); fixed-price menus 27€–42€ ($34–$52). AE, MC, V. Mon–Tues and Thurs–Fri noon–2pm and 7–10pm; Sat 7–10pm.

INEXPENSIVE

Amadeus 🞰 RIBS/CONTINENTAL   Sure, there are vegetarian and fish plates, but all of Ghent comes here for the all-you-can-eat spareribs dinner: a slab of cooked ribs with a choice of sauces and a baked potato. If you're up to it, you can order another and another and another. A bottle of wine is on the table, and you pay for what you drink from it. The decor is a sumptuous mix of Old Flemish and Art Nouveau with burnished wood, mirrors, and colored glass, and the ambience is relaxed.

Plotersgracht 8. 🕐 **09/225-13-85.** Spareribs dinner 18€ ($23). MC, V. Daily 6pm–midnight.

GHENT AFTER DARK
THE PERFORMING ARTS

From October to mid-June, international opera is performed in the 19th-century **De Vlaamse Opera,** Schouwburgstraat 3 (🕐 **09/225-24-25;** www.vlaamseopera.be). Ghent venues for those marvelous Belgian puppet shows are the folklore museum **Het Huis van Alijn,** Kraanlei 65 (🕐 **09/269-23-50**), and **Teater Taptoe,** Forelstraat 91C (🕐 **09/223-67-58**).

BARS & TAVERNS

In typical Flemish fashion, Ghent's favorite after-dark entertainment is frequenting atmospheric cafes and taverns. You should have a memorable evening in any one you choose. **De Witte Leeuw,** Graslei 6 (🕐 **09/233-37-33**), has a 17th-century setting and more than 300 varieties of beer. At the Old Flemish tavern **Dulle Griet,** Vrijdagmarkt 50 (🕐 **09/224-24-55**), also known as **Bieracademie,** you'll be asked to deposit one of your shoes before being given a potent Kwak beer in the too-collectible glass with a wood frame that allows the glass to stand up—you, too, might need artificial support if you drink too many of this or any of the other 250 different beers in stock. The smallest building on Graslei, the former Toll House, is now a nice little tavern called **Het Tolhuisje,** Graslei 10 (🕐 **09/224-30-90**).

Groentenmarkt, near the Gravensteen, makes for a good pub crawl in an easily navigable area. In an old canal house, **Het Waterhuis aan de Bierkant,** Groentenmarkt 9 (🕐 **09/225-06-80**), has more than 100 different Belgian beers, including locally made Stopken. Of all the gin joints in town, **'t Dreupelkot,** Groentenmarkt 12 (🕐 **09/224-21-20**), has to be the best. Ask owner Paul to recommend one of his 100 or so varieties of *jenever* (a stiff spirit similar to gin), served in tiny (but deadly) glassfuls. Or walk straight in and boldly go for a 64-proof Jonge Hertekamp or a 72-proof Pekèt de Houyeu. If they don't knock you down, you may be up for an 8-year-old 100-proof Filliers Oude Graanjenever or a 104-proof Hoogspanning. Across the tramlines,

Het Galgenhuisje, Groentenmarkt 5 (© 09/233-42-51), the oldest drinking spot in town, is an intimate place popular with students.

2 Antwerp ✮✮

48km (30 miles) N of Brussels; 51km (31 miles) NE of Ghent

Antwerp is one of western Europe's most hidden gems. Its reputation as a port and diamond trade center is well deserved, but that's not all there is to say about this easy-going and stylish city. Considering that Antwerp (pop. 470,000) boasts monuments from the wealthy medieval and Renaissance periods, a magnificent cathedral, a fine-arts museum full of Old Flemish masterpieces, a maze of medieval streets in the center city, and a vibrant nightlife and cultural scene, it's amazing that more tourists don't visit.

Home to the world's fifth-largest port, Antwerp (Antwerpen in Dutch; Anvers in French) is lively, sophisticated, and occasionally seedy. As the "Diamond Center of the World," it's the leading market for cut diamonds and second only to London as an outlet for raw and industrial diamonds. The diamond business is worth a sparkling $12.5 billion a year to the city, which swamps Amsterdam's $1 billion—though you would never guess as much from the way the Dutch capital flaunts its jewels and the discreet character maintained by the Belgians.

ESSENTIALS

GETTING THERE   By Plane   Brussels National Airport is the main international airport for Antwerp (see "Orientation," in chapter 5). A few scheduled international flights arrive at **Antwerp International Airport** (© 03/285-65-00; www.antwerp airport.be) at Deurne, 7km (4½ miles) east of the city. De Lijn bus no. 16 shuttles between the airport and Antwerp Centraal Station. Taxi fare to downtown is around 12€ ($15).

By Train   Antwerp's two stations are **Centraal Station,** 1.5km (1 mile) east of the Grote Markt, on the edge of the center city, and **Berchem,** 4km (2½ miles) south of the center city. Antwerp is on the **Thalys** high-speed train network that connects Paris, Cologne, Brussels, and Amsterdam; most Thalys trains stop at Berchem, but a few go to Centraal Station. For schedule and fare information, and for all train reservations, call © 02/528-28-28.

> **Impressions**
>
> *This goodly ancient City methinks looks like a disconsolate Widow, or rather some super-annuated Virgin that hath lost her Lover . . .*
>
> —English author
> James Howell (1619)

By Bus   Eurolines international buses arrive and depart from a **bus stop** at Van Stralenstraat 8, a short distance northwest of Centraal Station.

By Car   Major roads connecting to Antwerp's R1 Ring Expressway (beltway) are A1/E19 from Brussels via Mechelen and from Amsterdam; A12 from Brussels via Laeken; A14/E17 from Ghent; and N49 from Knokke, Bruges, and Zeebrugge.

VISITOR INFORMATION   Toerisme Antwerpen, Grote Markt 13, 2000 Antwerpen (© 03/232-01-03; fax 03/231-19-37; www.visitantwerpen.be; tram: 2, 3, 4, 8, or 15). The office is open Monday to Saturday from 9am to 5:45pm, Sunday and holidays from 9am to 4:45pm (closed Jan 1 and Dec 25). An **Info Desk** at Centraal Station is open the same hours as the main tourist office.

Antwerp

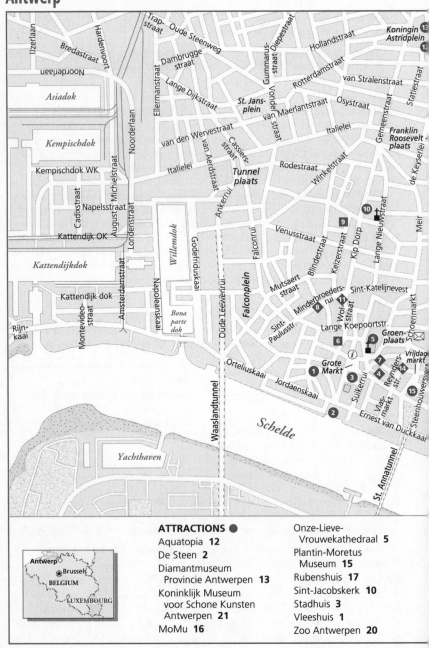

ATTRACTIONS ●

Aquatopia **12**

De Steen **2**

Diamantmuseum
Provincie Antwerpen **13**

Koninklijk Museum
voor Schone Kunsten
Antwerpen **21**

MoMu **16**

Onze-Lieve-
Vrouwekathedraal **5**

Plantin-Moretus
Museum **15**

Rubenshuis **17**

Sint-Jacobskerk **10**

Stadhuis **3**

Vleeshuis **1**

Zoo Antwerpen **20**

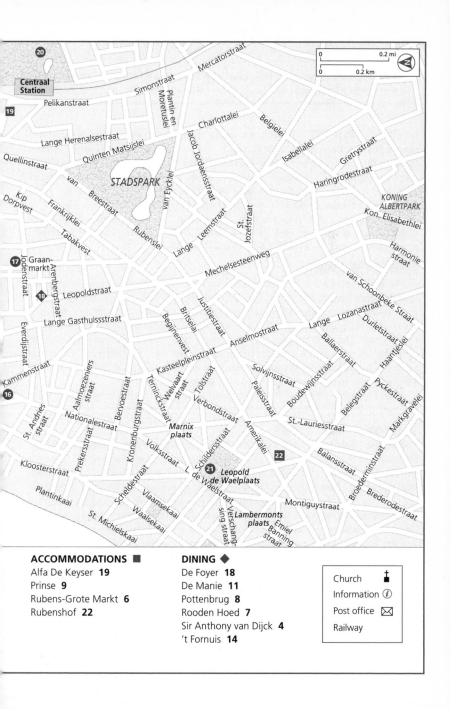

ACCOMMODATIONS ■
Alfa De Keyser **19**
Prinse **9**
Rubens-Grote Markt **6**
Rubenshof **22**

DINING ◆
De Foyer **18**
De Manie **11**
Pottenbrug **8**
Rooden Hoed **7**
Sir Anthony van Dijck **4**
't Fornuis **14**

Church ♁
Information ⓘ
Post office ✉
Railway

Tips **Mean Streets**

The area around Centraal Station, east of De Keyserlei and Koningin Astridplein, is more than a little seedy and has problems with drug-dealing and prostitution.

GETTING AROUND Antwerp is a good city for pedestrians, its major attractions easily reached from one major street, which changes its name as it goes along. Besides walking, the tram is the best way to get around the city; a single fare is 1.50€ ($1.90); a *lijnkaart* (line card), purchased before boarding the vehicle, costs less; a *dagkaart* (day card) is 6€ ($7.50) for 1 day and 18€ ($23) for 5 days. The most useful trams for tourists are lines 2 and 15 that run between Groenplaats, near the cathedral, to Centraal Station. Public transportation information is available from a kiosk inside Centraal Station and from **De Lijn** (✆ 070/22-02-00; www.delijn.be). The numbers to call for a taxi are ✆ **03/646-83-83** and **03/238-38-38**.

SEEING THE SIGHTS

Antwerp is a good place to walk around. Its major sightseeing attractions are easily reached from one major street that changes its name as it goes along: Italiëlei, Frankrijklei, Britselei, and Amerikalei. Most sights are within easy walking distance of the center, but if the cobblestone streets start to bother your feet, you can always hop onto a tram. The most colorful part of Antwerp is the medieval center that fans out from the Grote Markt in a warren of winding streets. South of there, on the streets around Vlaamsekaai and Waalsekaai, is a fascinating district of shipping warehouses renovated into trendy bars, restaurants, and art galleries.

Note: For many of the museums and churches in Antwerp (including some of those reviewed below), go to **http://museum.antwerpen.be** and **www.topa.be**.

THE TOP ATTRACTIONS

Koninklijk Museum voor Schone Kunsten Antwerpen (Antwerp Royal Museum of Fine Arts) ✮✮✮ Housed in this impressive neoclassical building is the KMSKA's world-class collection of paintings by Flemish Masters. More Rubens masterpieces are here than anywhere else, including frescoes by the artist in the marble entrance hall. To view Rubens's paintings, pass through the ground-floor exhibits of modern artists' canvases (including works by Magritte, Ensor, Permeke, and Delvaux) and ascend to the second floor, where you'll find Rubens, Jan van Eyck, Rogier van der Weyden, Dirck Bouts, Hans Memling, the Brueghel family, Rembrandt, and Frans Hals. All told, these walls hold paintings spanning 5 centuries.

Leopold de Waelplaats 2. ✆ 03/238-78-09. http://museum.antwerpen.be/kmska. Admission 6€ ($7.50) adults, 4€ ($5) seniors and students, free for children under 18; free admission for all last Wed of month. Tues–Sat 10am–5pm; Sun 10am–6pm. Closed Jan 1–2, May 1, Ascension Day, Dec 25.

Onze-Lieve-Vrouwekathedraal (Cathedral of Our Lady) ✮✮✮ A masterpiece of Brabant Gothic architecture, this towering edifice is the largest church in the Low Countries. Begun in 1352 and completed by around 1520, it stands on the site of a 10th-century chapel dedicated to the Virgin that later grew to be a church in the Romanesque style. There are seven aisles and 125 pillars in the cathedral, but of the original design's five towers, only one was completed. This one is the tallest church spire in the Low Countries, 123m (403 ft.) high, and the idea that the designers could have planned to construct five such behemoths is a graphic indication of the wealth and power of Antwerp at that time.

The cathedral's history includes a destructive fire in 1533, devastation by Protestant rebels during the religious wars of the 16th century, deconsecration by anticlerical French revolutionaries in 1794 (resulting in the removal of its Rubens paintings), and a slow rebirth that began after Napoleon's final defeat in 1815. Its interior embellishment is a mix of baroque and neoclasssical. Today the cathedral houses four Rubens masterpieces, all of them altarpieces: *The Raising of the Cross* (1610), *The Descent From the Cross* (1614), *The Resurrection* (1612), and *Assumption of the Virgin* (1626). Also outstanding is Nicolas Rombouts's *Last Supper* (1503), an impressive stained-glass window. Among many other notable works of art is a superb *Madonna and Child* (ca. 1350) in Carrrara marble by the anonymous Master of the Maasland Marble Madonnas. During July and August, the cathedral bells peal out in a carillon concert on Sunday from 3 to 4pm and on Monday from 8 to 9pm.

Handschoenmarkt (off Grote Markt). ☎ 03/213-99-51. www.dekathedraal.be. Admission 2€ ($2.50), free for children under 12. Mon–Fri 10am–5pm; Sat 10am–3pm; Sun and religious holidays 1–4pm. Closed to tourist visits during services. Metro: Groenplaats.

Rubenshuis (Rubens House) ★★

Touch Antwerp's cultural heart at the house where Antwerp's most illustrious son, the artist Peter Paul Rubens (1577–1640), lived and worked. Far from being the stereotypical starving artist, Rubens amassed a tidy fortune from his paintings that allowed him to build this impressive mansion in 1610, along what was then a canal, when he was 33. Today you can stroll past the baroque portico into its reconstructed period rooms and through a Renaissance garden, and come away with a good idea of the lifestyle of a patrician Flemish gentleman of that era. Examples of Rubens's works, and others by master painters who were his contemporaries, are sprinkled throughout. In the dining room, look for a self-portrait painted when he was 47 years old, and in another room a portrait of Anthony van Dyck as a boy. Rubens collected Roman sculpture, and some of the pieces in his sculpture gallery appear—reproduced in amazing detail—in his paintings. Don't just stay inside the house: The superb, restored ornamental garden from 1615 is well worth a stroll around, and a nice place to take a breather in fine weather.

Wapper 9–11 (a short walk east of the center). ☎ 03/201-15-55. http://museum.antwerpen.be/rubenshuis. Admission 6€ ($6.25) adults; 4€ ($3.15) those ages 19–26; free for seniors, visitors with disabilities and companion, and children under 19. Tues–Sun (also Easter Monday, Pentecost Monday) 10am–5pm. Closed Jan 1–2, May 1, Ascension Day, Nov 1–2, Dec 25–26. Tram: 2, 3, or 15 to Meir; 4, 7, or 8 to Meirbrug/Katelijnevest; 12 or 24 to Frankrijklei.

AROUND THE GROTE MARKT

A lively 16th-century square lined with sidewalk cafes and restaurants, the Grote Markt, though not quite as dramatic as Brussels's Grand-Place, is no less the focus of the city's everyday life. The fountain in the center recalls the city's founding legend of Druon and Brabo.

Stadhuis (City Hall) ★

The Renaissance City Hall (1561–65), designed by Cornelius Floris, is an outstanding example of the Flemish mannerism that replaced the formerly supreme Gothic style. It was burned by the Spanish in 1576 and rebuilt as you see it now. Look for the frescoes by Hendrik Leys, a 19th-century Antwerp painter; murals; and, in the burgomaster's chamber, an impressive 16th-century fireplace.

Grote Markt. ☎ 03/221-13-33. Guided tours 1€ ($1.25). Mon–Wed and Fri–Sat 11am, 2pm, and 3pm (council business permitting).

Vleeshuis (Butcher's Hall) Around the square and on the surrounding streets are excellent examples of 16th-century guild houses. One worth a visit is this magnificent Gothic structure. A short walk from the Stadhuis, it functions as a museum of archaeology, ceramics, arms, religious art, sculpture, musical instruments, coins, and medieval furnishings. The collections give a good general idea of daily life in Antwerp during the 16th century, as do the historical paintings (look for the striking *The Spanish Fury*, picturing Antwerp's darkest hour). There's also an Egyptian section.

Vleeshouwersstraat 38–40. ✆ 03/233-64-04. www.museum.vleeshuis.be. Admission 5€ ($6.25) adults; 3€ ($3.75) those ages 19–26; free for seniors, visitors with disabilities and companion, and children under 19. Tues–Sun (also Easter Monday, Pentecost Monday) 10am–5pm. Closed Jan 1–2, May 1, Ascension Day, Nov 1–2, Dec 25–26.

MORE ATTRACTIONS WORTH A VISIT

De Steen 🏛 Antwerp's oldest building, dating from the early 13th century, is this medieval fortress on the banks of the Schelde. The glowering fortress has served a number of purposes over the centuries. Today it houses the **Nationaal Scheepvaartmuseum (National Maritime Museum)** 🏛. There's an extensive library on river navigation and almost every nautical subject, and exhibits about the development of the port and maritime history in general. The most eye-catching are models of old-time sailing ships, like those of the Belgian East India Company clippers. You can walk into the courtyard even when the museum is closed.

Next to the museum there's an industrial archaeological division with the remains of the old Antwerp port; this division is open from Easter to November 1.

Steenplein 1 (at the Schelde River). ✆ 03/201-93-40. http://museum.antwerpen.be/scheepvaartmuseum. Admission 4€ ($5) adults; 3€ ($2.50) those ages 19–26; free for seniors, visitors with disabilities and companion, and children under 19. Tues–Sun (also Easter Monday, Pentecost Monday) 10am–5pm. Closed Jan 1–2, May 1, Ascension Day, Nov 1–2, Dec 25–26. Metro: Groenplaats.

MoMu 🏛 The collections of the Antwerp Fashion Museum consist of clothing, lace, embroidery, fabrics, and tools for textile processing, dating back to the 16th century, complemented with pieces by contemporary Belgian designers. MoMu combines a varied exhibits policy, with publications, a library and spacious public reading room, lectures, conferences, workshops, and movies. Together with the Flanders Fashion Institute (FFI) and the renowned fashion department of the Antwerp Royal Academy of Fine Arts, MoMu is housed in the beautifully restored 19th-century ModeNatie building in the cultural and historical heart of town.

Nationalestraat 28 (at Drukkerijstraat). ✆ 03/470-27-70. www.momu.be. Admission 6€ ($7.50) adults; 4€ ($5) students, seniors, and those 12–25; free for children under 12. Tues–Sun 10am–6pm (1st and 3rd Thurs of month 9pm). Closed Jan 1, July 21, Aug 15, Dec 25. Tram: 2 or 8.

Plantin-Moretus Museum 🏛 In 1555, Christoffle Plantin established a printing workshop in this stately patrician mansion. Its output included an astonishing multilanguage (Hebrew, Greek, Syriac, Latin, and Aramaic) edition of the Bible, and translations of other great works of literature. His grandson, Balthasar Moretus, was a contemporary and close friend of Rubens, who illustrated many of the books published by the Plantin-Moretus workshop and painted the family portraits you see displayed here. The museum's exhibits include an antique *Librorium Prohibitorum*, a catalog of books proscribed by the church as being unfit for the pious.

Vrijdagmarkt 22–23. ✆ 03/221-14-50. http://museum.antwerpen.be/plantin_moretus. Admission 6€ ($7.50) adults; 4€ ($5) those ages 19–26; free for seniors, visitors with disabilities and companion, and children under 19. Tues–Sun (also Easter Monday, Pentecost Monday) 10am–5pm. Closed Jan 1–2, May 1, Ascension Day, Nov 1–2, Dec 25–26.

Sint-Jacobskerk (St. James's Church) ✯   This flamboyant Gothic church with a baroque interior is the final resting place of Rubens. His vault is in the Rubens Chapel, one of seven chapels bordering the opulent semicircular ambulatory behind the high altar. Several of Rubens's works are here, and some by van Dyck and other prominent artists. Rubens is joined in his eternal slumber by a glittering collection of Antwerp's one-time high and mighty, and by a glittering collection of gold and silver and religious objects.

Lange Nieuwstraat 73–75 (a short walk east of the center city, north of the Rubens House). ℂ **03/225-04-14**. www.topa.be. Admission 2€ ($2.50) adults, 1.50€ ($1.90) students, free for children under 12. Apr–Oct daily 2–5pm; Nov–Mar Wed–Mon 2–5pm. Closed to tourist visits during services.

Zoo Antwerpen ✯ *Kids*   This fine (but expensive) 10-hectare (25-acre) zoo is a great place to take the kids. Its large collection of animals from around the world roam through spaces bounded for the most part by artificial reproductions of natural barriers. There's an aquarium, winter garden, Egyptian temple (which houses elephants), anthropoid house, museum of natural history, deer parks, Kongo peacock habitat, and planetarium. The zoo is something of an Art Nouveau masterpiece, though whether or not the animals appreciate this is hard to say.

Koningin Astridplein 26 (just east of Centraal Station). ℂ **03/202-45-40**. www.zooantwerpen.be. Admission 16€ ($20) adults; 11€ ($14) seniors, children 3–11, and visitors with disabilities and companion; free for children under 3. Daily from 10am; closing time: Jan–Feb and Nov–Dec 4:45pm; Mar–Apr and Oct 5.30pm; May–June and Sept 6pm; July–Aug 7pm. Metro: Centraal Station.

ANTWERP'S PORT

When you come down to it, if there were no Schelde River, there would be no Antwerp. The city's prime location just above the point where the river meets the tidal Schelde Estuary made it an important port as far back as the 2nd century B.C. For many centuries after that, Antwerp attracted a bevy of covetous invaders. Antwerp was a trading station of the powerful medieval Hanseatic League, but unlike Bruges, did not have the status of a full-fledged *Kontor*. In the early days, ships moored along the center city; nowadays the port has moved some 13km (8 miles) downstream to the huge excavated Zandvliet docks that jam up against the Dutch border.

The port is well worth a visit, if only to appreciate its vast size. The entire harbor/dock complex covers 65 sq. km (25 sq. miles). Each year, 16,000 ships visit, transporting 100 million metric tons of cargo. Port enterprises employ 57,000 people and add more than $6 billion to the national economy.

ESPECIALLY FOR KIDS

Futuristic **Aquatopia** ✯, Koningin Astridplein 7 (ℂ **03/205-07-40;** www.aquatopia.be; Metro: Centraal Station), in the Astrid Park Plaza Hotel building, has 40 aquaria filled with around a million liters (264,200 gal.) of salt water and houses 3,500 marine creatures, from sea horses to sharks. Tropical rainforests, mangroves, wetlands, coral reefs, the ocean floor—all, and more, are featured. No doubt your biggest thrill will be walking through a clear-walled "shark tunnel," while watching smallish examples of these toothy fish swimming around you. Multimedia applications and interactive computer displays complement the live action; even Nemo puts in an appearance. You may want to spend at least 2 hours here. Aquatopia is open daily from 10am to 6pm. Admission is (weekday/weekend) 11€/12€ ($14/$16) for adults; 8€/9€ ($10/$11) for seniors, visitors with disabilities, and children ages 4 to 12; and free for children under 4.

The Diamond Trade

The raw facts and figures are sparkling enough: Some 85% of the world's rough diamonds, 50% of its cut diamonds, and 40% of its industrial diamonds are traded here annually—together they're valued at more than $12.5 billion. The diamond cutters of Antwerp are renowned for their skill, which you can admire in the **Diamant Kwartier (Diamond Quarter),** a surprisingly down-at-the-heels-looking area, only steps away from Centraal Station. More than 12,000 expert cutters and polishers are at work in the Diamond Quarter at 380 workshops, serving 1,500 firms and 3,500 brokers and merchants. The trade is supervised by Antwerp's Hoge Raad voor Diamant (Diamond High Council).

In addition to perusing the stores and visiting a workshop (see "Shopping," below), a good place to get close to the city's diamond trade is the **Diamantmuseum Provincie Antwerpen (Antwerp Province Diamond Museum),** Koningin Astridplein 19–23 (© **03/202-48-90;** www.diamantmuseum.be; Metro: Centraal Station). Exhibits trace the history, geology, mining, and cutting of diamonds. Diamond-cutting and polishing demonstrations are on Saturday afternoon from 1:30 to 4:30pm. The museum is open February to December, Thursday to Tuesday (and Wed when national holiday) from 10am to 5:30pm (closed Dec 25–26). Admission is 6€ ($7.50) for adults, 4€ ($5) for seniors and ages 12 to 25, and free for children under 12.

ORGANIZED TOURS

WALKING TOURS   From July to September, a daily guided tour of the center city, in English (and French), departs at 2pm from the tourist office; the cost is 6€ ($7.50) for adults, and 3€ ($3.75) for accompanied children under 12. The tourist office can arrange for a qualified guide to accompany you on private walking tours around the city at a set rate of 50€ ($63) for the first 2 hours and 25€ ($31) for each additional hour. There are also clearly marked self-guided walks, with brochures available from the tourist office.

BY BOAT   Try to take a cruise around Antwerp's awesome harbor. Most departures are from the Schelde waterfront next to the Steen. **Rederij Flandria** (© **03/231-31-00;** www.flandriaboat.com) runs a 2½-hour harbor cruise for 12€ ($15) for adults, 10€ ($13) for seniors and children ages 3 to 12, and free for children under 3. A 50-minute excursion on the river is less interesting but still worthwhile, with half-hourly departures during summer months, for 7.50€ ($9.40) for adults, 6€ ($7.50) for seniors and children ages 3 to 12, and free for children under 3. In July and August, there's a delightful harbor dinner cruise from 8 to 10:30pm for 65€ ($81) for adults, 62€ ($78) for seniors, 45€ ($56) for children ages 3 to 12, and free for children under 3.

BY BUS   The **Antwerp Diamond Bus** is a double-decker bus that tours the city's main sights on a regular circuit. You can hop on and hop off at various stops along the way. Tickets, valid for 24 hours, are 10€ ($13) for adults, 9€ ($11) for seniors and students, and 5€ ($6.25) for children.

WHERE TO STAY
EXPENSIVE
Rubens-Grote Markt ★★   Only steps away from the Grote Markt, this comfortable hotel combines the classical elegance of a 16th-century mansion with plush, modern furnishings. The spacious rooms are individually decorated. Shady rooms are perked up with bright, tropical colors, and sunny rooms have more muted tones. Some of the rooms overlook an enclosed garden where breakfast is served in the summer.

Oude Beurs 29 (1 block north of the Grote Markt), 2000 Antwerpen. © **03/222-48-48.** Fax 03/225-19-40. www. hotelrubensantwerp.be. 36 units. 145€–255€ ($164–$556) double; 445€ ($556) suite. Rates include buffet breakfast. AE, DC, MC, V. Parking 15€ ($19). Tram: 10 or 11 to Wolstraat. **Amenities:** Bar; limited room service; laundry service. *In room:* A/C, TV, dataport, minibar, hair dryer, safe.

MODERATE
Alfa de Keyser   This well-located, seven-story hotel features some rooms stylized with a pastel color scheme and others in more classic tones (warmer, wine-red colors). The front lobby is dark and quiet, with plants, a piano, and luxurious sofas. Guests can enjoy the fine Chagall restaurant and Paint Pot bar.

De Keyserlei 66–70 (beside Centraal Station), 2018 Antwerpen. © **03/206-74-60.** Fax 03/232-39-70. www. nh-hotels.com. 123 units. 110€–190€ ($138–$238) double. AE, DC, MC, V. Limited street parking. Tram: Centraal Station. **Amenities:** Restaurant (French); bar; heated indoor pool; health club; Jacuzzi; 24-hr. room service; laundry service; dry cleaning. *In room:* A/C, TV, minibar, hair dryer.

Prinse ★   Although some guests might find the modern rooms—with their black leather-and-wood decor—a bit impersonal, others will appreciate their sophistication. This hotel in a restored 16th-century residence has a pleasant terrace and is on a quiet street between Centraal Station and the town center.

Keizerstraat 63 (at Prinsesstraat), 2000 Antwerpen. © **03/226-40-50.** Fax 03/225-11-48. www.hotelprinse.be. 33 units. 116€–122€ ($145–$153). Rates include continental breakfast. AE, DC, MC, V. Parking 8€ ($10). Tram: Meir. *In room:* TV.

INEXPENSIVE
Rubenshof ★★   This small family-owned hotel was once a residence of the Belgian cardinal—perhaps that explains the heavenly atmosphere. The place has a remarkably beautiful interior, with painted ceilings, chandeliers, and a great deal of ornamentation, some of it Art Nouveau. The guest rooms are somewhat plainer than the public spaces, but they're still comfortably and adequately furnished.

Amerikalei 115–117 (across from the Royal Museum of Fine Arts), 2000 Antwerpen. © **03/237-07-89.** Fax 03/ 248-25-94. www.rubenshof.be. 22 units (14 with bathroom). 44€ ($55) double without bathroom; 69€ ($86) double with bathroom. Rates include continental breakfast. AE, MC, V. Limited street parking. Tram: 12 or 24 to Brederodestraat. *In room:* No phone.

WHERE TO DINE
VERY EXPENSIVE
't Fornuis ★★ FRENCH   Behind the heavy doors of a 16th-century stone house, this Michelin two-star restaurant offers the finest dining in town in an intimate room furnished in oak. Chef Johan Segers comes to your table to explain each succulent dish. Although you can't go wrong with anything on the menu, the sole with rhubarb is particularly outstanding. Guests are invited to visit the superb wine cellar, which contains 4,000 bottles of wine.

Reyndersstraat 24. © **03/233-62-70.** Reservations required. Main courses 22€–52€ ($28–$65). AE, DC, MC, V. Mon–Fri noon–3pm and 7–10pm.

EXPENSIVE

De Manie ❀ FRENCH   This bright, modern restaurant serves innovative dishes that change every 6 months. Recent specialties included an appetizer of quail salad with goat cheese and artichoke; filet of hare with cranberries, chicory, and juniper sauce; and grilled wood pigeon with gratinéed Brussels sprouts. The food is excellent, and the setting is laid-back.

Hendrik Conscienceplein 3 (near Sint-Katelijnevest). ✆ **03/232-64-38.** Main courses 23€–33€ ($29–$41); fixed-price menus 24€–46€ ($30–$58). AE, MC, V. Mon–Tues and Thurs–Sat noon–2:30pm and 6:30–9:30pm; Sun 6:30–9:30pm. Metro: Groenplaats.

Sir Anthony Van Dijck ❀❀ BELGIAN/CLASSIC FRENCH   A location amid the delightful 16th-century Vlaeykensgang courtyard's jumble of cafes, restaurants, and antique apartments all but guarantees a pleasant atmosphere here. This used to be a Michelin Star–rated restaurant, until owner and chef Marc Paesbrugghe got tired of staying on the Michelin treadmill and chose to do something less stressful and more fun. He reopened this place as a relaxed brasserie/restaurant in an elegantly minimalist setting flooded with natural light from the old-world courtyard. It doubles as a contemporary art gallery but retains a commitment to good food.

Oude Koornmarkt 16. ✆ **03/231-61-70.** www.siranthonyvandijck.be. Main courses 29€–35€ ($36–$44). AE, DC, MC, V. Mon–Sat noon–1:30pm and 6:30–9:30pm.

MODERATE

Pottenbrug ❀ FRENCH/MEDITERRANEAN   The casual, relaxed atmosphere in this place, where you eat in cozy proximity with fellow diners, works well with the timber floorboards, the stove in full view, and a menu chalked on boards. The formula has changed little since Philip and Brigitte De Naeyer opened a quarter-century ago, even though the area has gone from seedy to chic, and it still appeals to a similar, arty clientele. But the menu, though it still offers traditional Flemish dishes with Italian accents, has moved with the times. Among the best choices are the *parelhoen met balsamico* (stuffed guinea-fowl in a balsamic sauce), the simple but refreshing *zomerse pastasla van de chef* (chef's summer pasta salad), and salmon or lobster accompanied by fresh pasta and cherry butter. An unusual and delicious dessert choice is the *olijfolieijs met witte truffelchocolade* (olive-oil ice cream and white truffle chocolate).

Minderbroedersrui 38. ✆ **03/231-51-47.** www.pottenbrug.com. Main courses 14€–21€ ($18–$26); *dagschotel* 14€ ($18). AE, MC, V. Tues–Fri noon–2pm and 6:30–10pm; Sat 6:30–11pm. Metro: Groenplaats.

Rooden Hoed ❀ BELGIAN/FRENCH   This pleasant, old-fashioned restaurant is the oldest in Antwerp, having been in business for more than 250 years. It serves hearty food—a mix of regional cuisine and trendy new forms—at moderate prices. Mussels, a delicious *choucroute d'Alsace* (sausages with sauerkraut and mashed potatoes), chicken *waterzooï*, and fish specialties are all featured on the menu. Try an aperitif, or a snack, in the medieval cellar under the restaurant.

Oude Koornmarkt 25 (near the Cathedral). ✆ **03/233-28-44.** www.roodenhoed.be. Main courses 12€–20€ ($15–$25); fixed-price menus 25€–40€ ($31–$50). AE, MC, V. Daily noon–2:30pm and 6–11pm.

INEXPENSIVE

De Foyer ❀ INTERNATIONAL   One of Antwerp's most popular dining addresses, this magnificent brasserie is in the foyer of the 19th-century Bourla Theater. With its ornately painted dome, potted palms, red velvet drapes, and marble columns, you would expect prices to be a lot higher than they are. The daily lunch buffet is a bargain;

it includes an array of fish and vegetable salads, soup, several hot dishes, cheese, and pastries. At least try to stop in for tea or drinks, if only to bask in the opulence.

Komedieplaats 18. ℂ 03/233-55-17. www.defoyer.be. Reservations recommended on weekends. Light meals 8€–16€ ($10–$20). Lunch buffet 18€ ($23). MC, V. Mon–Fri noon–midnight; Sat 11am–midnight; Sun 11am–6pm.

SHOPPING

Antwerp yields not an inch to Brussels in the style wars—in fact, Antwerp is the more fashion-conscious of the two. During the '80s and '90s, youthful local fashion designers, graduates of the city's Fine Arts Academy, made a major and enduring impact within Belgium, and established a substantial international reputation.

Expensive, upmarket stores, boutiques, and department stores abound in De Keyserlei and the Meir. For haute couture, go to Leopoldstraat; for lace, the streets surrounding the cathedral; for books, Hoogstraat; for electronics and antiques, Minderbroedersrui; and for diamonds, Appelmansstraat and nearby streets, all near Centraal Station.

WHERE TO SHOP

A top Belgian fashion designer keeps shop at **Ann Demeulemeester's** ★★, Verlatstraat 38 (ℂ **03/216-01-33;** tram: 8), in front of the Royal Fine Arts Museum. You can purchase complete lines of clothes, shoes, and accessories for both men and women by Demeulemeester, one of the "Antwerp Six." Space for displaying them is not a problem at this former seaman's academy, a 19th-century listed building. It's open Monday to Saturday from 10am to 7pm.

Treat your feet to shoes by Anne Demeulemeester, and other top Flemish designers Dries Van Noten and Dirk Bikkembergs, at **Coccodrillo,** Schuttershofstraat 9A (ℂ **03/233-20-93**). **Gozo,** Steenhouwersvest 63 (ℂ **03/226-24-58**), serves up chic, affordable women's fashion, including Belgian designer Olivier Strelli's moderately priced 22 Octobre line.

For diamonds, visit the glittering jewelry and gold stores of the **Diamond Quarter,** around Centraal Station. At **Diamondland,** Appelmansstraat 33A (ℂ **03/229-29-90;** www.diamondland.be; Metro: Centraal Station), it's fascinating to watch expert cutters and polishers transform undistinguished stones into gems of glittering beauty—the "Antwerp cut" is said to give them more sparkle. This luxurious showplace, the city's biggest, provides a firsthand look at the process on a guided tour of its workrooms, and you can take home a souvenir of lasting value for a price considerably lower than you'd pay elsewhere (tax-free for residents of countries outside the European Union). The store is open normal business hours Monday to Saturday, and on Sunday and holidays April to October.

MARKETS

Antwerp's famed street markets are fun and good bargain-hunting territory. If you're in town on a Saturday from April to September, shop for a steal (that'll be the day!) at the **Antiques Market,** Lijnwaadmarkt, Saturdays from Easter to October, from 10am to 6pm. The outstanding **Bird Market** is a general market that features live animals, plants, textiles, and foodstuffs; it takes place Sunday mornings in Oude Vaartplaats near the City Theater. At the **Friday Market,** on Wednesday and Friday mornings on Vrijdagmarkt facing the Plantin-Moretus Museum, household goods and secondhand furniture are put on public auction.

ANTWERP AFTER DARK

Antwerp is as lively after dark as it is busy during the day. To check what's going on while you're in the city, pick up a copy of *Antwerpen,* a monthly publication available at the tourist office.

The main entertainment zones are Grote Markt and Groenplaats, which both contain concentrations of bars, cafes, and theaters; High Town (Hoogstraat, Pelgrimstraat, Pieter Potstraat, and vicinity) for jazz clubs and bistros; Stadswaag for jazz and punk; and the Centraal Station area for discos, nightclubs, and gay bars. The red-light district here, concentrated in Riverside Quarter, is much seedier and less tourist-oriented than the one in Amsterdam (see chapter 12).

THE PERFORMING ARTS

Antwerp takes pride in being a citadel of Flemish culture. Two of the region's stellar companies are based here: the **Vlaamse Opera (Flanders Opera),** Frankrijklei 3 (© 03/233-66-85), and the **Koninklijk Ballet van Vlaanderen (Royal Flanders Ballet),** Kattendijkdok-Westkaai 16 (© 03/234-34-38; www.koninklijkballetvan vlaanderen.be).

To house its vibrant cultural life, the city has no shortage of performance venues. Top of the line for theater and classical music is the **Het Paleis,** Theaterplein 1 (© 03/ 202-83-11; Ticketline © 0900/00-311; www.hetpaleis.be). For music and ballet, there's the classically orientated **Queen Elisabeth Concert Hall,** Koningin Astridplein 26 (© 03/203-56-00; www.elisabethzaal.be), and the more modernist **deSingel,** Desguinlei 25 (© 03/248-28-28; www.desingel.be).

BARS

No city watering hole has a better outlook than **In Den Engel** ⊛, Grote Markt 3 (© 03/233-12-52), an old-style cafe dating from 1579 that's said never to close, on the main square, beside the fountain-sculpture of Silvius Brabo, where a round glass called a *bolleke* (little ball) of Antwerp's very own yeasty, copper-toned De Koninck beer becomes a work of liquid art. **Paeters Vaetje,** Blauwmoezelstraat 1 (© 03/231-84-76), below the cathedral's soaring spire, is a great place for listening to the Monday-evening carillon concert, and serves up 100 different brews.

Get into the abbey habit at **De Groote Witte Arend (The Great White Eagle),** Reyndersstraat 12–18 (© 03/226-31-90), a cafe in a 17th-century former monastery, where customers are serenaded by classical music. Go underground to **De Pelgrom,** Pelgrimstraat 15 (© 03/234-08-09), in a candlelit, brick-arched cellar, where you can get convivial at long wood benches.

A huge selection of beers, including virtually every Belgian brand, is displayed behind glass and served at candlelit tables in **Kulminator,** Vleminckveld 32 (© 03/ 232-45-38). Hot and cool at the same time, **Het Zottekot,** Vlaamse Kaai 21 (© 03/ 237-99-07), a wide step away from old-Antwerp style, is a wild, youth-oriented den where anything can happen—and generally does.

Kids The Belgian Muppets

Take the kids to the delightful **Van Campen Royal Puppet Theater,** Lange Nieuwstraat 3 (© 03/237-37-16), where the plot lines are always easy to understand (even if the language isn't).

An altogether different kind of drinking experience is to be had at **De Vagant** ✦, Reyndersstraat 25 (☎ **03/233-15-38**). It deals exclusively in *jenever* and has 220 varieties of this stiff grain spirit. An upstairs restaurant specializes in dishes with *jenever*-based sauces and its walls are a gallery of *jenever* memorabilia.

SIDE TRIPS FROM ANTWERP
LIER
16km (10 miles) SE of Antwerp

A pretty, small town on the banks of the Nete River, Lier (Lierre in French) has canal-side scenes reminiscent of Bruges.

Essentials
GETTING THERE   Trains for Lier depart hourly from Antwerp Centraal Station. There are buses every half-hour or so from the **bus** station in front of Centraal Station, but they take longer. To go by **car,** take N10.

VISITOR INFORMATION   Toerisme Lier, Stadhuis (Town Hall), Grote Markt 57 (☎ **03/800-05-55;** fax 03/488-12-76; www.lier.be).

What to See & Do
Don't miss the town's 14th-century **Zimmertoren (Zimmer Tower)** ✦, Zimmerplein (☎ **03/800-03-95**). It's equipped with the remarkable Centenary Clock and Wonder Clock, which were installed by astronomy enthusiast Lodewijk Zimmer to explain the workings of space and time to his fellow citizens. The clocks show the sun, moon, signs of the zodiac, seasons, and tides on the Nete River. The tower is open April to September daily from 9am to noon and 1:30 to 6pm, and October to March daily from 9am to noon and 1:30 to 5:30pm. Admission is 2€ ($2.50) for adults, 1€ ($1.25) for children ages 6 to 16, and free for children under 6.

If you have time, visit the **Stedelijk Museum (Municipal Museum),** Florent van Cauwenberghstraat 14 (☎ **03/800-03-96**), just off the Grote Markt in the center of town. The art collections here include paintings by Rubens, Jan and Pieter Brueghel, David Teniers the Younger, and local artist Isidore Opsomer. The museum is open Tuesday to Sunday from 10am to noon and 1 to 5pm. Admission is 1€ ($1.25) for adults and 0.50€ (65¢) for school students.

HASSELT
77km (48 miles) SE of Antwerp

The heart of Belgium's potent *jenever* industry, Hasselt is a center for touring the Kempen moorland.

Essentials
GETTING THERE   The town is easily reached by hourly **train** from Antwerp or by a leisurely **drive** east on N10 and N2.

VISITOR INFORMATION   In&Uit Hasselt, Lombaardstraat 3 (☎ **011/23-95-40;** fax 011/22-50-23; www.inenuithasselt.be).

What to See & Do
Centuries of the loving care devoted to the fiery drink *jenever* are recalled in the exhibits of the **Nationaal Jenevermuseum (National Jenever Museum),** Witte Non-nenstraat 19 (☎ **011/23-98-60;** www.jenevermuseum.be). These include its distillation, bottling, labeling and, of course, drinking. The *jenever* has the last word in a free

sample that rounds off the visit with an appropriate glow. The museum is open April to October, Tuesday to Sunday (also Mon July–Aug) from 10am to 5pm; November to March, Tuesday to Friday from 10am to 5pm, and Saturday and Sunday from 1 to 5pm (closed Jan 1 and rest of Jan, except school vacation days; Dec 24, 25, and 31). Admission is 3€ ($3.75) for adults (1 drink included), 1€ ($1.25) for children ages 12 to 18, and free for children under 12.

A nearby attraction, which is especially interesting for children, is the **Domein Bokrijk (Bokrijk Estate)** ★★ (© 011/26-53-00; www.bokrijk.be), 8km (5 miles) northeast of town. On the grounds of the large wooded estate is the **Openluchtmuseum (Open-Air Museum),** consisting of old houses that provide detailed reconstructions of everyday Flemish life in pre-modern times. In some, craftspeople work at traditional trades. Although all of the buildings and village sites are clearly marked, I suggest you purchase the English-language guide, which is an education in itself. In addition, the estate incorporates a big nature reserve. The museum is open April to September daily from 10am to 6pm; the rest of the estate is open the same hours year-round. Admission Monday to Saturday (Apr–May and June–Sept) is 7€ ($8.75) for adults, 6€ ($7.50) for seniors and visitors with disabilities, 3.50€ ($4.40) for children ages 6 to 12, and free for children under 6; Sunday and holidays (and daily July–Aug) 10€ ($8.75) for adults, 8.50€ ($7.50) for seniors and visitors with disabilities, 5€ ($5) for children ages 6 to 12, and free for children under 6. There's regular bus service from Hasselt, and train service from Brussels via Hasselt (Bokrijk has its own rail station). By car, take N75 from Hasselt; parking at the estate costs 3€ ($3.75).

TONGEREN ★
88km (55 miles) SE of Antwerp

Belgium's oldest town (Tongres in French), with a history dating back to Roman times, is at the eastern end of the Kempen, close to the Dutch border. Ambiorix, chief of the ancient Eburones, whipped one of Julius Caesar's legions here, earning himself a martial statue on the town's Grote Markt.

Essentials
GETTING THERE   There's frequent **train** service from Antwerp to Tongeren via Hasselt. By **car,** take N20 southeast from Hasselt.

VISITOR INFORMATION   **Toerisme Tongeren** is at Stadhuisplein 9, 3700 Tongeren (© 012/39-02-55; fax 012/39-11-43; www.tongeren.be).

What to See & Do
Tongeren is home to the imposing **Onze-Lieve-Vrouwebasiliek (Basilica of Our Lady)** ★, a Gothic church with a Brabantine tower and a Romanesque cloister. Its rich *schatkamer* (treasury) contains rare religious objects from the Merovingian era (6th–8th c. A.D.) up to the 18th century. The basilica is open daily from 9am to 4pm (the treasury Apr–Sept). Admission to the basilica is free. Admission to the treasury is 2.50€ ($3.15) for adults; 1.50€ ($1.90) for seniors, students, and children ages 12 to 18; 0.50€ (65¢) for children ages 5 to 12; and free for children under 5.

Also worth a visit is the **Gallo-Romeins Museum (Gallo-Roman Museum)** ★, Kielenstraat 15 (© 012/67-03-33; www.limburg.be/galloromeinsmuseum), which contains 18,000 objects, from prehistoric times through the Roman and Merovingian periods. The Roman period, when the town was known as Atuatuca Tungrorum, is well represented and includes huge and important collections of relics—pottery, glass objects, bronze articles, terra cotta, and sculptures—from its cemetery and the surrounding countryside. These are organized by theme to illustrate everyday life both in the town and in the country, and include exhibits on religious practices and traditions. *Note:* The museum is closed for expansion until 2008; the following practical information was in effect until the closure began and shouldn't be too far out when it reopens: The museum is open Monday from noon to 5pm, Tuesday to Friday from 9am to 5pm, and Saturday and Sunday from 10am to 6pm. It's closed on January 1 and December 25. Admission is 5€ ($6.25) for adults; 2€ ($2.50) for seniors, visitors with disabilities, and students; 2€ ($1.55) for children ages 7 to 14; and free for children under 7.

8

The Belgian Coast & Ypres

Belgium's 70km (44 miles) of North Sea coast is one continuous vista of beaches backed by sand dunes and speckled with resort towns. Except for De Haan, each resort is encumbered with a dense waterfront lineup of hotels, restaurants, and apartment buildings. Together, these have been dubbed the "Atlantic Wall," after Hitler's World War II fortifications, and they all but neutralize the coast's natural beauty.

Most visitors don't seem too concerned. Even those who might be a bit perturbed can find compensation in superb seafood dining, good shopping, and general vacation hustle and bustle. Kids love the seacoast. For adults, it offers several vacation styles—sea, sand, and sun; casino and nightclub action; gustatory gluttony; or a series of sightseeing expeditions. It's possible to cover all of these options in an incredibly short amount of time.

The beaches reach back up to 500m (1,626 ft.) at low tide, and their gentle slope into the sea makes for generally safe swimming—warnings are in force against swimming along isolated stretches. Just remember that this is the North Sea, not the Caribbean—the water is gray and pretty darn cold. You can skim along the sand on wind-blown sail carts (there's no shortage of wind), pedal beach buggies, or join the ever-hopeful sun worshipers in search of that perfect tan.

Accommodations can be hard to come by in July and August, despite the presence of thousands of vacation homes, apartments, and private homes offering bed-and-breakfast. You should reserve well ahead for this period, either through the local tourist office or directly with your chosen lodging. Don't worry too much if you can't do this—you'll always be able to get something, but it might not be what you want, where you want, and for the price you want.

⟨Moments⟩ Tracks Along the Coast

You won't need a car for sightseeing if you ride the **Kusttram (Coast Tram;** ℂ **070/22-02-00;** www.dekusttram.be), which runs the length of the seacoast between Knokke-Heist and De Panne in 2 hours, and stops at 70 places along the way. The tram is an attraction on its own. Departures are every 10 to 20 minutes in summer, and every 30 minutes in winter, in both directions. In addition to one-way tickets of varying price, special 1-, 3-, and 5-day unlimited-travel passes are available for 5€ ($6.25), 10€ ($13), and 15€ ($19), respectively, for adults; and 1.50€ ($1.90) per day for children ages 6 to 11; free for children under 6. These prices are for passes purchased before boarding the tram; for passes purchased onboard the tram, the cost is 6€ ($7.50), 12€ ($15), 18€ ($23), and 2€ ($2.50), respectively.

The Belgian Coast

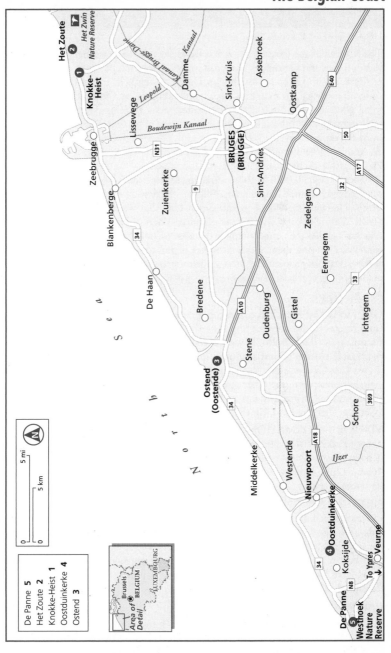

De Panne **5**
Het Zoute **2**
Knokke-Heist **1**
Oostduinkerke **4**
Ostend **3**

Area of Detail

Brussels

BELGIUM

LUXEMBOURG

0   5 mi
0   5 km

Het Zwin
Nature Reserve

Het Zoute

Knokke-
Heist

Kanaal Brugge-Damme

Damme Kanaal

Lissewege

Leopold

Boudewijn Kanaal

Sint-Kruis

Assebroek

Oostkamp

E40

Zeebrugge

N31

BRUGES
(BRUGGE)

50

Sint-Andries

A17

Zuienkerke

9

Zedelgem

32

Blankenberge

34

Eernegem

De Haan

Bredene

A10

Oudenburg

Gistel

33

Ichtegem

Stene

N
o
r
t
h

S
e
a

Ostend
(Oostende)

34

A18

Schore

369

Middelkerke

Westende

Nieuwpoort

IJzer

Oostduinkerke

Veurne

Koksijde

To Ypres

34

De Panne

N8

Westhoek
Nature
Reserve

167

1 Ostend ✦✦

110km (69 miles) NW of Brussels; 20km (12 miles) W of Bruges

The "Queen of the Coast's" glitter has faded since its 19th-century heyday as a royal vacation spot and prestigious European watering hole, but plenty of reasons remain to justify a visit to Ostend (Oostende in Dutch; Ostende in French): Great beaches, a casino, a racetrack, art museums, a spa, good shopping, an Olympic-size indoor swimming pool, outdoor pools filled with heated seawater, sailing and windsurfing, and, last but by no means least, a legitimate reputation of being a seafood cornucopia. This lively recreational haven is very much a people's queen now, welcoming all income levels, and has little of the posh exterior that's so much a part of Knokke-Heist and Het Zoute farther up the coast.

Ostend (pop. 70,000) has been attracting seawater enthusiasts since 1784 when the town council allowed Englishman William Hesketh to set up a drinks kiosk on the beach. He later introduced mobile beach huts that were hauled into the water by horses. Before World War II, the elevated Albert I Promenade and Zeedijk that together parallel the entire length of the 6km (4 miles) of beach were lined with elegant villas, among them vacation homes of European royalty. Wartime destruction and postwar "improvements" brought down many of these fine old houses. From the debris sprung character-free modern hotels and apartment buildings.

ESSENTIALS

GETTING THERE   Trains depart hourly from Brussels for the 70-minute trip, and from Bruges at least every half-hour for the 15-minute trip, to **Oostende station,** Stationsplein (✆ **02/528-28-28;** www.sncb.be), a neo-baroque edifice (1913) at the harbor. The **Kusttram (Coast Tram)** has fast, frequent service connecting all the seacoast resorts (see "Tracks Along the Coast," above). By car from Brussels and Bruges, take A10/E40 west; from the other coast resorts, take the N34 coast road.

You can sail in from Ramsgate in south England with **TransEuropa Ferries** (see "Getting There by Boat," in chapter 2).

VISITOR INFORMATION   **Toerisme Oostende** is at Monacoplein 2, 8400 Oostende (✆ **059/70-11-99;** fax 059/70-34-77; www.toerisme-oostende.be). The office is open May to October, Monday to Saturday from 9am to 7pm, and Sunday from 10am to 7pm; November to April, Monday to Saturday from 10am to 6pm, and Sunday from 10am to 5pm.

GETTING AROUND   Most points of interest in the town are close together. You can easily reach them by foot or by renting a bicycle from the rail station for 9€ ($11) a day. **De Lijn** bus lines 5, 6, and 39 go along the seafront to the west; if you want to get to points farther along the coast, in either direction, take the **Coast Tram** from a stop next to the rail station; for bus and tram information, call (✆ **070/22-02-00;** www.delijn.be). You can pick up a **taxi** at the rail station or the Casino-Kursaal, or call **Taxibond** (✆ **059/70-27-27**).

WHAT TO SEE & DO

With its Albert I Promenade and Zeedijk, which together form a kind of Boardwalk, along with its casino and beaches, Ostend is the nearest thing Belgium has to Atlantic City. But there's culture here, too, in notable art museums and links with modern artists. The long beach west of the harbor has stretches that are under lifeguard

Ostend

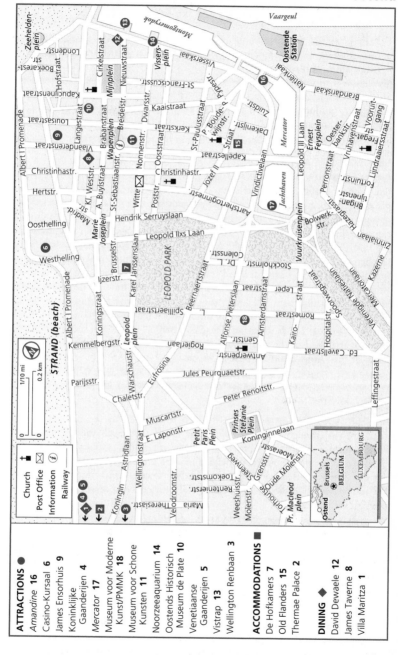

Vaargeul

Oostende Station

ATTRACTIONS ●

Amandine **16**
Casino-Kursaal **6**
James Ensorhuis **9**
Koninklijke
Gaanderijen **4**
Mercator **17**
Museum voor Moderne
Kunst/PMMK **18**
Museum voor Schone
Kunsten **11**
Noorzeeaquarium **14**
Oostends Historisch
Museum de Plate **10**
Venetiaanse
Gaanderijen **5**
Vistrap **13**
Wellington Renbaan **3**

ACCOMMODATIONS ■

De Hofkamers **7**
Old Flanders **15**
Thermae Palace **2**

DINING ◆

David Dewaele **12**
James Taverne **8**
Villa Maritza **1**

Church ✝
Post Office ⊠
Information ⓘ
Railway

STRAND (beach)

LEOPOLD PARK

Fun Fact **The Fat Lady**

A large statue of a reclining, generously endowed nude woman, outside Leopold Park, is formally entitled *De Zee* (The Sea), but it's known locally as *Dikke Mathille* (Fat Matilda).

---

surveillance in summer from 10:30am to 6:30pm, and some stretches where swimming is not permitted at any time. Look for the signs that indicate both of these, and for the green, yellow, or red flags that tell you whether the sea conditions permit swimming.

THE TOP ATTRACTIONS

James Ensorhuis (James Ensor House) ✦   The house where Anglo-Belgian artist James Ensor (1860–1949) lived from 1916 has been restored to its condition when his aunt kept a ground-floor shells-and-souvenir store here, and transformed into a museum of his life. Ensor's studio and lounge are on the second floor. Only reproductions are displayed, but if you're familiar with his paintings, you'll recognize some of the furnishings and views from the windows. Born in Ostend, the son of a Belgian mother and an English father, and little understood or appreciated during his lifetime for his fantastical, hallucinatory, and sexually ambiguous visions, the pre-Expressionist painter is considered a founder of modern art. *The Entry of Christ into Brussels* (1889), first exhibited in 1929 and now in California's Getty Museum, is his most famous work. Ostend appreciates him just as much for his carnival masks inspired by the town's annual *Bal du Rat Mort* (Dead Rat Ball).

Ensor is buried in the churchyard of **Onze-Lieve-Vrouw ter Duinenkerk (Our Lady of the Dunes Church)** on Dorpstraat.

Vlaanderenstraat 27 (off Wapenplein). © **059/80-53-35.** Admission 2€ ($2.50) adults, 1€ ($1.25) seniors and students, free for children under 18. June–Sept and Easter vacation week Wed–Mon 10am–noon and 2–5pm; Nov–May Sat–Sun 2–5pm. Closed Oct.

Museum voor Moderne Kunst (Modern Art Museum) ✦   Known by its initials, PMMK (though they've discarded the word "Provincial" the "P" stands for) is set in a former department store. Its paintings, sculptures, graphics, video, and films provide a wide-ranging picture of Belgian modern art from its beginnings to the present day. There are frequent international exhibits, a children's museum, a workshop for youngsters, slide shows, and educational projects. The museum's **Art Café** is a pleasant setting for lunch.

Romestraat 11 (at Amsterdamstraat). © **059/50-81-18.** www.pmmk.be. Admission 5€ ($6.25) adults, 4€ ($5) seniors and those 19–25, 2.50€ ($3.75) children 13–18, free for children under 13. Tues–Sun 10am–6pm.

Museum voor Schone Kunsten (Fine Arts Museum) ✦✦   Paintings by native sons James Ensor, Jan de Clerck, Constant Permeke, and Léon Spilliaert, and by Belgian Impressionists, are featured at this museum in the Municipal Festival and Culture Palace in the center of town. Among the Ensors is his racy *Bathing at Ostend* (1899), a work that scandalized polite Belgian society, though the amorous King Léopold II could appreciate its pointed humor; it is interesting to compare the beach scene then with today's.

Stedelijk Feest en Kultuurpaleis, Wapenplein. © **059/80-53-35.** Admission 2.50€ ($3.15) adults, 1€ ($1.25) children 14–18, free for children under 14. Wed–Mon 10am–noon and 2–5pm.

Oostends Historisch Museum De Plate (De Plate Ostend Historical Museum)

Housed in King Léopold I's restored, 19th-century summer residence, the museum holds displays of Neolithic and Roman objects excavated in the vicinity and exhibits depicting Ostend traditional dress, folklore, and history. There's a re-created fisherman's pub, a fisherman's home, and an old tobacco store. The Marine section deals with shipbuilding and fishing boats, and covers the Ostend–Dover scheduled ferry service, which started in 1846 and ended in 2002.

Langestraat 69 (close to Wapenplein). 𝄢 **059/80-02-89**. www.deplate.be. Admission 2€ ($2.50) adults, 1€ ($1.25) seniors and children 14–18, free for children under 14. Sat 10am–noon and 2–5pm; school vacations Wed–Mon 10am–noon and 2–5pm.

LEISURE ATTRACTIONS

Belgium's largest casino, **Casino Oostende** ✦, Oosthelling (𝄢 **059/70-51-11;** www. cko.be), has gaming rooms for roulette, blackjack, craps, and stud poker, along with slot machines. There's been a casino at this spot since 1852, but the elegant original was unlucky enough to occupy a prime spot for a concrete bunker in Adolf Hitler's Atlantic Wall seacoast defenses—you might think the restored 1953 postmodern replacement isn't much of an improvement over the bunker. The gaming rooms are open daily (minimum age 21) from 3pm to 7am. Admission is free and a passport or identity card is required. See "After Dark," below, for the attached Kursaal concert hall.

The **Wellington Renbaan (Wellington Racetrack),** Koningin Astridlaan (𝄢 **059/ 80-60-55**), close to the Royal Arcades, is the only racetrack on the seacoast. A post–World War II successor to an 1856 original, it has a grass track for flat and hurdle racing and a lava track for the trotters. Racing takes place May to September; call for race times (the tourist office can furnish a detailed schedule). Admission to grandstand seats is 12€ ($15) Monday to Friday, and 15€ ($19) on weekends and holidays; admission to the field opposite the grandstand is free.

ROYAL OSTEND

Made fashionable by King Léopold I's decision to establish a vacation residence here in 1834, Ostend soon became a magnet for blue-blooded vacationers from Britain and the Continent. You can view remnants of this vanished glory scattered around town. The **Venetiaanse Gaanderijen (Venetian Galleries),** now an exhibits hall, is on the seafront Albert I Promenade. The **Koninklijke Gaanderijen (Royal Galleries),** 400m (1,300 ft.) long, from 1906, constructed under Léopold II's tutelage, connected the Royal Villa with the racetrack. These galleries protected the king and his entourage

---

Impressions

"You had some fun there, I suppose?" I put in, thinking of—well, of Ostend in August.
"Fun! A filthy hole I call it . . . there was nothing to do on shore."
                    —Erskine Childers, *The Riddle of the Sands* (1903)

Ostend is now one of the most fashionable and cosmopolitan watering-places in Europe.
                    —*Baedeker Belgium and Holland* (1905)

from sun, wind, and rain during their promenades. In 1930, the Thermae Palace (see "Where to Stay," below) was constructed at its center.

At the entrance to Venetian Galleries stands a sympathetic bronze sculpture (2000) of King Baudouin (1951–93). When compared with the resort's haughty sculptures of King Léopold I (1831–65) and King Léopold II (1865–1909), it shows how times have changed for the royal family. **Léopold I,** the first king of the Belgians, adopts a heroic nationalistic pose in an equestrian sculpture on Léopold I Plein, and **Léopold II,** a pompous imperialistic pose in an equestrian sculpture on the seafront Zeedijk at the Venetian Galleries (see above). **Baudouin,** the "people's king," is depicted strolling in Ostend, wearing a raincoat.

The **summer residence** of Léopold I, a surprisingly ordinary-looking town house at Langestraat 69, abandoned by the royals and fallen into a crestfallen state, has been restored and now houses the **Ostend Historical Museum** (see "The Top Attractions," above). Its 1954 waterfront replacement as the Royal Villa, close to the Casino, later became the plush Oostendse Compagnie Hotel, which closed in 2005, and the building now is privately owned.

Léopold II earned a reputation for allowing the royal libido free rein. He supposedly stashed one of his mistresses, a Hungarian baroness, at the grand **Villa Maritza,** Albert I Promenade 76, one of a group of three surviving 19th-century waterfront villas, now the upscale eponymous restaurant (see "Where to Dine," below).

The vast, neo-Gothic **Sint-Petrus-en Pauluskerk (St. Peter and Paul Church),** from 1907, on Sint-Petrus-en-Paulusplein, has a suite of stained-glass windows and a memorial chapel dedicated to Belgium's first queen, Marie-Louise of Orléans, who died in Ostend in 1850.

MARINE THEMES

There's plenty of sea-related stuff to see and do in Ostend. Kids will likely appreciate a ramble through the **Driemaster *Mercator* (Three-Master *Mercator*),** Mercatordok (© 059/70-56-54), moored in a dock facing the rail station. Formerly a Belgian merchant marine training ship, the *Mercator,* a white-painted, three-masted schooner, is now a floating maritime museum. The ship is open May, June, and September, daily from 9am to noon and 1 to 6pm; July and August, daily from 9am to 7pm; April to June and September, daily from 10am to 1pm and 2 to 6pm; and October to March, weekends and holidays from 11am to 1pm and 2 to 5pm. Admission is 3.50€ ($4.40) for adults, 2.75€ ($3.45) for seniors, 1.60€ ($2) for children ages 5 to 14, and free for children under 5.

Another worthwhile old sea dog is the **Museumschip (Museum Ship)** *Amandine,* Vindictive-laan 35Z (© 059/23-43-01; www.museum-amandine.be). Launched in 1961, the trawler was the last Ostend *IJslandvaarder* (Iceland Fishing Boat) to work the rich Iceland fishing grounds. She now sits in a dry basin on a plastic "sea," as a museum of the history and traditions of Ostend's Icelandic fishery. The ship can be visited Monday from 2 to 7pm, and Tuesday to Sunday from 10am to 7pm. Admission is 2.50€ ($3.15) for adults, and 1.25€ ($1.55) for children under 14.

Fun Fact **Gaye Old Time**

Marvin Gaye's 1982 classic soul torch song *Sexual Healing,* a million-selling Grammy winner, was written during an 18-month retreat in 1981 and 1982 the troubled singer took in the unlikely haven of Ostend.

Though popular with children, the small **Noordzeeaquarium (North Sea Aquarium),** Visserskaai (© **059/50-08-76**), by the old fishing harbor, is not exactly riveting. It features North Sea flora and fauna, including fish, mollusks, crustaceans, polyps, anemones, and shell and seaweed collections. The aquarium is open April to September, daily from 10am to noon and 2 to 6pm, and October to March, weekends from 10am to noon and 2 to 6pm. Admission is 2€ ($2.50) for adults, and 1.40€ ($1.75) for children under 14.

You need to be up early to watch the stands at the **Vistrap (Fish Market)** on Visserskaai being loaded up with North Sea fish fresh off the boats from the previous night's catch. Sole, plaice, whiting, cod, bream, brill, eels, and shrimps are the main species on view and for sale.

WHERE TO STAY

De Hofkamers   Under its new owners, the Pots family, the former Hotel Daniëlle continues to improve by leaps and bounds. The process of kitting out each guest room with new furnishings and decor is complete. Some rooms even include four-poster beds. These add to the attraction of this modern hotel in a convenient location, close to the beach and casino. All rooms are individually decorated, but in general feature bright colors and light-wood furnishings.

IJzerstraat 5, 8400 Oostende. © **059/70-63-49.** Fax 059/24-23-90. 25 units. www.dehofkamers.be. 75€–120€ ($94–$150) double. Rates include buffet breakfast. MC, V. Limited free parking. **Amenities:** Bike rental. *In room:* TV.

Old Flanders ✦   The cozy, country house–style guest rooms here are up-to-date and extensively furnished; each has a floor-to-ceiling, wall-to-wall wardrobe-and-shelves unit, on which the television stands. The bar has a cozy, antique feel, with a decor featuring a model sailboat and a model trawler and paintings of country scenes on the walls. The restaurant has an elegant look, with a marble mantel surrounding the fireplace, a timbered ceiling, and brick arches.

Jozef II Straat 49, 8400 Oostende. © **059/80-66-03.** Fax 059/80-16-95. 15 units. 75€–90€ ($94–$113) double. Rates include buffet breakfast. AE, DC, MC, V. Parking 8€ ($10). **Amenities:** Restaurant (Belgian); bar; babysitting. *In room:* TV, hair dryer.

Thermae Palace ✦✦   This slightly old-fashioned Art Deco hotel just off the beachfront is an integral part of the sprawling thermal-baths complex. Constructed in the 1930s, the building is still a prominent local landmark—a reminder of Ostend's previous glory as an exclusive resort. The hotel has comfortable, attractive, fairly standard guest rooms, many with a sea view. The French restaurant **Périgord** serves high-quality cuisine in a rather formal setting; the **Bistro Paddock** is more casual.

Koningin Astridlaan 7, 8400 Oostende. © **059/80-66-44.** Fax 059/80-52-74. www.thermaepalace.be. 159 units. 170€–220€ ($213–$275) double; 320€ ($400) suite. AE, DC, MC, V. Free parking. **Amenities:** 2 restaurants (French/Belgian); bar; lounge; health club; concierge; babysitting; laundry service; dry cleaning. *In room:* TV, minibar, hair dryer.

WHERE TO DINE

Diners pile into Ostend with fish on their mind. Visserskaai (Fishermen's Wharf), along the harbor, is lined with fish restaurants and is the most obvious setting for both sit-down dining in restaurants and for great snacks from waterside fish stands. Fine restaurants are sprinkled along the seafront Albert I Promenade and at spots hidden away in the old town. With 250 eateries in the vicinity, you'll have plenty of choices.

David Dewaele ⋆⋆ SEAFOOD/FRENCH   This family-owned restaurant has a strong local following. Chef Dewaele has worked at the highly regarded De Karmeliet in Bruges and the Sea Grill in Brussels. The exterior looks vaguely like a low ship's cabin on the outside, and a marine theme is maintained in the bright, elegant interior, with a decor of seashells, sailing ship photographs, and other nautical tokens. Most fish comes fresh from the North Sea and from the market across the street, with the more exotic red mullet and sea bass coming in from France. If you like tongue twisters, try to ask for *tongfilets met tomatenfonds en broodkruim van sjalotten* (sole filets on a base of tomato and crusted shallots). Alternatively, you can choose easier-to-say meat menu dishes like *pigeon de Bresse*.

Visserskaai 39 (opposite Fish Market). ✆ 059/70-42-26. Main courses 17€–36€ ($21–$45); fixed-price menus 27€–52€ ($34–$65). AE, DC, MC, V. July–Aug daily noon–3pm and 6:30–10:30pm; Sept–June Tues–Sun noon–3pm and 6:30–10:30pm.

James Taverne *Finds* TRADITIONAL FLEMISH   This Old Flemish tavern in an Art Deco shopping gallery is a good place to taste the humble North Sea shrimp, caught overnight, cooked in seawater on the boat, and eaten within the day on the sea-coast. It stars as *garnaalkroketten* (shrimp croquettes), accompanied by slices of lemon and a sprig of parsley, washed down with a glass of the local Wieze beer. The James serves these and other traditional Flemish dishes. Its cozy decor has marine paintings, antiques, and old photographs of both James Ensor and Ostend. I'd recommend this spot more for lunch than for dinner.

James Ensor Galerij 34 (off Vlaanderenstraat). ✆ 059/70-52-45. Main courses 9.50€–18€ ($12–$23). Wed–Mon 10am–10pm.

Villa Maritza ⋆⋆ SEAFOOD/FRENCH   In a waterfront villa (1885) that was the vacation home of an eponymous Hungarian baroness (reputedly one of footloose King Léopold II's mistresses), Ostend native Jacques Ghaye has created a sophisticated restaurant with an elegant cuisine. Seafood specialties vary with the season; all of them are culinary delights, but especially good options are the lobster with mixed vegetables and saffron, the lobster with red-wine sauce, and the pan-fried sole with green aspara-gus. Of the many ornate mansions that once lined the shore, this is one of the few that survived World War II bombings and destructive postwar "developers."

Albert I Promenade 76. ✆ 059/50-88-08. www.villa-maritza.be. Main courses 14€–36€ ($18–$45); fixed-price menus 53€–65€ ($66–$81). AE, DC, MC, V. Tues–Sat noon–2:30pm and 7–9:30pm; Sun 7–9:30pm.

Tips Musical Notes

Through the summer, carillon peals ring out periodically from the belfry tower of the Stedelijk Feest- en Kultuurpaleis (Municipal Festival and Culture Palace) on Wapenplein, and there are concerts at the painted wrought-iron bandstand (1895) on the square.

AFTER DARK

The concert hall of the **Kursaal Oostende** ✦, Monacoplein (℗ **070/22-56-00;** www. kursaaloostende.be), part of the Casino-Kursaal complex (see "Leisure Attractions," above) is a venue for symphonic concerts, operettas, and ballet. In its opulent interior are also a panoramic rooftop restaurant, the **Ostend Queen;** a coffee house; a snack bar; and the **Lounge Bar** nightclub.

If you want a quiet drink in the evening, visit the Old Flemish–style **Café Rubens,** Visserskaai 44 (℗ **059/80-85-08**), or one of the cafes with sidewalk terraces around Wapenplein. For late-night dance clubs, cabarets, and bars, head for Langestraat, which runs east from Monacoplein, in front of the Casino-Kursaal. Or take the kids for an ice cream at **George's Tearoom,** Adolf Buylstraat 15 (℗ **059/70-29-25**).

2 Knokke-Heist ✦

24km (14 miles) NE of Bruges; 35km (21 miles) NE of Ostend

Knokke is fashionable—not as exclusive as it once was, but still fashionable. You can tell by the very look of the place; its main shopping street features upscale jewelers, art galleries, and sporting stores adorned with internationally famous designer names. **Heist,** snuggled up close to the Dutch border, attracts average-income (*classy* average-income) families.

The winding residential streets of the nearby **Het Zoute** suburb fairly shriek "money," and big money by Belgian standards. The villas proclaim their owners to be people of both wealth and exquisite taste (or at any rate what they consider exquisite taste). Whether or not you fit easily into this moneyed environment, a drive, cycle, or walk through Het Zoute provides a glimpse of its inhabitants' wealthy lifestyle—and if that doesn't grab you as a worthwhile way to spend 15 minutes, you can pass right through to **Het Zwin Nature Reserve,** where the birds have worse table manners but more grace.

ESSENTIALS

GETTING THERE   There's frequent train and bus service from Bruges. To get here from Ostend and other seafront resorts, take the **Coast Tram** (see earlier in this chapter). The combination rail/bus/tram stations are at the south end of Lippenslaan, the main street. By car from Bruges, take N31 north; N34 runs the entire length of the coast, connecting all the resort towns.

VISITOR INFORMATION   The **Dienst voor Toerisme** is at Alfred Verweeplein 1, 8300 Knokke-Heist (℗ **050/63-03-80;** fax 050/63-03-90; www.knokke-heist.be).

WHAT TO SEE & DO

This area's list of attractions is topped by its fine beaches, where all manner of seaside sports are available. Beach activities range from half-hour sea trips in amphibious vessels launched right from the beach to sandcastle-building competitions and kite flying. In Knokke itself you can take a 30-minute ride through the streets in the **miniature train** that departs from Van Bunnenplein at the promenade.

For a different kind of fun, head to **Casino Knokke,** Zeedijk-Albertstrand 509 (℗ **050/63-05-05;** www.casinoknokke.be), across from the Albertstrand beach. This place, which dates from the 1920s, is the epitome of elegance, with plush gaming rooms, nostalgic bits of Art Deco, and glittering chandeliers illuminating a festive,

A Great (Small) Nature Reserve

Along this stretch of coast in the Middle Ages, the Zwin inlet met the sea and made Bruges a leading European port. The silting up of the inlet (leaving Bruges to settle into a landlocked prominence of quite another sort), created a salty, sandy marshland. It's now the **Natuurreservaat (Nature Reserve) Het Zwin** ⭐, Graaf Leon Lippensdreef 8 (𝄢 **050/60-70-86**; www. zwin.be), east of Het Zoute.

The reserve covers just 150 hectares (370 acres), yet it's one of the most important remaining wetland breeding zones for birds on Europe's northwest coast, and one of the Belgium's last scraps of coastal wilderness. Among the 100 migratory and indigenous species that enjoy the reserve's facilities are avocets, storks, snipes, plovers, geese, and ducks. The spongy soil nurtures an amazing variety of vegetation, making the reserve a colorful place to explore, especially in summer, when it's tinged with lavender.

There's an aviary near the entrance; the **Vlindertuin (Butterfly Garden);** a restaurant, the **Châlet du Zwin;** and a bookstore. The reserve is open from Easter to September daily from 9am to 7pm; and from October to Easter, Thursday to Tuesday from 9am to 5pm. Admission is 5.20€ ($6.50) for adults, 4.40€ ($5.50) for seniors, 3.20€ ($4) for children ages 6 to 11, and free for children under 6. Combination tickets are available for the reserve and the Butterfly Garden.

dressed-to-the-nines clientele. Two nightclubs and a ballroom feature leading European entertainers. The magnificent Salle Magritte dining room is a tribute to surrealist painter René Magritte, whose paintings have been transformed into gigantic murals that adorn the walls. You'll need to be decked out in dressy attire and bring your passport. The minimum age is 21 and admission is free.

A cure for all your ills may be awaiting you at **Thalassa Center** ⭐, a combination spa, fitness center, and gymnasium in the Hôtel La Réserve (see below), Elizabetlaan 158 (𝄢 **050/60-06-12;** www.la-reserve.be). In the "thermal institute," you can indulge in hot sea-mud baths and other seawater treatments, work out on a variety of exercise equipment, swim in the seawater pool, or laze in the sauna. If you're a guest at the hotel, admission to the fitness club comes with your room rate; others pay 9€ ($11) plus charges based on any additional treatments, which range from 31€ to 65€ ($39–$81).

Golfers should find they've come to the right place. The **Royal Zoute Golf Club,** Caddiespad 14, Knokke (𝄢 **050/60-12-27;** www.zoute.be), has two 18-hole courses beside the dunes and accepts visiting players. Greens fees (visitors must be a member of a golf club) are 95€ ($119) for the championship course, and 55€ ($69) for the executive course; players under 21 get a 50% discount.

WHERE TO STAY

Cosmipolis ⭐ Just a block from the beach, the elegant Cosmipolis rubs elbows with upper-stratosphere stores in Het Zoute. Its guest rooms have recently been refurbished in bright colors, with tartan-style curtains. There's a moderately priced restaurant and an attractive bar. Three of the rooms have kitchenettes. Most of the rooms have balconies.

Kustlaan 353, 8300 Knokke-Heist. © **050/61-16-17.** Fax 050/62-04-05. www.cosmipolishotel.be. 25 units. 136€–227€ ($170–$284) double. Rates include buffet breakfast. AE, DC, MC, V. Parking 10€ ($13). **Amenities:** Bar. *In room:* A/C, TV w/pay movies, dataport, minibar, hair dryer, safe.

Hôtel La Réserve ✨ Although this hotel near the beachfront is quite large, it manages to maintain a comfortable, almost country, air. It's home to Knokke's health spa, the **Thalassa Center** (see above). The guest rooms, 80 with balconies, are spacious, modern, and comfortable. The hotel has a very good restaurant, **La Sirène,** and a lounge bar.

Elizabetlaan 160 (facing the casino, at Albertstrand), 8300 Knokke-Heist. © **050/61-06-06.** Fax 050/60-37-06. www.la-reserve.be. 110 units. 237€–376€ ($296–$470) double; 460€–544€ ($575–$680) suite. AE, DC, MC, V. Free parking. **Amenities:** Restaurant (French); lounge; bar; indoor pool; tennis courts; health club and sauna. *In room:* TV, minibar.

Parkhotel The family-run Parkhotel, 2 blocks from the beach, offers well-appointed guest rooms that are furnished in a bright, modern style.

Elizabetlaan 204 (at Duinbergen), 8301 Knokke-Heist. © **050/60-09-01.** Fax 050/62-36-08. www.parkhotel knokke.be. 14 units. 78€–98€ ($98–$123) double. Rates include continental breakfast. AE, MC, V. Free parking. **Amenities:** Restaurant (French/Belgian); bar. *In room:* TV.

WHERE TO DINE

Aquilon ✨ FRENCH/SEAFOOD This ground-floor restaurant on Albertplein in the center city is the most outstanding and most elegant in the area. Allow plenty of time to savor such specialties as veal with mushrooms and truffles or lobster Marguerite.

Elizabetlaan 6. © **050/60-12-74.** www.aquilon.be. Reservations required. Main courses 15€–27€ ($19–$34); fixed-price lunch 25€ ($31); fixed-price menus 35€–71€ ($44–$89). AE, DC, MC, V. Thurs–Mon noon–2pm and 6:30–9pm (open Wed during school vacations).

Panier d'Or ✨ SEAFOOD/BELGIAN Seafood stars at this waterfront restaurant, a medium-size place with elegant decor that's reminiscent of an ocean liner's restaurant. Menu dishes range from straightforward steaks to expensive fish dishes; the fish soup is a local legend. Standard menu items include lobster, cod, sole, and North Sea shrimps, but if you're feeling aristocratic, try the caviar on toast.

Zeedijk-Knokke 659. © **050/60-31-89.** www.panierdor.com. Main courses 16€–46€ ($11–$18); fixed-price menus 25€–35€ ($31–$44). AE, DC, MC, V. June–Sept daily noon–2:30pm and 6:30–9pm; Oct–May Wed–Mon noon–2:30pm and 6:30–9pm.

Ter Dycken ✨ FRENCH/BELGIAN This farmhouse-style restaurant has a solid reputation on the coast. The wide-ranging menu emphasizes seafood. Even a straightforward dish like the *gebakken zeetong* (grilled sole) with french fries and salad comes out tasting pretty fine. Turbot, grilled lobster, and Iranian caviar are excellent seafood

---

Tips **Great Green Way**

From Knokke-Heist, you can drive or cycle the 48km (30-mile) *Riante Polder-route*, a signposted route that takes you through wooded parks, past the Zwin, into polder farm country and along canals, to Damme.

Tips The Sea on a Plate

Many seacoast restaurants specialize in seafood, fresh off the boats from catches landed daily and prepared by chefs who have a long tradition of treating the fruits of the sea with respect. Local specialties include *sole à l'Ostendaise* (Ostend sole), *waterzooï op Oostendse wijze* (a creamy, souplike fish stew), gray North Sea *garnaalen* (shrimps), and *garnaalkroketten* (croquettes made with those shrimps).

---

choices, while lamb cutlet is the best choice among the meats. A fireplace and filled bookcases add to the atmosphere.

Kalvekeetdijk 137. © 050/60-80-23. www.terdycken.be Main courses 20€–59€ ($25–$51); fixed-price menus 35€–72€ ($44–$90). AE, DC, MC, V. Wed–Sun 10am–3pm and 6–10pm.

3 Oostduinkerke

20km (12 miles) SW of Ostend

Oostduinkerke and the neighboring resorts of **Koksijde-Bad and Sint-Idesbald,** with 8km (5 miles) of beach between them, are family oriented yet hold much to interest art and nature lovers.

ESSENTIALS
GETTING THERE Ostend has the nearest **rail** station on the line from Brussels via Ghent and Bruges to the seacoast. Frequent **Coast Tram** service goes from Ostend. By **car,** take N34, which runs along the coast.

VISITOR INFORMATION **Toerisme Koksijde-Oostduinkerke** is at Leopold II Laan 2, 8670 Koksijde (© **058/53-21-21;** fax 058/53-21-22; www.koksijde.be).

WHAT TO SEE & DO
Oostduinkerke's chief attraction is its wide **beach** ⚓, the site of a special activity you find nowhere else along the coast: On days when the weather is reasonable, a group of stalwart, yellow-slickered gentlemen mount sturdy horses and wade into the surf at low tide to drag nets behind them, ensnaring large quantities of *garnaalen*—tiny but tasty gray North Sea shrimps. These *garnaalvissers* **(shrimp fishermen)** follow a tradition that dates back centuries. Much of their catch goes into the kitchens of cafes owned by these same horsemen, but if you go to the National Fishery Museum's next-door neighbor, cafe **De Peerdevisser,** Pastoor Schmitzstraat 5 (© **058/51-32-57**), soon after the fishermen return, you can purchase the just-caught, just-boiled delicacies by the sackful.

Sand-yachting—a form of overland sailing in a sailboat with wheels—is popular at Oostduinkerke. At several places on the beach you can rent the colorful vehicles and participate in the fun. Other beach activities include summer festivals (get a list from the tourist office to see what's on during your visit), **sandcastle competitions,** and **horseback riding** on the strand. Horses can be rented from **Hacienda,** Weststraat 9 (© **058/51-69-50**), for 20€ ($25) for 1½ hours.

Oostduinkerke's beach is backed by impressive sand dunes, one of which, De Hoge Blekker, is the highest dune in the country, at over 30m (100 ft.). Both **dune hiking** and **climbing** are popular.

Abdijmuseum Ten Duinen 1138 (Abbey of the Dunes 1138 Museum) 🔾 During much of the 12th century, this Cistercian abbey was a regional center of culture. The abbey lay in ruins for centuries. Excavations begun in 1949 have revealed objects that shed light on coastal history and the development of the abbey. A small museum presents exhibits displaying these finds. Nearby, the large abbey farmstead Ten Bogaerde includes a 12th-century barn that is now an agricultural school. It's typical of the large farm holdings of the ancient abbeys.

Koninklijke Prinslaan 6–8, Koksijde. ⓒ 058/53-39-50. www.tenduinen.be. Admission 5€ ($6.25) adults, 1€ ($1.25) children 6–18, free for children under 6. Mon–Fri 10am–6pm; Sun 2–6pm.

Nationaal Visserijmuseum (National Fishery Museum) This museum has maps of sea routes followed by local fishing fleets, and displays fishing implements used through the centuries, sea paintings, a fishing-harbor model, a North Sea aquarium, and a collection of fishing-boat models from A.D. 800 to the present. The interior of a typical fisherman's tavern is another highlight. *Note:* A new building to house the museum was being constructed at the time of writing, with no reopening time announced. Call ahead or check the website before visiting.

Pastoor Schmitzstraat 5 (in a small park at the rear of the Town Hall), Oostduinkerke. ⓒ 058/51-24-68. www.visserijmuseum.be. Admission 3€ ($3.75) adults, 1.50€ ($1.90) students, 1€ ($1.25) children 6–12, free for children under 6. Sept–June Tues–Sun 10am–noon and 2–6pm; July–Aug daily 10am–noon and 2–6pm.

Paul Delvaux Museum 🔾 The nephew of the surrealist artist Paul Delvaux has turned a Flemish farmhouse into a modernized museum displaying his uncle's works. Delvaux's adulation of the undraped female form is conveyed in many of the paintings, as is his love of trains and railway stations (though it's hard to see the connection).

Paul Delvauxlaan 42, Sint-Idesbald. ⓒ 058/52-12-29. www.delvauxmuseum.com. Admission 5€ ($6.25) adults, 4€ ($5) seniors and students, free for children under 10. July–Aug daily 10:30am–6:30pm; Apr–June and Apr–Sept Tues–Sun 10:30am–5:30pm; Oct–Dec Thurs–Sun and holidays 10:30am–5:30pm; Jan (school vacations only) 10:30am–5:30pm. Closed Jan 1, Dec 25.

WHERE TO STAY

Hotel Terlinck This modern hotel in the center of Koksijde offers a friendly welcome and a high level of comfort. Many rooms have a sea view, and all are furnished in a bright, contemporary style. The fine restaurant is popular locally.

Terlinckplein 17 (at Zeedijk), 8670 Koksijde. ⓒ 058/52-00-00. Fax 058/51-76-15. 37 units. 85€–115€ ($106–$144) double. Rates include buffet breakfast. AE, DC, MC, V. Free parking. **Amenities:** Restaurant (seafood); laundry service; dry cleaning. *In room:* A/C, TV, minibar, coffeemaker.

WHERE TO DINE

Bécassine 🔾 SEAFOOD This is a homey kind of place that serves great food at reasonable prices—but only as complete four- or five-course menus, not a la carte. Tasty North Sea shrimp is the star of the show. Try it in shrimp soup or stuffed in potatoes and pastries. The bouillabaisse is great, too. There are only seven tables here.

Rozenlaan 20, Oostduinkerke. ⓒ 058/52-11-00. Fixed-price menus 40€–50€ ($50–$63). Reservations not required. AE, DC, MC, V. Fri–Tues noon–2pm and 7–9pm.

4 De Panne

26km (16 miles) SW of Ostend; 7km (4 miles) SW of Oostduinkerke

De Panne, near Dunkirk, is Belgium's closest coastal point to France and England. During World War I, it was here that King Albert I clung to Belgian resistance against

---

Moments Sand-Yachting at De Panne

Just like at Oostduinkerke, the long wide beaches, firm sand, and frequent high winds at De Panne make for ideal conditions for sand-yachting. Rental companies on the beach outfit you in a wet suit and a crash helmet, give a few rudimentary tips on how to handle the vehicles, push you out into the wind— and off you go. The yachts are unwieldy to handle at first, and heavier than they look, so maintaining stability can be difficult until you get the hang of it. But once you do, it's exhilarating.

German occupying forces. But its most famous moment came in 1940, during World War II, when its sandy beach was the site of the massive evacuation of beleaguered Allied forces carried out by a makeshift armada of small craft gathered from boat own-ers around England. When "the miracle of Dunkirk" was over, almost all the soldiers were saved, and the 13km (7½-mile) stretch of beach between Dunkirk and De Panne was a mass of military litter. It's a little-recognized fact that the British commander, Lord Gort, was not headquartered in Dunkirk but here in De Panne.

Today, that wide beach—.5km (¼ mile) at low tide—and spectacular sand dunes bring hordes of visitors to De Panne each year. The dunes are made all the more sce-nic by wooded areas that turn them into a wonderland of greenery banding the white sands of the beach and the gray sea beyond.

ESSENTIALS

GETTING THERE   Ostend has the nearest **rail** station on the direct line from Brussels via Ghent and Bruges to the coast. A station just south of the town, at Adinkerke–De Panne, is served by trains from Bruges and Ypres. De Panne is the southern terminus of the **coast tram** line that extends north to Knokke-Heist. By **car,** take the N34 coast road from any of the coastal resorts; from Bruges, Ghent, and Brussels, take E40 to Veurne and then go north a short distance on N8.

VISITOR INFORMATION   **Toerisme De Panne** is at Stadhuis (Town Hall) Zee-laan 21, 8660 De Panne (© **058/42-18-18;** fax 058/42-16-17; www.depanne.be).

WHAT TO SEE & DO

A stroll through De Panne's tree-lined residential streets, with rows of delightful Art Nouveau villas left over from another era, and traditional fishermen's cottages still in use (on Veurnestraat), is a delight. But outdoors recreation is what people come to De Panne for. With all those dunes to explore and the beach for sunning, swimming, horseback riding, and sand-yachting, no one's ever short of things to do.

NATURE RESERVES

Four nature areas around De Panne are all free and open daily. The most important, **Westhoekreservaat (Westhoek Reserve)** ✦✦, 340 hectares (840 acres) on the west-ern edge of De Panne, is the largest dunes landscape on the Belgian coast. Although vacation developments squeeze right up against its boundary, once you're immersed in this broad vista of sand, dubbed "the Sahara," you'll find it hard to believe it's in the same country as the overdeveloped seacoast. Vegetation varies from full-grown trees to scrubby shrubs. In the springtime, wildflowers blossom among the sands; in winter, shallow rainwater pools accumulate. The dunes change both their shape and position as contrary winds imperceptibly move the grains beneath your feet.

You're obliged to tour on four signposted footpaths, because tramping on the dunes causes erosion, scares off nesting birds, and damages the fragile life-support system of rare indigenous plants, including orchids—sadly, many visitors ignore this stipulation. Archaeologists have found traces of a Roman saltworks, and at a closed animal reserve are Shetland ponies, Highland cattle, and wild horses, in an attempt to mimic the scene from a century ago. The dunes continue across the border into France, in an additional 225 hectares (555 acres) called Les Dunes de Perroquet.

The 93-hectare (230-acre) **Cabourduinen (Cabour Dunes),** straddling the French border, is another area that provides nature walks. **Calmeynbos (Calmeyn Wood),** which covers only 45 hectares (110 acres), is the loving legacy of one man, Maurice Calmeyn, who in 1903 began to plant trees here in order to preserve the dunes. Some 25 varieties of his trees are thriving today.

East of De Panne is the 60-hectare (150-acre) **Oosthoekduinen (Oosthoek Dunes),** which has more dunes and woods.

For detailed information about all these reserves, and for guided tours, go to the **Bezoekerscentrum De Nachtegaal (Nightingale Visitor Center),** Olmendreef 2, De Panne (© **058/42-21-51;** www.vbncdenachtegaal.be).

ESPECIALLY FOR KIDS

Plopsaland *Kids*   It's instant enchantment for children at this adventure park, where a multitude of delightful attractions will appeal to the whole family. There's Elfira (a fairy-tale wonderland), the animal park, a jungle fantasy parrot show, a water symphony, Carioca (all sorts of playground activities), and Phantom Guild, with three different fun fairs filled with rides.

De Pannelaan 68, Adinkerke. © **058/42-02-02.** www.plopsaland.be. Admission July–Aug, 14€ ($18) adults, 13€ ($16) seniors and visitors with disabilities, 5€ ($6.25) children under 1m (3 ft., 3in.). July–Aug daily 10am–6pm; other months generally Wed–Sun 10am–6pm, but with many variations; call ahead or check website for calendar.

WHERE TO STAY

Hotel Donny   Set among the dunes, about 150m (492 ft.) from the beach, the hotel attracts you by the scenery. Some of the rooms have balconies facing the sea, and all are comfortably furnished in a style that complements the contemporary look of the building.

Donnylaan 17. © **058/41-18-00.** Fax 058/42-09-78. 45 units. www.hoteldonny.com. 70€–125€ ($88–$156) double. Rates include buffet breakfast. AE, DC, MC, V. Free parking. **Amenities:** Restaurant (seafood); bar; lounge; outdoor pool; health club; Internet lounge. *In room:* TV, minibar, hair dryer.

WHERE TO DINE

Le Fox *★★* FRENCH/SEAFOOD   Although pricey, this is the best restaurant in town. The Buyens family has upheld the stellar reputation of its Michelin-star establishment into a second generation, with son Stéphane now at the helm in the kitchen.

Tips Cheap Eats

On Nieuwpoortlaan in De Panne there's a row of fast-food places that sell mussels and *frites* (fries) from 5€ ($6.25).

Most menu items change seasonally, but a strong contingent of seafood offerings is fairly stable. Turbot with a variety of minced mushrooms and a fennel-and-tomato ragout is a good choice; so are salmon-and-asparagus fondue, and one of the French regional meat courses. Unlike most restaurants along the coast, Le Fox leaves mussels off the menu but amply makes up for this omission with oysters, scampi, *langoustines* (spiny lobster), and shrimps. Thoughtfully selected French wines from admirable wineries fill the wine cellar. The rustic interior has an open fire.

In the Hostellerie Le Fox, Walckiersstraat 2 (off the seafront). ℰ 058/41-28-55. www.hotelfox.be. Main courses 25€–49€ ($31–$61); fixed-price menus 50€–125€ ($63–$156). AE, DC, MC, V. Wed–Sun noon–2:30pm; Tues–Sun 7–9:45pm.

5 Ypres *⚹*

110km (69 miles) W of Brussels; 45km (28 miles) SW of Bruges

Ypres (Ieper in Dutch), set among the low, gentle slopes of the West Flanders *Heuvelland* (Hill Country), owed its early prosperity to a textile industry that peaked in the 13th century. Over the centuries, the handsome town was victimized by one war after another and became a ghost of its former self. By far the most devastating was World War I (1914–18)—the "war to end all wars"—when hardly a brick was left standing after 4 years of violent bombardments. Many visitors come to Ypres (pronounced *ee-pruh*) to pay homage to those who fell on the surrounding battlefields and rest in the many military cemeteries on the green breast of the Heuvelland.

Brick by brick, the town's most important medieval buildings have been reconstructed exactly as they were, carefully following original plans. This accounts for the pristine look of venerable monuments, instead of the moldering stones you might expect.

ESSENTIALS

GETTING THERE   Because it lies in a corner of Belgium that's awkward to reach, some visitors combine a visit to Ypres with a trip to Bruges or the nearby seacoast resorts. **Trains** depart hourly from Bruges. Look out for the Dutch name, Ieper, on the station name board. The trip takes around 1 hour and you may need to change trains at Kortrijk. Going by **bus** from Bruges is a bad option unless you have time to take in every haystack and hamlet along the way. By **car** from Bruges, take A17/E403 south to the Kortrijk interchange, and then A19 west; from the coast at De Panne, take N8 south.

VISITOR INFORMATION   **Toerisme Ieper** is in the Lakenhalle, Grote Markt 34, 8900 Ieper (ℰ **057/23-92-00;** fax 057/23-92-75; www.ieper.be). The office is open April to September, Monday to Friday from 9am to 6pm, and weekends from 10am to 6pm; October to March, Monday to Friday from 9am to 5pm, and weekends from 10am to 5pm.

GETTING AROUND   Sights in the town are easily reached on foot, though if you're arriving by train you can save time by taking a **De Lijn** (ℰ **070/22-02-00;** www.delijn.be) bus to the Grote Markt from the bus station adjoining the rail station. Taxis often are available at the rail station, or call **Taxi Leo** (ℰ **057/20-04-13**). You can rent bicycles (Apr–Sept) from the rail station for 9€ ($11) daily.

SEEING THE SIGHTS

The gabled guild houses and patrician mansions around the Grote Markt are occupied now mostly by restaurants, cafes, and hotels. At the western end of this main central square, Ypres's medieval wealth is reflected in its extravagant Gothic **Lakenhalle (Cloth Hall)** 🏛️🏛️. The original, constructed between 1250 and 1304 along the Ieperlee River, which has long since been banished underground, was blown to bits between 1914 and 1918 and reconstructed with painstaking care in subsequent decades, though the work wasn't finished until 1967. Gilded statues adorn the roof, and a statue of Our Lady of Thuyne, the patron of Ypres, stands over the main entrance, the Donkerpoort. Inside, the spacious first-floor halls where wool and cloth were once sold are now used for exhibits; the upper-floor storage space houses the In Flanders Fields Museum (see below).

From the center of the Lakenhalle, the **Belfort (Belfry),** which has four corner turrets and a spire and encloses a 49-bell carillon, soars 70m (228 ft.). You get fine views over the town from here, provided you're willing and able to climb 264 interior steps to the upper gallery. Carillon concerts chime out on Saturday from 11am to noon and Sunday from 4 to 5pm.

A Flemish Renaissance extension at the eastern end, the arcaded Nieuwerck (1624), houses Ypres's **Stadhuis (Town Hall).** You can visit the council chamber and view its fine stained-glass window Monday to Friday from 8:30 to 11:45am when the council is not in session. Admission is free.

The graceful spire of the 13th-century Gothic **Sint-Martenskathedraal (St. Martin's Cathedral)** in Sint-Maartensplein is a town landmark. Inside is the tomb of Flemish theologian Cornelius Jansen (1585–1638), a bishop of Ypres whose doctrine of predestination, Jansenism, rocked the Catholic church and was condemned as heretical by the pope in 1642. Britain's armed forces donated the superb stained-glass rose window in honor of Belgium's King Albert I, the World War I "soldier king." Note the eight alabaster statues on the baptistery chapel screen. The cathedral is open to visitors daily from 8am to 8pm, except during services (when it's open to worshipers). Admission is free.

Behind St. Martin's, the Celtic cross **Munster Memorial** honors Irish soldiers killed in World War I. Across the way, British and Commonwealth veterans made the Anglican **St. George's Memorial Church,** Elverdingsestraat (📞 **057/21-56-85**), dating from 1929, a shrine to the memory of their fallen comrades. Wall-mounted banners and pew kneelers decorated with colorful corps and regimental badges add an almost festive air to what might otherwise be a somber scene. The church is open daily from 9:30am to dusk (4pm in winter). Admission is free.

At Meensepoort (Menen Gate), on the famous marble arch of the **Missing Memorial** 🏛️, you can read the names of 54,896 British troops who fell around Ypres between 1914 and August 15, 1917, and who have no known grave. Every evening at 8 o'clock, traffic through the gate is stopped while Ypres firefighters in dress uniform sound the plaintive notes of *The Last Post* on silver bugles donated by the British Legion, in a brief but moving ceremony that dates from 1928. Adjacent to this, the **Australian Memorial** honors the more than 43,000 Aussies killed in the Ypres salient.

The impressive 17th-century **ramparts** designed by the French military engineer Vauban, fronted by a moat that once surrounded the town, are among the few structures not demolished during World War I. You can reach them via stairs at the Menen Gate and walk around a pleasant park to **Rijselsepoort (Lille Gate)** to visit **Ramparts Cemetery,** a British war cemetery with a green lawn and just 193 headstones. Next to Rijselsepoort at Rijselsestraat 204 is a timber **house** from 1575; streets hereabouts are lined with reconstructed 17th-century facades.

A STANDOUT WAR (OR PEACE) MUSEUM

In Flanders Fields Museum ✮✮ "War is hell" is the clear message of this superb interactive museum. No series of dry and dusty historical exhibits, it is as much a peace museum as a war museum—it could scarcely be otherwise, considering the awesome slaughter on all sides that took place on the battlefields around the town, which makes any talk about winners and losers, or of glory, seem obscene. The museum won the 2000 Museum Award of the Council of Europe for its innovative presentation.

Lakenhalle, Grote Markt 34. ℂ 057/23-92-00. www.inflandersfields.be. Admission 7.50€ ($9.40) adults, 3.50€ ($4.40) children 7–15, free for children under 7. Apr–Sept daily 10am–6pm; Oct–Mar Tues–Sun 10am–5pm (closed for 3 weeks after New Year's). Closed Jan 1, Dec 25.

OTHER SIGHTS AROUND TOWN

The fine arts **Hotel-Museum Arthur Merghelynck,** Arthur Merghelynckstraat 2A (ℂ 057/22-85-84), in a rococo and neoclassical manor house from 1744, is furnished with Louis XV and XVI antiques. Its elegant rooms house a collection of silverware and Chinese and Japanese porcelain. Even the coach house is pressed into service, to exhibit items associated with the town's medieval cloth trade. A highlight of the collection is a painting, *The Vanity of Riches* (ca. 1637–38), attributed tentatively in part to Rubens, and equally tentatively believed to have been commissioned by Ypres's heretical Bishop Jansenius. It contains images depicting expensive objects and implying their transitory nature. The museum is open by appointment only, Monday to Saturday from 10am to noon and 2 to 5pm. Admission is 2.50€ ($3.15) for adults, 0.50€ (65¢) for children ages 7 to 15, and free for children under 7.

The **Godshuis Belle Museum,** Rijselsestraat 38 (ℂ 057/22-85-84), in an almshouse from 1276, counts among its treasures the *Virgin and Child* by the anonymous Master of 1420. Other exhibits include religious paintings from the 16th to the 19th centuries, by artists such as Nicolaas Van de Velde and Gilles Lamoot. In addition, you can view pewter, lace, and furniture. The museum is open April to October, Tuesday to Sunday from 10am to noon and 2 to 6pm. Admission is 2.50€ ($3.15) for adults and free for children under 15.

In the Sint-Jansgodshuis, a reconstructed almshouse from 1270, the **Stedelijk Museum (Municipal Museum),** Ieperleestraat 31 (ℂ 057/22-85-82), recounts the town's history through paintings, antique maps, and sculpture. A fine arts section has sculpture, silverware, porcelain, and more. The museum is open April to October

---

⟨Moments⟩ Flying Felines

Every 3 years on the second Sunday in May, Ypres celebrates a colorful pageant, the *Kattestoet* (Festival of the Cats) ✮, when hundreds of cats are thrown by the town jester from the Belfry to the crowds of people down below. Outraged cat lovers can simmer down; these days the flying felines are fluffy toys. The custom originated centuries ago when the great Lakenhalle attracted thousands of mice, and cats by the hundreds were imported to eliminate them. Once the cloth was sold, the cats themselves became a problem. After due consideration, officials came up with the brilliant solution of flinging them from the Belfry. That tradition evolved into the revelry of today's lively carnival and procession. The next *Kattestoet* is in 2009.

> (*Kids*) **A Great Theme Park**
>
> If you're traveling with children, check out **Bellewaerde Park** (⊛, Meenseweg 497, Ieper-Zillebeke (© **057/46-86-86;** www.bellewaerde.be). This theme park combines familiar white-knuckle rides like the Screaming Eagle with a wildlife reserve, various re-created natural environments, and a zone called Pepinoland for the tiniest tots. Ironically, Bellewaerde is set in what was once the wasteland of the World War I front lines. The park is open April to June, daily from 10am to 6pm (7pm weekends); July daily from 10am to 7pm; August daily from 10am to 9pm; September to mid-October, weekends from 10am to 6pm. Admission is 25€ ($31) for adults, 22€ ($27) for children between 1m and 1.4m (3 ft., 3 in.–4 ft., 7 in.), and free for children under 1m (3 ft., 3 in).

Tuesday to Sunday from 10am to 12:30pm and 2 to 6pm; November to March Tuesday to Sunday from 10am to 12:30pm and 2 to 5pm. Admission is 2.50€ ($3.15) for adults, 0.50€ (65¢) for children ages 7 to 15, and free for children under 7.

GUIDED TOURS

Local companies **Flanders Battlefield Tours,** Slachthuisstraat 58 (© **057/36-04-60;** www.ypres-fbt.be), and **Salient Tours,** c/o British Grenadier Bookshop, Meensestraat 5 (© **057/21-46-57;** www.salienttours.com), both run minibus tours of the battlefields and memorials, departing from the Grote Markt or the Menen Gate, and ranging from 2 hours to half a day. Prices are from 20€ to 25€ ($25–$31). The tourist office can furnish a package for the In Flanders Fields Route, a self-guided tour of 80km (50 miles) on signposted roads that covers all the main sights.

For a less ambitious, 1- to 2-hour self-guided tour by car, head out of town through the Menen Gate and take N8 to Canadalaan, close to Bellewaerde Park (see below), at the end of which is a preserved stretch of trenches complete with shell holes and shattered trees in **Sanctuary Wood.** Amazingly, there's almost no other remaining sign of that vast network of muddy, waterlogged trenches—the once-tortured landscape has been reclaimed by agriculture and nature. Nearby stands the **Canadian Monument** on **Hill 62.**

From here, return to N8. Then, take N332 and N303 through Zonnebeke in the direction of Passendale, to the **Tyne Cot Commonwealth Military Cemetery** and its 12,000 graves surmounted by a Cross of Remembrance in white Portland stone. Finally, to be evenhanded, head west from Zonnebeke to the far side of Langemark and the 44,000 graves at the **Deutscher Soldatenfriedhof (German Military Cemetery).** N313 from Langemark takes you straight back into Ypres.

WHERE TO STAY

Old Tom   This family-owned hotel has a prime location in the center of town and reasonable rates. With only nine rooms, it fills up fast in summer. The building has plenty of antique style and the guest rooms are comfortable and nicely, if plainly, furnished. A cafe-restaurant on the first floor has an outdoor terrace and serves regional specialties, like eels, in addition to common Flemish menu dishes.

Grote Markt 8, 8900 Ieper. ℂ **057/20-15-41**. Fax 057/21-91-20. www.oldtom.be. 9 units. 64€ ($80) double. Rates include continental breakfast. MC, V. Parking 7€ ($8.75). **Amenities:** Restaurant (Flemish); bar. *In room:* TV.

Regina ★ On the outside, the building that houses this small, neo-Gothic–style hotel looks as if it dates from Ypres's medieval heyday, but like most of the town it was raised anew out of the rubble left behind by World War I. When you enter, you leave the somber past at the door and step into an ambience as cool as a modern-art museum. The guest rooms actually do take modern artists and performers, like James Ensor, René Magritte, and Jacques Brel, as their theme. Those at the front have views of the Lakenhalle and the Grote Markt fountain. The invariably busy Regina restaurant serves West Flanders regional cuisine.

Koning Albert I 45 (at Grote Markt), 8900 Ieper. ℂ **057/21-88-88**. Fax 057/21-90-20. www.hotelregina.be. 17 units. 75€–100€ ($94–$125) double. Rates include buffet breakfast. AE, DC, MC, V. Limited street parking. **Amenities:** Restaurant (Flemish); bar. *In room:* TV, minibar (some rooms).

WHERE TO DINE

De Waterpoort ★ FLEMISH You'll find this stylish restaurant in the north of town beyond a moat. Decorated in a spare, modern style, it's quite different from the traditional type of eatery in Ypres. It has a light, open dining room and a garden with an alfresco terrace and a play area for children. The menu offers seafood and updated versions of Flemish dishes, some of them cooked on an open grill, and a fine Australian entrecôte steak and vegetarian options.

Brugseweg 43 (6 blocks north of Grote Markt on Diksmuidestraat and Arthur Stoffelstraat). ℂ **057/20-54-52**. www.waterpoort.be. Main courses 14€–23€ ($18–$29); fixed-price menu 32€ ($40). AE, MC, V. Thurs–Sat and Mon–Tues noon–2:30pm; Thurs–Tues 6–10:30pm.

Ter Posterie ★ FLEMISH This traditional cafe-restaurant, down a narrow alleyway off Arthur Merghelynckstraat, serves basic Flemish fare. Look out for mussels in season, sole, and steak with french fries. These are accompanied by no less than 170 different Belgian beers, including the local—and expensive—Poperings Hommelbier, and all six of Belgium's Trappist beers, among them Westmalle Dubbel, the only Trappist beer that's on tap. Weather permitting, you can dine and drink outdoors in the courtyard. The plainly furnished interior is convivial when it's busy but can seem somewhat gloomy out of season.

Rijselsestraat 57 (off Grote Markt). ℂ **057/20-05-80**. Main courses 8€–20€ ($10–$25). No credit cards. Thurs–Tues 11am–2am.

Liège, the Meuse River & Hainaut

The steep-sided Meuse River valley has long been an important tourist area. After rolling across northern France, the Meuse takes an L-shaped course through Belgium, and then crosses into Holland, where its name changes to the Maas. Along its Belgian banks are historic towns, strikingly situated châteaux and abbeys, impressive scenery—and aging industrial plants and smokestacks that spoil views, particularly around Liège.

It's best to do the Meuse Valley as a driving tour, beginning at Liège and heading upstream to Namur, Huy, and Dinant. But it's possible to tour by train and bus, thanks to frequent and fast connections. In that case, you should base yourself in either Liège or Namur.

From Dinant, you can head east into the Ardennes (see chapter 10), or go west across Hainaut, the "Green Province" that stretches along most of Belgium's border with France. Much of the landscape is lush and verdant. Hainaut has a rich history and is the repository of great art treasures from the past. Tournai and Mons, the sites of many antiquities and museums, draw visitors like magnets, as do the province's lovely lakes.

1 Liège ⓐ

89km (55 miles) SE of Brussels; 27km (17 miles) NE of Huy; 54km (33 miles) NE of Namur

Fervent, lively Liège (pop. 160,000) is known as *La Cité Ardente* (the Passionate City). Nowadays it exudes in part the aura of an aging industrial gloom, but that seems to fade next to its gracefully down-at-the-heels 19th-century monuments, and remnants from the time of its powerful ruling prince-bishops. Liège has always had an independent spirit. Its 12th-century charter decreed that the *pauvre homme en sa maison est roi* (the poor man is king in his home)—an attitude still vividly alive in Liège today. The city straddles the Meuse, with a backdrop of Ardennes foothills.

ESSENTIALS

GETTING THERE Trains frequently run to Liège from Brussels, Antwerp, Maastricht, Cologne, and Luxembourg; and on the Thalys high-speed train, via Brussels, from Paris, Amsterdam, and Cologne. Belgian Railways train information is available at ⓒ **02/528-28-28;** www.sncb.be. The main station is **Gare Guillemins,** rue des Guillemins, just south of the center city. The smaller, more centrally located Liège Palais station, on rue de Bruxelles, is used by some local and connecting trains.

The main bus station is outside Gare Guillemins. Regional **buses** arrive from other places along the Meuse, such as Namur and Dinant (and Maastricht in Holland), and

---

Fun Fact The Town Mascot

Liège's most beloved symbol is Tchantchès (François in Walloon dialect), a pup-pet who has been the spokesman of the streets since the 1850s. He's usually dressed in a blue smock, patched trousers, tasseled floppy hat, and red scarf, and he's constantly either grumbling or espousing every noble cause in sight—the personification of your average, everyday Liégeois. A statue of Tchantchès stands on place de l'Yser.

---

from points in the Ardennes, like Spa. Bus information is available from **TEC** (✆ **04/ 361-94-44;** www.infotec.be).

By **car** from Brussels, take A3/E40 east; from Namur, take either A15/E42 or the scenic riverside N90.

VISITOR INFORMATION   The city's **Office du Tourisme** is at Féronstrée 92, 4000 Liège (✆ **04/221-92-21;** fax 04/221-92-22; www.liege.be). It's open Monday to Friday from 9am to 5pm.

CITY LAYOUT   The **Old City,** which has most of Liège's sightseeing attractions, and nighttime entertainment in the student-filled **Carré** district, is on the west bank of the Meuse, bounded by rue de l'Université, boulevard de la Sauvenière, and rue Pont-d'Avroy. On the east bank, the **Outremeuse** ("Across the Meuse") district has a big choice of lively bars, discothèques, and cabarets. Along the river are tree-lined walkways.

GETTING AROUND   Sightseeing highlights in the Old City are close together, so downtown Liège is easily walkable, though traffic can be frenetic. **Buses,** useful for getting to sights outside the Old City, cost 1.30€ ($1.65) for a ride. You can buy dis-counted 8-ride tickets from booths at major route stops and at the rail stations. The excellent bus system is not hard to figure out, since many stops have network maps posted. Place St-Lambert, an important interchange point, is reached from Gare Guillemins by lines 1, 2, 3, and 4. City bus information is available from **TEC** (✆ **04/361-94-44;** www.infotec.be).

For a taxi, call **Liège-Tax** (✆ **0800-32-200** or 04/367-50-40).

WHAT TO SEE & DO

Monumental **place St-Lambert** and neighboring **place du Marché,** surrounded by buildings in the Mosan Renaissance style, are the hub of Liège's daily life. This is where you find the 1698-vintage **Perron Fountain,** the city's symbol of freedom; and the 18th-century **Hôtel de Ville (Town Hall),** which has sculptures by Jean Delcour in its lobby. French-inspired local revolutionaries in 1795 destroyed the sumptuous Gothic Cathédrale St-Lambert (St. Lambert's Cathedral) on place St-Lambert, a sym-bol of the prince-bishopric's hated *ancien régime.* Only its outline is preserved in mod-ern paving. Excavations on the square has revealed the foundations of a Roman villa and traces of the early medieval city, from the 7th century.

The prince-bishops, who ruled the city and the surrounding territory from 980 to 1794, constructed the world's largest secular Gothic building: the **Palais des Prince-Evêques (Prince-Bishops Palace),** on place St-Lambert. Of primary interest are the two inner courtyards, one lined with 60 carved columns depicting the follies of

Liège

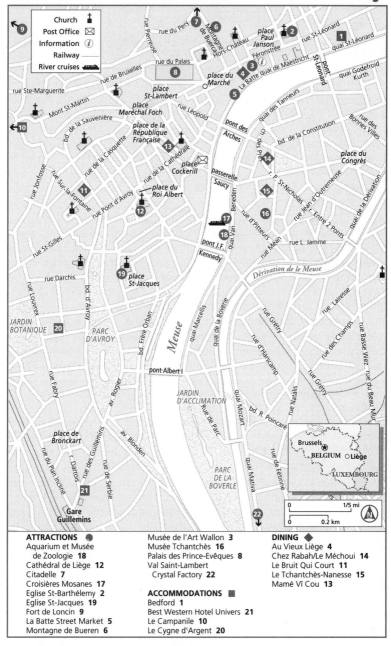

ATTRACTIONS ●
Aquarium et Musée
  de Zoologie **18**
Cathédral de Liège **12**
Citadelle **7**
Croisières Mosanes **17**
Eglise St-Barthélemy **2**
Eglise St-Jacques **19**
Fort de Loncin **9**
La Batte Street Market **5**
Montagne de Bueren **6**

Musée de l'Art Wallon **3**
Musée Tchantchès **16**
Palais des Prince-Evêques **8**
Val Saint-Lambert
  Crystal Factory **22**

ACCOMMODATIONS ■
Bedford **1**
Best Western Hotel Univers **21**
Le Campanile **10**
Le Cygne d'Argent **20**

DINING ◆
Au Vieux Liège **4**
Chez Rabah/Le Méchoui **14**
Le Bruit Qui Court **11**
Le Tchantchès-Nanesse **15**
Mamé Vî Cou **13**

> ## *Tips* Local Heroes
>
> For a feel of **Old Liège,** stroll through the narrow, twisting streets and stairways on Mont St-Martin, which are lined with fine old houses.

human nature, and the other housing an ornamental garden. Today, this historic building is Liège's **Palais de Justice (Palace of Justice),** housing courtrooms and lawyers' offices. The chambers, hung with antique Brussels tapestries, are not normally open to visitors, but it's sometimes possible to arrange a guided tour through the tourist office. You can visit the courtyards Monday to Friday from 10am to 5pm; admission is free.

MUSEUMS

Note: Three important Liège museums featured in previous editions of *Frommer's Belgium, Holland & Luxembourg* were closed for rebuilding at the time of writing. These are the Musée d'Armes, the Musée des Arts Décoratifs et d'Archéologie (formerly the Musée Curtius), and the Musée de la Vie Wallonne. None are scheduled to reopen before the second half of 2007, and it's quite possible that their due dates will slip back. In view of this, and the uncertainty about how the museums will be arranged when they reopen, I have decided to leave them out of this edition. Contact the tourist office for up-to-date information at the time of your visit.

Musée de l'Art Wallon (Museum of Walloon Art) ⟨✯⟩   Small but impressive, the collection of works by Walloon (French-speaking Belgian) artists and sculptors extends from the 16th century to the present. Paul Delvaux's *L'Homme de la Rue* (1940) is one of the premier works. Many other well-known, and not-so-well-known, artists from the 16th to the 21st centuries are represented, including Constant Meunier, Antoine Wiertz, Félicien Rops, René Magritte, Roger Somville, and Pierre Alechinsky.

Ilot St-Georges, Féronstrée 86 (by the river in the center city). ⟨✆⟩ **04/221-92-31.** Admission 3.80€ ($4.75) adults; 2.50€ ($3.15) seniors, students, and children 12–18; free for children under 12. Tues–Sat 1–6pm; Sun 11am–4:30pm. Closed Jan 1, May 1 and 8, Nov 11 and 15, Dec 24–26 and 31.

Musée Tchantchès (Tchantchès Museum) ⟨*Kids*⟩   If your children have fallen under the spell of the city's favorite puppet (see "The Town Mascot," above), come here to find a marvelous collection of his cohorts and their costumes, and to discover the remarkable history of this character, the intimate of emperors and bishops. Liège marionette-theater developed during the 19th century, the puppets having a limited range of gesture and movement that makes them particularly easy for children to appreciate. And the more important the character, the bigger the puppet. From mid-September to Easter, there are frequent marionette performances; call ahead for schedules.

Rue Surlet 56, Outremeuse. ⟨✆⟩ **04/342-75-75.** www.tchantches.be. Admission 2€ ($2.50) adults, 1€ ($1.25) children. Aug–June Tues and Thurs 2–4pm. Closed July.

SIGHTS OF RELIGIOUS SIGNIFICANCE

Cathédrale de Liège (Liège Cathedral) ⟨✯⟩   Ask the sacristan to show you the cathedral's priceless treasures. These include a white-marble-and-oak pulpit and the 13th-century polychrome *Madonna and Child* by the high altar. The **Trésor (Treasury)** in the cloisters (rue Bonne Fortune 6) holds a small but exquisite collection that includes a gold reliquary that was Burgundian Duke Charles the Bold's gift of "penance" after he wiped out the city and every able-bodied man in it in 1468. This masterpiece, the work of Charles's court jeweler, shows a repentant duke kneeling as St. George looks on (there's no word about whether the surviving populace were satisfied with this gesture). Nearby, a bas-relief depicting the Crucifixion is said to contain a piece of the True Cross. Equally impressive is the reliquary of St. Lambert, which dates from the early 1500s and holds the saint's skull.

Place Cathédrale. ℂ **04/232-61-32.** www.tresordeliege.be. Free admission to Cathedral. Treasury: 4€ ($5) adults, 2.50€ ($3.15) seniors and students, 1.50€ ($1.90) children 6–18, free for children under 6. Tues–Sun 2–5pm.

Eglise St-Barthélemy (Church of St. Bartholomew) ⊛   This twin-towered Romanesque church dates from 1108. Its **Fonts Baptismaux (Baptismal Font)** ⊛ is counted among Belgium's most important historical treasures, a masterpiece of the Mosan Art style that flourished in the Meuse Valley during the Middle Ages. The big copper-and-brass font, cast in the early 1100s by master metalsmith Renier de Huy, rests on the backs of 10 sculptured oxen and is surrounded by five biblical scenes.

Place St-Barthélemy. ℂ **04/221-89-44.** Admission 2.50€ ($3.15) adults, 1€ ($1.25) children. Mon–Sat 10am–noon and 2–5pm; Sun 2–5pm.

Eglise St-Jacques (Church of St. James)   A felicitous mixture of architectural styles, the church has a Gothic Flamboyant exterior, a Romanesque narthex, and a Renaissance porch. Its intricately designed vaulted ceiling makes this one of the most beautiful church interiors in Liège.

Place St-Jacques 8 (south of the Cathedral of St-Paul). ℂ **04/222-14-41.** Free admission. Mid-Sept to mid-June (except Easter vacation) Mon–Sat 8am–noon, Sun 10am–noon; Easter vacation and mid-June to mid-Sept Sun–Fri 10am–noon and 2–6pm, Sat 10am–noon and 2–4:15pm.

OTHER SIGHTS
Aquarium et Musée de Zoologie (Aquarium and Zoological Museum) ⊛ (Kids
Though owned by the University of Liège and housed in the university's neoclassical Zoological Institute, the **Aquarium** isn't a dry academic institution. Attractively

---

The Belgian Rome

The prince-bishops of Liège combined the roles of head of state and head of the church, but they were churchmen first and foremost—and unencumbered by the dynastic fixation of monarchs with blood lines to perpetuate.

Notger, at the end of the 10th century, was the first prince-bishop. Of Germanic origin, he had been an adviser to the Holy Roman Emperor Otto II and liked to keep up appearances in his new career. He constructed churches and other religious edifices, surrounded the city with a defensive wall, and in general acted to enhance the city-state's prestige. Thanks to Notger, Liège became a center of art, culture, and religion that fully deserved to be dubbed "Rome Beyond the Alps." A medieval chronicler commented that the city "owed Notger to Christ and the rest to Notger."

The prince-bishopric was finally overthrown with the help of the French revolutionary army in 1794.

presented underwater displays bring together 2,500 examples from 250 marine species. The exhibits cover a lot of ground—or water—in their 46 display tanks. Pride of place, for most younger visitors at any rate, goes to the 4,420-gallon shark tank. The Salle des Coraux (Coral Room) contains beautiful specimens collected from Australia's Great Barrier Reef by a university expedition in 1966 to 1967.

The ragged-looking **Zoological Museum** on the same premises has some 20,000 exhibits, including the skeleton of a 19m (62-ft.) whale. In its foyer is the mural *La Genèse* (*Genesis;* 1960) by Belgian artist Paul Delvaux, which depicts a kind of Garden of Eden scene, with smoke from volcanoes staining the skies of Creation.

Quai Van Beneden 22 (beside the Meuse at Pont Kennedy). ℂ 04/366-50-21. www.ulg.ac.be/aquarium. Admission 5€ ($6.25) adults; 4.20€ ($5.25) seniors, students, and children 13–18; 3.50€ ($4.40) children 6–12; free for children under 6. Sept–June (except Easter school vacation) Mon–Fri 9am–5pm, Sat–Sun and holidays 10:30am–6pm; Easter school vacation and July–Aug Mon–Fri 10am–6pm, Sat–Sun and holidays 10:30am–6pm. Closed Jan 1, Dec 24–25 and 31.

Val Saint Lambert Crystal Factory ⚓   This place would be interesting enough if only to watch the company's craftsmen at work making the renowned hand-blown crystal that bears the Val Saint Lambert label. But you'll find the remains of a 13th-century Cistercian abbey, a 16th-century Mosan Renaissance–style house, and examples of industrial archaeology from the 18th and 19th centuries. At an on-site store you can buy recently made crystal (the sales pitch is low-key), including slightly flawed examples at a considerable discount. You can visit the **Musée du Cristal (Crystal Museum)** and wander around the site.

Rue de Val 245, Seraing (southwest of Liège, beside the Meuse, on N90). ℂ 04/337-39-60. www.val-saint-lambert. com. Admission 6€ ($7.50) adults, 3€ ($3.75) children 5–16, free for children under 5. Mon–Thurs 10:30am and 2:30pm; Fri 10:30am.

THE CITADEL

For superb views of the city and the broad, curving Meuse, climb the 353 steps of the **Montagne de Beuren,** a street that ascends from rue Hors-Château. At the top of the hill, commanding panoramic views, is the site of the **Citadelle (Citadel),** which has been a setting for more than its share of the bloodier side of Liège's history. It was here on October 29, 1468, that 600 citizens made a heroic but ill-considered assault on Duke Charles the Bold of Burgundy, who had sparked a revolt by installing one of his cousins as prince-bishop, and was encamped with his Burgundian troops. They penetrated almost to Charles's tent before being beaten off and massacred to the man. Charles ordered the city's complete destruction, a task that continued for several weeks and left only the churches standing.

A decisive battle in Belgium's fight for independence took place here in 1830. In 1914, locals held German forces at bay long enough for the French to regroup and go on to a vitally important victory at the Battle of the Marne. German troops again met with typically stubborn resistance from the city's defenders in 1940. The Citadel Hospital now occupies the site.

For an idea of how Liège suffered in wartime, visit the ravaged World War I **Fort de Loncin,** route des Héros 15B (ℂ 04/246-44-25; www.fortdeloncin.be). The powerful Belgian fortress came under German artillery fire in August 1914, and an incoming shell detonated its magazine. The fort blew up, killing 350 of its 500 defenders, who are interred in a necropolis on the site, which otherwise remains as it was on that August day.

ORGANIZED TOURS

From April to October, hour-long **cruises** on the Meuse are operated by **Croisières Mosanes** (✆ **04/366-50-21**). They aren't wildly exciting, but they are an easy way to view the city along the river. They depart daily at 11am and at 1, 3, and 5pm, from Quai Van Beneden, outside the Aquarium (see above). Tickets are 6€ ($7.50) for adults; 5.50€ ($6.90) for seniors, students, and children ages 5 to 18; and free for children under 5.

WHERE TO STAY

Bedford   Located beside the Meuse and just a 10-minute walk away from the center city, this high-rise hotel is equipped to the latest business standards. Front-room windows overlook the river, and all rooms have comfortable armchairs along with firm beds.

Quai St-Léonard 36, 4000 Liège. ✆ **04/228-81-11**. Fax 04/227-45-75. www.hotelbedford.be. 149 units. 105€–273€ ($131–$341) double; 372€ ($465). Rates include buffet breakfast. AE, DC, MC, V. Free parking. **Amenities:** Restaurant (Belgian); bar; concierge; secretarial services; room service; babysitting; laundry service; nonsmoking rooms. *In room:* A/C, TV, minibar.

Best Western Hotel Univers ⭐   There's good value in this medium-size hotel, where the guest rooms are modest in decor but quite comfortable. Though there's no restaurant on the premises, several are within walking distance. A major renovation program, including new bathrooms, has recently been completed.

Rue des Guillemins 116 (close to Gare Guillemins), 4000 Liège. ✆ **04/254-55-55**. Fax 04/254-55-00. www.bestwestern.be. 51 units. 75€–95€ ($94–$119) double. AE, DC, MC, V. Parking 5€ ($6.25). *In room:* TV, hair dryer.

Le Campanile   Guest rooms are spacious and comfortable, if not inflected with much character, at this motel-style hotel, which has a reputation for its good quality/price ratio. All have en-suite bathrooms. This is a good choice if you're touring by car, as it's just 200m (645 ft.) from an expressway ramp—and just 5 minutes by bus to the center city.

Rue Jules de Laminne, 4000 Liège. ✆ **04/224-02-72**. Fax 04/224-03-80. www.campanile.fr. 50 units. 58€–73€ ($73–$91) double. AE, DC, MC, V. Free parking. **Amenities:** Restaurant (Belgian/Continental); bar; nonsmoking rooms. *In room:* TV, dataport.

Le Cygne d'Argent   A homey atmosphere pervades this small, family-owned hotel, on a quiet side street in a leafy neighborhood just south of the center city, between the Jardin Botanique and the Parc d'Avroy. The guest rooms vary in size, and were recently refurbished and refitted. A former bare-bones approach has given way to a smooth design that integrates new beds, closets, desks, drapes, and carpets into a restful ensemble of pastel tones and soft lighting, affording a tolerable approach to indulgence for a hotel in this price category.

Rue Beeckman 49 (close to Gare Guillemins), 4000 Liège. ✆ **04/223-70-01**. Fax 04/222-49-66. www.cygnedargent.be. 22 units. 69€–72€ ($86–$90) double. AE, DC, MC, V. Parking 9€ ($11). *In room:* TV, minibar.

WHERE TO DINE

Liège has a great diversity of restaurants, thanks in part to the various ethnic communities here. Italian, Spanish, Turkish, North African, Greek, and other immigrants have settled in the city and brought their favorite dishes with them. The popularity of Walloon cuisine (see "Local Heroes," below) adds regional specialties to the mix.

Local Heroes

The Liégeois are especially fond of their *boudin blanc de Liège* (white sausage); *grives* (thrushes) and goose; *boulet frites avec sirop de Liège* (meatballs in a sauce made from pear and apple syrup, served with french fries); *tarte au riz* (rice flan); *bouquette* (a kind of pancake); *botées aux carottes ou au chou* (a kind of stew made with potatoes, cabbage or carrots, and meat such as pork or sausage); and *salade liégeoise* (potatoes, onions, bacon pieces, vinegar, and beans).

Au Vieux Liège ⭐ SEAFOOD/CONTINENTAL   This marvelous restaurant is in the center city in a four-story 16th-century town house furnished with antiques of that era. Dinner is by candlelight, and the waiters wear formal attire; but the food out-shines even the excellent setting. Almost any fish dish is a good choice, but there's more experimental fare including rare-cooked *escargots niçoises* (snails) and lobster ravioli. More conventional diners can stick with Irish steak with bacon or grilled salmon.

Quai de la Goffe 41. ✆ **04/223-77-48**. www.vieux-liege.be. Reservations recommended on weekends. Main courses 25€–49€ ($21–$34); fixed-price menus 29€–40€ ($36–$50). AE, DC, MC, V. Mon–Sat noon–2:45pm and 6:30–9:45pm.

Chez Rabah/Le Méchoui ⭐ NORTH AFRICAN   In a rambling, informal setting, with open wood grills in two rooms, you'll dine among Arabic ornamentation that includes a gigantic brass teapot. The menu has just a handful of main options, such as couscous (the couscous royal is ace), mushrooms, and salad, with variations provided by grilled meats, including spicy sausage, and by scampi. Honey-suffused desserts lie in wait to tempt your sweet tooth. Friendly waitstaff ensure a constant supply of scented fruit tea, and you can drink little-known but surprisingly good Moroccan wines, in addition to French ones. If the restaurant is full, as it often is on weekends, similar North African eateries are close by.

Ch. des Prés 15 (Outremeuse). ✆ **04/343-38-56**. Main courses 9.50€–16€ ($12–$20); fixed-price menus 24€ ($30). MC, V. Daily 6pm–dawn.

Le Bruit Qui Court FRENCH/BELGIAN   An imposing 19th-century building, formerly a bank, confers a certain class on this establishment, which is matched by the refined cuisine. Light dishes, such as salads and quiches, predominate and often combine flavors in unexpected ways. You can dine in the ground-floor strong room, behind the original heavily armored door.

Bd. de la Sauvenière 142. ✆ **04/232-18-18**. www.bruitquicourt.be. Main courses 7.80€–15€ ($9.75–$18). AE, DC, MC, V. Mon–Thurs 8am–midnight; Fri–Sat 8am–2am; Sun 6pm–midnight.

Le Tchantchès-Nanesse WALLOON   Named after the local folk hero, this is one of the best addresses in town for plain Liège specialties, such as grilled *boudin* sausage with potatoes, the warm *salad liégeoise,* and the world-famous (in Liège) meatballs with french fries in syrup. The beer glasses hanging above the bar counter are "mail boxes"—every regular has his or her own glass in which other *habitués,* and you if you so desire, can leave messages.

Rue Grande-Bêche 35 (Outremeuse). ✆ **04/343-39-31**. Main courses 7€–12€ ($8.75–$14). V. Mon–Sat 6pm–midnight.

Mamé Vî Cou ⋆ WALLOON   "Mamé Vî Cou" is Walloon dialect for "A Nice Old Lady," and although I would never call Madame Dupagne old, her welcome is certainly nice enough. Her character-filled, oak-beamed restaurant is a Liège institution, serving traditional Walloon specialties such as pigs' kidneys flamed in *pekèt* (Belgian gin), chicken in beer, and hot black pudding with acid cherries.

Rue de la Wache 9. ℂ 04/223-71-81. www.mamevicou.be. Main courses 11€–20€ ($13–$24); fixed-price menus 18€–33€ ($23–$41). AE, DC, MC, V. Daily noon–2:30pm and 6:30–11:30pm.

SHOPPING

On Sunday mornings, what is said to be the oldest **street market** ⋆ in Europe—and surely one of the most colorful—is strung out for a mile along quai de la Batte on the city side of the Meuse. You'll find brass, clothes, flowers, foodstuffs, jewelry, birds, animals, books, radios, and . . . the list is simply endless. Shoppers from as far away as Holland and Germany join sightseers from overseas, and what seems to be at least half the population of Liège. If you're anywhere near Liège on a Sunday, plan to check out this marvelous shopping hodgepodge, if only to browse and people-watch.

Tip: You'll find good shopping in the several small pedestrian-only streets off place Saint-Lambert in the Old City.

LIEGE AFTER DARK

A short way from place Cathédrale, the pedestrians-only Carré district is the most animated part of town, a place for shopping during the day and stepping out after dark until the wee small hours.

THE PERFORMING ARTS

The highly acclaimed **Opéra Royal de Wallonie** performs at the Théâtre Royal de Liège, rue des Dominicains 1 (ℂ 04/223-59-10). The **Théâtre Royal de LAC,** near the Church of St. Jacques, presents concerts by the city's **Orchestre Philharmonique de Liège** (ℂ 04/220-00-00; www.opl.be), along with opera and ballet. Concerts are performed at the **Conservatoire Royal du Musique,** bd. Piercot 27–29 (ℂ 04/222-03-06). For schedules and prices of current performances, contact **Infor-Spectacles,** Feronstrée 92 (ℂ 04/222-11-11), Monday to Friday from 11am to 6pm.

Theaters staging puppet shows performed by the **Théâtre des Marionettes** ⋆ (in dialect, but easy to follow) are at the Museum of Walloon Art (see earlier in this chapter), the Tchantchès Museum (see earlier in this chapter), and the **Al Botroûle Museum,** rue Hocheporte 3 (ℂ 04/223-05-76). Liégeois wit is especially apparent in

The Prolific Touch of Georges Simenon

Liège will always be associated with one of the 20th century's most prolific and popular authors. Georges Simenon (1903–89), creator of the famed Paris police Inspector Maigret, was born at rue Léopold 24. He grew up here and did his first writing for the local newspaper, the *Gazette de Liège.* Though he later left to live in Paris and Switzerland, he never forgot his roots, and the atmosphere of Maigret's Paris owes a clear debt to the mean streets of Liège's Outremeuse district.

The Liège tourist office has marked out a Simenon itinerary, which takes you on a tour of places associated with the author.

The **Château de Jehay** ✿ (© 085/31-17-16; www.chateaujehay.be), at Jehay-Bodegnée, 18km (11 miles) southwest of Liège, dates from the 15th century and houses a remarkable museum of humankind's past in the Meuse Valley. Its lawns and gardens are beautified with sculptures and Italian fountains. Moats reflect a checkerboard pattern of light and dark stone, and round towers at each end/corner of a central rectangular block. Inside, the rooms are filled with paintings, tapestries, lace from the private collections of Liège prince-bishops, silver and gold pieces, jewels, porcelain and glass, antique furniture, and family heirlooms. A chapel adorns a small islet.

The château is open weekends and holidays in April to September, from 11am (or 2pm) to 6pm. Admission is 5€ ($6.25) for adults, 2.50€ ($3.15) for students and children ages 6 to 18, and free for children under 6. To get there, take N167 along the Meuse toward Huy, and go right at Amay toward Tongeren (Tongres).

the puppets' appearance; each puppet is sized according to its historical importance—for example, a huge Charles the Bold is attended by Lilliputian archers (though just how important Charles would have been without those archers is debatable!).

CAFES, TAVERNS & OTHER NIGHTSPOTS

When the sun goes down (and even when it's still up), the Liégeois head for their pick of the city's hundreds of **cafes** and **taverns** to quaff Belgium's famous beers and engage in their favorite entertainment—good conversation. If a quiet evening of the same appeals to you, you'll have no problem finding a locale. One of the best is **Tchantchès et Nanesse,** Grande-Bêche 35 (© 04/221-05-70) in the Outremeuse district. **Café Lequet,** quai sur Meuse 17 (© 04/222-21-34), a popular cafe/brasserie, is the place to encounter local characters speaking the Walloon dialect, in particular during the Sunday La Batte street market (p. 195).

La Notte, rue Tête de Bœuf 10 (© 04/223-07-32), close to place Cathédrale, has a group of eclectic musicians who seem equally at home with rock, samba, and French _chanson française._ If you're at all musical, they'll let you pick up an instrument and do your own thing. Thursday is jazz evening. **Le Pot au Lait,** rue Sœur de Hasque 9 (© 04/222-07-94), a cybercafe close to the university, is always pretty animated.

If beer is your pleasure, you can't go wrong at **Le Vaudrée II,** rue St-Gilles 149 (© 04/223-18-80; www.vaudree.be), which has a choice of some 900 different ales from around the world. If you're hungry, don't miss their delicious _pavé sur pierre_ (a tender beef filet roasted on a hot stone) and the variety of dishes served in beer sauces.

In spite of having a beer cornucopia right on their doorstep, the city's imbibers are just as likely to favor the stiff Belgian perfumed grain liquor, or gin, commonly called _jenever,_ and in Wallonia, _genièvre_ or _pekèt._ The table-topper in this league is the **Maison du Pekèt,** rue du Stalon 4 (© 04/250-67-83), a traditional old cafe off place Saint-Lambert, which has 200 varieties of _genièvre_ on its drinks list. The local favorite is Pekèt des Houyeux. In the same building, behind the cafe, is the restaurant **Amon Nanesse,** which dishes up Liège specialties.

For livelier nighttime fun, there are numerous nightspots in the Carré and along rue Roture in Outremeuse. Some good examples include **La Chapelle,** place St-Denis (✆ **04/223-26-85**); **Palace Club,** place St-Paul 8 (✆ **04/223-40-53**); **Le Premier,** rue du Pot d'Or (✆ **04/222-28-46**); and **Les Trois Frères,** rue d'Amay 3 (✆ **04/ 223-07-44**).

2 Huy

27km (17 miles) SW of Liège; 27km (17 miles) NE of Namur

The drive from Liège to Namur follows the Meuse River. Once you get beyond the city's industrial environs, the riverside scenery evolves into a picturesque landscape with small towns every few miles and one of many Meuse Valley castles never far away.

Charming Huy (pop. 18,000) on the Meuse started out as a center for tin, copper, and wine merchants, and was granted its town charter in 1066. It has a long tradition of metalwork. Its most famous native son, Renier de Huy, was the 12th-century gold-smith who designed the baptismal font in Liège's Eglise St-Barthélemy (Church of St. Bartholomew; see earlier). Today pewter is the alloy of choice, and Huy's stores are filled with pewter bowls, goblets, pitchers, and other items. The town has several notable examples of the 16th- and 17th-century architectural style known as Mosan Renaissance.

ESSENTIALS

GETTING THERE   There's frequent train service from Liège to Huy's **Gare du Nord,** place Zenobe Gramme. Across the square is the **bus station.** Bus information is available from **TEC** (✆ **04/361-94-44;** www.infotec.be). By **car** from Liège, take N90 southwest.

VISITOR INFORMATION   The **Maison du Tourisme** is at quai de Namur 1, 4500 Huy (✆ **085/21-29-15;** fax 085/23-29-44; www.pays-de-huy.be). It's open January to March and October to December, Monday to Friday from 9am to 4pm, and weekends and holidays from 10am to 4pm; April to September, Monday to Friday from 8:30am to 5:30pm, and weekends and holidays from 10:30am to 5:30pm (6pm July–Aug).

WHAT TO SEE & DO

Huy is dominated by a hilltop citadel, the **Fort de Huy,** chaussée Napoléon (✆ **085/21-53-34**), which affords marvelous views of the town, the river below, and the Roi Baudouin suspension bridge. The fort was constructed in 1818 on the site of earlier castles and forts that date back to the Gallo-Roman period at the very least. In World War II, the Nazis used it as a concentration camp; a museum on the site explains that history and also about the Belgian Resistance. You can reach the fort on foot or by *téléphérique* (cable car; ✆ **085/21-18-82**) from the riverside at the corner of rue d'Amérique and rue d'Arsin. Cable-car fare is 3.50€ ($4.40) for a one-way ticket and 4.50€ ($5.65) round-trip for adults; and 2€ ($2.50) one-way and 2.50€ ($3.15) round-trip for children. The fort is open from July to August, daily from 11am to 7pm; April to June and September, Monday to Friday from 9am to 12:30pm and 1 to 4:30pm, and weekends from 11am to 6pm. Admission is 3.50€ ($4.40) for adults, and 3€ ($3.75) for children.

The **Musée Communal (Town Museum),** rue Vankeerberghen 20 (✆ **085/23-24-35**), in a 17th-century former monastery of the Friars Minor, displays local metalwork and glass objects. Its finest single piece is the wood crucifix from 1240 known as the

---

Kids **High Times**

A welcome break for children awaits at the **Mont Mosan Leisure Park,** plaine de la Sarte (℃ **085/23-29-96;** www.montmosan.be), in the eastern suburbs, reachable by road and by the cable car to the Fort de Huy, referred to above. The park has sea lions, rides, games, and a resident clown. It's open April to September, daily from 10am to 8pm; October, weekends from 10am to 8pm. Admission is 6€ ($7.50) per person.

Beau Dieu de Huy (Good Lord of Huy). The museum is open May to September, Monday to Friday from 2 to 4pm, and weekends from 2 to 6pm; October, Monday to Friday from 2 to 4pm; November to mid-December and mid-January to April, Monday to Friday from 11am to 12:30pm and 1:30 to 3:30pm. Admission is 3€ ($3.75) for adults, 1€ ($1.25) for children ages 5 to 12, and free for children under 5.

On the Grand-Place, an 18th-century copper fountain known as **Li Bassinia** stands in front of the elegant neoclassical **Hôtel de Ville (Town Hall)** from the same period—with any luck you'll be on hand when the town hall carillon rings out *Brave Liégeois,* as it does every hour.

The vast 14th-century Gothic **Collégiale (Collegiate Church) Notre-Dame** ✦, parvis Théoduin de Bavière (℃ **085/21-29-15**), is famed for its magnificent stained-glass windows, including *Li Rondia,* a beautiful Gothic rose window, and other stained windows in the choir. Its **Trésor (Treasury)** contains the Romanesque reliquaries of St. Domitien and St. Mengold, and many items in chiseled copper. The Treasury is open Saturday to Thursday from 9am to noon and 2 to 5pm (except during services). Admission to the church is free; visiting the Treasury is 3€ ($3.75) for adults, 2€ ($2.50) for students, and free for children under 12.

Huy's quaint narrow streets are great for walking. Take note of the stone bas-reliefs on tiny arcaded rue des Cloîtres that runs along the side of Notre-Dame church. For a stroll through the town's history, start on Grand-Place and walk down rue des Rôtisseurs, rue des Augustins, and rue Vierset-Godin.

For an excursion on water, take a **river cruise** on the *Val Mosan* (℃ **085/21-29-15**), which sails from quai de Namur in front of the tourist office. Departures May to August are Tuesday to Sunday (and Mon on national holidays) at 2, 3, and 4:30pm; and September, Sunday at 2, 3, and 4:30pm. Tickets are 5€ ($6.25) for adults, 3€ ($3.75) for children.

3 Namur ✦✦

56km (35 miles) SE of Brussels; 27km (17 miles) SW of Huy; 54km (33 miles) SW of Liège

A handsome riverside town (pop. 40,000) at the confluence of the Meuse and Sambre rivers, the bustling capital of Belgium's French-speaking Wallonia region, has fine museums and churches, a casino, and an abundance of cafes and restaurants. You'll find many good places to eat and drink along the narrow, atmospheric alleyways of **Le Corbeil,** the old quarter of rows of 17th-century brick homes, squeezed into the angle between the Sambre and the Meuse.

The town is dominated by its brooding hilltop **Citadelle,** evidence of the strategic importance attached to Namur in centuries past.

ESSENTIALS

GETTING THERE   On average, there are two trains an hour from Huy and Liège, and one an hour from Brussels, to the **Gare de Namur,** square Léopold (© **02/528-28-28;** www.sncb.be), just north of the center city (which you can easily reach on foot). The **bus station** is out front (© **081/25-35-55;** www.infotec.be). By **car** from Liège, take N90 southwest via Huy; from Brussels, A4/E411 southeast.

VISITOR INFORMATION   The **Maison du Tourisme** is at square Léopold (also known as sq. de l'Europe Unie), 5000 Namur (© **081/24-64-49;** fax 081/26-23-60; www.namurtourisme.be), close to the rail station. The office is open daily from 9:30am to 6pm. There's a small **Tourist Information Center** on place du Grognon (© **081/24-64-48**), at the confluence of the Meuse and Sambre; it's open April to October, daily from 9:30am to 6pm.

WHAT TO SEE & DO

Cathédrale de St-Aubain (St. Aubain's Cathedral) ⓐ   The domed cathedral (1751) was designed by its Italian architect in the light, ethereal, Renaissance style of his native land, with columns, pilasters, cornices, and balustrades. It was constructed on the site of a 1047-vintage church of the same name that became the Namur cathedral in 1559; the old church's belfry still survives in the existing structure. The **Musée Diocésain et Trésor (Diocesan Museum and Treasury),** place du Chapitre 1 (© **081/44-42-85**), just outside the cathedral, holds a small but impressive collection of ecclesiastical relics, gold plate, and sculptures.

Place St-Aubain. © **081/22-03-20.** Free admission to church; admission to Diocesan Museum 2.50€ ($3.15) adults, 2€ ($2.50) seniors and students, 1€ ($1.25) children. Museum open Easter–Oct, Tues–Sat 10am–noon and 2:30–6pm, Sun 2:30–6pm; Nov to Easter Sunday, Tues–Sun 2:30–4:30pm.

Citadelle (Citadel) ⓐⓐ *Kids*   To reach the hilltop Citadel, you can drive or walk one of two scenic ways, route Merveilleuse and route des Panoramas, that wind up the steep cliffside. A fortification has stood atop this bluff since pre-Roman times, but the Dutch are responsible for the Citadel's present shape. Today the structure is part of a 6.5-hectare (16-acre) wooded estate that includes museums (including a forest museum), children's playparks, restaurants, cafes, and craft stores. Visitors are shown a film on the Citadel's history and given a tour of the fortifications. You can explore the intriguing underground caverns by torchlight on a 45-minute tour with a guide. A small excursion "train" runs through the extensive grounds on a 30-minute round-trip.

Route Merveilleuse. © **081/65-45-00.** www.citadelle-namur.be. Admission to Citadel free; to caverns and museums 7.50€ ($9.40) adults, 6€ ($7.50) children. Tues–Sun 11:30am–6pm.

Musée Archéologique (Archaeological Museum)   The 15th-century Renaissance-style building on the banks of the Sambre that houses this museum was Namur's former meat market. It displays important remains of the life and times of the Meuse Valley, from prehistoric ages through the Celtic, Roman, and Frank periods into the Middle Ages. The collections include Roman glassware, pottery, jewelry, and coins, and a relief map of the city dating from 1750.

Rue du Pont 21. © **081/23-16-31.** Admission 2€ ($2.50) adults, 1€ ($1.25) children 6–12, free for children under 6. Tues–Fri 10am–5pm; Sat–Sun 10:40am–5pm.

Musée Félicien Rops (Félicien Rops Museum) ⓐ   Namur sometimes seems unsure of what to make of one of its best-known sons, the bizarre and erotic 19th-century painter and engraver Félicien Rops. His museum is tucked away on a narrow side street, near the artist's birthplace in the old quarter of town—but inside, exposure is the name of the game. The perfection of Rops's soft-ground etchings and drypoint work is internationally recognized, and he was indisputably one of the most outstanding engravers of the late 19th century. Some important examples of his work on display are *Pornokratès* (1879), *Mors Syphilitica* (1866), and *The Beach at Heist* (1886).

Rue Fumal 12. (Ⓒ 081/22-01-10. www.ciger.be/rops. Admission 3€ ($3.75) adults; 1.50€ ($1.90) seniors, students, and children 12–18; free for children under 12. July–Aug daily 10am–6pm; Sept–June Tues–Sun 10am–5pm. Closed Jan 1, Dec 24–25 and 31.

Trésor du Prieuré d'Oignies (Treasury of the Oignies Priory) The Couvent des Soeurs de Notre-Dame (Convent of the Sisters of Our Lady), in the center of town, holds Namur's richest prize. The "treasures" are the work of 13th-century master goldsmith Brother Hugo of Oignies. His sumptuous, jewel-studded crosses, chalices, reliquaries, and other creations are decorated with forest motifs and hunting scenes.

Rue Julie Billiart 17. (Ⓒ 081/25-43-00. Admission 2€ ($2.50) adults, 1€ ($1.25) children ages 6–12, free for children under 6. Tues–Sat 10am–noon and 2–5pm; Sun 2–5pm. Closed holidays and Dec 11–27.

SIGHTSEEING TOURS

In July and August, the tourist office organizes a daily **guided tour** of the old town, the Citadel, and the riverside. This 1½-hour tour starts from the Maison du Tourisme (see "Visitor Information," above), at 11am. The tour is 3.75€ ($4.70) for adults, 3€ ($3.75) for seniors and students, and free for children under 12.

A variety of **river cruise** options is available from Namur, including trips to Dinant and Wépion, other tours of the Meuse and Sambre rivers, and a cruise called "Namur by Night." All of them depart from the junction of the Meuse and Sambre rivers, at boulevard Baron Louis Huart. The cruise line, **Croisières Mosanes** (Ⓒ **082/22-23-15**), is based in nearby Dinant (see below).

NAMUR AFTER DARK

Gamble the night away over the roulette and blackjack tables at the **Casino de Namur,** av. Baron de Moreau 1 (Ⓒ **081/22-30-21**). There's a fine French restaurant here, the **Casino Club.** Jackets and ties are required for men. The casino is open daily from 2pm to dawn.

NEARBY PLACES OF INTEREST

Abbaie de Maredsous (Maredsous Abbey) The twin towers of the neo-Gothic Benedictine abbey stand out clearly above the rugged, forested countryside outside the village of Denée. It is famed for its own beer, cheese, and bread, all of which can be consumed by visitors in a giant cafe on the grounds—and all of which are consumed in copious quantities at busy times. The abbey's third abbot, Dom Columba Marmion of Dublin, appointed in 1909, was beatified by Pope John Paul II in 2000.

Near Denée. (Ⓒ 082/69-81-11. www.maredsous.be. Free admission. Daily 9am–6pm. From Annevoie, take N932 for 4.8km (3 miles); then turn left on N971.

Jardins d'Annevoie (Annevoie Gardens) The ornamental gardens and fountains here, and the 18th-century château they surround, together make a splendid display that should top every regional sightseeing list. Annevoie is sometimes dubbed the "Belgian Versailles," and though these gardens indeed share similarities with their French cousins, and are also reminiscent of Italian and English gardens, they possess unique qualities. The fountains, waterfalls, lagoons, and canals are all engineered without the use of any artificial power. No throbbing pump or other machinery intrudes on their tranquillity and beauty. The grounds were laid out in the mid-1700s by a member of the de Montpellier family and have been tended and added to by successive generations. The present owner, Jean de Montpellier, lives here with his family. Inside the château are fine architectural details in the woodwork, stuccos, fireplaces, and family chapel. In addition to a gift store, there's a full-service restaurant and a rustic cafe decorated with ancient farming implements.

Rue des Jardins 37A, Annevoie. © 082/67-97-97. www.jardins.dannevoie.be. Admission 7.50€ ($9.40) adults, 5€ ($6.25) students and children 3–12, 4€ ($5) visitors with disabilities, free for children under 3. Gardens Apr–Oct daily 9:30am–5:30pm (July–Aug 6:30pm). Parking 1.25€ ($1.55).

WHERE TO STAY

Le Beau Vallon *(Finds)* This elegant *chambre d'hôtes* in a restored stone *château-ferme* (manor-farm), part of which dates from the 17th century and part from 1870, lies in a narrow, wooded valley outside Wépion, the "village of strawberries." This is one of the traditional properties that comes under the umbrella of the **Gîtes de Wallonie** organization (p. 57, chapter 4). Its hospitable proprietors, Marie-Jeanne and Denis de Ribaucourt, ensure that guests feel at home, for example, by serving guests wine or local Blanche de Namur beer at a garden table beside the pool. Rooms are furnished in a comfortable, rustic style, and an 18-hole golf course is across the road.

Chemin du Beau Vallon 38 (off N92 between Wépion and Profondeville), 5100 Wépion. ©/fax 081/41-15-91. 5 units. 50€–65€ ($63–$81) double. **Amenities:** Pool; golf course nearby. *In room:* No phone.

Les Tanneurs *(*)* This luxuriously appointed hotel occupies a character-rich cluster of restored 17th-century buildings, close to the confluence of the rivers Meuse and Sambre. The buildings in this area were falling down from neglect a few years ago, but an imaginative restoration program has recreated an old-world atmosphere. The guest rooms are individually decorated with an effective mix of antiques and modern fittings. Several have been fully renovated. The French restaurant, **L'Espièglerie,** has a strong local reputation.

Rue des Tanneries 13B, 5000 Namur. © 081/24-00-24. Fax 081/24-00-25. www.tanneurs.com. 28 units. 70€–215€ ($88–$269) double. AE, DC, MC, V. Limited street parking. **Amenities:** 2 restaurants (French/steakhouse). *In room:* TV, minibar.

Novotel Namur Despite its chain-hotel provenance and a look that seems more suited to business travel (a character that extends to the in-house restaurant), this is also a decent, up-to-date vacation lodging in a green and scenic spot along Meuse, next to a riverside walking path. There's plenty for children to do—besides the outdoor play

---

Moments Strawberry Fields

A few kilometers beyond Namur lies Wépion, a sleepy riverside village at the heart of Belgium's strawberry-growing district, and the country's self-appointed "Strawberry Capital." Wépion's **Musée de la Fraise (Strawberry Museum),** chaussée de Dinant 1037 (© 081/46-20-07), is devoted to the fruit. In summer, you can buy strawberries from local kiosks.

area, there are games, computer games, and sports like tennis and table tennis. The airy guest rooms are furnished in a functional style suited to a midlevel chain hotel, with writing desks and fine bathrooms. Ask for a room at the back, facing the river.

Chaussée de Dinant 1149 (less than 5km/3 miles from Namur), 5100 Wépion-Namur. ✆ **800/NOVOTEL** or 081/46-08-11. Fax 081/46-19-90. www.novotel.com. 110 units. 105€ ($131) double. AE, DC, MC, V. Free parking. Take E411 Brussels–Luxembourg to Exit 14. **Amenities:** Restaurant (Belgian); bar; indoor pool; outdoor pool; golf course nearby; children's play area. *In room:* TV, minibar, hair dryer.

WHERE TO DINE

Brasserie Henry ★★ FRENCH/BELGIAN   Get a feel for the new Namurois style at this trendy brasserie on a pretty square. It's informal but classy, and the food is excellent. A good bet is the *medaillons de sole, sauce onctueuse au champagne* (sole filets in a champagne sauce). You can pick up nine Normandy oysters, or go for Belgian specialties such as *asperges à la flamande* (asparagus in the Flemish style) and *waterzooï* (a souplike Flemish stew, traditionally made with freshwater fish but more often these days with chicken). In addition to the long and elegant main dining room, there's a plant-bedecked outdoor terrace at the back.

Place St-Aubin 3 (at St. Aubin Cathedral). ✆ **081/22-02-04.** Main courses 7.50€–18€ ($9.40–$22); fixed-price menus 21€–27€ ($26–$34). AE, DC, MC, V. Daily 8am–1am.

Château de Namur ★ FRENCH   There's no more refined place to locally dine than at this magnificent château restaurant. Its setting, up in the Citadel Park overlooking the town, has made it especially popular. In a light-filled arched dining room, try the *truite au bleu* (oven-baked trout).

Av. de l'Ermitage 1. ✆ **081/72-99-00.** www.chateaudenamur.com. Main courses 12€–20€ ($15–$25); fixed-price menus 25€–40€ ($31–$50). AE, DC, MC, V. Daily noon–2:30pm and 7–9:30pm.

La Petite Fugue ★ FRENCH   This intimate place at the heart of old Namur, in a converted 18th-century presbytery, has an interior typical of period bourgeois Namur houses, with a wood staircase and wooden fixtures and fittings. Try the salmon filet with cabbage, potatoes, and mushrooms, or the lobster in a Chablis butter sauce. Prices are reasonable considering the fine food and service (the three-course menu is an especially good deal), and the restaurant's 20 or so places fill up fast during its short open hours. There's a good wine selection and some decent advice to go with it.

Place Chanoine Descamps 5. ✆ **081/23-13-20.** www.lapetitefugue.be. Main courses 9.50€–18€ ($12–$23); fixed-price menus 26€–42€ ($30–$53). MC, V. Tues–Fri noon–1:30pm and 7–9:30pm; Sat 7–9:30pm; Sun noon–2:30pm.

4 Dinant ★

23km (14 miles) S of Namur

A bustling riverside resort town, Dinant (pop. 13,000) has suffered from history's turmoil. In 1466, in reprisal for a rebellion, duke of Burgundy Charles the Bold razed the town and drowned 800 citizens, tied up in pairs and thrown from the Citadel into the Meuse. In a chilling echo, the World War I German army executed 700 citizens when its troops were fired on in the town. A reminder of Dinant's military past is never far from view, for the Citadel dating from 1530 that crowns a bluff 100m (328 ft.) high dominates the skyline.

Despite all the bloodshed, the town developed such skill in working *Dinanderie* (hammered copper) that its engravings were widely sought after as early as the 13th century. Charles the Bold's ruthlessness put a stop to such artistry, but in recent years

Sax Appeal

Most people would call New Orleans the spiritual home of jazz. But Dinant can lay claim to a part of that heritage. In 1814, Adolphe Sax, inventor of the saxophone, was born here. Sax was a prolific instrument maker and designer. In 1838, he developed the bass clarinet, based on some of the same principles he later used for the saxophone. The first saxophone was made in 1841 or 1842. Sax patented his new instrument in 1846.

The saxophone was controversial from the start, never gaining wide acceptance in the orchestra, despite the support of composers Berlioz, Saint-Saens, and Massenet. Sax's saxophone class at the Paris Conservatory closed in the 1870s. Sax himself went bankrupt, and in 1894 he died a saddened man.

Salvation for the instrument came in the 1920s and 1930s, as the saxophone became popular in jazz, big band, and military music. The composer, looking down from the great sax jam in the sky, was vindicated in 1996, when his brainchild celebrated its 150th anniversary. Dinant was a throbbing, foot-tapping center of the festivities.

the skill has come back to life, and you'll find fine examples of engravings in town stores.

Just outside town is **Abbaye de Leffe (Leffe Abbey),** one of several Belgian abbeys that combine their spiritual calling with brewing beer.

ESSENTIALS

GETTING THERE   There are on average two trains an hour to Dinant from Namur, and regular bus service. The **rail** and **bus** stations are on rue de la Station on the west bank of the Meuse. By **car** from Namur, take N92 south.

VISITOR INFORMATION   The **Maison du Tourisme** is at av. Cadoux 8, 5500 Dinant (℃ **082/22-28-70;** fax 082/22-77-88; www.dinant-tourisme.be). The office is open in summer daily from 9am to 7pm; winter daily from 9am to 5pm (winter open hours may be shorter on occasion).

WHAT TO SEE & DO

Citadelle (Citadel) ⍟   The 16th-century Citadel, a fortress perched spectacularly on a cliff high above the town and river, can be reached by car or *téléphérique* (cable car). Alternatively, if you're feeling energetic or can't turn down the challenge, you can climb the 408 steep steps leading to the bluff top and spectacular views of the town and river. The **Musée d'Armes (Weapons Museum)** inside has cannon and other firearms, and there's an audiovisual historical presentation in three languages (including English). But it's the view that takes your breath away. You might want to spend an hour or two wandering around up here.

Le Prieuré 25. ℃ **082/22-36-70.** www.citadellededinant.be. Admission (includes the cable-car fare) 6.50€ ($8.15) adults, 5€ ($6.25) children. Apr–Sept daily 10am–6pm; Oct–Dec and Feb–Mar Sat–Thurs 10am–4:30pm; Jan Sat–Sun 10am–4:30pm.

Collégiale Notre-Dame (Collegiate Church of Our Lady)   Although this riverside church looks old, it was reconstructed twice during the last century, after being destroyed in both World War I and II. An original church gained collegiate status (through its chapter of canons) in 934. Its Romanesque successor bit the dust in 1228 when part of the neighboring cliff collapsed on top of it, and it was reconstructed in the Mosan Gothic style. The big bulbous spire from 1697 is a majestic sight beneath the looming presence of the Citadel. Points of interest inside are the baptismal font from 1472, the 1731 lectern made from local *Dinanderie,* and the fine stained-glass window that depicts scenes from the Bible. A brief visit here should suffice.

Place Astrid. © 082/22-22-07. Free admission. Daily 10am–5pm.

SIGHTSEEING TOURS

Dinant is the best place on the Meuse for cruising, along the scenic reaches upstream and downstream. River cruises are offered by **Croisières Mosanes,** boulevard Winston Churchill, Quai 5 (© 082/22-23-15; www.bateaux-meuse.be). The cruises run from Easter to October, and last 45 minutes to 3½ hours. Boats depart from the quay beside the road bridge in the center of town.

WHERE TO STAY

Hôtel de la Couronne ✦   This pleasant, classic-style family hotel, constructed after the war, stands right in the center of town. It has comfortable and attractive rooms, as well as a good, moderately priced restaurant and tavern. The traditional decor and furnishings lend a homey feeling to the place.

Rue Adolphe-Sax 1–3, 5500 Dinant. © 082/22-24-41. Fax 082/22-70-31. www.hotellacouronne.com. 20 units. 70€–77€ ($88–$96) double. Rates include continental breakfast. AE, MC, V. Limited street parking. **Amenities:** Restaurant (Belgian); bar. *In room:* TV.

L'Auberge de Bouvignes ✦   Right on the banks of the Meuse, in this rustic, country-style inn, are six charming guest rooms. Refurbished in 2006, the rooms are decorated in blue or pink and brightened with lots of flowers and photogravures (etched images from photographic negatives) of scenes along the river. Accommodations at the front have fine views of the Meuse.

Rue Fétis 112, rte. de Namur (3.2km/2 miles from Dinant center), 5500 Dinant. © 082/61-16-00. Fax 082/61-30-93. www.aubergedebouvignes.be. 6 units. 59€ ($74) double. AE, DC, MC, V. Limited street parking. **Amenities:** Restaurant (Belgian); bar. *In room:* TV.

WHERE TO DINE

Restaurant Thermidor ✦ FRENCH   An old-fashioned, family-run place in the center of town, Restaurant Thermidor is widely considered the best restaurant in Dinant. Specialties include *truite au bleu* (oven-baked trout) and a terrific country-style *pâté de canard* (duck pâté). You should try the grilled kidneys with mustard sauce, a local favorite.

Rue de la Station 3. © 082/22-31-35. Main courses 11€–21€ ($14–$26); fixed-price lunch 15€ ($19). AE, MC, V. Wed–Mon noon–2:30pm; Wed–Sun 6–10pm.

5 Mons ✦

51km (32 miles) SW of Brussels; 66km (41 miles) W of Namur; 43km (27 miles) SE of Tournai

Hainaut's provincial capital started out as a fortified camp constructed by Julius Caesar's Roman legions. Today, it's home to SHAPE (Supreme Headquarters Allied Powers Europe). Between those military bookends, it saw a rich and eventful history. The

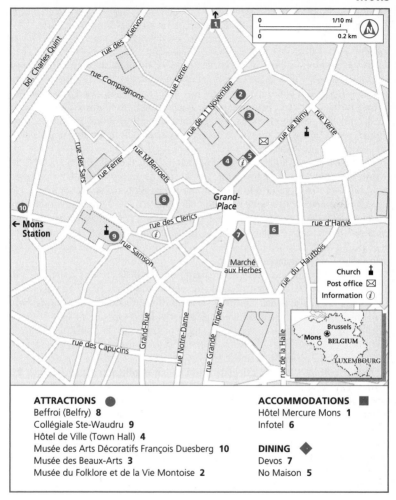

ATTRACTIONS ●
Beffroi (Belfry) **8**
Collégiale Ste-Waudru **9**
Hôtel de Ville (Town Hall) **4**
Musée des Arts Décoratifs François Duesberg **10**
Musée des Beaux-Arts **3**
Musée du Folklore et de la Vie Montoise **2**

ACCOMMODATIONS ■
Hôtel Mercure Mons **1**
Infotel **6**

DINING ◆
Devos **7**
No Maison **5**

Roman camp, set in a landscape of rolling hills (*mons* means "mount" in Latin), became a town when St. Waudru, daughter of a local nobleman, founded a convent here in the 600s. Mons was fortified in the 12th century by Count Baldwin IV of Flanders, and again by the Dutch in the early 1800s. Its present character reflects its more recent history as a center of industrialization and coal mining.

ESSENTIALS

GETTING THERE   Mons is an easy day trip from Brussels, with **train** service hourly. The station is on place Léopold, a short walk west from the center of town. To get to Mons by **car** from Brussels, take E19.

VISITOR INFORMATION   The **Office du Tourisme** is at Grand-Place 22, 7000 Mons (© **065/33-55-80;** fax 065/35-63-36; www.paysdemons.be). The office is open

Monday to Saturday from 9am to 6pm (5:30pm in winter), and Sunday from 1 to 6pm (5:30pm in winter).

WHAT TO SEE & DO

Almost everything you'll want to see here is on, or no more than a short walk from, the Grand-Place, which is lined by fine historic buildings and surrounded by steep, cobbled streets. But you don't have to walk—you can step on and off the free **Mons Intra Muros** minibuses. Two routes, Line A and Line B, run between the station and the Grand-Place every 6 minutes (every 3 min. on joint sections) daily from 7am to 9pm. If you're here when the weather is good, be sure to fit in some time at a sidewalk cafe on the Grand-Place.

The first thing you'll likely notice about Mons is the **Beffroi (Belfry),** a UNESCO World Heritage Site, at the highest point in town. Don't worry if you feel an urge to giggle at your first sight of this tower; it *does* look a bit comical, and as Victor Hugo remarked, somewhat like "an enormous coffee pot, flanked below belly-level by four medium-size teapots." Don't be perplexed if you hear the tower referred to as *le château*—it sits near the site of an old castle of the counts of Hainaut, and even though the castle was demolished in 1866, local people have never broken the habit of using the old designation.

A short distance across square du Château from the Belfry is the **Chapel St-Calixte** (© 065/35-12-08), the oldest structure in town, dating from 1051. The chapel holds the **Musée du Château des Comtes (Museum of the Castle of the Counts),** which contains relics, models, and archaeological finds. It's open May to mid-September, Tuesday to Sunday from 10am to 8pm; and mid-September to April, Tuesday to Sunday from 10am to 6pm. Admission is 2.50€ ($3.15) for adults, 1.25€ ($1.55) for seniors, and free for children under 13.

The remarkable Gothic **Collégiale Ste-Waudru (Collegiate Church of St. Waudru)** ★★, place du Chapitre (© 065/33-55-80; www.waudru.be), dating from 1450, honors the daughter of the count of Hainaut whose 7th-century convent marked the beginning of Mons as a town. The church stands below and a little to the west of the Belfry. Inside its vast vaulted space are 16th-century sculptures and wall carvings by Mons artist Jacques Du Broeuck. Around the choir, 16th-century stained-glass windows depict biblical scenes. At the entrance of the church, the **Car d'Or (Golden Coach)** waits for its annual spring outing (see box, "The Ducasse Festival on Trinity Sunday," above). The church is open Monday to Saturday from 9am to 6:30pm, and

---

Tips **The Ducasse Festival on Trinity Sunday**

Each year on Trinity Sunday—the eighth Sunday after Easter—Mons erupts in a burst of color, mock drama, and revelry, when it celebrates the **Ducasse de la Trinité Festival** ★. This begins with the Procession of the Golden Coach, when that vehicle from 1780 is drawn through the streets by a team of white horses, followed by richly dressed girls, and clerics bearing a gilded copper reliquary that holds the skull of St. Waudru. There follows a mock battle between St. George and the Dragon (known here as the *Lumeçon*). The evening performance of the Pageant of Mons by 2,000 musicians, singers, and actors brings the day to a close.

Fighting Talk

Mons has an important place in British military history, as the site of a stiff World War I battle on August 23 and 24, 1914. The greatly outnumbered British Expeditionary Force absorbed the pile-driver blows of the Kaiser's invading army, holding up the Germans on their advance to Paris.

Sunday from 7am to 6:30pm. Its **Trésor (Treasury)** is open March to November, Tuesday to Saturday from 1:30 to 6pm, and Sunday from 1:30 to 5pm (closed last week in May). Admission to both is free.

The centerpiece of the **Grand-Place** is the 15th-century **Hôtel de Ville (Town Hall).** Access is by a free guided tour from the tourist office, July to August daily at 2:30pm (at other times by arrangement). As you go through its main entrance, look to the left and perhaps stop to rub the head of "the monkey of the Grand-Garde," an iron monkey that's been granting good luck since the 15th century. Needless to say, by this time he has a very shiny pate. Inside the Town Hall are antique tapestries and paintings.

The Town Hall courtyard is occupied by the **Jardin du Mayeur (Mayor's Garden),** with fountains, trees, flowers, and plants. It's a good place to relax.

Musée des Arts Décoratifs (Museum of Decorative Arts) François Duesberg ✿

Housed in the 19th-century former National Bank of Belgium building, this museum has a fine collection of objects dating from 1775 to 1825, including exotic clocks, gilded bronzes, porcelain, crockery, gold, and silverwork. In addition, it displays 3,000 pieces of fine porcelain dating from the 17th to the 19th centuries.

Sq. Franklin Roosevelt 12 (entrance rue de la Houssière 2). © 065/84-16-56. Admission 4€ ($5) adults, free for children under 18. Apr–Dec Tues, Thurs, and Sat–Sun 2–7pm.

Musée des Beaux-Arts (Museum of Fine Arts) ✿

Despite its name, this museum in a side street off the Grand-Place occupies a remarkably ugly modern building. Its collections emphasize 19th- and 20th-century paintings and sculpture from Mons and Hainaut, and it displays older 15th- and 16th-century works such as *Ecce Homo* (1450) by Dirck Bouts. *Note:* The museum is closed for renovations until at least the spring of 2007.

Rue Neuve 8 (beside the Jardin du Mayeur). © 065/40-53-06. Admission (prices current when the museum closed for renovation; likely to increase when it reopens) 2€ ($2.50) adults; 1€ ($1.25) seniors, students, and children 13–18; free for children under 13. Tues–Sat noon–6pm; Sun 10am–noon and 2–6pm.

Musée du Folklore et de la Vie Montoise (Museum of Folklore and Life in Mons)

This 17th-century former convent hospital in the center of town houses collections of antique furniture, and folk and craft objects. The displays are organized according to themes, such as public welfare among the poor, religious observances, weights and measures, and Mons's Procession of the Golden Coach (see box "The Ducasse Festival on Trinity Sunday," above). *Note:* The museum, which stands in front of the Musée des Beaux-Arts (see above), has been affected by the work in progress there, and is closed until the spring of 2007.

Rue Neuve 8, in the Maison Jean Lescarts. © 065/31-43-57. Admission (prices current when the museum closed temporarily; likely to increase when it reopens) 2.50€ ($3.15) adults; 1.25€ ($1.55) seniors, students, and children 13–18; free for children under 13. Tues–Sat noon–6pm; Sun 10am–noon and 2–6pm.

NEARBY PLACES OF INTEREST

Grand-Hornu 🏛 This monument of industrial archaeology is a memorial to an idealistic—or paternalistic—employer. Mine-owner Henri de Gorge (1774–1832) constructed the complex between 1810 and 1830 in neoclassical style, and attached to it some 450 well-designed and well-equipped houses for his workers. Fallen into disuse and dereliction, Grand-Hornu was bought in the 1970s by a local architect and restored. It's a fascinating, unlikely mixture of antiquarian sensibility and gritty industrial reality that showcases the Victorian entrepreneurial tradition at its best.

Rue Ste-Louise 82, Hornu (13km/8 miles southwest of Mons). ℂ 065/65-21-21. www.grand-hornu.be. Admission 6€ ($7.50) adults; 4€ ($5) seniors, students, and ages 19–26; 2€ ($2.50) children 6–18; free for children under 6. Tues–Sun 10am–6pm. Closed Jan 1, Dec 25.

Maison Van Gogh (Van Gogh House) 🏛 During his days as a none-too-successful church missionary, the Dutch artist Vincent van Gogh lived in 1879 and 1880 in this miner's house in the Borinage coal-mining district. He preached the gospel to the mining families, while painting and drawing them and the bleak countryside. The house has been restored as a monument, with documents and an audiovisual presentation. *Note:* At this writing, the house was closed for renovations, and was expected to reopen in the spring of 2007.

Rue du Pavillon 3, Cuesmes (3km/2 miles south of Mons). ℂ 065/35-56-11. Admission (prices current at the time of the house's closure for renovations; these might change when it reopens) 2.50€ ($3.15) adults; 1.25€ ($1.55) seniors, students, and children 12–18; free for children under 12. Tues–Sun 10am–6pm. Closed Jan 1, Dec 25.

A NEARBY CASTLE

Château de Beloeil (Beloeil Castle) 🏛🏛 Beloeil Castle, the ancestral home of the prince de Ligne, has been called, with some justification, the "Versailles of Belgium." It is, quite simply, magnificent. The castle sits amid French-style gardens in its own park, on the shores of an ornamental lake. For more than a thousand years, the de Ligne family has lived in the grand style that pervades these vast rooms, filled with priceless antiques, paintings by the masters, historical mementos (among them a lock of Queen Marie Antoinette's hair), and more than 20,000 books, many of them rare editions.

Rue du Château 11, Beloeil (22km/14 miles northwest of Mons). ℂ 069/68-94-26. www.beloeil.be. Admission 6€ ($7.50) adults, 3.50€ ($4.40) children. Apr–May Sat–Sun 1–6pm; June–Sept daily 10am–6pm.

THE HAINAUT LAKES

Among several lakes in Hainaut are the artificial lakes of the **Barrages de l'Eau d'Heure** 🏛, at Boussu-lez-Walcourt in the Botte de Hainaut (Hainaut's Boot) district, south of Charleroi (off N798). The **Plate Taille** is Belgium's largest lake, covering 350 hectares (867 acres), and the entire area has been developed as a watersports center, with designated zones for windsurfing, jet-skiing, scuba diving, sailing, and water-skiing. For information on the area's ecology, go to the **Centre d'Acceuil** (ℂ 071/50-92-92; www.lacsdeleaudheure.be), the visitor center, beside the Plate Taille Dam. It's open daily from 10am to 6pm (7pm July–Aug). Admission is 5.50€ ($6.90) for adults, 4.50€ ($5.65) for seniors and children ages 6 to 12, and free for children under 6.

Farther south, near Chimay, are the **Etangs de Virelles (Virelles Lakes),** a protected nature reserve covering 100 hectares (247 acres) of natural lakes, wetlands, and forest. There are guided walking tours, and observation points for watching bird life. **Aquascope,** rue du Lac 42, Virelles-lez-Chimay (ℂ 060/21-13-63; www.aquascope. be), the lakes' nature park, has an exhibit and audiovisual presentation at its visitor center. It's open mid-March to June and September to mid-November, Tuesday to Sunday (and Mon during school vacations) from 10am to 5pm; July to August, daily from 10am to 7pm; and mid-November to mid-March, weekends, national holidays, and school vacations from 10am to 4pm; closed Jan 1, and Dec 24, 25, 31. Admission is 6€ ($7.50) for adults, 3.50€ ($4.40) for children ages 6 to 12, and free for children under 6; various activities in the reserve have additional charges.

WHERE TO STAY

Hôtel Mercure Mons   Lodging here only really makes sense if you're traveling by car or looking to sink a few putts at the local golf courses. The hotel is outside of Mons, in quiet, rural surroundings, and not well served by public transportation. Guest rooms at this business-traveloriented hotel, while affording tranquil views of woodlands and fields, don't have much in the way of local character, and their brown color palette is a shade downbeat. They are, however, spacious and have large beds and bathrooms.

Rue des Fusillées (off N56), 7020 Mons. ✆ **065/72-36-85.** Fax 065/72-41-44. www.mercure.com. 53 units. 110€–160€ ($138–$200) double. AE, DC, MC, V. Free parking. **Amenities:** Restaurant (Belgian); bar; outdoor pool. *In room:* TV, coffeemaker, safe.

Infotel   The centrally located Infotel, a welcome addition to Mons's hotel scene, has pretty guest rooms with thoughtful touches—wood furnishings offset by sky-blue curtains and salmon-pink walls, for example. The hotel offers a concierge, daytime room service, and laundry and dry-cleaning service.

Rue d'Havré 32, 7000 Mons. ✆ **065/40-18-30.** Fax 065/35-62-24. www.hotelinfotel.be. 25 units. 62€–93€ ($78–$116) double. Rates include continental breakfast. AE, DC, MC, V. Free parking. **Amenities:** Concierge; limited room service; laundry service; dry cleaning. *In room:* TV.

WHERE TO DINE

Devos ✿ FRENCH/BELGIAN   One of Mons's finest restaurants occupies a courtyard setting just off the Grand-Place. Seafood dishes are a specialty, and beef and veal are good backups. The chef will prepare a delicious roast duckling with black cherries if you request it when booking. Try some of the menu items cooked *à la bière* (in beer).

Rue de la Coupe 7 (off Grand-Place). ✆ **065/35-13-35.** www.restaurantdevos.be. Main courses 15€–23€ ($19–$29); fixed-price lunch 30€ ($38); fixed-price menus 50€–95€ ($63–$119). AE, DC, MC, V. Daily noon–2pm; Mon–Tues and Thurs–Sat 7–9:30pm. Closed 1 week in Feb, 3 weeks from mid-July.

No Maison BELGIAN   Thinking up a less promising name for a restaurant would be a tough proposition, but "no" is likely to become "yes" once you've tried it. A simple enough place, on three floors of an old patrician house, with a fine view over the Grand-Place from window tables, No focuses on Belgian and Mons specialties, such as *escavêche Montoise* (eel). Dark wood paneling is offset by colorful paintings of local festivals.

Grand-Place 21. ✆ **065/31-11-11.** www.nomaison.be. Main courses 9€–17€ ($11–$21); *plat du jour* 9€ ($11); *menu Montoise* 22€ ($28). MC, V. Daily 10am–2am.

6 Tournai ✿✿

72km (45 miles) SW of Brussels; 43km (27 miles) NW of Mons

Historic, handsome Tournai, on the Escaut River, is Belgium's second-oldest town (after Tongeren). During medieval and Renaissance times, it had a position of prominence as a European ecclesiastical center. Its importance in earlier centuries was forgotten until 1653, when a workman discovered the tomb of Childeric, king of the Franks, whose son, Clovis, founded the Merovingian dynasty that ruled for nearly 3 centuries. This led to the discovery that Tournai's predecessor, a Roman settlement known as Tornacum, was the first capital of the Frankish empire. The tomb yielded breathtaking royal treasures—the best of which, sadly, are now in Paris.

In World War II, a full 60% of the town's buildings were destroyed—it can only be deemed a miracle that the great cathedral emerged with little damage. Tournai still has magnificent works of art and architecture, the legacy of its painters, sculptors, goldsmiths, tapestry weavers, and porcelain craftsmen. Today, the town greets you with glorious monuments that are once more intact.

ESSENTIALS

GETTING THERE   A 1½-hour train ride from Brussels gets you here. The **Tournai station** is on the northern edge of town, on boulevard des Nerviens. By **car** from Brussels, Tournai is less than an hour's drive on A8/E429.

VISITOR INFORMATION   The **Office du Tourisme** is at Vieux Marché aux Poteries 14, 7500 Tournai (✆ **069/22-20-45;** fax 069/21-62-21; www.tournai.be), facing the Belfry. The center is open Easter to September, Monday to Friday from 8:30am to 6pm, and weekends from 10am to noon and 2 to 5pm; October to Easter, Monday to Friday from 8:30am to 5:30pm, Saturday from 10am to noon and 2 to 5pm, and Sunday and holidays from 2:30 to 6pm; closed January 1 and 2; November 1, 2, 11, and 15; and December 24 to 26 and 31.

SPECIAL EVENTS   Tournai celebrates amid splendid pageantry the Nativity of Our Lady on the second Sunday in September, with the religious **Procession of Tournai** through the city. On the **Days of the Four Parades,** during the second weekend in June, episodes from Tournai's history are reenacted in a series of folklore processions and events.

WHAT TO SEE & DO

To get an idea of how Tournai looked in medieval times, take a stroll along rue Barre St-Brice on the opposite side of the Escaut from the center city. **Pont des Trous (Bridge of Holes)** on quai Sakharov is an appropriate name for this 13th-century bridge. It has taken its lumps from any number of battles and sieges since then—most recently in 1944, when it was blown up. The bridge and its two anchoring towers once formed part of the city's defensive walls. Another military work, the 24m-high (80-ft.) **Tour Henry VIII,** in rue du Rempart, named for the notorious English king of the six-wives fame, dates from a period of English occupation from 1512 to 1518.

Beffroi (Belfry)   A UNESCO World Heritage Site, The Belfry dates from the late 1100s, making it Belgium's oldest. If you're up for it, climb the 265 steps to the top

---

⎛Moments Still Standing

Although you can't go inside, you can at least peruse in Tournai the exteriors of what are said to be some of the oldest private houses still in existence in Europe. Nos. 10 and 12 rue Barre Saint-Brice date from 1175. In the same neighborhood, 13th-century **Gothic houses** line rue des Jésuites.

Tournai

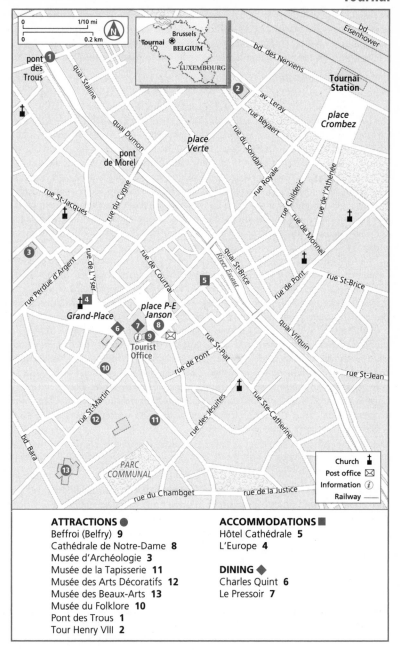

of this 72m (236-ft.) tower; you'll be rewarded with glorious views of the town and surrounding countryside. The 44-bell carillon plays Saturday-morning concerts.

Vieux Marché aux Poteries. ℂ **069/22-20-45.** Admission 2.50€ ($3.15). Mar–Oct Mon–Sat 10am–noon and 2–5:30pm, Sun 11am–1pm and 2–6:30pm; Nov–Feb Mon–Sat 10am–noon and 2–5pm, Sun 2–5pm.

Cathédrale Notre-Dame (Cathedral of Our Lady) ✸✸✸   This magnificent five-towered cathedral, a UNESCO World Heritage Site, is one of Europe's most striking examples of Romanesque architecture. Completed in the late 1100s, it's not the first place of worship to stand on this spot. There was a church here as early as A.D. 761, and it's thought there was a pagan temple before that. The 8th-century church was replaced by another in 850, which Viking raiders burned to the ground in 881. After fire again destroyed the replacement church in 1060, it was reconstructed by 1089 and became a place of refuge for a plague-stricken population. On September 14, 1090, after the dreaded disease had abated, the bishop led a great procession through the cathedral to honor Our Lady, who was credited with miraculous cures of sick pilgrims who had poured into the cathedral to pray before her statue. Since then, the **Procession of Tournai** has taken place every year, except 1559, when Calvinists broke into the cathedral in a destructive orgy.

The Romanesque style was, in the eyes of a 13th-century bishop, old-fashioned compared to the Gothic buildings that were then appearing all over Europe. Before his money ran out, he had added stained-glass windows and created a soaring, graceful Gothic choir adjoining the low Romanesque nave. There's no sense of disharmony, but rather a compatible marriage of the two styles.

Paintings by Rubens and Jordaens adorn the interior, along with 700-year-old murals, a Renaissance pulpit, and a stained-glass "rose window." Even these wonders pale before the display in the **Trésor (Treasury),** which houses a vast collection of priceless religious relics and antiquities. The centerpiece is a reliquary that takes the place of honor in the Procession of Tournai, the *Chasse de Notre-Dame,* with a gold covering created by Nicholas of Verdun in 1205. Other treasures include 15th-century tapestries (one 22m/72 ft. long), a jewel-encrusted 10th-century Byzantine cross, and a 14th-century ivory statue of the Virgin.

Place de l'Evêché (just off the Grand-Place). ℂ **069/22-31-91.** www.cathedrale-tournai.be. Free admission to Cathedral; Treasury 2€ ($2.50). Cathedral: Apr–Oct daily 9:15am–noon and 2–6pm; Nov–Mar daily 9:15am–noon and 2–5pm. Treasury: Apr–Oct daily 9:30am–noon and 2–6pm; Nov–Mar daily 9:30am–noon and 2–5pm.

Musée d'Archéologie (Archaeological Museum)   A 17th-century pawnshop in the center of town houses collections of Tournai relics covering virtually every period in its history. The Merovingian section features items recovered in and around the tomb of Childeric, including the skeletons of horses sacrificed during the 5th-century Frank king's funeral. There's a fine collection of glassware from the Gallo-Roman period of the 1st to the 4th century.

Rue des Carmes 8. ℂ **069/22-16-72.** Admission 4€ ($5) adults, 1€ ($1.25) students and children 6–18, free for children under 6. Apr–Oct Wed–Sun 9:30am–12:30pm and 2–5:30pm; Nov–Mar Wed–Sun 10am–noon and 2–5pm.

Musée des Arts Décoratifs (Museum of Decorative Arts)   This museum features examples of the exquisite porcelain and china made in Tournai in the 18th century, including the dinner service for the duc d'Orléans, and displays of fine silverware and historical coins.

Rue St-Martin 50. ℂ **069/33-23-53.** Admission 4€ ($5) adults, 1€ ($1.25) students and children 6–18, free for children under 6. Apr–Oct Wed–Sun 9:30am–12:30pm and 2–5:30pm; Nov–Mar Wed–Sun 10am–noon and 2–5pm.

Musée des Beaux-Arts (Museum of Fine Arts) ★★ It's hard to say which is more impressive: the museum's 700 works of art, or the building dating from 1928 that houses them. The star-shaped white stone structure, its interior illuminated by natural light, was designed by noted Art Nouveau architect Victor Horta. The art collections contain such outstanding works as *Virgin and Child* by 15th-century native son Roger de la Pasture (Rogier van der Weyden); and Edouard Manet's *Argenteuil* and *At Father Lathuille's*. Other Belgian artists represented include Pieter Brueghel the Younger, James Ensor, Henri de Braekeleer, and Sir Anthony van Dyck.

Enclos St-Martin (off rue St-Martin). ✆ 069/22-20-43. Admission 4€ ($5) adults, 1€ ($1.25) students and children 6–18, free for children under 6. Apr–Oct Wed–Sun 9:30am–12:30pm and 2–5:30pm; Nov–Mar Wed–Sun 10am–noon and 2–5pm.

Musée du Folklore (Folklore Museum) ★ Two marvelous 17th-century buildings in the center city, complete with gables and mullioned windows, provide just the right setting for a series of authentic re-creations of an ancient farmhouse, a tavern, a weaver's workroom, a blacksmith's forge, and many other old scenes, aimed at preserving the atmosphere of Tournai in times gone by. A fast-food stall shows how french fries were dispensed at the turn of the 20th century.

Réduit des Sions. ✆ 069/22-40-69. Admission 4€ ($5) adults, 1€ ($1.25) students and children 6–18, free for children under 6. Apr–Oct Wed–Sun 9:30am–12:30pm and 2–5:30pm; Nov–Mar Wed–Sun 10am–noon and 2–5pm.

Musée de la Tapisserie (Tapestry Museum) In the late Middle Ages, Tournai was one of the great European centers of tapestry making, and this museum reflects that heritage. Several historical tapestries are displayed, but the museum focuses more on contemporary works, including pieces by modern Belgian artists like Roger Somville.

Place Reine Astrid 9. ✆ 069/23-42-85. Admission 4€ ($5) adults, 1€ ($1.25) students and children 6–18, free for children under 6. Apr–Oct Wed–Sun 9:30am–12:30pm and 2–5:30pm; Nov–Mar Wed–Sun 10am–noon and 2–5pm.

SIGHTSEEING TOURS

From April until the end of August, **horse-drawn carriages** are available to roll you through Tournai cobblestone streets. They depart from the Grand-Place. A 30-minute ride for one to five people costs 20€ ($25).

The **Tournai from the River** boat cruise on the Escaut lasts about an hour and departs from the dock at Pont des Trous from May to August, Tuesday to Sunday at 11am, 2:30pm, and 4:15pm. Tickets are 8€ ($10) for adults, 5€ ($6.25) for children 3 to 10, and free for children under 3.

WHERE TO STAY

L'Europe This hotel right in the central square follows the rustic style common in Tournai—except that in this case the style of the building is rustic Spanish—with antique paintings and lots of flowers in the public spaces. The guest rooms, plain but comfortable, feature modern furnishings, and some of them overlook the Grand-Place. The ground-floor cocktail bar **Le Tam Tam** provides other views of the square.

Grand-Place 36, 7500 Tournai. ✆ 069/22-40-67. Fax 069/23-52-38. 8 units. 65€ ($81) double. Rates include continental breakfast. AE, DC, MC, V. Limited street parking. **Amenities:** Restaurant (Belgian); cocktail bar. *In room:* TV.

WHERE TO DINE

Charles Quint ★ BELGIAN It's nearly always crowded here at lunch, and deservedly so. The kitchen produces excellent fish, fowl, and meat dishes. Try the *foie* *de canard au chicon* (duck liver with chicory) or the exceptional beef filet with onions and bacon. The restaurant is in Art Deco style, with mixed brown and orange colors, and is located in the center city overlooking the Belfry.

Grand-Place 3. ⓒ **069/22-14-41**. www.charles-quint.be. Main courses 17€–24€ ($21–$29); fixed-price lunch 33€ ($41); fixed-price menu 47€ ($59). AE, DC, MC, V. Fri–Wed noon–2:30pm; Fri–Tues 7–10:30pm.

Le Pressoir CONTINENTAL   This elegant restaurant is in the 17th-century former winepress of Tournai Cathedral. It retains as much of its antique ambience as possible in its interior fittings and silver tableware. The setting is subdued and sophisticated, and the fare is mouthwatering. Look for the duck and fish specialties, and such dishes as grilled lobster with fresh herbs, oven-baked turbot with fried shallots, and kidney with orange sauce and herbs.

Vieux Marché aux Poteries 2. ⓒ **069/22-35-13**. Main courses 11€–23€ ($14–$28); fixed-price menu 35€ ($44). AE, DC, MC, V. Sun–Thurs noon–2:30pm; Fri–Sat noon–2:30pm and 6:30–9:30pm.

10

The Ardennes

A scenic and gastronomic delight, the Ardennes is a welcome respite from museum hopping. With the change in landscape comes a shift in emphasis, away from treasures hoarded indoors and toward the outdoor riches of bracing air, winding mountain roads, sparkling streams, and tranquil lakes. Add to that some pretty resort towns, nestled in steep river valleys, and fine old country inns—now you have an idea of the Ardennes.

The region offers a cornucopia of outdoor possibilities (though the landscape is one of hills, rather than genuine mountains): hiking, biking, canoeing, fishing, golf, hunting, horseback riding, skiing, swimming, tennis, and more. Tourist offices can point the way to any necessary rental equipment.

Recommending an itinerary for the Ardennes is difficult. I don't think you can do better than to follow your nose. Sooner or later you'll bump into some biggish place like Spa, Bouillon, Bastogne, or Durbuy where you can join other wanderers. If you stick to the back roads, you'll have fun getting lost among all the stone villages and farmhouses for which the region is justly famed. Many of these were reconstructed after being destroyed during the Battle of the Bulge in the winter of 1944 and 1945.

1 Bouillon ⓐ

60km (38 miles) SE of Dinant

At a strategic bend in the Semois River, this little town guarded the major route from the Eifel to Champagne for centuries. In addition to a spectacular location in the plunging river valley, Bouillon boasts the country's finest medieval castle. The awesome 10th-century feudal castle of Godefroy de Bouillon, leader of the First Crusade to the Holy Land, still stands over the town, crouching like a great stone dragon on a steep bluff.

Bouillon is also a scenic and gastronomic stronghold. Where better to try bouillon than in the place that gave it its name?

ESSENTIALS

GETTING THERE　Frequent **bus** service runs from the Libramont **rail** station. For bus information, call ⓒ **061/46-62-57.** By **car** from Dinant, take N95 southeast and then N89 south to Bouillon.

VISITOR INFORMATION　The **Maison du Tourisme du Pays de Bouillon,** Quai des Saulx 12, 6830 Bouillon (ⓒ **061/46-52-11;** fax 061/46-52-18; www.bouillon-tourisme.be), is open March to November, daily from 10am to 5pm; December to February, Monday to Friday from 1 to 5pm.

The Ardennes on a Plate
Food lovers rejoice! This region is home to the delicately smoked Ardennes ham (*jambon d'Ardenne*) proudly served all over Belgium, and of other regional specialties, including game and fresh trout and pike. The Ardennes is famed for its wealth of gourmet restaurants, many in country inns where the innkeeper doubles as a fine chef.

SEEING THE SIGHTS

Château de Bouillon (Bouillon Castle) ★★★   Once home to Duke Godefroy de Bouillon, this massive, sprawling castle is the town's dramatic centerpiece, floodlit every night during summer months. The worthy de Bouillon actually put the castle in hock in order to raise funds for his great venture, the First Crusade. The mortgaged castle passed by default into the hands of the prince-bishops of Liège, who continued to hold it for 6 centuries. After the 15th century, it was conquered and reconquered several times, as local rulers and invading forces fought over this strategic spot. Within the castle's thick walls, life during its turbulent history will come alive as you walk through the ruins and visit the old prisons and gallows and the so-called Hall of Justice.

Rue des Hautes-Voies 33. ℂ 061/46-62-57. Admission 5.20€ ($6.50) adults, 4.50€ ($5.65) seniors, 3.80€ ($4.75) students, 3.50€ ($4.40) children 6–12, free for children under 6. Combined tickets for Bouillon Castle and Ducal Museum 8€ ($10) adults, 4.80€ ($6) children 6–12, free for children under 6. Jan–Feb and Dec Mon–Fri 1–5pm, Sat–Sun 10am–5pm; Mar and Oct–Nov daily 10am–5pm; Apr–June and Sept Mon–Fri 10am–6pm, Sat–Sun 10am–6:30pm; July–Aug daily 10am–6:30pm (and visit at 10pm Wed and Fri–Sun).

Musée Ducal (Ducal Museum) ★   This museum, in an 18th-century house, contains exhibits on the region's archaeology, iron industry, and folklore. It includes the Godfrey of Bouillon Museum, which holds souvenirs of the Crusades and of gallant Godfrey, including a model of Godfrey's tomb in Jerusalem as well as armor, weapons, and religious objects of the period.

Rue du Petit 1–3. ℂ **061/46-41-89.** www.museeducal.be. Admission 4€ ($5) adults, 3.50€ ($4.40) seniors, 3€ ($3.75) students, 2.50€ ($3.15) children 6–12, free for children under 6. Combined tickets for Bouillon Castle and Ducal Museum 8€ ($10) adults, 4.80€ ($6) children 6–12, free for children under 6. Easter to mid-Nov and school vacations daily 10am–6pm (5pm Oct to mid-Nov).

WHERE TO STAY

Aux Armes de Bouillon   This large hotel in the town center has nicely appointed guest rooms. It offers an indoor heated swimming pool, private garden, sauna, whirlpool, and sun lamp. There's a bar and a moderately priced restaurant on the premises.

Rue de la Station 9–15, 6830 Bouillon. ℂ 061/46-60-79. Fax 061/46-60-84. 60 units. 65€–110€ ($81–$138) double. Rates include buffet breakfast. AE, DC, MC, V. Limited street parking. **Amenities:** Restaurant (Belgian); bar; lounge; heated indoor pool; sauna. *In room:* TV, minibar.

WHERE TO STAY & DINE NEARBY

Auberge du Moulin Hideux ★   Set beside an old water mill, with wooded hills almost at its doorstep, you'll find one of Belgium's prettiest country inns. A warm, subdued sophistication exudes from the decor. A focal point for guests is the crackling log fire, which is surrounded by luxurious leather furniture and touches of brass to complete the lounge scene. The glassed-in bar is decorated with plants. The 12 guest

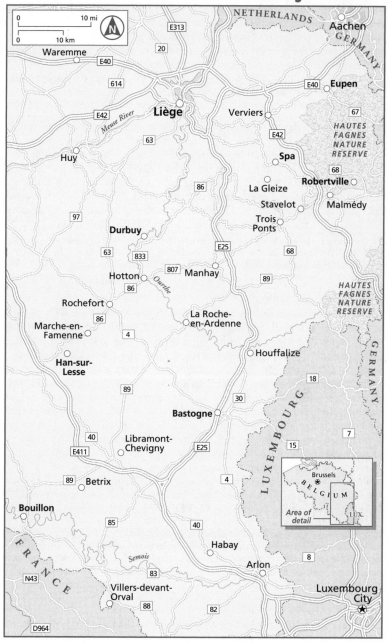

rooms are appointed with the same sense of style. Extras include beautiful forest walks and horse riding trails nearby. The hotel's notable restaurant serves meals that feature lamb, saddle of pork, game, and fish delicacies such as baby lobsters (which are kept in a tank out in the garden). Everything is cooked to order, so be prepared to wait a bit for your dinner—your patience will be rewarded.

Rte. de Dohan 1 (4km/2½ miles from Bouillon), 6831 Noirefontaine. © 061/46-70-15. Fax 061/46-72-81. www. moulinhideux.be. 12 units. 190€ ($238) double; 250€ ($313) suite. Rates include full breakfast. AE, DC, MC, V. Free parking. **Amenities:** Restaurant (Continental); bar; lounge; heated indoor pool; tennis courts. *In room:* TV, minibar.

Hostellerie du Prieuré de Conques ★   This is a great spot to enjoy perfect tranquillity on the edge of an Ardennes forest, in an atmospheric inn on the banks of the Semois River. This hotel is set in what was once a 7th-century convent (although the oldest remains go back only as far as the 12th c.). It overlooks green lawns, rose gardens, and the Semois River. The charming guest rooms are individual in shape and character—some have alcoves, some peek from beneath the eaves—and their comfort rates just as high as their charm. The vaulted main dining room is warmed by an open fire, and any overflow of diners spills into a bevy of smaller vaulted rooms.

Rue de Conques 2, Ste-Cécile, 6820 Florenville © 061/41-14-17. Fax 061/41-27-03. www.conques.be. 18 units. 110€–160€ ($138–$200) double. Rates include full breakfast. AE, DC, MC, V. Free parking. Take N83 about 23km (14 miles) south and east from Bouillon. **Amenities:** Restaurant (Continental); bar; lounge. *In room:* TV, minibar, hair dryer.

A SIDE TRIP TO ORVAL ★
A handful of monks administer the impressive **Abbaye Notre-Dame d'Orval (Abbey of Our Lady of Orval)** ★, Villers-devant-Orval (© 061/31-10-60; www.orval.be), set in a forest. The serene and fascinating abbey dates back to the coming of the first Cistercians in 1110, though much was left in ruins after a destructive visit from the French in 1793. Today the complex includes the old ruins and a church, its gardens, and a brewery that produces one of Belgium's finest beers. A visit to the abbey is an exercise in serenity, since there is now little to suggest the enormous power its Cistercian monks wielded in past centuries. The old ruins are fascinating. Legend has it that somewhere in the web of underground passages that connected the abbey to seven nearby lakes, a vast treasure lies hidden. The abbey is open daily: March to May and October, from 9:30am to 5:30pm; June to September, from 9:30am to 6:30pm; November to February, from 10:30am to 5:30pm. Admission is 4.50€ ($5.65) for adults, 4€ ($5) for seniors and students, 2.50€ ($3.15) for children ages 7 to 14, and free for children under 7. To get here by car from Bouillon, take the country road 27km (17 miles) southeast through Florenville; TEC bus no. 24 passes by the monastery.

2 Bastogne ★ & Han-sur-Lesse
These two towns offer dramatically different experiences, while sharing the scenic beauty and fresh air that are the Ardennes's strongest suit.

BASTOGNE
70km (44 miles) S of Liège

During the Battle of the Bulge in the bitter winter of 1944 and 1945, the U.S. 101st Airborne Division, outnumbered and surrounded, held the town and its vital road network until a relief force could break through to them. It was a hard, nip-and-tuck fight for the troopers of the 101st—the "Battered Bastards of Bastogne," they dubbed themselves. Their commander, Brig. Gen. Anthony MacAuliffe, answered German demands for surrender with a single word that became legend: "Nuts!" During the annual December memorial days, you'll see the division's Screaming Eagle emblem around town.

ESSENTIALS
GETTING THERE   Bastogne makes a good day trip from almost any point in the Ardennes, but it's a little out-of-the-way to use as a base for exploring. There are regular **buses** from Liège and other towns—take the Liège-Athus bus from Libramont rail station. By **car** from Liège, take Exit 53 or 54 off the A26/E25 Liège–Luxembourg City expressway.

VISITOR INFORMATION   The **Maison du Tourisme du Pays de Bastogne,** place MacAuliffe, 6600 Bastogne (℃ **061/21-27-11;** fax 061/21-27-25; www.paysde bastogne.be), is open daily from 9:30am to 12:30pm and 1 to 5:30pm.

EXPLORING BASTOGNE
American Memorial & Bastogne Historical Center ★★   A visit to the Historical Center will lay the groundwork for a better appreciation of the great battle fought here in December 1944. General MacAuliffe of the 101st Airborne Division and his opponent, Gen. Hasso von Manteuffel of the Fifth Panzer Army, both gave advice in putting together the film, dioramas, and commentary that tell the story of the siege of Bastogne. Afterward, visitors can climb to the gigantic star-shaped memorial to America's fallen on Mardasson Hill. Key points of the battlefield are clearly posted for those interested in retracing the course of the fighting.

Colline du Mardasson (1.6km/1 mile outside Bastogne). ℃ **061/21-14-13.** www.bastognehistoricalcenter.be. Admission 8.50€ ($11) adults, 7€ ($8.75) seniors, 6€ ($7.50) children 8–12, free for World War II veterans and children under 8. May–Sept daily 9:30am–6pm; Mar–Apr and Oct–Dec daily 10am–5:30pm; Jan–Feb by arrangement. Closed Dec 24, 25, and 31.

HAN-SUR-LESSE
40km (25 miles) NW of Bastogne; 25km (16 miles) SE of Dinant

This is a particularly good stop for those traveling with children, though the two places described below are very interesting for adults as well.

ESSENTIALS
GETTING THERE   **Trains** from Namur and Liège stop at nearby Jemelle, from where a **bus** service connects with Han-sur-Lesse. By **car** from Dinant, take N94 southeast to its junction with N86; then go northeast on this road for the last few miles.

VISITOR INFORMATION   The **Office du Tourisme** is at place Théo Lannoy, 5580 Han-sur-Lesse (℃/fax **084/37-75-76;** www.rochefort.be). The office is open in summer daily from 1:30 to 5:30pm; in winter Monday to Friday from 10am to 4pm.

WHAT TO SEE & DO
Grottes de Han (Han Caves) ★ *Kids*   Of the several cave complexes in the Ardennes, this one is probably the most spectacular and worth visiting. Only about one-fifth of the cave is open to the general public, though other parts are accessible to experienced speleologists. Guides take visitors on an hour-long tour to see the stalagmites and stalactites, marvel at the sometimes bizarre and sometimes graceful shapes taken on by the

The Battle of the Bulge

Hitler aimed his last great offensive squarely at the Americans, because he believed that if he hit them hard enough, their easygoing, multi-ethnic, citizen army would fall apart and run. By mid-December 1944, he had assembled his last reserves of men, tanks, and guns, including the elite SS Panzer divisions, in the hilly, misty Eifel region of Germany, opposite the thinly held American lines in the Ardennes. In one of the great failures of military intelligence, the American high command didn't know they were there.

On the morning of December 16, the German forces came charging out of the forests. Their aim was far-reaching: to smash straight through the American line, cross the Meuse River before Allied reinforcements had time to intervene, capture Brussels and the vital port of Antwerp, split the American army from the British and Canadians, and break the Allied coalition.

The Führer's ambition outstripped his means, but in the Ardennes he had overwhelming strength for the attack: 300,000 against 80,000 on the first day. A few of the hard-hit American defenders "bugged out," but most held their ground until forced back or overrun. Savage struggles all across the Ardennes in Belgium and Luxembourg propelled the names of obscure towns, villages, and places into the history books: Rocherath and Krinkelt, the Elsenborn Ridge, Malmédy, Stavelot, Trois Ponts, La Gleize, Sankt-Vith, the Skyline Drive, Clervaux, Wiltz, and, of course, Bastogne. The action came to be called the Battle of the Bulge, after the shape the front took as German forces pushed through the middle of the Ardennes.

The lightly armed U.S. 82nd and 101st Airborne divisions were rushed in to stem the German armored tide until heavier reinforcements could be brought to bear. While the 82nd fought no-quarter battles with SS troops

limestone rock of the caves, and listen to the echo in the great subterranean chambers carved out by the Lesse River. The highlight is a boat trip on an underground river.

Rue Joseph Lamotte 2. ℂ 084/37-72-13. www.grotte-de-han.be. Admission (guided tours only) 11€ ($13) adults, 7€ ($8.75) children 6–12, 6€ ($7.50) children under 6. Jan–Mar Sat–Sun 11:30am–1pm and 2:30–4:30pm; Apr–June daily 10am–noon and 1:30–4:30pm (5:30pm Sat–Sun and holidays); July–Aug daily 9:30am–noon and 1:30–5pm (5:30pm mid-June to mid-July); Sept–Oct daily 10am–noon and 1:30–4:30pm; Christmas week daily 11:30am and 1, 2:30, and 4pm.

Réserve d'Animaux Sauvages (Wildlife Reserve) ★ Kids
The Wildlife Reserve, which is part of the same tourist complex as the Grottes, gives you a breath of fresh air after the damp and chilly caves. You can take a guided tour by train through the scenic Massif du Boine estate, where you may see wild boars, wild horses, stags, fallow deer, wolves, bison, ibex, chamois, tarpans, lynx, brown bears, and other animals—many of them native to the area, but some imported.

Departures from rue Joseph Lamotte 2, Han-sur-Lesse. ℂ 084/37-72-12. Admission (guided tours only) 8.75€ ($11) adults, 5.25€ ($6.55) children 6–12, 4.50€ ($5.65) children under 6. Jan–Mar Sat–Sun 11:30am–1pm and 2:30–4:30pm; Apr–June daily 10am–noon and 1:30–4:30pm (5:30pm Sat–Sun and holidays); July–Aug daily 9:30am–noon and 1:30–5pm (5:30pm mid-June to mid-July); Sept–Oct daily 10am–noon and 1:30–4:30pm; Christmas week daily 11:30am and 1, 2:30, and 4pm.

who had massacred American prisoners and murdered Belgian civilians, the 101st found itself cut off in Bastogne, holding the vital road junction there.

On December 26, the enemy spearhead was destroyed just a few miles short of the Meuse. General George S. Patton's Third Army, counterattacking from the south, relieved Bastogne. More weeks of heavy fighting pushed the German army back to its start line. Hitler's great gamble had failed, with German casualties above 100,000 out of 500,000 engaged.

The victors were the ordinary GI's who, in the depths of winter, outnumbered, and faced with a surprise offensive by a still powerful foe, had refuted Hitler's contemptuous opinion of them in the only way that mattered. The price of victory was 81,000 American casualties out of 600,000 engaged: 19,000 killed, 47,000 wounded, and 15,000 captured. Memorials all over the Ardennes bear witness to their courage and sacrifice.

Those of the fallen not repatriated, or still lying somewhere among the Ardennes forests, rest at the military cemeteries of **Neuville-en-Condroz** and **Henri-Chapelle.** Both are U.S. soil, donated in perpetuity by the people of Belgium. So many names on the long rows of white crosses and Stars of David on the carefully tended lawns; and so many "known but to God."

If you want to know more, read Charles B. MacDonald's *A Time for Trumpets: The Untold Story of the Battle of the Bulge* (William Morrow, 1984). A company commander with the 2nd Infantry Division, MacDonald fought in the Ardennes and later became a U.S. Army historian. His book skillfully melds the strategic picture and the tactical ebb and flow with up-close-and-personal experiences of the men who did the fighting, the bleeding, and the dying.

3 Durbuy ⟨★

31km (19 miles) S of Liège

Durbuy makes an ideal touring base. A quaint, medieval town on a bend in the river, its narrow, twisting streets are lined with pretty, flower-trimmed stone houses. It even has an 11th-century castle to complete the scene.

ESSENTIALS

GETTING THERE In July and August only, there is one **bus** to Durbuy a day from Barvaux **rail** station. By **car** from Liège, take Exit 48 west from A26/E25.

VISITOR INFORMATION The **Syndicat d'Initiative** is at place aux Foires 25, 6940 Durbuy (© **086/21-24-28;** fax 086/21-36-81; www.durbuyinfo.be).

EXPLORING DURBUY

The village is pretty (though the main square is a big parking lot) without having any particularly outstanding sights. Wander around to peruse its medieval stone buildings, many of which house artists and craftspeople; or take a walk by the plunging valley of the Ourthe River or into the nearby forests. You get fine views of the town from scenic overlooks in the surrounding hills, and good exercise getting to them in the first place. Besides all that, there's crazy golf for the kids. Stores abound, selling antiques, pottery, handmade jewelry, and locally produced artisanal food and drink, including chocolates, liqueur, and beer.

WHERE TO STAY & DINE IN DURBUY

Le Clos des Récollets   In the heart of the old village, in a pedestrian zone fronted by 17th-century buildings, you'll come to Le Clos des Récollets. Housed in a structure that dates from the 17th century, it has 18th-century modifications. The interior conserves the style of the period, with oak doors, oil paintings, and wooden furnishings. Illumination is provided by candle, as much as possible. The guest rooms are rather plainly furnished, but quite comfortable. On the premises is a good, moderately priced restaurant, with umbrella tables on a terrace for outdoor dining. Menu items include game in season, such as pheasant, and lobster stew with vegetables.

Rue de la Prévôté 9, 6940 Durbuy. © **086/21-29-69.** Fax 086/21-36-85. www.closdesrecollets.be. 8 units. 80€ ($100) double. Rates include full breakfast. AE, DC, MC, V. Free parking. **Amenities:** Restaurant (Belgian); bar; lounge. *In room:* TV, minibar.

Le Sanglier des Ardennes ★★★   This stellar, centrally located hotel overlooking a shallow gorge offers comfortable rooms replete with old-fashioned charm. Those in the back overlook the Ourthe River; those in the front have a postcard-pretty view of the old town, with mountains in the background. The restaurant on the ground floor is internationally famous. In this cozy spot overlooking the Ourthe River on the main street in the town center, master chef Maurice Caerdinael creates internationally acclaimed classic dishes. Fish straight from the river outside come to the table full-flavored, with subtle sauces or seasonings that add to their delicacy. Regional specialties such as game and the famed smoked *jambon* (ham) take on new dimensions after passing through this extraordinary kitchen. The superb wine cellar reflects the chef's expertise. There's a covered terrace for outdoor dining.

Skiing the Ardennes

It may not be the Alps, and it sure ain't the Rockies, but Belgium's Ardennes region can be something of a skier's paradise—so long as the snow shows up. Therein lies the problem. In the low Ardennes hills—the highest point is a mere 694m (2,256 ft.) above sea level—snow's appearance is often brief and unpredictable. Some years it stays away altogether. Still, when the thermometer starts dropping, ski aficionados in Belgium take serious notice. Skiing is particularly popular on weekends.

Although there are some downhill slopes, cross-country is more usual. Traversing the gentle wooded hills or the high plateau of the Hautes Fagnes Nature Reserve can be a memorable experience. The main ski zones lie in the north of the Ardennes, around Botrange, Robertville, Bütgenbach, Spa, Stavelot, Vielsalm, La Roche-en-Ardenne, and Bastogne. Parts of Luxembourg and the neighboring Eifel district of Germany offer good facilities.

Detailed information is available from local tourist information offices for these places (some are listed in this chapter).

Rue Comte Théodule d'Ursel 14, 6940 Durbuy. © **086/21-32-62.** Fax 086/21-24-65. www.sanglier-des-ardennes.be. 45 units. 110€–240€ ($138–$300) double. AE, DC, MC, V. Free parking. **Amenities:** Restaurant (Continental); bar; lounge. *In room:* TV, minibar, hair dryer.

4 Spa ⋆⋆

28km (17 miles) SE of Liège

To uncover the origin of mineral springs, you need to go straight to the source. Where better to begin than Spa? The town virtually floats on some of the healthiest H_2O ever to gurgle up to the surface and has been a bustling resort ever since a medieval blacksmith from other parts bought up the land holding these wondrous springs (the Roman geographer Pliny the Elder, in the 1st c. A.D., might have been referring to these waters when he wrote about a curative spring in the country of the Tungri). The town that grew up around them has catered to the likes of Charles II of England, Montaigne, the queen of Sweden, and Czar Peter the Great of Russia. So universally was its name equated with the miracles of thermal springs and mineral waters that the word "spa" is now applied to health and fitness centers of every description.

In the 18th and 19th centuries, *curistes* came from all over Europe to take the waters, gamble their money in the casino founded in 1763 (and said to be the world's oldest) and, like Victor Hugo, stroll on the forested Promenade des Artistes just outside town. Nowadays, visitors pour in for the Formula One motor race at the nearby Spa-Francorchamps circuit, arguably the most scenic racetrack in the world.

ESSENTIALS

GETTING THERE   **Trains** frequently run to Spa from Liège, but you have to change at Verviers. Train information is available from **SNCB** (© **02/528-28-28;** www.sncb.be). Buses leave regularly from in front of Verviers rail station. For **bus** information, call © **04/361-94-44.** By **car** from Liège, take A26/E25 southeast to Exit 46, then follow the signs for Remouchamps, and from there take N697 east.

VISITOR INFORMATION   The **Spa Tourist Office** is at place Royale 41, 4900 Spa (© **087/79-53-53;** fax 087/79-53-54; www.spa-info.be), inside the 19th-century Pavillon des Petits-Jeux, in the center of town. The office is open April to September, Monday to Friday from 9am to 6pm, and weekends from 1 to 6pm; October to March, Monday to Friday from 9am to 5pm, Saturday from 10am to 5pm, and Sunday from 1 to 5pm (closed Jan 1).

WHAT TO SEE & DO

Visitors continue to gather in Spa both for the healing treatments and for its lively action at the **Casino de Spa,** rue Royale 4 (© **087/77-20-52;** www.casinodespa.be), in the center of town. The casino is open Monday to Friday from 11am to 4am, and weekends from 11am to 5am.

Another attraction in town is the **Pouhon Pierre le Grand (Peter the Great Spring),** place Pierre le Grand (© **087/79-53-53**), in what was formerly a winter garden and is now a small art gallery. The pavilion was constructed in the elegant Belle Epoque style, with lots of wrought iron and windows combining to give it a light, airy feel. The pavilion usually hosts small-scale exhibits and is open April to October, daily from 10am to noon and 1:30 to 5pm; November to March, Monday to Friday from 1:30 to 5pm, weekends from 10am to noon and 1:30 to 5pm.

There are numerous springs in the countryside around Spa, and at some of them you can draw as much water as you like for free (bring your own container). The water is said to be very healthy and full of iron, but most of it smells remarkably bad. To visit these springs, get a free description of the *Route des Fontaines* from the tourist office.

On Sunday, there's a flea market (8am–2pm) in the wrought-iron Galerie Léopold II arcade, behind the tourist office.

WHERE TO STAY

Hôtel la Heid des Pairs ✦ Surrounded by lawns dotted with ancient trees, this villa was constructed for Baron Nagelmackers, whose family founded the Orient Express. It still feels like a private home. A mixture of period and functional furnishings give the inn a welcoming, homey feel. Fruit and sweets greet you in your room on arrival. Three of the rooms have private balconies; you can elect to have your breakfast served there or on the terrace downstairs.

Av. Professor-Henrijean 143, 4900 Spa. ✆ 087/77-43-46. Fax 087/77-06-44. www.laheid.be. 7 units. 99€–139€ ($124–$174) double. Rates include full breakfast. AE, MC, V. Free parking. **Amenities:** Lounge; outdoor pool. *In room:* TV, hair dryer.

L'Auberge de Spa ✦ This attractive hotel in the town center opens onto a small square. Older rooms are comfortable and look out through casement windows to the town outside. Tastefully furnished luxury suites include a bedroom, a large living room, a fully equipped kitchen, and a bathroom. Each can accommodate up to four people. The hotel's ground floor houses a good restaurant.

Place du Monument 3–4, 4900 Spa. ✆ 087/77-48-33. Fax 087/77-48-40. www.auberge-spa.be. 17 units. 60€–90€ ($75–$113) double. Rates include continental breakfast. AE, DC, MC, V. **Amenities:** Restaurant (Belgian). *In room:* TV.

WHERE TO DINE

Brasserie du Grand Maur ✦ FRENCH/BELGIAN A 200-year-old building with creaky wooden floorboards and a cozy, U-shaped dining room is the graceful setting for a variety of seafood and regional dishes. You read the menu from a board that the owners prop beside your table, and choose from a wide-ranging, well-considered wine list—at prices, though, that can easily double your bill. Fresh lobster emerges from a big tank in the lobby, joining oysters, sole, and cod among seafood dishes; if the lobster is too expensive as a main course, you can at least taste it in the excellent and inexpensive lobster *bisque* (soup). The *pâté de foie gras* (duck-liver pâté) is excellent, as is the *côte d'agneau d'Ecosse* (Scottish side of lamb). There's a small bar where you can enjoy your aperitif and postprandial *pousse-café*. In the summer, you can dine on a garden terrace.

Rue Xhrouet 41 (behind Pouhon Pierre le Grand). ✆ 087/77-36-16. www.legrandmaur.com. Main courses 14€–28€ ($18–$35); fixed-price menu 39€ ($49). AE, DC, MC, V. Wed–Sun noon–2pm and 6:30–11pm.

MORE DINING OPTIONS

If you walk the 10km (6-mile) Route des Fontaines that connects the mineral springs in the countryside around Spa, you'll find rustic little restaurants conveniently located about 10 steps from each spring—you'd almost think it had been planned that way. The first spring on the route, the Fontaine de Barisart, has the least interesting eatery, a blocky, cafeteria-style place with all the charm of a missile silo. After that, things pick up. **La Géronstère,** route de la Géronstère 119 (✆ 087/77-03-72; www.lageronstere. com), is a stone farmhouse-style building that stocks good snacks, beside the Fontaine de la Géronstère; farmhouse-style **Le Relais de la Sauvenière,** rue de la Sauvenière 116 (✆ 087/77-42-04; www.lerelaisdelasauvenière.be), is at the Fontaine de la Sauvenière and the adjacent Fontaine de Groesbeeck; and Italian **La Fontaine du Tonnelet** ⍟, rue du Tonnelet 82 (✆ **087/77-26-03**), in a red-and-white pavilion, its interior decorated in the style of a Tuscan villa, is beside the Fontaine du Tonnelet. Back in Spa, **La Tonnellerie,** Parc des Sept Heures 1 (✆ **087/77-22-84;** www.latonnellerie.be), in the park just behind the tourist office, is a good place to dine in the open air when the weather is fine.

5 The Amblève Valley

LA GLEIZE

14km (9 miles) S of Spa

Sad to relate, but the main claim to fame of this village—other than a scenic location—is that it got blown to bits in December 1944 during the Battle of the Bulge. The fighting here was as important to the eventual U.S. victory in the Ardennes as the better-known struggle at Bastogne. La Gleize is on N633.

Spearheading the entire German offensive, *Kampfgruppe Peiper,* a powerful battle group from the 1st SS Panzer Division *(Leibstandarte Adolf Hitler),* under Oberstürmbannführer Joachim Peiper, broke through the thin American front in the Losheim Gap. Peiper's tanks and armored infantry smashed up rear-echelon units, and then drove west through Stavelot to Trois Ponts, where an American engineer detachment blew up the vital bridges over the Amblève in their faces. After penetrating deeper into the Amblève valley, the battle group was finally brought to La Gleize, cut off, and pounded relentlessly by artillery. Just 800 of Peiper's 6,000-strong force, minus all their tanks and other heavy equipment, made it back to German lines.

Musée Décembre 1944 (December 1944 Museum) ⍟⍟   There is no shortage of museums in the Ardennes to record its dark winter of World War II. This, one of the best, focuses on the battle waged by troops of the 82nd Airborne, 30th Infantry, and 3rd Armored divisions to eliminate Kampfgruppe Peiper. That battle reached its climax at La Gleize. In an old, reconstructed presbytery, signposted off the main street, are 15 dioramas stocked with 80 uniformed mannequins representing soldiers from both sides, along with military equipment, photographs, maps, and a half-hour film in four languages, including English, on the bitter fighting in and around La Gleize during which the village was entirely destroyed.

A rare German Royal Tiger tank, a shot-and-shell-scarred 68-ton behemoth with a high-velocity 88-millimeter cannon, stands guard outside, having been liberated from its original allegiance. Few American weapons could dent a Royal Tiger, far less knock one out, and a close-up view of this beast gives you some idea why. Historian and Bulge veteran Charles B. MacDonald recalled: "A Tiger advancing with machine-guns blazing or 88 blasting was a near-paralyzing sight."

> **Impressions**
>
> *No one could say they enjoyed being here during the Battle of the Ardennes. None of us wanted to be here. But we had a job to do. We hope that what happened here will not be forgotten, because we don't want a new generation to go through the same experience.*
> —Battle of the Bulge veteran Don Lassen, 82nd Airborne Division

Rue de l'Eglise 7. ✆ **080/78-51-91**. www.december44.com. Admission 5€ ($6.25) adults, 3€ ($3.75) children 5–10, free for children under 5. Apr to mid-Nov daily 10am–6pm; mid-Nov to Mar Sat–Sun 10am–6pm.

6 The Ostkantone ★★

This rugged frontier—where Belgium meets Holland, Germany, and Luxembourg—is arguably one of the prettiest places in western Europe. The dense pine forests of the Eifel-Ardennes region alternate with rolling hills and deeply gouged river valleys, creating an outdoor playground for ramblers, cyclists, and canoeists. Known as the East Cantons (*Ostkantone* in German; *Cantons de l'Est* in French), this district in the east of Belgium is home to the country's German-speaking minority. Of its population of 100,000, two-thirds speak German and the remainder French. The whole area is sparsely populated and wonderfully scenic, with no end in sight of hills, forests, and streams. Outdoor pursuits are a way of life here.

EUPEN
20km (12 miles) NE of Spa; 34km (21 miles) E of Liège

This handsome little town (pop. 17,000) is the capital of the East Cantons. It houses the German-speaking minority's local parliament, a prime minister, and a German-language television and radio station. The entire East Cantons district is a popular vacation zone and has an extensive array of hotels, guesthouses, and camping sites. Many people prefer to stay in the countryside, but for those who like the amenities of a small town, Eupen has some good lodging possibilities.

Hautes Fagnes: A Great National Park

Eupen's main tourist value—aside from its hotels, restaurants, cafes, and stores—is that it is a gateway to the wide green yonder. Outside the town lies the Hertogenwald Forest, with many marked walking and riding trails. Beyond the forest, in the direction of Malmédy, is Belgium's largest national park, **Hautes Fagnes Nature Reserve** ★★★, a high, boggy moorland plateau with unique subalpine flora, fauna, and microclimate. You can access the reserve through Baraque-Michel and Mont-Rigi, though sections of it are closed for some weeks in spring because of the breeding season for the endangered Fagnes *coq de bruyère* (capercaillie); they may be closed on occasion in summer due to the increased fire risk. At all other times you must stick to the boardwalks and signposted paths (unless accompanied by an official guide). A hike amid the stark beauty of the Hautes Fagnes (Höhes Venn in German) in the dead of winter is a memorable experience—but be aware that the subalpine climate can suddenly change to subarctic, so only do this if you are properly clad and equipped.

For the complete lowdown on the Hautes Fagnes, visit the **Centre Nature de Botrange** (✆ **080/44-03-00;** www.centrenaturbotrange.be), signposted off the road to Sourbrodt, which documents the history and ecology of the reserve. The center is open daily from 10am to 6pm. Admission to the center is free; to the museum it is 3€ ($3.75) for adults, 1.20€ ($1.50) for children ages 6 to 18, and free for children under 6.

Close by is the **Signal de Botrange,** a tower that marks the less-than-dizzying highest point in Belgium, 694m (2,276 ft.) above sea level.

ESSENTIALS

GETTING THERE   There are hourly **trains** to Eupen from Brussels and Liège, some direct and some involving a change at Verviers. By **car** from Liège, take Exit 38 off A3/E40.

VISITOR INFORMATION   The **Verkehrsamt Eupen** is at Marktplatz 7, 4700 Eupen (© **087/55-34-50;** fax 087/55-66-39; www.eupen-info.be). For information about the East Cantons in general, contact **Verkehrsamt der Ostkantone,** Mühlen-bachstrasse 2, 4780 Sankt-Vith (© **080/22-76-64;** fax 080/22-65-39; www.east belgium.com).

WHAT TO SEE & DO

The **Exekutive (Parliament)** of the East Cantons, Klötzerban 32 (© **087/55-34-50**), is in a handsome patrician mansion dating from 1761. Guided tours are free, but you can only make one by prior arrangement.

The baroque **Sankt-Nikolaus Pfarrkirche (Church of St. Nicholas),** Marktplatz (© **087/74-20-62**), incorporating part of a 14th-century church, dates mainly from 1720 to 1726. Its two bulbous spires from the late 1890s have become symbols of the town, and the Aachen style of the exterior contrasting with an interior design typical of Liège reflects Eupen's position on the frontier between the German and the Belgian cities. The church is open daily; admission is free.

WHERE TO STAY

Best Western Ambassador Hotel Bosten ✪   On the eastern edge of town, beside the road that leads uphill to the Hertogenwald Forest and the Hautes Fagnes National Park, this family-run hotel boasts a good location. The Weser River (Vesdre in French) nearly runs through it, and just across the street is a small park with a fountain. The guest rooms are spacious and have twin beds that can be rolled together to make a double, a comfortable sofa or armchair, and a large bathroom with a combined bathtub and shower. Every room has a balcony: Ask for one over the river, or if the sound of running water sets off your own waterworks, of the hills. The warm decor features peach-colored walls and lush floral patterns on the curtains and bedcovers. The hotel's classic French restaurant, **Le Gourmet,** is well regarded.

Haasstrasse 77–81 (in the Lower Town), 4700 Eupen. © **087/74-08-00.** Fax 087/74-48-41. www.bestwestern.com. 28 units. 95€–165€ ($119–$206) double. Rates include buffet breakfast. AE, DC, MC, V. Parking 8€ ($10). **Amenities:** Restaurant (French); lounge. *In room:* TV, minibar, hair dryer.

Rathaus Hotel ✪   Don't be put off by the name, which sounds just like "Rat House" in English. In German, "Rathaus" means Town Hall (come to think of it, the expression in English might have a certain validity). This fine hotel faces the flower-bedecked Town Hall, and offers a friendly welcome in the white-marble reception area. Some guest rooms have a balcony. Decor and furnishings are simple but bright and clean, with pine beds covered by colorful quilts, pine furnishings, gray carpeting, and walls adorned with floral paintings. There's no in-house restaurant, but the neighboring Italian restaurant **La Luna** does a good job of filling in.

Rathausplatz 13, 4700 Eupen. © **087/74-28-12.** Fax 087/74-46-64. www.rathaushotel.com. 18 units. 75€–80€ ($94–$100) double. Rates include buffet breakfast. AE, DC, MC, V. Free parking. *n room:* TV, minibar, hair dryer.

WHERE TO DINE

Fiasko ✪ CONTINENTAL   Despite the name, this family-owned restaurant is absolutely not a fiasco. Small and intimate, with attentive service, it brings a touch of

Gallant Stand

East of Robertville, in the center of a rotary on the road between Bütgenbach and Büllingen, stands a tall marble column inscribed with a big red numeral "1." It marks the spot where, in December 1944 during the Battle of the Bulge, the U.S. 1st Infantry Division (the Big Red One) stood in the way of the German 12th SS Panzer Division *(Hitlerjugend)*, which was trying to force a passage onto the high ground. "We fight and die here," battalion commander Lt. Col. Derrill M. Daniel told his men. Many of them did just that, but the storm troopers never got past them.

---

adventure to an area where, when it comes to cuisine, devotion to tradition is more usual. There's room for just 26 diners in a setting of timber beams and bare brick walls. The menu, handwritten on plates (and the drinks list on empty wine bottles), changes weekly depending on what's fresh at local markets, and seasonally to track Belgian manias such as the spring asparagus crop and the autumn game hunt in the Ardennes. But there are always likely to be items like steak filet with a cognac-and-cream sauce and potato gratin; *magret de canard au porto* (duck breast in a port-wine sauce) with vegetables of the day and pasta; and locally fished (or farmed) trout.

Bergstrasse 28 (at Am Clown, in the center of town). ℂ **087/55-25-50**. www.fiasko.be. Main courses 19€–26€ ($24–$33). AE, MC, V. Wed–Sun noon–2:30pm and 6–10:30pm.

Le Mont-Rigi ✦ BELGIAN   A few miles out of Eupen on the Malmédy road, this stone brasserie-restaurant is blessed with one of the finest outdoor terraces imaginable. It looks southward over the high, wide moorland bordered by forests of the Fagne de la Poleûr and acts as a sun trap in good weather. The place can get busy with hikers and day-trippers, especially on weekends in summer and during the winter ski season, but at other times it can be very quiet, which accounts for an uncertain but early closing time. Meals range from simple snacks of cheese and cold cuts, through the ubiquitous Belgian *steak-frites,* to lavish game dishes in season. Apart from on the terrace, you can eat either in the convivial main area at no-frills wooden tables, or in the formal restaurant section, where there are napkins and proper table settings.

Route de Botrange 135, Mont-Rigi (at Hautes Fagnes Nature Reserve). ℂ **080/44-48-44**. Main courses 7.50€–14€ ($9.40–$18); *menu du jour* 9.95€–18€ ($12–$23). MC, V. Tues–Sun 10am–8pm or 9pm.

ROBERTVILLE
20km (12 miles) S of Eupen; 18km (11 miles) E of Spa

Beyond the Hautes Fagnes, in the direction of the German border, is **Lac de Robertville,** a 62-hectare (153-acre) lake outside Robertville village that's a popular area for swimming and watersports in summer.

Burg Reinhardstein (Castle Reinhardstein) ✦   This is the very image of a fairy-tale castle, a little more homey than formidable in appearance. Nevertheless, its battlemented towers stand on a rugged rocky outcrop overlooking a forest and a plunging stream. After having tumbled into near ruin, it was saved from total destruction by a Belgian castle enthusiast, the late Prof. Jean Overloop, and fully restored. Now you can tour its towers and chambers in the company of guides who have inherited Overloop's love for the place.

Ovifat-Robertville (signposted from the village). © **080/44-68-68**. Admission (guided tours only) 5.50€ ($6.90) adults, 3.50€ ($4.40) students, 2.20€ ($2.75) children 6–14, free for children under 6. Mid-June to mid-Sept (also school vacations and national holidays during this period) Sun 2:15, 3:15, 4:15 and 5:15pm (July–Aug also Tues, Thurs, Sat 3:30pm).

WHERE TO STAY & DINE

Hôtel des Bains ✹   On the shores of Lac de Robertville, near Hautes Fagnes Nature Reserve, the rooms here are stylish yet cozy. They feature two twin beds and an overall sense of good taste. The hotel restaurant's classic French cuisine is served with a delicate touch. Pike from the lake comes poached and served on lettuce with a white butter sauce—*the* choice when it's available.

Lac de Robertville 2, 4950 Robertville. © **080/67-95-71**. Fax 080/67-81-43. www.hoteldesbains.be. 14 units. 95€–130€ ($119–$163). Rates include buffet breakfast. AE, V. Free parking. A short way from Spa on E5 to Exit A27, signposted MALMÉDY-WAIMES. **Amenities:** Restaurant (Belgian); lounge. *In room:* TV, minibar.

11

Planning Your Trip to Holland

Whether you choose to drive or use the excellent Dutch public transportation system, getting around is relatively easy in the Netherlands. But a few hints on how to plan and navigate your visit can help, so peruse this chapter for some practicalities.

To learn more about the Benelux countries in general, see chapter 2.

1 The Regions in Brief

Holland might be a small country, but it boasts one of Europe's most memorable cities: Amsterdam. Around Amsterdam, the old and historic province of Holland, now divided into separate northern and southern provinces, is the economic powerhouse of the nation, and its most heavily populated region. Beyond these are three more or less natural divisions—the northern, central, and southern Netherlands.

AMSTERDAM   The national capital—easygoing, prosperous, full of canals, bridges, and museums—is the natural focus of a visit to Holland. Few skyscrapers mar the clarity of the sky, and locals mostly walk or ride bicycles from place to place. The historic center recalls Amsterdam's 17th-century Golden Age, when it was the command post of a vast trading network and colonial empire, and wealthy merchants constructed gabled residences along neatly laid-out canals. A delicious irony is that some of the placid old structures now host brothels, smoke shops, and extravagant nightlife.

NOORD-HOLLAND   You can think of North Holland province as the environs of Amsterdam, because anywhere in the province is within easy reach of the capital. **Haarlem** is a graceful town of winding canals and medieval neighborhoods that hold several fine museums. A visit to the tradition-rich village of **Zaanse Schans,** on the banks of the Zaan River, makes a great short excursion. Among many other options, you can make day trips to brash **Zandvoort** on the North Sea coast and to the traditional IJsselmeer lakeside villages of **Volendam** and **Marken.**

ZUID-HOLLAND   South Holland contains an awesome amount of interest for visitors. Starting with the seat of government, **The Hague,** a graceful city separated from the North Sea only by its seacoast resort of Scheveningen, is far more than politics. Leading-edge **Rotterdam,** which sits on the delta where the Rhine, Maas, and Waal rivers meet the North Sea, is far more than a great port. **Delft** is the town of the famous blue-and-white porcelain; the cradle of the Dutch Republic and the traditional burial place of the royal family; and the birthplace and inspiration of the 17th-century master of light and subtle emotion, painter Jan Vermeer. Famous for its associations with the Pilgrim Fathers, **Leiden** was the birthplace of the Dutch tulip trade, and of the painters Rembrandt and Jan Steen, and is home to the oldest university in the country. **Gouda** is renowned for its cheese.

FRIESLAND, GRONINGEN & DRENTHE   Every one of the three sparsely populated northern provinces has a different character. With its own language, traditions,
and national history, lake-filled Friesland is a vacation area par excellence. Groningen
has its bustling university city of the same name, and Drenthe, Holland's "green
province," is dotted with prehistoric monuments.

UTRECHT, GELDERLAND, OVERIJSSEL & FLEVOLAND   Stretching
through the heartland, the four central provinces encompass a variety of scenery. The
three Great Rivers—the **Rhine, Maas,** and **Waal**—flow through here, creating the
country's greatest natural division. If it wasn't for the forests in Gelderland and
Utrecht, most of Holland would consist of the flat green fields dotted with farmhouses
so often depicted on the canvases of Dutch Masters. Overijssel is barely touched by
tourism, and Flevoland, built on land reclaimed from the **IJsselmeer** lake (the former
Zuiderzee) in recent decades, has only existed as a province since 1986.

ZEELAND, NOORD-BRABANT & LIMBURG   These three provinces consider
themselves the Burgundian part of the Netherlands, packed to their borders with
southern charm. Coastal Zeeland, the part of Holland most threatened by the sea, is
protected by the **Delta Works.** These massive dams and barriers also shelter many
coast resorts (and seafood restaurants). Noord-Brabant has most of the marshy **Biesbosch National Park** on its territory, and the city of **Eindoven,** home base of the
giant Philips electronics corporation. **Maastricht,** a city many Dutch consider the
country's second liveliest (after Amsterdam), and the country's highest "mountain,"
a peak that ascends a whole 321m (1,053 ft.), are both in the southeast province of
Limburg.

2 Visitor Information
VISITOR INFORMATION
International addresses for the Netherlands Board of Tourism are given in "Visitor
Information," in chapter 2.

Holland has a remarkably organized tourist organization. The **Vereniging voor
Vreemdelingenverkeer (Association for Tourist Traffic),** known simply as the **VVV**
(pronounced *vay-vay-vay*), has more than 400 offices around the country. VVV offices
can book accommodations, help with travel arrangements, tell you what's going on
where, and plenty more. The umbrella organization for the VVV offices is the **Netherlands Board of Tourism & Conven-
tions (NBTC),** Post Box 458, 2260
MG Leidschendam (© **070/370-5705;**
fax 070/320-1654; www.holland.com).

Anywhere you travel in the Netherlands, you can expect to find a local
VVV office, usually either near the rail
station or on the town's main square. If you're driving, you'll see blue-and-white VVV
signs posted along major routes into town to direct you to the office.

For tourist information when you arrive at Amsterdam's Schiphol Airport and to
make hotel reservations, go to the **Holland Tourist Information** desk in Schiphol
Plaza (© **0900/400-4040**), open daily from 7am to 10pm.

The Euro
Holland's currency is the euro (see
"Currency," in chapter 2).

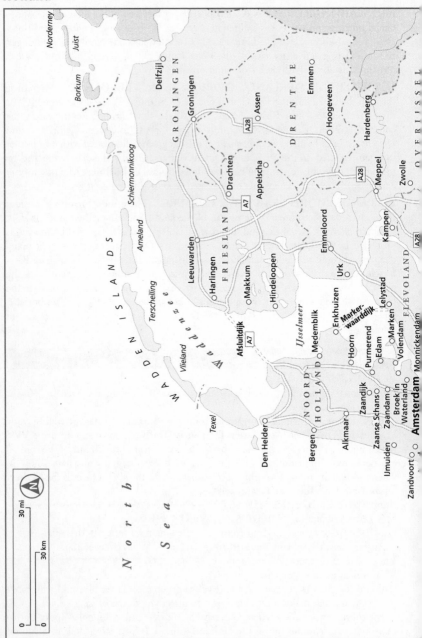

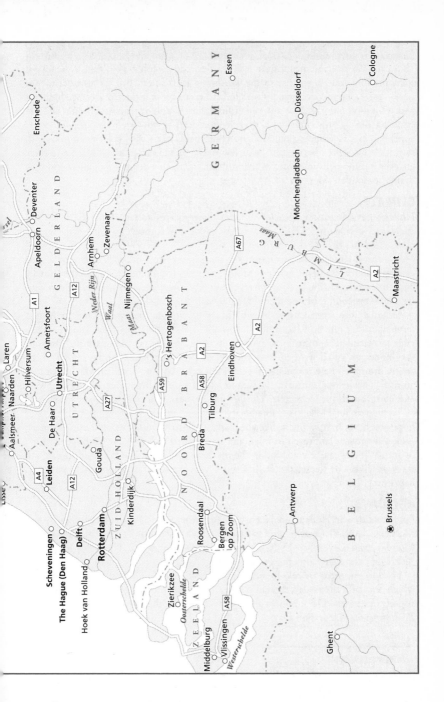

233

3 When to Go

"In season" in Holland means from mid-April to mid-October. The peak of the tourist season is July and August, when the weather is at its finest. But the weather here is never really extreme, and you'll find Holland every bit as attractive during shoulder- and off-season months. Not only are airlines, hotels, and restaurants cheaper and less crowded during this time (with more relaxed and personalized service), but some appealing events are going on. Holland's bulb fields burst with color from mid-April to mid-May; September usually has a few weeks of late summery weather; and there are even sunny spells in winter, when brilliant and crisp weather often alternates with dramatic clouded skies.

CLIMATE

Holland has a maritime climate. Summer temperatures average about 67°F (19°C); the winter average is 35°F (2°C). Winters, moderated a touch by the North Sea, are often rainy (it's driest Feb–May).

July and August are the best months to soak up rays on a sidewalk cafe terrace, dine at an outdoors restaurant in the evening, and head for the beach. September usually has a few weeks of fine late-summer weather; and there are even sunny spells in winter, when brilliant, crisp weather alternates with clouded skies.

Although the temperature doesn't always linger long below freezing in winter, remember that much of Holland is below sea level, making fog, mist, and dampness your too-frequent companions. This damp chill often seems to cut through to your very bones, so you'll want to layer yourself in Gore-Tex or something similar in the colder months. There are plenty of bright but cold days in winter, and if the temperature falls far enough, canals, rivers, and lakes freeze to become sparkling highways and playgrounds for ice skaters. Throughout the year, you can expect some rain.

To prepare for Holland's unpredictable weather, invest in a fold-up umbrella and hope you never have to use it; likewise, carry a raincoat (with a wool liner for winter); pack a sweater or two (even in July), and be prepared to layer your clothing any time of year. Winters can be cold, and in the northern provinces, like Friesland, canals and lakes are likely to freeze; the farther south you go, the less chance there is of this happening.

HOLIDAYS

Public holidays in Holland are January 1 (New Year); Good Friday; Easter Sunday and Monday; April 30 (*Koninginnedag*/Queen's Day); Ascension; Pentecost Sunday and Monday; and December 25 (Christmas) and December 26. The dates for Easter, Ascension, and Pentecost change each year.

In addition, there are two Remembrance Days related to World War II, neither of which is an official holiday, though you may find some stores closed: May 4, *Herdenkingsdag* (Memorial Day), honors all those who died in the war; and May 5 celebrates *Bevrijdingsdag* (Liberation Day).

Impressions

We can walk on water and see the lands we made with our own hands.
                              —Historian Herman Pleij (on skating frozen water-
                                       ways in winter), *National Geographic* (Jan 1998)

HOLLAND CALENDAR OF EVENTS

One of the biggest and most eagerly awaited events in Holland is the *Elfstedentocht,* the 11-cities race in which skaters compete over a 202km (125-mile) course through Friesland province. The first race was run in 1909, and it has been run only 13 times since. Perhaps the weather and ice conditions will allow the race to be held when you are visiting. If so, it's well worth going out of your way to see—or even to take part in. Contact VVV Friesland (© **0900/202-4060**).

January

Rotterdam International Film Festival. More than 300 indie films are screened at theaters around town. Contact © **010/890-9090;** www.film festivalrotterdam.com. January 24 to February 4, 2007; similar dates in 2008.

February

Carnival, Maastricht and Den Bosch ('s-Hertogenbosch). Contact **VVV Maastricht** (© **043/325-2121**) and **VVV Den Bosch** (© **0900/112-2334**). Seven weeks before Easter.

ABN AMRO World Tennis Tournament, Rotterdam. The world's top men tennis players converge on the port city for this ATP Tour event. Contact **Ahoy** (© **0900/235-2469;** www. ahoy.nl), or go to www.abnamrowtt.nl. February 19 to 25, 2007; similar dates in 2008.

March

Windmill Days, Zaanse Schans. All five working windmills at this recreated old village and open-air museum in the Zanstreek, just north of Amsterdam, are open to the public. Contact **VVV Zaanstreek/Waterland** (© **075/ 616-2221**). March to October.

The European Fine Art Fair, Maastricht. Top-rated international art and antiques fair at the Maastricht Exhibition and Congress Center (MECC). Art dealers from around the world present their finest objects. Jewelry, silver, carpets, Egyptian and classical antiquities, and 20th-century art are among the items on view. Contact © **0411/ 645-090;** www.tefaf.com. March 9 to March 18, 2007; March 7 to March 16, 2008.

Opening of Keukenhof Gardens, Lisse. The greatest flower show on earth blooms with a spectacular display of tulips and narcissi, daffodils and hyacinths, bluebells, crocuses, lilies, amaryllis, and many other flowers at this 28-hectare (70-acre) garden in the heart of the bulb country. There's said to be nearly eight million flowers. Contact © **025/246-5555;** www. keukenhof.nl. March 22 to May 20, 2007; similar dates in 2008.

April

National Museum Weekend. A weekend during which most museums in the Netherlands offer free or reduced admission and have special exhibits. April 14 to April 15, 2007; similar dates in 2008.

Bloemencorso van de Bollenstreek (Bulb District Flower Parade). Floats keyed to a different floral theme each year parade from Noordwijk, through Sassenheim, Lisse, and Bennebroek, to Haarlem. Call © **0252/434-710.** First Saturday after April 19: April 21-22, 2007; April 19-20, 2008.

Koninginnedag (Queen's Day). Countrywide celebration honoring the queen's official birthday, with parades, street fairs, and street entertainment. Throughout Holland, but best in Amsterdam. April 30.

May

Herdenkingsdag (Memorial Day). Countrywide observance for victims of World War II, principally marked by 2 minutes of silence at 8pm. May 4.

Bevrijdingsdag (Liberation Day). Commemorates the end of World War II and Holland's liberation from Nazi occupation. Throughout the country, but best in Amsterdam. May 5.

National Windmill Day, throughout Holland. Around two-thirds of the country's almost 1,000 working windmills spin their sails and are open to the public. Contact **Vereniging de Hollandsche Molen** (© **020/623-8703;** www.molens.nl). Second Saturday in May: May 12, 2007; May 10, 2008.

National Cycling Day, throughout Holland. On this day, Dutch people get on their bikes and pedal. So what else is new? Second Saturday in May: May 12, 2007; May 10, 2008.

June

Holland Festival, Amsterdam, The Hague, Rotterdam, and Utrecht. Each year, these four cities join forces to present a cultural buffet of music, opera, theater, film, and dance. The schedule includes all the major Dutch companies and visiting companies and soloists. Contact **Holland Festival** (© **020/530-7110;** www.hollandfestival.nl). May 29 to June 24, 2007; similar dates in 2008.

Vlaggetjesdag (Flag Day), Scheveningen. The fishing fleet opens the herring season with a race to bring the first *Hollandse Nieuwe* herring back to port (the first barrel is auctioned for charity). Contact **Stichting Vlaggetjesdag Scheveningen** (© **070/345-3267;** www.vlaggetjesdag.com). June 9, 2007; similar date in 2008.

Oerol Festival, Terschelling. Open-air performances by international theater companies on this island in the Wadden Sea. There was some doubt about financing for future events, so double-check that the festival is still happening. Contact **VVV Terschelling** (© **056/244-3000;** www.oerol.nl). June 15 to June 24, 2007; similar dates in 2008.

Amsterdam Roots Festival. Various venues. This festival features music and dance from around the world, along with workshops, films, and exhibits. One part is the open-air **Oosterpark Festival,** a multicultural feast of song and dance held at Oosterpark in Amsterdam-Oost (East). Contact **Amsterdam Roots Festival** (www.amsterdamroots.nl). June 16 to June 24, 2007; similar dates in 2008.

Canalhouse Gardens in Bloom, Herengracht, Keizersgracht, and Prinsengracht. If you wonder what the gardens behind the gables of those fancy canal-side houses look like, this is your chance to find out. A number of the best are open to the public for 3 days. Contact **Stichting De Amsterdamse Grachtentuin** (© **020/422-2379;** www.amsterdamsegrachtentuin.nl). Late June.

July

Amsterdam Arts Adventure, venues throughout the city. It includes offbeat and informal events across the full range of the arts. Contact **VVV Amsterdam** (© **0900/400-4040**) or **Amsterdam Uit Buro** (© **0900/0191**). July and August.

North Sea Jazz Festival, Ahoy, Rotterdam. One of the world's leading gatherings of top international jazz and blues musicians unfolds over 3 concert-packed days at the city's giant Ahoy venue. Last-minute tickets are scarce, so book as far ahead as you can. Contact **North Sea Jazz Festival** (© **015/214-8393;** www.northseajazz.nl). July 13 to July 15, 2007; similar dates in 2008.

Over Het IJ Festival. Avant-garde theater, music, and dance are performed in Amsterdam-Noord, beside the IJ channel, at the old NDSM Wharf, TT Neveritaweg 15. Contact **Over Het IJ**

Festival (© 020/492-2229; www.over hetij.nl). Middle 2 weeks of July.

Skûtsjesilen, the Frisian Lakes and the IJsselmeer. Sailing races feature traditional Frisian sailing ships, called *skûtsjes.* Contact **VVV Friesland** (© 0900/ 202-4060; www.skutsjesilen.nl). July 21 to August 3, 2007; similar dates in 2008.

August

Amsterdam Pride. This is a big event in Europe's most gay-friendly city. A crowd of as many as 150,000 people turns out to watch the highlight Boat Parade's display of 100 or so outrageously decorated boats cruising the canals. In addition, there are street discos, open-air theater performances, a sports program, and a film festival. (The entire festival's future is in the balance, subject to the City Council not revoking its permission on "public order" grounds.) Contact **Amsterdam Gay Pride** (www.amsterdamgaypride. nl). First weekend in August: August 3 to August 5, 2007 (Canal Parade Aug 4); August 1 to August 3, 2008 (Canal Parade Aug 2).

Grachten Festival. A 5-day festival of classical music, on a different theme each year, plays at various intimate and elegant venues along the city's canals and at the Muiziekgebouw aan 't IJ. There's always a performance or two designed for children. Part of the festival is the exuberant **Prinsengracht Concert,** which plays on a pontoon in front of the Hotel Pulitzer. Contact **Stichting Grachtenfestival** (© 020/ 421-4542; www.grachtenfestival.nl). August 11 to August 19, 2007; August 9 to August 17, 2008.

Holland Festival of Early Music, Utrecht. Concerts of music from the Middle Ages to the Romantic era. Contact **Stichting Organisatie Oude**

Muziek (© 030/232-9000; www. oudemuziek.nl). August 24 to September 2, 2007; August 29 to September 7, 2008.

Uitmarkt. Amsterdam previews the cultural season with this open market of information and free performances at impromptu outdoor venues, and at theaters and concert halls. Both professional and amateur groups take part in the shows, which run the gamut of music, opera, dance, theater, and cabaret. Contact **Amsterdam Uitmarkt** (© 020/626-2656; www.uitmarkt.nl). Usually the last weekend in August, but dates are not confirmed until the preceding March.

11 Steden Fiets 4 Daagse (11 Cities 4 Days Bicycle Tour), Friesland. The bicycling version of the famous Elfstedentocht ice-skating race through Friesland province (see introduction to the "Holland Calendar of Events," above), based on the idea that roads and bikes are more reliable than frozen canals and skates. Contact **VVV Friesland** (© 0900/202-4060). End of August.

September

Bloemencorso Aalsmeer. The Dam in Amsterdam is the final destination for the Flower Parade that originates in Aalsmeer. This parade features a large number of floats that carry a variety of in-season flowers (so no tulips). Contact **Stichting Bloemencorso** (© 0297/325-100; www.bloemencorso aalsmeer.nl). September 1, 2007. *Note:* Due to organizational, security, and traffic difficulties, the 2007 Bloemencosro will be the last one.

Open Monumentendag, all over the country. A chance to see historic buildings and monuments usually not open to the public—and to get in free as well. Contact **Vereniging Open Monumentendag** (© 020/470-1170).

Second Saturday: September 8, 2007; September 13, 2008.

State Opening of Parliament, The Hague. On *Prinsjesdag* (Princes' Day), Queen Beatrix rides in a splendid gold coach to the Knights' Hall in The Hague to open the legislative session by delivering the *Troonrede* (Speech from the Throne). Contact **VVV Den Haag** (© 0900/340-3505). Third Tuesday in September: September 18, 2007; September 16, 2008.

October

Leidens Ontzet, Leiden. Procession commemorating the anniversary of the raising of the 1574 Spanish siege. *Haring en witte brood* (herring and white bread) are distributed, just as they were on that day. Contact **VVV Leiden** (© 0900/222-2333). October 3 (Oct 4 when the 3rd is a Sun).

Leather Pride is a growing happening of parties and other events for gays who are into a leather lifestyle. Contact **Leather Pride Nederland** (© 020/422-3737; www.leatherpride.nl). Last weekend of October.

November

International Horti Fair, Amsterdam. The largest exhibit of autumn-blooming flowers in the Netherlands takes place at the RAI Convention Center. Contact © 0297/344-033; www.hortifair. nl. October 9 to October 12, 2007; October 13 to October 16, 2008.

Crossing Border Festival, Den Haag (The Hague). Literature, poetry, and music are combined in this festival. Contact **Crossing Border** (© 070/346-2355; www.crossingborder.nl). Mid-November.

Sinterklaas Arrives. Holland's "Santa Claus" (St. Nicholas) launches the Christmas season when he arrives in Holland from Spain, accompanied by black-painted assistants, called Zwarte Piet (Black Peter) who hand out sweets to kids. During the next 2 weeks he makes his way to towns across the land. Contact local VVV offices. Third Saturday in November: November 17, 2007; November 15, 2008. He arrives the next day in Amsterdam.

December

Sinterklaas, throughout Holland. St. Nicholas's Eve is the traditional day in Holland for exchanging Christmas gifts. Join some Dutch friends or a Dutch family if possible. December 5.

Gouda bij Kaarslicht (Gouda by Candlelight). Gouda. In the evening, all the electric lights are turned off around the Markt, and Gouda's main square, the 15th-century town hall, and a giant Christmas tree are all lit up by thousands of candles. Contact **VVV Gouda** (© 0900/468-3288; www. vvvgouda.nl). Second Tuesday before Christmas.

Tips Money-Savers

One way to save money, and not just on admission to museums and attractions, is to buy one—or more—of the visitor passes offered by some city and province VVV tourist offices, like the I amsterdam Card (see "Your Passport to Amsterdam," in chapter 12). Remember that many museums and other attractions offer reduced admission to seniors, students, and children.

If you're in Holland on **National Museum Weekend** (Apr 14–15, 2007; similar dates in 2008), you're really in luck. Many museums in Holland offer free admission over the weekend, and others charge reduced admission.

4 Getting Around

Holland is a great place to sightsee because it's so compact. Roads and expressways are excellent, and the rail network is one of Europe's finest. For public transportation information, call ✆ **0900/9292.**

BY TRAIN

All major tourist destinations in Holland are within 2½ hours of Amsterdam via **Nederlandse Spoorwegen/NS** (✆ **0900/9292;** www.ns.nl), Holland's national rail system. Generally clean and on time, the trains are a good way to travel with the Dutch, who use them even for short journeys to the next town up the line. In addition to Amsterdam, other destinations easily reached by train from Amsterdam Airport Schiphol include The Hague (40 min.), Rotterdam (45 min.), and Utrecht (40 min.). The trains run so often that you can just go to the station and wait for the next one— your wait will be short. At even the smallest stations, there is half-hour service in both directions, and major destination points have between four and eight trains an hour in both directions. Service begins as early as 5am (slightly later on Sun and holidays) and runs until around 1am. A special Night Train runs between Utrecht and Rotterdam, via Amsterdam, Schiphol, Leiden, and The Hague.

If all or most of your travel will be by rail, consider investing in one of the NS special programs, such as *Zomertour* **(Summer Tour),** or **Holland Rail Pass.** For instance, the Summer Tour pass, available between July 1 and September 9, permits unlimited 3-day travel in second class for one or two persons, over 10 consecutive days. *Zomertour Plus* **(Summer Tour Plus)** allows you to use other public transportation modes as well, such as the tram, bus, and Metro. The price ranges from 49€ ($61) for the basic pass for one, to 84€ ($105) for the Plus option for two.

In addition, there are hundreds of bargain-day and weekend fares called *RailIdee,* for trips to specific destinations, including picturesque walking and biking routes. These handy combination tickets include admission to attractions, maps, reduced hotel rates (if so desired), lunch packs, and bicycle hire. The family excursion fares are especially attractive. For information, pick up the *EropUit!* booklet, published by NS and available at tourist offices or major rail stations.

Dutch Railways has some handy arrangements for **bicycles;** you can pick up a bike at one station and drop it off at another.

BY BUS

Regional service is usually slow because buses stop at so many places en route, and you may have to change at an intermediate town or city on the way. Traveling by train is faster, but it is possible (and cheaper) to travel long distances using the bus. A *strippenkaart,* valid throughout the country, is a combined multi-journey public transport ticket costing 6.40€ ($8) for 15 strips and 19 € ($24) for 45 strips; fares are based on a zone system, and your ticket is stamped by the driver for the number of zones plus one extra strip. For more information on these tickets and how to use them, see "Getting Around," in chapter 12.

BY CAR

Driving in Holland is easy—except in the cities and towns where traffic congestion can be ulcer-inducing. Outside of these, major expressways and local roads are excellent; they're well planned (as you'd expect from the efficient Dutch), well maintained, and well signposted. However, they are often jampacked with traffic, particularly during the twice-daily rush hours, so avoid these times if possible.

Surprisingly enough, the biggest problem on the roads is other drivers: Many Dutch cast off their usual social skills and conscience when they get behind the wheel of a vehicle and become as bad-tempered, erratic, and downright dangerous as, well, as the Belgians, whose roadway recklessness is infamous.

RENTALS   Rental cars are available from desks at Schiphol Airport and from offices around the country (airport pickup and drop-off is available in most cases). All of the top international firms are represented: **Avis** (ⓒ 0800/235-2847 or 020/683-6061), **Budget** (ⓒ 0900/1576 or 020/612-6066), **Europcar** (ⓒ 070/381-1812 or 020/683-2123), and **Hertz** (ⓒ 020/201-3512). Expect to pay from 50€ ($63) a day, and 200€ ($250) a week, including insurance and other charges, and for unlimited mileage.

DRIVING RULES   To drive in the Netherlands, you need only a valid passport, a driver's license, and registration for the car you drive. The minimum age for drivers is 18. The speed limit is 120kmph (75 mph) on expressways; 100kmph (60 mph) on some marked stretches of expressway near cities; 50kmph (30 mph) in cities and urban areas; and 80kmph (48 mph) in the outskirts of towns and cities. Lower limits might be posted. Traffic approaching from the right has the right of way, unless the road you are on has signposts with an orange diamond. Pedestrians on the crosswalks always have the right of way. Watch out for bikers, who are vulnerable road users but don't always act like it.

ROAD MAPS   Adequate road maps for Holland, and street maps for major cities, are available from local VVV tourist information offices. Road maps are published by the **ANWB** and **KNAC** motoring organizations, and by various private concerns—among them the excellent Michelin map nos. 210 and 211, which cover the country and are available from bookstores and some news vendors.

BREAKDOWNS/ASSISTANCE   If you're a member of a national automobile club, like the American Automobile Association, you're automatically entitled to the services of **ANWB Royal Dutch Touring Club.** This organization sponsors a fleet of yellow *Wegenwacht* (ⓒ **080/000-0888**) vans, a sort of repair shop on wheels that you see patrolling the highways. There are special yellow call boxes on all major roads to bring them to your assistance. Emergency call boxes marked *Politie* will bring the police.

BY PLANE

Because Holland is so small, you really need to fly from one city to another only if you're extremely pressed for time (even then you might get there quicker by car or train). But if you must fly, **KLM Cityhopper** and **KLM Exel** (ⓒ **020/474-7474;** www.klm.nl) serve Amsterdam, Rotterdam, Eindhoven, Maastricht, Groningen, and Enschede.

BY BICYCLE

Holland has 16 million people and 11 million bicycles. To fully engage in the Dutch experience, you must climb aboard a bike at some point and head out into the wide green yonder. You can rent bikes at many railway stations around the country to tour the local highlights. Tourism authorities have marked out many biking tour routes and publish descriptive booklets and maps, available from VVV offices.

Biking in Holland is safe, easy, and pleasant. Almost all roads have designated bike paths, often separated from the road by a screen of trees or bushes, and there are separate traffic lights and signs for bikes. (Mopeds, called *brommers* in Holland, and motor scooters also use the bicycle paths.) An unpleasant surprise for those who think an absence of hills makes for easy riding is that in a totally flat landscape, nothing blocks the wind—which is great when the wind is behind you and not so great when it's blowing in your face.

FAST FACTS: Holland

Airport See "Orientation," in chapter 12.

American Express See "Fast Facts: Amsterdam," in chapter 12.

Area Codes See "Telephones," below.

Business Hours Banks are open Monday to Friday from 9am to 4pm (some stay open until 5pm). Some banks open on late-hour shopping nights and Saturday. Stores generally are open Monday from 10 or 11am to 6pm, Tuesday to Friday from 8:30 or 9am to 5 or 6pm, and Saturday to 4 or 5pm. Some stores close for lunch, and nearly all have one full closing day or one morning or afternoon when they're closed—signs are prominently posted announcing closing times. Many stores, especially in the larger towns, have late hours on Thursday and/or Friday evening. In the cities, stores along the main streets are open on Sunday.

Car Rentals See "Getting Around," above.

Climate See "When to Go," earlier in this chapter.

Currency See "Money" in chapter 2.

Driving Rules See "Getting Around," above.

Drugs The use of controlled narcotic drugs is officially illegal in the Netherlands, but Amsterdam and some other local authorities permit the sale in licensed premises of up to 5 grams (⅕ oz.) of hashish or marijuana for personal consumption, and possession of 30 grams (1⅕ oz.) for personal use. Not every local authority in the Netherlands is as liberal-minded as Amsterdam when it comes to smoking pot—and Amsterdam is not so tolerant that you should just light up on the street, in cafes, and on trams and trains (though enough dopey people do). The possession and use of hard drugs like heroin, cocaine, and ecstasy is an offense, and the police have swept most of the downtown heroin-shooting galleries away from the tourist centers. Drug abusers are considered a medical and social problem rather than a purely law-enforcement issue. On the other hand, peddling drugs *is* a serious offense.

Electricity The Netherlands runs on 220 volts electricity. You may need to take with you a small voltage transformer and a European-style adapter plug (available in drug and appliance stores and by mail order) that plugs into the round-holed European electrical outlet.

Embassies & Consulates **U.S.:** Lange Voorhout 102, Den Haag (© 070/310-2209; http://netherlands.usembassy.gov). **U.K.:** Lange Voorhout 10, Den Haag (© 070/427-0427; www.britain.nl). **Australia:** Carnegielaan 4, Den Haag (© 070/310-8200; www.australian-embassy.nl). **Canada:** Sophialaan 7, Den Haag (© 070/311-1600; www.canada.nl). **Ireland:** Dr. Kuijperstraat 9, Den Haag (© 070/363-0993; www.irishembassy.nl). **New Zealand:** Carnegielaan 10, Den Haag (© 070/346-9324; www.nzembassy.com).

For the U.S. and U.K. consulates in Amsterdam, see "Fast Facts: Amsterdam," in chapter 12.

Emergencies   For police assistance, an ambulance, or the fire department, call ⓒ **112.**

Language   The Dutch speak Dutch, of course. But English is the country's second language and it's taught in schools from the early grades; nearly everyone speaks it fluently.

Mail   Postage for a postcard or ordinary letter to the U.S., Canada, Australia, and New Zealand is 0.75€ (95¢); to the U.K. and Ireland it's 0.45€ (55¢).

Pharmacies   In the Netherlands, a pharmacy is called an *apotheek* and sells both prescription and nonprescription medicines. Regular open hours are Monday to Saturday from 9am to 5:30pm. Pharmacies post details of nearby all-night and Sunday pharmacies on their doors.

Police   In an emergency, call ⓒ **112.**

Post Office   Most post offices are open Monday to Friday from 9am to 5pm.

Restrooms   The most important thing to remember about public toilets in Holland—apart from calling them *toiletten (twa-lett-en)* or "the WC" *(Vay-say)* and not restrooms or comfort stations—is not the usual Male/Female *(Heren/ Dames)* distinction (important though that is), but to pay the attendant. He or she has a saucer where you put your money. Toilets usually cost only about 0.30€ (40¢), and the attendant generally ensures that they are clean.

Safety   See "Health & Safety," in chapter 2.

Taxes   There's a value-added tax (BTW) of 6% on hotel and restaurant bills (19% on beer, wine, and liquor), and 6% or 19% (the amount depends on the product) on purchases. This tax is always included in the price. People resident outside the European Union can shop tax-free in the Netherlands. Stores that offer tax-free shopping advertise with a Holland Tax-Free Shopping sign in the window, and they provide you with the form you need to recover value-added tax (BTW) when you leave the European Union. Refunds are available only when you spend more than 137€ ($171) in a store. (Note that at this writing, the minimum amount was expected to be cut to 50€/$63.)

Telephones   The country code for the Netherlands is **31.** When calling Holland from abroad, you do not use the initial **0** in the area code. For example, if you're calling an Amsterdam number (area code **020**) from outside Holland, you dial the international access code (which is **011** when calling from North America, and **00** from elsewhere in Europe) and then **31-20,** followed by the subscriber number. You only dial the initial **0** of the area code if you're calling within Holland.

When making local calls in Holland, you won't need to use the area codes shown in this book. You do need to use an area code between towns and cities. The two main formats for Dutch phone numbers are: for cities and large towns, a three-digit area code followed by a seven-digit number; and for small towns and villages a four-digit area code followed by a six-digit number.

For operator assistance: Call ⓒ **0800/0410.** For information inside Holland, dial ⓒ **0900/8008;** for international information, dial ⓒ **0900/8418** for multiple numbers, and **118** for a maximum one number per call. Numbers beginning with 0800 within Holland are toll-free, but calling a 1-800 number in the United States from Holland is not toll-free. In fact, it costs the same as an overseas call. Watch out for the special Dutch numbers that begin with 0900. Calls to these are charged at a higher rate than ordinary local calls. Depending who you call, they can cost up to 0.90€ ($1.15) a minute.

To make international calls from the Netherlands, first dial **00** and then the country code. To call the United States or Canada, dial **00** (the international access code) + **1** (the country code) + the area code + the number. For example, if you want to call the British Embassy in Washington, D.C., you dial 00-1-202-588-7800. Other country codes are: United Kingdom, **44;** Ireland, **353;** Australia, **61;** New Zealand, **64.** International calls, per minute, cost: **U.S.** and **Canada:** 0.30€ (40¢); **U.K.** and **Ireland:** 0.35€ (40¢); **Australia** and **New Zealand:** 0.40€ (50¢).

You can use pay phones with either a KPN or a Telfort *telekaart* (phone card)—but note that neither company's card works with the other company's phones. KPN cards are 5€ ($6.25), 10€ ($13), 20€ ($25), and 50€ ($63), from post offices, train ticket counters, VVV tourist information offices, GWK Travelex currency-exchange offices, and some tobacconists and newsstands. Telfort cards sell for 8€ ($10) and you get an additional 2€ ($2.50) worth of time free. Some pay phones take credit cards. A few take coins of 0.10€, 0.20€, 0.50€, 1€, and 2€. Use smaller coins whenever possible, at least until you are connected with the right person, as no change is given from an individual coin, and once the call has begun, excess coins will not be returned when you hang up. Both local and long-distance calls from a pay phone are 0.30€ (40¢) a minute.

There's a sustained dial tone, and a beep-beep sound for a busy signal. Should there be no answer, hang up and the coin comes back to you. On card and coin phones, a digital reading tracks your decreasing deposit so you know when to add another card or more coins. To make additional calls when you still have a coin or card inserted, briefly break the connection, and you will get a new dial tone for another call.

To charge a call to your calling card, call: **AT&T** (✆ 0800/022-9111); **MCI** (✆ 0800/022-9122); **Sprint** (✆ 0800/022-9119); **Canada Direct** (✆ 0800/022-9116); **British Telecom** (✆ 0800/022-0444); **Telecom New Zealand** (✆ 0800/022-4464).

Time Zone Holland is on Western European Time (WET), which is Coordinated Universal Time (UTC) or Greenwich Mean Time (GMT) plus 1 hour. Clocks are advanced by 1 hour for Western European Summer Time (WEST) between the last Sunday in March and the last Sunday in October.

Tipping The Dutch government requires that all taxes and service charges be included in the published prices of hotels, restaurants, cafes, discos, nightclubs, salons/barbershops, and sightseeing companies. Even taxi fare includes taxes and a standard 15% service. To be absolutely sure in a restaurant, for example, that tax and service are included, look for the words *inclusief BTW en service* (BTW is the abbreviation for the Dutch words that mean value-added tax), or ask the waiter.

Tips for extra service are always appreciated but not necessary. Dutch waiters and hotel staff often conveniently "forget" that service and tipping are essentially the same thing. If you ask them, they'll likely tell you a tip is not included in the bill—true, since it's not called a tip but a service charge. The customer pays 15% service (in most restaurants) whether they liked the service or not. Most Dutch either don't add an extra tip at all, or they leave a minimal amount. Being human, waitstaff and other service personnel appreciate tips. They know that foreigners often leave generous ones, and they want to encourage this practice.

To tip like the Dutch, in a cafe or snack bar, leave some small change; in a restaurant, leave 1€ to 2€ ($1.25–$2.50), and up to a generous 5€ ($6.25) or 10% if you think the service was particularly good; for expensive tabs and in expensive places, you may want to leave more—or maybe less! An informal survey (I asked a taxi driver) reveals that Americans and British are the best tippers; the worst are the Dutch themselves.

Transit Info For information regarding tram, bus, Metro, and train services around the Netherlands, call ✆ **0900/9292,** or visit **www.9292ov.nl**.

Water The water from the faucet in Holland is safe to drink. Many people drink bottled mineral water, called generically *spa* even though not all of it is the Belgian Spa brand.

Weather For weather information, call ✆ **0900/8003.**

12

Amsterdam

Live and let live. Easygoing. Liberal. Tolerant. These words are commonly used to describe Amsterdam.

For centuries, the city has been a magnet for the oppressed and persecuted. In the 17th century, it was a haven for Jewish and Protestant refugees from Catholic countries. Its tradition of acceptance has continued into the 21st century (though there are some signs the welcome mat may be fraying).

In the 1960s, the city was Europe's hippie capital. In the 1990s, Amsterdam took a leading role in liberalizing Dutch laws on homosexuality and gay marriages. Similar pragmatic attitudes help explain the existence of the Red Light District, as much a city attraction as the Rijksmuseum, the Van Gogh Museum, and the Anne Frankhuis.

It's surprising how many people still think of Holland's capital as being caught in a rose-tinted time warp of free love, free drugs, free everything. Truthfully, the heady heydays of the 1960s and 1970s have given way to new realities. The city government has worked hard to transform Amsterdam into an international business center, and it's certainly succeeding—if not all the way.

Amsterdam remains different. Its citizens, happily bubbling along in their multiracial melting pot, are not so easily poured into the restrictive molds dictated by trade and industry. Not only do free thinking and free living have their places here, they are the watchwords by which Amsterdam lives its collective life. But don't kid yourself. All this free-spirited existence is at least partially fueled by a successful economy, and not by the combustion of semilegal substances.

Amsterdam is undoubtedly magical, and it captures visitors in its spell. At night, the 1,200 bridges spanning 200 canals are lit with a zillion tiny lights that give them a fairy-tale appearance. In the morning, the cityscape slowly unfolds through a mysterious mist to reveal its treasures.

1 Orientation

ARRIVING
BY PLANE
For details on air travel to Holland, see chapter 2. The country's main international airport is **Amsterdam Airport Schiphol** (© **0900/0141** from inside Holland, and 31-20/794-0800 from outside, for both general and flight information; www.schiphol.nl; airport code: AMS), 13km (8 miles) southwest of the center city. After you deplane, moving sidewalks will take you to the main terminal building, where you pass through Passport Control, Baggage Reclaim, and Customs, into Schiphol Plaza. Tourist information is available from the **Holland Tourist Information** desk (daily 7am–10pm) in Schiphol Plaza.

Trains depart from Schiphol station, downstairs from Schiphol Plaza, for Amsterdam's Centraal Station. Departures range from one per hour at night to six per hour at peak times. The one-way fare is 3.60€ ($4.50), and the ride takes 20 minutes.

The **Connexxion Hotel Shuttle** (© 038/339-4741; www.schipholhotel shuttle.nl) runs daily every 10 to 30 minutes from 6am to 9pm, between the airport and around 100 Amsterdam hotels. No reservations are needed and buses depart from in front of Schiphol Plaza. Buy tickets from the Connexxion desk inside Schiphol Plaza or on board from the driver. The fare is 12€ ($15) one-way and 19€ ($24) round-trip; 5.50€ ($6.90) and 8.75€ ($11), respectively, for children ages 4 to 14.

Taxis from the airport are operated by **Schiphol Taxi** (© 0900/900-6666). They are metered and charge around 40€ ($50) to the center of Amsterdam.

BY TRAIN

Trains arrive at **Centraal Station,** on an artificial island on the IJ waterway. Centraal Station is the point of origin for most city trams (streetcars) and Metro trains, and a departure point for canalboat tours, passenger ferries on the IJ, taxis, water taxis, the Canal Bus, and the Museum Boat. It houses an office of the VVV Amsterdam tourist information organization (a second office is outside on Stationsplein) and a GWK Travelex currency-exchange office. Schedule and fare details on rail travel in Holland are available from the information office inside the station; information is also available by dialing © **0900/9292,** or visit www.9292ov.nl. Call © **0900/9296** for international travel. Each phone service costs 0.90€ ($1.15) per minute.

Tram stops are on either side of the main station exit. A **taxi stand** is in front of the station. (For details on transportation within the city, see "Getting Around," below.)

BY BUS

International buses arrive at Amstel bus station, outside Amstel rail station (Metro: Amstel). From here, there are Metro connections to Centraal Station; for the Leidseplein area, take the Metro toward Centraal Station and get out at the Weesperplein station; then go aboveground to take tram no. 7 or 10.

BY CAR

European expressways E19, E35, E231, and E22 reach Amsterdam from Belgium and/or Germany.

VISITOR INFORMATION

Amsterdam's tourist information organization is the **Amsterdam Tourism & Convention Board,** P.O. Box 3901, 1001 AS Amsterdam (Mon–Fri 9am–5pm; © **0900/ 400-4040,** or 31-20/551-2525 from outside the Netherlands; fax 020/201-8850; www.amsterdamtourist.nl). This organization operates four **VVV Amsterdam** tourist offices: one inside Centraal Station, on platform 2B, open Monday to Saturday from 8am to 8pm, and Sunday and holidays from 9am to 5pm; one in front of the station, at Stationsplein 10, open daily from 9am to 5pm (tram for both: 1, 2, 4, 5, 9, 13, 16,

Human Statistics

Amsterdam has a population of 740,000. By 2010, the native Dutch residents are expected to be a minority, outnumbered by ethnic minorities and foreign residents. The Old City, inside the arc of the Singelgracht canal, covers an area of 8 sq. km (3 sq. miles), containing 44,000 dwellings that house 80,000 people. The residents share this central space with 8,000 historical monuments, 2,000 stores, 1,500 cafes and restaurants, and 200 hotels. Every working day, more than two-thirds of a million people pour into the center by public transportation, bike, and car.

17, 24, 25, or 26); one at Leidseplein 1 (tram: 1, 2, 5, 7, or 10), on the corner of Leidsestraat, open Sunday to Thursday from 9:15am to 5pm, and Friday to Saturday from 9:15am to 7pm; and inside Passenger Terminal Amsterdam, the cruise-liner dock on Oostelijke Handelskade (tram: 25 or 26), a short distance east of Centraal Station.

VVV Amsterdam can help you with almost any question about the city. It also provides brochures, maps, and the like, and reserves hotel rooms. Pick up a copy of the VVV's *Amsterdam Day by Day* for 1.50€ ($1.90). This monthly magazine is full of details about the month's art exhibits, concerts, and theater performances, and lists restaurants, bars, dance clubs, and more. Handle the VVV's 0900 phone number with caution; it costs 0.40€ (50¢) a minute. Calls made from outside the Netherlands are at the usual international rate.

CITY LAYOUT

Amsterdam's center is small enough that its residents think of it as a village. Finding your way around can be confusing, however, until you get the hang of it. The concentric rings of major canals are the center city's defining characteristic, along with several important squares that act as focal points.

A map is essential. You need to know that in Dutch -*straat* means "street," -*gracht* means "canal," -*plein* means "square," -*markt* means market or market square, *dijk* means dike, and -*laan* means "boulevard." All of these are used as suffixes attached directly to the name of the thoroughfare (for example, Princes' Canal becomes *Prinsengracht*).

STREET MAPS   The most cost-effective map is Amsterdam Tourism & Congress Bureau's **Amsterdam City Map,** available from VVV Amsterdam offices for 2€ ($2.50). It shows every street and canal, tram routes and stops, museums and churches, and more. It goes about as far out as the ring road. For even more detailed coverage of the entire city and suburbs, buy the **Falk Amsterdam City Map** for 7.95€ ($9.95).

NEIGHBORHOODS IN BRIEF

The city of Amsterdam can be divided into six major neighborhoods and four lesser outlying districts.

The Old Center   The oldest part of the city, around the Dam and Centraal Station, includes the major downtown shopping areas and such attractions as the Royal Palace, the Amsterdam Historical Museum, and the canalboat piers.

The Waterfront   Centered on Centraal Station, and stretching east and west along both banks of the IJ channel, this fast-redeveloping area covers the artificial islands, warehouses, and installations of Amsterdam's old harbor (the new harbor lies west of the city).

The Canal Belt The semicircular, multistrand necklace of waterways constructed during the 17th century includes elegant gabled houses, many restaurants, antiques stores, and small hotels, plus such sightseeing attractions as the Anne Frankhuis and the canal-house museums.

Leidseplein The city's most happening nightlife square and its surroundings are a trove of performance venues, movie theaters, restaurants, bars, cafes, and hotels.

Rembrandtplein Like Leidseplein, but on a reduced scale, this lively square is home to hotels, restaurants, cafes, and nightlife venues.

The Jordaan This nest of small streets and canals is west of the center city, outside the major canals. Once a working-class neighborhood, it has become a fashionable residential area with a slew of upscale boutiques and restaurants. Its indigenous inhabitants are alive and well, and show no sign of succumbing to the gentrification going on around them.

Museum District & Vondelpark A gracious residential area surrounds three major museums: the Rijksmuseum, the Van Gogh Museum, and the modern-art Stedelijk Museum (the last-named has been rehoused temporarily in the TPG Post building near Centraal Station). The area includes Vondelpark, the Concertgebouw concert hall, many restaurants and small hotels, and Amsterdam's most elegant shopping streets, P. C. Hooftstraat and Van Baerlestraat.

Amsterdam South This very prestigious 20th-century residential area is the site of a number of hotels, particularly along Apollolaan, a boulevard the locals have dubbed the "Gold Coast" for its wealthy inhabitants and stately mansions.

Amsterdam East In this residential area on the far bank of the Amstel River, you'll find the maritime and tropical museums, and Artis, the local zoo.

Amsterdam West The district west of the Singelgracht canal covers a lot of ground but doesn't have much to recommend in the way of sights.

2 Getting Around

When you look at a map of Amsterdam, you may think the city is too large to explore on foot. This isn't true: It's possible to see almost every important sight on a 4-hour walk, and most people should be able to cover the center city on foot, though not all at once. Be sure to wear comfortable walking shoes, since those charming cobbles can get under your soles and on your nerves. When crossing the street, watch out for trams and bicycles; be particularly careful when crossing bike lanes.

BY PUBLIC TRANSPORTATION

Note: By the end of 2007 (or a bit later), all public transportation in Amsterdam and around the Netherlands should be using the new electronic **OV-chipkaart,** which is being field-tested at the time of this writing. You load up this smart card with a selected amount of euros, and these are reduced automatically by electronic readers as you ride. A transition period will ensure that the information below on the existing cards and fares remains valid during the lifetime of this book.

FARE INFORMATION & DISCOUNT PASSES   There are 11 public transportation fare zones in Greater Amsterdam, though tourists rarely travel beyond the center-city zone 5700 (Centrum). The central information and ticket sales point for GVB Amsterdam, the city's public transportation company, is **GVB Tickets & Info,**

Stationsplein (℃ **0900/9292;** www.gvb.nl), in front of Centraal Station. Most cards are valid on buses, trams, and the Metro. A **day card** *(dagkaart)* is valid for the day of purchase and the following night, and can be bought from any bus or tram driver, conductor, or card dispenser for 6.30€ ($7.90). Also available (from GVB Tickets & Info and other sales points) are day cards valid for **2** and **3** days, for 10€ ($13) and 13€ ($16).

A **single-journey card** *(enkeltje)* is 1.60€ ($2) for one zone and 2.40€ ($3) for two zones. For multiple journeys, buy a **national strip card** *(nationale strippenkaart)*. An 8-strip card is 6.40€ ($8) from the driver or conductor. Discount strip cards are available at train and Metro station ticket counters, GVB Tickets & Info, post offices, and many news vendors, where you pay 6.70€ ($8.40) for a card with 15 strips, and 20€ ($25) for 45 strips. The more strips you buy, the less each one costs. Try to avoid buying while onboard vehicles if you can avoid it; it's more expensive and time-consuming.

Children ages 4 to 11 ride on reduced-rate cards; children under 4 ride free.

TICKET VALIDATION   Bus and tram cards in Amsterdam need to be validated when you board. Use the card-validating machines on Metro-station platforms and on trams, or visit the conductor at the back of the tram, and be sure to keep your card with you until it's no longer valid. To use the machine, fold the card at the line and punch in; you don't need to punch in each individual strip—just count down the number of strips you need and punch in the last one. Most Amsterdam trams either have a conductor or operate on the honor system, but teams of roving inspectors do their best to keep everyone honest. The fine for riding without a card or not having one properly stamped is 30€ ($38), plus the fare for the ride, payable on the spot. On buses, the driver stamps your card.

Note that the "national" part of the strip card's name means just that—the card is valid for use on trams, buses, trolley buses, Metro trains, and some local train services anywhere in the land.

BY TRAM & BUS   An extensive bus network complements 16 tram lines, 10 of which begin and end at Centraal Station (another one passes through). Most tram/bus shelters have transit maps that show the entire system. A detailed map is available from the GVB Tickets & Info office.

BY METRO   Four lines—nos. 50, 51, 53, and 54—run partly aboveground and bring people in from the suburbs.

BY TAXI

Officially, you can't hail a cab from the street, but often taxis will stop if you do. If you're having trouble, find one of the strategically placed taxi stands sprinkled around the city or call **Taxi Centrale Amsterdam** (℃ **020/677-7777**). Taxis are metered. Fares, which include a service charge, begin at 3.40€ ($4.25) when the meter starts. They run up at the rate of 1.95€ ($2.45) per kilometer, and after 25km, 1.40€ ($1.75) per kilometer. The fare includes service; you can round it up if want to, or tip for an extra service.

ON THE WATER

With all the water in Amsterdam, it makes sense to use it for transportation. As a side benefit, this affords the unique view of the city from the water.

BY WATER BUS   Two separate services bring you to many of the city's top museums and other attractions. **Canal Bus** (℃ **020/623-9886;** www.canal.nl) operates three routes—Green, Red, and Blue. A day pass, valid until noon the next day and affording reduced admission to some museums and attractions, is 16€ ($20) for adults, 11€ ($14) for children ages 4 to 12, and free for children under 4. The **Museumboot** (*(Ⓒ)* **020/530-1090;** www.lovers.nl)—pronounced "museum boat"—operates a scheduled service every 30 to 45 minutes from Centraal Station to Prinsengracht, Leidseplein, Museumplein, Herengracht, the Muziektheater, and the Eastern Dock. A day ticket is 15€ ($19) for adults, 13€ ($12) for children ages 4 to 12, and free for children under 4; after 1pm, tickets are, respectively, 13€ ($16) and 7.25€ ($9.05). Tickets afford reduced admission to some museums and attractions.

BY WATER TAXI   Water taxis do more or less the same thing as landlubber taxis, except they do it on the water. To order one, call **Watertaxi** (*(Ⓒ)* **020/535-6363;** www.water-taxi.nl), or pick one up from the dock outside Centraal Station (near the VVV office). For up to 40 passengers, the cost is 30€ ($38) per boat per quarter-hour, and 10€ ($13) per quarter-hour for pickup in the center city.

BY FERRY   Free **ferries** for passengers and two-wheel transportation connect the center with Amsterdam-Noord (North), across the IJ channel. These short crossings are ideal micro-cruises for the cash-strapped; they afford fine views of the harbor. Ferries depart from the Waterplein-West dock on De Ruijterkade behind Centraal Station. Other ferries, for which you pay (though they don't always bother to collect the money), sail to Java Island in the Eastern Docks and then cross over to the north shore; and also sail west to NDSM Island.

BY BICYCLE

Follow the Dutch example and rent a bicycle—there are more than 550,000 on the streets of Amsterdam to keep you company. Bike-rental rates are around 5€ to 8€ ($6.25–$10) a day or 25€ to 40€ ($31–$50) a week; a deposit is required. **MacBike** (*(Ⓒ)* **02/620-0985;** www.macbike.nl) rents a range of bikes, including tandems and six-speed touring bikes. Rental outlets are: Stationsplein 12 (tram: 1, 2, 4, 5, 9, 13, 16, 17, 24, 25, or 26), at Centraal Station; Mr. Visserplein 2 (tram: 9 or 14), at Waterlooplein; and Weteringschans 2 (tram: 1, 2, 5, 7, or 10), at Leidseplein. **Bike City,** Bloemgracht 70 (*(Ⓒ)* **020/626-3721;** tram: 13, 14, or 17), is near the Anne Frankhuis.

Tips   **Bicycling in Amsterdam**

It takes a while to get used to moving smoothly and safely through the whirl of trams, cars, buses, trucks, fellow bikers, and pedestrians, particularly if you're on a typically ancient and much-battered *stadfiets* (city bike), also known as an *omafiets* (grandmother bike)—the only kind that makes economic sense here, since anything fancier will attract a crowd of people wanting to steal it. It's better to develop your street smarts slowly.

The first rule: Don't argue with trams—they bite back, hard. The second rule: Cross tram tracks perpendicularly so your wheels don't get caught in the grooves, which could pitch you out of the saddle. And the third rule: Don't crash into civilians (pedestrians). That's about it. Like everyone else, you'll likely end up making up the rest of the rules as you go along.

Damstraat Rent-a-Bike, Damstraat 20–22 (© **020/625-5029;** tram: 4, 9, 14, 16, 24, or 25), has a central location near the Dam.

Warning: Bicycle theft is common. Always lock both your bike frame and one of the wheels to something solid and fixed.

BY CAR

Don't rent a car to get around Amsterdam. You'll regret both the expense and the hassle. The city is a jumble of one-way streets, narrow bridges, and no-parking zones. Parking fees are expensive, and street parking is hard to come by. **Dienst Parkeerbeheer (Parking Service Authority;** © **020/553-0333**), with offices around the city, is responsible for the clamping and/or towing of illegally parked cars. The service's staff is efficient, hardworking, and enthusiastic, and the cost of transgression is high. If you are driving and want to avoid parking headaches, leave your car at the free Park & Ride car parks at some of the outer Metro and train stations (directions are indicated with blue-and-white P+R signs on the way).

Outside the city, driving is a different story and you may want to rent a car to tour the nearby countryside.

RENTALS   See "Getting Around" in chapter 11 for details.

FAST FACTS: Amsterdam

Airport See "Orientation," earlier in this chapter.

American Express The office at Damrak 66 (© **020/504-8770;** tram: 4, 9, 14, 16, 24, or 25), is open Monday to Friday from 9am to 5pm and Saturday from 9am to noon.

ATMs You'll find automated teller machines (ATMs) at Schiphol Airport, Centraal Station and other main rail stations, and throughout the city. Among the centrally located ATMs accessible by cards linked to the Cirrus and PLUS networks, and by the major credit cards and charge cards, are those at **ABN AMRO Bank,** Dam 2 (tram: 4, 9, 14, 16, 24, or 25) and Leidsestraat 1 (tram: 1, 2, or 5) at Leidseplein; **Rabobank,** Dam 16 (tram: 4, 9, 14, 16, 24, or 25); and **Fortis Bank,** Singel 548 (tram: 4, 9, 14, 16, 24, or 25), at the Flower Market.

Babysitters Many hotels can arrange babysitters. A reliable local organization is **Stichting Oppascentrale Kriterion** (© **020/624-5848;** www.kriterionoppas. org), which has vetted babysitters who are students over 18. Its rates are 6€ to 7€ ($7.50–$8.75) an hour, with extra charges for administration, for Friday and Saturday evening reservations, and for hotels.

Business Hours See "Fast Facts: Holland," in chapter 11. Thursday is *koopavond* (late shopping evening) in Amsterdam, when many stores stay open to 9pm.

Car Rentals See "Getting Around," in chapter 11 for details.

Currency Exchange The best options for changing money are the VVV tourist offices, banks and, if you carry American Express traveler's checks, **American Express** (see above). A fair-dealing option is **GWK Travelex,** which has currency-exchange offices at Schiphol Airport (© **020/653-5121**); Centraal Station (© **020/627-2731;** tram: 1, 2, 4, 5, 9, 13, 16, 17, 20, 24, 25, or 26); Damrak 125 (© **020/620-3236;** tram: 4, 9, 14, 16, 29, 24, or 25), Dam 23–25 (© **020/625-0922;**

tram: 4, 9, 14, 16, 24, or 25), and Leidseplein 31A (© **020/626-7000;** tram: 1, 2, 5, 7, or 10). See "Money," in chapter 2.

Doctors & Dentists For 24-hour emergency medical and dental service, call the **Central Doctors Service** (© **020/592-3434**).

Drugs See "Fast Facts: Holland," in chapter 11.

Drugstores See "Fast Facts: Holland," in chapter 11, and "Pharmacies," below.

Electricity See "Fast Facts: Holland," in chapter 11.

Embassies & Consulates **U.S. Consulate:** Museumplein 19 (© **020/575-5309;** http://netherlands.usembassy.gov; tram: 3, 5, 12, or 16), open Monday to Friday from 8:30am to noon and 1:30 to 3:30pm. **U.K. Consulate:** Koningslaan 44 (© **020/676-4343;** www.britain.nl; tram: 2), open Monday to Friday from 9am to noon and 2 to 4pm. For embassies in The Hague, see "Fast Facts: Holland," in chapter 11.

Emergencies For police assistance, an ambulance, or the fire department, call © **112.**

Hospitals Two hospitals with emergency service are the **Onze-Lieve-Vrouwe Gasthuis,** Oosterpark 9 (© **020/599-9111;** www.olvg.nl; tram: 3, 7, or 10), in Amsterdam Oost; and the **Academisch Medisch Centrum (AMC),** Meibergdreef 9 (© **020/566-3333;** www.amc.uva.nl; Metro: Holendrecht), in Amsterdam-Zuidoost.

Internet Access In the city center, **easyInternetcafe,** Damrak 33 (www.easy internetcafe.com; tram: 4, 9, 14, 16, 24, or 25), is open daily from 9am to 10pm, and access is 2€ ($2.50) per hour. For an alternative, try the smoking "coffeeshop" **Freeworld Internetcafé,** Nieuwendijk 30 (© **020/620-0902;** www. freeworld-internetcafe.nl; tram: 1, 2, 5, 13, or 17). Or try the **Lost in Amsterdam Lounge Café,** Nieuwendijk 19 (© **06/2547-7333;** www.lostinamsterdam.com; tram: 1, 2, 5, 13, or 17), where you can smoke a water pipe before or after you surf; access is 3€ ($3.75) an hour.

Mail See "Fast Facts: Holland," in chapter 11.

Narcotics The use of narcotic drugs is officially illegal in the Netherlands, but Amsterdam allows the sale in licensed premises of up to 5 grams (⅕ oz.) of hashish or marijuana for personal consumption, and possession of 30 grams (⅕ oz.) for personal use. Not every local authority in the Netherlands is as liberal-minded as Amsterdam when it comes to smoking pot—and Amsterdam is not so tolerant that you should just light up on the street, in cafes, and on trams and trains (though enough dopey people do).

Pharmacies See "Fast Facts: Holland," in chapter 11. A centrally located pharmacy is **Dam Apotheek,** Damstraat 2 (© **020/624-4331;** tram: 4, 9, 14, 16, 24, or 25), close to the Nationaal Monument on the Dam.

Police Holland's emergency number for the police *(politie)* is © **112.** For routine matters, visit a district police office; a centrally located one is at Lijnbaansgracht 219 (© **0900/8844;** tram: 1, 2, 5, 7, or 10), off Leidseplein.

Post Office Most **TPG post offices** are open Monday to Friday from 9am to 5pm. The office at Singel 250, at the corner of Raadhuisstraat (tram: 13, 14, or

17), is open Monday to Friday from 9am to 6pm, and Saturday from 10am to 1:30pm.

Restrooms See "Fast Facts: Holland," in chapter 11. Should you have a toilet emergency in Amsterdam, a comfortable place to find relief is the NH Grand Hotel Krasnapolsky, across the square from the Royal Palace on the Dam. Just breeze in as if you own the "Kras," swing left past the front desk and along the corridor, pass the Winter Garden restaurant, and then go up a short stairway.

Safety In Amsterdam, if it isn't bolted to the floor, somebody will try to steal it—and even if it is bolted to the floor, somebody will try to steal it. Watch out for pickpockets on trams, buses, and the Metro, and in train and Metro stations. Constant public announcements at Centraal Station and Schiphol Airport warn about pickpockets, and signs on the trams say in a multitude of languages ATTENTION: PICKPOCKETS. Consider wearing a money belt. Women should wear their purses crossed over their shoulders so they hang in front, with the clasps or zippers facing in.

Violence does occasionally occur in Amsterdam, but it's not a violent city. Drug-related crime is prevalent. Most crime, like pickpocketing, is nonviolent, relatively minor, and opportunistic. Stolen bicycles are a big problem here! Mugging and armed robbery do happen, though incidents are not common.

There are some risky areas, especially in and around the Red Light District. Be leery of walking alone after dark through narrow alleyways and along empty stretches of canal. Don't use ATMs at night in quiet areas. It's wise to stay out of Vondelpark at night, but there are cafes on the edge of the park that are busy until closing time.

The rules about not walking alone in poorly lit and unpeopled areas at night apply here, especially to women. Although Amsterdam is generally safe, incidents of harassment do occur, and rape isn't unheard of. Public transportation is usually busy even late at night, so you generally won't have to worry about being alone in a tram or Metro train. But if you feel nervous, sit close to the driver when possible. Many local women go around by bicycle at night.

Note: Listing some of the possible dangers together like this can give a misleading impression of the threat from crime in Amsterdam. There is no need to be afraid to do the things you want to do. Amsterdammers aren't afraid. Just remember to exercise the usual rules of caution and observation that apply in any big city. Report any crime committed against you to the police, most of whom speak English.

See "Health & Safety," in chapter 2.

Taxes See "Fast Facts: Holland," in chapter 11.

Telephone See "Fast Facts: Holland," in chapter 11. The area code for Amsterdam is **020**. When making local calls in Amsterdam, simply leave off the area code and dial only the phone number. If you're calling from within the Netherlands but not in Amsterdam, use **020**. When you're calling from outside the Netherlands, the area code for Amsterdam is **20**.

Tipping See "Fast Facts: Holland," in chapter 11.

Transit Info For information regarding tram, bus, Metro, and train services, call ℭ **0900/9292**, or visit **www.9292ov.nl**.

3 Where to Stay

Is your preference old-world charm combined with luxurious quarters? Glitzy modernity with every conceivable amenity? Small family-run hotels? A bare-bones room that frees up scarce cash for other purposes? Amsterdam has all of these, and more. Many hotels offer significant rate reductions between November 1 and March 31, with the exception of the Christmas and New Year periods. The city has many charms in the off season, when the calendar is full of cultural events. Traditional Dutch dishes are offered that aren't available in warm weather; and the streets, cafes, restaurants, and museums are filled more with locals than with visitors.

RESERVATIONS   Should you arrive without a reservation, VVV Amsterdam will help you for a moderate charge of 3.50€ ($4.40), plus a refundable room deposit. They'll find you something, even at the busiest periods, but it may not be exactly what, or where, you want. You can reserve ahead of time for Amsterdam with **Amsterdam Tourism & Convention Board,** P.O. Box 3901, 1001 AS Amsterdam (© **020/551-2525;** fax 020/201-8850; www.amsterdamtourist.nl); and for all of the Netherlands, with the free **Netherlands Reservations Center,** Plantsoengracht 2, 1441 DE Purmerend (© **0299/689-144;** fax 0299/689-154; www.hotelres.nl).

THE OLD CENTER
VERY EXPENSIVE
Hotel de l'Europe ✦✦   Occupying a stretch of prime waterfront—where the Amstel River flows into the city's canal net—this grande dame from 1896 is at once homey and dignified. Its *fin de siècle* style hides behind a pastel-red and white facade. Guest rooms and marble bathrooms are spacious and bright, furnished in classic style, but some could do with having those classics updated a notch or two. Try to get a room with a mini-balcony overlooking the river; you'll have great views. The **Excelsior** (see "Where to Dine," later, for details) is among the toniest restaurants in town. In the summer, drinks are served on **La Terrasse,** an outdoor cafe beside the Amstel.

Nieuwe Doelenstraat 2–8 (facing Muntplein), 1012 CP Amsterdam. © 800/223-6800 in the U.S. and Canada, or 020/531-1777. Fax 020/531-1778. www.leurope.nl. 100 units. 365€–445€ ($456–$556) double; from 525€ ($656) suite; add 5% city tax. AE, DC, MC, V. Valet and self-parking 40€ ($50). Tram: 4, 9, 14, 16, 24, or 25 to Muntplein. **Amenities:** 2 restaurants (French, Continental); 2 bars; heated indoor pool; health club; sauna; concierge; 24-hr. room service; massage; babysitting; laundry service; dry cleaning; nonsmoking rooms. *In room:* A/C, TV w/pay movies, dataport, minibar, hair dryer, safe.

EXPENSIVE
Die Port van Cleve ✦✦   One of the city's oldest hotels, Die Port van Cleve actually started life in 1864 as the first Heineken brewery. It stands across the street from the Royal Palace on the Dam, and its original ornamental facade with turrets and alcoves has been fully restored. Likewise, the interior was completely renovated a few years back. The guest rooms are relatively small, and in general are furnished in a plain way that doesn't quite complement the building's handsome looks. Watch out for noise from the busy (or bustling, if you prefer) street, in rooms at the front, especially in summer when you may want the windows open due to the absence of air-conditioning. You won't eat much more traditionally Dutch than in the **Brasserie de Poort,** and you can drink in the **Bodega de Blauwe Parade** watched over by a feast of Delft Blue tiles.

Nieuwezijds Voorburgwal 176–180 (behind the Royal Palace), 1012 SJ Amsterdam. © 020/622-6429. Fax 020/ 622-0240. www.dieportvancleve.com. 120 units. 235€–305€ ($294–$381) double; from 450€ ($563) suite; add 5%

city tax. AE, DC, MC, V. No parking. Tram: 1, 2, 5, 13, 14, or 17 to the Dam. **Amenities:** Restaurant (Dutch/international); 2 bars; cafe; concierge; business center; limited room service; babysitting; laundry service; dry cleaning; executive rooms; nonsmoking rooms. *In room:* TV w/pay movies, hair dryer, safe.

Hotel Amsterdam-De Roode Leeuw ✿   Close to Centraal Station, this hotel, founded in 1911 and still owned by descendants of the original proprietors, has an 18th-century facade. Its guest rooms are supermodern, and have thick carpets and ample wardrobe space. The entire hotel underwent a renovation completed in April 2001. Those at the front of the hotel tend to get more light, but are subjected to more street noise; some have balconies. The award-winning in-house **De Roode Leeuw** restaurant serves typical Dutch cuisine, and a glassed-in heated terrace (open daily 11am–11:30pm) overlooking the Dam is a pleasant and relaxing spot for a beer.

Damrak 93–94 (beside the Dam), 1012 LP Amsterdam. ✆ **800/44-UTELL** in the U.S. and Canada, or 020/555-0666. Fax 020/620-4716. www.hotelamsterdam.nl. 79 units. 225€–310€ ($281–$388) double. AE, DC, MC, V. No parking. Tram: 4, 9, 14, 16, 24, or 25 to the Dam. **Amenities:** Restaurant (Dutch); cafe; business center; 24-hr. room service; nonsmoking rooms; executive rooms. *In room:* A/C, TV w/pay movies, dataport, minibar, coffeemaker, hair dryer, safe.

MODERATE
Sint-Nicolaas ✿   Named after Amsterdam's patron saint, this hotel is near the Centraal Station, in a prominent corner house with a dark facade. It's a typical family hotel with an easygoing atmosphere, and children are welcome. Originally, the building was occupied by a factory that manufactured ropes and carpets from sisal imported from the Dutch colonies. It was converted into a hotel in 1980. The basic furnishings are more than compensated for by the ideal location and the Mesker family's friendliness.

Spuistraat 1A (at Nieuwendijk), 1012 SP Amsterdam. ✆ **020/626-1384.** Fax 020/623-0979. www.hotelnicolaas.nl. 24 units. 95€–120€ ($119–$150) double. Rates include continental breakfast. AE, DC, MC, V. Limited street parking. Tram: 1, 2, 5, 13, or 17 to Martelaarsgracht. **Amenities:** Bar. *In room:* TV, hair dryer, safe.

INEXPENSIVE
St. Christopher's at the Winston   Maybe too close to the Red Light District for some people's taste, and on a slightly seedy street, this is a step up from grunge-class, with a hang-loose, alternative rep. You might even hear some (pretty fanciful) comparisons with New York's Chelsea. Local artists have created paintings, photographs, and other works of what you might call art for the hallways and guest rooms. Sparely furnished, the rooms vary in size, holding from two to six beds, and are tolerably clean and well maintained. None have a view worth looking out the window for. Bathrooms are small but have most of the necessary bits and pieces in them, and those rooms that don't have a bathtub do have a shower. The downstairs bar is a fun meeting place and it has live music on weekends.

Warmoesstraat 129 (off Damrak), 1012 JA Amsterdam. ✆ **020/623-1380.** Fax 020/639-2308. www.winston.nl or www.st-christophers.co.uk. 69 units. 85€–105€ ($106–$131) double. Rates include buffet breakfast. AE, DC, MC, V. No parking. Tram: 4, 9, 14, 16, 24, or 25 to the Dam. **Amenities:** Restaurant (snacks/burgers); bar; lounge. *In room:* TV (some rooms), no phone.

THE WATERFRONT
EXPENSIVE
Lloyd Hotel ✿   Opened in 2004 on the waterfront redevelopment zone of the old steamship docks east of Centraal Station, the Lloyd was originally an emigrants' hotel between 1921 and 1935. The standout Amsterdam School of architecture building then served sequentially as a prison, a house of corrections for young offenders, and studio space for hard-up artists. Every one of its thoroughly renovated guest rooms has

Where to Stay in Amsterdam

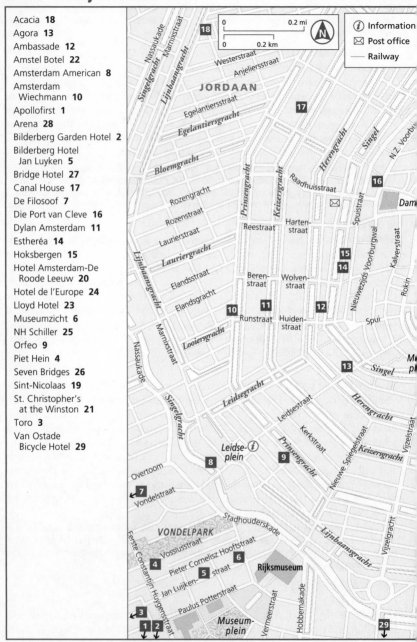

(i) Information

✉ Post office

---- Railway

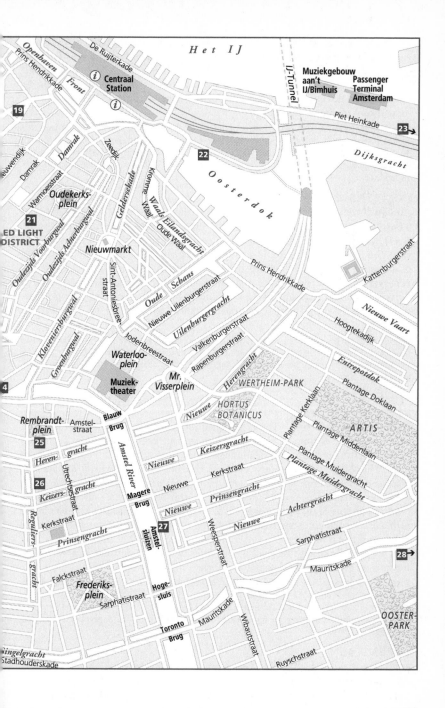

Het IJ

Openhaven
Prins Hendrikkade
Front
De Ruijterkade

ⓘ Centraal
Station
ⓘ

19

Muziekgebouw
aan't
IJ/Bimhuis

**Passenger
Terminal
Amsterdam**

IJ-Tunnel

Piet Heinkade

23→

ieuwendijk
Damrak
Warmoesstraat
Damrak

Oudekerks-
plein

Zeedijk

Kromme
Waal
Oude Waal

Waals Eilandsgracht

22

Oosterdok

Dijksgracht

21
**ED LIGHT
DISTRICT**

Oudezijds Voorburgwal
Oudezijds Achterburgwal

Geldersekade

Nieuwmarkt

Sint-Antoniesbree-
straat

Oude Schans

Nieuwe Uilenburgerstraat

Uilenburgergracht

Prins Hendrikkade

Kattenburgerstraat

Nieuwe Vaart

Hoogtekadijk

Kloveniersburgwal
Groenburgwal

Jodenbreestraat

Valkenburgerstraat
Rapenburgerstraat

Waterloo-
plein

**Muziek-
theater**

Mr.
Visserplein

Herengracht

WERTHEIM-PARK

Entrepotdok

Plantage Doklaan

4

Nieuwe

*HORTUS
BOTANICUS*

Plantage Kerklaan

ARTIS

Rembrandt-
plein
25

Amstel-
straat

**Blauw
Brug**

Amstel River

Plantage Middenlaan

Heren-
gracht

Keizersgracht

Nieuwe

Kerkstraat

Plantage Muidergracht

Plantage Muidergracht

26

Keizers-

Utrechtsestraat

Nieuwe

Prinsengracht

Achtergracht

**Magere
Brug**

Nieuwe

Reguliers-
gracht

Kerkstraat

Prinsengracht

27
Amstel-
sluizen

Weesperstraat

Nieuwe

Sarphatistraat

28→

Falckstraat

**Frederiks-
plein**

Sarphatistraat

Hoge-
sluis

Mauritskade

Mauritskade

**OOSTER-
PARK**

Singelgracht
Stadhouderskade

Toronto
Brug

Wibautstraat

Ruyschstraat

a different shape, style, and modern decor. The most expensive are the largest and have views on the water or specially designed interiors (or both). Beds are new and mattresses firm, but only a few rooms have king-size doubles. You can "improve" yourself by a visit to the in-house Culturele Ambassade art center, or a glance at one of the modern artworks scattered around. The two restaurants, **Snel** and **Sloom,** aim to make it cool to dine in a hotel.

Oostelijke Handelskade 34, 1019 BN Amsterdam (at IJhaven). ℂ 020/561-3636. Fax 020/561-3600. www.lloyd hotel.com. 120 units (106 with bathroom). 95€–295€ ($119–$369) double with bathroom; 80€ ($100) double without bathroom. AE, DC, MC, V. Parking 20€ ($25). Tram: 10 or IJtram to Rietlandpark. **Amenities:** 2 restaurants (Continental); bar; bike rental; secretarial services; 24-hr. room service; in-room massage; babysitting. *In room:* TV, dataport.

INEXPENSIVE

Amstel Botel ⚐ *Kids*   Where better to experience a city-on-the-water than aboard a boat hotel? This moored floating hotel on the sheltered waters of the inner harbor, where waves—and therefore possible problems with seasickness—never reach, has cabins on four decks, connected by an elevator. Be sure to ask for a room with a view of the water, not of the uninspiring harbor wall. Bright, modern guest rooms are nononsense but comfortable. The showers are small. This hotel is popular largely because of its location and rates, and the rare experience of sleeping on a boat. To get here, turn left out of Centraal Station, pass the bike rental, and you'll see it floating in front of you.

Oosterdokskade 2–4 (at Centraal Station), 1011 AE Amsterdam. ℂ 020/521-0350. Fax 020/639-1952. www.amstel botel.com. 175 units. 84€–92€ ($105–$115) double. AE, DC, MC, V. Limited parking on quay. Tram: 1, 2, 4, 5, 9, 13, 16, 17, 24, 25, or 26 to Centraal Station. **Amenities:** Bar; Internet access; concierge; dry cleaning. *In room:* TV w/inhouse movie channel, safe.

THE CANAL BELT
VERY EXPENSIVE

Dylan Amsterdam ⚐⚐   The exceptional service at this intimate boutique hotel wins justified raves from its primarily American and British guests, and a splendid location hasn't hurt any. Its Asian-influenced decor is arguably the most stylish in town. Housed in a 17th-century landmark that began as a theater, it has a serene black-and-white lounge that still sports the theater's original brick floor. All of the guest rooms and suites have an array of luxury amenities and are individually decorated in different colors and themes; no. 5, for example, is a blue Japanese-style room with a deep soaking tub and traditional sliding screens. Only three rooms have canal views, so if this is important to you, you'd better specify it. My one complaint: Style here occasionally trumps substance—the water fountain–style sinks in a few of the rooms look grand, but the design makes them somewhat hard to use.

Keizersgracht 384 (at Runstraat). 1016 GB Amsterdam. ℂ 020/530-2010. Fax 020/530-2030. www.dylanamsterdam. com. 41 units. 390€–690€ ($488–$863) double; from 990€ ($1,238) suite; add 5% city tax. AE, DC, MC, V. Limited street parking. Tram: 1, 2, or 5 to Spui. **Amenities:** Restaurant (Asian/international); bar; lounge; bike rental; boat rental; concierge; 24-hr. room service; laundry service; dry cleaning. *In room:* A/C, TV/VCR w/pay movies, minibar, hair dryer, safe.

EXPENSIVE

Ambassade ⚐⚐   Housed in 10 canal houses dating from the 17th and 18th centuries on Herengracht and Singel, Ambassade recreates the feeling of living in a homey canal-side setting. The pastel-toned guest rooms are individually styled and their size and shape vary according to the character of the individual houses. Everyone who stays here should enjoy the view each morning with breakfast in the bi-level, chandeliered breakfast room, or each evening in the adjoining parlor, with its Persian rugs and a stately grandfather clock ticking away. To get to some rooms, you cope with a typically Dutch steep and skinny staircase, though other rooms are accessible by elevator. For the nimble-footed who can handle the stairs, the reward is a spacious room with large multipane windows overlooking the canal. There's a library decorated in Empire style and an Internet room (no charges).

Herengracht 341 (near Spui), 1016 AZ Amsterdam. ✆ 020/555-0222. Fax 020/555-0277. www.ambassade-hotel.nl. 59 units. 185€–225€ ($231–$281) double; 270€–305€ ($338–$381) suite. AE, DC, MC, V. Limited street parking. Tram: 1, 2, or 5 to Spui. **Amenities:** Lounge; bike rental; 24-hr. room service; massage at nearby float center; babysitting; laundry service; dry cleaning. *In room:* TV, hair dryer, safe.

Estheréa 🅐🅐 *Kids* Owned by the same family since its beginnings, this elegant, not-too-big hotel is built within the walls of neighboring 17th-century canal houses. The family touch shows in careful attention to detail and a breezy but professional approach. In the 1930s, the proprietors spent a lot of money on wood paneling and other structural additions; recent proprietors have had the good sense to leave all of it in place. While it might look dated to some, the wood bedsteads and dresser-desks lend warmth to the guest rooms. These vary considerably in size depending on their location in the canal houses, and a few are quite small. Most of the rooms will accommodate two, but some have more beds, which make them ideal for families.

Singel 305 (near Spui), 1012 WJ Amsterdam. ✆ 800/223-9868 in the U.S. and Canada, or 020/624-5146. Fax 020/623-9001. www.estherea.nl. 71 units. 174€–294€ ($218–$368) double; add 5% city tax. AE, DC, MC, V. Limited street parking. Tram: 1, 2, or 5 to Spui. **Amenities:** Bar; lounge; bike rental; concierge; limited room service; babysitting; laundry service; dry cleaning; nonsmoking rooms. *In room:* TV, dataport, minibar, hair dryer, safe.

MODERATE

Agora 🅐 Old-fashioned friendliness is the keynote at this efficiently run and well-maintained lodging, a block from the Flower Market. The hotel occupies a canal house built in 1735 that has been fully restored. Furniture from the 1930s and 1940s mixes with fine mahogany antiques. Bouquets greet you as you enter, and a distinctive color scheme creates an effect of peacefulness and drama at the same time. They have installed an abundance of overstuffed furniture, and nearly every guest room has a puffy armchair you can sink into after a day of sightseeing. Those with canal views cost the most, but the extra few euros are worth it, though the hustle and bustle out on the street can make them somewhat noisy by day. The large family room has three windows overlooking the Singel. Those rooms that don't have a canal view look out on a pretty garden. There's no elevator.

Singel 462 (at Koningsplein), 1017 AW Amsterdam. ✆ 020/627-2200. Fax 020/627-2202. www.hotelagora.nl. 16 units. 92€–140€ ($115–$175) double. Rates include buffet breakfast. AE, DC, MC, V. Limited street parking. Tram: 1, 2, or 5 to Koningsplein. *In room:* TV, dataport, hair dryer, safe.

Amsterdam Wiechmann 🅐 It takes only a moment to feel at home in the antique-adorned Wiechmann, a classic, comfortable, casual sort of place. Besides, the location is one of the best you'll find in this or any price range: 5 minutes in one direction is the Kalverstraat shopping street; 5 minutes in the other, Leidseplein. Most of the guest rooms—all of them nonsmoking—are standard, with good-size twin beds or double beds, and some have big bay windows. Furnishings are elegant, and Oriental rugs grace many of the floors in the public spaces. The higher-priced doubles with views on the canal have antique furnishings, and many have a view of the Prinsengracht.

The breakfast room has hardwood floors, lots of greenery, and white linen cloths on the tables. There's no elevator.

Prinsengracht 328–332 (at Looiersgracht), 1016 HX Amsterdam. 📞 **020/626-3321.** Fax 020/626-8962. www.hotel wiechmann.nl. 37 units. 125€–145€ ($156–$181) double. Rates include continental breakfast. MC, V. Limited street parking. Tram: 1, 2, or 5 to Prinsengracht. **Amenities:** Lounge; Internet access; nonsmoking rooms. *In room:* TV, wireless Internet access, safe.

Canal House 🌟🌟 A contemporary approach to reestablishing the elegant canal-house atmosphere has been taken by the proprietor of this small hotel. Three adjoining houses dating from 1630 were gutted and rebuilt to provide private bathrooms and an interior filled with antiques, quilts, and Chinese rugs. The elevator does not stop at every floor, so you may have to walk a short distance up or down a (steep) staircase that still has its carved old balustrade. Overlooking the back garden, which is illuminated at night, the magnificent breakfast room seems to have been untouched since the 17th century. On the parlor floor is a cozy Victorian-style salon.

Keizersgracht 148 (near Leliegracht), 1015 CX Amsterdam. 📞 **020/622-5182.** Fax 020/624-1317. www.canalhouse.nl. 26 units. 150€–190€ ($188–$238) double. Rates include continental breakfast. DC, MC, V. Limited street parking. Tram: 13, 14, or 17 to Westermarkt. **Amenities:** Lounge; limited room service. *In room:* Hair dryer.

Seven Bridges 🌟🌟 Proprietors Pierre Keulers and Gunter Glaner have made the Seven Bridges, which gets its name from its view of seven arched bridges, one of Amsterdam's canal-house gems. Each guest room is individual, with antique furnishings from the 17th to the 20th centuries, plush carpets, handmade Italian drapes, hand-painted tiles and wood-tiled floors, and Impressionist art posters. The biggest room, a quad on the first landing, has high ceilings, a big mirror over the fireplace, an Empire onyx table, antique leather armchairs, an array of potted plants, and a huge bathroom with marble floor, double sinks, a fair-size shower, and a separate area for the lavatory (the sink and shower even have gold-plated taps). Attic rooms have sloping ceilings and exposed wood beams, and there are big basement rooms. Rooms at the front overlook a canal, and those at the rear overlook a garden. There's no elevator.

Reguliersgracht 31 (at Keizersgracht), 1017 LK Amsterdam. 📞 **020/623-1329.** No fax. www.sevenbridgeshotel.nl. 8 units. 110€–200€ ($138–$250) double. Rates include full breakfast. AE, MC, V. Limited street parking. Tram: 4 to Keizersgracht. *In room:* TV, dataport, hair dryer.

INEXPENSIVE

Hoksbergen 🌟 *Kids* At a tranquil point on the historic Singel canal, this inexpensive hotel in a 300-year-old canal house is not flashy or elegant, but it is bright and fresh, which makes it appealing to budget-conscious travelers who don't want to swap creature comforts for euros. Its central location makes it easy to get to all the surrounding sights and attractions. Rooms at the front have a canal view. There's no elevator.

Singel 301 (near Spui), 1012 WH Amsterdam. 📞 **020/626-6043.** Fax 020/638-3479. www.hotelhoksbergen.com. 19 units. 72€–90€ ($90–$113) double. Rates include continental breakfast. AE, DC, MC, V. Limited street parking. Tram: 1, 2, or 5 to Spui. *In room:* TV.

Orfeo One of the city's longest-standing gay lodgings has, for more than 30 years, been providing basic, practical facilities and friendly, helpful service. The front desk is in a cozy and sociable lounge, and there is a marble-floored breakfast room. Only three guest rooms have a full bathroom, some with beamed ceilings; others share shower and/or toilet. One of the perks is a small in-house Finnish sauna. The largest concentration of center-city restaurants is right at the doorstep.

Leidsekruisstraat 14 (off Leidseplein), 1017 RH Amsterdam. ⓒ 020/623-1347. Fax 020/620-2348. www.hotelorfeo. com. 19 units, 3 with bathroom. 115€–122€ ($144–$153) double with bathroom; 50€–97€ ($63–$121) double without bathroom. Rates include continental breakfast. AE, MC, V. Limited street parking. Tram: 1, 2, or 5 to Prinsengracht. **Amenities:** Restaurant (Italian); bar. *In room:* TV, minibar, hair dryer, safe.

LEIDSEPLEIN
EXPENSIVE
Amsterdam American 🏨🏨   A fanciful, castlelike mix of Venetian Gothic and Art Nouveau, the American has been both a prominent landmark and a popular meeting place for Amsterdammers since 1900. While the exterior must always remain a protected architectural treasure of turrets, arches, and balconies, the interior (except that of the cafe, which is protected) is modern and chic. Guest rooms are subdued, refined, and superbly furnished. While some have views of Singelgracht, others overlook kaleidoscopic Leidseplein. Many are pink-toned and bright, which perhaps appeals to the international rock stars who often stay here. The location, in the thick of the action and near many major attractions, is one of the best in town. In the **Café Américain,** the hotel has one of the most elegant eateries in Europe (see "Where to Dine," later).

Leidsekade 97 (at Leidseplein), 1017 PN Amsterdam. ⓒ **020/556-3000.** Fax 020/556-3001. www.amsterdamamerican. com. www.amsterdam-american.crowneplaza.com. 190 units. 110€–270€ ($138–$338) double; 385€–470€ ($481–$588) suite; add 5% city tax. AE, DC, MC, V. No parking. Tram: 1, 2, 5, 7, or 10 to Leidseplein. **Amenities:** Restaurant (Continental); bar; exercise room; sauna; concierge; 24-hr. room service; in-room massage; laundry service; same-day dry cleaning. *In room:* A/C, TV w/pay movies, dataport, minibar, coffeemaker, hair dryer, iron, safe.

REMBRANDTPLEIN
EXPENSIVE
NH Schiller 🏨🏨   An Amsterdam gem from 1912, now fully restored, this hotel boasts a blend of Art Nouveau and Art Deco in its public spaces that is reflected in tasteful decor and furnishings in the guest rooms. Its sculpted facade, wrought-iron balconies, and stained-glass windows stand out on the often brash Rembrandtplein. Café Schiller, next door to the hotel, is one of the trendiest watering holes in town. The hotel takes its name from the painter Frits Schiller, who built it in 1912, and whose outpourings of artistic expression, in the form of 600 portraits, landscapes, and still lifes, are displayed in the halls, rooms, stairwells, and public areas. Brasserie Schiller is a gracious oak-paneled dining room and Café Schiller is one of Amsterdam's few permanent sidewalk cafes.

Rembrandtplein 26–36, 1017 CV Amsterdam. ⓒ **800/327-1177** in the U.S. and Canada, or 020/554-0700. Fax 020/626-6831. www.nh-hotels.com. 92 units. 295€ ($369) double (add 5% city tax). AE, DC, MC, V. Limited street parking. Tram: 4, 9, or 14 to Rembrandtplein. **Amenities:** Restaurant (Dutch); 2 bars; health club; 24-hr. room service; babysitting; laundry service; dry cleaning. *In room:* TV, minibar, coffeemaker, hair dryer.

THE JORDAAN
INEXPENSIVE
Acacia 🏨   Not on one of the major canals, but facing a small canal, just a block from Prinsengracht, the Acacia is shaped like a slice of cake. It's run by Hans and Marlene van Vliet, a friendly couple who have worked hard to make their hotel welcoming, clean, and well kept, and are justifiably proud of the result. Simple, clean, and comfortable, the guest rooms have new beds, writing tables, and chairs, and they all have canal views. Breakfast is served in a cozy Old Dutch breakfast room with windows on two sides, and a nice view of the canal. There's no elevator. Two houseboats

for guests on nearby Lijnbaansgracht add an authentic local touch—but what might seem like the earth moving for you may be only the wake from a passing boat setting your houseboat bobbing on the water.

Lindengracht 251 (at Lijnbaansgracht), 1015 KH, Amsterdam. ℂ **020/622-1460.** Fax 020/638-0748. www.hotel acacia.nl. 20 units (including 2 houseboats and 2 studios). 80€–90€ ($100–$113) double; 95€–110€ ($119–$138) houseboat double. Rates include continental breakfast. MC, V (5% charge). Limited street parking. Tram: 3 or 10 to Marnixplein. *In room:* TV.

MUSEUM DISTRICT & VONDELPARK
EXPENSIVE
Bilderberg Hotel Jan Luyken ★★ One block from the Van Gogh Museum and from the elegant Pieter Cornelisz Hooftstraat shopping street, this is best described as a small hotel with many of the amenities and facilities of a large one—though without the large guest rooms. Everything is done with perfect attention to detail. The Jan Luyken maintains a balance between its sophisticated lineup of facilities (double sinks and bidets, elevator, lobby bar with fireplace, and meeting rooms for business) and an intimate and personalized approach that's appropriate to a 19th-century neighborhood. That residential feel extends to the rooms, which look much more like those in a well-designed home than in a standard hotel.

Jan Luijkenstraat 58 (near the Rijksmuseum), 1071 CS Amsterdam. ℂ **020/573-0730.** Fax 020/676-3841. www. janluyken.nl. 62 units. 120€–220€ ($150–$275) double; add 5% city tax. AE, DC, MC, V. Limited street parking. Tram: 2 or 5 to Hobbemastraat. **Amenities:** Wine bar; spa; concierge; 24-hr. room service; in-room massage; babysitting; laundry service; dry cleaning; nonsmoking rooms. *In room:* A/C, TV, dataport, minibar, hair dryer, iron, safe.

MODERATE
De Filosoof ★★ *Finds* On a quiet street facing Vondelpark, this hotel might be the very place if you fancy yourself something of a philosopher. One of the proprietors, a philosophy professor, has chosen posters, painted ceilings, framed quotes, and displayed unusual objects to represent philosophical and cultural themes, and the garden is a kind of grove of academe. Each guest room is dedicated to a mental maestro—Aristotle, Plato, Goethe, Wittgenstein, Nietzsche, Marx, and Einstein are among those who get a look-in—or are based on motifs like Eros, the Renaissance, astrology, and women. You can even consult your private bookshelf of philosophical works or join in a weekly philosophy debate. Rooms in an annex across the street are larger; some open onto a private terrace.

Anna van den Vondelstraat 6 (off Overtoom, at Vondelpark), 1054 GZ Amsterdam. ℂ **020/683-3013.** Fax 020/ 685-3750. www.hotelfilosoof.nl. 38 units. 112€–150€ ($140–$188) double. Rates include buffet breakfast. AE, MC, V. Limited street parking. Tram: 1 to Jan Pieter Heijestraat. **Amenities:** Lounge. *In room:* TV, hair dryer, safe.

Piet Hein ★ Facing Vondelpark, and close to the city's most important museums, this appealing, well-kept hotel is in a villa named after a 17th-century Dutch admiral who captured a Spanish silver shipment. Its spacious guest rooms are well furnished and the staff is friendly and professional. Half the rooms overlook the park, two second-floor double rooms have semicircular balconies, and the honeymoon suite has a water bed. The lower-priced rooms are in an annex behind the main hotel. Hair dryers are available on request.

Vossiusstraat 52–53 (off Van Baerlestraat), 1071 AK Amsterdam. ℂ **020/662-7205.** Fax 020/662-1526. www. hotelpiethein.nl. 65 units. 118€–160€ ($148–$200) double. Rates include continental breakfast. AE, DC, MC, V. Limited street parking. Tram: 3, 5, or 12 to Van Baerlestraat. **Amenities:** Bar; concierge; limited room service; laundry service; dry cleaning; nonsmoking rooms. *In room:* TV w/pay movies, dataport, safe.

Kids Family-Friendly Hotels

Amstel Botel (p. 258)   Although it's more common to find youthful spirits traveling alone or in small groups here, there's no reason why the Amstel Botel wouldn't work for families, and there's the added interest for the kids of being on a ship, even if it isn't going anywhere.

Estheréa (p. 259)   Most of the guest rooms in this canal-house hotel are rather small, but all are tastefully furnished, and a few, ideal for families, are equipped with bunk beds.

Hoksbergen (p. 260)   Children under 4 years of age stay free at this centrally located hotel. The simple but comfortable atmosphere is ideal for allowing the kids some informal vacation freedom.

Toro ✮   On the fringes of Vondelpark in a quiet residential district, this beautiful hotel in a completely renovated mansion dating from 1900 is a good, moderately priced choice. Both on the inside and the outside, it is as near as you can get in Amsterdam to staying in a country villa. The house is furnished and decorated with taste, combining Louis XIV and Liberty styles and featuring stained-glass windows and Murano chandeliers, and affords guests a private garden and terrace. It's about a 10-minute walk through Vondelpark to Leidseplein.

Koningslaan 64 (off Oranje Nassaulaan), 1075 AG Amsterdam. ✆ 020/673-7223. Fax 020/675-0031. www.hotel toro.nl. 22 units. 125€–240€ ($156–$300) double. AE, MC, V. Limited street parking. Tram: 2 to Valeriusplein. **Amenities:** Laundry service; dry cleaning; nonsmoking rooms. *In room:* TV w/pay movies, dataport, minibar, hair dryer, safe.

INEXPENSIVE
Museumzicht   This hotel in a Victorian house across from the back of the Rijksmuseum is ideal for museum-goers on a budget. The breakfast room commands an excellent view of the museum with its numerous stained-glass windows. Robin de Jong, the proprietor, has filled the guest rooms with an eclectic furniture collection, from 1930s English wicker to 1950s pieces. There's no elevator, and the staircase up to reception is pretty steep.

Jan Luijkenstraat 22 (facing the Rijksmuseum), 1071 CN Amsterdam. ✆ 020/671-2954. Fax 020/671-3597. www. hotelmuseumzicht.nl. 14 units, 3 with bathroom. 95€ ($119) double with bathroom; 75€ ($94) double without bathroom. Rates include continental breakfast. AE, DC, MC, V. Limited street parking. Tram: 2 or 5 to Hobbemastraat. **Amenities:** Lounge; limited room service (coffee and tea). *In room:* No phone.

AMSTERDAM SOUTH
EXPENSIVE
Bilderberg Garden Hotel ✮✮✮   This is the smallest and most personal five-star hotel in town. Because of its excellent restaurant, the Garden considers itself a "culinary hotel," an idea that extends to the guest rooms, whose color schemes are decorated in salad-green, salmon-pink, cherry-red, and grape-blue tones—choose whichever suits you best. The rooms themselves are furnished with refined taste and equipped to the highest standards; only executive rooms have coffeemakers. Bathrooms are in marble and are equipped with Jacuzzi tubs. The Garden's spectacular lobby has a wall-to-wall fireplace with a copper-sheathed chimney. The French restaurant **Mangerie de**

Kersentuin (Cherry Orchard), a member of Les Etappes du Bon Goût, boasts an international reputation.

Dijsselhofplantsoen 7 (at Apollolaan), 1077 BJ Amsterdam. (C) 020/570-5600. Fax 020/570-5654. www.garden hotel.nl. 124 units. 249€–325€ ($311–$406) double; 274€–350€ ($343–$438) executive rooms; add 5% city tax. AE, DC, MC, V. Limited street parking. Tram: 5 or 24 to Apollolaan. **Amenities:** Restaurant (French/Mediterranean); bar; access to nearby health club; concierge; business center; 24-hr. room service; in-room massage; babysitting; laundry service; same-day dry cleaning; executive rooms; nonsmoking rooms. *In room:* A/C, TV w/pay movies, fax, dataport, minibar, hair dryer, safe.

MODERATE
Apollofirst ⭐   The small, elegant Apollofirst, a family-owned hotel set amid the Amsterdam school architecture of Apollolaan, advertises itself as the "best quarters in town in the town's best quarter." Their claim may be debatable, but the Venman family's justifiable pride in their establishment is not. All the accommodations are quiet, spacious, and grandly furnished. Bathrooms are fully tiled. Rooms at the back overlook the well-kept gardens of the hotel and its neighbors, and the summer terrace where guests can have a snack or a cocktail. The hotel's elegant **Restaurant Chambertin** is a French *fin de siècle* affair.

Apollolaan 123 (off Minervalaan), 1077 AP Amsterdam. (C) 020/673-0333. Fax 020/675-0348. www.apollofirst.nl. 40 units. 165€ ($206) double; 250€ ($313) studio. Rates include continental breakfast. AE, DC, MC, V. Limited street parking. Tram: 5 or 24 to Apollolaan. **Amenities:** Bar; 24-hr. room service; babysitting; laundry service; dry-cleaning; nonsmoking rooms. *In room:* TV, wireless Internet, hair dryer, safe.

INEXPENSIVE
Van Ostade Bicycle Hotel ⭐⭐   The young owners of this establishment have found a niche, catering mainly to visitors who wish to explore Amsterdam on bicycles. They help guests plan biking routes through and around the city. You can rent bikes for 5€ ($6.25) daily, no deposit, and stable your trusty steed indoors. The guest rooms have new carpets and plain but comfortable modern furnishings; some have kitchenettes and small balconies, and there are large rooms for families. The hotel is a few blocks from the popular Albert Cuyp street market, in the somewhat raggedy De Pijp neighborhood. Two old bicycles hang 6m (20 ft.) high on the hotel's facade, and there are always bikes parked in front. There's no elevator.

Van Ostadestraat 123 (off Ferdinand Bolstraat), Amsterdam 1072 SV. (C) 020/679-3452. Fax 020/671-5213. www. bicyclehotel.com. 16 units, 8 with bathroom. 70€–105€ ($88–$131) double with bathroom; 50€–65€ ($63–$81) double without bathroom. Rates include continental breakfast. AE, MC, V. Parking 17€ ($21). Tram: 3, 12, or 25 to Ceintuurbaan-Ferdinand Bolstraat. **Amenities:** Lounge; bike rental. *In room:* TV.

AMSTERDAM EAST
MODERATE
Arena ⭐   A converted Roman Catholic orphanage from 1890 houses this friendly, stylish, youth-oriented hotel. Monumental marble staircases, cast-iron banisters, stained-glass windows, marble columns, original murals—all have been faithfully restored. Spare modern guest rooms, some sporting timber roof beams and wooden floors, line long, high-ceilinged corridors on two floors. Each room is individually decorated and styled by up-and-coming young Dutch designers. Some are split-level. You still see kids toting backpacks, but they're a better class of backpack than those that clog corridors in the city's hostels and cheap hotels. Hotel guests get discounts on concerts and dance nights in the nightclub called Tonight, in the old orphanage chapel. The Arena is a bit removed from the center city but the traffic is two-way, with youthful revelers heading out here to the nightspot and the outdoor cafe.

's-Gravesandestraat 51 (at Mauritskade), 1092 AA Amsterdam. ℂ **020/850-2410.** Fax 020/850-2415. www.hotel arena.nl. 127 units. 80€–150€ ($100–$188) double; 175€–275€ ($219–$344) suite. Rates include buffet breakfast. AE, DC, MC, V. Free parking. Tram: 7 or 10 to Korte 's-Gravesandestraat. **Amenities:** Restaurant (Continental); bar; executive rooms. *In room:* TV.

Bridge Hotel 🏨🏨 The bridge in question is the celebrated Magere Brug (Skinny Bridge) over the Amstel River. This small and tastefully decorated hotel likely provides its guests with more space per euro than any other hotel in town. Its pine-furnished guest rooms seem like studio apartments, with couches, coffee tables, and easy chairs arranged in lounge areas in such a way that there's plenty of room left between them and the beds for you to do your morning exercises. There's no elevator.

Amstel 107–111 (near Theater Carré), 1018 EM Amsterdam. ℂ **020/623-7068.** Fax 020/624-1565. www.thebridge hotel.nl. 36 units. 85€–130€ ($106–$163) double; 150€–275€ ($188–$344) apt. Rates include continental breakfast. AE, DC, MC, V. Limited street parking. Tram: 7 or 10 to Weesperplein. **Amenities:** Lounge; laundry service. *In room:* TV.

NEAR THE AIRPORT
VERY EXPENSIVE
Sheraton Amsterdam Airport 🏨 If you were sleeping any closer to the airport, you'd be lodging on the runway. There's all the comfort you would expect of a top-flight Sheraton, including soundproof guest rooms with big, comfortable beds, marble bathrooms with separate shower, and a well-equipped health club and fitness center. That said, the Sheraton is no fount of Dutch tradition. Blocky and modern is the kindest thing I can say about the exterior, which is about what you'd expect of a hotel in this location. The inside story is better, with rooms that bring a touch of style to their mis-

> **Impressions**
> *I had in my mind's eye a perfect bed in a perfect hostelry hard by the Amstel River.*
> —Erskine Childers, *The Riddle of the Sands* (1903)

sion of lodging itinerant businesspeople. Room styles range from modern and functional to unashamed luxury in the suites. The **Voyager** restaurant has an international, a la carte menu. The **Dutch Runway Café** serves drinks and delicatessen snacks.

Schiphol Blvd. 101 (outside Schiphol Plaza), 1118 BG Amsterdam. ℂ **800/325-3535** in the U.S. and Canada, or 020/316-4300. Fax 020/316-4399. www.sheraton.com/amsterdamair. 408 units. 140€–300€ ($175–$375) double; from 890€ ($1,113) suite; add 5% city tax. AE, DC, MC, V. Parking 30€ ($38). **Amenities:** 2 restaurants (international/Dutch); 2 bars; heated indoor pool; health club; sauna; concierge; business center; 24-hr. room service; babysitting; laundry service; dry cleaning; nonsmoking rooms; executive rooms. *In room:* A/C, TV w/pay movies, dataport, minibar, coffeemaker, hair dryer, safe.

---

4 Where to Dine

If cities get the cuisine they deserve, Amsterdam's ought to be liberal, multiethnic, and adventurous. Guess what? It is. A trading city with a true melting-pot character, Amsterdam has absorbed culinary influences from far and wide, and rustled them all up to its own satisfaction. You can find just about every international cuisine type on the city's restaurant roster—in Amsterdam, they say, you can eat in any language. Better yet, many of these eateries satisfy the sturdy Dutch insistence on getting maximum value out of every euro. Dutch cooking, of course, is part of all this, naturally, but you won't be stuck with *biefstuk* (beefsteak) and *kip* (chicken) every day, unless you want to be.

Where to Dine in Amsterdam

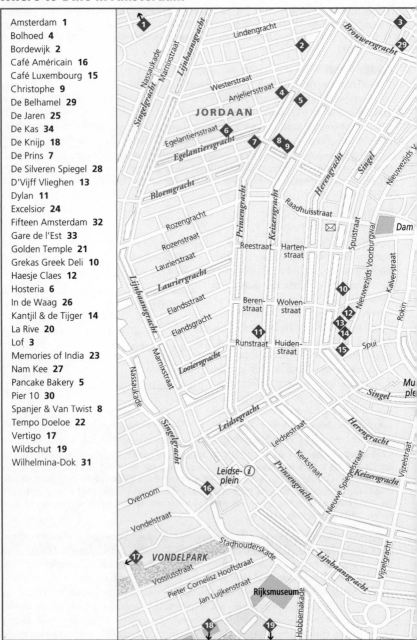

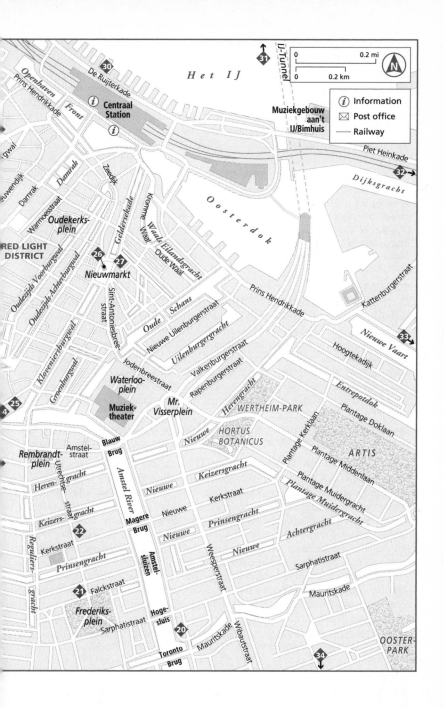

Het IJ

31

IJ-Tunnel

0 — 0.2 mi
0 — 0.2 km

N

ⓘ Information
✉ Post office
— Railway

30

De Ruijterkade

Openhaven

Prins Hendrikkade

Front

ⓘ Centraal
Station

ⓘ

Zeedijk

Muziekgebouw
aan't
IJ/Bimhuis

Piet Heinkade

...gwal

Damrak

Damrak

Warmoesstraat

Nieuwendijk

Oudekerks-
plein

RED LIGHT
DISTRICT

Oudezijds Voorburgwal

Oudezijds Achterburgwal

Geldersekade

Kromme
Waal

Waals Eilandsgracht

Oude Waal

Oosterdok

Dijksgracht

32

26

27

Nieuwmarkt

Sint-Antoniesbree-
straat

Oude

Schans

Nieuwe Uilenburgerstraat

Prins Hendrikkade

Kattenburgerstraat

Nieuwe Vaart

33

Klovenniersburgwal

Groenburgwal

Uilenburgergracht

Hoogtekadijk

Jodenbreestraat

Valkenburgerstraat

Rapenburgerstraat

Waterloo-
plein

Muziek-
theater

Mr.
Visserplein

Herengracht

WERTHEIM-PARK

Entrepotdok

Plantage Doklaan

4 25

Amstel-
straat

Blauw
Brug

Nieuwe

HORTUS
BOTANICUS

ARTIS

Rembrandt-
plein

Heren-
gracht

Utrechtse-

Keizers-
gracht

Amstel River

Nieuwe

Keizersgracht

Plantage Kerklaan

Plantage Middenlaan

22

Kerkstraat

Nieuwe

Kerkstraat

Plantage Muidergracht

Plantage Muidergracht

Magere
Brug

Prinsengracht

Reguliers-
gracht

Prinsengracht

Nieuwe

Nieuwe

Achtergracht

Weesperstraat

Sarphatistraat

Amstel-
sluizen

21

Falckstraat

Frederiks-
plein

Sarphatistraat

Hoge-
sluis

20

Mauritskade

Wibautstraat

Mauritskade

OOSTER-
PARK

Toronto
Brug

34

267

THE OLD CENTER
VERY EXPENSIVE

Excelsior ★★★ CONTINENTAL   One of Amsterdam's most eminent restaurants derives its reputation from critically acclaimed cuisine and superb service. It's more than a little formal—especially by Amsterdam standards. Crystal chandeliers, elaborate moldings, crisp linens, fresh bouquets of flowers, and picture windows with great views on the Amstel River help give this refined place a baronial atmosphere. Respectable attire (jackets for men) is required. If your budget can't quite compete with that of the royalty and showbiz stars who dine here, try the three-course *middag-menu* (lunch menu), or the *menu du théâtre* in the evening, which make fine dining more affordable. The menu includes such choices as smoked eel with dill (a Dutch specialty) or marinated sweetbreads of lamb with salad for starters, and filet of halibut with caper sauce, or filet of veal with leek sauce as main courses.

In the Hotel de l'Europe, Nieuwe Doelenstraat 2–8 (facing Muntplein). ℰ 020/531-1705. www.leurope.nl. Reservations recommended on weekends. Main courses 28€–44€ ($35–$55); fixed-price menus 56€–79€ ($70–$99). AE, DC, MC, V. Mon–Fri 7–11am, 12:30–2:30pm, and 7–10:30pm; Sat–Sun 7–11am and 7–10:30pm. Tram: 4, 9, 14, 16, 24, or 25 to Muntplein.

EXPENSIVE

De Silveren Spiegel ★ DUTCH/FRENCH   The twin houses that form the premises of this elegant restaurant were built in 1614 for a wealthy soap maker, Laurens Jansz Spieghel. It's Old Dutch–style inside, with the bar downstairs and more dining rooms where the bedrooms used to be. The whole place emanates a traditionally Dutch tidiness that's very welcoming. There's a garden in back. The menu has been updated and now offers new, finely prepared seafood and meat dishes, such as baked sole filets with wild spinach, and trilogy of lamb with ratatouille—but just as in the old days, the lamb is Holland's finest, from the island of Texel, and accompanied by tangy Zaanse mustard.

Kattengat 4–6 (off Singel). ℰ 020/624-6589. www.desilverenspiegel.com. Main courses 22€–35€ ($28–$44); fixed-price menus 29€–46€ ($36–$58). AE, MC, V. Mon–Sat 5:30–10:30pm. Tram: 1, 2, 5, 13, or 17 to Martelaarsgracht.

D'Vijff Vlieghen ★★ MODERN DUTCH   Touristy? Yes. The "Five Flies" is a kind of Old Dutch theme park, with nine separate dining rooms in five canal houses decorated with objects from Holland's Golden Age. Each room has a different character. For example, the Rembrandt Room has four original etchings by the artist; the Glass Room has a collection of Golden Age handmade glassware; and the Knight's Room is adorned with 16th-century armor and accouterments. The chef is out to convey the culinary excellence inherent in many traditional Dutch recipes and products, in an updated, "New Dutch" form, employing organic ingredients when possible. You can enjoy quite a mouthful by choosing the *geroosteerde tamme eend op een bedje van appeltjes en tuinboontjes overgroten met een vinaigrette van rode en groene pepers* (roasted tame duck on a layer of apples and broad beans drizzled with a vinaigrette of red and green peppers).

Spuistraat 294–302 (at Spui; entrance at Vliegendesteeg 1). ℰ 020/530-4060. www.d-vijffvlieghen.com. Main courses 21€–29€ ($26–$36); seasonal menu 31€–51€ ($39–$64). AE, DC, MC, V. Daily 5:30pm–midnight. Tram: 1, 2, or 5 to Spui.

MODERATE

Haesje Claes ★ DUTCH   If you're yearning for a cozy Old Dutch environment and hearty Dutch food at moderate prices, try this inviting place. Lots of nooks and crannies decorated with wood paneling, Delftware, wooden barrels, brocaded benches, and traditional Dutch hanging lamps with fringed covers give an intimate, comfortable feel to the setting. The menu covers a lot of ground, from canapés to caviar, but you have the most luck with Dutch stalwarts ranging from omelets to tournedos. Try *hutspot* (stew), *stampot* (mashed potatoes and cabbage), and various fish stews, including those with IJsselmeer *paling* (eel).

Spuistraat 273–275 (at Spui). ℂ 020/624-9998. www.haesjeclaes.nl. Main courses 15€–26€ ($19–$33); tourist menu 20€ ($25). AE, DC, MC, V. Daily noon–10pm. Tram: 1, 2, or 5 to Spui.

In de Waag ℱ CONTINENTAL   Dissections were once carried out on the top floor of De Waag, the public weigh house, which had earlier been the Sint-Antoniespoort Gate in the city walls. Nowadays, dissections are of a culinary nature. This castlelike structure holds one of Amsterdam's most stylish cafe-restaurants, in an area that's becoming hipper by the minute. It's an indelibly romantic place, the long banquet-style tables ablaze with light from hundreds of candles in the evening. You can mix easily with other diners. The breast of Barbary duck with sesame-cracker and sherry dressing is pretty good, as is the vegetarian Kashmir bread with braised vegetables and coriander-yogurt sauce. If you're not hungry, you can just drop by for a coffee or a drink.

Nieuwmarkt 4. ℂ 020/422-7772. www.indewaag.nl. Main courses 15€–25€ ($19–$31). AE, DC, MC, V. Sun–Thurs 10am–1am; Fri–Sat 10am–2am. Metro: Nieuwmarkt.

Kantjil & de Tijger ℱ INDONESIAN   Unlike the many Indonesian restaurants in Holland that wear their ethnic origins on their sleeves, literally, with waitstaff decked out in traditional costume, the "Antelope and the Tiger" is chic, modern, and cool. Moreover, it attracts customers who like their Indonesian food not only chic, modern, and cool, but good as well. The two bestsellers in this popular place are *nasi goreng Kantjil* (fried rice with pork kabobs, stewed beef, pickled cucumbers, and mixed vegetables) and the 20-item *rijsttafel* for two. Other choices include stewed chicken in soy sauce, tofu omelet, shrimps with coconut dressing, Indonesian pumpkin, and mixed steamed vegetables with peanut-butter sauce. Finish off your meal with the multilayered cinnamon cake or (try this at least once) the coffee with ginger liqueur and whipped cream.

Spuistraat 291–293 (beside Spui). ℂ 020/620-0994. www.kantjil.nl. Reservations recommended on weekends. Main courses 11€–16€ ($14–$20); budget meal (4:30–6:30pm) 9€ ($11); rijsttafel 40€–50€ ($50–$63) for 2. AE, DC, MC, V. Daily 4:30–11pm. Tram: 1, 2, or 5 to Spui.

Lof ℱℱ *Finds* CONTINENTAL   It's hard to pin down this fashionable, vaguely French/Italian eatery. For one thing, there's no menu. Its youthful chefs describe their creations as *cuisine spontane*—they go to the markets, spontaneously pick out whatever's fresh, and equally spontaneously figure out what to do with it back at base. But the name means "praise" in Dutch, and that sounds about right, since the results are invariably admirable. The choice is deliberately limited, not quite take-it-or-leave-it, but not too far away. Oysters are a regular feature among two or three starters; then, choose from three main courses: meat, fish, and vegetarian; and finish with a *torte*. You dine on one of two levels, at plain tables in a cozy setting with bare brick walls and a view of proceedings in the open kitchen.

Haarlemmerstraat 62 (west of Centraal Station). ℂ 020/620-2997. Main courses 12€–22€ ($15–$28); fixed-price menu 35€ ($42). No credit cards. Tues–Sun 7–11pm. Tram: 1, 2, 5, 13, or 17 to Maartelaarsgracht.

Moments Secrets of the Rijsttafel

The Indonesian feast **rijsttafel** is Holland's favorite meal and has been ever since the United East India Company sea captains introduced it to the wealthy burghers of Amsterdam in the 17th century. The rijsttafel (literally "rice table") originated with Dutch plantation overseers in Indonesia, who liked to sample selectively from Indonesian cuisine.

The basic concept of a rijsttafel is to eat a bit of this and a bit of that, blending the flavors and textures. A simple, unadorned bed of rice is the base and the mediator between spicy meats and bland vegetables or fruits, between sweet-and-sour tastes, soft-and-crunchy textures. Although a rijsttafel for one is possible, this feast is better shared by two or by a tableful of people. In the case of a solitary diner or a couple, a 17-dish rijsttafel will be enough food; for four or more, order a 24- or 30-dish rijsttafel and you can experience the total taste treat.

Among the customary dishes and ingredients of a rijsttafel are *loempia* (classic Chinese-style egg rolls); *satay*, or *sateh* (small kabobs of pork, grilled and served with a spicy peanut sauce); *perkedel* (meatballs); *gado-gado* (vegetables in peanut sauce); *daging smoor* (beef in soy sauce); *babi ketjap* (pork in soy sauce); *kroepoek* (crunchy, puffy shrimp toast); *serundeng* (fried coconut); *roedjak manis* (fruit in sweet sauce); and *pisang goreng* (fried banana). Beware of one very appealing dish of sauce with small chunks of what looks to be bright-red onion—that is *sambal badjak*, or simply *sambal*, and it's hotter than hot.

INEXPENSIVE

Café Luxembourg 𝒢𝒢 INTERNATIONAL   "One of the world's great cafes," wrote the *New York Times* about this bohemian, see-and-be-seen grand cafe, where the waitstaff wear starched white aprons. Unlike other cafes in Amsterdam, which often draw a distinctive clientele, the Luxembourg attracts all kinds of people because it offers amazingly large portions of food at reasonable prices. Soups, sandwiches, and such dishes as meatloaf are available. Special attractions often include choices like Chinese dim sum and *satay ajam* (Indonesian grilled chicken in a peanut sauce). Sunday in particular, but also on other days, it's a good place to do breakfast over the day's papers and a cup of strong coffee. You're encouraged to linger and relax. In summer, there's sidewalk dining.

Spui 24 (at Spui). 🕐 **020/620-6264.** www.cafeluxembourg.nl. Salads and specials 7.50€–12€ ($9.40–$15); lunch 4.50€–9.75€ ($5.65–$12); main courses 8.50€–15€ ($11–$19). AE, DC, MC, V. Sun–Thurs 9am–1am; Fri–Sat 9am–2am. Tram: 1, 2, or 5 to Spui.

De Jaren 𝒢 CONTINENTAL   If you admire picturesque surroundings, you'll love this large cafe-restaurant. Fashionable without being pretentious, it occupies a solid-looking, spacious building (which was once a bank) on two stories, with unusually high ceilings and a multicolored tiled mosaic floor. De Jaren's unique selling point is not so much the fashionable set that hangs out here, but its two marvelous open-air terraces beside the Amstel River, places in the sun that are in high demand in fine weather. Occupants of these prime-time seats display a firmness of purpose as if they mean to settle there permanently. You can enjoy everything from a cup of coffee, a beer, or a *jenever* (gin), to ham and eggs for breakfast, a salad from the extensive salad bar, spaghetti bolognese, couscous, and rib-eye steak. And you can peruse the English-language newspapers while you do it.

Nieuwe Doelenstraat 20–22 (near Muntplein). ℂ 020/625-5771. www.cafe-de-jaren.nl. Main courses 9.50€–18€ ($12–$23); lunch menu 9.50€ ($12). V. Sun–Thurs 10am–1am; Fri–Sat 10am–2am. Tram: 4, 9, 14, 16, 24, or 25 to Muntplein.

Nam Kee ☆ CHINESE   In the heart of the city's small but growing Chinatown, Nam Kee has a long interior with few obvious graces, little in the way of decor, and no plastic Ming Dynasty knickknacks. People come here to pay modestly for food that is both authentic and excellent, from a menu of around 140 items. The steamed oysters with black-bean sauce and the duck with plum sauce are to die for. Judging by the number of ethnic Chinese customers clicking chopsticks around, Nam Kee does okay when it comes to homeland credibility. The service is fast—not quite so fast you'll still be eating off your plate while the waitperson is bringing it to the dishwasher, but close. On the bright side, you don't have to wait long for a table, even when it's crowded.

Zeedijk 111–113 at Nieuwmarkt. ℂ 020/624-3470. www.namkee.nl. Main courses 5.75€–16€ ($7.20–$20). AE, DC, MC, V. Daily 11:30am–midnight. Metro: Nieuwmarkt.

THE WATERFRONT
EXPENSIVE
Fifteen Amsterdam ☆ FUSION/ITALIAN   British celeb chef Jamie Oliver brought his unique restaurant concept from London to Amsterdam in 2004, when he opened a branch of the budding Fifteen chain in the old Brazilië building in the harbor redevelopment zone east of Centraal Station. Oliver presents an internationally syndicated BBC cookery show, *The Naked Chef,* his cookbooks sell like hot cakes, and he likes to tool around in his Maserati. His cool London Fifteen eatery took on unemployed kids and trained them up to be more than acceptable chefs and waitstaff, and his Amsterdam venture adopts the same approach. Even though Oliver doesn't often preside in person, you can try out his eclectic, fun-cooking concept in the vast main restaurant, and in the more intimate trattoria—on risottos, pasta dishes, and other Italian fare—where prices are more like moderate. There's outdoors dining on a water-side terrace.

Pakhuis Amsterdam, Jollemanhof 9, Zeeburg (at Oostelijke Handelskade). ℂ 0900/FIFTEEN (0900/343-8336). www.fifteen.nl. Reservations recommended on weekends. Main courses 17€–35€ ($21–$44); tasting menu 44€ ($55). AE, MC, V. Restaurant: Mon–Sat 6pm–1am; trattoria: daily 5:30pm–1am. Tram: 26 to Kattenburgerstraat.

MODERATE
Gare de l'Est ☆☆ FRENCH/MEDITERRANEAN   Originally a coffeehouse for workers at the docks, this distinctive detached house—with a conservatory extension and a large sidewalk terrace—is reason enough to make a trip to this part of town. As the restaurant's name indicates, the cuisine is French traditional, though you'll notice Mediterranean touches. Service is both relaxed and knowledgeable, and the fixed-price menu is an excellent value. The strict five-course formula (starter, salad, main course of meat or fish, cheese, and dessert) leaves no room for choice—except for the main course—but plenty for market-fresh ingredients and culinary creativity. How does this sound: *pulpo estofado et risotto nero* (ink-fish stew and black rice) as a starter, and roast lamb with gazpacho and farfalle as a main course?

Cruquiusweg 9 (at the Eastern Harbor). ✆ **020/463-0620**. www.garedelest.nl. Reservations recommended on weekends. Fixed-price menu 30€ ($38). No credit cards. Daily 6–11pm. Tram: 7 or 10 to Zeeburgerdijk.

Pier 10 FRENCH/INTERNATIONAL   Perched on an old pier on Het IJ behind Centraal Station (but set back far enough that you won't be bothered by the noise), this restaurant can't help being romantic. It has great views of the IJ waterway from its big outdoor terrace and from the "serre" (glassed-in room) at the end of the pier. The coming and going of harbor ferries, cruise liners, and workaday barges on the ship channel adds a dash of nautical bustle to the scene, making this one of only a few restaurants where you're aware of the sea and port traffic that was once Amsterdam's lifeblood. Candlelight softens the funky diner decor, and the fanciful international-eclectic food—salads of all kinds, new herring, steak, and fish—ebbs and flows like the tides in Het IJ.

De Ruyterkade, Steiger 10 (behind Centraal Station). ✆ **020/427-2310**. www.pier10.nl. Reservations recommended on weekends. Main courses 15€–24€ ($20–$30). AE, DC, MC, V. Daily noon–3pm and 6:30pm–1am. Tram: 1, 2, 4, 5, 9, 16, 17, 24, 25, or 26 to Centraal Station.

Wilhelmina-Dok CONTINENTAL   Just across the IJ channel from Centraal Station, this waterside eatery has an old-fashioned maritime look from its plain wood tables, wood floors, and oak cabinets, and large windows serve up views across the boat-speckled waterway. Breezy is one way to describe the impact of the prevailing westerlies, but tables on the outdoor terrace are sheltered from the wind. The menu favors plain cooking and organic products. A couple of good choices are the *zwaard-vis van de grill met saffranrisotto* (grilled swordfish with saffron rice) and the *kalfslende van de grill met gemarineerde aubergine en flageolottensalade en pesto* (grilled veal cutlets with marinated aubergines, flageolet salad, and pesto). Or you can settle back with just a beer and a snack. On Monday evenings in August, movies are shown on an outdoor screen.

Nordwal 1 (at IJplein). ✆ **020/632-3701**. www.wilhelmina-dok.nl. Reservations recommended on weekends. Main courses 16€–21€ ($20–$26). AE, DC, MC, V. Mon–Fri noon–midnight; Sat–Sun noon–1am. Ferry: IJveer from Waterplein-West behind Centraal Station to the dock at IJplein; then go right, along the dike-top path.

THE CANAL BELT
EXPENSIVE
Dylan CONTINENTAL/FUSION   If you dress up in black to celebrate, and I don't mean a tux, then head for this ultra-hip and hyper-pricey Zen-like restaurant in the converted bakery of an 18th-century almshouse, of the ultra-chic designer hotel of the same name. This is where neo-millionaires, jet-setters, and media tycoons go to check out each other's black duds, in a setting that shares some of the mother ship's

---

Tips **An Amsterdam Dinner Cruise**

A dinner cruise is a delightful way to combine sightseeing and leisurely dining. During these 2½-hour canal cruises, you can enjoy a five-course dinner that includes a cocktail, wine with dinner, coffee with bonbons, and a glass of cognac or a liqueur to finish. Reservations are required. The cruises cost around 69€ ($86) for adults, and 45€ ($56) for children ages 4 to 12. See "Organized Tours," later in this chapter, for details on the tour-boat lines.

black-and-white themes, while feeding on skate filet with squid ink sauce, or chicken Fabergé with lobster, ginger, and lemon-grass sauce. Affable celeb chef Schilo van Coevorden numbers among Amsterdam's hottest culinary properties and is a proficient practitioner of a number of ethnic cuisines. He cooks up Thai/Italian/French–inspired delicacies. Asian combinations predominate at lunchtime, and Mediterranean themes edge them out in the evening.

In Dylan Amsterdam Hotel, Keizersgracht 384 (at Runstraat). *C* 020/530-2010. www.dylanamsterdam.com. Reservations required. Main courses 29€–43€ ($36–$54); fixed-price menu 45€ ($56). AE, DC, MC, V. Mon–Fri 7–11am, noon–2pm, and 6:30–11pm; Sat 7–11am and 6:30–11pm. Tram: 13, 14, or 17 to Westermarkt.

MODERATE

Bolhoed *(R)(R)* VEGETARIAN   Forget the corn-sheaf 'n' brown-rice image affected by so many vegetarian restaurants. Instead, garnish your healthful habits with tangy flavors and a dash of zest. Latin style, world music, ethnic exhibits, evening candlelight, and a fine view of the canal from each of the two plant-bedecked rooms in this former hat store—*bolhoed* is Dutch for bowler hat—distinguish a restaurant for which *vegetarian* is a tad too wholesome-sounding. Service is delivered with equal amounts of gusto and attention. Try the pumpkin soup, *ragoût croissant* (pastry filled with leeks, tofu, seaweed, and curry sauce), a variety of salads, and *zarzuela*. If you want to go the whole hog, so to speak, and eat vegan, most of Bolhoed's dishes can be so prepared, and most are made with organic produce; the wine is organic, too. In fine weather, you can dine right beside the canal.

Prinsengracht 60–62 (near Noordermarkt). *C* **020/626-1803.** Main courses 12€–15€ ($15–$19); 3-course menu 19€ ($24). No credit cards. Sun–Fri noon–11pm; Sat 11am–11pm. Tram: 13, 14, or 17 to Westermarkt.

De Belhamel *(R)(R) Finds* CONTINENTAL   Classical music complements a graceful Art Nouveau setting at this two-level restaurant overlooking the photogenic junction of the Herengracht and Brouwersgracht canals. The tables fill up quickly most evenings, so make reservations or go early. The menu changes seasonally (game is a big deal here in the fall), but here's a sampling of dishes that recently appeared: puffed pastries layered with salmon, shellfish, crayfish tails, and chervil beurre blanc to start; and beef tenderloin in Madeira sauce with zucchini *rösti* and puffed garlic for a main course. You can also order vegetarian dishes. Try for a window table and take in the superb canal views. The waitstaff is occasionally a bit too laid-back, and when it's full, the acoustic peculiarities of the place can drive the noise level up to that of a boiler factory.

Brouwersgracht 60 (at Herengracht). *C* 020/622-1095. www.belhamel.nl. Main courses 19€–21€ ($24–$26); fixed-price menu 32€ ($40). AE, MC, V. Sun–Thurs 6–10pm; Fri–Sat 6–10:30pm. Tram: 1, 2, 5, 13, or 17 to Martelaarsgracht.

Spanjer & Van Twist *(R) Finds* CONTINENTAL   This place would almost be worth the visit for its name alone, so it's doubly gratifying that the food is good, too. The interior is typical neighborhood-*eetcafé* style, with the day's specials chalked on a blackboard, a long table with newspapers at the front, and the kitchen visible in back. High standards of cooking put this place above others of its kind. The eclectic menu changes seasonally, but to give you an idea of its range, I've come fork-to-face here with Thai fish curry and *pandan* rice; *saltimbocca* of trout in white-wine sauce; and artichoke mousseline with tarragon sauce and green asparagus. In fine weather, you can eat under the trees on an outdoor terrace beside the tranquil Leliegracht canal.

Leliegracht 60 (off Keizersgracht). ✆ **020/639-0109.** Reservations not accepted. Main courses 11€–16€ ($13–$20). MC, V. Sun–Thurs 10am–1am; Fri–Sat 10am–2am (only light snacks after 11pm). Tram: 13, 14, or 17 to Westermarkt.

Tempo Doeloe ✿✿ INDONESIAN For authentic Indonesian cuisine, this place is hard to beat. You dine in a *batik* ambience that's Indonesian, but restrained. The attractive decor and the fine china are unexpected pluses. Try the small meat, fish, and vegetable dishes of three different *rijsttafel* (rice table) options, from the 15-plate vegetarian rijsttafel *sayoeran* and the 15-plate rijsttafel *stimoelan,* to the sumptuous 25-plate rijsttafel *istemewa.* You get dishes like *gadon dari sapi* (beef in a mild coconut sauce and fresh coriander), *ajam roedjak* (chicken in a strongly seasoned sauce of chiles and coconut), *sambal goreng oedang* (small shrimps with Indonesian spices), and *atjar* (sweet-and-sour Indonesian salad). For great individual dishes, go for the *nasi koening* or any of the vegetarian options. One caution: When something on the menu is described as *pedis,* meaning hot, that's *exactly* what it is.

Utrechtsestraat 75 (between Prinsengracht and Keizersgracht). ✆ **020/625-6718.** www.tempodoeloerestaurant.nl. Reservations recommended on weekends. Main courses 14€–25€ ($18–$31); rijsttafel 27€–35€ ($34–$44); fixed-price menu 27€–43€ ($34–$54). AE, DC, MC, V. Mon–Sat 6–11:30pm. Tram: 4 to Keizersgracht.

INEXPENSIVE

De Prins ✿✿ *Value* DUTCH/FRENCH This cozy *eetcafé* housed in a 17th-century canal house across the water from the Anne Frankhuis, has a smoke-stained, brown-cafe style, but its food could easily grace a much more expensive restaurant. De Prins offers an unbeatable price-to-quality ratio for typically Dutch/French menu items, and long may it continue to do so. The youthful clientele is loyal and enthusiastic, quickly filling up the relatively few tables. This is a quiet neighborhood place—nothing fancy or trendy, but very appealing in a local way. There's a bar on a slightly lower level than the restaurant. From March to September, De Prins spreads a terrace along the canalside.

Prinsengracht 124 (at Egelantiersgracht). ✆ **020/624-9382.** www.deprins.nl. Main courses 7.50€–15€ ($9.40–$19); *dagschotel* 10€ ($13); specials 11€–16€ ($14–$20). AE, DC, MC, V. Daily 10am to 1 or 2am (kitchen to 10pm). Tram: 13, 14, or 17 to Westermarkt.

Golden Temple ✿ VEGETARIAN This temple of taste is one of the best vegetarian (and vegan) options in town. Its limpid, nonsmoking atmosphere is a tad too hallowed, an effect enhanced by an absence of decorative flourishes that may be Zen-like in its purity but leaves you wishing for something, anything, to look at other than your fellow veg-eaters. The menu livens things up, with its unlikely roster of Indian, Middle Eastern, and Mexican dishes, and the food is delicately spiced and flavored. Multiple-choice platters are a good way to go. For the Indian *thali,* you select from choices like *sag paneer* (homemade cheese in a spinach and onion sauce), vegetable *korma,* and *raita* (cucumber and yogurt dip); the Middle Eastern platter has stalwarts like falafel, chickpea-and-vegetable stew, and vegetable *dolmas.* Side dishes are as varied as guacamole, couscous, and *pakora.*

Utrechtsestraat 126 (2 blocks south of Prinsengracht). ✆ **020/626-8560.** Main courses 10€–14€ ($13–$17); mixed platter 14€ ($18). MC, V. Daily 5–10pm. Tram: 4 to Prinsengracht.

Grekas Greek Deli ✿ GREEK With just five tables and a small sidewalk terrace in summertime, Grekas would be more of a frustration than anything else, except that its main business is its takeout service. The food is fresh and authentic, and you can choose your meal like you would on Mykonos, by pointing to the dishes you want. If there are no free tables, you can always take your choices back to your room, or eat alfresco on the canalside. Menu items are standard Greek but with a freshness and taste that are hard to beat. The moussaka and pasticcio are heavenly; the roast lamb with wine, herbs, olive oil, and bouillon is excellent; the calamari in the salad seems to have come straight out of Homer's wine-dark sea; and there's a good Greek wine list. Takeout dishes are a euro or two less than eat-in.

Singel 311 (near Spui). ℂ 020/620-3590. No reservations. Main courses 9.50€–14€ ($12–$18). No credit cards. Wed–Sun 5–10pm. Tram: 1, 2, or 5 to Spui.

Pancake Bakery ⋇ *(Kids)* PANCAKES   In a 17th-century canal warehouse, this two-story restaurant with winding staircases and exposed beams serves some of the most delicious and unusual pancakes you'll ever taste. There are several dozen varieties, and almost all constitute a full meal. The satisfyingly large—you might even find them heavy—pancakes come adorned with all sorts of toppings, both sweet and spicy. Choices include salami and cheese, cheese and ginger, curried turkey with pineapple and raisins, honey nuts and whipped cream, and ice cream and *advokaat* (a Dutch eggnoglike cocktail). One of the bestsellers is the "American" pancake: with fried chicken, sweet corn, peppers, carrots, Cajun sauce, and salad. In summer, a few tables are placed in front overlooking the canal, but beware: All the syrup, honey, and sugar being passed around tends to attract bees and hornets.

Prinsengracht 191 (at Prinsenstraat). ℂ 020/625-1333. www.pancake.nl. Reservations required for large groups. Pancakes 4.75€–11€ ($5.95–$14). AE, MC, V. Daily noon–9:30pm. Tram: 13, 14, or 17 to Westermarkt.

LEIDSEPLEIN
MODERATE
Café Américain ⋇ CONTINENTAL   The lofty dining room here—restored in 2005—is a national monument of Art Nouveau and Art Deco. Since its opening in 1900, the place has been a hangout for Dutch and international artists, writers, dancers, and actors. Seductress/spy Mata Hari held her wedding reception here in her pre-espionage days. *Tout* Amsterdam once liked to be seen here (and some of it still does), but now it's mostly for tourists. Don't let that worry you: It's still great. Leaded stained-glass windows, newspaper-littered reading tables, bargello-patterned velvet upholstery, frosted-glass Tiffany chandeliers from the 1920s, and tall carved columns are all part of the dusky sit-and-chat atmosphere. Seafood specialties include monkfish, perch, salmon, and king prawns; meat dishes include rack of Irish lamb and rosé breast of duck with creamed potatoes. Jazz lovers can stock up on good music and food at the Sunday jazz brunch.

> **Fun Fact Real Cutups**
>
> In the 1960s, satirist Gerrit Komrij described the Café Américain's notoriously brusque waiters as "unemployed knife-throwers."

In the Amsterdam American Hotel, Leidsekade 97 (at Leidseplein). ℂ 020/556-3116. www.amsterdamamerican. com. Main courses 16€–21€ ($20–$26). AE, DC, MC, V. Daily 10:30am–midnight. Tram: 1, 2, 5, 7, or 10 to Leidseplein.

REMBRANDTPLEIN
MODERATE
Memories of India ⋇ INDIAN   The Khan family proprietors earned their spurs in the crowded and intensely competitive London market for Indian cuisine and then

---

Tips **Local Heroes**

You'll have no trouble finding *broodjes* (small sandwiches) on menus all over Amsterdam, but to eat a *broodje* in a real *broodjeswinkel* (sandwich shop), head to the ever-crowded **Eetsalon Van Dobben,** Korte Reguliersdwarsstraat 5–9 (✆ **020/624-4200**), just off Rembrandtplein; or to **Broodje van Kootje,** Leidseplein 20 (✆ **020/623-2036**), and Spui 28 (✆ **020/623-7451**).

---

brought their award-winning formula to Amsterdam. That formula is simple, really: Serve top-flight Indian food in a setting that gives traditional Indian motifs a modern slant, charge moderate prices, and employ an attentive waitstaff. The menu is pretty straightforward, with the usual tandoori and curry dishes, but it pushes the boat out a bit with some fish items, like the Indian Ocean pomfret in a roasted coriander-seed sauce. Takeout service is available.

Reguliersdwarsstraat 88 (at Vijzelstraat). ✆ **020/623-5710.** www.memoriesofindia.nl. Main courses 12€–23€ ($15–$29); fixed-price menus 18€–28€ ($23–$35) a head. AE, DC, MC, V. Daily 5–11:30pm. Tram: 4, 9, or 14 to Rembrandtplein.

THE JORDAAN
EXPENSIVE

Bordewijk ✿✿ FRENCH   This restaurant is often regarded as one of the best in the city. The decor is tasteful, with green potted plants offsetting the severity of the white walls and metallic black tables. Service is relaxed yet attentive, and on mild summer evenings you can't beat dining alfresco on the canal-side terrace. But the real treat is the food. An innovative chef accents French standards with Mediterranean and Asian flourishes to create an elegant fusion of flavors. The menu changes often, but might include something like these: Roman-style artichokes with wontons, herbs, and a South Seas sauce; salted rib roast with bordelaise sauce; Serrano ham marinated in wine and vinegar and served with fresh pasta; pigeon cooked in the style of Bresse; or even Japanese-style raw fish.

Noordermarkt 7 (at Prinsengracht). ✆ **020/624-3899.** www.bordewijk.nl. Reservations recommended on weekends. Main courses 24€–30€ ($30–$38); fixed-price menu 37€–52€ ($46–$65). AE, MC, V. Tues–Sun 6:30–10pm. Tram: 1, 2, 5, 13, or 17 to Martelaarsgracht.

MODERATE

Hostaria ✿ ITALIAN   Owners Marjolein and Massimo Pasquinoli have transformed this tiny space on a lively Jordaan street into a piece of authentic Italy, and a showcase for the kind of cuisine Italian mothers wish they could equal. When you sit down, Marjolein brings a dish of garlicky *tapenade* and warm bread. As an appetizer you might select a balanced fish soup with a slice of salmon or lightly grilled eggplant slices with fresh herbs. The *zuppa di gamberone con l'acquetta,* a plate of prawns and shellfish from the market, is terrific. Choose from a variety of wonderful homemade pastas—the tagliatelle with arugula and truffles is a particular treat—and of *secondi piatti,* such as veal stuffed with Italian sausage or duck cooked Roman style.

Tweede Egelantiersdwarsstraat 9 (off Egelantiersgracht). ✆ **020/626-0028.** Reservations recommended on weekends. Main courses 15€–19€ ($19–$24); fixed-price menu 24€ ($30). No credit cards. Tues–Sun 7–10pm. Tram: 13, 14, or 17 to Westermarkt.

MUSEUM DISTRICT & VONDELPARK
MODERATE

De Knijp ⊛ DUTCH/FRENCH   One of the advantages of this fine restaurant is that it's open late—its kitchen is still taking orders when chefs at many other Amsterdam restaurants are sound asleep back home. This wouldn't count for much if the food weren't good. De Knijp is definitely worth staying up late for, or worth stopping by for after a taking in a performance at the nearby Concertgebouw, and many concert-goers and assorted other late-nighters do so. The menu is not wildly inventive, but you might try such specialties as carpaccio with pesto, poached salmon with tarragon sauce, or goose breast with pink pepper sauce. Look for friendly (if at times a little worn-out) service and an intimate bistro ambience, with lots of wood and tables on two levels. There's a sidewalk terrace in the summer.

Van Baerlestraat 134 (near the Concertgebouw). ℭ 020/671-4248. www.deknijp.nl. Reservations required for lunch and for more than 5 people. Main courses 14€–22€ ($19–$25). AE, DC, MC, V. Mon–Fri noon–3pm; daily 5:30pm–1:30am. Tram: 3, 5, 12, or 24 to Museumplein; 16 to Concertgebouwplein.

Vertigo ⊛ MEDITERRANEAN   In the vaulted basement of a monumental, late-19th-century villa, Vertigo shares premises with the Film Museum; hence the portraits of screen legends on the walls and the classic scenes of movie dining on the menu, and the name is a reference to Hitchcock's classic movie. On summer days, the outside terrace on the edge of Vondelpark is a favored time-out spot for in-line skaters and joggers, and on hot days a restricted menu is served here. At other times, you can enjoy the southern-European-inspired cuisine in an intimate, candlelit setting inside. The menu, which changes often, has fish, meat, and vegetarian options, plus some fresh pastas.

Vondelpark 3 (at the Film Museum). 020/612-3021. www.vertigo.nl. Reservations recommended on weekends. Main courses 19€–23€ ($24–$29); fixed-price menu 24€ ($30). AE, MC, V. Daily 10am–1am. Tram: 1 or 6 to Eerste Constantijn Huygensstraat; 2, 3, 5, or 12 to Van Baerlestraat.

Wildschut ⊛ CONTINENTAL   One of those places that keeps its chic reputation through thick and thin, this cafe-restaurant occupies a curved dining room at the junction of Van Baerlestraat and Roelof Hartstraat, not far from the Concertgebouw. During the summer, Amsterdam's bold and beautiful come to see and be seen on the terrace. It gets crowded here on Friday and Saturday evenings, so be prepared to join the standing throng while waiting for a table. The food is straightforward but good, ranging from BLTs, to vegetarian lasagna, to American rib-eye with green pepper sauce.

Roelof Hartplein 1–3 (off Van Baerlestraat). ℭ 020/676-8220. www.goodfoodgroup.nl. Main courses 12€–15€ ($15–$19). MC, V. Mon–Thurs 9am–1am; Fri 9am–3am; Sat 10:30am–3am; Sun 9:30am–midnight. Tram: 3, 5, 12, or 24 to Roelof Hartplein.

AMSTERDAM SOUTH
MODERATE

De Kas ⊛⊛ CONTINENTAL   Despite a precocious, aren't-we-fabulous house style, this eatery merits a traipse out to the edge of town. The converted 1926 greenhouse with smokestack, on open ground in South Amsterdam, is light, breezy, and spacious. You get just a couple of variations on a three-course, daily changing fixed menu, with cheeseboard extra. Organic Mediterranean-style greens and herbs come fresh from an adjacent working hothouse and the restaurant's own farm, and meat is

---

Tips   Picnic Picks

You can pick up almost anything you might want for a picnic—from cold cuts to freshly packed sandwiches to a bottle of wine—at the **Albert Heijn super-market,** at the corner of Leidsestraat and Koningsplein, near Spui (tram: 1, 2, or 5), open Monday to Friday from 9am to 8pm and Saturday from 9am to 6pm. Then head over to Vondelpark, only a 10-minute walk. In summertime, you might even catch a free concert at the outdoor theater there.

At the branch of **Albert Heijn** on Museumplein, across the street from the Concertgebouw (tram: 3, 5, 12, or 16), you can haul your brown bag right up onto the sloping, grass-covered roof, which is a prime spot for sunbathing, hanging out, and picnicking, and has a great view on Museumplein.

---

sourced daily from nearby animal-friendly eco-producers. Persnickety attention to detail is the norm in the kitchen, and service is attentive enough that the waitstaff seem to be acquainted personally with every item on your plate.

Kamerlingh Onneslaan 3 (close to Amstel station). ✆ 020/462-4562. www.restaurantdekas.nl. Reservations required. Fixed-price lunch 33€ ($41); fixed-price dinner 45€ ($56). AE, DC, MC, V. Mon–Fri noon–3pm and 6:30–10pm; Sat 6:30–10pm. Tram: 9 to Hogeweg.

AMSTERDAM EAST
VERY EXPENSIVE
La Rive ✦✦✦ REGIONAL FRENCH/MEDITERRANEAN   Amsterdam's high temple of the culinary arts combines French cuisine with influences from around the Mediterranean, and a taste for adventure from even farther afield. Royalty, leading politicians, show business stars, and captains of industry all show up here. The dining room overlooks the Amstel, and in summer opens onto a terrace along the embankment with superb views on the river. The interior atmosphere suggests a private library called into service for a dinner party, its walls paneled in cherry and punctuated with cabinets filled with books and brass objects. Along one wall, private booths overlook the other tables and provide views through the French windows to the water. Specialties include grilled baby abalone with citrus-pickled onion purée and garlic juice, turbot and truffles with trimmings, and grill-roasted rack of lamb with dates and Zaanse mustard.

In the Amstel Inter-Continental Amsterdam Hotel, Professor Tulpplein 1 (off Weesperstraat). ✆ 020/520-3264. www.restaurantlarive.com. Main courses 33€–55€ ($41–$69); fixed-price menus 85€–98€ ($106–$123). AE, DC, MC, V. Mon–Fri noon–2pm; Mon–Sat 6:30–10:30pm. Tram: 7 or 10 to Sarphatistraat.

AMSTERDAM WEST
MODERATE
Amsterdam ✦ *Finds* CONTINENTAL   Based in a century-old water-pumping station, complete with diesel-powered engine, the inventively named Amsterdam has taken a monument of Victorian industrial good taste and transformed it into a model of contemporary good eats. You dine amid a buzz of conviviality in the large, brightly lit, former pumping hall, which had been so carefully tended by the water workers that some of its elegant decoration didn't even need repainting. Service is friendly and the good food is moderately priced. The fried sweetbreads are popular. If you're feeling

flush, spring for a double starter of half lobster with six Zeeland oysters. The Amsterdam is a little bit out from the center city, but easily worth the tram ride.

Watertorenplein 6 (off Haarlemmerweg). ℂ **020/682-2666.** www.cradam.nl. Reservations recommended on weekends. Main courses 10€–20€ ($13–$25). AE, DC, MC, V. Sun–Thurs 11am–1am; Fri–Sat 11am–2am (meals served to 11:30pm). Tram: 10 to Van Hallstraat.

5 Seeing the Sights

For sightseers in Amsterdam, the question is not simply what to see and do, but rather how many of this intriguing city's marvelous sights you can fit into the time you have. There are miles and miles of canals to cruise, hundreds of narrow streets to wander, countless historic buildings to visit, more than 40 museums holding collections of everything from artistic wonders to obscure curiosities, not to mention all the diamond cutters and craftspeople to watch as they practice generations-old skills . . . the list is as long as every tourist's individual interests.

Your very first stop on any sightseeing excursion, of course, should be the **VVV** tourist office—the staff there has information on anything you might want to know and some things you might not even have known you wanted to know. One absolute must-do in Amsterdam is a **canalboat cruise** (see "Organized Tours," later). The view of the elegant canal houses from the water is unforgettable.

THE TOP ATTRACTIONS

Anne Frankhuis ✹✹✹   In the summer, you may have to wait an hour or more to get in, but you shouldn't miss seeing and experiencing this house. It's a typical Amsterdam canal house, with very steep interior stairs where eight people from three separate families lived together in silence for more than 2 years during World War II. This

---

Your Passport to Amsterdam

To get the most out of your trip, consider buying the **I amsterdam Card.** The card is valid for 1 day for 33€ ($41), 2 days for 43€ ($54), and 3 days for 53€ ($66). It affords free travel on public transportation; free admission to more than 20 museums and attractions, including the Rijksmuseum or the Van Gogh Museum (not both) and the Stedelijk Museum, and discounted admission to more museums and attractions; a free canalboat cruise; discounted excursions, including reduced rates on the Museum Boat and the Canal Bus; and discounts at some restaurants and stores. Total possible savings are about 150€ ($188).

Before purchasing one, however, think about whether you'll get your money's worth. Remember, this is Holland, where the local fondness for the coin of the realm is proverbial and killer bargains are thin on the ground. You'll have to work yourself pretty hard to come out ahead on the cost of the card, jumping on and off trams, buses, and canalboats, and running into and out of museums that fall mostly into the solid-culture class.

The card is available from Holland Tourist Information at Schiphol Airport and from VVV tourist information offices in the city.

What to See & Do in Amsterdam

Canal tour boats

(i) Information

Post office

Railway

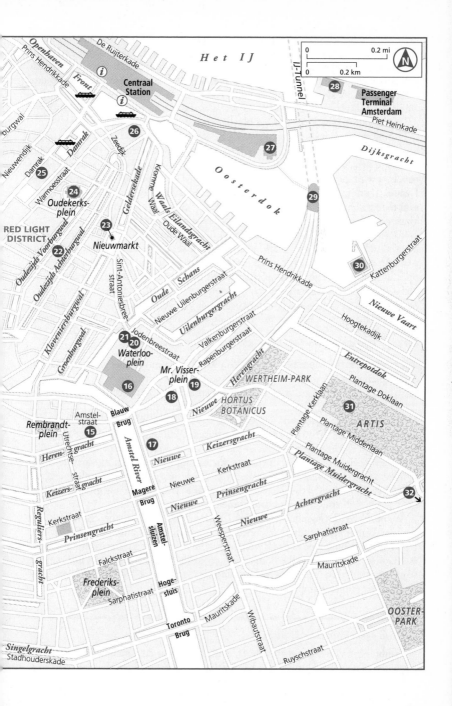

Openhaven
Prins Hendrikkade
Front
De Ruijterkade
Het IJ
IJ-Tunnel

0   0.2 mi
0   0.2 km
N

28
Passenger Terminal Amsterdam
Piet Heinkade

ⓘ
Centraal Station
ⓘ

Dijksgracht

26

27

burgwal
Nieuwendijk
Damrak
Warmoesstraat
25
Zeedijk
Kromme Waal
Geldersekade
Waals Eilandsgracht

Oosterdok

29

24
Oudekerks-plein
Oude Waal

RED LIGHT DISTRICT
Oudezijds Voorburgwal
Oudezijds Achterburgwal
22
23
Nieuwmarkt

Sint-Antoniesbree-straat
Oude   Schans
Nieuwe Uilenburgerstraat
Uilenburgergracht

Prins Hendrikkade

Kattenburgerstraat

30

Klovniersburgwal
Groenburgwal
Jodenbreestraat
Valkenburgerstraat
Rapenburgerstraat

Nieuwe Vaart

Hoogtekadijk

21
20
Waterloo-plein

16

Mr. Visser-plein
19

18

Nieuwe
HORTUS BOTANICUS

Herengracht
WERTHEIM-PARK

Entrepotdok
Plantage Doklaan

Plantage Kerklaan
31
ARTIS

Amstel-straat
Blauw Brug

Rembrandt-plein
15
Heren-gracht
Utrechte-straat

17
Keizersgracht
Nieuwe
Kerkstraat

Plantage Middenlaan
Plantage Muidergracht

Keizers-straat
Keizers-gracht
Amstel River

Nieuwe
Nieuwe
Prinsengracht
Achtergracht

32

Reguliers-gracht
Kerkstraat
Magere Brug
Nieuwe

Weesperstraat

Sarphatistraat

Prinsengracht
Amstel-sluizen

Mauritskade

Falckstraat
Frederiks-plein
Sarphatistraat
Hoge-sluis

Wilbautstraat

OOSTER-PARK

Singelgracht
Stadhouderskade
Toronto Brug
Mauritskade

Ruyschstraat

281

hiding place that Otto Frank found for his family, the Van Pels family, and Fritz Pfeffer kept them safe until it was raided by Nazi forces—tragically close to the end of the war—and its occupants were deported to concentration camps. It was in this house that Anne, whose ambition was to be a writer, kept her famous diary as a way to deal with both the boredom and her youthful array of thoughts, which had as much to do with personal relationships as with the war and the Nazi terror raging outside. Visiting the rooms in which she hid is a moving and eerily real experience.

During the war, the building was an office and warehouse, and its rooms are still as bare as they were when Anne's father returned, the only survivor of the eight *onderduikers* (divers, or hiders). Nothing has been changed, except that protective Plexiglas panels now protect the wall on which Anne pinned up photos of her favorite actress, Deanna Durbin, and of the little English princesses Elizabeth and Margaret. As you tour the small building, it's easy to imagine Anne's experience growing up in this place, awakening as a young woman, and writing down her secret thoughts.

To avoid lines, get here early—this advice isn't as useful as it used to be, because everybody is both giving it and heeding it, but it should still save you some waiting time. An even better strategy is to go in the evening on a night when the museum stays open until 9pm—it's generally quieter and less crowded at that time. Next door at no. 265–267 is a new wing for temporary exhibits.

Prinsengracht 263 (at Westermarkt). ℂ 020/556-7105. www.annefrank.org. Admission 7.50€ ($9.40) adults, 3.50€ ($4.40) children 10–17, free for children under 10. Mid-Mar to mid-Sept daily 9am–9pm; mid-Sept to mid-Mar daily 9am–7pm; Jan 1 and Dec 25 noon–7pm; May 4 and June 24 9am–7pm; Dec 25 noon–5pm, Dec 31 (and 1 variable day in Dec) 9am–5pm. Closed Yom Kippur. Tram: 13, 14, or 17 to Westermarkt.

Rijksmuseum De Meesterwerken ⭐⭐⭐   The country's premier museum, the Rijksmuseum, is still working through a 5-year mission to refit itself for the 21st century. Until renovations are done (they're expected to be completed in 2008), most of the museum is closed, but key paintings and other works from the 17th-century Dutch Golden Age collection can be viewed in the Philips Wing, under the banner of The Masterpieces. Even in its drastically reduced circumstances, the "State Museum" is still one of the leading museums in the land—and even of Europe as a whole. The three-star rating given here is justified by the highlights of Golden Age art alone. But remember: Most of the museum's collection, which totals some seven million individual objects (only a small fraction of which would be displayed at any given time), will be "invisible" to visitors for at least another year or so.

Architect Petrus Josephus Hubertus Cuypers (1827–1921), the "grandfather of modern Dutch architecture," designed the museum in a monumental Dutch neo-Renaissance, gabled style in brick. Cuypers, a Catholic, slipped in more than a dab of neo-Gothic, too, causing the country's thoroughly Protestant King William III to scorn what he called "that cathedral," and the building opened in 1885 to a less-than-enthusiastic public reception.

Fun Fact **The Day Watch?**

Rembrandt's *The Night Watch* (1642) actually shows a daytime scene. Centuries of grime dulled its luster until restoration revealed sunlight glinting on the militia company's arms and accouterments.

Impressions

What other place in the world could you choose where all of life's comforts, and all novelties that man could want are so easy to obtain as here and where you can enjoy such a feeling of freedom.
—René Descartes, French philosopher (1634)

While Amsterdam may box your Puritan ears, this great, historic city is an experiment in freedom.
—ABCNEWS.com (2000)

The Rijksmuseum contains the world's largest collection of paintings by the Dutch Old Masters, including the most illustrious of all, a single work that all but defines the Golden Age. The painting is ***The Shooting Company of Captain Frans Banning Cocq and Lieutenant Willem van Ruytenburch*** (1642), better known as ***The Night Watch,*** by Rembrandt. The scene it so dramatically depicts is surely alien to most of the people who flock to see it: gaily uniformed militiamen checking their weapons and accouterments before moving out on patrol.

Artists van Ruisdael, van Heemskerck, Frans Hals, Paulus Potter, Jan Steen, Vermeer, de Hooch, Terborch, and Gerard Dou are also represented in the museum. The range is impressive—individual portraits, guild paintings, landscapes, seascapes, domestic scenes, medieval religious subjects, allegories, and the incredible (and nearly photographic) Dutch still lifes.

Two rare furnished 17th-century dollhouses should be a highlight for children, by bringing the Dutch Golden Age to life for them in a way no amount of "real" stuff could. In addition, some of the museum's finest pieces of antique Delftware and silver are exhibited.

Philips Wing, Jan Luijkenstraat 1B (at Museumplein). ⓒ 020/647-7047. www.rijksmuseum.nl. Admission 10€ ($13) adults, free for those under 19. Daily 9am–6pm. Closed Jan 1. Tram: 2 or 5 to Hobbemastraat.

Van Gogh Museum ✦✦✦   Walking through the rooms of this rather stark contemporary building is a moving experience. The museum displays, in chronological order, more than 200 van Gogh paintings. As you move through the rooms, the canvases reflect the artist's changing environment and much of his inner life, so gradually van Gogh himself becomes almost a tangible presence standing at your elbow. You'll see the early, brooding *The Potato Eaters* and *The Yellow House,* and the painting known around the world simply as *Sunflowers,* though van Gogh actually titled it *Still Life with Fourteen Sunflowers.* By the time you reach the vaguely threatening painting of a flock of black crows rising from a waving cornfield, you can almost feel the artist's mounting inner pain.

In addition to the paintings, there are nearly 600 drawings by van Gogh, on permanent display in the museum's new wing. This free-standing, multistory, half-oval structure, designed by the Japanese architect Kisho Kurokawa, is constructed in a bold combination of titanium and gray-brown stone, and is connected to the main building by a subterranean walkway.

Note: Lines at the museum can be long, especially in summer—try going on a weekday morning. Allow 2 to 4 hours to get around once you're inside.

Tips Don't "Go"

Gogh is not pronounced *go,* as Americans incorrectly say it, nor is it *goff,* as other English speakers would have it, but *khokh* (the *kh* sounds like the *ch* in the Scottish pronunciation of *loch*—a kind of clearing-your-throat sound). If you can pronounce van Gogh correctly, you should be able to manage Schiphol (*skhip*-ol), Scheveningen (*skheven*-ingen), and 's-Gravenhage (ss-*khraven*-hakhe, the full name of Den Haag/The Hague).

Paulus Potterstraat 7 (at Museumplein). ✆ 020/570-5200. www.vangoghmuseum.nl. Admission 10€ ($13) adults, 2.50€ ($3.15) children 13–17, free for children under 13. Sat–Thurs 10am–6pm; Fri 10am–10pm. Closed Jan 1. Tram: 2, 3, 5, or 12 to Van Baerlestraat.

MORE MUSEUMS & GALLERIES

Amsterdams Historisch Museum (Amsterdam Historical Museum) 🏛🏛🏛 To better understand what you see as you explore the city, a visit to this brilliantly executed museum is especially worthwhile. Its location, the restored 17th-century former Burger Weeshuis (City Orphanage), is already notable. Gallery by gallery, century by century, you learn how a small fishing village founded around 1200 became a major sea power and trading center. The main focus is on the city's 17th-century Golden Age, when Amsterdam was the wealthiest city in the world, and some of the most interesting exhibits are of the trades that made it rich. You can also view famous paintings by the Dutch Old Masters in the context of their time.

There are plenty of hands-on exhibits and some neat video displays. A scale model from around 1677 shows a then-new Stadhuis (Town Hall) on the Dam, now the Royal Palace. Some outer walls and the roof have been removed to allow you a bird's-eye look inside, which makes a later visit to the palace that much more enjoyable.

When you leave the museum, be sure to cut through the **Schuttersgalerij (Civic Guards Gallery),** a narrow, two-story sky-lit covered passageway that leads to the Begijnhof (p. 288), bedecked with 15 enormous 17th-century paintings of the Amsterdam Civic Guards. The open hours are the same as for the museum and admission is free.

Kalverstraat 92, Nieuwezijds Voorburgwal 357, and Sint-Luciënsteeg 27 (next to the Begijnhof). ✆ 020/523-1822. www.ahm.nl. Admission 6€ ($7.50) adults, 4.50€ ($5.65) seniors, 3€ ($3.75) children 6–18, free for children under 6. Mon–Fri 10am–5pm; Sat–Sun and holidays 11am–5pm. Closed Jan 1, Apr 30, Dec 25. Tram: 1, 2, 4, 5, 9, 14, 16, 24, or 25 to Spui.

Hermitage Amsterdam   The Amsterdam branch of Russia's celebrated State Hermitage museum of art and fine arts in St. Petersburg recalls links between the two canal-threaded cities that date back centuries. During a visit to Amsterdam in 1697, Czar Peter the Great, a great admirer of Holland, visited the Amstelhof, which dates from 1681 to 1683 and was built as a home for seniors (at first only for Protestant women). Laid out around a central courtyard, it's flanked on two sides by canals and on a third by the Amstel River. Exhibits here change twice a year, at first in six galleries on the two floors of the renovated and modernized Neerlandia Building, which was built next to the Amstelhof in 1888 as a home for indigent married couples. In addition to works from the Russian museum, modern art from New York's Guggenheim Museum is exhibited here. The full Amstelhof complex is expected to open by 2007, with the Neerlandia section repurposed as a "Children's Hermitage."

Nieuwe Herengracht 14 (at the Amstel River). © 020/530-8751. www.hermitage.nl. Admission 7€ ($8.75) adults, free for children under 17. Daily 10am–5pm. Closed Jan 1, Dec 25. Tram: 9 or 14 to Waterlooplein.

Joods Historisch Museum (Jewish Historical Museum) ★

In the heart of what was once Amsterdam's thriving Jewish Quarter, this museum is housed in the restored Ashkenazi Synagogue complex—a cluster of four former synagogues. It contains a collection of paintings, decorations, and ceremonial objects confiscated during World War II and patiently reestablished in the postwar period. Through its objects, photographs, artworks, and interactive displays, the museum tells three intertwining stories—of Jewish identity, Jewish religion and culture, and Jewish history in the Netherlands. Extended in 2006, it presents the community in both good times and bad and provides insights into the Jewish way of life over the centuries. Leave time to appreciate the beauty and size of the buildings themselves, which include the oldest public synagogue in Europe. This is a museum for everyone—Jewish or otherwise. There are frequent temporary exhibits of international interest.

The museum cafe is a great place to have a cup of coffee and a pastry, or a light meal (kosher, too). It's quiet and inexpensive, and the food is good.

Jonas Daniël Meyerplein 2–4 (at Waterlooplein). © 020/626-9945. www.jhm.nl. Admission 6.50€ ($8.15) adults, 4€ ($5) seniors, 3€ ($3.75) children 13–17, 2€ ($2.50) children 6–12, free for children under 6. Daily 11am–5pm (Jan 1 noon–5pm). Closed Jewish New Year (2 days) and Yom Kippur. Tram: 9 or 14 to Waterlooplein.

Museum Het Rembrandthuis (Rembrandt House Museum)

This isn't the place to see Rembrandt's greatest masterpieces. Those are at the Rijksmuseum. But without a doubt, this is the best place to get an intimate sense of the artist himself. Bought by Rembrandt in 1639 when he was Amsterdam's most fashionable portrait painter, the house, which has 10 rooms, is a shrine to one of the most remarkable artists the world has ever known. In this house, Rembrandt's son Titus was born and his wife, Saskia, died. The artist was bankrupt when he left it in 1658. Not until 1906 was the building rescued from a succession of subsequent owners and restored as a museum.

More recent restoration has returned the old house to the way it looked when Rembrandt lived and worked here. The rooms are furnished with 17th-century objects and furniture that, as far as possible, match the descriptions in Rembrandt's 1656 petition for bankruptcy. His printing press is back in place, and you can view 250 of his etchings and drawings hanging on the walls. Temporary exhibits are mounted in a modern wing next door.

Jodenbreestraat 4–6 (at Waterlooplein). © 020/520-0400. www.rembrandthuis.nl. Admission 7.50€ ($9.40) adults, 5€ ($6.25) students, 1.50€ ($1.90) children 6–15, free for children under 6. Mon–Thurs and Sat–Sun 10am–5pm; Fri 10am–9pm; Sun and holidays 11am–5pm. Closed Jan 1. Tram: 9 or 14 to Waterlooplein.

Museum Van Loon

This magnificent patrician house was owned by the Van Loon family from 1884 to 1945. On its walls hang more than 80 family portraits, including those of Willem van Loon, one of the founders of the United East India Company; Nicolaes Ruychaver, who liberated Amsterdam from the Spanish in 1578; and another, later, Willem van Loon, who became mayor in 1686. Among other treasures are a family album in which you can see tempera portraits of all living Van Loons painted at two successive dates (1650 and 1675), and a series of commemorative coins struck to honor seven different golden wedding anniversaries celebrated between the years 1621 and 1722. The house's restored period rooms are filled with richly decorated paneling, stucco work, mirrors, fireplaces, furnishings, porcelain, medallions, chandeliers, rugs, and more. The garden has carefully tended hedges and a coach house modeled on a Greek temple.

Keizersgracht 672 (near Vijzelstraat). © 020/624-5255. www.museumvanloon.nl. Admission 6€ ($7.50) adults, 4€ ($5) students and children 6–18, free for children under 6. Sept–June Fri–Mon 11am–5pm; July–Aug daily 11am–5pm. Tram: 16, 24, or 25 to Keizersgracht.

Museum Willet-Holthuysen

This museum offers another rare opportunity to visit an elegant 17th-century canal house, with an ornamental garden. This particular house, built in 1687, was renovated several times before its last inhabitant gave it and its contents to the city in 1889. Among the most interesting rooms are a Victorian-era bedroom on the second floor, a large reception room with tapestry wall panels, and an 18th-century basement kitchen that's still so completely furnished and functional you could swear the cook had merely stepped out to go shopping. In the dining salon, the table under the chandelier is set for a meal being served some 300 years too late.

Herengracht 605 (near the Amstel River). © 020/523-1822. www.willetholthuysen.nl. Admission 4€ ($5) adults, 3€ ($3.75) seniors, 2€ ($2.50) children 6–18, free for children under 6. Mon–Fri 10am–5pm; Sat–Sun 11am–5pm. Closed Jan 1, Apr 30, Dec 25. Tram: 4, 9, or 14 to Rembrandtplein.

Scheepvaartmuseum (Maritime Museum) ★★ Kids

A bonanza for anyone who loves ships and the sea, the Scheepvaartmuseum is housed in a former arsenal of the Amsterdam Admiralty dating from 1656, and overlooks the busy Amsterdam harbor. Surrounding the inner courtyard are 25 rooms with ship models, charts, instruments, maps, prints, and paintings—a chronicle of Holland's abiding ties to the sea through commerce, fishing, yachting, navigational development, and war. Brief texts explain each exhibit, and desks with more extensive information are found in every room.

A full-size replica of the *Amsterdam,* a three-masted United East India Company sailing ship that foundered off Hastings in 1749 on her maiden voyage to the fabled Spice Islands (Indonesia), is moored at the museum's wharf. Other ships that can be seen include a steam icebreaker, a motor lifeboat, and a herring lugger. Environmentalists will want to go aboard Greenpeace's retired environmental combatant *Rainbow Warrior.* You can reach this museum by taking a 20-minute walk along the historical waterfront, the Nautisch Kwartier (Nautical Quarter).

Kattenburgerplein 1 (in the Eastern Dock). © 020/523-2222. www.scheepvaartmuseum.nl. Admission 9€ ($11) adults, 7€ ($8.75) seniors, 4.50€ ($5.65) children 6–17, free for children under 6. Tues–Sat 10am–5pm (also Mon during school vacations); Sun noon–5pm. Bus: 22, 42, or 43 to Kattenburgerplein.

Stedelijk Museum CS ★★

The Stedelijk Museum of modern art's permanent premises, on Paulus Potterstraat at Museumplein, have shut entirely for a period of refurbishment, which is expected to continue until 2008. But lovers of modern art can catch the latest show at Stedelijk Museum CS, its temporary quarters just east of Centraal Station (hence the "CS"). This is the place to see works by such Dutch painters as Karel Appel, Willem de Kooning, and Piet Mondrian, alongside works by the French artists Chagall, Cézanne, Picasso, Renoir, Monet, and Manet; and by the Americans Calder, Oldenburg, Rosenquist, and Warhol. The Stedelijk centers its collection around the De Stijl, Cobra, post-Cobra, Nouveau Réalisme, pop art, color-field painting, zero, minimalist, and conceptual schools of modern art. It houses the largest collection outside Russia of the abstract paintings of Kasimir Malevich.

Oosterdokskade 5 (just east of Centraal Station). © 020/573-2911. www.stedelijk.nl. Admission 9€ ($11) adults; 3.50€ ($4.40) seniors, students, and children 7–16; free for children under 7. Daily 10am–5pm. Closed Jan 1. Tram: 1, 2, 4, 5, 9, 13, 16, 17, 24, 25, or 26 to Centraal Station.

Tropenmuseum (Tropical Museum) ★★ *Kids*   One of Amsterdam's more intriguing museums is run by the Royal Tropical Institute, a foundation devoted to the study of the cultures of tropical areas around the world. The building complex alone is worth the trip to Amsterdam East and the Oosterpark (East Park); its heavily ornamented facade is an amalgam of Dutch architectural styles—turrets, stepped gables, arched windows, and delicate spires—and the monumental galleried interior court is one of the most impressive spots in town.

The most interesting exhibits are the walk-through model villages and city-street scenes that capture moments in the daily lives of such places as India and Indonesia; the exhibit on the tools and techniques used to produce *batik,* the distinctively dyed Indonesian fabrics; and the displays of the tools, instruments, and ornaments that clutter a tropical residence. There's a permanent exhibit on people and the environment in West Asia and North Africa. Part of the premises is given over to the children-only Kindermuseum—the Tropical Museum Junior—with its educational and interactive exhibits.

Linnaeusstraat 2 (at Mauritskade). 𝄪 020/568-8215. www.tropenmuseum.nl. Admission 7.50€ ($9.40) adults, 6€ ($7.50) seniors and students, 4€ ($5) children 6–17, free for children under 6. Daily 10am–5pm (to 3pm Dec 5, 24, 31). Closed Jan 1, Apr 30, May 5, Dec 25. Tram: 7, 9, 10, or 14 to Mauritskade.

HISTORICAL BUILDINGS & MONUMENTS

A massive edifice of colored brick and stone enclosing three arcades roofed in glass and iron, **Beurs van Berlage,** Beursplein 1 (𝄪 020/530-4141; www.beursvanberlage.nl; tram: 4, 9, 14, 16, 24, or 25), at Damrak, was originally the city's Stock Exchange. Completed in 1903, architect Hendrik Petrus Berlage's building was a revolutionary break with 19th-century architecture and is well worth visiting as a prime example of the Amsterdam School, contemporaneous with the work of Frank Lloyd Wright in America. Today, the Beurs is used as a space for concerts, conferences, and exhibits. Admission and open hours vary.

Constructed in the 14th century, **De Waag (Weigh House)** Nieuwmarkt (𝄪 020/ 557-9898; www.waag.org; Metro: Nieuwmarkt), is the city's only surviving medieval fortified gate. It later became a guild house. Among the guilds lodged here was the Surgeon's Guild, immortalized in Rembrandt's painting *The Anatomy Lesson of Dr. Nicolaes Tulp* (1632), which depicts a dissection being conducted in the upper-floor Theatrum Anatomicum. Most of De Waag now houses a specialized educational and cultural institute and is rarely open; admission (when it's possible at all) is free (except in the case of occasional special exhibits). You can, however, visit the exceptional cafe-restaurant **In de Waag** (p. 269) on the ground floor.

A PALATIAL RESIDENCE

Koninklijk Paleis (Royal Palace) ★★   Dominating the Dam is the 17th-century, neoclassical facade of the Royal Palace. The building was originally designed by Jacob van Campen as a town hall, but in 1808, when Napoleon Bonaparte's younger brother Louis reigned as king of the Netherlands, it became a palace and was filled with Empire-style furniture. During the summer, you can visit the high-ceilinged Citizens' Hall, the Burgomasters' Chambers, and the Council Room. Since the return to the throne of the Dutch House of Orange, this has been the official palace of the reigning king or queen of the Netherlands. However, it's only used for occasional state receptions or official ceremonies (Queen Beatrix lives at Huis ten Bosch in The Hague).

Finds **Gay Remembrance**

The *Homomonument,* Westermarkt (tram: 13, 14, or 17), a sculpture group of three pink granite triangles near the Anne Frankhuis, is dedicated to the memory of gays and lesbians killed during World War II, or as a result of oppression and persecution because of their sexuality. People visit to remember those who have died of AIDS.

Note: The palace is closed for renovations until fall 2007; in the meantime, you can only view the exterior.

Dam. ☎ 020/620-4060. www.koninklijkhuis.nl. Tram: 1, 2, 4, 5, 9, 13, 14, 16, 17, 24, or 25 to the Dam.

SIGHTS OF RELIGIOUS SIGNIFICANCE

A cluster of small homes around a garden courtyard, the **Begijnhof** ★★, Spui (☎ **020/625-8853;** tram: 1, 2, or 5), dates from the 14th century and is one of the best places to appreciate the earliest history of the city, when Amsterdam was a destination for religious pilgrims and an important center of Catholic nunneries. The Begijnhof itself was not a convent, but an almshouse for pious laywomen—*begijnen*—involved in religious and charitable work. It remained in operation even after the about-face changeover of the city from Catholicism to Protestantism in the late 16th century. The last of the *begijnen* died in 1971, but you can still pay homage to these pious women by pausing for a moment at the small flower-planted mound that lies just at the center garden's edge across from the English Church. Opposite the front of the church is a secret Catholic chapel built in 1671 and still in use. In the southwest corner of the cloister, at no. 34, stands **Het Houten Huys,** one of Amsterdam's pair of surviving timber houses, built around 1425. You're welcome to visit the Begijnhof daily from 8am to 1pm. Seniors now reside in the 47 old homes, and their privacy and tranquillity must be respected. Access is on Gedempte Begijnensloot, an alleyway off Spui. Admission is free.

Nieuwe Kerk (New Church)   This beautiful church was built in the last years of the 14th century, when the Oude Kerk (see below) had become too small to accommodate its congregation. Many of the Nieuwe Kerk's priceless treasures were removed or painted over in 1578 when it passed into Protestant hands, but much of the church's original grandeur has since been recaptured. In 1814, the king first took the oath of office and was inaugurated here (Dutch royalty are not crowned). The church has a stately arched nave, an elaborately carved altar, a great pipe organ that dates from 1645, several noteworthy stained-glass windows, and sepulchral monuments for many of Holland's most revered poets and naval heroes. Afterward, take the weight off your feet on the sidewalk terrace of the fine cafe, the attached Nieuwe Kafé, which has a fine view on the Dam.

Dam (next to the Royal Palace). ☎ 020/638-6909. www.nieuwekerk.nl. Admission varies with different events; free when there's no exhibit. Daily 10am–6pm (Thurs to 10pm during exhibits). Tram: 1, 2, 4, 5, 9, 13, 14, 16, 17, 24, or 25 to the Dam.

Oude Kerk (Old Church) ★★   Construction on this late-Gothic church began in 1250. On its southern porch, to the right of the sexton's house, you'll see a coat of arms belonging to Maximilian of Austria who, with his son Philip, contributed to the porch's construction. Rembrandt's wife Saskia is buried here. The church contains a magnificent organ from 1724 and is used regularly for organ recitals. Nowadays, the pretty little gabled almshouses around the Oude Kerk feature red-fringed windows through which the scantily dressed ladies of the Red Light District can be seen. You can climb the 70m (230-ft.) church tower, which holds a carillon of 17th-century Hemony bells, on an hourly guided tour for great views of Old Amsterdam.

Oudekerksplein (at Oudezijds Voorburgwal). ℂ 020/625-8284. www.oudekerk.nl. Church: Admission 5€ ($6.25) adults, 4€ ($5) seniors and students, free for children under 12; rates may vary for special exhibits. Mon–Sat 11am–5pm; Sun 1–5pm. Tower: Visits for pre-arranged groups only, maximum 25 persons, 40€ ($50) per hour; call ℂ 020/689-2565. Closed Jan 1, Feb 3, Apr 18–24 and 30. Metro: Nieuwmarkt. Tram: 1, 2, 4, 5, 9, 13, 14, 16, 17, 24, or 25 to the Dam.

Portugees-Israëlietische Synagoge (Portuguese-Israelite Synagogue)
Sephardic Jews fleeing Spain and Portugal during the 16th and early 17th centuries established a neighborhood east of the center known as the Jewish Quarter. In 1665, they built an elegant Ionic-style synagogue within an existing courtyard facing what is now a busy traffic circle. The building was restored in the 1950s. Today it looks essentially like it did 320 years ago, with its women's gallery supported by 12 stone columns to represent the Twelve Tribes of Israel, and the large, low-hanging brass chandeliers that together hold 1,000 candles, all of which are lighted for the private weekly services.

Mr. Visserplein 3 (at Waterlooplein). ℂ 020/624-5351. www.esnoga.com. Admission 6.50€ ($8.15) adults, 5€ ($6.25) children 10–15, free for children under 10. Apr–Oct Sun–Fri 10am–6pm; Nov–Mar Sun–Thurs 10am–6pm, Fri 10am–3pm. Closed Jewish holidays. Tram: 9 or 14 to Mr. Visserplein.

Westerkerk (West Church)
The Dutch Renaissance–style Westerkerk is where Rembrandt was buried, and it holds the remains of his son, Titus. This is also where Queen Beatrix said her marriage vows in 1966. Hendrick de Keyser designed the building and construction began in 1620, but he died a year later. His son Pieter took over, and the building opened in 1631. Get the best views of Amsterdam by climbing the 186 interior steps or taking the elevator to the top of the Westertoren on a guided tour; the 85m (277-ft.) church tower, dubbed "Lange Jan" (Long John), is Amsterdam's tallest. On its top is the blue, red, and gold imperial crown of the Holy Roman Empire, a symbol bestowed by the Habsburg emperor Maximilian. The tower's carillon is among the city's most lyrical.

Westermarkt. ℂ 020/624-7766. www.westerkerk.nl. Church: Free admission. Apr–June and Sept Mon–Fri 11am–3pm; July–Aug Mon–Sat 11am–3pm. Tower: Admission 5€ ($6.25). Apr–Sept Mon–Sat 10am–5:30pm; tours every 30 min. Tram: 13, 14, or 17 to Westermarkt.

OTHER SITES & ATTRACTIONS

Artis Kids   For something to do with the kids, Artis is a safe bet. Established in 1838, the oldest zoo in the Netherlands houses more than 6,000 animals—including, of course, the usual tigers, leopards, elephants, camels, and peacocks. But, for no extra charge, there's much more here. You can visit the excellent Planetarium (closed Mon morning), and the Geological and Zoological Museum. The Aquarium is superbly presented, particularly the sections on the Amazon River, coral reefs, and Amsterdam's own canals. Finally, there's a children's farm, where kids help tend to the needs of resident sheep, goats, chickens, and cows. An Insectarium opened in 2005 and a Butterfly Garden in 2006. For a snack or lunch, try the Artis Restaurant.

Plantage Kerklaan 38–40 (at Plantage Middenlaan). ℂ 020/523-3400. www.artis.nl. Admission 16€ ($20) adults, 15€ ($19) seniors, 13€ ($16) children 3–9, free for children under 3. May–Oct daily 9am–6pm (Sat to sunset); Nov–Apr daily 9am–5pm. Tram: 9 or 14 to Plantage Kerklaan.

Heineken Experience   The experience unfolds inside the former Heineken brewing facilities, which date from 1867. Before the brewery stopped functioning in 1988, it was producing more than 100 million liters (26 million gal.) annually. The fermentation tanks, each capable of holding a million glassfuls of Heineken, are still there, along with the multistory malt silos and all manner of vintage brewing equipment and implements. You "meet" Dr. Elion, the 19th-century chemist who isolated the renowned Heineken "A" yeast, which gives the beer its taste. In one amusing attraction, you stand on a moving floor, facing a large video screen, and get to see and feel what it's like to be a Heineken beer bottle—one of a half-million every hour—careening on a conveyor belt through a modern Heineken bottling plant. Best of all, in another touchy-feely presentation, you "sit" aboard an old brewery dray-wagon, "pulled" by a pair of big Shire horses on the video screen in front of you, that shakes, rattles, and rolls on a minitour of Amsterdam.

Stadhouderskade 78 (at Ferdinand Bolstraat). ☎ 020/523-9666. www.heinekenexperience.com. Admission 10€ ($13); under 18 admitted only with parental supervision. Tues–Sun 10am–6pm. Closed Jan 1, Dec 25. Tram: 16, 24, or 25 to Stadhouderskade.

Holland Experience *(Overrated*   This multidimensional film and theater show takes you through the landscapes and culture of Holland at different periods of its history and today. If you've ever nervously wondered what would happen to the city if all that seawater should ever break through the defensive dikes, Holland Experience will give you an idea. Other exhibits include farming and fishing scenes. The show isn't as good as they could make it, or as the steep admission suggests, but it does give you a nutshell picture of Holland.

Waterlooplein 17 and Jodenbreestraat 8–10 (next door to the Rembrandthuis). ☎ 020/422-2233. www.holland-experience.nl. Admission 8.50€ ($11) adults, 7.25€ ($9.05) seniors and children 5–16, free for children under 5. Daily shows 10:30am–4:45pm. Closed Jan 1, Dec 25 and 26. Tram: 9 or 14 to Waterlooplein.

Madame Tussaud's 😱 *(Kids*   The Amsterdam version of the famed London attraction has its own cast of Dutch characters (Rembrandt, Queen Beatrix, Mata Hari), among a parade of international names (Churchill, Kennedy, Gandhi). Exhibits bring you "face to face" with the powerful and famous and let you step into the times, events, and moments that made them so. In the Grand Hall, styled to look like a reception room in a Dutch manor around 1700, are images of world leaders, royalty, artists, writers, and religious leaders. Those portrayed are brought to life with memorabilia such as paintings, smoking cigarettes, or pictures of the most memorable moments of their lives.

Dam 20. ☎ 020/522-1010. www.madametussauds.nl. Admission 18€ ($22) adults, 20€ ($25) seniors, 13€ ($16) children 5–16, free for children under 5. July–Aug daily 10am–9pm; Sept–June daily 10am–6:30pm. Closed Apr 30. Tram: 4, 9, 14, 16, 24, or 25 to the Dam.

The Narrow View

You can see the **narrowest house** in Amsterdam at **Singel 7.** It's just 1m (3.3 ft.) wide—barely wider than the front door. However, it's a cheat. Only the front facade is really so narrow; behind this it broadens out to more usual proportions. The *genuine* narrowest house is **Oude Hoogstraat 22,** near Nieuwmarkt. With a typical Amsterdam bell gable, it's 2m (6½ ft.) wide and 6m (20 ft.) deep. A close rival is nearby at **Kloveniersburgwal 26,** the cornice-gabled **Kleine Trippenhuis,** 2.4m (8 ft.) wide.

NEMO Science Center ⊛ *Kids*   A paean of praise to science and technology, NEMO is in a strikingly modern building in the Eastern Dock, designed by Italian architect Renzo Piano, which seems to reproduce the graceful lines of an ocean-going ship. The center is a hands-on experience as much as a museum, with games, experiments, demonstrations, workshops, and theater and film shows. You learn how to steer a supertanker safely into port, boost your earnings on the floor of the New York Stock Exchange, and execute a complicated surgical procedure. One exhibit will even try to make you understand the basis of sexual attraction. Internet-linked computers on every floor help provide insights. IStudio Bits & Co is NEMO's digital world, in which you can play with images, sounds, text websites, and your own imported material.

Oosterdokskade 2 (off Prins Hendrikkade, over the south entrance to the IJ Tunnel). ℂ **020/531-3233**. www.e-nemo.nl. Admission 12€ ($14), free for children under 4. July–Aug daily 10am–5pm; Sept–June Tues–Sun 10am–5pm (also Mon during school vacations). Closed Jan 1, Apr 30, Dec 25. Bus: 22 to Kadijksplein.

AN ALTERNATIVE MUSEUM

Hash Marihuana & Hemp Museum ⊛   Well, it wouldn't really be Amsterdam, would it, without its fascination with intoxicating weeds? This museum will teach you everything you ever wanted to know, and much you maybe didn't, about hash, marijuana, and related products. The museum does not promote drug use but aims to make you better informed before deciding whether to light up and, of course, whether to inhale. One way it does this is by having a cannabis garden in the joint . . . sorry, on the premises. Plants at various stages of development fill the air with an unmistakable, heady, resinous fragrance. Hemp, not plastic, could be the future if the exhibit on the multifarious uses of the fiber through the ages is anything to go by. Some exhibits shed light on the medicinal uses of cannabis and on hemp's past and present-day uses as a natural fiber. Among several notable artworks in the museum's collection is David Teniers the Younger's painting, *Hemp-Smoking Peasants in a Smoke House* (1660).

Oudezijds Achterburgwal 130 (Red Light District). ℂ **020/623-5961**. www.hashmuseum.com. Admission 5.70€ ($7.15). Daily 11am–10pm. Closed Jan 1, Apr 30, Dec 25. Tram: 4, 9, 14, 16, 24, or 25 to the Dam.

THE JORDAAN

Few traditional sights clutter the beguiling old Jordaan district—just west of the northern reaches of the Canal Belt—though 800 of its buildings are protected monuments. This neighborhood of narrow streets and canals, and tightly packed houses, was built in the 17th century for craftsmen, tradesmen, and artists. Some streets used to be canals, until these were filled in during the 19th century. The charming area provides an authentic taste of Old Amsterdam.

Its modest nature remains even though renewal and gentrification proceed apace, bringing an influx of offbeat boutiques, quirky stores, cutting-edge art galleries, and trendy restaurants. The name Jordaan may have come from the French *jardin* (garden), from Protestant French Huguenot refugees who settled here in the late 17th century. Indeed, many streets and canals are named for flowers, trees, and plants.

RED LIGHT DISTRICT

This warren of streets and old canals (known as De Rosse Buurt or De Wallen in Dutch) around Oudezijds Achterburgwal and Oudezijds Voorburgwal by the Oude Kerk, a testament to the city's tolerance and pragmatism, is on most people's sightseeing agenda. However, a visit to this area is not for everyone, and if you're liable to be offended by the sex industry exposed in all its garish colors, don't go. If you do choose to go, exercise some caution because the area is a center of crime, vice, and drugs. As always in Amsterdam, there's no need to exaggerate the risks, and in fact the night-clubs' own security helps keep the brightly lit areas quite safe. Plenty of tourists visit the Red Light District and suffer nothing more serious than a come-on from one of the prostitutes.

It's extraordinary to view the hookers in leather and lace sitting in their storefronts with their radios and TVs blaring as they do their knitting or adjust their makeup, waiting patiently for customers. The district seems to reflect Dutch pragmatism; if you can't stop the oldest trade in the world, you can at least confine it to a particular area and impose health and other regulations on it. And the fact is that underneath its tacky glitter, the Red Light District contains some of Amsterdam's prettiest canals and loveliest old architecture, plus some excellent bars and restaurants, secondhand book-stores, and other specialty stores (not all of which work the erogenous zones). To get there, take tram no. 4, 9, 14, 16, 24, or 25 to the Dam, and then pass behind the Grand Hotel Krasnapolsky.

GREEN AMSTERDAM

Amsterdam is not a notably green city, particularly in the old center. Still, the city as a whole has plenty of parks, including the celebrated **Vondelpark** 🍀🍀. You'll find Frisbee flipping, in-line skating, pickup soccer and softball, open-air performances, smooching in the undergrowth, and picnics. Best of all, it's free, or as the Dutch say, *gratis*. The Vondelpark lies southwest of Leidseplein, with the main entrance adjacent to the Leidseplein, on Stadhouderskade.

To enjoy scenery and fresh air, head out to the giant **Amsterdamse Bos (Amsterdam Wood)** 🍀, in the southern suburb of Amstelveen. This is nature on the city's doorstep. The park was laid out during the Depression years as a public works project. The **Bezoekerscentrum (Visitor Center;** ℂ **020/545-6100;** www.amsterdam sebos.nl), at the main entrance on Amstelveenseweg, traces the park's history and gives information about its wildlife; it's open daily (except Dec 25–26) from noon to 5pm, and admission is free. At a large pond called the **Grote Vijver** you can rent small boats (ℂ **020/644-5119**). The **Openluchttheater (Open-Air Theater)** often has perform-ances on summer evenings. The best way to get to the **Amsterdamse Bos** from the center is to take Connexxion bus no. 170 or 172 from outside Centraal Station.

ORGANIZED TOURS

BY BOAT   **Canalboat cruises** 🍀🍀 last approximately an hour. Boats depart at regu-lar intervals from *rondvaart* (excursion) piers in key locations around town. The major-ity of launches are docked along Damrak and Prins Hendrikkade near Centraal Station, on Rokin near Muntplein, and at Leidseplein. Tours leave every 15 to 30 minutes dur-ing the summer season (9am–9:30pm), every 45 minutes in winter (10am–4pm). A basic 1-hour tour is around 8€ ($10) for adults, 5€ ($6.25) for children ages 4 to 12, and free for children under 4 (prices may vary from company to company).

The canal tour-boat lines are: **Amsterdam Canal Cruises** (ℂ 020/626-5636); **Canal Company** (ℂ 020/626-5574); **Holland International** (ℂ 020/622-7788; www. hir.nl); **Meijers Rondvaarten** (ℂ 020/623-4208); **Rederij Boekel** (ℂ 020/612-9905); **Rederij Hof van Holland** (ℂ 020/623-7122); **Rederij Lovers** (ℂ 020/530-1090; www.lovers.nl)—despite its heart-shaped logo, Lovers is not necessarily for lovers only, but is named after the man who started up the company; **Rederij Noord-Zuid** (ℂ 020/ 679-1370; www.canal-cruises.nl); **Rederij P. Kooij** (ℂ 020/623-3810); and **Rederij Plas** (ℂ 020/624-5406).

BY WATER BIKE   If the canalboat cruise whets your appetite to ramble the canals on your own, you can rent sturdy paddleboats, called canal bikes, from (by a strange coincidence) **Canal Bike,** Weteringschans 24 (✆ **020/626-5574**). Canal bikes seat two or four and come with a detailed map, route suggestions, and a bit of information about the places you pedal past. The four Canal Bike moorings are at Leidseplein (tram: 1, 2, 5, 7, or 10); Westerkerk, near the Anne Frankhuis (tram: 13, 14, or 17); Stadhouderskade, beside the Rijksmuseum (tram: 7 or 10); and Toronto Bridge on Keizersgracht, near Leidsestraat (tram: 1, 2, or 5). You can rent a canal bike at one mooring and leave it at another. The canals can be busy with tour boats and other small craft, so go carefully, particularly under bridges. Rental is 8€ ($10) per person hourly for one or two people; 7€ ($8.75) per person hourly for three or four people. You need to leave a deposit of 50€ ($63).

BY BICYCLE   You're going to look pretty conspicuous taking one of the guided tours offered by **Yellow Bike,** Nieuwezijds Kolk 29, off Nieuwezijds Voorburgwal (✆ **020/620-6940**). Why? Because you'll be biking on a yellow bicycle along with a dozen other people on yellow bikes, that's why. In partial compensation, you'll have a close encounter with Amsterdam or the nearby countryside.

BY BUS   For many travelers, a quick bus tour is the best way to launch a sightseeing program in a strange city, and though Amsterdam offers its unique alternative—a canalboat cruise—you might want to get your bearings on land. A basic 2½-hour bus tour is around 17€ ($21); on most tours children ages 4 to 13 are charged half fare, and children under 4 go free. Major sightseeing lines offering these and other motorcoach tours are **The Best of Holland,** Damrak 34 (✆ **020/623-1539**); **Holland International,** Prins Hendrikkade 33A (✆ **020/625-3035**); **Holland Keytours,** Dam 19 (✆ **020/624-7304**); and **Lindbergh Excursions,** Damrak 26 (✆ **020/622-2766**). In addition, these lines provide a variety of half- and full-day tours into the surrounding area, particularly between April and October, and there are special excursions at tulip time and at the height of the summer season. Rates vary from company to company and with the particular tour on offer. Typical half-day tours are around 25€ ($31), full-day tours 38€ ($48); children ages 4 to 13 are charged half fare, and children under 4 go free.

BY FOOT   **Amsterdam Walking Tours** (✆ **020/640-9072**) leads guided strolls through historic Amsterdam on Saturday and Sunday at 11am.

6 Sports & Recreation

AMERICAN FOOTBALL   Amsterdam has its own franchise, the Amsterdam Admirals, Amsterdam ArenA, ArenA Boulevard 73–75 (✆ **020/465-4545;** Metro: Strandvliet/ArenA), complete with cheerleaders.

BASEBALL   Honk if you like baseball (the game is called *honkbal* in Holland). The Amsterdam Pirates aren't the greatest practitioners of the sport, but they have their moments, as you can see at the **Sportpark Ookmeer,** Herman Bondpark 5 (✆ **020/616-2151;** bus no. 19 or 192).

BASKETBALL   Demon Astronauts Amsterdam (✆ **020/671-3910;** www. astronauts.nl), turn out at **Sporthallen Zuid,** Burgerweeshuispad 54 (✆ **020/305-8305;** tram: 16).

BOWLING   Try **Knijn Bowling,** Scheldeplein 3 (© **020/664-22-11;** tram: 12 or 25).

FITNESS CENTERS   Among the many centers you can try are **Fitness Aerobic Center Jansen,** Rokin 109–111 (© **020/626-9366**); **Garden Gym,** Jodenbreestraat 158 (© **020/626-8772;** tram: 9 or 14); and **A Bigger Splash,** Looiersgracht 26–30 (© **020/624-8404;** tram: 7, 10, or 17).

GOLF   There are public golf courses in or near Amsterdam at the **Golf Center Amstelborgh,** Borchlandweg 6 (© **020/697-5000**); **Sloten,** Sloterweg 1045 (© **020/614-2402**); **Waterland Golf Course,** Buikslotermeerdijk 141 (© **020/636-1010**); and **Spaarnwoude Golf Course,** Het Hogeland 2, Spaarnwoude (© **020/538-5599**). Call ahead for greens fees and tee times.

HORSEBACK RIDING   Riding, both indoor and outdoor, is offered at **Amsterdamse Manege,** Nieuwe Kalfjeslaan 25 (© **020/643-1342**); indoor riding only is available at **Nieuw Amstelland Manege,** Jan Tooropplantsoen 17 (© **020/643-2468**). Horses rented at **De Ruif Manege,** Sloterweg 675 (© **020/615-6667**), can be ridden in Amsterdamse Bos.

ICE SKATING   Skating on Amsterdam's ponds and canals (see the box "Skating on the Canals," below) won't be easy unless you're willing to shell out for a new pair of skates—there are very few places that rent them. One that does is **Jaap Edenbaan,** Radioweg 64 (© **020/694-9894;** tram: 2); here you can rent skates November to February.

IN-LINE SKATING   **Rent A Skate** has a rent shop for in-line skates in Vondelpark, at the Amstelveenseweg entrance (© **020/664-5091**).

JOGGING   The two main jogging areas are Vondelpark in the center city and Amsterdamse Bos on the southern edge of the city. You can run along the Amstel River. If you choose to run along the canals, as many do, watch out for uneven cobbles, loose paving stones, and dog poop.

SOCCER   Soccer (known as football in Europe, and *voetbal* in Dutch) is absolutely the biggest game in Holland. Ajax Amsterdam is invariably the best team in the land and often is among the best in Europe. Ajax plays home matches at a fabulous modern stadium with a retractable roof, the **Amsterdam ArenA,** ArenA Blvd. 1, Amsterdam Zuidoost (© **020/311-1333;** Metro: Strandvliet/ArenA). There's an on-site Ajax Museum.

SWIMMING   Amsterdam's state-of-the-art swimming facility is **Het Marnix,** Marnixplein 1 (© **020/524-6000;** tram: 3 or 10), which opened in 2006 and has two heated pools along with a fitness center and spa, and a cafe-restaurant. **De Mirandabad,** De Mirandalaan 9 (© **020/546-4444;** tram: 25), features an indoor pool with wave machines, slides, and other amusements, and an outdoor pool that's open May to September. A handsome, refurbished place from 1911, close to the Rijksmuseum, the **Zuiderbad,** Hobbemastraat 26 (© **020/679-2217;** tram: 2 or 5), has times set aside for those who like to swim in their birthday suit.

TENNIS   You'll find indoor courts at **Frans Otten Stadion,** Stadionstraat 10 (© **020/662-8767;** tram: 16). For both indoor and outdoor courts, try **Gold Star,** Karel Lotsylaan 20 (© **020/644-5483;** tram: 5); and **Tenniscentrum Amstelpark,** Koenenkade 8, Amsterdamse Bos (© **020/301-0700;** bus: 170 or 172), which has 36 courts.

Moments Skating on the Canals

In winter, the Dutch watch the falling thermometers as avidly as people in Aspen and Chamonix. When it drops low enough for long enough, the landscape becomes a big icemaker, and rivers, canals, and lakes become sparkling highways through the countryside. This doesn't happen very often, but if you're lucky enough to be here at such a time, the best experience of your whole trip may be skating on the canals of Amsterdam. Classical music plays over the ice, and little kiosks are set up to dispense heart-warming liqueurs. Just be cautious when skating under bridges, and in general don't go anywhere the Dutch themselves don't.

7 Shopping

Bargain-hunters won't have much luck (except at the flea markets), but shopping in Amsterdam definitely has its rewards. Best buys include diamonds and traditional Dutch products, such as Delftware, pewter, crystal, and old-fashioned clocks. No matter what you're looking for, you're sure to be impressed with the range of possibilities Amsterdam offers. Shopping can easily be integrated into your Amsterdam experience because the center city is small enough that stores and other attractions are often right beside each other.

THE SHOPPING SCENE

Major shopping streets in Amsterdam, many of which are closed to traffic, include **Kalverstraat,** from the Dam to Muntplein (inexpensive and moderately priced stores); **Rokin,** parallel to Kalverstraat (quality fashions, art galleries, antiques stores); **Leidsestraat** (upmarket stores for clothing, china, gifts); **P. C. Hooftstraat** and **Van Baerlestraat,** near Museumplein (designer fashions, accessories, china, gifts); and **Nieuwe Spiegelstraat,** near the Rijksmuseum (art and antiques).

Malls have sprung up across the city. **Magna Plaza** has filled the former main post office, just behind the Dam, with four floors of exclusive and useful stores. The **Kalvertoren** occupies a prime site at the corner of Kalverstraat, near the Munt; a cafe at the top offers a bird's-eye view of Amsterdam's rooftops.

STORE HOURS   Regular open hours are Monday from 10 or 11am (some stores don't open at all in the morning) to 6pm; Tuesday, Wednesday, and Friday from 9am to 6pm; Thursday from 9am to 9pm; and Saturday from 9am to 5pm. Many stores stay open on Sunday as well, usually from noon to 5pm. Many supermarkets are open daily from 8am to 8pm, or even 10pm.

SHOPPING A TO Z
ANTIQUES

Amsterdam's antiques stores rank among the finest in Europe. The best places to look for them are around **Nieuwe Spiegelstraat** and **Kerkstraat,** and in the **Jordaan.** The **Kunst- & Antiekcentrum de Looier,** Elandsgracht 109 (© **020/624-9038;** www. looier.nl), is an indoor antiques market spread through several old warehouses, where hundreds of individual dealers rent small stalls and corners to show their wares.

ART

Paintings large and small, originals and reproductions, peer out of every other store window. For quality reproductions of works by the Dutch Old Masters, **museum shops** are your best bet. For ceramics and glassware, **Galerie Carla Koch,** Prinsengracht 510 (℃ **020/639-0198;** www.carlakoch.nl), employs some of the raciest design talent in Amsterdam.

BOOKS

For English-language publications, there's the **American Book Center** ✦, Spui 12 (℃ **020/625-5537;** www.abc.nl); **Waterstone's,** Kalverstraat 152 (℃ **020/638-3821;** www.waterstones.com); and **Athenaeum Boekhandel & Nieuwscentrum,** Spui 14–16 (℃ **020/514-1460;** www.athenaeum.nl), which carries a big selection of international magazines and newspapers, and books.

CIGARS, PIPES & SMOKING ARTICLES

Run by the same family since 1826, warm, wood-paneled **P. G. C. Hajenius,** Rokin 92–96 (℃ **020/623-7494;** www.hajenius.com), is virtually a museum of antique tobacco humidors (not for sale), and has a beautiful selection of distinctively Dutch blends for sale. Pipes of all description are displayed, and fine Sumatra and Havana cigars are kept in a room-size glass humidor.

CLOCKS

A small store across the street from Centraal Station, **B. V. Victoria,** Prins Hendrikkade 47 (℃ **020/427-2051;** www.victoriagifts.nl), has traditional Dutch clocks—soft-toned chimes, handcrafted cases, covered with tiny figures and mottoes, insets of hand-painted porcelain, and hand-painted Dutch scenes—along with Delftware, chocolates, and other gift items.

CRAFTS & CURIOS

In the **Blue Gold Fish,** Rozengracht 17 (℃ **020/623-3134**), there's no real rhyme or reason behind the items for sale. Still, there's unity in its diversity and in the more-or-less fantastic design sensibility that goes into each piece. For more traditional choices, **'t Curiosa Winkeltje,** Prinsengracht 228 (℃ **020/625-1352**), sells assorted knickknacks

---

Tips **The Lowdown on Delftware**

Those ubiquitous earthenware items in the familiar blue-and-white "Delft" colors have almost become synonymous with Holland. Souvenir stores, specialty stores, and department stores have Delftware products in the widest variety of forms imaginable. If an object has particular appeal, by all means buy it—but be aware that unless it meets certain specifications, you are not carting home an authentic piece of the hand-painted earthenware pottery that has made the Delft name illustrious. A wide selection of hand-painted Delftware of every conceivable type from De Koninklijke Porcelyne Fles can be found at the well-stocked emporium **Galleria d'Arte Rinascimento,** Prinsengracht 170 (℃ **020/622-7509**), across the canal from the Anne Frank House.

Tips **Tax Return**

If you live outside the European Union, you're entitled to a refund of the value-added tax (BTW) you pay on purchases of 137€ ($171) or more in a day at a store that subscribes to the system. (*Note:* at this writing, the minimum amount was expected to be cut to 50€/$63.) Subscribing stores are identified by a TAX-FREE SHOPPING sticker. On high-ticket items, the savings of 13.5% can be significant. You must export the purchases within 3 months.

To obtain your refund, ask for a **global refund check** from the store. When you are leaving the EU, present this check, your purchases, and receipts to Customs. They will stamp the check. You can get the refund in cash or paid to your credit card at an International Cash Refund Point. At Schiphol Airport, this is the Global Refund Cash Refund Office; refunds are also available from the airport's branch of ABN-AMRO bank.

For more information, contact **Europe Tax-Free Shopping**, Leidsevaartweg 99, 2106 AS, Heemstede, Netherlands (ⓒ **023/524-1909;** fax 023/524-6164; www.globalrefund.com).

such as colored bottles and glasses, modern versions of old tin cars and other children's toys from the 1950s and earlier, big plastic butterflies, lamps shaped like bananas, and many other such useful things.

DEPARTMENT STORES

De Bijenkorf ✪, Dam 1 (ⓒ **0900/0919;** www.bijenkorf.nl), Amsterdam's largest department store, holds a vast array of goods in all price ranges and a couple of good eateries. Other well-stocked warehouses, as the Dutch call department stores, include **Vroom & Dreesmann (V&D),** Kalverstraat 203 (ⓒ **0900/235-8363;** www.vroom endreesmann.nl.), at Muntplein; and **HEMA,** the Dutch Woolworth's (ⓒ **020/ 422-8988;** www.hema.nl), in the Kalvertoren mall near the Munt.

The store of choice for Amsterdam's power shoppers, **Metz & Co** ✪✪, Leidsestraat 34–36 (ⓒ **020/520-7020;** www.metzandco.com), sells modern furniture, fabrics, kitchenware, and other such items. The in-store rooftop cafe Metz, designed by De Stijl architect Gerrit Rietveld in 1933, affords a spectacular panoramic view across the rooftops of Amsterdam.

DIAMONDS

Amsterdam diamond cutters have an international reputation for high standards. When you buy from them, you'll be given a certificate listing the weight, color, cut, and identifying marks of the gem you purchase. The following stores offer diamond-cutting and -polishing tours, and sales of the finished product: **Amsterdam Diamond Center,** Rokin 1–5 (ⓒ **020/624-5787;** www.amsterdamdiamoncenter.com); **Coster,** Paulus Potterstraat 2–8 (ⓒ **020/305-5555;** www.costerdiamonds.com); **Gassan,** Nieuwe Uilenburgerstraat 173–175 (ⓒ **020/622-5333;** www.gassandiamonds.com); **Stoeltie,** Wagenstraat 13–17 (ⓒ **020/623-7601;** www.stoeltiediamonds.com); and **Van Moppes,** Albert Cuypstraat 2–6 (ⓒ **020/676-1242;** www.moppesdiamonds. com).

FASHIONS

Alongside the standard designer emporia on **Rokin** and **P. C. Hooftstraat** are more exclusive, often homegrown designer clothes stores in the small streets running across the main canals, such as **Herenstraat, Hartenstraat, Wolvenstraat,** and **Huidenstraat.**

FLOWER BULBS

Gardeners will find it well-nigh impossible to leave Amsterdam without at least one purchase from the **Flower Market** ✸, on Singel Canal at Muntplein, open daily year-round. Just be certain the bulbs you buy carry with them the obligatory phytosanitary certificate clearing them for entry into the U.S. and other countries.

FOOD & DRINK

Jacob Hooy & Co., Kloveniersburgwal 10–12 (✆ **020/624-3041**; www.jacobhooy. nl.), opened in 1743 and operated for the past 130 years by the same family, is a wonderland of fragrant smells that offers more than 500 different herbs and spices and 30 different teas, sold loose by weight, plus health foods, homeopathic products, and natural cosmetics. In a store from 1839, **Simon Levelt,** Prinsengracht 180 (✆ **020/622-8428**; www.simonlevelt.nl), specializes in coffee and tea. Devotees of the legal "narcotic" from Columbia and other coffee-producing nations will be tempted by the smell of freshly roasted coffee beans at **Geels & Co.** ✸, Warmoesstraat 67 (✆ **020/624-0683**; www.geels.nl), a coffee-roasting and tea-importing establishment that has been going strong since 1864.

   H. P. de Vreng en Zonen, Nieuwendijk 75 (✆ **020/624-4581**; www.oudamsterdam. nl), has an extensive selection of special Dutch liqueurs and gins. To recover from the aftereffects of these fine distilled spirits, head for **De Waterwinkel,** Roelof Hartstraat 10 (✆ **020/675-5932**; www.dewaterwinkel.nl.), a one-of-a-kind store that stocks a massive range of mineral waters from around the world. Fresh, handmade pralines in a plethora of shapes and styles—pure, milk, and white chocolate—are laid out for perusal at the two branches of **Puccini Bomboni,** Singel 184 (✆ **020/427-8341**; www.puccinibomboni.com), and Staalstraat 17 (✆ **020/626-5474**).

JEWELRY

Marvelous contemporary designs and materials turn jewelry into an art form at **Galerie Ra,** Vijzelstraat 90 (✆ **020/626-5100**; www.galerie-ra.nl). Owner Paul Derrez specializes in stunning modern jewelry in gold and silver, and goes a bit farther, turning feathers, rubber, foam, and other materials into pieces he describes as "playful." **BLGK Edelsmeden,** Hartenstraat 28 (✆ **020/624-8154**; www.blgk.nl), sells affordable designer jewelry. Some of their pieces represent a fresh spin on classic forms; others are more innovative.

MARKETS

Awnings stretch over 15 stalls of brightly colored blossoms, bulbs, and potted plants at the **Bloemenmarkt (Flower Market)** ✸, Singel, between Koningsplein and Muntplein. Partly floating on a row of permanently moored barges, this is one of Amsterdam's stellar spots, the most atmospheric place to buy fresh-cut flowers, bright- and healthy-looking plants, ready-to-travel packets of tulip bulbs, and all the necessary accessories for home gardening. The market is open daily from 8am to 8pm.

   At the **Albert Cuypmarkt,** Albert Cuypstraat, you find just about anything and everything your imagination can conjure up. It's open Monday to Saturday from 9am to 6pm. Every Friday from 10am to 6pm, there's a **Book Market** on Spui. The **Farmer's Market,** also known as the Bio Market, takes place every Saturday from 9am to 5pm on Noordermarkt, and caters to Amsterdam's infatuation with health foods and natural products. Thorbeckeplein hosts a **Sunday Art Market** April to October, Sunday from 11am to 6pm, with local artists showing their wares.

The **Waterlooplein Flea Market** ✦ is Amsterdam's classic market, offering everything from cooking pots to mariner's telescopes to decent historical prints of Dutch cities. It's open Monday to Saturday from 10am to 5pm.

8 Amsterdam After Dark

Nightlife is centered on the **Leidseplein** and **Rembrandtplein** areas, both of which have a large and varied selection of restaurants, bars, and nightspots. The **Rosse Buurt (Red Light District)** serves up its unique brand of nightlife, and adjoining this is **Nieuwmarkt,** which is rapidly becoming a popular, alternative hangout. Check out *Amsterdam Day by Day* (p. 247) to see what's happening around town.

If you want to attend any of Amsterdam's theatrical or musical events (including rock concerts), getting tickets should be your first task upon arrival. **Amsterdam Uit Buro (AUB) Ticketshop,** Leidseplein 26 (✆ **0900/0191** or 020/621-1288; www.aub.nl; tram: 1, 2, 5, 7, or 10), at the corner of Marnixstraat, can reserve tickets for almost every venue in town, for a reservations charge of 2€ ($2.50) per ticket at their office, 2.50€ ($3.15) online, and 3€ ($3.75) by phone. In addition, if you are under age 26, you

> **Impressions**
>
> I often think the night is more richly colored than the day.
> —Vincent van Gogh, 1888

can pick up a **Cultural Youth Pass (CJP)** for 15€ ($19). This pass will get you reduced admission to many museums and cultural events. The AUB office is open Monday to Wednesday and Saturday from 10am to 6pm, Thursday from 10am to 9pm, and Sunday from noon to 6pm. The VVV Amsterdam tourist information office can reserve performance tickets, and charges 2.50€ ($3.15) for the service. Most upmarket and many midlevel hotels will reserve tickets.

Prices for after-dark entertainment in Amsterdam tend to be modest. Many nightspots only charge for drinks, though others have a nominal cover charge.

THE PERFORMING ARTS
CLASSICAL MUSIC

Amsterdam's top orchestra—indeed one of the world's top orchestras—is the famed **Royal Concertgebouw Orchestra** (www.concertgebouworkest.nl) whose home is the **Concertgebouw** ✦✦✦, Concertgebouwplein 2–6 (✆ **020/671-8345** daily 10am–5pm, 24-hr. information line 020/675-4411; www.concertgebouw.nl; tram: 3, 5, or 12). World-class orchestras and soloists are only too happy to appear at The Grote Zaal (Great Hall) of the Concertgebouw because of its perfect acoustics. No matter where you sit, the listening is impeccable. Chamber and solo recitals are given in the Kleine Zaal (Little Hall). Tickets are from 15€ to 100€ ($19–$125). The main concert season is from September to mid-June, but during July and August there's the Robeco Summer Series, world-class but with a more friendly price tag—all seats are just 30€ ($38).

Tips After-Dark Attire

If you intend to go to the opera, a classical music concert, or the theater, don't worry about what to wear. Amsterdam has a very informal dress code—no code at all, really. Of course, you might want to dress up, and in fact many people do, but you won't be turned away for being "improperly" dressed.

The city's other symphony orchestra, the **Netherlands Philharmonic Orchestra** (www.orkest.nl), doesn't lag far behind its illustrious cousin. The orchestra's official home is the **Beurs van Berlage,** Damrak 213 (© **020/521-7250;** www.berlage.com; tram: 4, 9, 14, 16, 24, or 25), formerly the Amsterdam Stock Exchange. This venue hosts chamber music concerts and recitals in the large hall that was once the trading floor. Tickets are 8€ to 25€ ($10–$31).

At the other end of the musical spectrum, lovers of avant-garde and experimental music should head to the **Muziekgebouw aan 't IJ,** Piet Heinkade 1 (© **020/788-2000;** www.muziekgebouw.nl; tram: 25 or 26), which opened in 2005 in a spectacular piece of modern architecture on the IJ waterfront, just east of Centraal Station. You can savor electronic adventurism and contemporary use of the standard instrumentarium, along with modern and old jazz, non-Western music, small-scale musical theater, opera, and dance. The waterside terrace of the cafe-restaurant here is one of the most idyllic in town. Tickets are 10€ to 20€ ($13–$25).

A next-door annex to the Muziekgebouw is the equally new home of the Bimhuis jazz and improvised music club (see below).

OPERA & DANCE

Artistic director Pierre Audi has built up the **Netherlands Opera** (www.dno.nl) and its repertoire. The company performs at the superb modern **Muziektheater,** Waterlooplein 22 (© **020/625-5455,** 24-hr. information line 020/551-8100; www.hetmuziektheater.nl; tram: 9 or 14). This theater is also used by the **National Ballet** (www.het-nationale-ballet.nl), which performs large-scale classical ballet repertoire and contemporary work, and by the **Netherlands Dance Theater** (www.ndt.nl), which is based in The Hague and is noted for its groundbreaking contemporary repertoire. Most performances begin at 8:15pm; opera tickets cost 20€ to 80€ ($25–$100), and ballet tickets slightly less.

THEATER

Homegrown theater productions are almost always in Dutch, with the main city venue being the **Stadsschouwburg,** Leidseplein 26 (© **020/624-2311;** www.stadsschouwburgamsterdam.nl; tram: 1, 2, 5, 7, or 10). Tickets are 10€ to 50€ ($13–$63).

Because English is so widely spoken, Amsterdam is a favorite venue for road shows from the United States and England. Theaters that often host English-language productions include: **Felix Meritis,** Keizersgracht 324 (© **020/626-2321); Frascati,** Nes 63 (© **020/626-6866),** which focuses on modern theater; **Carré,** Amstel 115–125 (© **020/622-5225);** and **Nieuwe de la Mar,** Marnixstraat 404 (© **020/623-3462).** Showtime is usually 8:15pm, and ticket prices vary widely.

Comedy

Boom Chicago ☆, Leidsepleintheater, Leidseplein 12 (© **020/423-0101;** www.boomchicago.nl; tram: 1, 2, 5, 7, or 10), brings delightful English-language improvisational comedy to Amsterdam. *Time* magazine compared it to Chicago's celebrated Second City comedy troupe. Dutch audiences don't have much problem with the English sketches; they often seem to get the point ahead of the native English-speakers in attendance. Spectators are seated around candlelit tables for eight people, and you can have dinner and a drink while you enjoy the show. Tickets are 13€ to 23€ ($15–$39), not including dinner. The restaurant is open at 7pm. The box office is open daily from noon to 8:30pm.

THE CLUB & MUSIC SCENE
JAZZ & BLUES
In Amsterdam, jazz and blues groups hold forth in bars, and the joints start jumping at around 11pm. **Bimhuis** ✵, Piet Heinkade 3 (© 020/788-2188; www.bimhuis.nl; tram: 25 or 26), at the new Muziekgebouw aan 't IJ, on the waterfront, just east of Centraal Station, is for the serious contemporary jazz connoisseur. Tickets are 10€ to 25€ ($13–$31).

The **Joseph Lam Jazz Club,** Diemenstraat 8 (© 020/622-8086), plays Dixieland; **Bourbon Street Jazz & Blues Club,** Leidsekruisstraat 6–8 (© 020/623-3440), hosts a mix of local and traveling talent; also recommended is **Alto,** Korte Leidsedwarsstraat 115, off the Leidseplein (© 020/626-3249). At Amsterdam's "home of the blues," **Maloe Melo** ✵, Lijnbaansgracht 163 (© 020/420-4592), the music's quality varies from sounds lovingly created by capable amateurs to those cooked up by an occasional big name.

DANCE CLUBS
Amsterdam's dance scene embraces every type of ambience and clientele, from sophisticated rooms in large hotels to underground alternative spots. The scene isn't wildly volatile, but places do come and go, so check the listings in *Amsterdam Day by Day* for current addresses. Leading dance clubs include **Mazzo,** Rozengracht 114 (© 020/626-7500), for trance and techno; **Akhnaton,** Nieuwezijds Kolk 25 (© 020/624-3396), for African music and salsa; and **Paradiso,** Weteringschans 6–8 (© 020/626-4521), which has live music followed by dance parties.

Other good locations are **Amnesia,** Oudezijds Voorburgwal 3 (© 020/638-1461) for trance-house and hard-core; **Escape,** Rembrandtplein 11 (© 020/622-1111; www.escape.nl and www.chemistry.nl), a large venue with a choice of several dance floors, and a great sound system; **Odeon,** Singel 460 (© 020/521-8555), serving up '50s to '80s "credible classics," in the graceful surroundings of a converted 17th-century canal house; and the seriously trendy **Sinners,** Wagenstraat 3–7 (© 020/620-1375; www.sinners.nl), where the big names in the Dutch film, theater, and TV scene like to see and be seen (especially seen).

Melkweg: A Multidimensional Venue
A sometime hippie haven in an old dairy factory, **Melkweg,** Lijnbaansgracht 234A (© 020/531-8181; tram: 1, 2, 5, 7, or 10), near Leidseplein, houses an art center, dance floor, cinema, theater, concert hall, photo gallery, and exhibit space. The cover charge is 5€ to 10€ ($6.25–$13) plus 3€ ($3.75) monthly club membership. The box office is open Monday to Friday from 1 to 5pm, and Saturday and Sunday from 4 to 6pm.

The most popular gay dance venue in town, **Cockring,** Warmoesstraat 96 (© **020/ 623-9604**), in the Red Light District, generally lays down no-nonsense, hard-core, high-decibel dance and techno music on the dance floor. More relaxed beats in the sociable upstairs bar make a welcome break.

THE BAR & CAFE SCENE
BROWN CAFES

You'll see brown cafes *(bruine kroegen)* everywhere: on street corners, at canal intersections, and down narrow little lanes. They look as if they've been there forever. These are the favorite local haunts and are quite likely to become yours as well—they're positively addicting. Brown cafes will typically sport lace half-curtains at the front window and ancient Oriental rugs on tabletops (to sop up any spills from your beer). Wood floors, overhead beams, and plastered walls blend into a murky brown background, darkened by centuries of smoke from Dutch pipes. Frequently there's a wall rack with newspapers and magazines, but they get little attention in the evening, when conversations flow as readily as *pils* (beer). *Jenever,* the potent Dutch gin, is on hand in several different flavors, some served ice-cold—but never on the rocks. Excellent Dutch beers, and expensive imported brews, are available as well.

Your hotel neighborhood is sure to have at least one brown cafe close at hand. Far be it for me to set any sort of rigid itinerary for a *kroegentocht* (pub crawl), but you might want to look into the following: **Hoppe,** Spui 18–20 (© **020/623-7849**), a student and journalist hangout since 1670, which still has sawdust on the floor and is always packed; **Kalkhoven,** at Prinsengracht and Westermarkt (© **020/624-9649**), a

Smoking Coffeeshops

Tourists often get confused about "smoking" coffeeshops and how they differ from "nonsmoking" ones. Well, to begin with, "smoking" and "nonsmoking" don't refer to cigarettes—they refer to hashish and marijuana.

Smoking coffeeshops not only sell cannabis, most commonly in the form of hashish, they provide a place where patrons can sit and smoke it all day long if they so choose. Generally, these smoking coffeeshops are the only places in Amsterdam called "coffeeshops"—regular cafes are called cafes or *eetcafés*—so chances are if you want to smoke, you'll be able to find what you're looking for without too much difficulty.

You're allowed to possess up to 5 grams of hashish or marijuana for personal use, and coffeeshops are forbidden to sell more than this amount to each customer. Each coffeeshop has a menu listing the different varieties of hashish and marijuana it stocks. Hash comes in two varieties: light pollen and oily black. Connoisseurs say the best stuff has a stronger smell and is soft and sticky. The bright green weed called Skunk has an extra high content of THC (the active ingredient in cannabis). A 5-gram bag costs from 4€ to 10€ ($5–$13), depending on the quality. Coffeeshops have joints (stickies) for sale, rolled with tobacco. Officially, coffeeshops are not allowed to sell alcohol, so they sell coffee, tea, and fruit juices. You're even allowed to bring along and smoke your own stuff, so long as you buy a drink.

serious drinker's bar that dates back to 1670; **Cafe 't Smalle,** Egelantiersgracht 12 (*©* **020/623-9617**), in the Jordaan district on the canalside, a bar in a former distillery and tasting house that dates from 1786; **Café Chris,** Bloemstraat 42 (*©* **020/624-5942**), a tap house since 1624; **Gollem,** Raamsteeg 4 (*©* **020/626-6645**), which sells more than 200 different beers; **De Karpershoek,** Martelaarsgracht 2 (*©* **020/624-7886**), which dates from 1629 and was once a favorite hangout of sailors; and **Papeneiland,** Prinsengracht 2 (*©* **020/624-1989**), a 300-year-old establishment filled with character and a secret tunnel leading under the Brouwersgracht that was used by 17th-century Catholics.

TASTING HOUSES

The decor will still be basically brown and typically Old Dutch—and the age of the establishment may be even more impressive than that of its beer-swilling brown-cafe neighbors—but in a *proeflokaal* (tasting house) you usually order *jenever* (Dutch gin, taken neat, without ice) or another product of the distillery that owns the place. To drink your choice of spirit, custom and ritual decree that you lean over the bar, with your hands behind your back, to take the first sip from your well-filled *borreltje* (small drinking glass).

Tasting houses to look for include: **De Admiraal,** Herengracht 319 (*©* **020/625-4334**); **De Drie Fleschjes,** Gravenstraat 18 (*©* **020/624-8443**), behind the Nieuwe Kerk; **De Ooievaar,** Sint Olofspoort 1 (*©* **020/625-7360**), on the corner with Zeedijk near Centraal Station; and **Het Proeflokaal,** Pilsteeg 35 (*©* **020/622-5334**), a wonderful little place that undoubtedly looks much as it did when it opened in 1680.

TRENDY CAFES

Every city has its hip venues, where those out to impress can preen their feathers against a fitting backdrop. Amsterdam is no exception. The places listed below offer contemporary designs and often cocktails instead of beer. Some of them function as grand cafes. **Café Dante,** Spuistrat 320 (*©* **020/638-8839**), is an artists' hangout with an exhibit space, close to the Spui; **Seymour Likely,** Nieuwezijds Voorburgwal 250 (*©* **020/627-1427**), behind the Royal Palace at the Dam, has a constantly changing decor; and **Café Schiller** , Rembrandtplein 36 (*©* **020/624-9864**), has enduringly attracted artistic and literary types to its stunning Art Nouveau setting.

GAY & LESBIAN BARS

The gay scene in Amsterdam is strong, and there is no lack of gay bars and nightspots in town. Below are listings of some of the most popular spots for gay men. For lesbians, the scene is a little more difficult to uncover. Places that are hot now might not be later, so you might want to call or visit **COC,** Rozenstraat 14 (*©* **020/623-4079**), the office/cafe headquarters of the Organization of Homosexuals in the Netherlands. The office and telephone lines are open daily from 10am to 5pm. More information should be available from the **Gay and Lesbian Switchboard** (*©* **020/623-6565**). *Frommer's Gay & Lesbian Europe* devotes a chapter to Amsterdam.

Most of the city's gay bars are in well-defined areas. For frivolous, old-style camp, look along the Amstel near Muntplein and on Halvemaansteeg. Trendier places are along Reguliersdwarsstraat. Casual locals head for Kerkstraat, on both sides of the crossing with Leidsestraat.

One of the city's oldest, most traditional gay bars, **Amstel Taveerne,** Amstel 54 (*©* **020/623-4254**), off Rembrandtplein, is the kind of place where about an hour after happy hour everyone starts singing popular songs in Dutch. It's said every gay visitor to Amsterdam goes to **Café April,** Reguliersdwarsstraat 37 (© **020/625-9572**), near the Flower Market, at least once, so you'll likely make friends from around the world. **April's Exit,** Reguliersdwarsstraat 42 (© **020/625-8788**), an affiliated dance club, is close by, and many people from Café April head over after happy hour.

Getto, Warmoesstraat 51 (© **020/421-5151**), in the Red Light District, attracts an equal mix of boys and girls with its hip interior and such events as "Club Fu" karaoke (first Mon of every month) and bingo (every Thurs). There is an eclectic dinner menu inspired by food from around the world, whether vegetarian or a Cajun crocodile steak. **Spijker,** Kerkstraat 4 (© **020/620-5919**), on the corner with Leidsegracht, attracts a casual crowd who extend a friendly welcome to visitors. The pinball machine and pool table are focal points, and video screens show an amusing juxtaposition of cartoons and erotica. Lively bar staffers keep the atmosphere relaxed with a varied selection of music and stiff drinks, and happy hour draws the crowds in daily from 5 to 7pm.

Once a female-only enclave with a feisty atmosphere, **Saarein,** Elandsstraat 119 (© **020/623-4901**), in the Jordaan, is now open to both genders. Attractions include pool, darts, pinball, and Continental food. Lesbian bar **Vive-la-Vie,** Amstelstraat 7 (© **020/624-0114**), off Rembrandtplein, attracts a young, lively crowd prior to club-hopping time, and lipstick isn't forbidden. The sidewalk terrace offers summertime relaxation and a fine view of tourists in neighboring Rembrandtplein.

MORE ENTERTAINMENT
MOVIES
In Amsterdam you'll find a dozen or more first-run features, most of them Hollywood's finest, in English with Dutch subtitles. Admission prices are around 10€ ($13), depending on the day, the time, and the movie. The **Tuschinski Theater,** Reguliersbreestraat 26–34 (© **0900/1458; tram: 4, 9, or 14**), is worth a visit to view its restored Art Deco style from 1921, when it first opened as a variety theater. On the upper balconies you sit on plush chairs and can sip champagne during the movie.

CASINO
Visit **Holland Casino Amsterdam,** in the Lido, Max Euweplein 62 (© **020/521-1111; tram: 1, 2, 5, 7, or 10**), at Leidseplein, for European gambling, with emphasis on the quiet games of roulette, baccarat, punto banco, blackjack, and others, though there are abundant one-armed bandits, which the Dutch call "fruit machines," and blackjack, poker, and bingo machines (start saving your euro coins!). You need correct attire to get in (jacket and tie or turtleneck for men), and you have to bring your passport to register at the door. The minimum age is 18. The casino is open daily (except May 4 and Dec 31) from 1:30pm (slot machines from 11am) to 3am. Admission is 4€ ($5).

13

Haarlem & Noord-Holland

The landscape around Amsterdam in the province of Noord-Holland (North Holland) affords a taste of the cultural and natural variety of the Netherlands. There are the dikes that brought this improbable country into being, windmills, wooden shoes, tidy farms, tiny yacht-filled harbors overlooking IJsselmeer Lake, flower fields reaching to the broad Dutch horizon, and sandy beaches looking out to the North Sea.

In the west is the venerable and graceful city of Haarlem; in the east are remnants of strategic fortifications that protected medieval crossing points. In other places, you can climb tall towers and view museums that recreate the local life of yesteryear, ride a steam train, eat fish by the harbor, and see giant locks and tiny canals.

Everything in Noord-Holland is an easy day trip from Amsterdam, but there's so much to see that you need to make several trips to do the region justice.

For details of tours from Amsterdam by bus, and out-of-town trips by bicycle, see "Organized Tours," in chapter 12.

1 Haarlem ★★

18km (11 miles) W of Amsterdam

Some visitors to Amsterdam prefer to "commute" from Haarlem. The small city (pop. 150,000) has a similar 17th-century ambience, but gets along nicely without the many hassles that go with the nearby capital's famously tolerant and often eccentric lifestyle. You can easily get around this quaint, quiet center of music and art on foot. Haarlem is home to one of Holland's premier art museums. Besides, it's close to the North Sea beaches and to the bulb fields, at the heart of an area dotted with elegant manor houses and picturesque villages.

ESSENTIALS

GETTING THERE Trains depart at least every half-hour from Amsterdam Centraal Station for Haarlem; the trip takes 15 minutes, and a round-trip ticket is 6.20€ ($7.75). **Buses** depart every 15 minutes or so from outside Amsterdam Centraal Station, but take longer than the train. By **car** from Amsterdam, take N5 and A5.

VISITOR INFORMATION VVV Haarlem, Stationsplein 1, 2011 LR Haarlem (© 0900/616-1600; fax 023/534-0537; www.vvvzk.nl), is just outside the rail station. The office is open January to March and October to December, Monday to Friday from 9:30am to 5:30pm and Saturday from 10am to 2pm; April to September, Monday to Friday from 9:30am to 5:30pm and Saturday from 10am to 4pm.

SEEING THE SIGHTS

Haarlem is the little sister city of Amsterdam. Granted municipal status by Count Willem II of Holland in 1245, it was where Frans Hals, Jacob van Ruisdael, and Pieter

Saenredam were living and painting their famous portraits, landscapes, and church interiors during the same years that Rembrandt was living and working in Amsterdam.

THE GROTE MARKT & STADHUIS

The old center is a 5- to 10-minute walk from the graceful Art Nouveau rail station from 1908 (which is decorated with painted tiles and has a fine station restaurant), most of it via pedestrian-only shopping streets. First-time visitors generally head straight for the **Grote Markt** ✶✶✶, the beautiful central market square, adjacent to the **Sint-Bavokerk (Church of St. Bavo;** see below). Most points of interest in Haarlem are within easy walking distance of the Grote Markt. The monumental buildings around the tree-lined square, which date from the 15th to the 19th centuries, are a visual minicourse in the development of Dutch architecture. Here stands Haarlem's 14th-century **Stadhuis (Town Hall),** Grote Markt 2 (✆ 023/511-3000), a former hunting lodge of the counts of Holland rebuilt in the 17th century, and containing a magnificent tapestry of the *Crusades* (1629) by Josef Thienpont of Oudenaerde—just one of Haarlem's many historical connections with the Belgian region of Flanders.

OTHER TOP SIGHTS

Frans Hals Museum ✶✶✶   The finest attraction in Haarlem, this may be a high point of your trip to Holland. The galleries here are the halls and furnished chambers of the Oudemannenhuis (1608), a home for retired gentlemen designed by Ghent architect Lieven de Key, with a courtyard garden. The famous paintings by Frans Hals (ca. 1580–1666) and other Masters of the Haarlem School hang in settings that look like the 17th-century houses they were intended to adorn. Hals is best known for works such as *The Laughing Cavalier* (1624) and *The Gypsy Girl* (1630)—neither of which is in the museum—but he earned his bread and butter by painting portraits of members of the local Schutters (Musketeers) Guild. Typified by his *Officers of the Militia Company of St. George* (ca. 1627), five such works, whose style inspired van Gogh, hang in the museum, along with six more paintings by Hals.

Look out for a peculiar painting, *The Monk and the Beguine* (1591) by Cornelisz van Haarlem: It depicts a monk touching a beguine nun's bare breast, and has been interpreted variously as a satire on lecherous behavior in cloisters, or as being symbolic of purity and virginity.

You'll see fine collections of antique silver, porcelain, and clocks. Among other pieces is a superb dollhouse from around 1750—though "dollhouse" seems an inadequate description for an exquisitely detailed miniature replica of a merchant's house.

Groot Heiligland 62. ✆ 023/511-5775. www.franshalsmuseum.com. Admission 7€ ($8.75) adults, free for those under 19. Tues–Sat 11am–5pm; Sun and holidays noon–5pm. Closed Jan 1, Dec 25.

Sint-Bavokerk ✶✶   Walking to the center of town from Haarlem station, you catch only glimpses of the high-towered St. Bavo's Church, also known as the Grote Kerk (Great Church), looming above the narrow streets. But the moment you reach the Grote Markt, it's revealed in all its massive splendor. The colossal late-Gothic church was begun in 1445 under the direction of Antwerp's city architect Evert Spoorwater. It was basically complete by 1520 and so has a rare unity of structure and proportion. The interior is light and airy, with tall whitewashed walls and sandstone pillars. Its elegant wooden tower is covered with lead sheets and adorned with gilt spheres.

Look for the tombstone of painter Frans Hals, who was probably born in Antwerp around 1580 and who lived and worked for most of his life in Haarlem, where he died in 1666. Search, too, for a cannonball that has been embedded in the wall ever since

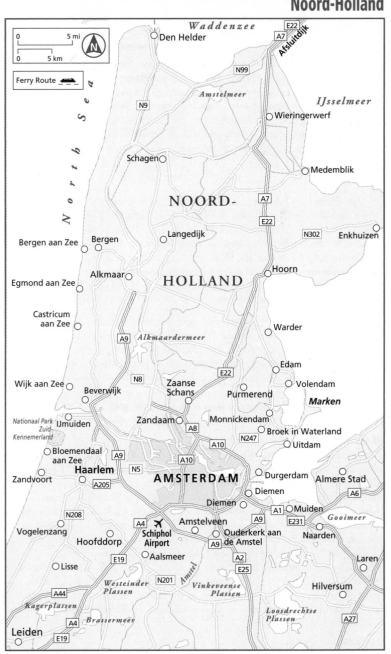

Waddenzee

Den Helder

E22
A7
Afsluitdijk

N99

Amstelmeer

IJsselmeer

N9

Wieringerwerf

Schagen

Medemblik

North Sea

NOORD-

A7

E22

N302

Enkhuizen

Bergen aan Zee

Bergen

Langedijk

Egmond aan Zee

Alkmaar

HOLLAND

Hoorn

Castricum
aan Zee

Warder

A9

Alkmaardermeer

Edam

Wijk aan Zee

N8

E22

Beverwijk

Zaanse
Schans

Volendam

Purmerend

Marken

Nationaal Park
Zuid-
Kennemerland

IJmuiden

Zandaam

A8

Monnickendam

Broek in Waterland

N247

A10

Uitdam

Bloemendaal
aan Zee

A9

A10

Zandvoort

Haarlem

N5

AMSTERDAM

Durgerdam

Almere Stad

A205

Diemen

A6

Diemen

A1

Muiden

Gooimeer

N208

A4

Amstelveen

A9

E231

N201

Schiphol
Airport

A9

Ouderkerk aan
de Amstel

Naarden

Vogelenzang

Hoofddorp

Aalsmeer

A2

Laren

E19

E25

Lisse

Amstel

Westeinder
Plassen

Vinkeveense
Plassen

Hilversum

A44

Kagerplassen

Brassermeer

Loosdrechtse
Plassen

A27

Leiden

A4

E19

0   5 mi

0   5 km

Ferry Route

> **_Moments_ Canalboat Trips**
>
> An ideal way to view Haarlem is by canalboat. The boats are operated by **Woltheus Cruises** (© 072/511-4840; www.woltheuscruises.nl) from a dock on the Spaarne River at the Gravenstenenbrug, a handsome lift bridge. Boats depart April to October, every hour from noon to 5pm for a 50-minute cruise around the canals. Cruises are 6.50€ ($8.15) adults, 3.50€ ($4.40) children 4 to 11, and free for children under 4. In addition, candlelight cruises and longer cruises outside town are offered.

it came flying through a window during the Spanish siege of Haarlem (1572–73). Don't miss the famous Christian Müller Organ, built in 1738. Mozart played this magnificent instrument in 1766 when he was just 10 years old and is said to have shouted for joy—when you see it, you may be struck dumb at the thought of little Wolfie reaching for one of the 68 stops. You can hear it at one of the free concerts given on Tuesday and Thursday from April to October.

Oude Groenmarkt 23. © 023/553-2040. www.bavo.nl. Admission 2€ ($2.50) adults, 1.25€ ($1.55) children 12–16, free for children under 12. Mon–Sat 10am–4pm.

Teylers Museum The oldest public museum in the Netherlands was established here in 1784 by a private collector. It contains a curious collection of displays: drawings by Michelangelo, Raphael, and Rembrandt (which are exhibited in rotation); fossils, minerals, and skeletons; and instruments of physics and an odd assortment of inventions, including the largest electrostatic generator in the world (1784) and a 19th-century radarscope.

Spaarne 16. © 023/531-9010. www.teylersmuseum.nl. Admission 5.50€ ($6.90) adults, 2.75€ ($3.45) students, 1€ ($1.25) children 5–18, free for children under 5. Tues–Sat 10am–5pm; Sun and holidays noon–5pm. Closed Jan 1, Dec 25.

MORE PLACES OF INTEREST

Belgium's French-speaking Walloons weren't left out of Haarlem's feast of Flemish history and culture, as may be seen in the 16th-century **Waalse Kerk (Walloon Church),** at the Begijnhof. Built by Walloon and French Protestant refugees so they could practice their religion in peace and in French, the church is surrounded by the Begijnhof, a cluster of little houses that started out as a Catholic foundation for pious laywomen. Its rooms have been put to use by less-pious modern laywomen—they host the minimally clad working girls of Haarlem's small *rosse buurt* (red light district).

Haarlem counts one of the finest tallies of *hofjes* (almshouses) of any Dutch city. These charitable establishments around secluded courtyards were constructed from medieval times onward to house poor and retired persons. There are 20 of them scattered around town. Two worth visiting in the central zone close to the Grote Markt are the **Hofje van Oorschot,** in Kruisstraat; and the **Bakenesserhofje,** founded in 1395, in Wijde Appelaarsteeg.

WHERE TO DINE

Jacobus Pieck 🍴 DUTCH/INTERNATIONAL   This popular cafe-restaurant on one of Haarlem's best shopping streets has a lovely shaded terrace in the garden for fine-weather days. Inside, it's bustling and stylish. Outside or in, you get excellent

Haarlem

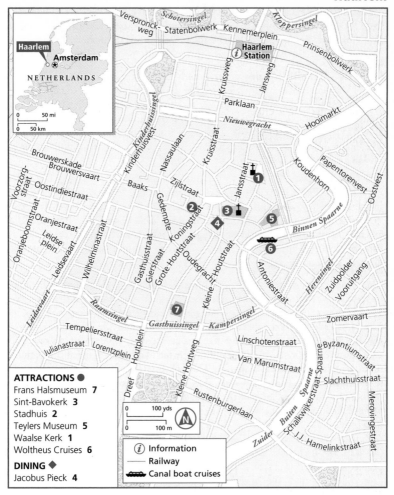

ATTRACTIONS ●
Frans Halsmuseum **7**
Sint-Bavokerk **3**
Stadhuis **2**
Teylers Museum **5**
Waalse Kerk **1**
Woltheus Cruises **6**

DINING ◆
Jacobus Pieck **4**

ⓘ Information
— Railway
🚢 Canal boat cruises

food from the open kitchen for reasonable prices, and friendly, mostly efficient service, though at the busiest times it can be slow. At lunchtime, try one of the generous sandwiches, burgers, or particularly good salads. At dinner, a daily changing menu typically includes dishes ranging from pastas and Middle Eastern dishes to wholesome Dutch standards.

Warmoesstraat 18. ℂ **023/532-6144.** www.jacobuspieck.nl. Main courses 8€–15€ ($10–$19); *dagschotel* 11€ ($14). AE, MC, V. Mon 11am–4pm; Tues–Sat 11am–4pm and 5:30–10pm.

2 Zandvoort

24km (15 miles) W of Amsterdam; 7km (4½ miles) W of Haarlem

If you feel like drawing a breath of fresh sea air and you don't have much time for it, do what most Amsterdammers do: Head for Zandvoort (*Zand*-fort). On the North Sea coast just west of Haarlem, the resort is brash and brassy in the summer, though it often looks forlorn out of season. Even in winter, locals and visitors take the train here, stroll along the shore for an hour or so, and then repair to one of the resort's cafes.

ESSENTIALS

GETTING THERE   **Trains** depart hourly from Amsterdam Centraal Station for Zandvoort. You transfer at Haarlem (where the Zandvoort train is usually waiting on the adjacent platform). During summer months extra trains go direct from Centraal Station. In either case, the trip time is around 30 minutes, and a round-trip ticket is 8.30€ ($10). **Buses** depart every 30 minutes from outside Centraal Station, but they take longer than the train. By **car** go via Haarlem, on N5, A5, and N200, but be ready for long traffic lines in summer.

VISITOR INFORMATION   VVV Zandvoort, Schoolplein 1, 2042 VD Zandvoort (© 023/571-7947; fax 023/571-7003; www.vvvzk.nl), is opposite the bus station in the center of town. The office is open October to March, Monday to Friday from 9:30am to 12:30pm and 1:30 to 5pm, Saturday from 10am to 12:30pm and 1:30 to 3:30pm; April to mid-July and mid-August to September, Monday to Saturday from 9am to 5pm; mid-July to mid-August, Monday to Saturday from 9am to 7pm.

WHAT TO SEE & DO

There's not much more to Zandvoort than its **beach,** but what a beach! In summer, this seemingly endless stretch of smooth sand is lined with dozens of temporary beach cafe-restaurants *(paviljoenen)*. Adjoining the mainstream section of the beach is a naturist stretch, where the shocking sight of a clothed individual can generate considerable moral outrage; and a stretch that has been ceded, more or less, to gays.

Windsurfing is pretty good at Zandvoort, which hosts international competitions in this sport and in catamaran sailing. The Dutch Formula One Grand Prix motor race used to be run at **Circuit Park Zandvoort,** Burg van Alphenstraat 63 (© 023/574-0740), in the north of the town. For now the circuit hosts only smaller events. If you come on a summer weekend, you might find a Formula Three training session or a Porsche meeting underway.

Equally racy, though less noisy, is **Holland Casino Zandvoort,** Badhuisplein 7 (© 023/574-0574; www.hollandcasino.com), in the center behind the seafront promenade. There's roulette, blackjack, punto banco, fruit machines, and more. The dress code is "correct" (collar and tie for men), and the minimum age is 18. You need

---

Tips Hot Jets

How about a jetfoil ride to the seacoast? **Connexxion Fast Flying Ferries** (© 020/639-2247; www.fastflyingferries.nl), runs a scheduled service on the North Sea Canal between Amsterdam and Velsen-Zuid. At the nearby seaport of IJmuiden (connected by frequent bus service), you can view the three great locks of the **North Sea Canal,** and visit the **fish auctions** at Halkade 4, Monday to Friday from 7 to 11am. Jetfoils depart from a dock behind Amsterdam Centraal Station, Monday to Friday every half-hour from 7am to 8pm, and Saturday and Sunday hourly; the trip takes 30 minutes. Fares are 8.30€ ($10) round-trip for adults, and 4.85€ ($6.05) round-trip for children ages 4 to 11; children under 4 ride free.

your passport to get in. The casino is open daily (except May 4 and Dec 31) from 1:30pm to 3am. Admission is 4€ ($5).

Solitude amid surroundings of natural beauty can be found by walking among the 2,500 hectares (6,200 acres) of sand dunes, deciduous and pine forest, grassland, and small lakes in the **Nationaal Park Zuid-Kennemerland** (www.npzk.nl), north of town. Reinforced by native vegetation, the dunes play an important part in the sea defense system and have been designated nature reserves. You can have an active fresh-air experience here, strolling along pathways—once used by fishermen's wives bringing their menfolks' catch from the coast to market—through the woods on the landward side and westward across the dunes toward the sea. A variety of plants, some of them rare, occupies this relatively small area, and you can spot up to 230 species of birds, including rare crossbills and sea eagles. The beach is never far away.

Adjoining the national park is a quiet beach resort called **Bloemendaal aan Zee.** It's only 4km (2½ miles) from Zandvoort, so you can walk there—along the beach or on the diketop promenade. You can also take the bus that departs every half-hour or so from outside Zandvoort rail station. Hot spot **Grand Café-Restaurant Tropen aan Zee,** Zeeweg 80 (© 023/573-1700; www.tropenaanzee.nl), is the place to people-watch, do lunch, sip a sundowner, and loosen up to DJ beats after dark. You can munch on snacks or dine on full meals.

3 The Western IJsselmeer Shore ★★

Some of Holland's most emblematic places—Hoorn, Edam, Marken, Urk, Stavoren—lie along the shores of the great lake called the IJsselmeer. Painterly light washes through clouds and luminous mists that seem to merge water and sky. Cyclists test both speed and endurance against its 400km (250-mile) circumference, zipping round in bright Lycra blurs, or plodding along on the dike-top, immersed in wind, rain, or shine. The IJsselmeer (pronounced *Eye*-sselmeer) has a surface area of around 1,200 sq. km (460 sq. miles), and hosts fleets of traditional *boter* and *skûtsje* sailing ships, fishing smacks, modern sailboats, powerboats, and canoes. Its waters are an important feeding ground for migrating and resident birds.

This section covers the IJsselmeer's western shore, the part that lies in Noord-Holland province. To complete the "Golden Circle" of the great lake, see "The Eastern IJsselmeer Shore," in chapter 15; and "Lelystad & the Noordoostpolder," in chapter 16.

VOLENDAM, MARKEN ★ & MONNICKENDAM
18km (11 miles), 16km (10 miles), and 14km (9 miles) NE of Amsterdam

Volendam and Marken have long been combined on bus-tour itineraries from Amsterdam as a kind of "packaged Holland and costumes to go." Many people would even attach that damning label "tourist trap" to these two lakeside communities. Yes, they're touristy (in particular during summer months), but it's possible to have a delightful day in the bracing air here, where a few residents (fewer all the time) may be seen in traditional dress. Monnickendam is between them.

ESSENTIALS
GETTING THERE   You get to Volendam and Monnickendam by **buses** that depart every 15 to 30 minutes from outside Amsterdam Centraal Station. Lines 110, 112, and 116 stop in Volendam; 111 goes to Marken via Monnickendam; and 115 goes to Monnickendam. Trip time to Volendam is 35 minutes; to Monnickendam 30 minutes; to Marken 45 minutes. The fare is around 4.50€ ($5.65) round-trip.

By the Side of the Zuiderzee

Only in Holland could you say, "This used to be a sea." The IJsselmeer actually was once a sea, until the Dutch decided they didn't want it to be one any longer, since it was always threatening to flood Amsterdam and other towns and villages along its low-lying coastline.

For centuries the Dutch have been protecting themselves from encroaching seas, and snatching more land to accommodate their expanding population. One of their most formidable challenges was the Zuiderzee (Southern Sea), an incursion of the North Sea that washed over Frisian dunes to flood vast inland areas between A.D. 200 and 300. Over the centuries, the Zuiderzee continued to expand, and in the 1200s a series of storms drove its waters far inland.

As early as the 1600s, there was talk of driving back the sea and reclaiming the land it covered. Parliament got around to authorizing the project in 1918, and in the 1920s, work was begun. In 1932, in an unparalleled feat of engineering, the North Sea was sealed off, from Noord-Holland to Friesland, by the 30km (19-mile) Afsluitdijk (Enclosing Dike), and the saltwater Zuiderzee became the freshwater IJsselmeer. Since then, a vast area has been pumped dry, converting fishing villages into farming villages, and joining islands to the mainland.

When **driving** to Marken, which was once an island, you cross a 3km (2-mile) causeway from Monnickendam. You must leave your car in a parking lot outside the main village in Marken before walking through the narrow streets to the harbor. From April to October, the **Marken Express** (© **0299/363-331;** www.markenexpress.nl), a passenger-and-bike ferry, sails every hour or so between Volendam and Marken from 11am to 6pm; the trip takes around 30 minutes, and costs 4€ ($5) for adults, 3.25€ ($4.05) for children under 12.

VISITOR INFORMATION   VVV Volendam is at Zeestraat 37, 1131 AA Volendam (© **0299/363-747;** fax 0299/368-484; www.vvvvolendam.nl), next to the harbor. VVV Monnickendam/Marken is at Nieuwpoortslaan 15, 1141 BT Monnickendam (© **0299/651-998**). Open hours for both offices are Monday to Friday from 9am to 5pm, and Saturday from 9am to 4pm.

WHAT TO SEE & DO

A small, Catholic town on the mainland, **Volendam** lost most of its fishing industry to the enclosure of the Zuiderzee. It is geared now for tourism in a big way and has souvenir stores, boutiques, gift stores, cafes, and restaurants. Lots of people come to town to pig out on the town's near-legendary *gerookte paling* (smoked eel), and to visit such attractions as the **fish auction, diamond cutter, clog maker,** and **house** with a room entirely wallpapered in cigar bands. Still, Volendam's boat-filled harbor, tiny streets, and traditional houses have an undeniable charm. If you must have a snapshot of yourself in the traditional Dutch costume—local women wear white caps with wings—this is a good place to do it.

Volendam's rival, **Marken,** is Protestant and was an island until a narrow causeway connected it to the mainland in 1957. It remains insular. Smaller and less rambunctious than Volendam, it is rural, with clusters of farmhouses dotted around the polders. Half of Marken village, Havenbuurt, consists of green-and-white houses on stilts grouped around a tiny harbor. A **clog maker** works in summer in the village car park. Four old smokehouses in the other half of the village, Kerkbuurt, serve as the **Marker Museum,** Kerkbuurt 44–47 (© 0299/601-904; www.markermuseum.nl), which covers traditional furnishings, costumes, and more. The museum is open April to September, daily from 10am to 5pm; and October daily from 11am to 5pm. Admission is 2.50€ ($3.15) for adults, and 1.25€ ($1.55) for children ages 5 to 12.

For a pleasant stroll (in fine weather) of an hour or two, take the road that leads past Havenbuurt, through the peaceful heart of the former island, to a white-painted **lighthouse** on the IJsselmeer shore. Then, go left along the dike, all the way back to Havenbuurt—where you arrive conveniently right next to the harborfront cafe-restaurant De Taanderij (see below).

Marken does not go gushy for the tourists. It merely feeds and waters them, and allows them to wander its pretty streets gawking at the locals as they go about their daily routines of hanging out laundry, washing windows, and shopping for groceries. Some residents occasionally wear traditional dress—for women, caps with ribbons and black aprons over striped petticoats—but as much to preserve the custom as for the tourists.

In contrast to its two neighbors, **Monnickendam** doesn't pay much attention to tourists at all, but gets on with its own life as a boating center and with what's left of its fishing industry, as you can see in its busy **harbor.** Take a walk through streets lined with gabled houses and make a stop to admire the 15th-century late Gothic **Sint-Nicolaaskerk (St. Nicholas's Church),** at Zarken 2. Be sure to visit the **Stadhuis (Town Hall),** at Noordeinde 5, which began as a private residence in 1746 and has an elaborately decorated ceiling.

Across the street, a 15th-century tower, the **Speeltoren,** Noordeinde 4 (© 0299/652-203; www.despeeltoren.nl), has a carillon that chimes every hour, accompanied by a parade of mechanical knights. The museum is open early April to May and mid-September to mid-October, Saturday and Sunday from 10am to 4pm; and June to mid-September, Tuesday to Sunday from 10am to 4pm. Admission is 1.50€ ($1.90) for adults, and 0.50€ (65¢) for children.

WHERE TO STAY
Hotel Spaander ⭐   This old-fashioned hotel has a real harbor flavor to go with its waterfront location. The public spaces have an Old Dutch interior look, and the

---

⌜Finds⌝ At Home in Waterland

Midway along the road from Amsterdam to Monnickendam, the pretty village of **Broek in Waterland** is worth a stop for its charming green- and gray-painted 17th- and 18th-century timber houses clustered around a church and the little Havenrak lake. In the 18th century, so obsessive were the locals about cleanliness, that they were even to be seen scrubbing the trees. During summer months, visit the Jakob Wiedermeier farmhouse, to watch Edam cheeses being produced. Look, too, for the pagoda-style Napoléonhuisje from 1656, a lakeside pavilion named for a visit by Napoleon in 1811.

(*Moments*   **Perchance to Dream**

To overnight in style in Volendam and Monnickendam, ask at the VVV offices about sleeping aboard one of the old wooden IJsselmeer *boters* and *skûtsjes* (sailing ships) in the harbor (this option is not available in Marken). It makes for a romantic, if somewhat cramped, way to spend the night.

paintings on the walls were accepted in times past as payment by visiting artists—but I wouldn't try that today. The rooms are modern, brightly furnished, and comfortable. Around 30 recently upgraded rooms have minibars and dataports. Two dining rooms, an old-style inn and an elegant sun lounge, serve local IJsselmeer and other Dutch specialties, and the outside terrace cafe is great in good weather.

Haven 15–19 (north end of the harbor), 1131 EP Volendam. (C) **0299/363-595.** Fax 0299/369-615. www.spaander.com. 80 units. 75€–120€ ($94–$150) double. Rates include continental breakfast. AE, DC, MC, V. **Amenities:** Restaurant (Dutch); bar; heated indoor pool; fitness center. *In room:* TV, hair dryer.

WHERE TO DINE

De Taanderij ⚸ DUTCH/FRENCH   For lunch, try this little *eethuis* at the end of the harbor. Seafood dishes are served. Especially good for snacks are the traditional Dutch treats—*koffie en appelgebak met slagroom* (coffee with apple pie and cream) and *poffertjes* (small fried pancake "puffs" coated with confectioners' sugar and filled with syrup or liqueur). The inside is an elegant and cozy interpretation of Old Marken style. When the weather is good, a terrace will be spread at the harborside, where you can absorb the sunshine, the tranquil view over the IJsselmeer and, of course, the luscious goodies on the menu.

Havenbuurt 1, Marken. (C) **0299/602-206.** Main courses 15€–19€ ($19–$24); snacks 4€–13€ ($5–$16). AE, MC, V. Apr–Sept Tues–Sun 11am–10pm; Oct–Mar Tues–Sun 11am–7pm.

EDAM ⚸

18km (11 miles) NE of Amsterdam; 2km (1 mile) N of Volendam

Just inland from the IJsselmeer, Edam (pronounced *Ay*-dam) has given its name to one of Holland's most famous cheeses. Don't expect to find it in the familiar red skin, however—that's for export. In Holland, the cheese's skin is yellow. This pretty little town (pop. 7,000), a whaling port during Holland's Golden Age in the 17th century, is centered around canals you cross by way of drawbridges, with views on either side of canal houses, gardens, and canal-side teahouses.

ESSENTIALS

GETTING THERE Bus nos. 114 and 116 depart every half-hour or so from outside Amsterdam Centraal Station. By **car** from Amsterdam, drive via Monnickendam and Volendam.

VISITOR INFORMATION VVV Edam is at the Stadhuis (Town Hall), Damplein 1, 1135 BK Edam ((C) **0299/315-125;** fax 0299/374-236; www.vvv-edam.nl), in the center city. Should you wish to tour a local Edammer cheese factory, this is where you get the details. The office is open May to October, Monday to Saturday from 10am to 5pm; November to April, Monday to Saturday from 10am to 3pm.

WHAT TO SEE & DO

If you've arrived here after mingling with the floods of tourists in Volendam, Monnickendam, and Marken, Edam will make a pleasant change of pace. Except during the Wednesday cheese market, it's not a huge draw for tourists. You get to explore a pretty canal-side town with some handsome old buildings without this distraction, and Edam is well worth a few hours of strolling.

This was once a port of some prominence, and a visit to the **Edams Museum,** Damplein 8 (© **0299/372-644;** www.edamsmuseum.nl), opposite the Town Hall (and with a section in the Town Hall), gives you a peek not only at its history but also at some of its most illustrious citizens of past centuries. Look for the portrait of Pieter Dirkszoon, a one-time mayor and proud possessor of what is probably the longest beard on record anywhere. An intriguing feature of this merchant's house from around 1530 is the cellar, which is actually a box floating on water, constructed that way so changing water levels wouldn't upset the foundations of the house. The museum is open April to October, Tuesday to Saturday from 10am to 4:30pm, and Sunday from 1 to 4:30pm. Admission is 3€ ($3.75) for adults, 1.50€ ($1.90) for seniors, and 1€ ($1.25) for children ages 5 to 17.

Take a look at the lovely "wedding room" in the **Stadhuis (Town Hall).** The **Speeltoren (Carillon Tower)** from 1561 tilts a bit and was very nearly lost when the church to which it belonged was destroyed.

The Cheese Market

Edam wouldn't really be Edam without a *kaasmarkt* (cheese market)—and the cheese in question is Edammer, naturally. The market takes place each Wednesday in July and August, from 10:30am to 12:30pm, in Kaasmarkt, outside the gaily decorated **Kaaswaag (Cheese Weigh House)** from 1592, which features a cheese-making display during these months.

WHERE TO STAY & DINE

Hotel-Restaurant De Fortuna   Most of the modern, comfortable rooms in this hotel look out on a quiet garden and the canal in back. Weather permitting, you can lounge on the canal-side terrace. The step-gabled main house, where you eat breakfast, features country-style furnishings and exposed beams. The on-site restaurant serves specialties of game and fish; its three-course dinner menu is 33€ ($41).

Spuistraat 3, 1135 AV, Edam. © 0299/371-671. Fax 0299/371-469. www.fortuna-edam.nl. 23 units. 90€–108€ ($113–$135) double. AE, DC, MC, V. **Amenities:** Restaurant (Dutch); bar; lounge. *In room:* TV, minibar, hair dryer.

HOORN ✶✶

32km (20 miles) NE of Amsterdam; 17km (11 miles) N of Edam

Hoorn (pronounced *Hoarn*) is one of the legendary names in Dutch maritime history. Even now, with the open sea no longer on its doorstep, it remains orientated toward the water and is a busy IJsselmeer sailing center. While touring the graceful streets of the Golden Age town, in particular those around the central square, the Rode Steen, be sure to visit the old harbor, the Binnenhaven. Hoorn (pop. 62,000) was the hometown of Willem Cornelisz Schouten, who in 1616 rounded South America's southernmost tip, which he promptly dubbed Kap Hoorn (Cape Horn) in the town's honor.

ESSENTIALS

GETTING THERE   Trains depart at least every hour from Amsterdam Centraal Station to Hoorn; trip time is 40 minutes, and a round-trip ticket is 13€ ($16). **Buses**

depart every hour or so from outside Centraal Station, but they take longer than the train. By **car** from Amsterdam, take E22/A7 north.

VISITOR INFORMATION   **VVV Hoorn** is at Veemarkt 4, 1621 JC Hoorn (✆ **072/ 511-4284;** fax 0229/215-023; www.vvvhoorn.nl), between the rail station and the center of town. The office is open May to August Monday from 1 to 6pm, Tuesday to Wednesday and Friday from 9:30am to 6pm, Thursday from 9:30am to 9pm, and Saturday from 9:30am to 5pm; and September to April, Monday from 1 to 5pm, and Tuesday to Saturday from 9:30am to 5pm.

WHAT TO SEE & DO

The **Westfries Museum,** Rode Steen 1 (✆ **0229/280-022;** www.wfm.nl), in a building from 1632, contains a wide-ranging historical collection that includes armor, weapons, paper cuttings, costumes, toys, naive paintings (these embody a style that is deliberately "childlike"), coins, medals, jewels, civic guards' paintings, and porcelain. A second-floor exhibit details the town's maritime history, with an emphasis on ships and voyages of the United East India Company (V.O.C.). There are tapestries and 17th- and 18th-century period rooms. A collection of Bronze Age relics is exhibited in the basement. The museum is open Monday to Friday from 11am to 5pm, Saturday and Sunday from 2 to 5pm; closed January 1, April 30, the third Monday in August, and December 25. Admission is 3.50€ ($4.40) for adults, and 1.50€ ($1.90) for seniors and children ages 5 to 16.

Every Wednesday in July, an interesting **craft market** is held in the marketplace.

During summer months, an antique steam tram, the **Museumstoomtram Hoorn- Medemblik** (✆ **0229/214-862;** www.museumstoomtram.nl), transports visitors through the pretty West Friesland farm country between Hoorn and Medemblik (see below), a 1-hour trip. It departs from a station at Van Dedemstraat 8 in Hoorn. Tickets are 17€ ($21) round-trip for adults, 13€ ($16) for children ages 4 to 11, and free for children under 4.

WHERE TO DINE

De Hoofdtoren ✦ DUTCH   Boat-lovers will want to sit on the terrace of this cafe-restaurant in an old defense tower, in the midst of the busy harbor, surrounded by traditional IJsselmeer sailing ships and by pleasure boats large and small. The tower, which dates from about 1500, protected the harbor entrance, and its interior retains many antique features. Traditional Dutch fare and grilled specialties, both meat and fish, are served at dinner. During the day, you can order lunch or snacks.

Hoofd 2. ✆ **0229/270-344.** www.hoofdtoren.nl. Main courses 11€–27€ ($14–$34). AE, DC, MC, V. Daily 10am–10pm.

De Waag ✦ FRENCH   This grand cafe in the monumental Weigh House from 1609 is open for breakfast, lunch, and dinner. It stands on a square that is among the finest in the country, surrounded by 17th-century buildings from the town's heyday. You can still see the antique weighing scales in the wood-beamed interior.

Rode Steen 8. ✆ **0229/215-195.** www.dewaaghoorn.nl. Main courses 13€–23€ ($16–$29). MC, V. Daily 10am–1am.

ENKHUIZEN ✦

44km (27 miles) NE of Amsterdam; 15km (9 miles) NE of Hoorn

A 400-boat herring fleet once sailed out of Enkhuizen, and so important was this fish to the town's prosperity that images of three herring grace its coat of arms. Then in 1932 came the Enclosing Dike (see below), closing off the North Sea. Enkhuizen's population has declined from 30,000 in its 17th-century heyday to 16,000 today, and the town looks to pleasure boating, tourism, and bulb-growing for its livelihood. It does pretty well in all three respects, and boasts one of the country's most fascinating open-air museums, a must-see sight on any itinerary that passes this way.

ESSENTIALS

GETTING THERE   Trains depart hourly from Amsterdam Centraal Station for **Enkhuizen station,** Stationsplein 2 (© **0228/321-002**), beside the harbor; trip time is 1 hour, and a round-trip ticket is 17€ ($21). **Buses** depart every half-hour or so from outside Hoorn rail station. By **car** from Amsterdam, drive to Hoorn, and then take N302 northeast.

VISITOR INFORMATION   VVV Enkhuizen is at Tussen Twee Havens 1, 1601 EM Enkhuizen (© **0228/313-164;** fax 0228/315-531; www.vvvenkhuizen.nl), at the harbor. The office is open April to October, daily from 9am to 5pm.

WHAT TO SEE & DO

The town is orientated toward its harbors, Oosterhaven, Oudehaven, Buitenhaven, and Spoorhaven, protected by the 16th-century **Drommedaris** defense tower, which now houses a restaurant. Behind the waterfront, the handsome old center is worth a leisurely stroll along Westerstraat between the 15th- to 16th-century **Westerkerk,** also known as the **Sint-Gomaruskerk,** and the 17th-century **Stadhuis (Town Hall).** You can do a pleasant walk along the moated 16th- to 17th-century defense walls on the west side of town, along Vest.

Enkhuizen is connected by road across the IJsselmeer, 31km (19 miles) atop the Markerwaarddijk to Lelystad (see "Lelystad & the Noordoostpolder," in chapter 16). This dike originally was built to enclose a vast drainage project, the Markerwaard Polder, in the southwestern reaches of the lake, but the plan was canceled for financial and environmental reasons, and the Markermeer is still open water. In summer months, you can go by passenger boat from Enkhuizen's Veerhaven up the coast to Medemblik (see below), or across the IJsselmeer to Stavoren (see "The Eastern IJsselmeer Shore," in chapter 15) and Urk (see "Lelystad & the Noordoostpolder," in chapter 16).

An Outstanding Museum of Tradition

Zuiderzeemuseum ★★★ *Kids*   Take a step back in time at this remarkable museum, and come face to face with bygone ways of life in the fishing ports around the old Zuiderzee from 1880 until the sea was transformed into the freshwater IJsselmeer in 1932. It's in two sections, the Binnenmuseum (Indoor Museum) and the Buitenmuseum (Outdoor, or Open-Air Museum), and you'll need to set aside a half-day at least to get the most out of them. Information desks, restrooms, souvenir stores, and restaurants are on-site.

You go by boat from a dock in Veerhaven beside Enkhuizen rail station, or from another dock beside the dike road from Enkhuizen to Lelystad, for the short trip across to the **Open-Air Museum.** This stands on the IJsselmeer shore at the northeast edge of town and can be accessed only by way of these boats. It contains 130 complete old buildings, including farmhouses, public buildings, stores, and a church, all furnished in period style and some of them with beautifully tiled interiors. These buildings have been shipped intact from lakeside villages or rebuilt on-site and combined to form a cobblestone-street village. The boat docks beside a pair of bottle-shaped limekilns, which employed seashells as the raw material for making quicklime.

Then, you set off by foot to explore the scene, beginning with transplanted houses from the village of Zoutkamp.

To the north, a working windmill twirls its sails atop the dike. Nearby is a functioning smokehouse, where workers preserve herring by smoking them over smoldering wood chips before packing them in barrels. The village church hails from the former island of Wieringen, which now lies inland surrounded by polders northwest of Enkhuizen. In the sail maker's store, you can watch sails being made that later will fill with wind aboard traditional Zuiderzee *boter* and *skûtsje* sailing ships. In a group of houses from Urk on the IJsselmeer's eastern shore, daily scenes from around 1905 are reenacted. Don't miss the apothecary and its ornamental "gapers"—painted heads with open mouths—in the window. Among other buildings, all of them functioning concerns, are a grocery store, a cheese warehouse, a post office, a bakery, a painter's store, and a steam laundry.

Between the Open-Air Museum and the Indoor Museum is a recreation of the harbor at Marken, with smokehouses for preserving herring and eels standing on the dike, and fishing boats tied up at the dock. From here, you can walk a short way to the **Indoor Museum,** housed in the Peperhuis (Pepper House), a Dutch Renaissance building from 1625 that was used as offices and a warehouse by the Enkhuizen Chamber of the United East India Company (V.O.C.). In a former warehouse, you'll see numerous examples of the old fishing boats that provided the incomes on which Zuiderzee villagers largely depended, and old sailboats (including one that the kids can play on). Other rooms have been fitted out in the varied styles of houses from villages around the Zuiderzee and from other parts of Holland.

Wierdijk 12–22. ℂ 0228/351-111. www.zuiderzeemuseum.nl. Admission: mid-Apr to Oct 12€ ($14) adults, 7€ ($8.75) children 4–12, free for children under 4; Nov–Mar 7€ ($8.75) adults, 6.50€ ($8.15) children 4–12, free for children under 4. Outdoor Museum: mid-Apr to Oct daily 10am–5pm; Indoor Museum: daily 10am–5pm. Closed Jan 1, Dec 25.

MEDEMBLIK

46km (29 miles) NE of Amsterdam; 14km (9 miles) NW of Enkhuizen

A small IJsselmeer town with busy twin harbors that already was a going concern by the year 700, Medemblik later joined the powerful Hanseatic League trading federation.

There are two fun ways to reach Medemblik in summer. One is onboard the 1956 passenger-and-bike ferry *Friesland* from Enkhuizen (see above). Another is by antique steam tram from Hoorn (see above). Tram tickets are 8.35€ ($10) round-trip for adults, 6.35€ ($7.95) for children ages 4 to 11, and free for children under 4. Tourist information is available from **VVV Medemblik,** Kaasmarkt 1, 1671 BH Medemblik (ℂ **072/511-4284;** fax 072/511-7513; www.vvvmedemblik.nl).

Adjacent to Medemblik's Oosterhaven (East Harbor)—its twin is called the Westerhaven (West Harbor)—is the moated **Kasteel Radboud,** Oudevaartsgat 8 (ℂ **0227/ 541-960;** www.kasteelradboud.nl), an originally 8th-century castle refortified by the count of Holland in 1289 against a possible rebellion by the troublesome Frisians. The remaining section has been restored to its 13th-century state and is well worth a visit. The castle is open May to mid-September, Wednesday to Monday from 11am to 5pm, and Sunday from 2 to 5pm; and mid-September to April, Sunday from 2 to 5pm (during school vacations as for summer open hours). Admission is 4€ ($5) for adults, 2€ ($2.50) for seniors and children ages 5 to 13, and free for children under 5.

AFSLUITDIJK (ENCLOSING DIKE) 🔾

62km (38 miles) N of Amsterdam; 19km (12 miles) N of Medemblik

It's hard to grasp what a monumental work the great barrier that separates the salty Waddenzee from the freshwater IJsselmeer is until you drive its 30km (19-mile) length. The Afsluitdijk connects the provinces of Noord-Holland and Friesland. Dr. Cornelis Lely came up with the plans in 1891, but construction was delayed for 25 years while he tried to convince the government to allocate funding.

Massive effort went into building the dike, which is 100m (330 ft.) wide and stands 7m (23 ft.) above mean water level. Many communities around the shores of what used to be the saltwater Zuiderzee lost their livelihood when access to the open sea was shut off. Some of the fishing boats that now sail the IJsselmeer hoist dark-brown sails as a sign of mourning for their lost sea fishing.

Midway along the dike's length, at the point where it was completed in 1932, stands a **monument** to the men who put their backs to the task, and a memorial to Dr. Lely. You can stop for a snack at the cafe in the monument's base and pick up an illustrated booklet that explains the dike's construction. For those crossing over by bicycle or by foot, there's a bike path and a pedestrian path.

4 The Zaanstreek

Also known as Zaanstad, this district occupies both banks of the Zaan River north of Amsterdam. The industrial towns of the Zaanstreek are not greatly worth visiting in their own right, but they contain a number of embedded pearls that are worth seeking out. Timber was the foundation of wealth along the Zaan in the 16th and 17th centuries. A burgeoning Dutch merchant marine and navy needed the wood, and the invention of a wind-powered sawmill here in 1592 provided the power. The timber was used to build the Zaanstreek's distinctive green-painted houses.

ZAANSE SCHANS 🔾🔾

16km (10 miles) NW of Amsterdam

On the northern edge of the Zaanstreek, on the east bank of the Zaan River, this living-history experience is a replica 17th- to 18th-century village made up of houses, windmills, and workshops that were moved to the site when industrialization leveled their original locations. The aim is to re-create the way of life along the Zaan in the 17th century. Pictures of the windmills and the green-painted houses grace many a Holland brochure. Most of the buildings on the 8-hectare (20-acre) site are inhabited by people who can afford and appreciate their antique timbers, and who have the patience for the summertime crowds that pour from fleets of tour buses.

ESSENTIALS

GETTING THERE   Trains depart every 20 minutes from Amsterdam Centraal Station via Zaandam to Koog-Zaandijk station, from where Zaanse Schans is around 1km (½ mile) distant; you can take bus no. 88 from outside the station. By **car** from Amsterdam, take A8 north and then switch to A7/E22 north to Exit 2, from where you follow the signs to Zaanse Schans.

VISITOR INFORMATION   VVV Zaanstreek/Waterland is at Gedempte Gracht 76, 1506 CJ Zaandam (© **075/616-2221;** fax 075/670-5381; www.zaanstreekwaterland.nl), between Zaandam rail station and the center of town. The office is open Monday to Friday from 9am to 5:30pm and Saturday from 9am to 4pm.

Get Your Clogs On

Clogs are still a fixture in many farming areas, where they're much more effective against wetness and cold than leather shoes or boots. They are, too, a tourist staple, and if you plan to buy a pair, **Zaanse Schans** is a good place to do it. Traditionally, those with pointed toes are for women and rounded toes are for men. All must be worn with heavy socks, so when buying, add the width of one finger when measuring for size.

WHAT TO SEE & DO

From the **Zaanse Schans Visitor Center,** Schansend 7 (✆ **075/616-8218;** www. zaanseschans.nl), inside the Zaans Museum, pick up a brochure that features an artist's-impression bird's-eye view of the entire site, with each important location identified. This makes self-guided exploration a snap. The district's fascinating history is told in the **Zaans Museum** (✆ **075/616-2862;** www.zaansmuseum.nl), which is open daily from 9am to 5pm (closed Jan 1 and Dec 25). Admission is 4.50€ ($5.65) for adults, 2.70€ ($3.40) for seniors, and free for children under 18.

You then enter the village, which is crisscrossed by canals and paths that cross over the water on bridges. To the pleasure of walking, you can add a visit to one or more of the five working industrial windmills here, lined up along the Zaan shore. From south to north from the boat dock, these are **Mosterdmolen De Huisman,** where the renowned Zaanse mustard is produced; a sawmill, **Houtzaagmolen De Gekroonde Poelenburg; Werfmolen De Kat,** which specialized in producing paint; and two mills that produce vegetable oil, **Oliemolen De Zoeker** and **Oliemolen De Bonte Hen.** By the end of the 17th century, the Zaanstreek sported more than 500 windmills spinning their sails in the breeze and providing plenty of free power. An even dozen have survived intact, including these five, and a short tour of one shows you just how these wind machines worked.

Visit, too, **Museumwinkel Albert Heijn,** Kalverringdijk 5, a working reconstruction, with old-style candies and other items for sale, of an Oostzaan store from 1887 that was the beginning of Holland's largest supermarket chain. If you are at all interested in cookies and candy and in old recipes for the same, step inside the **Bakkerijmuseum (Bakery Museum),** Zeilenmakerspad 4, in an old house called De Gecroonde Duykevater. And to get an idea of how a well-heeled Zaan resident lived, visit **Museum Het Noorderhuis,** Kalverringdijk 17, a merchant's house from 1670 containing furnishings, utensils, and costumes that date from a period 2 centuries later.

Even if you are in a hurry, you should make time for the **Nederlandse Uurwerk (Dutch Clock) Museum,** Kalverringdijk 3, which displays timepieces from the period 1500 to 1900, and a workshop. Then there's the **Klompenmakerij (Clog Maker's Workshop),** a workshop where wooden *klompen* (clogs) are made and sold; and **De Catherina Hoeve Kaasmakerij,** which does likewise with cheese.

Most of these mini-museums and other attractions are open March to October, daily from 10am to 5 or 6pm; and November to February, Saturday and Sunday from around 11am to 4pm. Open hours for other sites are more restricted. Admission (sometimes free) varies from to 1€ to 2.50€ ($1.25–$3.15) for adults, 0.50€ to 1€ (65¢–$1.25) for children ages 5 to 12, and free for children under 5.

For a view from a different perspective, take a 1-hour **cruise** on the Zaan River aboard a tour boat of **Rederij De Schans** (✆ **075/614-6762;** www.rederijdeschans.nl). Boats depart from a dock on the Zaan River next to the De Huisman windmill, April to September, hourly from 10am to 4pm. Cruises are 5€ ($6.25) for adults, 4€ ($5) for seniors, 2.50€ ($3.15) for children ages 3 to 12, and free for children under 3.

De Hoop op d'Swarte Walvis ✾ FRENCH   A stellar restaurant with a mouthful of a name, the "Hope for the Black Whale" stands amid the green-painted houses of Zaanse Schans, with a glass pavilion and an outdoor terrace overlooking the Zaan River and the waterside villas on the far bank. You can expect an unforgettable treat, with subtle mixtures of superior ingredients cooked and prepared to perfection. The restaurant is owned by the same company as Holland's biggest supermarket chain, Albert Heijn.

Kalverringdijk 15, Zaanse Schans. ⓒ 075/616-5629. www.dewalvis.nl. Main courses 14€–27€ ($18–$21); lunch menu 45€ ($56); dinner menu 60€–70€ ($74–$87). AE, DC, MC, V. Mon–Fri noon–2:30pm and 6–10pm; Sat 6–10pm.

NEARBY PLACES OF INTEREST
Across the river from the Zaanse Schans, in **Zaandijk,** riverside Lagedijk is a well-preserved example of an old-style Zaanstreek street. At its northern end, in a merchant's house from 1706 furnished in the old Zaan style, is the **Zaans Historisch Museum,** Lagedijk 80 (ⓒ **075/621-7626**). Paintings, furnishings, religious items, traditional costumes, Chinese porcelain, and more afford an idea about life in the Zaan district around this period. The museum is open Tuesday to Friday from 10am to noon and 1 to 5pm, and Saturday and Sunday from 1 to 5pm.

Adjoining Koog aan de Zaan to the south, **Zaandam,** the main town of the Zaanstreek, was an important shipbuilding center in the 17th century. In 1697, Czar Peter the Great of Russia worked incognito as "Peter Mikhailov" for a few days at a Zaandam shipyard, studying the shipbuilding methods of Dutch craftsmen, whom that

Windmill Ways

Picture Holland in your mind. Now try to picture it without windmills. See? It's almost impossible. The Netherlands isn't the only country to harness passing wind in this way, but it seems to have secured exclusive worldwide rights to the image. Tulips, clogs, and cheese all have their places in Dutch mythology, but without windmills much of this low-lying country would not even exist.

Windmills first appeared in the 13th century, transforming the rotation of their sails into mechanical energy via a system of cogs and gears. They were employed to grind wheat, barley, and oats; crush seeds to create mustard and vegetable oil; hull rice and peppercorns; and power sawmills and other industrial machinery. Most important of all, windmills kept the fertile polder land dry by pumping away surplus water and draining it into the rivers by way of a network of stepped canals.

Of the many thousands that once stood in towns and villages, and in rows on the dikes, fewer than a thousand working examples survive today. The two most famous multiple-windmill scenes in the country are the industrial windmills at Zaanse Schans (see above) and the polder-drainage windmills at Kinderdijk (see "Windmills of Kinderdijk," in chapter 14).

avid nautical student considered the world's finest. He stayed at the humble timber home of a local blacksmith, Gerrit Kist. The **Czaar Peterhuisje,** Krimp 23–24 (✆ **075/ 616-0390**), is the oldest surviving house of the Zaan district. In 1895, Czar Nicholas II had it enclosed inside a brick shelter. It contains souvenirs of Peter's stay, including an exhibit on his life, the small bed into which the Czar of All the Russias squeezed his 2.1m (7-ft.) frame, and displays recounting the history of the district and of shipbuilding on the Zaan. Peter visited Zaandam again in 1698 and twice in 1717, each time paying Kist a visit. The house is open Tuesday to Friday from 10am to 1pm and 2 to 5:30pm, and Saturday and Sunday from 1 to 5pm. Admission is 2€ ($2.50) for adults, and 1€ ($1.25) for children under 13. A **statue** of Peter at work on a ship stands on Damplein, the town's main square.

5 Tulips & Cheese

After windmills come tulips and the cheeses of Edam and Gouda, as standard-bearers of Dutch national pride. The places to see tulips in their full glory are in the extensive bulb fields of the **Bollenstreek** and at **Keukenhof,** where vast numbers of tulips and other flowers create a dazzling tapestry of color. (Keukenhof is actually just across the province line in neighboring Zuid-Holland, so strictly speaking it belongs in chapter 14.) Edam (see "The Western IJsselmeer Shore," earlier in this chapter) and Gouda (see chapter 14) have more than cheese-making to occupy their time, but the town of Alkmaar is a pretty good stand-in, for the sheer and unabashed hokum of its weekly cheese market.

Keukenhof 𝕶𝕶   Flowers at their peak and these gardens both have short seasons, but if you're here in the spring, you'll never forget a visit to this park. A meandering, 32-hectare (70-acre) wooded green in the heart of the bulb-producing region is planted each fall by the major Dutch growers (each plants his own plot or establishes his own greenhouse display). Then, come spring, the bulbs burst forth and produce not hundreds of flowers, or even thousands, but millions (almost eight million at last count) of tulips and narcissi, daffodils and hyacinths, bluebells, crocuses, lilies, amaryllis, and many others. The blaze of color is everywhere in the park and in the greenhouses, beside the brooks and shady ponds, along the paths and in the neighboring fields, in neat little plots and helter-skelter on the lawns. Keukenhof claims to be the greatest flower show on earth—and it's Holland's annual spring gift to the world. *Tip:* There are four cafes on-site where you can grab a quick bite to eat.

Stationsweg 166A, Lisse. ✆ **0252/465-555**. www.keukenhof.nl. Admission 17€ ($21) adults, 15€ ($18) seniors, 9€ ($11) children 4–11, free for children under 4. Late Mar to late May daily 8am–7:30pm. Special train/bus connections via Haarlem and Leiden.

BULB FIELDS

The heaviest concentration of bulb fields is in the **Bolenstreek (Bulb District)** 𝕶, a strip of land 16km (10 miles) long and 6km (4 miles) wide, between Haarlem and Leiden. In the spring, it's a kind of a Dutch rite of passage to take a traipse through this colorful district and view the massed, varicolored regiments of tulips on parade. Each year from around the end of January to late May, the fields are covered at various times with tulips, crocuses, daffodils, narcissi, hyacinths, lilies, and more.

Viewing the flowers is easy. Just follow the signposted **Bollenstreek Route** (60km/37 miles) by car or bike. Stalls along the roads sell flower garlands—do as the natives do and buy one for yourself and another for the car. VVV tourist information

---

Fun Fact **Flower Power**

During Holland's 17th-century "Tulip Mania," when trading in bulbs was a lucrative business and prices soared to ridiculous heights, a single tulip bulb could be worth as much as a prestigious Amsterdam canal house, with garden and coach house thrown in.

---

offices in the area can provide detailed information about the route. To get to the bulb fields from Amsterdam, you can drive first to Haarlem; then south on N206 through De Zilk and Noordwijkerhout, or on N208 through Hillegom, Lisse, and Sassenheim. Alternatively, go south from Amsterdam on A4/E19, past Schiphol Airport, to Exit 4 (Nieuw-Vennep), and then northwest on N207 for 8km (5 miles) until you hit N208.

Other bulb-growing centers are scattered around Noord-Holland, with an important concentration in the Hoorn-Medemblik area. If you are interested in the original plants, **Hortus Bulborum,** Zuidkerkenlaan 23A, Limmen (© 0251/231-286; www.hortus-bulborum.nl), a specialized tulip garden 30km (18 miles) northwest of Amsterdam, has re-created some of the older varieties. Here you can see the flowers that are so prominent in the floral still-lifes painted by 17th-century artists, fancifully shaded in flaming patterns and with names like Semper Augustus and Bruin Anvers. The garden is open early April to mid-May, Monday to Saturday from 10am to 5pm and Sunday from noon to 5pm. Admission is 2.50€ ($3.15) for adults, 1.75€ ($2.20) for seniors, and free for children under 12.

A GARGANTUAN FLOWER AUCTION

Selling flowers and plants nets 1.5€ billion ($1.88 billion) a year at the **Bloemenveiling (Flower Auction)** ☆, Legmeerdijk 313 (© 0297/392-185; www.vba.nl), in the lakeside community of Aalsmeer, 18km (11 miles) southwest of Amsterdam, close to Schiphol Airport. Every day, the auction sells 19 million cut flowers and two million plants, in 12,000 varieties, from 7,000 nurseries, representing 30% of the trade worldwide. So vast is the auction "house" that 120 soccer fields would fit inside.

Get here early to see the biggest array of flowers in the distribution rooms and to have as much time as possible to watch the computerized auctioning process. The bidding on flowers goes from high to low. Mammoth bidding clocks are numbered from 100 to 1. As many as 1,500 buyers sit in rows in the five auditorium-style auction halls; they have microphones to ask questions and buttons to push to register their bids in the computer. As bunches of tulips, daffodils, whatever, go by the stand on carts, they are auctioned in a matter of seconds. The first bid, which is the first one to stop the clock as it works down from 100 to 1, is the only bid.

The auction is open Monday to Friday from 7:30 to 11am. Admission is 5€ ($6.25) for adults, 2.50€ ($3.15) for children ages 6 to 11, and free for children under 6. Connexxion bus no. 172 goes there from outside Amsterdam Centraal Station. By car, take A4/E19 south to the Hoofddorp junction, and then go southeast on N201.

ALKMAAR

30km (19 miles) N of Amsterdam

GETTING THERE   **Trains** depart at least every hour from Amsterdam Centraal Station to Alkmaar; the trip takes around 30 minutes by fast train, and a round-trip ticket is 12€ ($15). By **car** from Amsterdam, take A8, N246, N203, and A9 north.

VISITOR INFORMATION **VVV Alkmaar** is at Waagplein 2, 1811 JP Alkmaar (© **072/511-4284;** fax 072/511-7513; www.vvvalkmaar.nl), in the center city. The office is open Monday from 10am to 5:30pm, Tuesday and Wednesday from 9am to 5:30pm, Thursday from 9am to 9pm, Friday from 9am to 6pm, and Saturday from 9:30am to 5pm.

WHAT TO SEE & DO

At the Friday morning **Kaasmarkt (Cheese Market)** ☞ in Waagplein, yellow-skinned Edam, Gouda, and Leidse (Leiden) cheeses are piled high on the cobblestone square. The carillon in the 16th-century **Waaggebouw (Weigh House)** tower hourly showers the streets with tinkling Dutch folk music, accompanying a jousting performance of attached mechanical knights. The square is filled with sightseers, barrel organs, souvenir stalls, and a tangible excitement. White-clad *kaasdragers* (cheese porters) dart around, wearing colored lacquered straw hats in red, blue, yellow, or green as a sign of which of four sections of their more than 400-year-old guild they belong to. Porters, who are not permitted to smoke, drink, or curse while on duty, are so proud of their standards that every week they post on a "shame board" the name of any carrier who has indulged in profanity or has been late arriving at the auction.

> **Impressions**
>
> *Aalsmeer is an auction house in the sense that Shanghai is a city or Everest a mountain.*
>
> *—National Geographic (Apr 2001)*

The bidding process is carried on in the traditional Dutch manner of hand clapping to bid the price up or down, and a good solid hand clap to seal the deal. Then, once a buyer has accumulated his lot of cheeses, teams of porters move in with their shiny, shallow barrows and, using slings that hang from their shoulders, carry the golden wheels and balls of cheese to the scales in the Weigh House for the final tally of the bill. The market is held from the first Friday of April to the first Friday of September, from 10am to 12:30pm; art and craft markets piggyback on the cheese market but run longer.

The history of Dutch cheese and how the various cheeses are produced is the theme of the **Hollands Kaasmuseum,** in the Waaggebouw, Waagplein 2 (© **072/511-4284**). It's open April to October, Monday to Thursday and Saturday from 10am to 4pm, and Friday from 9am to 4pm; Christmas and New Year holidays from 10am to 4pm; and Easter, Pentecost, and Ascension Day holidays from 10:30am to 1:30pm. Admission is 2.50€ ($3.15) for adults, 1.50€ ($1.90) for children ages 4 to 12, and free for children under 4.

6 Den Helder & Texel

These two places are connected like sea-going Siamese twins. Den Helder, a harbor town on the tip of the Noord-Holland peninsula, with the North Sea on one side and the Wadden Sea on the other, is the gateway to the vacation island of Texel.

DEN HELDER

67km (42 miles) N of Amsterdam; 31km (19 miles) NW of Medemblik

Den Helder holds the country's most important navy base. It still is home to its Royal Naval College (the Dutch Annapolis), and host of the annual Navy Days, the national fleet festival, in July. It's a reasonably endowed resort in its own right, with plenty of adjacent beach space, and takes delivery of more hours of sunshine annually than any other place in the country.

ESSENTIALS

GETTING THERE   **Trains** depart at least every hour from Amsterdam Centraal Station for Den Helder; the trip takes around 65 minutes, and a round-trip ticket is 22€ ($27). By **car** from Amsterdam, take A8, A9, and N9 north.

VISITOR INFORMATION   **VVV Den Helder,** Bernhardplein 18, 1781 HH Den Helder (© 0223/625-544; fax 0223/614-888; www.vvvkopvannoordholland.nl), is next to the rail station. The office is open Monday from 1 to 6pm; Tuesday to Friday from 9:30am to 6pm; and Saturday from 9:30am to 5pm.

WHAT TO SEE & DO

Marinemuseum (Navy Museum) ⭐   For an insight into the Royal Netherlands Navy's illustrious past, by way of models, marine paintings, weapons and equipment, and some real live warships, visit this extensive facility just 200m (656 ft.) west of the Texel ferry dock. Among several retired combatants on display is the steam-and-sail ram *De Schorpioen,* built in France for the Dutch navy in 1868. Now tied to a dock, the *"Scorpion"* was once a vessel with a sting in its bow, where a below-the-water-line ram could deal fatal blows to enemy ships—not that it ever did. The steam engine still works, and you can visit the captain's cabin and crew's quarters. Equally fascinating is the dry-landed coastal attack submarine *Tonijn (Tunny),* which has a torpedo emerging from its front tube and which you can board to experience the claustrophobic quarters of a submariner's world.

Hoofdgracht 3. © 0223/657-534. www.marinemuseum.nl. Admission 4.50€ ($5.65) adults, 4€ ($5) seniors, 3.50€ ($4.40) children 5–15, free for children under 5. May–Oct Mon–Fri 10am–5pm, Sat–Sun and holidays noon–5pm; Nov–Apr Tues–Fri 10am–5pm, Sat–Sun and holidays noon–5pm. Closed Jan 1, Dec 25.

Other Attractions

While you're in navy mode, visit the **Nationaal Reddingmuseum Dorus Rijkers (Dorus Rijkers National Lifeboat Museum),** Oude Rijkswerf, Willemsoord 60G (© 0223/618-320; www.reddingmuseum.nl), which chronicles the history of the service. The museum is open April to October, daily from 10am to 5pm; and November to March, Tuesday to Sunday from 10am to 5pm (open Mon during school vacations; closed Jan 1 and Dec 25). Admission is 5€ ($6.25) for adults, 4.50€ ($5.65) for seniors, 4€ ($5) for children ages 5 to 15, and free for children under 5.

The Bulb District between Leiden and Haarlem (see above) may be better known, but the largest area of bulb fields in the country is in the hinterland of Den Helder—and the serried ranks of spring tulips look as colorful here as there.

(Fun Fact Ice Hazard

Den Helder has the dubious distinction of being possibly the only port in the world that ever lost a fleet to a company of horsemen. That unique event took place in January 1794, when the Dutch navy found itself stuck fast in the frozen waters of the roads between Den Helder and Texel. French cavalry simply rode out to the ships and captured them.

TEXEL ★
69km (43 miles) N of Amsterdam; 4km (2½ miles) N of Den Helder

A short ferry trip from Den Helder, family-orientated Texel (pronounced *Tess*-uhl) is the largest and most populated of the Wadden Islands archipelago. With just 14,000 permanent inhabitants (outnumbered three to two by sheep that are the source of the prized Texel lamb), that's not saying much. Texel, 24km (15 miles) long and a maximum of 9km (6 miles) wide, has a varied landscape of tidal gullies, sand dunes, and rolling meadows, and its entire North Sea shoreline is one long beach. It has the serenity intrinsic to islands, even allowing for the many visitors who pour in during summer months to fill up the island's extensive roster of hotels, vacation homes, apartments, and camping sites.

For the other Wadden Islands—Vlieland, Terschelling, Ameland, and Schiermonnikoog—which lie in Friesland province, see chapter 15.

ESSENTIALS
GETTING THERE The **TESO** line (ⓒ **0222/369-691;** www.teso.nl) operates car-ferry service from Den Helder (a connecting bus shuttles between Den Helder rail station and the ferry dock) across the Marsdiep Strait to 't Horntje on Texel—a 20-minute crossing. Ferries depart hourly at peak times and reservations are not accepted. Round-trip fares for cars, including passengers, are April to October, Friday to Monday 35€ ($44), and all other days 25€ ($31). For passengers without cars, round-trip fares are 3€ ($3.75) for adults, 1.50€ ($1.90) for children ages 4 to 11, and free for children under 4. Bicycles and mopeds cost 2.50€ ($3.15).

May to September, a passengers-only tourist boat operates between De Cocksdorp in the north of Texel and neighboring Vlieland, a 25-minute crossing that opens up the possibility of island-hopping through the Wadden chain.

VISITOR INFORMATION VVV Texel, Emmalaan 66, 1791 AA Den Burg (ⓒ **0222/314-741;** fax 0222/310-054; www.texel.net), lies just off the main road into town from the ferry harbor. The office is open Monday to Friday from 9am to 5:30pm; and Saturday from 9am to 5pm.

GETTING AROUND **Cars** are permitted on Texel, and **buses** connect the villages and the main beaches, but there's no doubt that the best way to get around and to respect the island's environment is to go by **bicycle.** These can be brought over free on the ferry, or rented from dozens of outlets around the island.

WHAT TO SEE & DO
Beaches, sailing, biking, hiking, and bird-watching are the big attractions on Texel, yet eating, drinking, and partying have a place, too. The main village, **Den Burg,** is a bustling settlement near the center of the island. For a glimpse of past island life, visit its moderately interesting, centrally located **De Oudheidkamer,** Koogerstraat 1 (ⓒ **0222/ 313-135**). The house dates from 1599 and is the island's oldest, furnished in a style from around 1900. The museum is open April to October, daily from 10am to 12:30pm and 1:30 to 3:30pm. Admission is 2€ ($2.50) for adults, and 1€ ($1.25) for children.

Areas of dune and forest belonging to the **Staatsbosbeheer (State Forest Authority)** may be freely visited so long as you stick to the marked trails. Guided tours of some of these areas are conducted by wildlife biologists from **EcoMare,** Ruijslaan 92 (ⓒ **0222/ 317-741;** www.ecomare.nl), a Wadden Islands research center, located amid the sand dunes just south of the main coastal village, De Koog. EcoMare's visitor center houses a small natural history museum that features the geology and plants of Texel, and its wildlife of land, sea, and air. The Wadden Sea is rich in seals, and EcoMare has a seal rehabilitation facility that cares for weak and injured seals until they are strong enough to be returned to the sea. An additional rehabilitation project cares for birds affected by pollution and other hazards. The center is open daily from 9am to 5pm. Admission is 7.75€ ($9.70) for adults, and 4.75€ ($5.95) for children ages 4 to 13.

Some 300 bird species have been observed on Texel, of which around 100 breed on the island. Among the avian stars are oyster-catchers, Bewicks swans, spoonbills, eider ducks, Brent geese, avocets, marsh harriers, snow buntings, ringed plovers, kestrels, short-eared owls, and bar-tailed godwits. You can observe these and more in **De Schorren, De Bol,** and **Dijkmanshuizen,** three protected nature reserves that may be entered only on tours conducted by guides from EcoMare.

WHERE TO DINE

Het Vierspan DUTCH/FRENCH   The warm welcome here, on a pretty corner occupied by the island's top restaurants, is complemented by a homely interior and well-prepared dishes based on local ingredients. Don't miss out on the local Texel lamb, succulent and salty from grazing the sea-sprayed grass. Other specialties here include game and mushrooms.

Gravenstraat 3, Den Burg. ⓒ **0222/313-176.** Main courses 13€–18€ ($16–$23). AE, MC, V. Wed–Mon 6–11pm.

7 Castle Country

In earlier times, the territory southeast of Amsterdam was a place of strategic importance, as evidenced by the grand military constructions still standing today, such as the 13th-century Muiderslot moated castle in Muiden—itself a handsome village of gabled houses along the waterfront at the mouth of the Vecht River—and the star-shaped fortifications of Naarden.

Muiderslot ✦   A 14th-century, fairy-tale castle with a moat, turrets, and stout walls with crenellations, Muiderslot perches on the bank of the Vecht River, just outside the small IJsselmeer harbor town of Muiden, 13km (8 miles) southeast of Amsterdam. Count Floris V of Holland, who in 1275 granted toll privileges to the vibrant new settlement of Aemstelledamme (Amsterdam), built the castle around 1280, and was murdered here by rival nobles in 1296. Muiderslot is where poet Pieter Cornelisz Hooft found both a home and employment—and inspiration for romantic and lofty phraseology—when he served here as castle steward and local bailiff for 40 years in the early 17th century. The castle is furnished essentially as Hooft and his artistic friends, known in Dutch literary history as the *Muiderkring* (Muiden Circle), knew it. You'll find distinctly Dutch carved cupboard beds, heavy chests, fireside benches, and mantelpieces.

Muiden. ⓒ **0294/261-325.** www.muiderslot.nl. Admission 8.50€ ($11) adults, 6€ ($7.50) children ages 4 to 12, free for children under 4. Apr–Oct Mon–Fri 10am–5pm, Sat–Sun and holidays noon–6pm; Nov–Mar Sat–Sun noon–6pm (last tour 5pm at all times). By car from Amsterdam, take A1/E231 east.

NAARDEN

19km (12 miles) E of Amsterdam

The highlight of this small town is that it has one of Holland's best-preserved rings of old military fortifications.

ESSENTIALS

GETTING THERE   Trains depart every hour or so from Amsterdam Centraal Station to Naarden-Bussum station; the trip takes around 20 minutes, and a round-trip ticket is 7.20€ ($9). By **car** from Amsterdam, take E231/A1 east.

An American Life

American artist William Henry Singer (1868–1943) chose to live and paint in the clear light of Holland rather than follow his family's traditional path to fame and fortune via the steel mills of Pittsburgh. He settled in suburban Laren, a haven for artists of the Laren, Hague, and Amsterdam schools, 26km (16 miles) southeast of Amsterdam. Among the town's star residents was Dutch Impressionist Anton Mauve (1838–88), an uncle of Vincent van Gogh.

Singer's home, a 1911 villa he called The Wild Swans, is now the **Singer Museum,** Oude Drift 1 (© **035/531-5656;** www.singerlaren.nl). It houses Impressionist-influenced paintings by Singer and his collection of works by American, Dutch, French, and Norwegian artists. The museum is open Tuesday to Sunday from 11am to 5pm (closed Jan 1, Dec 25). Admission is 10€ ($13) for adults, and free for children under 13. To get here from Naarden, take bus no. 109, which stops at the museum.

VISITOR INFORMATION   VVV Naarden, Adriaan Dortsmanplein 1B, 1411 RC, Naarden (© **035/694-2836;** fax 035/694-3424; www.vvvhollandsmidden.nl), is located inside the walls of the old town. The office is open May to October, Monday to Saturday from 10am to 5pm, Saturday from 10am to 3pm, and Sunday from noon to 3pm; November to April, Monday to Saturday from 10am to 2pm.

WHAT TO SEE & DO
Much in the spirit of locking the barn door after the horse had bolted, the surviving inhabitants of Naarden erected their double fortifications, in the shape of a beautiful 12-pointed-star, after the town was brutally sacked and its populace put to the sword by Don Frederick of Toledo and his Spanish troops in 1572. The inhabitants might have spared themselves the trouble, since the French were able to storm the works in 1673.

Beneath the Turfpoort, one of six bastions, you can visit the casemates (artillery vaults) which house the **Nederlands Vestingmuseum (Dutch Fortification Museum),** Westwalstraat 6 (© **035/694-5459;** www.vestingmuseum.nl), filled with cannon, muskets, accouterments, and documentation. The museum is open mid-March to October, Tuesday to Friday from 10:30am to 5pm, and Saturday, Sunday, and holidays from noon to 5pm; November to mid-March, Sunday, and Saturday before Christmas to Sunday after New Year, Tuesday to Friday from 10:30am to 5pm, and Sunday from noon to 5pm; closed January 1, December 25 and 31. Admission is 5€ ($6.25) for adults, 3€ ($3.75) for children 5 to 16, and free for children under 5.

Take in the town's 15th-century late-Gothic **Grote Kerk (Great Church),** Marktstraat (© **035/694-9873**), noted for its 45m-high (148-ft.) tower, fine acoustics, and annual pre-Easter performances of Bach's *St. Matthew Passion*. The church is open June to September, daily from 1 to 4pm. Admission is free.

14

The Hague, Rotterdam & Zuid-Holland

Zuid-Holland (South Holland) province takes in a cluster of important cities and towns, all within about an hour's drive or train ride from Amsterdam. Roads pass through a landscape straight out of a painting by one of the Dutch Masters. You'll see flat green fields ribboned with canals and distant church spires piercing a wide sky.

Stately and dignified, **The Hague** is the Dutch government's home. Technically, it's not a true city—never having been granted a charter or city rights—but such a triviality is brushed off with disdain. The Hague's seacoast resort, **Scheveningen,** makes something of a stab at being Holland's Deauville or Biarritz.

Brash **Rotterdam** has been commercial to the core from the beginning. Most of its historically significant buildings, along with most of the city, were destroyed in World War II Nazi bombings. Rebuilding was a remarkable feat of modern urban planning. High-rise towers, with straight lines and right angles—features that until recently were considered anathema in most parts of the country—mold an oddly attractive open cityscape. Rotterdam's port boasts the world's highest annual shipping tonnage.

The Hague and Rotterdam, for all their geographical proximity, are about as different as two cities easily could be. Zuid-Holland's trio of venerable art towns have more in common. The triangle formed by **Delft, Gouda,** and **Leiden** makes for leisurely sightseeing, with distances short enough to allow you to visit all three from a base in Amsterdam, The Hague, or Rotterdam. Better yet, you can overnight in any one of the three.

1 The Hague ✶✶✶

50km (31 miles) SW of Amsterdam; 22km (14 miles) NW of Rotterdam; 54km (33 miles) W of Utrecht

The Hague is an easy day trip from Amsterdam, but some travelers prefer it as a more relaxed sightseeing base. 's-Gravenhage, to give the city its full name, or more commonly Den Haag, is a cosmopolitan center bursting with style and culture, full of parks and elegant homes. Its 18th-century French look suits its role as a diplomatic center and the site of the International Court of Justice, housed in the famous Peace Palace.

Amsterdam might be the national capital, but The Hague (pop. 463,000) has always been the seat of national government and the official residence of the Dutch monarchs, whether or not they chose to live there. Three royal palaces grace the city.

In the beginning, the counts of Holland chose a small village named Haag (from the Dutch for "hedge") as the setting for their hunting lodge, which was why the town was later called 's-Gravenhage (the count's hedge). By the time Count Willem II was crowned king of the Romans in 1248, in the German city of Aachen, his father, Floris IV, had already begun construction of the Binnenhof, which Willem appointed the

---

(*Fun Fact* **Hard-Handed Boosters**

In an ironic counterpoint to The Hague's genteel image, supporters of the city's soccer club, FC Den Haag, have about the worst reputation in the land for hooliganism.

---

official royal residence, thereby providing the city with what is now considered its foundation year. Willem's son, Floris V, added the massive Ridderzaal (Hall of the Knights) in 1280, thereby expanding a complex that is today the heart of the country's government. Lush greenery from the original hunting grounds remains in the city's parks, gardens, and forests.

ESSENTIALS

GETTING THERE **By Plane** Amsterdam's **Schiphol Airport,** 40km (25 miles) away, also serves The Hague (see "Getting There," in chapter 2 and "Orientation," in chapter 12). Train service frequently runs from the airport to The Hague, with up to six trains an hour during the day and one an hour at night; the trip time is 30 minutes, and a one-way ticket costs 7€ ($8.75). A taxi from Schiphol to The Hague center takes 30 minutes in light traffic and costs around 60€ ($75).

By Train The Hague has excellent rail connections from around the Netherlands, with up to six trains arriving hourly from Amsterdam, Rotterdam, and Utrecht. Intercity trains take around 50 minutes from Amsterdam and Utrecht, and 25 minutes from Rotterdam. A round-trip ticket from Amsterdam is 18€ ($22). Note that the city has two main stations: **Centraal Station** (CS) and **Hollands Spoor** (HS). Most city sights are closer to Centraal Station, but many trains, among them Thalys and other international trains from France and Belgium, stop only at Hollands Spoor. Both stations are well served by public transportation.

By Car From Amsterdam and the north, take A4/E19; from Rotterdam and the south, take A13/E19; and from Utrecht and the east, take A12/E30. You'll want to avoid all three *snelwegen* (expressways) during the morning and evening peak hours, when the name can seem like a bad joke. At other times, you should be able to go from both Amsterdam and Utrecht in under an hour, and from Rotterdam in around 20 minutes.

VISITOR INFORMATION VVV **Den Haag,** Hofweg 1 (mailing address: Postbus 85456, 2500 CD Den Haag; ℭ **0900/340-3505;** fax 0900/352-0426; www.den haag.com; tram: 1 or 16), outside the Binnenhof (Parliament). The office is open Monday to Friday from 10am to 6pm, Saturday from 10am to 5pm, and Sunday from noon to 5pm.

GETTING AROUND Public transportation in the city is operated by **HTM** (ℭ **0900/9292;** www.htm.net). Centraal Station (tram: 2, 3, 6, 9, 10, 15, 16, or 17) is the primary interchange point for bus and tram routes, and Hollands Spoor station (tram: 1, 9, 11, 12, 16, or 17) the secondary node. Going by tram is the quickest way to get around town, but some points are served only by bus. Note that on tram line 1 you can go from the North Sea coast at Scheveningen, through The Hague, and all the way to Delft. Regional bus service is handled by **Connexxion** (ℭ **0900/266-6399;** www. connexxion.nl).

In addition to the various types of *strippenkaart* (see "Getting Around," in chapter 12 for how to use these tickets), which are valid nationally, two day tickets—**Dagkaart Den Haag** (5.90€/$7.40) and **Dagkaart Den Haag Plus** (7.90€/$9.90)—are available. These cover the city and its environs, respectively.

Taxis operated by **HTMC** (© **070/390-7722;** www.htmc.nl), wait at stands outside both main rail stations and at other strategic points around town.

The best thing about going by car in The Hague is that it's not as bad as in Amsterdam. But tight restrictions on parking and vigorous enforcement of the rules make using public transportation a better option.

SPECIAL EVENTS The **State Opening of Parliament,** during which the queen delivers a speech from the throne in the Hall of the Knights (see below), is worth being in town for. On *Prinsjesdag* (Princes' Day), the third Tuesday in September, she arrives and departs in her golden coach—like Cinderella—drawn by high-stepping royal horses.

WHAT TO SEE & DO

One of the pleasures of spending a day or more in The Hague is walking through its pleasant streets, matching your pace to the unhurried leisure that pervades the city. Stroll past the mansions that line Lange Voorhout, overlooking a broad avenue of poplar and elm trees, and notice how these spacious, restrained structures differ from

Amsterdam's gabled, ornamented canal houses. Window-shop or get down to serious buying in the covered shopping arcades and store-lined pedestrians-only streets. Take time to loiter in the more than 30 sq. km (12 sq. miles) of parks, gardens, and other green spaces within the city limits. To go farther, hop on a tram for the short ride out to The Hague's seacoast resort, Scheveningen, or to nearby Delft.

THE TOP ATTRACTIONS

Binnenhof & Ridderzaal (Inner Court & Hall of the Knights) ★★   The magnificent Binnenhof, the 13th-century hunting lodge of the counts of Holland, is the center of Holland's political life. It now houses the First and Second Chamber of the Staaten-Generaal (States General), an equivalent to the U.S. House of Representatives and Senate, respectively. At the heart of the cobblestoned courtyard is the beautiful, twin-towered Hall of the Knights, measuring 38×18m (126×59 ft.) and soaring 26m (85 ft.) to its oak roof. Since 1904, its immense interior, adorned with provincial flags and leaded-glass windows depicting the coats of arms of Dutch cities, has hosted the queen's annual address to Parliament (third Tues in Sept) and official receptions. Adjacent to the Ridderzaal are the former quarters of the *Stadhouder* (Head of State).

You can visit the Parliament exhibit in the reception room of the Hall of Knights, and join a guided tour to visit the Hall and, government business permitting, one of the chambers of Parliament. Book in advance by phone for the tour, and call ahead to make sure tours are going on the day you intend to visit. It's worthwhile to visit the courtyard and the Hall of the Knights, which you can do easily in an hour; the tour of Parliament isn't all that exciting, so don't fret if you miss it. Be sure to check out the view from the outside the Binnenhof, across the rectangular **Hofvijver (Court Lake)** pond, which has a fountain and a tiny island.

Binnenhof 8A. ℰ **070/364-6144.** www.binnenhofbezoek.nl. Admission to courtyard and Ridderzaal reception hall free; guided tours 5€ ($6.25) or 6€ ($7.50) adults, 4€ ($5) or 3€ ($3.75) seniors/students/children under 14, depending on the tour offered at the time; book in advance by phone for the guided tour—call ahead in any case to make sure tours are going on the day you intend to visit. Mon–Sat 10am–4pm. Closed holidays and during special events. Tram: 10, 16, or 17 to Buitenhof.

Gemeentemuseum Den Haag (The Hague Municipal Museum) ★   Housed in a honey-toned brick building (1935) by architect Hendrik Petrus Berlage, this fine museum has plenty to see. Top billing goes to the world's most comprehensive collection—more than 50 works—by De Stijl artist Piet Mondrian, among them his last painting, the unfinished *Victory Boogie Woogie* (1944), an abstract representation of New York. Other rooms cover 19th-century Dutch Romantic art, the Impressionist Hague School, and 20th-century art, and there are a few works by van Gogh, Monet, and Picasso, and prints and drawings by Karel Appel and Toulouse-Lautrec. For decorative arts, there's ceramics from Delft, China, and the Middle East; Dutch and Venetian glass; silver; period furniture; and an intricate 1743 dollhouse. The music department has antique instruments from Europe—harpsichords, pianos, and more—and from around the world, and an impressive library of scores, books, and prints. New underground rooms are used for temporary fashion exhibits. Plan to spend a couple hours here.

Stadhouderslaan 41 (close to the Nederlands Congres Centrum, north of the center). ℰ **070/338-1111.** www.gemeentemuseum.nl. Admission 8€ ($10) adults, 6€ ($7.50) seniors, 5€ ($6.25) students, free for those under 19. Tues–Sun 11am–5pm. Closed Jan 1, Dec 25. Tram: 10 or 17 to Gemeentemuseum.

Mauritshuis ★★   Once the residence of Count Johan Maurits van Nassau-Siegen, court dandy, cousin of the ruling Oranje-Nassaus, and governor-general of Dutch

The Hague & Scheveningen

ATTRACTIONS ●
Beelden aan Zee **5**
Binnenhof & Ridderzaal **32**
Escher in Het Paleis **25**
Galerij Prins Willem V **29**
Gemeentemuseum Den Haag **10**
Holland Casino Scheveningen **3**
Madurodam **12**
Mauritshuis/Koninklijk Kabinet van Schilderijen **33**
Museum Meermanno **24**
Muzee Scheveningen **7**
Omniversum **11**
Paleis Huis ten Bosch **34**

Paleis Noordeinde **21**
Panorama Mesdag **15**
Scheveningen Pier **1**
Sea Life Scheveningen **4**
Vredespaleis (Peace Palace) **13**

ACCOMMODATIONS ■
De Seinduin **6**
Delta Hotel **14**
Golden Tulip Corona **31**
Le Méridien Hotel des Indes **22**
Parkhotel Den Haag **27**
Paleis Hotel **28**
Steigenberger Kurhaus Hotel **2**

DINING ◆
Café-Restaurant Greve **20**
De Wankele Tafel **17**
Ducdalf **8**
Garoeda **19**
Het Brouwcafe **9**
Le Bistroquet **26**
Le Haricot Vert **18**
Plato **16**
Saur **23**
Stadsherberg 't Goude Hooft **30**

Brazil, this small but delightful neoclassical mansion from 1637 rises out of the Hofvij-ver pond. It houses the **Koninklijk Kabinet van Schilderijen (Royal Cabinet of Paintings),** a stunning collection of 15th- to 18th-century Low Countries art, given to the nation by King Willem I in 1816. The intimate rooms, set on two floors, were restored after a fire in 1704. Some have illuminated ceilings. It almost feels like you're viewing a private collection.

Famous works include pieces by Rembrandt, Frans Hals, Johannes Vermeer, Jan Steen, Peter Paul Rubens, and Hans Holbein the Younger. Highlights are Rembrandt's *The Anatomy Lesson of Dr. Nicolaes Tulp* (1632); Vermeer's meticulous *View of Delft* (ca. 1660), in which cumulous clouds roil the skies above the neat little town; and his first stab at a movie script: *Girl With a Pearl Earring* (ca. 1660).

The first floor is mainly given over to Dutch and Flemish religious paintings, and por-traits by Holbein and Rubens. Look out in particular for Rogier van der Weyden's dis-turbingly realistic *The Lamentation* (ca. 1450), depicting Christ being taken down from the cross. As the first of the "Flemish Primitives," Van der Weyden did more than his share of setting off the whole Low Countries art boom. Works by Rembrandt, Vermeer, and a riotous Steen are upstairs. You could easily spend a day here, but a morning or after-noon provides a powerful impression of the wealth and breadth of a great art tradition.

Korte Vijverberg 8 (next to the Binnenhof). © **070/302-3435.** www.mauritshuis.nl. Admission 4.75€ ($5.95) adults, free for those under 19; note that during special exhibits the admission for adults can double; tickets are valid also in the Galerij Prins Willem V (see below). Apr–Sept Mon–Sat 10am–5pm, Sun and holidays 11am–5pm; Oct–Mar Tues–Sat 10am–5pm, Sun and holidays 11am–5pm. Closed Jan 1, Dec 25. Tram: 10, 16, or 17 to Buitenhof.

Vredespaleis (Peace Palace)   This imposing building—constructed between 1907 and 1913, largely due to donations made by Andrew Carnegie—houses the Interna-tional Court of Justice, the Permanent Court of Arbitration, the International Law Academy, and an extensive library. Its furnishings were donated by countries around the world. The palace is open for guided tours only. Reserve a tour at least a day or two ahead of time (© **070/302-4137;** fax 070/302-4234; guidedtours@planet.nl). If you can do it a week ahead, you'll have a better chance of getting a place. English is sure to be spoken by the guide but it can't hurt to confirm this for your chosen time, and note that the Peace Palace's museum is only visited on the 11am and 3pm tours.

Carnegieplein 2. © **070/302-4242.** www.vredespaleis.nl Tours last 50 min. without the museum visit and 1½ hr. with. Admission 5€ ($6.25) adults, 3€ ($3.75) children 5–12, free for children under 5; add 3€ ($3.75) per person for the museum visit. Guided tours Mon–Fri 10am, 11am, 2pm, 3pm, and 4pm (there isn't always a 4pm tour). Tram: 1 or 10 to Vredespaleis.

THE ROYAL PALACES

The working palace for Queen Beatrix and her staff, the splendid neoclassical **Paleis Noordeinde,** Noordeinde (tram: 1 or 10), west of Lange Voorhout, dates from 1553. It was elegantly furnished when William of Orange's widow was in residence, but it became almost derelict by the beginning of the 19th century. In 1815, restoration brought it back to a state suitable for the residence of King Willem I. Extensive reno-vation followed fire damage in 1948, and in the early 1980s additional restoration was begun. It is from here that Queen Beatrix and Prince Claus, on the third Tuesday of September each year, depart in a golden coach drawn by eight horses, escorted by mil-itary corps, bands, local authorities, and a blaze of street pageantry, to proceed to the Binnenhof, where the queen officially opens Parliament with an address to both houses of the States General in the Ridderzaal.

<table>

Tips **A Right Royal Bus Route**

If you're interested in royalty and palaces, take a ride on city bus no. 4. Its route passes by four Dutch palaces built during the 16th and 17th centuries, including Huis ten Bosch, the home of Queen Beatrix, in the Haagse Bos (Hague Woods); no visits are permitted.

When Queen Juliana abdicated the Dutch throne in 1980, her daughter, Queen Beatrix, moved her family and the official royal residence from a palace near Utrecht to the **Paleis Huis ten Bosch (House in the Woods Palace),** in the beautiful Haagse Bos (Hague Woods; bus no. 4 or 43). For many years, it had been the royal family's summer residence, and originally a small, rather plain structure consisting of several rooms opening from a domed central hall. Prince Willem IV added the two large side wings in the 1700s. *Note:* The palace isn't open to visitors, but you can view it from the park.

OTHER ATTRACTIONS
Madurodam *Kids*   To see "Holland in a Nutshell," head to the wooded dunes linking The Hague and the coastal resort of Scheveningen. This enchanting display of a miniature, fictitious city sprawls over 25,600 sq. m (275,560 sq. ft.), amid the trees of the Scheveningse Bosjes (Scheveningen Woods). Typical Dutch townscapes and famous landmarks are replicated on a scale of 1 to 25—you feel a bit like Gulliver viewing Lilliput. The wonder of it all is that this is a working miniature world: Trains run, ships move, planes taxi down runways, bells ring, the barrel organ plays, there's a town fair in progress, and thousands of tiny lamps light up when darkness falls. Children love it—but surprisingly, 75% of the 1.2 million annual visitors are adults.

George Maduroplein 1. © **070/416-2400.** www.madurodam.nl. Admission 13€ ($15) adults, 12€ ($14) seniors, 9€ ($11) children 3–11, free for children under 3. Apr–June daily 9am–8pm; July–Aug daily 9am–10pm; Sept–Mar daily 9am–6pm. Tram: 9 to Madurodam.

Omniversum *Kids*   This globe-shaped construction contains a digital planetarium and various multimedia theaters that explain humankind, the universe, foreign cultures, and space travel.

President Kennedylaan 5. © **070/307-3456.** www.omniversum.nl. Admission 9€ ($11) adults, 7.50€ ($9.40) children 4–11, free for children under 4. Mon 10am–3pm; Tues–Wed 10am–5pm; Thurs–Sun 10am–10pm; public holidays and school vacations daily 10am–10pm (note that the times are from the first to the last screening). Tram: 10 or 17 to Gemeentemuseum.

MORE MUSEUMS & GALLERIES
Escher in Het Paleis (Escher at the Palace)   The small Paleis Lange Voorhout, dating from 1764, in the heart of the old city, was the home of Emma, Queen Beatrix's grandmother, from 1901 to 1934. Since 2002, it has housed a museum honoring the Dutch graphic artist M. C. Escher (1898–1972), who in his lifetime produced 448 lithographs, woodcuts, and engravings, and more than 2,000 drawings and sketches. The museum doesn't have them all, but it has a fair sampling, and a computer-animation section on the top floor. Plus, you get to see inside one of The Hague's royal palaces (see "The Royal Palaces," above), and even if it's a small, second-tier one, a visit is still worthwhile.

Lange Voorhout 74. © **070/427-7730.** www.escherinhetpaleis.nl. Admission 7.50€ ($9.40) adults, 5€ ($6.25) children 7–15, free for children under 7. Tues–Sun 11am–5pm. Closed Jan 1, Sept 19, Dec 25. Tram: 16 or 17 to Korte Voorhout.
</table>

(Moments **Rising Roses**

In the **Rosarium** in Westbroekpark, more than 20,000 roses from 300 different varieties bloom each year between July and September. The grounds are open daily from 9am to 1 hour before sunset.

Galerij Prins Willem V   This elegant little gallery is a kind of separate annex of the Mauritshuis (see above), and if you have a ticket to that museum you'll get in here free. The country's first purpose-built art gallery, it opened to the public in 1774 to display the private collection of Prince of Orange Willem V. Most of the 150 paintings from the Dutch Golden Age are the original occupants of the gallery, arranged in the cluttered style of the time. There are few internationally known works, but all the paintings are interesting and have a cumulative impact. Look out for Jan Steen's shiver-inducing *The Toothpuller* (1651), and give thanks for modern dentistry. An hour here should do it.

Buitenhof 35 (across from the Binnenhof). 𝒞 070/302-3435. www.gemeentemuseum.nl. Admission 3€ ($4.50) adults, 1€ ($1.25) seniors, free for visitors under 19, free for visitors with a Mauritshuis ticket. Tues–Sun 11am–4pm. Closed Jan 1, Dec 25. Tram: 10, 16, or 17 to Buitenhof.

Museum Meermanno   This charming museum occupies a spacious 19th-century town house with formal garden. Part of the collection was assembled by the 19th-century collector Baron W. van Westrenen, who resided here. His book collection includes rare medieval manuscripts, religious and secular, and early examples of the printed book; it integrated the collection of his second cousin Johan Meerman. On his travels, van Westrenen amassed a charming collection of artifacts from ancient Egypt, Rome, and Greece that includes mummies, small statues of deities, and coins. In the garden house are temporary exhibitions of modern typography and displays explaining the printing process. The museum's subsequent curators have nursed a special interest in book design from the 1850s to the present.

Prinsessegracht 30. 𝒞 070/346-2700. www.meermanno.nl. Admission 4€ ($5) adults, free for those under 19. Tues–Fri 11am–5pm; Sat–Sun and holidays noon–5pm. Closed Jan 1, Dec 25. Tram: 9 to Malieveld.

Panorama Mesdag ⚘ (Kids   If you don't have time to visit Scheveningen, you can sort of see the seacoast resort here. The panoramic painting, with a circumference of 119m (395 ft.), may take your breath away, and in any case it feels like a breath of fresh sea air. You walk through a dark passageway, up a stairway, and out onto a circular platform—and suddenly you're in the fishing village of Scheveningen in 1880. Its dunes, beach, fishing boats, and everything else in the village are three-dimensional, an illusion enhanced by the artificial dunes that separate you from the painting. The panorama was the work of The Hague school artist Hendrik Willem Mesdag, with the assistance of his wife and two other prominent artists.

Zeestraat 65. 𝒞 070/364-4544. www.panorama-mesdag.com. Admission 5€ ($6.25) adults, 4€ ($5) seniors, 2.50€ ($3.15) children 3–13, free for children under 3. Mon–Sat 10am–5pm; Sun and holidays noon–5pm. Closed Jan 1, Dec 25. Tram: 1 or 10 to Mauritskade.

WHERE TO STAY
VERY EXPENSIVE
Le Méridien Hotel des Indes ⚘⚘   Highly recommended for its elegant accommodations and a location in the center of the oldest part of the city, this old-world hotel recently underwent a top-to-bottom renovation and modernization that was

completed in 2005. It began as the residence of Baron van Brienen, and became a hotel in 1881. Since then it has welcomed royalty, diplomats, celebrities, and tourists, and has held a consistently prominent place in the social life of The Hague. Its classically decorated guest rooms are the ultimate in comfort. Some bathrooms contain a whirlpool. Public rooms are lavishly fitted with marble, polished wood, chandeliers, and velvet upholstery. The gracious lobby lounge is a favorite place for residents of The Hague to meet for tea and other refreshments. Continental **Le Restaurant,** a stylish setting for good eating, is as popular with locals as it is with visitors and guests.

Lange Voorhout 54–56, 2514 EG Den Haag. 🕾 070/361-2345. Fax 070/361-2350. www.lemeridien.com/hague. 92 units. 190€–425€ ($238–$531) double; from 495€ ($619) suite. AE, DC, MC, V. Tram: 1 or 10 to Kneuterdijk. **Amenities:** Restaurant (Continental); bar; lounge; health club; concierge; secretarial services; 24-hr. room service; in-room massage; babysitting; laundry service; dry cleaning; nonsmoking rooms. *In room:* A/C, TV, dataport, minibar, coffeemaker, hair dryer, iron, safe.

EXPENSIVE

Parkhotel Den Haag   This pleasant, centrally located hotel is on a quiet street, with doors opening from the spacious entrance lobby to a walled-in street-side terrace in fine weather. The grandiose breakfast room overlooks the gardens of the Noordeinde royal palace. The early-20th-century monument has original yellow brick and tile features on the staircases that demand a constant process of preservation. Its spacious and attractive guest rooms have full marble bathrooms.

Molenstraat 53, 2513 BJ Den Haag. 🕾 070/362-4371. Fax 070/361-4525. www.parkhoteldenhaag.nl. 116 units. 170€–300€ ($213–$375) double; from 475€ ($594) suite. Rates include buffet breakfast. AE, DC, MC, V. Tram: 1 or 10 to Kneuterdijk. **Amenities:** Bar; 24-hr. room service; laundry service; dry cleaning; nonsmoking rooms. *In room:* TV, dataport, minibar, safe.

MODERATE

Golden Tulip Corona 🖈🖈   Once a lively coffeehouse, this charming hotel is opposite the House of Parliament and between the Binnenhof and the Passage (a large covered shopping center). In the 18th century, the middle one of the three buildings that form the hotel was known as the Koffyhuys van Dalen, which in 1783 became De Beurs van Amsterdam. The name Corona was given to it in 1945. Public rooms feature contemporary decor, with touches of handsome marble and mahogany in the lobby. The guest rooms are done in soft pastel colors with graceful window drapes. The hotel's popularity dates back to the early 1900s. Today, politicians, antiques dealers, and gourmets still congregate here. The elegant restaurant—full of French Provincial furnishings, soothing ecrus, and brushed blues—is a favorite retreat for the good and the great in government circles. In balmy weather, part of the restaurant becomes a sidewalk terrace.

Buitenhof 39–42, 2513 AH Den Haag. 🕾 070/363-7930. Fax 070/361-5785. www.corona.nl. 36 units. 110€–175€ ($138–$219) double. Rates include buffet breakfast only at weekends. AE, DC, MC, V. Tram: 10, 16, or 17 to Buitenhof. **Amenities:** 2 restaurants (French, brasserie); bar; 24-hr. room service. *In room:* TV, minibar, hair dryer.

Paleis Hotel 🖈   The spacious guest rooms in this intimate boutique hotel are furnished with soft chairs and settees. The beds are very comfortable and some rooms are air-conditioned. Bathrooms are a bit small but beautifully fitted. There's a lavish breakfast buffet. The quiet city-center setting is convenient for shopping (the pedestrian shopping promenade is nearby) and sightseeing.

Molenstraat 26 (behind Paleis Noordeinde), 2513 BL Den Haag. 🕾 070/362-4621. Fax 070/361-4533. www.paleishotel.nl. 20 units. 110€–150€ ($138–$188) double. AE, DC, MC, V. Limited street parking. Tram: 17 to Gravenstraat. **Amenities:** Bar; sauna. *In room:* TV, dataport, minibar, coffeemaker, hair dryer, safe.

INEXPENSIVE

Delta Hotel   Here you'll find a smart designer feel without the stiff price tag; the walls here often host exhibitions by local artists. The reception is open to 11pm, and room service is available during the day. Other services include dry cleaning, and all rooms are equipped with a hair dryer. In one of The Hague's nicest neighborhoods, there's a good selection of local bars and restaurants.

Anna Paulownastraat 8, 2518 BE Den Haag. ℂ 070/362-4999. Fax 070/345-4440. 11 units. 85€–95€ ($106–$119) double. Rates include continental breakfast. AE, DC, MC, V. Limited street parking. Tram: 1 or 10 to Mauritskade. *In room:* TV.

WHERE TO DINE
EXPENSIVE

Saur 🕊 FRENCH/SEAFOOD   The Saur, which overlooks a beautiful square in the center city, has been a favorite of residents of The Hague since 1928. In 2001, it was voted Best Restaurant of the Year in The Hague by the local newspaper, the *Haagse Courant*. The traditional French cuisine is superb, and the service is impeccable.

Lange Voorhout 47. ℂ 070/346-2565. www.saur.nl. Reservations recommended on weekends. Main courses 27€–45€ ($34–$56); fixed-price menus 30€–50€ ($37–$63). AE, DC, MC, V. Mon–Fri noon–2:30pm and 6–10:30pm; Sat 6–10:30pm. Tram: 10, 16, or 17 to Korte Voorhout.

MODERATE

Café-Restaurant Greve 🕊 MEDITERRANEAN/INTERNATIONAL   This former car showroom is now a popular cafe-restaurant. The large windows of the cafe look out on the lively Torenstraat; the restaurant, however, is more intimate, with its low ceiling, candles, and wooden tables. You can choose a dish as a starter or a main course, which is an ideal solution for small appetites (or when you want a taste of everything!). Fish and lamb dishes, such as bouillabaisse or lamb cutlets with feta cheese and ouzo sauce, are popular.

Torenstraat 138 (at Veenkade). ℂ 070/360-3919. www.greve.nl. Main courses 12€–15€ ($14–$19). AE, DC, MC, V. Cafe daily 10am–1am; restaurant Mon–Sat 6–11pm, Sun 6–10pm. Tram: 17 to Noordwal.

Garoeda INDONESIAN   If it's *rijsttafel* you're hankering for, you couldn't find better than what's served at this pleasant, very popular Indonesian restaurant in the center city. The waitstaff are dressed smartly in traditional Javanese silks, adding a classy touch to the authentic cooking. Lunch gets especially crowded, so make a reservation or come early or late.

Kneuterdijk 18A. ℂ 070/346-5319. www.garoeda.nl. Reservations recommended for lunch. Main course items 5.75€–14€ ($7.20–$18); rijsttafel 50€–75€ ($63–$94). AE, DC, MC, V. Mon–Sat 11am–11pm; Sun 4–11pm. Tram: 1 or 10 to Kneuterdijk.

Le Bistroquet 🕊 FRENCH/INTERNATIONAL   This small restaurant in the center city is one of The Hague's best, with lovely table settings in a quietly elegant setting. The menu is mostly French. Lamb, fish, and fresh vegetables are featured. Good choices include Irish salmon with lobster ravioli in a Thai curry sauce, and lamb filet with cashews, French beans, and a marjoram sauce.

Lange Voorhout 98. ℂ 070/360-1170. www.bistroquet.nl. Reservations recommended on weekends. Main courses 23€–35€ ($29–$42). AE, DC, MC, V. Mon–Fri noon–2pm and 6–10pm; Sat 6–10pm. Tram: 10, 16, or 17 to Kneuterdijk.

Le Haricot Vert 🕊 BELGIAN/FRENCH   A warm ambience awaits visitors to this long-standing favorite. In the summertime, tables are set outside on the sidewalk of the narrow pedestrians-only street. Indulge in the three-course "Verwen Menu" and you'll be spoiled with enormous plates holding tasty selections of the best seasonal meat, fish, or vegetable dishes.

Molenstraat 9A. ✆ **070/365-2278**. Reservations recommended on weekends. Main courses 15€–25€ ($19–$31); fixed-price menus 27€–35€ ($34–$44). AE, DC, MC, V. Daily 6–11pm. Tram: 1 or 10 to Kneuterdijk.

Plato INTERNATIONAL   Plato has perfected its formula and hums every night with keen return visitors. Most dishes on the menu can be ordered in small or large portions, according to your capacity or appetite, and you can choose the most appropriate from a list of five combo possibilities. For example, start with a soup and have two small-size dishes instead of a full main course. I go back just for the Greek-style succulent stewed lamb shank. Other appetizing (and unusual) menu dishes include ostrich tournedos.

Frederikstraat 32. ✆ **070/363-6744**. www.restaurant-plato.nl. Main courses 9€–14€ ($11–$18); fixed-price menus 16€–27€ ($20–$34). AE, DC, MC, V. Daily 3–10:30pm. Tram: 9 to Dr. Kuyperstraat.

Stadsherberg 't Goude Hooft ★★ DUTCH/CONTINENTAL   There's a definite Old Dutch flavor to this wonderful, large, happy cafe-restaurant overlooking the city's old market square. But its 1600s exterior cloaks a 1939 interior installed after a disastrous fire. In fact, the establishment's history dates back to 1423. Originally, it was a tavern. In 1660, it was transformed into a coffeehouse and then in 1939 into a cafe-restaurant. The wooden beams, brass chandeliers, and rustic chairs and tables blend harmoniously with the stained-glass windows, medieval banners, and wall murals. Some of the rooms that divide the interior are nonsmoking. There's a large, pleasant sidewalk cafe on the "Green Market" square. An extensive menu ranges from snacks to light lunches to full dinners. Look out for fine menu dishes like the guinea fowl with thyme sauce and the red perch with saffron sauce. This is a good place to drop by for a cocktail and snack, a beer, or a coffee.

Dagelijkse Groenmarkt 13 (at the Grote Kerk). ✆ **070/346-9713**. www.tgoudehooft.nl. Main courses 14€–20€ ($18–$25); fixed-price menus 16€–24€ ($20–$30). AE, DC, MC, V. Mon noon–6pm; Tues–Wed and Fri–Sat 10am–7pm; Thurs 10am–9:30pm; Sun 11am–6pm. Tram: 17 to Gravenstraat.

INEXPENSIVE
De Wankele Tafel VEGETARIAN   Organic-food fanatics and vegetarians will love chowing down at the casual "Wobbly Table." Start with a delicious soup of the day, followed by a tasty whole-grain pancake generously filled with tofu or tempeh and a variety of fresh vegetables and salad.

Mauritskade 79. ✆ **070/364-3267**. Main courses 8€–14€ ($10–$17). No credit cards. Mon–Sat 4:30–11pm. Tram: 1 or 10 to Mauritskade.

SHOPPING
Interesting shopping areas include Oude Molstraat and Denneweg in the center city, with a concentration of authentic Dutch stores. Connected to Centraal Station, the modern Babylon shopping mall has two floors with more than 60 stores, restaurants, and a luxury hotel.

A network of pedestrian streets offers a big selection of stores on Spuistraat, Vlamingstraat, Venestraat, and Hoogstraat. The covered **Passage** is a beautiful 19th-century arcade running from Spuistraat to Gravenstraat, though the stores it contains are nothing to write home about.

De Bijenkorf, Wagenstraat 32 (✆ **070/426-2700**), in a stunning example of functional early-20th-century architecture, stands on Grote Marktstraat; and the stiffly chic **Maison de Bonneterie,** Gravenstraat 2 (✆ **070/330-5300**), stands on Buitenhof.

Noordeinde and Oude Molenstraat are home to fashion boutiques, antiquarian booksellers, and expensive delicatessens. Leading off from Lange Voorhout, Denneweg and Frederikstraat are lined with high-priced antiques, interior design stores, and boutiques catering to specialties such as fashion for pregnant women. One of the largest interior-design stores is the multi-location **Loft Interiors,** part of which is in a stunning 1899 iron-and-glass showroom at Denneweg 56.

Among the top shopping attractions are a number of fine antiques stores and a weekly **antiques and curios market** under the beautiful canopy of trees on Lange Voorhout. The market runs May to September on Thursday from 9am to 7pm and Sunday from 10am to 5pm; and October to May, on Thursday from noon to 5pm. Year-round, on Wednesday, there's an **organic farm market** on the square around the Grote Kerk from 10am to 4pm.

THE HAGUE AFTER DARK

There's nearly always something going on after dark. The monthly publication *The Hague Agenda,* available at the VVV offices and many hotels and restaurants, lists up-and-coming concerts and other cultural events. Spui, just behind Centraal Station, is the city's modern cultural square. Here you find **Dr. Anton Philips Concert Hall,** Spui 150 (✆ **070/360-9810**), home to the Residentie Orchestra; and the **AT&T Dance Theater,** Spui 152 (✆ **070/360-4930**), where the three companies of the renowned Netherlands Dance Theater perform their virtuoso contemporary productions. If you're more into jazz and pop music, check out **'t Paard,** Prinsengracht 12 (✆ **070/360-1618**).

The Hague doesn't have a big student population, and the city's natural formality somewhat subdues its nightlife, but there is a thriving bar and cafe culture. The Plein, a large square in front of the Tweede Kamer (lower house of Parliament), is a favorite for recess with politicians and civil servants. If you want to combine eating and drinking, and hide from the masses in a quiet walled garden, head for close-by **Schlemmer,** Lange Houtstraat 17 (✆ **070/360-9000**). The Grote Markt square is lined with busy bars and restaurants, ranging from traditional brown cafes to trendy designer spots. **De Zwarte Ruiter,** Grote Markt 27 (✆ **070/364-9549**), is a popular drinking and eating place that makes a good starting point. Another lively area is the narrow **Maliestraat,** just off Denneweg, behind the Hotel Des Indes, where you find great bars such as **Ca l'Emile,** De Maliestraat 16 (✆ **070/365-5400**), in which a more mature but lively professional crowd likes to greet the evening. One of The Hague's oldest lesbian and gay bars, **Cafe De Landman,** Denneweg 48 (✆ **070/346-7727**), is close by.

For a casino and other nightspots, head to nearby Scheveningen.

2 Scheveningen ⟨⁂

5km (3 miles) NW of The Hague center

A chic beach resort with a notoriously hard-to-pronounce name, Scheveningen is virtually a part of The Hague. It sports a cast of upscale restaurants, accommodations in all price ranges, designer boutiques, and abundant nighttime entertainment. Visitors often stay at Scheveningen, and make the 10-minute drive or tram ride into The Hague.

Until early in the 19th century, this was a sleepy fishing village set amid the dunes on the North Sea coast. But as its beaches began to attract vacation crowds, Scheveningen evolved into an internationally known watering hole. The magnificent and beautifully restored 19th-century waterfront Kurhaus Hotel still draws celebrities

---

Fun Fact   **Code Name: Scheveningen**

Just try to pronounce Scheveningen (skh-*ay*-vening-uhn) correctly! The name is so difficult to say that during World War II the Dutch underground used it as a code name for identification—the Germans just couldn't get it right.

---

from around the globe. Gamblers flock to the resort's casino, where tuxedoed croupiers ply their craft nightly.

ESSENTIALS

GETTING THERE   There is frequent **tram** service from The Hague by lines 1 and 9 to the seafront at Gevers Deynootplein in front of the Kurhaus Hotel; 11 to the beach between the Kurhaus and the fishing harbor; and 10 and 17 to the harbor area. Although there's no real reason to choose the **bus** over the tram, bus line 22 goes to the resort from outside Den Haag Centraal station.

By **car** from The Hague, you can take numerous alternative routes to the resort; the most direct is on Scheveningseweg from the Peace Palace, through the Scheveningen Woods. Going by **bicycle** is even better, and there are several special signposted bicycling routes.

VISITOR INFORMATION   VVV Scheveningen, Gevers Deynootweg 1134 (mailing address: Postbus 85456, 2500 CD Den Haag; © **0900/340-3505;** fax 070/352-0426; www.denhaag.com; tram: 1 or 9), is at the Palace Promenade mall. The office is open Monday to Friday from 9:30am to 5:30pm, Saturday from 10am to 5pm, and Sunday from 11am to 4pm.

SPECIAL EVENTS   The harbor, crowded with fishing boats and lined with restaurants that serve up just-caught seafood, is where the Dutch herring fleet is launched with a colorful *Vlaggetjesdag* (Flag Day) celebration each year on the first or second Saturday in June. Fishermen's wives dress up in their traditional costume. The fleet then returns with the new season's herring catch. Amid much fanfare, they rush the first batch off to the queen and conduct a lively auction with leading restaurateurs for the rest.

WHAT TO SEE & DO

The **Scheveningen Pier** *F* (© **070/306-5500;** www.pier.nl; tram: 1 or 9)—a wide, sand beach bordered by a 3km (2-mile) Promenade that juts into the North Sea—is one of this area's highlights. It first opened in 1901 and was rebuilt in 1961 after being destroyed in World War II. The walkway is covered for all-weather use. Adults and kids will be amused here. The choices range from a cafe-restaurant and indoor gaming arcades to an unusual inverted bungee-jump that throws you into the air on an industrial-size rubber band (see "Sea Sports & Recreation," below). The pier is open daily from 10am to midnight. Admission is 1€ ($1.25), and free for children under 4.

In the **Muzee Scheveningen,** Neptunusstraat 92 (© **070/350-0830;** www.museum scheveningen.nl; tram: 1 or 9), you can learn about the history of a former fishing village. The museum is open Tuesday to Saturday from 11am to 5pm, and Sunday from 1 to 5pm. Admission is 4€ ($5) for adults, 2.50€ ($3.15) for seniors and children.

You go under the sea, in a manner of speaking, at **Sea Life Scheveningen,** Strandweg (aka the Boulevard) 13 (© **070/354-2100;** www.sealife.nl; tram: 1 or 9), an aquarium with a walk-through underwater tunnel from where you can observe the denizens of the deep, including sharks, swimming around above your head. The aquarium is just west of the Kurhaus Hotel and is open August, daily from 10am to 7pm; and September to July, daily from 10am to 6pm (closed Dec 25). Admission is 12€ ($14) for adults, 11€ ($13) for seniors and visitors with disabilities, 8€ ($10) for children ages 3 to 11, and free for children under 3.

A few blocks away from the Kurhaus, a museum inside the dunes, almost hidden by giant masks looking out to sea, offers a peaceful oasis amid the seaside entertainment. This museum, **Beelden aan Zee (Sculptures on the Seafront),** Harteveltstraat 1 (© 070/358-5857; www.beeldenaanzee.nl; tram: 1), just off the seafront Boulevard, is dedicated to sculptures of the human body. There are changing exhibitions by modern sculptors from around the world, and an impressive permanent collection. The halls are different shapes, and some exhibits are outside on the patios. Wherever you are in the museum, you'll be aware of the surrounding dunes and the wind playing in the grass. From the highest terrace, you can even glimpse the sea. The museum is open Tuesday to Sunday from 11am to 5pm. Admission is 7€ ($8.75) for adults, 3.50€ ($4.40) for children ages 5 to 18, and free for children under 5.

Scheveningen's southern neighboring beach resort, **Kijkduin,** is quieter and more family-oriented. Its main attractions are the sea and dunes.

SEA SPORTS & RECREATION

The North Sea's fair-to-middling waves make surfing fun for both the initiated and the uninitiated, who might prefer boogie boards. A wet suit is not an option but a necessity, unless you want to experience hypothermia. You can rent surfboards and wet suits at **Hart Beach Shop,** Vissershavenweg 55B (© 070/358-5900), which runs a beach hut during the summer season. The unfortunately named **Go Klap,** Dr. Lelykade 44 (© 070/354-8679), rents surfboards, other windsurfing gear, and sea kayaks.

You can head out from the harbor for a deep-sea fishing day trip aboard a converted trawler, operated by **Rederij Groen,** Dr. Lelykade 1D (© 070/355-3588).

Windsurfers congregate at the **Windsurfvereniging** beach hut opposite the lighthouse. For windsurfing and kite-surfing lessons, in and out of season, contact instructor **Harry Vogelezang** (© 065/132-3547).

Are you up for a plunge into the cold gray waters of the North Sea? **Bungy Jump** (© 070/310-6242) can accommodate you, with a 60m (262-ft.) freefall from their jump point on Scheveningen Pier. Jump times (weather permitting) are May to June

---

Kids A Great Theme Park

For a theme park with rides galore—roller coasters, carousels, treetop cable cars, and Europe's largest tropical water paradise, head for **Duinrell** ⭐, Duinrell 1 (© 070/515-5255; www.duinrell.com), at Wassenaar, 5km (3 miles) north of The Hague. Water activities include luge runs, a centrifugal "Waterspin," and floating plastic frogs. In addition to the amusement park, covered tropical swimming pools are ideal for wet-weather days with kids. The park is open April to October, daily from 10am to 5pm; the pool is open throughout the year. September to March, you can ski on an outdoors artificial ski slope. Admission is 19€ ($23), and free for children under 4. Bus no. 491 goes to the park from The Hague Centraal station and other points in the center city.

and September, weekends from noon to 8pm; and July and August, Wednesday to Sunday from noon to midnight.

WHERE TO STAY

De Seinduin   This rather plain, small hotel has clean, simply furnished guest rooms. Some large rooms are especially suitable for groups or families—the hotel offers a special group discount. The beach is just around the corner, and the beach-front is lined with cafes and restaurants where you can relax after a plunge in the sea.

Seinpostduin 15, 2586 EA Scheveningen. ℭ **070/355-1971.** Fax 070/350-5829. www.hotelseinduin.nl. 18 units. 70€–110€ ($88–$138) double. Rates include continental breakfast. AE, DC, MC, V. Tram: 1 to Gevers Deynootweg. *In room:* TV, minibar.

Steigenberger Kurhaus Hotel ✮✮✮   The five-star Kurhaus is the undisputed grande dame of the North Sea coast. Its leather-bound guest register, which opens with the signature of the 13-year-old Queen Wilhelmina, is filled with the names of the world's greats and illustrated by leading artists who embellished their signatures with original drawings. The Kurhaus's Kurzaal concert hall has seen performances by leading musical artists as disparate as violinist Yehudi Menuhin and the Rolling Stones. The guest rooms, many with balconies facing the sea, are spacious and have elegant decor and furnishings, including trouser presses. The splendid **Kandinsky** restaurant, where the dining room walls are "decorated" with signed lithographs by abstract artist Wasily Kandinsky (1866–1944), has earned an international reputation. The **Kurzaal** has lavish lunch and dinner buffets, and even more lavish ones on week-ends, spread in the gorgeous Kurzaal area, with after-dinner dancing on Friday and Saturday nights. The Kurzaal Café is for drinks and light meals.

Gevers Deynootplein 30, 2586 CK Scheveningen. ℭ **070/416-2636.** Fax 070/416-2646. www.kurhaus.nl. 255 units. 245€–345€ ($306–$431) double; from 495€ ($619) suite. Rates include full breakfast. AE, DC, MC, V. Tram: 1 or 9 to Circustheater. **Amenities:** 2 restaurants (French, Continental); bar; lounge; access to nearby health club and spa; concierge; secretarial services; 24-hr. room service; in-room massage; babysitting; dry cleaning; laundry service. *In room:* TV, minibar, hair dryer, safe.

WHERE TO DINE

Ducdalf ✮ SEAFOOD   On a street by the wharf, you can rest assured that the fish you order here isn't long out of local waters. The menu also lists an amazingly varied selection of main courses, including steak, veal, and chicken for non-seafood lovers. There's a very good mixed grill, and filet of sole appears in no fewer than 11 different guises. For dessert, try the *appelgebak* (apple pie); it's a contender for the best in Holland.

Dr. Lelykade 5. ℭ **070/355-7692.** www.ducdalf.com. Main courses 16€–40€ ($20–$50). AE, DC, MC, V. Tues–Sat 5–10:30pm; Sun noon–10:30pm. Tram: 11 to Dr. Lelykade.

Het Brouwcafe DUTCH/SEAFOOD   This microbrewery puts up three or four of its house-brand beers, depending on the season, and an impressive selection of domes-tic and foreign beers. The atmosphere is lively thanks to all this free-flowing beer, and the food is scrumptious and filling, too. The fixed-price three-course menu changes weekly and might include mouthwatering lasagna with tuna and lemon sole as a main course. Many dishes can be ordered as a starter or a main course, and alongside fish dishes, there are meat and vegetarian choices.

Dr. Lelykade 28. ℭ **070/354-0970.** www.hetbrouwcafe.nl. Main courses 9€–16€ ($11–$20); fixed-price menu 16€ ($20). AE, MC, V. Tram: 11 to Dr. Lelykade.

Herring Days

Scheveningen may be the place most obsessed with herring in this herring-obsessed land. On the last Saturday in May, fishing boats compete to land the season's first *nieuwe haring* (new herring) during the annual, colorful *Vlaggetjesdag* (Flag Day) event. The fresh-caught fish is considered a delicacy; it's eaten whole (minus the head and the tail!), or chopped with minced onion if you're squeamish. Year-round, the fish are pickled as *maatjes.* You can get herring from sidewalk vendors, beachfront fish stands, and trailers towed onto the beach. See "A Taste of Holland," in appendix B.

SCHEVENINGEN AFTER DARK

Tuxedoed croupiers provide blackjack and roulette at **Holland Casino Scheveningen,** Kurhausweg 1 (© **070/306-7777;** www.hollandcasino.com; tram: 1 or 9), across from the restored 19th-century Kurhaus Hotel. There's also punto banco, fruit machines, and more. The dress code here is "correct" (collar and tie for men), and the minimum age is 18. You need your passport to get in. The casino is open daily (except May 4 and Dec 31) from 1:30pm to 3am. Admission is 4€ ($5).

Look for nightclubs at Gevers Deynootplein in front of the Kurhaus, and for theater productions at the **Circustheater,** which may include opera, ballet, and musical theater.

3 Rotterdam

58km (36 miles) SW of Amsterdam; 23km (16 miles) SE of The Hague

Rotterdam is only 30 minutes from The Hague and an hour from Amsterdam, but it's centuries away from them in both appearance and personality. Here, instead of the usual Dutch web of little streets, alleyways, and winding canals, there's a spacious and elegant shopping mall and the world's busiest ocean harbor. Rotterdam is a fascinating place to see, particularly when you consider that this city was a living monument to Holland's Golden Age until it was bombed to rubble during World War II. The city retains traces of its long history in only two areas—Delfshaven (Delft Harbor) and Oude Haven (Old Harbor).

At the war's end, rather than try to recreate the old, Rotterdammers looked on their misfortune as an opportunity and approached their city as a clean slate. They relished the chance to create an efficient, workable modern city. The results, though they're not always elegant, are a testimony to their ability to find impressive solutions to their problems.

Today this bustling metropolis (pop. 600,000) has the world's biggest port, created when its several harbors were opened directly to the sea, 32km (20 miles) away, by the dredging of a deepwater channel that accommodates even the largest oil tankers. **Europoort** (pronounced the same as "port" in English) handles more ships and more cargo every year than any other port in the world.

ESSENTIALS

GETTING THERE Rotterdam's **Zestienhoven Airport** (© **010/446-3455;** www.rotterdam-airport.nl), 4km (2½ miles) north of the city, has scheduled flights from a few places in the Netherlands and Europe. Bus no. 33 goes from the airport to

Rotterdam

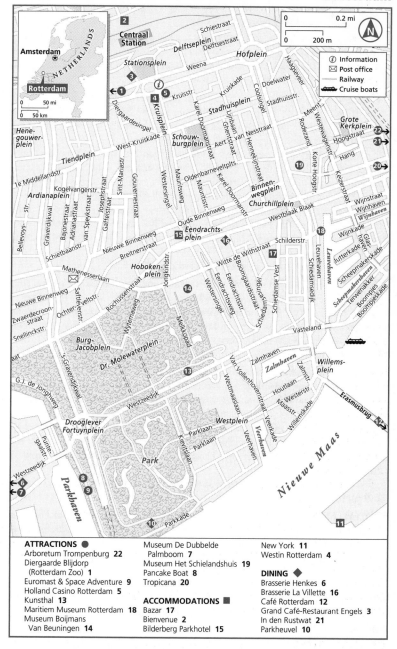

ATTRACTIONS ●
Arboretum Trompenburg **22**
Diergaarde Blijdorp
  (Rotterdam Zoo) **1**
Euromast & Space Adventure **9**
Holland Casino Rotterdam **5**
Kunsthal **13**
Maritiem Museum Rotterdam **18**
Museum Boijmans
  Van Beuningen **14**

Museum De Dubbelde
  Palmboom **7**
Museum Het Schielandshuis **19**
Pancake Boat **8**
Tropicana **20**

ACCOMMODATIONS ■
Bazar **17**
Bienvenue **2**
Bilderberg Parkhotel **15**

New York **11**
Westin Rotterdam **4**

DINING ◆
Brasserie Henkes **6**
Brasserie La Villette **16**
Café Rotterdam **12**
Grand Café-Restaurant Engels **3**
In den Rustwat **21**
Parkheuvel **10**

> *Fun Fact* **Working People**
>
> The citizens of Rotterdam are so hardworking that they're said to be "born with their sleeves already rolled up."

the center city in 20 minutes for 2.70€ ($3.40); a taxi to downtown is around 20€ ($25). If, as is far more likely, you fly into Amsterdam's **Schiphol Airport** (see "Orientation," in chapter 12), Netherlands Railways has fast train service (45 min.) from Schiphol to Rotterdam, for a fare of 10€ ($13) one-way.

There's frequent **train** service to Rotterdam Centraal station from around the Netherlands, and from Paris and Brussels. From Amsterdam, there are two to six trains each hour round-the-clock; the trip takes around 1 hour, and a round-trip ticket is 23€ ($28). For information on train schedules, call ✆ **0900/9292.**

The Hoek van Holland sea-ferry terminal, for **car ferries** from Harwich in England, is 20km (13 miles) away, and there are good bus and train connections. Rotterdam's Europoort, the terminal for P&O Ferries car ferries from Hull in England, is about a 30-minute drive.

By **car** from Amsterdam, take A4/E19, and then A13/E19.

VISITOR INFORMATION VVV **Rotterdam**'s mailing address is: Postbus 30235, 3001 DE Rotterdam (✆ **0900/403-4065;** fax 010/413-3124; www.vvvrotterdam.nl). You can visit the **VVV Rotterdam Store,** Coolsingel 5 (at Hofplein), open Monday to Thursday from 9am to 6pm, Friday from 9am to 9pm, Saturday from 9am to 5:30pm, and (Apr–Sept) Sunday from 10am to 5pm.

GETTING AROUND Rotterdam's sprawling size makes it a city to be explored on foot one area at a time, using a taxi or the extensive **RET** (✆ 010/447-6911; www.ret.nl) public transportation network of bus, tram, and Metro (which runs on north-south and east-west axes) to move from one area to another. The VVV can furnish a map of public transportation routes.

In addition to the various types of *strippenkaart* (see "Getting Around," in chapter 12 for how to use these tickets), which are valid nationally, day tickets for 1, 2, and 3 days are available, covering the city. These cost 6.40€ ($8), 9.60€ ($12), and 13€ ($16) respectively.

Taxi stands are sprinkled throughout the city; or call **Rotterdamse Taxi Centrale** (✆ 010/462-6060).

SPECIAL EVENTS The festival year kicks off with the **International Film Festival** (✆ 010/890-9090), which has established a reputation over 3 decades for presenting quality independent films. During 10 days in late January/early February, huge numbers of film buffs find their way to cinemas around the center city to watch one or more of about 300 films shown on 15 screens.

Each year, for 3 days every July, jazz greats from around the world gather in Holland for the **North Sea Jazz Festival** (✆ 015/214-8393; www.northseajazz.nl). This nonstop extravaganza features star performances by internationally acclaimed musicians, in some 200 concerts of jazz, free jazz, blues, Be Bop, and world music, at the giant Ahoy venue.

Another festival worth looking out for is the multicultural **Summer Carnival** (✆ 010/414-1772) and its colorful street parade, on the last weekend of July.

WHAT TO SEE & DO

Rotterdam's modern urban planning has resulted in an unusually effective use of city-center space. Particularly attractive are the shingle paths and lazy lawns in the landscaped **Museumpark,** which serves as a central focus for two of the museums mentioned below. Between visits you can stretch your legs or sit down and have a picnic.

THE TOP ATTRACTIONS

Euromast and Space Adventure ★★ *Kids*   This slender tower, 188m (611 ft.) tall, is indisputably the best vantage point for an overall view of Rotterdam and its environs. More than that, though, the tower contains interesting exhibitions, a restaurant, and an exciting Space Cabin ride that emulates a rocket takeoff. A super-fast elevator brings you up to the viewing platforms.

Parkhaven 20. ✆ 010/436-4811. www.euromast.nl. Admission 8€ ($10) adults, 5.20€ ($6.50) children 4–11, free for children under 4. Apr–Sept daily 9:30am–11pm; Oct–Mar daily 10am–11pm. Tram: 8 to Euromast.

Maritiem Museum Rotterdam ★ *Kids*   Devoted entirely to the history of Rotterdam Harbor, this marvelous museum consists of two sections: the main building, and *De Buffel,* a beautifully restored 1868 warship. Constantly changing exhibits give you new insight into the close relationship between the Dutch and the sea. In the museum harbor basin, some 20 vessels—dating from 1850 to 1950—are moored. There's a bookstore and a coffeeshop.

Leuvehaven 1 (at the harbor). ✆ 010/413-2680. www.maritiemmuseum.nl. Admission 5€ ($6.25) adults, 3€ ($3.75) children 4–16, free for children under 4. Tues–Sat 10am–5pm (also Mon July–Aug and school vacations); Sun and holidays 11am–5pm. Closed Jan 1, Apr 30, Dec 25. Metro: Beurs, Churchillplein.

Museum Boijmans Van Beuningen ★★★   Art lovers will enjoy this collection of works by 16th- and 17th-century Dutch and Flemish artists, such as Rubens, Hals, Rembrandt, and Steen. They share wall space with an international contingent that includes Salvador Dalí and Man Ray, Titian and Tintoretto, Degas and Daumier. Other galleries hold international modern art, sculpture, porcelain, silver, glass, and Delftware, and regular exhibits of prints and drawings. It's particularly enjoyable to walk among the modern sculptures in the gardens.

Museumpark 18–20. ✆ 010/441-9400. www.boijmans.rotterdam.nl. Admission 8€ ($10) adults, free on Wednesday and for children under 18. Tues–Sat 10am–5pm; Sun and holidays 11am–5pm. Closed Jan 1, Apr 30, Dec 25. Tram: 4 or 5 to Witte de Withstraat.

Museum Het Schielandshuis ★   Lost between towering office blocks is the Schielandshuis, the city's sole survivor from the 17th century. The building has been gloriously restored and now shows off Rotterdam's cultural heritage. Period rooms are filled with furnishings rescued from mansions destroyed during World War II. The Atlas Van Stolk, a vast collection of prints and drawings relating to Dutch history,

---

⌜Fun Fact **Dutch Heights**

Maybe it's nature's way of compensating for their country being altitudinally challenged, but the Dutch are TALL. The average man is 1.8m (6 ft.) and the average woman is 1.7m (5 ft., 7 in.), which in both cases is 5 centimeters (2 in.) more than the European average. Not only that, but a government study showed that the average height of the Dutch increases by 1.5 centimeters (½ in.) every decade.

---

occupies an entire floor. An interesting minor exhibit is Holland's second-oldest clog shoe (the oldest was found in Amsterdam), dating from the second half of the 13th century and made from alder wood.

Korte Hoogstraat 31. ℂ **010/217-6767**. www.hmr.rotterdam.nl. Admission 2.70€ ($3.40) adults, 1.35€ ($1.70) children 4–16, free for children under 4. Tues–Fri 10am–5pm; Sat–Sun and holidays 11am–5pm. Closed Jan 1, Apr 30, Dec 25. Metro: Beurs.

OTHER MUSEUMS & ATTRACTIONS

Arboretum Trompenburg ★ *Finds* This gorgeous garden has evolved from a family-owned 19th-century estate into a peaceful oasis east of the center city that is kept in good order by an army of gardeners. Originally landscaped as an English country garden, the arboretum today has more than 4,000 trees, bushes, and perennials. Oak, pine, cedar, hostas, and rhododendron are particularly well represented, and there are a rose garden, goldfish pond, aviary, and glasshouse full of cacti and succulents. With a variety of bridges and benches, the garden is a perfect antidote to exhaustion-inducing sightseeing.

Honingerdijk 86. ℂ **010/233-0166**. www.trompenburg.nl. Admission 3.75€ ($4.70) adults, free for children under 13. Apr–Oct Mon–Fri 9am–5pm, Sat–Sun 10am–4pm; Nov–Mar Mon–Fri 9am–5pm, Sat 10am–4pm, Sun noon–4pm. Closed Dec 23–Jan 7 (the closed dates might vary by a few days). Tram: 21 to Woudestein.

Museum De Dubbelde Palmboom ★ On Voorhaven, in the old port district, is this historical museum, which consists of twin converted warehouses. Craftspeople work in the old Zakkendragershuisje (Grain Sack Carriers Guild House), using copies of 17th- and 18th-century molds to cast beautiful plates, bowls, tea urns, and other utensils—their products make great gifts.

Voorhaven 12, Delfshaven (at the harbor). ℂ **010/476-1533**. www.hmr.rotterdam.nl. Admission 3€ ($3.75) adults, 1.50€ ($1.90) seniors/children 4–16, free for children under 4. Tues–Fri 10am–5pm; Sat–Sun and holidays 11am–5pm. Closed Jan 1, Apr 30, Dec 25. Metro: Delfshaven.

MODERN ARCHITECTURE

Rotterdam has some spectacular modern architecture. Just outside Centraal station you encounter the office of the **Nationale Nederlanden** insurance corporation, the city's highest skyscraper at 152m (495 ft.). Down Coolsingel is the bottle-green **World Trade Center;** and east of this, on Overblaak, is a geometric chaos of quirky, cube-shaped apartments balancing atop tall concrete stalks. One of them, the **Kijk-Kubus,** Overblaak 70 (ℂ **010/414-2285;** www.kubuswoning.nl; Metro: Blaak), is open for visits March to December, daily from 11am to 5pm; January to February, Friday to Sunday from 11am to 5pm. Admission is 2€ ($2.50) for adults, 1.50€ ($1.90) for seniors and children ages 4 to 12, and free for children under 4.

Two prominent bridges span the Nieuwe Maas River, the dark red **Nieuwe Willemsbrug,** and a single-span suspension bridge called the **Erasmusbrug** and nick-named "The Swan" (or, if you're not quite as charmed by its looks, "The Dishwash-ing Brush").

To see a splendid surviving corner of Old Rotterdam, take the Metro to **Delfshaven** which, many years ago, was Delft's harbor. Of special interest to Americans is the old **Pilgrim Fathers Church,** on Voorhaven, in which the Pilgrims said their last prayers before setting off for the New World aboard the *Speedwell.* The *Speedwell* didn't prove to be very seaworthy, though, so after crossing the English Channel, the Pilgrims boarded another ship in Southampton—the *Mayflower.* The Pilgrims are remembered in special services every Thanksgiving Day.

ESPECIALLY FOR KIDS

Diergaarde Blijdorp (Blijdorp/Rotterdam Zoo) ⭐⭐ *Kids*   A large enclosed plaza contains elephants, crocodiles, reptiles, amphibians, and tropical plants and birds. An Asian section houses Javanese monkeys, a bat cave, and exotic birds. The newly opened Oceanium section presents a submarine world inhabited by sharks, jellyfish, and other creatures of the deep brought here from around the world.

Abraham van Stolkweg. ✆ 010/443-1495. www.rotterdamzoo.nl. Admission 16€ ($19) adults, 14€ ($17) seniors, 13€ ($16) children 3–11, free for children under 3. Oct–Mar daily 9am–5pm; Apr–Sept Mon–Fri 9am–5pm; Sun, holidays, and school vacations 9am–6pm. Bus: 32, 33, or 39 to Diergaarde Blijdorp.

Tropicana *Kids*   This water-based amusement park simulates a luxuriant tropical setting. It has recreational facilities such as a swimming pool, a wave pool, a sauna, water slides, hot whirlpools, a wild-water strip, and a swimmers' bar.

Maasboulevard 100. ✆ 010/402-0700. www.tropicana.nl. 15€ ($18) adults, 12€ ($14) children 4–12, free for children under 4. Mon–Fri 10am–10pm; Sat–Sun and holidays 10am–8pm. Closed Jan 1, Apr 30, Dec 25. Tram: 1 to Oostplein.

ORGANIZED TOURS

One of the best things to do in Rotterdam is to take a **harbor cruise** ⭐⭐ from Spido Rondvaarten, Leuvehaven (✆ **010/275-9988;** www.spido.nl; Metro: Leuvehaven). Departures are April to September daily every 30 to 45 minutes from 9:30am to 5pm; October to March two to four times per day. The season of the year determines how much of the vast port you're able to see, but it's an unforgettable experience. The basic cruise, offered year-round, is a 75-minute tour of the city's waterfront. There are also extended tours; all-day excursions to the sluices of the Delta Works and along the full length of Europoort; music and dinner cruises; and more. Tours are from 8.75€ ($11) for adults, 5.40€ ($6.75) for children ages 4 to 11, and free for children under 4.

A big treat awaits your family aboard the **Pannenkoekenboot (Pancake Boat)** ⭐, Parkhaven (✆ **010/436-7295;** www.pannenkoekenboot.nl; tram: 8), moored at the foot of Euromast. As soon as the boat weighs anchor, it's a free-for-all at the pancake buffet, with as many plain, bacon, or apple pancakes as you can eat during the 1-hour

---

Grand Harbor

A dredged deepwater channel connects Rotterdam with the North Sea and forms a 32km-long (20-mile) harbor known as **Europoort**. This seaport handles more ships and more cargo every year than any other port in the world—20,000 ships and 310 million metric tons of cargo. Holland owes a fair piece of its prosperity to these statistics, but the port has a dark side, too: Rotterdam is a center for big-time international drug-dealers and gun-runners.

You may think visiting a harbor is boring business on a vacation, but Rotterdam's is one of the most memorable sights in Holland. Container ships, bulk carriers, tankers, sleek greyhounds of the sea, and careworn tramps are waited on by a vast retinue of machines and people. Trucks, trains, and barges, each carrying its little piece of the action, hurry into and out of the hub. You feel dwarfed by the hulking oil tankers and container ships that glide like giant whales into their berths along the miles of docks.

trip. Departures are Saturday and Sunday at 1:30, 3, 4:30, and 6pm; and Wednesday and Friday at 4:30 and 6pm. The cost is 14€ ($17) for adults, 8.50€ ($11) for children ages 3 to 12, and free for children under 3.

WHERE TO STAY

Bazar 𝒦𝒦   On a busy street near the main museums, the main floor of this place oozes with the atmosphere of *1,001 Nights*—golden pillars, frilly textiles, open-worked shutters, Persian rugs, stained-glass lamps, and brass fittings. By way of thematic variation, there's an African floor and a South American floor. The rooms follow these cues in both design and spirit, making for a distinctive experience, so long as you feel comfortable in whichever ambience you're given. If not, ask to change. The ground-floor international cafe-restaurant Bazar doubles as hotel reception, and the staff comprises more than a dozen nationalities—which is nice, but reportedly leads to mixed standards of service.

Witte de Withstraat 16, 3012 BP Rotterdam. 𝒸 **010/206-5151.** Fax 010/206-5159. www.hotelbazar.nl. 27 units. 75€–125€ ($94–$156) double. Rates include Middle Eastern breakfast. AE, DC, MC, V. Limited street parking. Tram: 5, 20, or 23. **Amenities:** Restaurant (international); bar. *In room:* TV, minibar.

Bienvenue   This small, budget hotel is one of the best in its price range. The bright guest rooms have soft red carpets, comfortable beds, and clean showers (two bathrooms have tubs). There's a canal in front of the hotel, and rooms at the back open onto the terrace. The hotel offers a tasty breakfast buffet.

Spoorsingel 24 (behind Centraal station), 3033 GL Rotterdam. 𝒸 **010/466-9394.** Fax 010/467-7475. www.hotel bienvenue.nl. 10 units, 7 with bathroom. 75€ ($94) double with bathroom; 65€ ($81) double without bathroom. Rates include continental breakfast. AE, DC, MC, V. Limited street parking. Metro: Centraal station. *In room:* TV.

Bilderberg Parkhotel Rotterdam 𝒦   For city-center convenience, you can't do better than this modern high-rise, set in a private garden. The spacious guest rooms (some of which are air-conditioned) are luxurious, furnished with soft couches, comfortable beds, and elegant bathrooms. The **Empress** restaurant is open for breakfast, lunch, and dinner.

Westersingel 70, 3015 LB Rotterdam. 𝒸 **010/436-3611.** Fax 010/436-4212. www.parkhotelrotterdam.nl. 189 units. 175€–320€ ($219–$400) double; from 795€ ($994) suite. AE, DC, MC, V. Parking 15€ ($19). Metro: Eendrachtplein. **Amenities:** Restaurant (Continental); bar; lounge; health club and sauna; 24-hr. room service; laundry service; dry cleaning; nonsmoking rooms; executive rooms. *In room:* TV w/pay movies, dataport, minibar, hair dryer, safe.

New York 𝒦   This building, one of Europe's first skyscrapers, was constructed at the beginning of the 20th century to house the headquarters of the Holland-America shipping line, which sailed to New York. Many of the city's emigrants passed through these portals with their trunks. The reception rooms retain some of their original features. In the bright guest rooms, stylish furnishings combine the old and the new; some rooms have stunning balcony views. The downstairs cafe-restaurant has a great view over the river and docklands. Open all day, it serves both teatime treats and dinner.

Koninginnenhoofd 1, 3072 AD Rotterdam. 𝒸 **010/439-0500.** Fax 010/484-2701. www.hotelnewyork.nl. 72 units. 95€–210€ ($119–$263) double. AE, DC, MC, V. Limited street parking. Tram: 5 to Westplein. **Amenities:** Restaurant (international/seafood); bar; limited room service; laundry service; dry cleaning. *In room:* TV, minibar.

Westin Rotterdam 𝒦   Welcome to a lodging where the "heavenly bed" was specially designed, the minibar is called an "electronic refreshment center," and laptop safes are provided. Shiny, modern, and somewhat impersonal, the hotel, which takes up the first 14 floors of the 32-story Millennium Tower, is the latest in five-star accommodations. It stands at the heart of a district of theaters, restaurants, stores, and a casino. In typical Westin fashion, the rooms are hushed oases of relative luxury. Rooms are big—in some of the upper-floor rooms you might need a bullhorn to cast your voice into the remotest nooks and crannies. The **Lighthouse Bar and Restaurant** is open for breakfast, lunch, and dinner.

Weena 686 (opposite Centraal station), 3012 CN Rotterdam. ✆ **010/430-2000.** Fax 010/430-2001. www.westin.com. 231 units. 315€–350€ ($394–$438) double; from 525€ ($525) suite. AE, DC, V. Valet parking 25€ ($31). Metro: Centraal station. **Amenities:** Restaurant (Continental); bar; health club and sauna; concierge; business center; 24-hr. room service; laundry service; dry cleaning; nonsmoking rooms; executive rooms. *In room:* TV w/pay movies, dataport, minibar, hair dryer, safe.

WHERE TO DINE
VERY EXPENSIVE

Parkheuvel FRENCH/INTERNATIONAL   With three Michelin stars to his credit, patron/chef Cees Helder will amuse your palate with luxurious dishes made from the freshest ingredients. The seafood dishes are particularly astounding: Try the starter of *carpaccio* of sea bass, or a lobster salad with sun-dried tomatoes and rucola. Main courses range from *turbot gratinée* to poached filet of beef with truffles.

Heuvellaan 21. ✆ 010/436-0766. www.parkheuvel.nl. Reservations recommended on weekends. Main courses 30€–40€ ($38–$50); fixed-price menus 40€–50€ ($50–$63). AE, DC, MC, V. Mon–Fri noon–2:30pm and 6:30–10pm; Sat 6:30–10pm. Tram: 5.

EXPENSIVE

In den Rustwat 𝕳𝕳 FRENCH   You'd swear you're in the country at the "Rest Some," but then, back in the 16th century, this thatched farmhouse-style restaurant used to be an inn. Patron/cuisinier Marcel van Zomeren has turned it into one of the city's top establishments. Using only the freshest organic ingredients, he keeps himself and his staff inspired by constantly adapting the menu to seasonal produce. A salad of Bresse pigeon breast with poached quail's eggs and a ravioli of pigeon and gooseliver is an example of a starter, which might be followed by crisp sautéed sea bass filet on a bed of warm tomatoes and young vegetables. Van Zomeren insists he has no specialties, and that everything he prepares meets his high standards.

Honingerdijk 96 (beside the Arboretum Trompenburg). ✆ 010/413-4110. www.indenrustwat.nl. Reservations recommended on weekends. Lunch menu 33€ ($41); fixed-price dinner menus 43€–58€ ($54–$73). AE, DC, MC, V. Tues–Fri noon–3pm and 6–10pm; Sat 6–10pm. Tram: 1.

MODERATE

Brasserie Henkes 𝕳𝕳 DUTCH/CONTINENTAL   The interior of the old Henkes *jenever* (Dutch gin) distillery has been completely transformed with the furnishings of a 19th-century Belgian insurance bank. Warm woodwork and brass chandeliers create a dining room on a grand scale. And this is an ideal place to appreciate the special atmosphere of old Delfshaven. The waterside terrace invites you to while away a sunny afternoon; later, you can take a leisurely stroll down to the harbor and then return for dinner. You can enjoy seafood and meat dishes or seasonal specialties like venison with a chocolate-and-port sauce.

Voorhaven 17 (at Delfshaven). ✆ 010/425-5596. www.henkes.nl. Main courses 15€–20€ ($19–$25); fixed-price menu 28€ ($35). AE, DC, MC, V. Daily 11:30am–midnight; kitchen closes at 10pm. Metro: Delfshaven.

Brasserie La Vilette 𝕳 CLASSIC FRENCH   Elegant and filled with potted plants and flowers, this center-city oasis has soft rose-colored walls and starched white table linen. Service is both polished and friendly. For starters, try the filet of beef *carpaccio.*

The grilled sea bass with lobster sauce makes a fine main course, and the crème brûlée with ice cream flavored with sweet Pedro Ximenez sherry is a tempting dessert. This member of the Alliance Gastronomique is much favored by leading business executives.

Westblaak 160. ℂ 010/414-8692. Main courses 24€–29€ ($30–$36); fixed-price menu 45€ ($56). AE, DC, MC, V. Mon–Sat noon–2pm and 6–9:30pm. Tram: 4 or 5.

Café Rotterdam 👍👍 DUTCH   As I savored the delicious flavors of skin-fried cod with truffle purée and spinach, a dramatic sunset lit up the low-lying barges gliding down the Nieuwe Maas outside. You might not be so lucky, but this cafe/restaurant—a jewel in Rotterdam's crown where royalty, dockworkers, and visitors can feel equally at home—is a good choice at any time. The architecture of the old cruise-ship terminal and the potted olive trees give its four floors a special atmosphere. Chef Albert Kooy recommends the shellfish platter as a starter, and caramelized apple pie with calves' liver, bacon, and onion for a main course.

Wilhelminakade 699. ℂ 010/290-8442. www.caferotterdam.nl. Main courses 13€–19€ ($16–$23); fixed-price menu 23€ ($29). AE, DC, MC, V. Mon–Thurs 11am–midnight; Fri–Sat 11am–1am; Sun 10am–midnight. Metro: Wilhelminaplein.

SHOPPING

You can shop till you drop in Rotterdam. On Lijnbaan, Holland's first car-free shopping promenade, which recently got a face-lift, you'll find dozens of small fashion boutiques. If you're pressed for time, the nearby **De Bijenkorf** department store, Coolsingel 105 (ℂ **010/282-3700**), sells a variety of designer labels under one roof. On one side, it opens onto the new Beurstraverse shopping mall, which runs below street level and has a mix of chain stores and small stores.

On the trendy south bank, the **Entrepot,** a 19th-century bonded warehouse, enjoys a new lease on life. In a place that defines the idea of fun shopping, you find distinct colonial overtones at **Konmar,** Vijf Werelddelen 33 (ℂ **010/280-9888**), the city's largest supermarket. A colonnade of diverse restaurants overlooks a small marina and faces a row of interior design stores.

Back in the center city, a huge **general market** brings alive the Binnenrotte area on Tuesday and Saturday. Part of the market (still 200 stalls!) opens from May to December on Sunday afternoon. Lovers of antiques, bric-a-brac, and old books should make their way to the **Sunday market** on Schiedamsedijk.

ROTTERDAM AFTER DARK

The world-class **Rotterdam Philharmonic Orchestra** plays at **De Doelen** concert hall, at Kruisstraat 2 (ℂ **010/217-1717**). If you want to see a global pop star, take a ride to **Ahoy** 👍, Zuiderparkweg 20 (ℂ **0900/235-2469**). Megastars perform here to capacity audiences of 10,000.

You can try your luck at **Holland Casino Rotterdam,** Plaza Complex, Weena 624 (ℂ **010/206-8206;** Metro: Centraal station). There's roulette, blackjack, punto banco, fruit machines, and more. The dress code here is "correct" (collar and tie for men), and the minimum age is 18. You need your passport to get in. The casino is open daily (except May 4, Dec 31) from 1:30pm to 3am. Admission is 4€ ($5).

After nightfall, a multitude of establishments in Rotterdam come alive with guests eager to eat, drink, and be merry. Along with drinking and dancing, late-night dining is on the menu in the 50m-long (164-ft.) tunnel called **De Blauwe Vis,** Weena Zuid 33 (ℂ **010/213-4243**). The close-by **Baja Beach Club,** Karel Doormanstraat 12 (ℂ **010/213-0534;** www.baja.nl), guarantees a sunny ambience even when it rains,

Windmills of Kinderdijk

The sight of windmill sails spinning in the breeze stirs the soul of a true Hollander. Kinderdijk (www.kinderdijk.nl), a tiny community between Rotterdam and Dordrecht, on the south bank of the Lek River, has 19 water-pumping windmills; that means 76 mill sails, each with a 14-yard span, all revolving on a summer day. It's a spectacular sight, and one important enough for Kinderdijk to have been placed on UNESCO's World Heritage list.

By regulating the level of water, Kinderdijk's windmills guarded the fertile polders (reclaimed land) of the Alblasserwaard, which were constantly at risk of returning to the water. The Windmill Exposition Center at Kinderdijk treats its subjects as more than just pretty faces and gives a detailed explanation of windmills' technical characteristics and the part they played in the intricate system of water control. It also looks at the people and the culture that developed on the polders.

The mills operate on Saturday afternoons in July and August from 2:30 to 5:30pm; the visitors' mill is open April to October, Monday to Saturday from 9:30am to 5:30pm. To get to Kinderdijk from Rotterdam, take bus no. 154 from outside Zuidplein Metro station. If you're driving, take N210 east to Krimpen aan de Lek, from where a ferry crosses over to Kinderdijk.

and the tanned, muscular bar staff effortlessly slip into the role of entertainers. A younger crowd frequents **Nighttown,** West-Kruiskade 26 (© 010/436-1210), for dancing and lounging and for hard-core and mellow music, both live and recorded.

If it can be played on a piano, you might hear it at **Crazy Pianos,** Maasboulevard 300 (© 010/280-0238), whose gaudy neon signs attract revelers under the ramp leading up Willemsbrug. The formula, which includes eating, drinking, and dancing, appeals to patrons of all ages.

Jazz cats should make their way to **Dizzy** , 's Gravendijkwal 127 (© 010/477-3014; www.dizzy.nl), an informal, long-established cafe where live music is the name of the game. **Maastheater,** Boompjes 751 (© 010/413-4091), a waterside disco where DJs dictate the music styles, is popular with students. Some nights are hosted by Rotterdam's party organizer, Ted Langenbach, who is associated with the ultra-cool **Now and Wow Club,** Lloydstraat 30 (© 010/476-2452).

A place where the Rotterdam gay scene parties the nights away is the **Gay Palace,** Schiedamsesingel 139 (© 010/414-1486).

4 Delft

10km (6 miles) SE of The Hague; 14km (9 miles) NW of Rotterdam; 35km (22 miles) W of Gouda; 30km (19 miles) SW of Leiden; 55km (34 miles) SW of Amsterdam

Delft is perhaps the prettiest little town in all of Holland. The facades of the Renaissance and Gothic houses here reflect age-old beauty, and a sense of tranquillity pervades the air. Indeed, it's easy to understand why Vermeer chose to spend most of his life surrounded by Delft's gentle beauty. It remains quiet, with flower boxes (and plenty more in the flower market on Hippolytusbuurt) and linden trees bending over its gracious canals.

A good part of Holland's history is preserved in the tombs of Delft. William the Silent, who led the Dutch insurrection against Spanish rule, was assassinated in the Prinsenhof and now rests in a magnificent tomb in the Nieuwe Kerk; and every member of the House of Orange-Nassau since King Willem I has been brought here for burial as well. Delft is the final resting place of someone named Karl Naudorff, who is suspected of being Louis XVII, dauphin of France. And two of Holland's greatest naval figures, admirals Tromp and Heyn, are entombed in the Oude Kerk.

Of course, to many visitors, Delft means just one thing—the distinctive blue-and-white earthenware still produced by the meticulous methods of old. Every piece of true Delftware is hand-painted by skilled craftspeople. A different Delft exists on the modern campus of the town's Technical University, noted for the excellence of its scientist and engineer graduates, among the latter being many of the world-class Dutch hydraulic engineers.

ESSENTIALS

GETTING THERE   **Trains** frequently run from Amsterdam and Rotterdam to Delft. The trip is 55 minutes and 15 minutes, respectively, costing 20€ ($25) and 4.80€ ($6) round-trip. From The Hague you can go by tram; it's a three-zone, 20-minute ride that costs four strips on a *strippenkaart,* or the equivalent of about 1.25€/$1.70). By **car,** the town is just off A13/E19, the expressway from The Hague to Rotterdam.

VISITOR INFORMATION   **Tourist Information Delft,** Hippolytusbuurt 4, 2611 HN Delft (© 015/215-4051; www.delft.nl), is in the center of town. The office is open April to September, Sunday and Monday from 10am to 6pm, Tuesday to Friday from 9am to 6pm, and Saturday from 10am to 5pm; October to March, Sunday from 11am to 4pm, and Tuesday to Saturday from 10am to 4pm.

WHAT TO SEE & DO

The best way to absorb Delft's special ambience is by strolling the streets. Around every corner and down every street, you step into a scene that might have been composed for the canvas of a great artist. Supplement your walks with a leisurely tour of the canals via the numerous water taxis that operate during the summer. The town's large main square, the Markt, is a zoo on market day (Thurs), but on quieter days you get space to see how picturesque it is.

THE TOP ATTRACTIONS

De Koninklijke Porceleyne Fles ✿   The Delft Blue stamped with the "De Porceleyne Fles" stamp you came to town to find is made here by a traditional and painstaking method. You can watch the hand-painting of each item and see an audiovisual show that explains the entire process. Delft potters have been at it since the 1640s, when they met the competition of Chinese porcelain imported by the East India Company. And, if you thought the trademark blue-and-white colors were the only Delft, here is where you see exquisite multicolored patterns. Your purchases can be packed carefully and shipped home directly from this factory.

Rotterdamseweg 196. © 015/251-2030. www.royaldelft.com Admission 4€ ($5) adults, free for children under 12 (except for group visits, when it is 2.50€/$3.15). Apr–Oct daily 9am–5pm; Nov–Mar Mon–Sat 9am–5pm. Closed Dec 25–Jan 1. Bus: 63, 121, or 129 to Jaffalaan.

Museum Lambert van Meerten   You'll find the most fascinating collection of Delft earthenware, including old Delft tiles, in this industrialist's mansion from 1893.

Delft

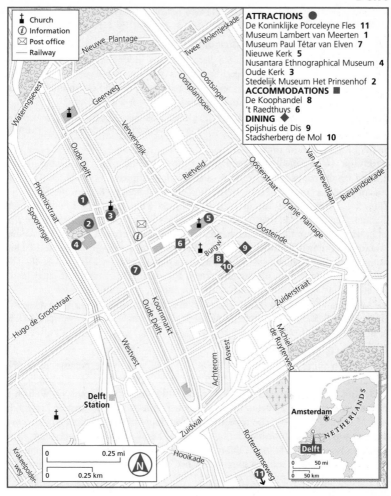

Church
ⓘ **Information**
✉ **Post office**
— **Railway**

ATTRACTIONS ●
De Koninklijke Porceleyne Fles **11**
Museum Lambert van Meerten **1**
Museum Paul Tétar van Elven **7**
Nieuwe Kerk **5**
Nusantara Ethnographical Museum **4**
Oude Kerk **3**
Stedelijk Museum Het Prinsenhof **2**
ACCOMMODATIONS ■
De Koophandel **8**
't Raedthuys **6**
DINING ◆
Spijshuis de Dis **9**
Stadsherberg de Mol **10**

Oude Delft 199 (north of Markt, near Prinsenhof). © 015/260-2358. www.lambertvanmeerten-delft.nl. Admission 3.50€ ($4.40) adults, 3€ ($3.75) children 12–16, free for children under 12. Tues–Sat 10am–5pm; Sun 1–5pm. Closed Jan 1, Dec 25.

Museum Paul Tétar van Elven ✦ *Finds*

The 19th-century artist van Elven (1823–96) lived and worked here, and the furnishings are just as he left them. The 17th-century-style studio looks like it's ready for the artist to enter and pick up his brushes. Van Elven was a noted copyist, and a lot of his reproductions hang on the walls. Except for a lousy Vermeer on the second floor, most of them are excellent, especially the Rembrandts and the Paulus Potter on the first floor. The furniture and porcelain collections are interesting, too. Watch your step on the exceptionally narrow and steep stairs going up to the attic exhibition room.

Koornmarkt 67 (just south of the Markt). ℗ 015/212-4206. Admission 2.50€ ($3.15) adults, free for children under 13. Mid-Apr to Oct Tues–Sun 1–5pm.

Nusantara Ethnographical Museum   A stunning collection of ethnographical objects from Indonesia is displayed here. Because Indonesia was a Dutch colony, Dutch academics have been specialists in this area for many years. The collection includes such beautiful objects as *wayang* shadow puppets and ceremonial attributes. The benches in the museum gardens are a nice place for a picnic lunch.

Sint-Agathaplein (north of Markt, near Oude Kerk). ℗ 015/260-2358. www.prinsenhof-delft.nl. Admission 3.50€ ($4.40) adults, 3€ ($3.75) seniors/children 12–16, free for children under 12. Tues–Sat 10am–5pm; Sun 1–5pm. Closed Jan 1, Dec 25.

Stedelijk (Municipal) Museum Het Prinsenhof ★   The Prinsenhof (Prince's Court), on the banks of Delft's oldest canal, Oude Delft, dates from the late 1400s and was originally a convent. This is where William I of Orange (William the Silent) lived from 1572 and had his headquarters in the years when he helped found the Dutch Republic, and where an assassin's bullets ended his life in 1584 (you can still see a pair of bullet holes from the fusillade that felled him in the stairwell). The interior William would have known has been recreated, and a museum preserves the record of Dutch struggles to throw off the yoke of Spanish occupation between 1568 and 1648. There are impressive tapestries, silverware, pottery, and paintings—among the latter are five other versions of the *View of Delft,* painted by contemporaries of Vermeer.

Sint-Agathaplein 1 (north of Markt, near Oude Kerk). ℗ 015/260-2358. www.prinsenhof-delft.nl. Admission 5€ ($6.25) adults, 4€ ($5) seniors and children 12–16, free for children under 12. Tues–Sat 10am–5pm; Sun 1–5pm. Closed Jan 1, Dec 25.

HISTORIC CHURCHES

Two church spires grace the Delft skyline. One belongs to the **Nieuwe Kerk (New Church)** ★★, Markt (℗ 015/212-3025), which isn't all that new, since it was begun in 1383 and finally completed in 1510. Inside is the magnificent tomb of William the Silent, surrounded by 22 columns and decorated with figures representing Liberty, Justice, Valor, and Religion. The royal dead of the House of Oranje-Nassau lie in a crypt beneath the remains of the founder of their line. There's a marvelous panoramic view of the town from the 109m-high (357-ft.) church tower, the second tallest in the country.

The other, slightly leaning spire is attached to the **Oude Kerk (Old Church)** ★, Heilige Geestkerkhof (℗ 015/212-3015), founded around 1200, and dating mostly from the 13th and 14th centuries. The tower is embellished with four corner turrets and is noted for its 27 stained-glass windows by Joep Nicolas. Inside are the tombs of the artist Jan Vermeer and his family, and his friend Antoni van Leeuwenhoek, the inventor of the microscope (and perhaps on occasion Vermeer's model).

Both churches are open April to October, Monday to Saturday from 9am to 6pm; November to March, Monday to Friday from 11am to 4pm and Saturday from 11am to 5pm. Admission is 3€ ($3.75) for adults, 2.50€ ($3.15) for seniors, 1.50€ ($1.90) for children ages 5 to 14, and free for children under 5. Tickets are valid in both churches. Separate admission to the Nieuwe Kerk tower is 2.50€ ($3.15) for adults, 1€ ($1.25) for children ages 5 to 14, and free for children under 5.

WHERE TO STAY   In a pinch, try the pensions near the railway station, but they fill up fast in summer. Another possibility is **'t Raedthuys,** Markt 38–40, 2611 GV Delft (℗ 015/212-5115; fax 015/213-6069; www.raedthuys.nl), with nine units (some with en-suite bathroom). Singles are 40€ ($46) without bathroom and 55€

($63) with bathroom, doubles are 45€ ($52) without bathroom and 65€ ($75) with bathroom, breakfast included. American Express, Diners Club, MasterCard, and Visa are accepted. Slightly more expensive is **De Koophandel,** Beestenmarkt 30, 2611 GC Delft (© **015/214-2302;** fax 015/214-0674; www.hoteldekoophandel.nl), which has 21 units for 70€ ($81) single, 85€ ($98) double, breakfast included. American Express, Diners Club, MasterCard, and Visa are accepted.

WHERE TO DINE

Spijshuis de Dis 🕈🕈 DUTCH   Some of the best Dutch cooking in the country is dished up at this atmospheric restaurant east of the market. Look for traditional plates presented in modern variations. These include *Bakke pot*—a stew made from three kinds of meat (beef, chicken, and rabbit) in beer sauce, served in the pan; V.O.C. mussels (named after the Dutch initials for the East India Company), prepared with garlic and spices such as ginger and curry; and asparagus in season (May–June). Steaks and lamb filet are other specialties. If you're feeling especially decadent, opt for dessert; we especially like the luscious vanilla ice cream with hot cherries, whipped cream, and cherry brandy.

Beestenmarkt 36 (2 blocks from the Markt). © **015/213-1782.** www.spijshuisdedis.com. Main courses 18€–25€ ($23–$31); fixed-price menu 30€ ($38). AE, DC, MC, V. Thurs–Tues 5–9:30pm.

Stadsherberg De Mol TRADITIONAL DUTCH   Food is served here in the medieval manner—in wooden bowls from which you eat with your hands. Prices are moderate and quantities copious. Live music and dancing add to the fun.

Molslaan 104 (off Beestenmarkt). © **015/212-1343.** www.stadsherbergdemol.nl. Fixed-price menu 65€ ($81). MC, V. Tues–Sun 6–11pm.

5 Gouda 🕈

40km (25 miles) S of Amsterdam; 25km (17 miles) NE of Rotterdam

You may know about its cheeses, but did you know that in Dutch its name is pronounced "*khow*-dah"?

ESSENTIALS

GETTING THERE   Trains depart every hour from Amsterdam Centraal Station, via Leiden or Rotterdam, for Gouda. On the fastest trains, the trip takes just under an hour; a round-trip ticket is 17€ ($22). By **car** from Amsterdam, take A4/E19 and N207 south.

VISITOR INFORMATION   VVV Gouda is at Markt 27, 2801 JJ Gouda (© **0900/ 4683-2888;** fax 0182/583-210; www.vvvgouda.nl). The office is open Monday from 1 to 5:30pm, Tuesday to Saturday from 9:30am to 5:30pm, and Sunday from 10am to 4pm.

WHAT TO SEE & DO

Try to come here on a Thursday morning between 10am and 12:30pm from about the third week in June to the first week in September, when the lively **Goudse kaasmarkt (Gouda cheese market)** 🕈 brings farmers driving farm wagons painted with bright designs and piled high with round cheeses in orange skins. Walk to the back of the **Stadhuis (Town Hall)** to sample the Gouda cheese. This gray stone building, with stepped gables and red shutters, is reputed to be Holland's oldest Town Hall, and parts of its Gothic facade date from 1449.

Gouda is noted for its **candles.** Every year from the middle of December, the Markt and the Town Hall are festively lit by candles.

Molen De Roode Leeuw (Red Lion Windmill) ⍟

This 1727 grain mill has been completely renovated and is now grinding away again. It's an impressive sight to see the mill at work—you can go out on the platform and watch the vanes swish past, while inside, the huge wooden cogwheels and beams work the millstones. There's a store where you can buy all kinds of flour ground here.

Vest 65 (west of Markt). ⓒ 0182/522-041. Admission 1.50€ ($1.90) adults, 0.50€ (65¢) children. Thurs–Sat 9am–4pm.

Museum Het Catharina Gasthuis ⍟

The jewel of the collections at this 1665 mansion, a former hospital near Sint Janskerk, is a gold chalice that Countess Jacqueline of Bavaria presented to the Society of Archers in 1465. Its whereabouts were unknown for over a century before it was recovered in the Town Hall's attic and brought here. The collections of the town's recently closed Museum De Moriaan have been brought here, adding displays of antique pipes and *plateel*, a colorful pottery that is Gouda's answer to Delftware. There are colorful guild relics, antique furniture, and a terra-cotta plaque whose Latin inscription proclaims that the humanist Erasmus may have been born in Rotterdam but was conceived in Gouda. There's limited wheelchair access.

Achter de Kerk 14 (at Oosthaven). ⓒ 0182/588-440. Admission 4€ ($5) adults, free for those under 19. Ticket also valid in Museum De Moriaan. Mon–Sat 10am–5pm; Sun noon–5pm. Closed Jan 1, Dec 25.

Sint-Janskerk (Church of St. John) ⍟

Holland's longest church, this majestic 15th-century building holds some of Europe's most beautiful stained-glass windows— 64 in all, with a total of 2,412 panels. Some date back as far as the mid-1500s. To see the contrast between that stained-glass art of long ago and the work being carried out today, take a look at the most recent window, no. 28A, commemorating the World War II years in Holland.

Achter de Kerk 16 (south of Markt). ⓒ 0182/512-684. www.st-janskerkgouda.nl. Admission 2.50€ ($3.15) adults, 2.25€ ($2.80) seniors/students, 2€ ($2.50) school students, 1.75€ ($2.20) children ages 5 to 12, free for children under 5. Mar–Oct Mon–Sat 9am–5pm; Nov–Feb Mon–Sat 10am–4pm.

Waag (Weighing House) ⍟ *Kids*

This monumental Weighing House, dating from 1669, is the pride of the town. An exhibit inside tells the story of cheese using interactive audiovisual media. You'll get to know all about the manufacturing process, from grass through cow through milk to cheese, and have a chance to taste the finished product. The museum explains the importance of Gouda as a center of Dutch dairy production.

Markt 35–36. ⓒ 0182/529-996. www.goudakaas.nl. Admission 3.50€ ($4.40) adults, 2€ ($2.50) children under 12, free for children under 5. Apr–Oct Tues–Wed and Fri–Sun 1–5pm, Thurs 10am–5pm.

WHERE TO DINE

Mallemolen ⍟ CLASSIC FRENCH   This excellent traditional restaurant is on what's known as "Rembrandt's corner." There's an antique windmill on the same street. The restaurant has an Old Dutch look, though the cuisine is chiefly French. Dishes include tournedos with gooseliver in a red-wine sauce.

Oosthaven 72. ⓒ 0182/515-430. www.mallemolen.com. Reservations recommended on weekends. Main courses 20€–25€ ($25–$31); fixed-price menu 28€ ($35). AE, DC, MC, V. Tues–Fri noon–2pm; Tues–Sun 5pm–midnight.

Gouda

ATTRACTIONS ●
Molen De Roode
  Leeuw **5**
Museum Het Catharina
  Gasthuis **4**
Sint-Janskerk **3**
Stadhuis **2**
Waag **1**
DINING ◆
De Mallemolen **6**

ⓘ Information
✉ Post office
— Railway
🚤 Canal boat
  cruises

6 Leiden ⍟

36km (23 miles) SW of Amsterdam; 20km (12 miles) NE of The Hague

A visit to Leiden is in the nature of a pilgrimage (pardon the pun) for Americans. It was here that the Pilgrim Fathers found refuge during the long years they waited to sail to a fresh beginning in the New World. Their sojourn was, however, but one small incident in Leiden's long history.

For the Dutch, the high point in Leiden's history is surely its display of heroism during the 5-month siege by the Spanish in 1574. Thousands of its residents perished, and the food situation became so intolerable that the mayor offered his own body to be used as nourishment for the starving population—talk about sacrifice! His offer wasn't accepted, but his memory is honored by a statue in a town park.

The Dutch fleet finally rescued Leiden on October 3, after a dramatic advance over flooded fields as dikes were broken to open up a watery route to the beleaguered citizens. From that terrible siege came one of Holland's most beloved national dishes, *hutspot* (stew), so named for the bubbling kettle of stew left behind by fleeing Spaniards (the kettle is now ensconced in the Lakenhal Museum). If you should be in Leiden on October 3, you'll see the anniversary of the Spanish defeat observed when *haring en witte brood* (herring and loaves of white bread) are distributed just as they were in 1574.

> **(Fun Fact** Intelligence Test
>
> As a reward for their heroic resistance during the 1574 Spanish siege, Prince William of Orange offered the people of Leiden a choice—a tax break or a university. They chose the university.

Leiden is known as the birthplace of Rembrandt (who was born at Galgewater on the Rhine River, just inside the city walls in the west of town, hence his surname "van Rijn"), Jan Steen, and Lucas van Leyden.

ESSENTIALS

GETTING THERE   There are frequent **trains** from Amsterdam Centraal Station. The ride takes around 35 minutes and is 14€ ($17) round-trip. Leiden station is about a 10-minute walk northwest of the center. By **car,** take A4/E19.

VISITOR INFORMATION   **VVV Leiden,** Stationsweg 2D, 2312 AV Leiden (② **0900/222-2333;** fax 071/516-1227; www.leidenpromotie.nl), is just opposite the rail station. The office is open Monday from 11am to 5:30pm, Tuesday to Friday from 9:30am to 5:30pm, and Saturday from 10am to 4:30pm, and (Apr–Aug) Sunday from 11am to 3pm.

SEEING THE SIGHTS

With 14 museums, ranging from those for antiquities, natural history, and anatomy, to those for clay pipes and coins, this canal-side town seems perfectly justified in calling itself the *Museumstad* (Museum Town). A 13th-century citadel, **De Burcht,** still stands on a mound of land in the town center between two branches of the Rhine, Oude and Nieuwe, providing a great view of the rooftops around.

THE TOP MUSEUMS

Leiden American Pilgrim Museum ✰   This museum occupies a 16th-century house where one of the Pilgrim families may have lodged. Here you can study a variety of documents relating to the Pilgrims' 11 years of residence in Leiden. The museum supplies a brochure that describes a self-guided walking tour of the city. The tour takes about an hour and leads you to the most important sites and monuments.

Beschuitsteeg 9. ② 071/512-2413. www.pilgrimhall.org/leidenmuseum. 2€ ($2.50) adults, free for children under 6. Wed–Sat 1–5pm.

Naturalis (National Museum of Natural History) ✰   If you follow the signposting around the modernistic hospital, behind it you'll find the old sanatorium, with the entrance, store, and courtyard cafe of Naturalis. From here, you can take displays, many with text in English and Dutch, that trace and explain the development of the natural world, from its mineral treasures to ecosystems to modern energy generation. Pickled specimens sit alongside stuffed and painted ones in the overview of plant and animal life. Kids love the simpler displays that let them look at topsoil through a periscope, and there's plenty of computer-based interactivity, too. Adults will enjoy anthropological displays comparing cultural views of nature: Ancient Egypt, the post-Renaissance western world, China, and Islam. Equally intriguing is the Treasure Room on the fifth floor, open under guard from 1:30 to 4:30pm. Cases of precious stones include cut examples from the historical collection of William I, and examples of extinct animals and birds that fell into taxidermists' hands.

Leiden

ATTRACTIONS ●
De Burcht **12**
Hortus Botanicus **9**
Leiden American Pilgrim
  Museum **11**
Lodewijkskerk **10**
Molenmuseum De Valk **4**
Naturalis **1**

Rijksmuseum van
  Oudheden **7**
Rijksmuseum Voor
  Volkenkunde **2**
Sint-Pieterskerk **8**
Stedelijk Museum De
  Lakenhal **5**

ACCOMMODATIONS ■
Hotel De Doelen **6**

DINING ◆
Annie's Verjaardag **13**
Stadscafé Van der Werff **3**

Darwinweg 2 (close to the rail station). © **071/568-7600.** www.naturalis.nl. Admission 9€ ($11) adults, 5€ ($6.25) children 4–18, free for children under 4. Tues–Sun 10am–6pm (summer school vacation daily 10am–6pm). Closed Jan 1, Dec 25.

Rijksmuseum van Oudheden (National Museum of Antiquities) ★★   No visit to Leiden is complete without seeing this museum, the most comprehensive of its kind in the Netherlands. It opened in 1818, and over the years it has acquired an impressive collection of Egyptian, Near East, Greek, and Roman artifacts. It's still a center for archaeological research. The first exhibit to catch your eye will be the magnificent Egyptian Temple of Taffeh from the 1st century A.D.—the museum's pride and glory. Greek and Roman sculpture are well represented, and there are some beautiful examples of Greek decorated ceramics. The top floor provides an overview of the archaeological finds in the Netherlands from prehistoric times to the early Middle Ages.

Walking in Fathers' Footsteps

To touch base with the Pilgrim Fathers, who lived in Leiden between 1609 and 1620, pick up the VVV brochure *A Pilgrimage Through Leiden: A Walk in the Footsteps of the Pilgrim Fathers.* The walk starts at the **Lodewijkskerk (Louis Church),** which was used as a meeting place by the cloth guild. William Bradford, who became the governor of New Plymouth, was a member of this guild.

The walk takes you past the **Groenehuis (Green House)** on William Brewsterssteeg, where in an attached printing shop William Brewster's and Thomas Brewer's Pilgrim Press published the religious views that so angered King James and the Church of England. Plaques at the brick **Sint-Pieterskerk (St. Peter's Church),** in a small square off Kloksteeg, memorialize the Pilgrims, who worshiped here and who lived in its shadow. Special Thanksgiving Day services are held each year in honor of the little band of refugees.

An almshouse, the **Jean Pesijnhofje,** now occupies the restored **Groene Port (Green Door)** house on Kloksteeg in which Rev. John Robinson and 21 Pilgrim families lived. Robinson was forced to stay behind because of illness and is buried in the church. The almshouse is named for Jean Pesijn, a Belgian Protestant who joined the Leiden community along with his wife Marie de la Noye, and whose son Philip would sail for North America in 1621, where his surname would in time contract to Delano.

On July 21, 1620, the 66 Pilgrims who were leaving boarded barges at Rapenburg Quay for the trip by canal from Leiden to the harbor of Delft, now Delfshaven in Rotterdam. From there they sailed on the *Speedwell* for England, where the *Mayflower* awaited them.

Rapenburg 28. ⓒ **071/516-3163.** www.rmo.nl. Admission 7.50€ ($9.40) adults, 6.50€ ($8.15) children 6–18, free for children under 6. Tues–Fri 10am–5pm; Sat–Sun and holidays (also Easter Monday and Pentecost Monday) noon–5pm. Closed Jan 1, Oct 3, Dec 25.

Rijksmuseum voor Volkenkunde (National Ethnography Museum) ⭐   Japan has pride of place in a museum that is the legacy of German-born Philipp Franz von Siebold. Between 1823 and 1830 von Siebold collected 5,000 varied objects from a Japan that was still closed to the outside world, except for the Dutch trading post on Deshima island in Nagasaki Bay, where he was post physician. From this basis, the collection has grown to take in much of the world outside of Europe. Von Siebold differed from other collectors by his passion for understanding and identifying with the Japanese way of life, which adds a social dimension that has been continued for other lands and cultures.

Steenstraat 1. ⓒ **071/516-8800.** www.rmv.nl. Admission 7.50€ ($9.40) adults, 4€ ($4) seniors, children 4–12, free for children under 4. Tues–Sun (and a few Mon in year) 10am–5pm. Closed Jan 1, Oct 3, Dec 25.

Stedelijk Museum De Lakenhal ⭐   This fine 17th-century guildhall is now home to Leiden's municipal museum. Its collection of paintings by Dutch artists of the 16th and 17th centuries includes works by Lucas van Leyden, Rembrandt, Steen, and Dou. Temporary modern art exhibitions are organized regularly. The cloth merchants' guild (the original occupants of the building) is represented in historical exhibits; the guild's splendid meeting hall is on the first floor.

Oude Singel 32. 🕐 071/516-5360. www.lakenhal.nl. Admission 4€ ($5) adults, 2.50€ ($3.15) seniors, free for children under 18. Tues–Sun 10am–5pm. Closed Jan 1, Dec 25.

OTHER ATTRACTIONS

Hortus Botanicus der Rijksuniversiteit (University Botanical Garden) ✦

The first tulip bulbs were brought to Holland in 1593 by the botanist Carolus Clusius, who planted them at the Hortus Botanicus in Leiden. Tulips soon became highly popular, especially among the aristocracy. The Hortus is near the Weddesteeg, the small street where Rembrandt was born. This garden was established by students and professors of the University of Leiden in 1590. Researchers grew tropical trees and plants such as banana plants, ferns, and flesh-eating plants in greenhouses. Many of the old specimens are still thriving today. The original garden has been reconstructed in the Clusius Garden. There's a minimalist Japanese garden.

Rapenburg 73. 🕐 071/527-7249. www.hortus.leidenuniv.nl. Admission 5€ ($6.25) adults, 3€ ($3.75) children 4–12, free for children under 4. May–Sept daily 10am–6pm; Oct–Apr daily 10am–4pm. Closed Jan 1 and last week Dec.

LEIDEN & REMBRANDT

In 1606, the great artist Rembrandt van Rijn was born in Leiden. He later moved to Amsterdam, where he won fame and fortune—and later suffered bankruptcy and obscurity. In his hometown, a **Rembrandt Walk** takes in the site of the house (since demolished) where he was born; the Latin School he attended as a boy; and the first studio where he worked. A descriptive booklet is available from VVV Leiden for 3.50€ ($4.40).

Molen Museum (Windmill Museum) De Valk

This small museum, in a monumental windmill nicknamed "The Falcon," which sticks up like a sore thumb on Molenwerf in the middle of town, contains exhibits dedicated to various types of windmills. The focus is on the history of grinding grain and on the construction and workings of a corn mill.

Tweede Binnenvestgracht 1. 🕐 071/516-5353. www.home.wanadoo.nl/molenmuseum. Admission 2.50€ ($3.15) adults, 1.50€ ($1.90) seniors and children 6–15, free for children under 6. Tues–Sat 10am–5pm; Sun and holidays 1–5pm.

WHERE TO STAY

Hotel de Doelen   This hotel is situated on one of the most beautiful and stately canals in Old Leiden. Part of the building was formerly a patrician's house, dating from 1435. The higher-priced rooms have open hearths; with their high ceilings,

Roots of a Love Affair

In the spring of 1594, a highly respected yet perennially disgruntled botanist, Carolus Clusius, strode purposefully into the Hortus Botanicus, his research garden at the University of Leiden. He stopped beside a flower bed where an experiment begun the year before was coming to fruition, and cast a critical eye over splashes of color nodding their heads in the spring breeze. Clusius was no great admirer of humanity, but flowers were something else, so we may suppose that his dyspeptic disposition softened for a moment as he paused to admire the first tulips ever grown in Holland. A nation's love affair with a flower had begun.

they're grand and comfortable. A wonderful painted ceiling fresco is in the breakfast room.

Rapenburg 2, 2311 EV Leiden. ⓒ **071/512-0527.** Fax 071/512-8453. www.dedoelen.com. 16 units. 90€–105€ ($113–$131) double. AE, DC, MC, V. Limited street parking. *In room:* TV, minibar.

WHERE TO DINE

Annie's Verjaardag DUTCH/CONTINENTAL   This lively restaurant at water level has vaulted cellars that are a favorite eating spot for both students and locals, who spill out onto the canal-side terrace in fine weather. When the canals are frozen, the view is enchanting, as skaters practice their turns. The dinner menu is simple but wholesome. During the day, you can enjoy sandwiches or tapas.

Hoogstraat 1A (at Oude Rijn). ⓒ 071/512-6358. www.anniesverjaardag.nl. Main courses 11€–14€ ($14–$18). No credit cards. Sun–Thurs 10am–1am; Fri–Sat 10am–2am.

Stadscafé van der Werff ✯ CONTINENTAL   A relaxed cafe-restaurant in a grand 1930s villa on the edge of the old town, this place is popular with the town's students and ordinary citizens alike. Even if you're not enjoying dinners like Indonesian satay or surf-and-turf *kalfsbiefstukje met gebakken gambas en een kreeftensaus* (beefsteak with fried prawns in a lobster sauce), you can while away your evening just having a drink and reading a paper. The cafe is open until 1am.

Steenstraat 2 (off Beestenmarkt). ⓒ 071/513-0335. www.stadscafevanderwerff.nl. Main courses 12€–19€ ($15–$24). AE, DC, MC, V. Daily 9am–1am.

15

Friesland, Groningen & Drenthe

The nation's three northern provinces were home to the earliest settlers of what is now the Netherlands. Almost another world, **Friesland** (pronounced *freess-luhnd*) has customs and a language all its own. Which is not to say the people are not Dutch; they are, but *first* they are Frisian. In the windmill-speckled north of the province are ancient earth dwelling mounds, or *terpen,* constructed on land that was subject to frequent floods before dike-building began. In the southwest is a cluster of lakes, and in the southeast are woodlands and moorlands covered in heather. Four of Holland's five Wadden Islands belong to Friesland.

Although not as varied, **Groningen** has its share of historical sites, among them its own mound villages. The provincial capital, the city of Groningen, has the vibrant atmosphere of a university town, with

architectural touches from a history that stretches back beyond the 12th century. The past is most eloquent at places like the 15th-century Menkemaborg manor house in Uithuizen, the fortress town of Bourtange, a 15th-century monastery, and any number of picturesque old villages.

Sparsely populated **Drenthe** is a green, tranquil, rural haven. The Dutch call this land of deep forests, broad moors, small lakes, and villages *Mooi Drenthe* (Beautiful Drenthe). It hosts prehistoric *hunebedden* (giants' beds), huge megalith constructions that served early inhabitants as burial sites. Farming provides a satisfactory living in Drenthe, to judge from the size of farmhouses and barns. Church spires, which elsewhere stick up through the haze on the horizon, are mostly hidden behind trees, in a province that hosts two national parks, Dwingelderveld and Drents-Fries Forest.

1 Leeuwarden (Ljouwert)

168km (105 miles) NE of Amsterdam

Be sure to take time to look around Friesland's pleasant, unostentatious capital. But don't make a visit to Leeuwarden a substitute for getting out into the province's wide-open spaces. It may be the provincial center, but the town's burghers themselves affirm

Independent Spirits

Frisian *(Frysk)* is spoken by two-thirds of the 600,000 inhabitants of Friesland, which is known to the natives as Fryslân. Road signs are in both Dutch and Frisian (I've put the Frisian name for localities in parentheses after the Dutch). These highly independent folk have their own flag, their own coat of arms, their own national anthem, and their own sense of belonging to a nation that long predated the Netherlands. They even have their own *nasjonale slokje* (national drink): potent, heart-warming Beerenburger herbal bitter.

Moments   **Tale from the Crypt**

Care for a gruesome moment? The crypt of the village church in Wiuwert, 12km (7½ miles) southwest of Leeuwarden, evidently has the power to prevent corpses from decomposing. Eleven naturally mummified bodies dating from the early 17th century can be seen. The church is open April to September, Monday to Friday from 10 to 11:30am and 1 to 4:30pm; admission is 1.50€ ($1.90).

wryly that visitors wash up on their doorstep only when it rains. An important trading town as far back as the 11th century, on a gulf of the Wadden Sea that has since been drained, Leeuwarden (pop. 85,000) is a university town and has a large student community.

ESSENTIALS

GETTING THERE   Leeuwarden is the hub of Friesland's thin rail network and has good connections from around the country. **Trains** arrive hourly from Amsterdam. The rail and bus stations are both on Stationsplein, south of the center. By **car** from Amsterdam, take A1/E231 southeast to the Muiderberg intersection and then A6 north. Continue on a brief segment on A7/E22 east to Heerenveen, and then drive north on N32 and A32. An alternative route is A7/E22 north across the Afsluitdijk, and then north and east on N31 and A31.

VISITOR INFORMATION   VVV **Leeuwarden,** Sophialaan 4, Leeuwarden (© **0900/202-4060;** fax 058/234-7551; www.vvvleeuwarden.nl), is 2 blocks north of the rail station. The office is open Monday to Friday from 9am to 5:30pm, and Saturday from 10am to 2pm. Pick up here a *Passpoart voor Fryslân* (Friesland Passport), which affords users discounted admissions and special offers around the province.

WHAT TO SEE & DO

Fries Museum *✦*   Friesland's "national" museum started in 1881 in the Eysinga House, the 18th-century home of a local nobleman, which has since been extended several times. The ground-floor rooms have been restored to their appearance when Mr. Eysinga lived here with his family. On the second floor is a series of stylized 19th-century period rooms and folk costumes. The third floor holds a collection of colorfully painted traditional Hindeloopen furniture. A gallery of paintings includes Rembrandt's portrait of his wife, Saskia, the mayor's daughter—they were married in 1634 in the nearby village of Sint-Anna Parochie (St. Anne). Finally, don't miss the exhibit on the World War I spy Mata Hari (see "Mata Hari," below), the highlight of which is a period recreation of a Parisian salon.

A subterranean tunnel leads to a museum annex in the Renaissance **Kanselarij (Chancellery)** from 1571, the seat of the Frisian High Court of Justice during the reign of King Philip II of Spain (1555–81). Here you can trace the history of the Frisians by way of prehistoric objects dating back to the Ice Age, and by medieval and Renaissance treasures, and peruse a collection of modern Frisian art. A statue of Emperor Charles V adorns the roof. In the Kanselarij attic is the moving **Verzetsmuseum Friesland/Frisian Resistance Museum** (© **058/213-2271;** same admission and hours). A collection of photos, personal mementos, and other items documents the bravery of the Frisian Resistance in World War II and the daily rigors of life under Nazi occupation.

Friesland, Groningen & Drenthe

Turfmarkt 11 (east of the Stadhuis, across the canal). ☎ **058/255-5501**. www.friesmuseum.nl. Admission 6€ ($7.50) adults, 3€ ($3.75) children 13–17, free for children under 13. Free admission for all on Wed. Tues–Sun 11am–5pm. Closed Jan 1, Dec 25. Bus: 2, 3, or 8 to Oosterkade.

Princessehof Leeuwarden/Nationaal Keramiekmuseum Het (Dutch Ceramics Museum)
In the 18th century, this elegant neoclassical building in the town center was the home of Princess Maria van Hessen-Kassel, the mother of William IV and widow of *Stadhouder* Jan Willem Friso. One of the rooms is preserved just as it was in her time. The museum holds what's said to be the world's largest collection of tiles, among them Dutch, Spanish, Portuguese, and Persian work, and a marvelous collection of Chinese porcelain and ceramics.

Grote Kerkstraat 11 (3 blocks northwest of the Stadhuis). ☎ **058/294-8958**. www.princessehof.nl. Admission 6€ ($7.50) adults, 3€ ($3.75) seniors and children 13–18, free for children under 13. Tues–Sun 11am–5pm. Closed Jan 1, Dec 25.

MORE PLACES OF INTEREST
A bronze plaque placed by the DeWitt Historical Society of Ithaca, New York State, adorns Friesland's **Provinciehuis (Provincial House),** Tweebaksmarkt 52. The house dates from 1570 with a 1784 facade and is a few blocks south of the Fries Museum. The plaque was presented in 1909 to the people of Leeuwarden in gratitude for their having been the first to vote for recognition of the fledgling United States in 1782.

Mata Hari

The most famous figure in Leeuwarden's history was born here in 1876 as Margaretha Geertruida Zelle, but gained notoriety as Mata Hari. Margaretha grew up in a wealthy family, and at the age of 19 married an army officer and left for the Dutch East Indies. She returned to Holland in 1902.

With her marriage falling apart, Margaretha left for Paris, where she performed as an Asian dancer. There she adopted the name "Mata Hari"—meaning "eye of the day" or "sun" in Malaysian. Her nude dancing became a sensation. During World War I, she had affairs with high-ranking Allied officers, and allegedly passed pillow-talk military secrets to the Germans. In any case, her naiveté and yarn-spinning led to her downfall. She was executed by the French in 1917.

(Holland was the first country to extend recognition to the U.S.) A letter written by John Adams in 1783 expresses his personal thanks. Another document of interest relates to Petrus Stuiffsandt, the same Peter Stuyvesant who had such an important role in America's beginnings, and who was born in Friesland. The Provinciehuis is open at variable times; inquire at the VVV office. Admission is free.

Just west, beside the canal at Korfmakerspijp, is a statue of **Mata Hari.**

WHERE TO STAY

Eden Oranje Hotel ⭐   You'd never suspect this beautiful hotel is actually over a century old. Within an easy walk of nearly everything you'll want to see in Leeuwarden, this modernized hotel has a great location. Plus, the management and staff go out of their way to make you feel at home. The guest rooms are quite luxurious. Lots of locals come to the bright, moderately priced restaurant and cozy bar. There's also a sophisticated French restaurant, **l'Orangerie.**

Stationsweg 4 (facing the rail station), 8911 AG Leeuwarden. © 800/641-0300 in the U.S. and Canada, or 058/212-6241. Fax 058/212-1441. www.edenhotelgroup.com. 78 units. 125€ ($156) double. AE, DC, MC, V. Limited street parking. **Amenities:** 2 restaurants (French); bar; executive rooms. *In room:* A/C, TV w/pay movies.

Hotel de Pauw   This budget hotel features Old Dutch lobby furnishings and a wood-paneled bar. Its basic rooms come with and without private showers (all toilets are down the hall). The rooms are adequate, but of varying standards.

Stationsweg 10 (across the street from the rail station), 8911 AH Leeuwarden. © 058/212-3651. Fax 058/216-0793. 30 units, none with private bathroom. 50€–80€ ($63–$100) double. MC, V. Limited street parking. **Amenities:** Restaurant (Dutch); bar. *In room:* No phone.

WHERE TO DINE

De Waag ⭐ FRISIAN/INTERNATIONAL   In the atmospheric 16th-century Weigh House, on a canalside packed with inexpensive eateries, this bistro serves local specialties and international fare. During the summer, you can dine on a terrace overlooking the canal that runs along the town's main shopping street.

Nieuwestad 148B (at Waagplein). © 058/213-7250. Main courses 9.50€–18€ ($12–$22). MC, V. Mon–Sat 10am–9:30pm.

A LUXURY CHATEAU-HOTEL NEARBY

Bilderberg Landgoed Lauswolt ⭐⭐   On the edge of the typically Frisian village of Beetsterzwaag (Beetstersweach) is this gracious three-story château. Green lawns

> ## *Tips* Of Blades & Ice
>
> Ice skating stirs the blood of a true Frisian, and no event stirs it more than the **Elfstedentocht (Eleven Cities Tour),** a tough ice-skating hypermarathon that follows the canals on a 210km (130-mile) loop through 11 medieval Frisian towns, beginning in Bolsward. The first race was run in 1909, and it has been run only 13 times since, when the canals freeze solidly enough. When it was last run, in 1997, it drew 16,000 skaters and a half million onlookers. In 1985, skater Evert van Benthem clocked a record time for the tour, getting around in 6 hours and 47 minutes.

and huge shady trees surround the lovely place. The grounds contain beautiful forest walks, and the decor—in both public rooms and guest rooms—is elegant. The high level of service, swimming pool, and sauna just add to the attractions here. The restaurant, where you dine by candlelight in a gracious paneled dining room overlooking a garden, enjoys a top reputation throughout this part of Holland and is a member of the prestigious Alliance Gastronomique Néderlandaise.

Van Harinxmaweg 10, 9244 CJ Beetsterzwaag, 45km (28 miles) southeast of Leeuwarden. © 0512/381-245. Fax 0512/381-496. www.bilderberg.nl. 58 units. 118€–190€ ($148–$238) double. AE, DC, MC, V. Take N31 from Leeuwarden to Drachten, then join Expwy. A7, heading toward Heerenveen, and take the Beetsterzwaag exit. Pass through the center of Beetsterzwaag, and look for the hotel on its outskirts, on the right. **Amenities:** Restaurant (French); heated indoor pool; golf course; tennis courts; sauna. *In room:* TV.

FRANEKER (FRJENTSJER)
17km (11 miles) W of Leeuwarden

Once an important Frisian cultural and trading center, Franeker is today an enchanting small town. A young Peter Stuyvesant, who would later govern the Dutch New Netherland (New York State) colony from 1646 to 1664, studied at the now-closed university here. In the center of town, stop to admire the **Stadhuis (Town Hall),** from 1591, a fine example of Northern Dutch Renaissance architecture.

Eise Eisinga Planetarium ✿ Franeker's highlight is this simple, restored period house of wool comber Eise Eisinga. Over a period of 7 years between 1774 and 1781, he spent his leisure hours building a scale representation of the solar system on his ceiling. An amateur astronomer, he wanted to prove to fearful neighbors that the planetary conjunction of May 8, 1774,

> **Impressions**
>
> *To be in nature with the cold and the silence and the elegant movement of skates, it's like flying. You feel free.*
>
> —Dutch ice-skating champion Riva Visser, *National Geographic,* January 1998

didn't mean the end of the world was nigh. Guides are on hand to explain the mechanism, which still functions and was accurate for the knowledge of that time, before the discovery of Uranus, Neptune, and Pluto.

Eise Eisingastraat 3. © 0517/393-070. www.planetarium-friesland.nl. Admission 3.50€ ($4.40) adults, 3€ ($3.75) seniors, 2.75€ ($3.45) children 4–14, free for children under 4. Apr–Oct Tues–Sat 10am–5pm, Sun–Mon 1–5pm; Nov–Mar Tues–Sat 10am–5pm, Sun 1–5pm.

2 The Eastern IJsselmeer Shore ★★★

From the long barrier of the Afsluitdijk, the east shore of Holland's great lake curves south through a string of historic towns that shelter behind the coastal dike. To complete the "Golden Circle" of the IJsselmeer, see "The Western IJsselmeer Shore," in chapter 13, and "Lelystad & the Noordoostpolder," in chapter 16.

MAKKUM
30km (19 miles) W of Leeuwarden; 17km (11 miles) SW of Franeker

A small harbor town 8km (5 miles) south of the Afsluitdijk, Makkum has been home to tile makers and ceramics craftspeople since the 1500s.

ESSENTIALS
GETTING THERE   By public transportation, take the hourly local **train** from Leeuwarden to Sneek, and then **bus no. 98** from outside the station.

VISITOR INFORMATION   **VVV Makkum,** Pruikmakershoek 2, 8754 ET Makkum (✆ **0900/540-0001;** fax 0515/232-920; www.friesekust.nl), is in the old Weigh House in the town center.

WHAT TO SEE & DO
Connoisseur, polychrome Makkumware ceramics—fully the equal of (some would say superior to) Delft Blue from Koninklijke Porcelyne Fles—are produced at the workshop of **Koninklijke Tichelaars Makkumer Aardewerk-en Tegelfabriek,** Turfmarkt 63 (✆ **0515/231-341**), founded in 1594 and now in its 10th generation of family management. Guides take you through the entire production process, in which craftspeople employ the same procedures as in the 17th century. You can watch the exquisite designs being painted by hand. Tichelaars is sold in specialized stores all over the country. At the salesroom, you can buy anything from a simple tile to a larger piece with an elaborate design.

In the **Waag (Weigh House),** dating from 1698, is the **Fries Aardewerkmuseum (Frisian Earthenware Museum),** Pruikmakershoek 2 (✆ **0515/231-422**). Its five rooms are filled with examples of Makkum, majolica, and earthenware tiles from the 17th to the 19th centuries. The building itself—a square, towerlike structure, constructed of brick and topped with an elegant steeple—was used for weighing cheese and butter. The ground floor has quaint, oval windows; the upper floors have shuttered windows. The museum is open April to October, Monday to Saturday from 10am to 5pm; November to March, Monday to Friday from 10am to noon and 1 to 4pm. This building houses the VVV office (see above).

Continuing south from Makkum to **Workum (Warkum),** take in the intriguing modern art of beloved local artist Jopie Huisman (1922–2000). The **Jopie Huisman Museum,** Noard 6 (✆ **0515/543-131;** www.jopiehuismanmuseum.nl), is open April to October, Monday to Saturday from 10am to 5pm, and Sunday and holidays from 1 to 5pm; March and November, daily from 1 to 5pm. Admission is 4€ ($5) for adults, 1.50€ ($2.50) for children ages 4 to 12, and free for children under 4.

HINDELOOPEN (HYLPEN) ★★
39km (24 miles) SW of Leeuwarden; 20km (12 miles) S of Makkum

Like something out of a Dutch fairy tale, this tiny 13th-century Hanseatic League trading port on the IJsselmeer is filled with charming houses and crisscrossed by small canals with wooden bridges. Talented craftspeople from the village have for centuries

A Heritage Trail

The engaging **Aldfaers Erf (Forefathers' Heritage) Route** passes through a trail of restored antique buildings—a grocery, schoolhouse, bakery (which serves Frisian pastries), church, bird museum, farm, and more—in the villages of Exmorra, Allingawier, Ferwoude, and Piaam, which lie in the triangle formed by Makkum, Workum, and Bolsward. The route is clearly signposted on minor roads and through villages, and the buildings are open May to September, daily from 10am to 5pm. A map and a ticket for all sights cost 18€ ($23) for adults, 9€ ($11) for children ages 5 to 14, and free for children under 5. You can purchase the map and ticket from any of the sights and from **Stichting Aldfaers Erf,** Kanaalweg 4, Allingawier (© **0515/231-631;** www.aldfaerserf.nl), open April to October, daily from 10am to 5pm.

adorned their homes, furniture, constructed-in cupboard beds, and even wooden coat hangers with the vivid colors and intricately entwined vines and flowers often associated with the Pennsylvania Dutch in America. It's thought the designs were originally brought from Scandinavia by Hindeloopen sailors who sailed the North Sea in the days when the IJsselmeer was the Zuiderzee.

ESSENTIALS

GETTING THERE   Hourly **trains** go from Stavoren and Leeuwarden to Hindeloopen station, just outside the village. **Cars** are not allowed in many of the village's narrow streets.

VISITOR INFORMATION   **VVV Hindeloopen,** Nieuwstad 26, 8713 JL Hindeloopen (© **0900/540-0001;** www.friesekust.nl), is in the village center.

WHAT TO SEE & DO

A good place to view Hindeloopen's decorative designs is the **Hidde Nijland Museum Hindeloopen,** Dijkweg 1 (© **0514/521-420**), across from the village's 17th-century **Grote Kerk (Great Church),** on the northwest edge of town. Each room presents a varied collection of period furniture and local costumes. There's a splendid selection of Dutch tiles, and every wooden surface seems covered in bright designs. The museum is open March to October, Monday to Saturday from 10am to 5pm, and Sunday and holidays from 1:30 to 5pm. Admission is 3.50€ ($4.40) for adults, 2€ ($2.50) for children ages 6 to 16, and free for children under 6.

Alternatively, you could visit one of the village workshops and see for yourself how the furniture is decorated. **Het Roosje,** Nieuwstad 19 and 44 (© **0514/521-251**), is a workshop established in 1894 that specializes in woodcarving.

⌐Fun Fact Clogged Up

Friesland is great country for clogs. Farmers, country folk, and even some townspeople wear the genuine—as distinct from the tourist—version of these traditional shoes, made from poplar wood and leather. They do so not as an affectation but as plain, functional footgear.

STAVOREN (STARUM) 🕊

46km (29 miles) SW of Leeuwarden; 7km (4½ miles) SW of Hindeloopen

Founded in 500 B.C. and once a capital of the ancient Frisian kings, then a medieval mercantile center and member of the powerful Hanseatic League, Stavoren has shriveled considerably from those heady days. Yet it remains a handsome small harbor town, for fishing boats and pleasure craft. Small boats and antique Frisian *skûtsje* sailing vessels shuttle through the town's Johan Friso Canal between the IJsselmeer and the Frisian lakes.

An hourly **train** from Leeuwarden stops in end-of-the-line Stavoren. In summer months, you can make a 90-minute trip by passenger-and-bike ferry, operated by **Rederij V&O** (© **0228/326-667;** www.veerboot.info), to and from Enkhuizen on the IJsselmeer's western shore, from where there are train connections with Amsterdam (see "The Western IJsselmeer Shore," in chapter 13). One-way fares are 8.50€ ($11) for adults, 5€ ($6.25) for children ages 4 to 11, and free for children under 4.

Visitor information is available from **VVV Stavoren,** Stationsweg 7, 8715 ES Stavoren (© **0900/540-0001;** www.friesekust.nl).

3 Sneek 🕊

20km (12 miles) SW of Leeuwarden; 26km (16 miles) NE of Stavoren

The placid inland waterways—lakes, canals, and rivers—around Sneek (pronounced *snayk,* like "snake") have made this Friesland's most important sailing center, with a marina and sailing schools in the bustling town (pop. 27,000).

ESSENTIALS

GETTING THERE   Hourly **trains** go from Leeuwarden to Sneek. By **car** from Leeuwarden, take A32 south to junction 15, and then go west on N354.

VISITOR INFORMATION   **VVV Sneek,** Marktstraat 18, 8601 CV Sneek (© **0515/ 414-096;** fax 0514/423-703; www.vvvsneek.nl), is in the town center.

WHAT TO SEE & DO

In the old, canal-ringed center of town, note the rococo facade on the 16th-century **Stadhuis (Town Hall)** on Marktstraat, which is close to the landmark **Martinikerk (St Martin's Church),** from the same century.

Interested in ships and the sea? Spare some time for the **Fries Scheepvaartmuseum en Sneker Oudheidkamer (Frisian Maritime Museum and Sneek Antiques Gallery),** Kleinzand 14 (© **0515/414-057;** www.friesscheepvaartmuseum.nl), in a

---

Sailing Days

During 2 weeks in July and August, Friesland falls under the spell of the *Skûtsjesilen* (Skûtsje Sailing) races between traditional flat-bottomed sailing barges. These boats, 20m (65 ft.) long, once used for transporting goods on the Zuiderzee, race on the lakes around Sneek, and on the IJsselmeer from Stavoren. More than a dozen boats compete, dating from 1910 to 1930. They don't look too maneuverable, but the crews have an arsenal of tricks designed to outwit their rivals. **VVV IJsselmeergebied Friesland** (© **0900/540-0001**) can provide information on dates and places, and you can visit the race organizers at **www.skutsjesilen.nl.**

canal-side house from 1844 east of Markstraat. The first part focuses on Friesland's maritime traditions on the sea, lakes, and inland waterways. Models of old sailing ships, marine paintings, reconstructed boat interiors, and more allow you to just about smell the salt tang of the sea. Antique local silver, paintings, and re-created house interiors are in the second part. The museum is open Monday to Saturday from 10am to 5pm, and Sunday from noon to 5pm (closed Jan 1 and Dec 25). Admission is 3€ ($3.75) for adults, 2.50€ ($3.15) for seniors, 1€ ($1.25) for children ages 6 to 12, and free for children under 6.

Astride the entrance to the port in the south of the old town rise the twin octagonal turrets of the brick Renaissance **Waterpoort,** a gate from 1613 and the only remains of the town's defense walls, which were razed in the 18th century.

THE FRIESE MEREN (FRISIAN LAKES) ⚓

The constellation of lakes south of Sneek—Pikmeer, Sneekermeer, Heegermeer, Slotermeer, and Tjeukemeer—is the main tourism region in Friesland. In the summer, you can rent powerboats, sailboats, rowboats, and canoes. The lakes are connected by rivers and canals so you can easily move between them.

Among the most attractive places around is **Sloten (Sleat),** beautifully sited on a tree-fringed canal south of the Slotermeer. The village's narrow streets lined by 17th-century houses make for a pleasant stroll. Just west of here is the forested **Gaasterland** district, which contains a hamlet called Nieuw Amerika and is good for hiking.

Southeast of the lakes, at **Wolvega (Wolvegea),** you can snap a picture of the statue of Peter Stuyvesant, the governor of New Netherland (New York State), who was born in 1592 at the hamlet of Scherpenzeel (Skerpenseel), 10km (6 miles) west.

4 The Waddenzee Coast

Traveling north through Friesland along the Waddenzee coast, you won't actually see much of the sea unless you climb onto the sea dike from time to time for a better view. The sea is an important European staging area on bird migration routes, a stopover zone where waterfowl as well as shore and wading birds rest and feed.

HARLINGEN (HARNS)

24km (15 miles) W of Leeuwarden

This bustling seaport and former whaling center (pop. 16,000), founded in the 9th century, hunkers down behind a dike on the Wadden Sea. Fishing boats, cargo ships, and ferries to the offshore Wadden Islands shuttle in and out of the busy harbor, and canalboats and recreational craft ply the Van Harinxma Canal that leads east to Leeuwarden.

ESSENTIALS

GETTING THERE   Frequent **trains** go from Leeuwarden to Harlingen and connect with ferries to Vlieland and Terschelling (see "The Wadden Islands," below); shuttle buses operate between the rail station and the ferry dock. By **car** from Leeuwarden, take N383 and N31 west.

VISITOR INFORMATION   VVV **Harlingen,** Noorderhaven 50, 8861 BL Harlingen (℡ **0900/540-0001;** fax 0517/415-176; www.friesekust.nl), is on the main shopping street in the center.

WHAT TO SEE & DO

Harlingen is a maze of canals filled with fishing boats and recreational craft, and lined with gabled 16th- to 18th-century houses and warehouses in its carefully preserved old center. Close to the ferry dock is one of several statues around Holland that represent the legend of the boy who saved the community from a calamity by sticking his finger in a leaking dike.

Moderately interesting seafaring and whaling exhibits, ship models, seascape paintings, antiques, porcelain, and silver are all to be seen in the **Gemeentemuseum Het Hannemahuis,** Voorstraat 56 (© **0517/413-658**), in the 18th-century Hannemahuis. The municipal museum is open April to June and mid-September to mid-November, Tuesday to Saturday from 1:30 to 5pm; July to mid-September, Tuesday to Saturday from 10am to 5pm and Sunday from 1:30 to 5pm. Admission is 1.80€ ($2.25) for adults, 1.20€ ($1.50) for children ages 5 to 12, and free for children under 5.

Since 1973, craftspeople have produced and painted by hand traditional-style Frisian pottery and tiles at the **Harlinger Aardewerk en Tegelfabriek,** Voorstraat 84 (© **0517/415-362**), open during store hours through the year. Should you need to choose between a visit to this workshop or to Tichelaars in Makkum (see above), Tichelaars produces the more prestigious wares, but Harlinger's are perhaps more individual.

WHERE TO STAY & DINE

Hotel Anna Casparii   This charming canal-house hotel on the edge of the yacht harbor has comfortable and attractive guest rooms. Ask for one with a view of the boat dock. The moderately priced restaurant specializes in seafood fresh off the boats that sail into the town's harbor.

Noorderhaven 67–71 (4 blocks east of the island ferry terminal), 8861 AL Harlingen. © **0517/412-065**. Fax 0517/414-540. 15 units, 11 with bathroom. 100€ ($125) double with bathroom; 80€ ($100) double without bathroom. AE, DC, MC, V. Limited street parking. **Amenities:** Restaurant (seafood/Dutch); lounge. *In room:* TV, minibar.

DOKKUM

19km (12 miles) NE of Leeuwarden; 42km (26 miles) NE of Harlingen

The northernmost terminus of the Eleven Cities Tours (see box "Of Blades & Ice," earlier), Dokkum is a pleasant small town, constructed on two *terpen* (earthen mounds). Remnants of its 16th-century walls and moat date from a period when the town was a seaport. St. Boniface, the English monk Wynfryth, was murdered here in 754 while on a mission to convert the pagan Frisians. That's about it history-wise until 1618 when Dokkum was made headquarters of the Friesland Admiralty.

In the restored former Admiralty building from 1618, the **Museum Het Admiraliteitshuis** (© **0519/293-134**) exhibits a mixed bag of antiquities, antiques, and Frisian folk art and traditional costumes. The museum is open April to September, Tuesday to Saturday from 10am to 5pm; October to March, Tuesday to Saturday from 2 to 5pm. Admission is 2€ ($2.50) for adults, 1€ ($1.25) for children ages 5 to 12, and free for children under 5.

AROUND DOKKUM

The scenic north Friesland country around Dokkum is speckled with windmills, and with villages and farmhouses constructed atop *terpen.* Friesland makes a big deal of its hundreds of *terpen,* but you'd have to be a genuine enthusiast for these small man-made hillocks to want to go out of your way to visit more than a few. **Hoogebeintum (Hegebeintum),** 10km (6 miles) west, boasts the highest *terp,* 9m (30 ft.) above sea

Moments **Frisian High**

In the Fochtelooërveen fenlands, near Appelscha (Appelskea) in southeast Friesland, you can climb the highest natural elevation in the entire province. Unless you have a bad case of vertigo, you won't get dizzy up there—it's just 26m (87 ft.) above sea level.

level—most are between 2 and 6m (6½ and 20 ft.) high—and a beautiful 17th-century church.

Southeast of Dokkum is the neat little village of **Veenklooster,** with thatched cottages around a *brink* (green), and a nearby abbey, the **Fogelsanghstate,** from 1725, which houses a branch of Leeuwarden's Fries Museum. **Bergumermeer** and Klein Zwitserland (Little Switzerland) are to the south.

THE LAUWERSMEER

Going northeast from Dokkum brings you to the **Lauwersmeer,** a man-made freshwater lake that was an inlet of the Waddenzee until it was cut off in 1969 by a barrier dam. Its sheltered waters provide a haven for birds, and for sailing and other watersports. Cross the dam-top road to Lauwersoog in Groningen province, from where ferries sail to Schiermonnikoog (see below). At **Expozee,** Strandweg 1 (*©* **0519/349-045**), a visitor center on the Lauwersmeer shore beside the village, you can learn about the natural history of both the Waddenzee and the lake. It's open Monday to Saturday from 10am to 5pm, and Sunday from 11am to 5pm.

5 The Wadden Islands ★★

Like North Carolina's Outer Banks, Holland's Waddeneilanden (Wadden Islands) are low-lying, dune-laden, windswept barrier islands. The five beautiful and highly individual islands are connected by ferry across the Waddenzee (Wadden Sea) from adjacent mainland harbors. This shallow sea's depth ranges from about 1m (3 ft.) to 3m (10 ft.), and at low tide it virtually disappears. The Dutch treasure these small islands as romantic getaways. On a line curving north and east, they are: Texel, Vlieland, Terschelling, Ameland, and Schiermonnikoog. Texel belongs to Noord-Holland and is covered separately (see "Den Helder & Texel," in chapter 13). The remaining four belong to Friesland.

These havens of wild natural beauty encompass miles of white sand on wide beaches along the North Sea coasts, marshes, and wetlands that are sanctuaries for thousands of migratory seabirds, seals sunning on sandbanks, rare plants, old villages, and museums connected with the sea and seafarers. Most vacationers visit between the spring and fall; only a hardy few brave the winter gales.

The best way to get around is by bike. You can rent bikes on the islands, though they can get scarce during the busiest periods. The island VVV offices have information on bungalows, campsites, bed-and-breakfasts, and hotels.

VLIELAND (FLYLÂN)

A thin strip of beach and dunes, 19km (12 miles) long and a maximum of 3km (2 miles) wide, Vlieland (pop. 1,200) is an ideal hide-out. Carefree and almost car-free, Vlieland is virtually deserted, except in summer. The only disturbance here is the cries of seabirds—and an occasional howling fly past by Royal Netherlands Air Force F16 jets on training sorties.

ESSENTIALS

GETTING THERE **Rederij Doeksen** (ⓒ 0900/363-5736; www.rederij-doeksen.nl) operates passenger-ferry service from Harlingen (see above), and additional fast service for passengers by jet-catamaran. Private cars are not transported to Vlieland. The ferry trip takes 1¾ hours one-way. A round-trip ticket is 20€ ($25) for adults, 18€ ($22) for seniors, 10€ ($12) for children ages 4 to 11, and free for children under 4. The jet-cat crosses over in 45 minutes, for an additional 3.95€ ($4.95) one-way; there is also jet-cat service from Terschelling (25 min.). In addition, a passenger boat sails from Texel, crossing over in 25 minutes (see "Den Helder & Texel," in chapter 13).

VISITOR INFORMATION **VVV Vlieland,** Hafenweg 10, 8899 BB Vlieland (ⓒ 0562/451-111; fax 0562/451-361; www.vlieland.net), is beside the ferry terminal.

WHAT TO SEE & DO

There's not a lot to see and do; that's the main attraction here. Sunbathing—the island has what's said to be Europe's longest nudist beach—bird-watching (at least they're *supposed* to be watching birds through those binoculars), biking, and walking among the dunes and forests are the key activities. An important bird sanctuary is the **Natuurgebied De Kroonpolders;** look out for **De Posthuys,** a cafe from 1837, on the edge of the reserve.

In the old-time whaling port of **Oost-Vlieland (East-Flylân),** the island's only village (its one-time sister village West-Vlieland vanished beneath the waves in 1736), the 16th-century **Trompshuys,** Dorpstraat 99 (ⓒ 0562/451-600), named for the 17th-century admiral Cornelis Tromp (though the house never belonged to him), hosts a local history museum, with a collection of antique clocks and other items. The museum is open May to September, Monday to Friday from 10am to noon and 2 to 5pm; April and October, Monday to Saturday from 2 to 5pm; and November to March, Wednesday and Saturday from 2 to 5pm. Admission is 2€ ($2.50).

The **Noordwester Visitor Center,** Dorpstraat 150 (ⓒ 0562/451-700), has displays on the island's flora and fauna, and can give advice on the best places for observing the hundred or so species of birds that show up here. The center is open May to September, daily from 10am to noon and 2 to 5pm; October to April, Wednesday and Saturday from 2 to 4pm. Admission is 2€ ($2.50).

The VVV office organizes guided tours on an observation vehicle, the **Vliehorsexpres.**

TERSCHELLING (SKYLGE) ☆☆

The most accessible of Friesland's four Wadden Islands, Terschelling (pop. 5,000) is a strip of beach, dunes, nature reserves, and pine forest. It's 29km (18 miles) long and a maximum of 4km (2½ miles) wide. Large and popular enough to have some things for visitors to do besides soak up sun and admire the natural beauty, the island can be quite busy, though not crowded, in summer.

Fun Fact **For Whom the Bell Tolls**

Lloyds of London's famous Lutine Bell, rung when a vessel insured by the company was reported missing, came from the British bullion ship *HMS Lutine,* which shipwrecked on Vlieland in 1799.

ESSENTIALS

GETTING THERE   **Rederij Doeksen** (© 0900/363-5736; www.rederij-doeksen.nl) operates car-ferry service from Harlingen (see above), and additional fast service for passengers by jet-catamaran. The ferry trip takes 2 hours one-way. A round-trip ticket is 20€ ($25) for adults, 18€ ($22) for seniors, 9.85€ ($12) for children ages 4 to 11, and free for children under 4. Taking a car is possible but not encouraged—the fare for the vehicle alone begins at 70€ ($88) round-trip, and goes up in stages to 260€ ($325) for a large auto and trailer, plus charges for above-average height and width; reservations are essential. The jet-cat crosses over in 45 minutes, for an additional 3.95€ ($4.95) per passenger one-way; there is also jet-cat service from Vlieland (25 min.). In addition, a passenger boat sails from Ameland (3 hr.).

VISITOR INFORMATION   **VVV Terschelling,** Willem Barentszkade 19A, 8881 BC Terschelling-West (© 0562/443-000; fax 0562/442-875; www.vvv-terschelling.org), overlooks the harbor.

WHAT TO SEE & DO

West-Terschelling (West-Skylge), the island's main village, a former whaling center set in a sheltered bay on the coast facing the mainland, is dominated by the square, yellowish-colored **Brandaris Lighthouse,** 54m (177 ft.) high and constructed in 1594. A look into the lives of the islanders of yesteryear is available at **'t Behouden Huys Museum,** Commandeurstraat 30–32 (© 0562/442-389), in the gabled houses constructed in 1668 for two sea captains. You'll find period rooms and displays about whaling and other local traditions. The museum is open April to October, Monday to Friday from 10am to 5pm (July–Aug also Sat 1–5pm). Admission is 3.50€ ($4.40) for adults, 2.50€ ($3.15) for seniors and children ages 5 to 12, and free for children under 5.

To learn more about local geography, wildlife, and plants, visit the **Centrum voor Natuur en Landschap,** Burgemeester Reedekkerstraat 11 (© 0562/442-390). A small aquarium recreates North Sea and Wadden Sea environments. The center is open April to October, Monday to Friday from 9am to 5pm, and weekends from 2 to 5pm. Admission is 4€ ($5) for adults, 2€ ($2.50) for children ages 5 to 12. An important nature reserve and bird sanctuary, **De Boschplaat Nature Reserve** ⚘, occupies the eastern half of the island (access is restricted during the breeding season, mid-Mar to mid-Aug).

More thrilling is sand-sailing on the North Sea beaches, aboard a wheeled sand-yacht that can sail along at an impressive clip when the wind is strong, as it often is. Rent one from **Strandzeilschool Beausi** (© 0562/448-055).

AMELAND (IT AMELÂN)

Ameland (pop. 3,500), 24km (15 miles) long and a maximum of 4km (3 miles) wide, can be thought of as the "median" Wadden Island—not as busy nor as varied as Texel and Terschelling; not as quiet and remote as Vlieland and Schiermonnikoog, but every bit as scenic as the other four. For many visitors, it's the ideal compromise.

ESSENTIALS

GETTING THERE   **Wagenborg Passagiersdiensten** (© 0900/455-4455 information, 0519/546-111 reservations; www.wpd.nl) operates car-ferry service from a dock 4km (2½ miles) north of Holwerd (Holwert), which is itself 22km (14 miles) north of Leeuwarden. April to September, the 45-minute trip is 11€ ($14) for adults,

> *Fun Fact*   **A Gift from America**
>
> Cranberry pie and cranberry wine are Terschelling specialties. These are pro-
> duced from berries originally brought from America, allegedly by way of a bar-
> rel washed up after a North Sea storm and tossed away in disgust by its finder,
> who had hoped for something stronger.

10€ ($13) for seniors, 5.95€ ($7.45) for children ages 4 to 11, and free for children
under 4; fares from October to March are around 10% cheaper; at all times, only
round-trip tickets are available. Taking a car is possible but not encouraged; the summer fare for an ordinary car is 76€ ($95); reservations are required. In addition, pas-
senger boats sail from both Terschelling and Schiermonnikoog (3 hr. in each case).

Buses connect both Groningen and Leeuwarden rail stations with the ferry dock.
Going by **car** from Leeuwarden, take N357 north.

VISITOR INFORMATION   **Ameland,** Bureweg 2, 9163 KE Nes (② **0519/546-546;**
fax 0519/546-547; www.vvvameland.nl), is close to the ferry terminal.

WHAT TO SEE & DO

The main village and ferry port, **Nes,** in the middle of the south coast, has 17th- to 18th-
century sea-captains' houses. In Nes, the **Natuurcentrum,** Strandweg 38 (② **0519/
542-737**), takes you close to the island's natural history. It has a weather station and an
aquarium containing denizens of the North Sea and Wadden Sea. The center is open
April to October, daily from 10am to 5pm and 7 to 9pm. Admission is 4€ ($5) for
adults, 2€ ($2.50) for children ages 5 to 12, and free for children under 5.

In **Hollum,** on the west coast, the **Cultuur-Historischmuseum Sorgdrager,**
Herenweg 1 (② **0519/554-477**) is in a sea captain's house from 1751. It employs cultural history as a cover for what's essentially a museum of whaling, an industry that
once was the island's bread and butter. The museum is open April to October, daily
from 1:30 to 5pm. Admission is 2€ ($2.50) for adults, 1€ ($1.25) for children ages
5 to 12, and free for children under 5. Check out the cemetery of the village's old
church for gravestones decorated with images of whaling ships.

Nearby, the **Reddingsmuseum Abraham Fock,** Oranjeweg 18 (② **0519/542-737**),
takes as its theme the sometimes grim, sometimes buoyant, but always uplifting history
of the local lifeboats and the crews who risked—and often enough, lost—their lives.
The museum is open April to October, daily from 1:30 to 5pm. Admission is 2€
($2.50) for adults, 1€ ($1.25) for children ages 5 to 12, and free for children under 5.

Birds do their avian thing in the **Oerduinen** and **Het Hon** nature reserves on the
east coast. You can get your own bird's-eye view aboard a light aircraft from an **air-
field** (② **0519/554-644**) just north of **Ballum,** a village between Nes and Hollum.
The 15-minute flights cost 36€ ($45).

SCHIERMONNIKOOG (SKIERMÛNTSEACH) ⍟

Wild, scenic, remote, and invariably all but deserted, the easternmost and smallest of
the Wadden Islands, Schiermonnikoog (pop. 1,000), 17km (11 miles) long and a
maximum of 6km (4 miles) wide, was declared a national park in 1988.

ESSENTIALS

GETTING THERE **Wagenborg Passagiersdiensten** (© 0900/455-4455 information, 0519/546-111 reservations; www.wpd.nl) operates ferry service from **Lauwersoog,** 36km (22km) northeast of Leeuwarden. April to September, the 45-minute trip is 12€ ($15) for adults, 11€ ($14) for seniors, 6.55€ ($8.20) for children ages 4 to 11, and free for children under 4. Fares from October to March are around 10% cheaper. At all times, only round-trip tickets are available. A bus meets the ferry and takes passengers to the island's only village, also called Schiermonnikoog. In addition, a passenger boat sails from Ameland (3 hr.).

If you're **driving,** you'll have to leave your car at Lauwersoog (only residents are permitted to ship their cars across). Buses connect both Leeuwarden and Groningen rail stations with Lauwersoog.

VISITOR INFORMATION **VVV Schiermonnikoog,** Reeweg 5, 9166 PW Schiermonnikoog (© **0519/531-233;** fax 0529/531-325; www.vvvschiermonnikoog.nl), is on the village's main street.

WHAT TO SEE & DO

On the sheltered Wadden Sea coast, **Schiermonnikoog** village dates from the early 18th century, and life here doesn't seem to have speeded up much since then. A statue known as the *Schiere Monnik (Gray Monk)* recalls the island's early history as a refuge

Walking on Water

At low tide, the Wadden Sea virtually disappears, the seabed becomes visible, and seabirds feast on mollusks in the sand. Then the Wadden Islands seem even closer to the mainland, and if you feel like walking the mud flats, from May to October you can join a *Wadlopen* (Wadden Walking) trip and plow across to one of the islands. *Note:* **Don't attempt this without an official guide—there is a real danger of being caught by a fast-incoming tide.** With a guide, it is safe, but every once in a while a group needs to be rescued by lifeboat.

Weather permitting, you start walking at ebb tide. Soon the mainland looks far away, and you feel lost in the middle of a salty mire trying to suck your feet in deeper with every step. But your attention will be drawn to the unusual landscape as you realize you're actually walking on the bottom of a sea, and in a few hours all this will disappear under water again. If you're lucky, you'll see seals disporting in pools or soaking up rays on a sandbar. When you reach the island, you need to wait for high tide to be able to go back by boat.

Tours cost 12€ to 30€ ($17–$38) a head and range from an easy round-trip of a few hours on the flats to difficult hikes to the islands lasting around 8 hours (including the wait for the boat). Wear shorts and close-fitting, ankle-high shoes or boots. The trips are popular; groups may be as large as 75 to 100 people, so you need to book ahead. Contact **Wadloop-centrum Fryslân** (© **0518/451-491;** www.wadlopen.net), in Holwerd; or **Stichting Wadloopcentrum Pieterburen** (© **0595/528-300**), in Pieterburen.

of Cistercian monks, and two nearby complete whale jawbones, its 18th-century hey-day as a whaling center.

Schiermonnikoog was made a national park partly because of its isolation, wild scenery, and migratory birds, and partly because of its flora—half of all native Dutch plant species can be found here. Housed in an old lighthouse, a short walk or bike ride from the village, Schiermonnikoog National Park's **Visitor Center** and **Natuurhistorische Museum,** Torenstreek 20 (*℃* **0519/531-641**), can provide information about wildlife on the island and offer guided tours. The center and museum are open April to October, Monday to Saturday from 10am to noon and 1:30 to 5:30pm; November to March, Saturday from 1:30 to 5:30pm. Admission is 4€ ($5) for adults, and free for children under 12.

A great way to get around the island's dunes, beaches, woodlands, and polders is aboard the **Balgexpress,** a tractor-drawn observation trailer, which departs from the Visitor Center.

WHERE TO STAY & DINE

Graaf Bernstorff Hotel/Apartments   This hotel and apartment complex opened in 1998, with luxuriously appointed rooms and apartments. The on-site restaurant has a more Continental feel than the traditionally Dutch Van der Werff. Main courses start at 16€ ($20). During the day you can get snacks on the terrace or at the bar.

Reeweg 1, 9166 PW Schiermonnikoog. *℃* **0519/532-000.** Fax 0519/532-050. 69 units. 125€–160€ ($156–$200) double. AE, DC, MC, V. **Amenities:** Restaurant (Continental); bar. *In room:* TV, minibar.

Hotel-Restaurant Van der Werff *✦*   There's a sort of stuffiness here, which some-how lends to this hotel's charm. Games and sagging leather armchairs are in the lounge. Guest rooms are up-to-date, with some elegant features. The restaurant, with its wood-paneled walls and rich decor, is like a colonial officers' dining room. Guests can take the free hotel shuttle—sometimes an old charabanc is pressed into service—to and from the ferry dock.

Reeweg 2, 9166 PX Schiermonnikoog. *℃* **0519/531-203.** Fax 0519/531-748. 55 units. 65€ ($81) double. Rates include buffet breakfast. DC, MC, V. **Amenities:** Restaurant (Dutch); bar; lounge. *In room:* TV.

6 Groningen *✦*

144km (90 miles) NE of Amsterdam; 51km (32 miles) E of Leeuwarden

The capital of Groningen province is commercially and industrially important, and sits at the heart of one of the world's largest natural gas fields. Cars are banned from the old center, which is enclosed by a moat. Part of the center was destroyed during World War II, but much of its medieval and 16th- and 17th-century heritage survived and has been preserved. The University of Groningen was founded in 1614, and a student population of 20,000 gives the town a lively character.

ESSENTIALS

GETTING THERE   There are **trains** every hour or so to Groningen from Amsterdam Centraal Station (trip time 3 hr.). The rail and bus stations adjoin each other about 1km (½ mile) south of the center of town. By **car** from Amsterdam, take A1/E231 southeast to the Muiderberg intersection, switch to A6 north to its intersection with A7/E22, and then take this expressway northeast to Groningen. An alternative route is A7/E22 north across the IJsselmeer dike, north and east on N31 and A31 to Leeuwarden, and then east on N355.

VISITOR INFORMATION VVV **Groningen,** Grote Markt 25, 9712 HS Groningen (© **0900/202-3050;** fax 050/311-3855; www.vvvgroningen.nl), is opposite the Martinitoren in the center of town. The office is open Monday to Wednesday and Friday from 9am to 6pm, Thursday from 9am to 8pm, and Saturday from 10am to 5pm; in July and August, also Sunday from 11am to 3pm.

WHAT TO SEE & DO

Among Groningen's highlights is its handsome central square, the **Grote Markt,** graced by the 1810 neoclassical **Stadhuis (Town Hall).** Adjacent to this, at Waagplein 1, is the sparkling 1635 Renaissance **Goudkantoor (Gold Office),** which first housed a tax office, then a hallmarking bureau for precious metals, and is now a restaurant. Should your Latin be rusty, the inscription on the building, *DATE CAESARI QUARE SUNT CAESARIS,* was spoken by Jesus and translates as: "Give unto Caesar that which is Caesar's."

THE TOP ATTRACTIONS

Groninger Museum ❤ Emerging like some exotic alien plant out of the gray waters of the Verbindingskanaal, this museum added a surprising touch to this sober northern city when it opened in 1994. Italian architect Alessandro Mendini dreamed up a structure as quirky and varied as the contents. Playful, garish, disjointed, all jutting beams and cantilevered panels, each of the four pavilions has a different style, thanks to designers as varied as Philippe Starck, Michele de Lucchi, and Vienna bureau Coop Himmelbau. One appears to be the victim of an exploded paint box, and another, as the locals say, of a plane crash. These surround a golden tower in which a spiral staircase leads upward, its walls and balustrade a mosaic of small, vari-colored tiles. After all this, you might find it hard to focus your attention on the collection. Each pavilion pursues a different theme: local archaeological finds and the history of the city and province; Eastern ceramics; decorative arts; and paintings—including works from the Expressionists of the Groningen school, and a watercolor by Vincent van Gogh, *Drawbridge in Nieuw-Amsterdam* (1883)—prints, and sculpture from the 16th century to the present. A visit here should last 2 hours and 5 minutes: 2 hours for looking around, and 5 minutes for gazing slack-jawed in front of the building before you enter.

Museumeiland 1 (opposite the rail station). © **050/366-6555.** www.groningermuseum.nl. Admission 8€ ($10) adults, 7€ ($8.75) seniors and students, 4€ ($5) children 12–16, 2€ ($2.50) children 6–11, free for children under 6. Sept–June Tues–Sun 10am–5pm; July–Aug Tues–Sun 10am–5pm, Mon 1–5pm. Closed Jan 1, Dec 25.

Martinitoren ❤ The 15th-century **Martinikerk (St. Martin's Church),** across from the Grote Markt, is not easily missed, thanks to its lofty tower. Begun in 1469, completed in 1482, and reworked in 1627, the church is 97m (318 ft.) high from its base to the tip of a weather vane in the shape of St. Martin's horse, and that makes it the fourth tallest in Holland. You can climb most of *D'Olle Grieze* (The Old Gray Man), as the tower is known locally, for fine panoramic views over the city and the low-lying country roundabout. A 17th-century Hemony carillon frequently rings out. Inside the church are 16th-century frescoes depicting the Christmas and Easter stories, and an impressive organ from 1480.

Martinikerkhof 3 (© **050/311-1277).** Tower: Admission 3€ ($3.75) adults, 1.50€ ($1.90) children 5–12, free for children under 5. Apr–Oct daily 11am–5pm; Nov–Mar daily noon–4pm (school vacations 11am–5pm). Church: Admission 1€ ($1.25). June–Aug Tues–Fri noon–5pm.

Noordelijk Scheepvaart en Niemeyer Tabaksmuseum (Northern Maritime and Niemeyer Tobacco Museum) ❤ Housed in two medieval buildings, the first

---

Fun Fact **Comfort Station**

If you find yourself caught short in Groningen, relax, and take some time to appreciate a modern-design masterpiece. The *Urinoir* (1996), by Rem Koolhaas, in Kleine der A-straat, may not attract the same crowds as the *Mona Lisa,* but those who pass this way might well derive an equal satisfaction from the experience.

---

part of this interesting twin museum traces the rich history of Groningen's shipping industry, through models, instruments, charts, paintings, and more. There's a fine section on Groningen's medieval Hanseatic trading period. Smokers and maybe even nonsmokers can revel in the tobacco museum's collection, which covers Holland's long involvement with the tobacco trade.

Brugstraat 24. ✆ 050/312-2202. www.noordelijkscheepvaartmuseum.nl. Admission 3€ ($3.75) adults, 1.60€ ($2) seniors and children 7–15, free for children under 7. Tues–Sat 10am–5pm; Sun and holidays 1–5pm. Closed Jan 1, Apr 30, Aug 28, Dec 25.

ALMSHOUSES

With more than 30 *hofjes* (almshouses) within the city limits, Groningen shares with Amsterdam and Leiden the distinction of hosting the greatest number of these charitable medieval institutions in the country. Constructed around courtyards, these clusters of small cottages still provide homes for the poor and the aged. The **Heilige Geestgasthuis (Holy Ghost Guesthouse),** Pelsterstraat 43, dating from 1267, is the oldest in town. Founded in 1405, the **Sint-Geertruidsgasthuis (St. Gertrude's Guesthouse),** Peperstraat 22, started out as a lodging for pilgrims who came to Groningen to pay homage to a relic—a supposed arm of John the Baptist in the Martinikerk—and later became homes for seniors. There's a handsome courtyard garden behind the gate. Until midway through the 17th century, the **Sint-Anthonygasthuis (St. Anthony's Guesthouse),** Rademarkt 29/1–30, functioned in part as an asylum for the mentally ill. Its red-brick and sandstone gate dates from 1644.

PARKS & GARDENS

The beautiful Renaissance **Prinsenhof Garden** was established in 1625 behind the Prinsenhof building at Martinikerkhof 23, which was a monastery before becoming the seat of the bishop of Groningen in 1568. Later taken over for a royal residence, it now houses a television and radio studio. The hedges surrounding the herb beds, the rose garden, and a sundial are the result of more than 250 years of topiary. The garden is open April to mid-October, daily from 10am to sundown; admission is free.

When the city fortifications were demolished in the 19th century, part of the terrain in the north of town was given over to a pretty park, the **Noorderplantsoen,** laid out in the English landscape style.

TWO SCENIC LAKES NEARBY

The **Paterswoldsemeer,** a lake on Groningen's southern edge, is a sailing and watersports center with a vacation village on its shores. Just 8km (5 miles) southeast of here, the **Zuidlaardermeer** attracts watersports enthusiasts. In October, the nearby village of **Zuidlaren** is the setting for one of Holland's largest horse fairs.

WHERE TO STAY

De Doelen   De Doelen, on the bustling Grote Markt square, is about as centrally located as you can get. The attractive guest rooms are done in muted colors, and feature soft carpets and a mixture of period and modern furniture. The Croissanterie Cave du Patron is a convenient drop-in spot for inexpensive sandwiches, salads, light meals, and snacks priced at 8€ ($10) and under. There's a moderately priced steakhouse restaurant on the premises.

Grote Markt 36, 9711 VL Groningen. ✆ **050/312-7041**. Fax 050/314-6112. 59 units. 110€ ($138) double. AE, MC, V. Limited street parking. **Amenities:** Restaurants (light meals/steakhouse). *In room:* TV, minibar.

Golden Tulip Hotel Paterswolde   To get to this lovely lakeside hotel, take A28 toward Assen, and then at the Haren intersection follow the signs for Paterswolde. From there the route to the hotel is signposted. The Paterswolde is set on 30 wooded acres and provides a respite from the center city. It offers spacious guest rooms, good wheelchair access, babysitting, a beauty salon, an indoor swimming pool, tennis courts, and bikes for hire. There's a nice bar and restaurant.

Groningerweg 19 (a 10-min. drive from Groningen), 9765 TA Paterswolde. ✆ **050/309-5400**. Fax 050/309-1157. www.goldentuliphotels.nl. 71 units. 125€–175€ ($156–$219) double. AE, DC, MC, V. Free parking. **Amenities:** Restaurant (Dutch); bar. *In room:* TV, minibar.

Hotel de Ville 🍃   Three old houses have been converted into this stylish, up-to-date hotel. Many rooms overlook the quiet gardens at the rear of the block. The breakfast room/bar is in a glass conservatory. Next door to the hotel is the excellent brasserie-style restaurant Bistro 't Gerecht, which will even deliver dinner to your room.

Oude Boteringstraat 43, 9712 GD Groningen. ✆ **050/318-1222**. Fax 050/318-1777. www.hoteldeville.nl. 43 units. 110€–195€ ($138–$244) double. Rates include breakfast. AE, DC, MC, V. Limited street parking. *In room:* TV, minibar.

Schimmelpenninck Huys 🍃🍃   This grand mansion was transformed from a derelict pile into an elegant hotel in the late 1980s, but it still retains many historical features, and has been extended into neighboring buildings. The light, spacious rooms have modern furniture that blends with the classical atmosphere. There is a snug bar in a 14th-century wine cellar, and a spacious and beautiful Jugendstil lounge. The elegant restaurant **Empire Room** has a French-style garden terrace in the summer, and is well worth visiting even if you are not a guest here.

Oosterstraat 53, 9711 NR Groningen. ✆ **050/318-9502**. Fax 050/318-3164. www.schimmelpenninckhuys.nl. 26 units. 130€–175€ ($163–$219) double. AE, DC, MC, V. Free parking. **Amenities:** Restaurant (Dutch/French); lounge; bar. *In room:* TV, minibar, coffeemaker.

Moments **Canal Tours**

From June to September, the *rondvaartboten* (tour boats) of **Rederij Kool** Stationsweg (✆ **050/312-8379**) operate regular 1-hour cruises through the canals of Groningen. These depart from a dock outside Groningen rail station, beside the Groninger Museum. Or, during the same months, you can propel yourself around on a canoe or a water bike from **'t Peddeltje** (✆ **050/318-0330**), from a dock under the Herebrug bridge, just east of the Groninger Museum.

WHERE TO DINE

Binnenhof DUTCH/INTERNATIONAL   This relaxed and friendly restaurant is part of an arts center in a former ballroom. It serves sandwiches and snacks throughout the day, and in the evening a range of entrees, including vegetarian options. In summer, you can take advantage of a quiet, shady terrace.

Oosterstraat 7A (in a courtyard near the Grote Markt). ℂ **050/312-3697.** Main courses 9.50€–17€ ($12–$21). MC, V. Daily noon–1am.

Muller ✿✿ FRENCH   For an exquisite experience amid classic French surroundings, come to Muller. Chef Jean Michel Hengge is the proud owner of a Michelin star. He uses local produce as often as possible, including game in season. The six-course chef's menu makes good use of the day's best market finds. Menu items include pumpkin soup, clams in cream sauce, and filet of lamb en croûte. There's also a vegetarian option.

Grote Kromme Elleboog 13. ℂ **050/318-3208.** Fixed-price menus 55€–64€ ($69–$72). AE, DC, MC, V. Tues–Sat 6–10pm.

7 Exploring Around Groningen

The towns and places below can easily be visited on day trips from Groningen by car or bus, some by train, and others by bike or canoe if you have the time and energy for it.

WARFFUM

20km (12 miles) N of Groningen

Warffum is typical of the "mound villages" constructed above flood level in past centuries. Before local people became expert at building dikes to hold back the water, they constructed mounds to provide places of safety for their families and livestock. These mounds, known as *terpen,* and sometimes in Groningen as *wierden* or *warften,* often hold the oldest settlements in the area and look like islands rising a little way above the surrounding polders.

There are local trains and buses from Groningen to Warffum; by car, go north on N361 to Winsum, and then north and east on N363.

Just outside the village, **Openluchtmuseum Het Hoogeland,** Schoolstraat 4 (ℂ **0595/422-233;** www.hethoogeland.com), is an open-air museum that holds fascinating relics from the mound settlements, medieval costumes, and other objects. It's open mid-February to early November, Tuesday to Saturday from 10am to 5pm and Sunday from 1 to 5pm. Admission is 4.80€ ($6) for adults, 3.20€ ($4) for seniors, 2€ ($2.50) for children ages 6 to 11, and free for children under 6.

UITHUIZEN

23km (14 miles) N of Groningen; 8km (5 miles) E of Warffum

A mound village with a 13th-century church that contains a beautiful organ from 1700 at its heart, Uithuizen is worth a quick look just for itself. But the main reason for coming here is to visit the nearby Menkemaborg manor house. There are frequent trains and buses from Groningen; by car, take N46 north and then N999.

Menkemaborg ✿✿   A double-moated fortified manor house that dates back to the 14th century, this is the finest surviving example of such a *borg,* as the country seats of the local lords of Groningen were called. It was extensively reconstructed in the early 18th century and its interior has changed little since then, though the elegant furnishings,

---

Fun Fact **Deathly Silence**

In the countryside just south of Uithuizen is a tiny hamlet with a name that says it all. It's called Doodstil (Dead Quiet).

---

paintings, and fittings are a combination of Menkemaborg's own from this period and notable antiques drawn from other manors. Five rooms in which the upper crust could live in style are open to view, as is the kitchen where the lower orders labored with a mass of cooking utensils to keep things that way. The **1939–1945 Museum** on the grounds evokes the World War II period through a collection of armaments and military vehicles. The estate's formal gardens, which include a rose garden and a labyrinth, are a compelling attraction. A pancake restaurant occupies the old carriage house.

Menkemaweg 2 (1km/½ mile east of Uithuizen). ✆ **0595/431-970.** www.menkemaborg.nl. Admission: Mansion and gardens 4.50€ ($5.65) adults, 2€ ($2.50) children 6–12, free for children under 6; gardens only 3€ ($3.75) adults, 1.50€ ($1.90) children 6–12, free for children under 6. May–Sept daily 10am–5pm; Oct–Dec Tues–Sun 10am–noon and 1–4pm.

DELFZIJL
26km (16 miles) NE of Groningen; 19km (12 miles) SE of Uithuizen

The port town of Delfzijl has a busy, colorful harbor and looks out across the Eems estuary to Germany. From here, seagoing vessels sail up the Eems Canal to Groningen.

There are frequent trains and buses from Groningen; by car, go northeast on N360. Tourist information is available from **VVV Delfzijl,** Kornputplein 1, Delfzil (✆ **0596/ 618-104).**

In the town is the **Museum AquariOm,** Zeebadweg 7 (✆ **0596/612-318;** www. aquariom.nl). Here you find North Sea aquatic life, corals, shells, and a geological museum with fossils, minerals, and archaeological and maritime exhibits. The aquarium is open Monday to Saturday from 10am to 7pm; admission is 4€ ($5) for adults, 3.25€ ($4.05) for seniors, and free for children under 4.

East of Delfzijl, the shore of the **Dollard,** a wide bay rimmed by mud flats, is a great place to observe wading birds.

WHERE TO STAY & DINE
Hotel Du Bastion   Rooms at this small hotel in the town center are comfortable, clean, and bright, with whitewashed walls and period furniture. On the premises is a good, moderately priced restaurant that features traditional Dutch dishes and a tourist menu.

Waterstraat 74–78, 9934 AX Delfzijl. ✆ **0596/618-771.** Fax 0596/617-147. www.dubastion.nl. 40 units. 75€ ($94) double. Rates include continental breakfast. AE, DC, MC, V. Limited street parking. **Amenities:** Restaurant (Dutch). *In room:* TV.

SLOCHTEREN
16km (10 miles) E of Groningen

This village is at the center of Groningen's natural gas field. Its star attraction is the lovely Fraeylemaborg estate. To get here by car from Groningen, take N360 toward Delfzijl, turn right onto N986 just outside the city, and then take N387. Bus no. 78 goes from Groningen bus station.

Fraeylemaborg ⊛   Comparable with Menkemaborg (see above), this 16th-century moated manor house, surrounded by attractive woods and gardens in the 19th-century

English landscape style, is a fine surviving example of a Groningen *borg*. The interior has a wealth of richly decorated period rooms from the 18th and 19th centuries. You'll find collections of Asian porcelain and an exhibit about the Dutch royal house of Oranje-Nassau.

Hoofdweg 30 (on the eastern edge of Slochteren). (℃ **0598/421-568**. www.fraeylemaborg.nl. Admission 4.50€ ($5.65) adults, 2€ ($2.50) children 6–12, free for children under 6. Mar–Dec Tues–Fri 10am–5pm, Sat–Sun and holidays 1–5pm.

HEILIGERLEE

30km (19 miles) E of Groningen

The village of Heiligerlee is known to every Dutch schoolchild because one of the most famous battles in the country's history was fought here. On May 23, 1568, Count Louis of Nassau defeated a Spanish army in a battle that sparked the Eighty Years War, which in turn led to the formation of the free Republic of the Netherlands.

To get here from Groningen by car, take A7/E22 east to Exit 46. Local trains and buses go from Groningen to nearby Winschoten.

A multimedia exhibit at the **Museum Slag bij Heiligerlee (Battle of Heiligerlee Museum),** Provincialeweg 55 ((℃ **0597/418-199**), takes you back to the famous battle of 1568 and the war that ensued. The museum is open April, Tuesday to Sunday from 1 to 5pm; May to September, Tuesday to Saturday from 10am to 5pm, Sunday from 1 to 5pm; and October, Tuesday to Friday and Sunday from 1 to 5pm. Admission is 4€ ($5) for adults, 2.50€ ($3.75) for children ages 6 to 13, and free for children under 6.

Just across the road, in the former Van Bergen Bell Foundry from 1795, which cast more than 10,000 bells, ranging from the smallest of dinner bells to massive church and carillon bells, is the **Klokkengieterijmuseum,** Provincialeweg 46 ((℃ **0597/418-199**). Exhibits explain the history of bell casting, and there are demonstrations (by appointment only) and carillon concerts. The museum has the same open hours as the Battle of Heiligerlee Museum.

LEEK

14km (8½ miles) SW of Groningen

Just northeast of this small town stands the wooded estate of **Landgoed Nienoord** ((℃ **0594/512-604;** www.nienoord-leek.nl). It's on the border of the Leekstermeer, a lake that offers swimming and sailing. At the heart of the estate, **Kasteel Nienoord,** a handsome manor house that was reconstructed in 1887 after fire and general deterioration had all but ruined the 1525 original, houses the **Nationaal Rijtuigmuseum (National Carriage Museum),** Nienord 1 ((℃ **0594/512-260;** www.rijtuigmuseum.nl). It holds a wonderful collection of antique horse-drawn carriages, stagecoaches, and sleighs; the uniforms and accessories of their drivers; and related paintings and prints. There's a restaurant on the premises. The museum is open April to October, Tuesday to Friday from 10am to 5pm, and weekends from 1 to 5pm. Admission is 4.50€ ($5.65) for adults, 3.60€ ($4.50) for seniors, and free for children under 13.

Moments Pedaling Pleasure

Groningen province's tranquil Waddenzee coastline—from Lauwersoog to Eemshaven, it's a distance of around 50km (31 miles)—makes a fine setting for a bicycling tour. From the dike, you get views offshore to Schiermonnikoog and the low-lying, uninhabited islets of Rottumerplaat and Rottumeroog.

Illustrious Son

Abel Tasman (1603–59), one of the greatest Dutch navigators, was born in the village of Lutjegast, 20km (12 miles) west of Groningen. In 1642, he discovered Tasmania and New Zealand, and the following year he reached Tonga and Fiji.

Around the estate, you'll find several other attractions. **Familiepark Nienoord,** Nienoord 10 (© **0594/512-230**), is a park with rides and other activities for children. And you can swim both indoors and outdoors in a "subtropical pool" at **Nienoord Zwemkasteel,** Nienoord 12 (© **0594/517-500**).

HAREN

6km (3½ miles) S of Groningen

The premier attraction of Haren is its excellent botanical garden.

Hortus Haren Exotic flowers and plants of all climates, from alpine to tropical, are collected at the botanical garden of the University of Groningen, which has been here since the middle of the 17th century. You can visit a greenhouse where plants from the tropical rainforests are kept, and a section devoted to tropical insects. Among different European gardens is a re-creation of a Celtic garden. The Hidden Kingdom of Ming is a replica of a Ming dynasty (1368–1644) Chinese imperial garden. You can even sip Chinese tea in the teahouse.

Kerklaan 34. © **050/537-0053.** www.hortusharen.nl. Admission 4.50€ ($5) adults, 3.50€ ($4.40) seniors, 2€ ($2.50) children 4–13, free for children under 4. Daily 9:30am–5pm. Closed Jan 1, Dec 25.

8 Assen

24km (15 miles) S of Groningen

With all due respect to the capital of Drenthe province, Assen (pop. 55,000) is a pleasant enough town but contains little of historical importance or unmissable visitor interest. It is, though, a good base from which to make forays into Drenthe's rural tranquillity—an ancient landscape in which life flourished long before the land on which most Dutch now live was reclaimed from the sea.

ESSENTIALS

GETTING THERE   There's frequent service by **train** and **bus** from Groningen to Assen station, a little way east of the center. By **car,** take A28/E232 south, or the parallel and more scenic N372.

VISITOR INFORMATION   VVV Assen, Marktstraat 8–10, 9401 JH Assen (© **0900/202-2293;** fax 0592/241-852; www.vvvassen.nl), is in the town center.

WHAT TO SEE & DO

Drents Museum The provincial museum is spread out over five neighboring historic buildings on the town's main square, including the church of the Cistercian Convent of Maria-in-Campis from 1260, and the former provincial Gouvernementsgebouw (Government Building) from 1885. Among many archaeological finds on display are Stone Age objects from Drenthe's *hunebedden* (megaliths), weapons, pottery, Roman sarcophagi, and Celtic and Merovingian jewelry. Among the well-preserved items recovered from Drenthe's peat bogs is the mummified corpse of *Het Meisje van Yde* (The Yde

A Moving Side Trip from Assen

After the German army occupied the Netherlands in World War II, **Camp Westerbork,** a refugee camp for German Jews south of Assen, became a transit center for Jews, Gypsies, Resistance fighters, and other victims on their way to the Nazi death camps. In memory of the 102,000 people transported from here, an equal number of stones have been laid out on the camp's parade ground, and at the **Memorial Center** (✆ 0593/592-600; www.kamp westerbork.nl), exhibits and film footage afford some idea of their fate. Among those who "transited" through Westerbork were Anne and Margot Frank, en route to Bergen-Belsen.

The camp terrain is open permanently; the museum is open Monday to Friday from 10am to 5pm, and Saturday, Sunday, and holidays from 1 to 5pm (closed Jan 1, Dec 25). Admission to the camp is free; to the museum it is 4.50€ ($5.65) for adults, 2.25€ ($2.80) for children ages 8 to 18, and free for children under 8. To drive there from Assen, take the minor road parallel to A28/E232 south to Hooghalen and then turn east for 4km (2½ miles). Or go by train to Beilen and then take bus no. 22 from outside the station to the center of Hooghalen, from where the camp is signposted, a 15-minute walk.

The nearby **National Radio Astronomy Center,** where an array of 19 radio telescopes tunes in to the music of the spheres, is a fantastic and—after the sad experience of visiting the camp—uplifting sight.

Girl). The highlight of the art collection is Vincent van Gogh's oil painting *Peat Boat With Two Figures* (1883).

Brink 1. ✆ 0592/377-773. www.drentsmuseum.nl. Admission 6€ ($7.50) adults, 4€ ($5) seniors, 3€ ($3.75) children 5–15, free for children under 5. Tues–Sun 11am–5pm (Mon when national holiday). Closed Jan 1, Dec 25.

MORE PLACES OF INTEREST

A brief visit to the **Draaiorgelmuseum (Barrel Organ Museum),** Rode Heklaan 3 (✆ 0592/345-885), gets you close to some beautiful examples of these old music-makers, similar to those you might see grinding away on town streets across the land. Tours are guided and by appointment only.

Just south of the center, the large **Asserbos** public park contains the remnants of an ancient oak forest, though only around one-tenth of the park's area is covered by original forest, the remainder having been planted in 1760. On the grounds is a children's farm.

Farther south, just outside of town, is Holland's national **TT (Tourist Trophy) Circuit,** where the annual Dutch grand prix motorcycle race takes place on the last Saturday in June. On preceding days, Assen's peaceable streets fill up with leather-clad bikers and fab-looking bikes from around Europe.

9 Emmen

32km (20 miles) SE of Assen

Drenthe's largest town (pop. 55,000) is a delightful mix of old buildings left over from its village origins and new ones reflecting its prosperity in recent years. It has dubbed

> *Moments* **Biking the Wide Green Yonder**
>
> The bicycle might have been invented with Drenthe in mind. A myriad of bike paths, signed routes, and remote byways lead deep into the heart of farming country, heathland, and forest. Local tourist offices have details of suggested bicycling routes. Other routes touch the main towns, Assen and Emmen, and yet others weave in and out of *hunebed* territory.

itself *Vlinderstad* (Butterfly Town), by way of drawing attention to some of the most notable denizens of its large zoo (see below).

ESSENTIALS

GETTING THERE   **Buses** frequently run from Assen to Emmen. By **car,** take N376 east from Assen to Rolde, and then go southeast through scenic country to its intersection with N381; go east on this highway and its continuation, N364, into Emmen.

VISITOR INFORMATION   **VVV Emmen,** Hoofdstraat 22, 7811 EP Emmen (✆ **0900/202-2393;** fax 0591/644-106; www.vvvemmen.nl), is in the town center. The office is open Monday from 1 to 5:30pm, Tuesday to Friday from 9:30am to 5:30pm, and Saturday from 10am to 4pm.

A GREAT ZOO

Noorder Dierenpark (Northern Zoo) ✮ *Kids*   Animals from around the world roam freely at this large zoo, in habitats that have been made as natural as can be for a park in the middle of Drenthe. For instance, cliffs, pebble beaches, and realistic underwater scenery are the setting in which Humboldt penguins disport. Among the nearly 500 different species here, you'll see elephants, tigers, white rhinoceroses, giraffes, hippopotamuses, impalas, apes, baboons, kangaroos, and snakes. On the children's farm, there are a bunch of cute domesticated animals. Emmen takes its moniker of "Butterfly Town" from the magnificent tropical *vlindertuin* (butterfly garden).

Hoofdstraat 18. ✆ 0591/850-850. www.noorderdierenpark.nl. Admission 15€ ($18) adults; 13€ ($17) seniors, 12€ ($15) children 3–9, free for children under 3. Mar–May and Oct daily 10am–5pm; June–Aug daily 10am–6pm; Sept daily 10am–5:30pm; Nov–Feb daily 10am–4:30pm.

SIDE TRIPS FROM EMMEN

BOURTANGE ✮

31km (19 miles) NE of Emmen; 17km (11 miles) NE of Ter Apel

This unique fortress village has been restored to its former glory. Constructed from 1580 onward, it withstood many battles over the centuries, only to fall into disrepair as methods of warfare changed. Two wooden drawbridges span a star-shaped moat and lead to traffic-free streets within the ramparts, where you can visit barracks, gunpowder storage rooms, a synagogue, and officers' quarters. Various relics of military life are displayed. The fortress is permanently open and admission is free. Its museums are open April to October, Monday to Friday from 10am to 5pm and Saturday and Sunday from 11am to 5pm; November to March, Saturday and Sunday from 12:30 to 4:30pm. Admission to the museums is 6€ ($7.50) for adults, 4€ ($5) for children ages 6 to 12, and free for children under 6. Bourtange's **Visitor Center** is at Willem Lodewijkstraat 33 (✆ **0599/ 354-600;** www.bourtange.nl), on the west side of the village. In July and August, military living-history events take place. The highlight is a uniformed re-enactment of the 1640 Battle of Bourtange during the Eighty Years War of liberation from Spain.

BARGER-COMPASCUUM
10km (6 miles) E of Emmen

Set outside this village, on 1.6 sq. km (⅔ sq. mile) of the peat moors along the German border, is the **Open-Air Museum Veenpark (Peat Park),** Berkenrode 4 (© **0591/324-444;** www.veenpark.nl). At a reconstructed peat cutters' village, 't Aole Compas, you can watch demonstrations of peat cutting, butter churning, weaving, and clog making, as they were done at the end of the 19th century. There are nostalgic stores and an antique barbershop, and you can take a short canal trip onboard a turf boat. The park is open April to June and September to October, daily from 10am to 5pm; and July to August, daily from 10am to 6pm. Admission is 11€ ($14) for adults, 9.25€ ($12) for seniors, and free for children under 5. To get there, take bus no. 45 from outside Emmen rail station to Barger Compascum, or drive on minor roads via Nieuw Dordrecht.

SCHOONOORD
12km (7½ miles) NW of Emmen

Named after Ellert and Brammert, two giants who once upon a time robbed travelers in these parts, the **Open-Air Museum Ellert en Brammert,** Tramstraat 73 (© **0591/ 382-421;** www.ellertenbrammert.nl), is a trip down Drenthe's memory lane. Sculptures

---

Stone Age Giants

Drenthe can count more than 50 Stone Age chambered tombs or temples called *hunebedden* on its territory. These fascinating monuments consist of large, free-standing stones, or megaliths, often capped by lateral stones. They are scattered along a stretch of scenic, relatively high ground known as the *Hondsrug* (Dog's Back). The terminal moraine of a long-vanished Ice Age glacier, the Hondsrug's rugged spine angles northwest from Emmen to the south-eastern edge of Groningen. Discoveries of pottery, tools, jewelry, and other items have enabled archaeologists to date the tombs to around 3400 B.C., and to attribute their construction to the farming communities of the Funnel-beaker Culture, so-called after the characteristic style of pottery they created.

The most interesting hunebedden are along N34, the Emmen-Groningen highway, in the northern reaches of Emmen itself and around the pretty Hondsrug villages of Odoorn, Borger, Rolde, Eext, Annen, and Anloo. The VVV tourist offices in Emmen and Assen have details on where they are and how to get to them. Equally worth a visit is the **National Hunebedden Information Center,** Bronnegerstraat 12 (© **0599/236-374;** www.hunebedcentrum.nl), in Borger, open May to September, Monday to Saturday from 10am to noon and 1 to 5pm; and October to April, Monday to Saturday from 10am to noon and 1 to 4pm. Close to the center is the largest hunebed, #D27, which has nine capstones still in place.

Vincent's Vision of Drenthe

It would take a van Gogh to capture Drenthe's many moods of landscape and light, especially when the summer fields are heavy with ripening crops. The traditional lives of this area's peasant farmers and peat cutters actually drew Vincent to the province for a 3-month sojourn in 1883, early in his career as a painter. "I am in a wonderful country," he wrote to his brother Theo.

Vincent lodged for 2 months at a ferry-house-cafe in the village of Nieuw-Amsterdam, 8km (5 miles) south of Emmen. He had to leave because he couldn't afford the rent. Then owned by Hendrik Scholte, the **Van Gogh House,** in Van Goghstraat (© 0591/555-600), has been restored to its 1883 condition and contains archival material on the artist. It's open Tuesday to Sunday from 1 to 5pm. Admission is 4.50€ ($5.65) for adults, and 3.50€ ($4.40) for children under 13.

Among the works Vincent created during his Drenthe period is an oil painting, *Peat Boat With Two Figures,* which you can view at the Drents Museum in Assen; and a watercolor, *Drawbridge in Nieuw-Amsterdam,* on display at the Groninger Museum in Groningen.

of Ellert and Brammert stand guard at the gates, behind which are sod huts, a Saxon farmhouse, a tollhouse, an old school, a prison, a smithy, a sawmill, an apiary (bee farm), geological exhibits, and a children's farm. You can watch living crafts, like pottery making, and the re-created farming methods of yesteryear, and then enjoy a snack and a drink at an old country inn. Children can relive the legend of the two bandits in their cave hideaway. You'll need a couple of hours to make a visit here worthwhile. The museum is open April to October, daily from 9am to 6pm. Admission is 4.50€ ($5.65) for adults, 3.50€ ($4.40) for seniors and children ages 4 to 11, and free for children under 4.

To get to Schoonoord, take bus no. 21 from outside Emmen rail station. By car, go west on N364 and north on N376.

ORVELTE
18km (11 miles) NW of Emmen; 6km (3½ miles) W of Schoonoord

In a beautiful, forested landscape, **Museumdorp Orvelte** ⊀ is a genuine old village, but one that has been preserved as a living-history monument that gives a fine insight into the way things once were in Drenthe. Rustic, thatched-roof buildings are grouped around the village square, the Brink. Real people live here and go about their daily lives, and though you can visit some houses and buildings that have been opened for display by masters of traditional crafts and trades, like the clog maker, the blacksmith, and the carpenter, others are private and can't be visited. There's an old-fashioned country cafe and a restaurant. For more information, call by the **Visitor Center,** Schapendrift 3 (© 0593/322-288).

You can reach Orvelte by signposted country roads off N364 (leave your car at one of the car parks just outside the village), and by bus from Emmen, Assen, and the rail station in nearby Beilen.

16

Utrecht, Gelderland, Overijssel & Flevoland

The four central provinces form a tapestry of history, scenic beauty, and feats of civil engineering. **Utrecht** is the smallest of the nation's 12 provinces, and elegant châteaux speckle the landscape. The provincial capital, the 2,000-year-old city of Utrecht, is a center of learning and religion, while Amersfoort and Oudewater evoke medieval times.

To the east is the country's largest province, **Gelderland.** The banks of the Rhine, Maas, and Waal rivers, along with national parks, nature reserves, and recreation centers, are vacation venues for the Dutch. Gelderland's towns beckon with attractions like the Het Loo royal palace museum at Apeldoorn and Arnhem's Netherlands Open-Air Folklore Museum. Also noteworthy is that the World War II

airborne battle for the Rhine bridge at Arnhem—the famous "bridge too far"—was fought here.

A parklike landscape of beautiful forests, meadows, and lakes distinguishes rural **Overijssel.** These are punctuated by châteaux, steep-roofed and half-timbered farmhouses, tranquil villages, and picturesque medieval and Hanseatic towns.

Holland's newest province, **Flevoland,** was created on land reclaimed in recent decades from the IJsselmeer and was officially inaugurated in 1986. The new polders cover some 1,800 sq. km (695 sq. miles), sprinkled with oddly integrated old villages that were once islands and with shiny modern towns like Lelystad. Straight roads run through flat fields traversed by equally straight canals.

1 Utrecht ★★

42km (26 miles) SE of Amsterdam

A good starting point for exploring this province is the capital city, with its thriving cultural life. Utrecht's modern face hits you right between the eyes when you arrive by train at Centraal station, in the multitiered Hoog Catherijne mall that spreads over a 6-block area to the edge of the Old Town. But don't let that dampen your interest in visiting this well-preserved city, Holland's fourth largest (pop. 240,000). Utrecht was founded by the Romans as the fortress of Trajectum ad Rhenum (Ford on the Rhine) in A.D. 47.

When the Dutch Republic was established here in 1579, Utrecht had already been a powerful political player from the earliest days of Christianity in the Low Countries, since the English missionary St. Willibrord founded a bishopric here around 690. As a result, this is a city of churches, with many restored medieval religious structures in the old heart of town.

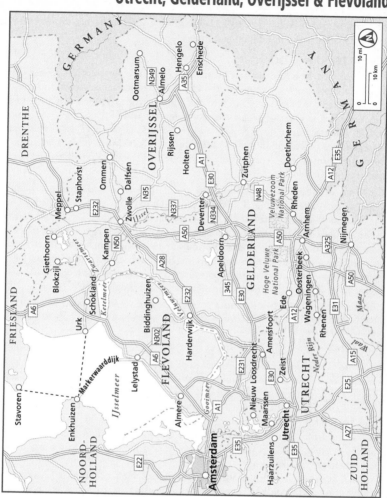

ESSENTIALS

GETTING THERE   **Trains** arrive every 15 minutes or so from Amsterdam, and about as frequently from many other places around the country. By **car,** take A2/E35 southeast from Amsterdam.

VISITOR INFORMATION   **VVV Utrecht** is at Domplein 9, 3512 JC Utrecht (© **0900/128-8732;** www.12utrecht.nl). The office is open Monday from noon to 6pm, Tuesday to Friday from 10am to 6pm (Thurs to 9pm), Saturday from 9:30am to 5pm, and Sunday (May to Sept) 10am to 2pm.

SPECIAL EVENTS   Every year, during the last week of August (and sometimes into the first few days of Sept), concert halls, churches, and ad hoc venues in Utrecht are filled with the sounds of Renaissance and baroque music during the **Holland Festival**

of Early Music Utrecht (© 030/232-9000; www.oudemuziek.nl), an international event that attracts the world's top performers.

WHAT TO SEE & DO

Unique to Utrecht is its tree-shaded wharf, 5m (17 ft.) below street level, along **Oudegracht,** a canal that winds through the Old Town. Restaurants, stores, and sidewalk cafes have replaced the hustle and bustle of the wharfside commercial activity of former times, when Utrecht was a major port along an arm of the Rhine—the adjacent sunken **Nieuwegracht** canal follows a former course of the river—and these quays were used for offloading into the vaulted storage cellars. Much of the Old Town has been transformed into a pedestrians-only zone, with many secondhand bookstores and antiques dealers.

Centraal Museum ☆ The emphasis at this convent-turned-museum is on an impressive collection of Dutch modern art and Dutch 20th-century applied art from the De Stijl group, displayed in the former stables on the grounds. Elsewhere are historical displays about Utrecht, including a preserved Viking longboat found in the city that dates from around 1100, and an exquisite dollhouse from 1680. Then there are paintings by artists of the 16th-century Utrecht school, in particular those of Jan van Scorel (1495–1562), whose group portraits planted the seeds of a genre that would flower in Holland in the next century. A 2-hour visit should suffice.

Nicolaaskerkhof 10. © 030/236-2362. www.centraalmuseum.nl. Admission 8€ ($10) adults; 5€ ($6.25) seniors, students, and children 13–17; 2€ ($2.50) for children 5–12; free for children under 5. Tues–Sun noon–5pm (Fri to 9pm). Closed Jan 1, Apr 30, Dec 25. Bus: 2.

Domkerk (Cathedral) ☆☆ This magnificent cathedral took almost 3 centuries to build, from 1254 to 1517. The original Romanesque structure was replaced bit by bit; first the choir, then the tower, and finally the nave and transepts. The nave collapsed during a violent storm in 1674 and was never reconstructed; the choir and transepts survived and remain disconnected from the tower (see below). The cathedral interior bears traces of the fierce wave of iconoclasm that spread over Holland in the second half of the 16th century. There's a battered altarpiece in one of the side chapels. A sandstone Holy Sepulcher, dated 1501, shows a defaced Christ in a tomb under a badly damaged Gothic arch.

Other worthwhile sights nearby are **Bisschopes Hof,** or Bishop's Garden (daily 11am–5pm); and **Dom Kloostergang,** a cloister arcade constructed in the 15th century, with magnificent stained-glass windows depicting scenes from the legend of St. Martin. The cathedral cloisters are connected to the former **Hall of the Chapter,** where the signing of the 1579 Union of Utrecht (which united the seven Protestant Dutch provinces in their rebellion against Catholic Spanish rule) took place.

Achter de Dom 1. www.domkerk.nl. © 030/231-0403. Free admission. Sun 2–4pm year-round; May–Sept Mon–Fri 10am–5pm, Sat 10am–3:30pm, Sun 2–4pm; Oct–Apr Mon–Fri 11am–3:30pm, Sat 11am–3:30pm, Sun 2–4pm. Bus: 2 or 22.

Domtoren ☆ The cathedral's 110m (365-ft.) tower, constructed between 1321 and 1383, dominates Utrecht's skyline and is the tallest in the Netherlands. It stands on the site of St. Willibrord's original 8th-century church and across a square from its mother building, since the nave collapsed during the great storm of 1674, leaving the tower unharmed. In the paving on the square, you can see the outline of the missing section. One of the best views of Utrecht is from the top of the tower, a climb of 465 steps if you have the stamina and the inclination (about halfway up is the 14th-c.

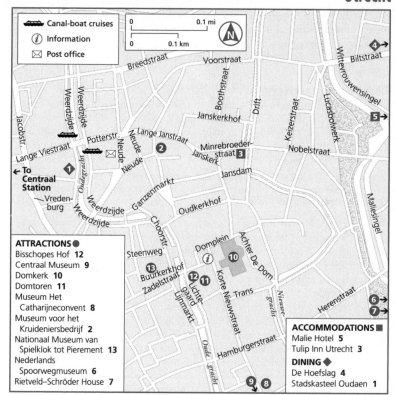

St. Michael's Chapel where you can stop and ease the panting!). The climb goes past the church carillon's 50 massive bells you hear all through your stay in Utrecht. Restored and extended in 1999, the carillon has since then been Europe's largest. Its bourdon (largest bell) weighs 10,000 kilograms (9.8 tons) and has a diameter of 2.7m (9 ft.).

Domplein 9–10. ℂ 030/233-3036. www.domtoren.nl. Admission 7.50€ ($9.40) adults, 6.50€ ($8.15) students, 4.50€ ($5.65) children 5–12, free for children under 5. Sun–Mon noon–5pm; Fri–Sat 10am–5pm. Bus: 2 or 22.

Museum Het Catharijneconvent   Housed in the old **St. Catherine's Convent,** this exceptional collection of medieval religious art—paintings, relics, carvings, and church robes—helps illustrate the development of Christianity in Holland from the 8th century onward. The courtyard of the convent where the museum is housed has a cafe terrace where you can take a meditative pause.

Lange Nieuwstraat 38. ℂ 030/231-3835. www.catharijneconvent.nl. Admission 8.50€ ($11) adults, 7.50€ ($9.40) seniors, 4.50€ ($5.65) children 6–17, free for children under 6. Tues–Fri 10am–5pm; Sat–Sun and holidays 11am–5pm. Closed Jan 1, Apr 30. Bus: 2.

Nationaal Museum van Speelklok tot Pierement (National Museum from Chimes to Barrel Organs) *(Kids*   Six hundred mechanical music machines from the 17th century to the present—including fairground organs and those barrel organs you see on Dutch streets—are housed in this 13th-century former church. A player piano is controlled by punched rolls. The most overwhelming exhibits are the music-hall organs of yesteryear, with which you can sing and dance at the end of your tour.

Steenweg 6. (✆ 030/231-2789. www.museumspeelklok.nl. Admission 7€ ($8.75) adults, 6€ ($7.50) seniors, 4€ ($5) children 4–12, free for children under 4. Tues–Sun and holidays 10am–5pm; guided tours on the hour. Closed Jan 1, Apr 30, Dec 25. Bus: 2.

Nederlands Spoorwegmuseum (Dutch Railway Museum) ★ *Kids*   You don't have to be a rail buff to be fascinated by this former rail station and its marvelous collection of more than 60 steam engines, carriages, and wagons. There are moving models, paintings, and films relating to train travel. The multimedia section should have you and the kids stuck to your seats with presentations on the latest high-speed trains, such as the Thalys and the TGV.

Maliebaanstation. (✆ 030/230-6206. www.spoorwegmuseum.nl. Admission 13€ ($10) adults, 11€ ($14) seniors, 9.50€ ($6.25) children 3–12, free for children under 3. Tues–Sun (also Mon during school vacations) 10am–5pm. Closed Jan 1, Apr 30. Bus: 3 to Maliebaan.

Rietveld–Schröder House ★   Constructed in 1924, this family home was something of a shocker at the time and represents a high point of the De Stijl movement that so influenced contemporary art. It was designed by Utrecht architect and designer Gerrit Rietveld (1888–1964)—famous for his angular, red-and-blue chair (1918)—and a female would-be architect, Truus Schröder (at the time it was virtually impossible for a woman to work as an architect). The plaster exterior bears De Stijl's signature red, yellow, blue, and gray tones, and the innovative interior is a model of space-saving and efficiency. Rietveld and Schröder both lived here until their deaths. The house was restored in 1985 and is now a UNESCO World Heritage Site, owned by the Centraal Museum. The tour operated by the museum takes in the Rietveld Model Home, at Erasmuslaan 9 in Utrecht.

Prins Hendriklaan 50. (✆ 030/236-2310. www.rietveldschroderhuis.nl. Admission (includes tour bus) 16€ ($20) adults; 13€ ($16) seniors, students, and children 13–18; 8€ ($10) children 5–12; free for children under 5. By appointment for guided tours only, at Centraal Museum (see above), Tues–Sun (reservations recommended). Tour bus from Centraal Museum: 11:45am, 12:45, 1:45, and 2:45pm.

BOAT TOURS

One-hour **cruises** on Utrecht's canals are available year-round from **Rederij Lovers** (✆ 030/231-6468) and **Rederij Schuttevaer** (✆ 030/272-0111; www.schuttevaer. com); both lines' boats depart from Nieuwekade. Tours are daily every hour on the hour from 11am to 5pm, and are 7€ ($8.75) for adults, 5.50€ ($6.90) for children ages 4 to 12, and free for children under 4. From mid-May to September, there are cruises on the Vecht River to the pretty village of Loenen aan de Vecht, with a stop to

Moments **Sweet Satisfaction**

Tucked away in a courtyard, the **Museum voor het Kruideniersbedrijf**, Hoogt 6 (✆ 030/231-6628), a grocers' museum upstairs in a tiny grocery store, is the place to satisfy your sweet tooth. The interior and equipment are original; an aroma of cinnamon, ginger, and other spices pervades the air; and the ladies behind the counter serve with old-fashioned friendliness. It's difficult not to buy an ounce or two of each kind of candy or cookie. The museum is open Tuesday to Saturday from 12:30 to 4:30pm. Admission is free.

visit the Terra Nova estate. Another cruise goes along the Kromme Rijn to the Rhijnauwen estate.

WHERE TO STAY

Malie Hotel   Two 19th-century mansions in a quiet residential neighborhood near the university Uithof complex are the setting for this lovely small hotel. The small lobby is furnished with modern black leather chairs. The guest rooms have large windows and are very bright. Both the breakfast room and the **Imperator** bar overlook the peaceful garden at the back.

Maliestraat 2, 3581 SL Utrecht. ✆ 030/231-6424. Fax 030/234-0661. www.hampshirehotels.nl. 29 units. 95€–125€ ($119–$156) double. Rates include buffet breakfast. AE, DC, MC, V. Bus: 4 or 11. **Amenities:** Bar. *In room:* TV, minibar.

Tulip Inn Utrecht ✿   This excellent hotel is literally in the shadow of the cathedral and within a 2-minute walk of the canal, with its bi-level wharf, restaurants, and stores. The intimate guest rooms have comfortable wooden furniture and large beds. Some windows still retain the original early-20th-century stained glass.

Janskerkhof 10, 3512 BL Utrecht. ✆ 030/231-3169. Fax 030/231-0148. www.goldentulip.com. 45 units. 130€ ($163) double. Rates include buffet breakfast. AE, DC, MC, V. Bus: 3. **Amenities:** Restaurant (Dutch). *In room:* TV.

WHERE TO DINE

De Hoefslag ✿✿ INTERNATIONAL/FRENCH   This beautiful dining spot, on wooded grounds northeast of Utrecht, is considered by many to be Holland's top restaurant. There's a Victorian-garden feel to the lounge, while the dining room is reminiscent of an upscale hunting lodge, with lots of dark wood, an open hearth, and ceiling-to-floor doors opening to the terrace. The De Hoefslag changes its menu daily, deciding on specials after the chef has returned from the market. The seafood is superb, as are pork, lamb, and game dishes.

Vossenlaan 28, Bosch en Duin. ✆ 030/225-1051. www.hoefslag.nl. Fixed-price menus 30€–75€ ($38–$94). AE, DC, MC, V. Mon–Sat noon–2:30pm and 5:30–9:30pm.

Stadskasteel Oudaen CONTINENTAL   This medieval fortified town house from 1320 has been transformed into a culinary palace. Downstairs, in what was the main hall, you can sit in the cafe and savor beer brewed on the premises according to medieval recipes. Upstairs is the restaurant "Tussen hemel en aarde" ("Between heaven and earth"), with its original fireplace still intact and a rustic tile floor. The menu changes weekly, according to what is freshest and in season.

Oudegracht 99. ✆ 030/231-1864. www.oudaen.nl. Main courses 20€–24€ ($25–$30); fixed-price menus 35€–40€ ($44–$50). AE, DC, MC, V. Cafe daily 10am–2am; restaurant Mon–Sat 5:30–9pm.

SIDE TRIPS FROM UTRECHT

At the **Loosdrechtse Plassen (Loosdrecht Lakes)** ✿, 8km (5 miles) north of Utrecht, old peat diggings brim with water and the land has been reduced to straggly ribbons between a checkerboard of lakes. These have become popular recreational sailing and watersports zones, based on the busy harbor at Oud-Loosdrecht. A handsome old village off the western end of the lakes is **Loenen aan de Vecht,** on the bank of the Vecht River.

NEARBY CASTLES

In and around the area between Utrecht and the Loosdrecht lakes are three of the finest castles and stately châteaux in the province of Utrecht.

Fun Fact **The Breukelen Bridge**

Noo Yawkers might want to take in Breukelen, a tiny village on the Vecht River northwest of Utrecht. Treat yourself to crossing the *original* Brooklyn Bridge— all of 6m (20 ft.) long, one car wide, and definitely not for sale!

Kasteel De Haar 🌟🌟 If you have time for only one castle jaunt, make it to richly furnished De Haar. Like most castles, it has had its ups and downs—fires and ransackings and the like—over the centuries, but thanks to an infusion of Rothschild money in the early 1900s, it now sits in all its 15th-century moated splendor in the middle of a gracious Versailles-like formal garden. After a disastrous fire in the 1800s it was reconstructed in 1892 to the designs of the neo-Gothic architect, Petrus Josephus Hubertus Cuypers—who was responsible for Amsterdam's Centraal Station and Rijksmuseum. Cuypers's craftsmen worked with medieval techniques to an extraordinary degree of detail. The trouble now is that the weight of this construction atop the original foundations is making them subside into the moat! The castle's owners, who use the place as their primary residence, had to hold a sale of family heirlooms in 1998 to fund measures to prevent more subsidence. Its walls are, however, still hung with many fine paintings and precious Gobelin tapestries of the 14th and 15th centuries; its floors are softened with Persian rugs; and its chambers are furnished in the styles of Louis XIV, XV, and XVI of France. Don't miss the magnificent formal gardens, for which a whole village was transported down the road to afford better views.

Kasteellaan 1, Haarzuilens. 𝄞 **030/677-8515**. www.kasteeldehaar.nl. Castle and park: 8€ ($10) adults, 5€ ($6.25) children 5–12, free for children under 5. Open hours: a mind-bogglingly complex schedule exists for both the castle and the park, and for guided tours of various types; either call ahead or visit the website, which has full details in English. The castle is 10km (6 miles) northwest of Utrecht off Junction 6, A2/E35 Amsterdam–Utrecht.

Kasteel-Museum Sypesteyn A castle turned art gallery and museum, Sypesteyn was reconstructed in the early 1900s on the foundations of a late-medieval manor house destroyed about 1580. Today it holds some 80 paintings dating from the 16th, 17th, and 18th centuries, representing the work of artists such as Moreelse, Maes, and Mierevelt. There are collections of old weapons, glassware, silverware, pottery, porcelain, and furnishings dating from the 16th to the 18th centuries. The parklike grounds are laid out in 17th-century landscape style, and include a colorful rose garden.

Nieuw Loosdrechtsedijk 150, Nieuw Loosdrecht (a few km/miles northeast of Maarssen). 𝄞 **035/582-3208**. www.sypesteyn.nl. Admission 7.50€ ($9.40) adults, 4.50€ ($5.65) children 4–16, free for children under 4. May–Sept Tues–Thurs 10am–5pm, Sat–Sun noon–5pm; Oct–Apr Sat–Sun noon–5pm. Tours Tues–Thurs at 11am, 12:30pm, 2pm, and 3:30pm; Sat–Sun at 1, 2, 3, and 4pm. Train to Hilversum, and then Treintaxi (a shared taxi that picks up train passengers).

Slot Zuylen 🌟 One of Holland's best examples of a medieval castle was constructed in the late 13th century and inhabited until the early 1900s. Since 1952 it has been a museum. Period rooms are furnished in 17th- to 19th-century styles, along with family portraits. A special feature in the landscaped gardens is a so-called "snake wall" that creates a sun trap, protecting southern fruit trees from the harsher northern European climate.

Tournooiveld 1, Oud-Zuilen, near Maarssen, 5km (3 miles) north of Utrecht. ⓒ 030/244-0255. www.slotzuylen.com. Admission 6€ ($7.50) adults, 5€ ($6.25) seniors, 4€ ($5) children 4–16, free for children under 4. Mid-Mar to mid-Nov Sat 2–4pm, Sun 1–4pm; mid-May to mid-Sept Tues–Thurs 11am–4pm. Guided tours hourly. Bus: 36.

OUDEWATER
18km (11 miles) SW of Utrecht

Back in the 1500s, this charming little village was the scene of some of Europe's most bizarre witch trials. Accused women were weighed on scales in the **Heksenwaag (Witches' Weigh House),** Leeuweringerstraat 2, to determine whether or not they were witches who, it was believed, lacked souls and so weighed little enough to fly through the air supported on a broomstick. So many women were weighed and convicted of witchcraft that the town's reputation for having accurate scales was in jeopardy. To remedy this, the town fathers devised a system of judging accused witches by having them stand on scales clad only in a paper costume and carrying a paper broom. Present were the mayor, the alderman, the weighmaster, and the local midwife. When the weighmaster had finished juggling his weights and balancing the scales, he could then proclaim with confidence that the accused could not possibly be a witch, and a certificate was issued to that effect. Europe's accused witches flocked here in droves. Nowadays, you can step on the Heksenwaag scales and—provided you're not too skinny—walk away with your very own certificate.

As you walk through the quaint village streets, take a look at the storks' nests on the **Stadhuis (Town Hall)** roof. The big birds, traditionally associated with the arrival of a new child, have been nesting here for over 3 centuries.

ZEIST
9km (6 miles) E of Utrecht

Set in a green landscape, this village gem was once a fashionable country retreat for Utrecht's wealthy nobility. There are frequent **buses** from Utrecht. By **car,** take N225 east then south, or A28/E34 northeast, from Utrecht. The tourist information office, **VVV Zeist,** Het Rond 1, Zeist (ⓒ **0900/109-1013;** fax 030/692-0017), has details on walking and biking tours through the parks and forests surrounding Zeist.

Slot Zeist ⓡ   This castle was constructed between 1677 and 1687 for Willem Adriaan van Nassau. Its plain brick facade conceals a lavish interior designed by French architect Daniël Marot, who was responsible for decorating Het Loo palace (see below). Many of his baroque murals and ceiling paintings have survived, and ornate gilded wood paneling and stucco. The grand drive is lined by elegant houses belonging to the Hernhutters, a Protestant religious order that had its origins in Switzerland in the first half of the 18th century. The vast formal gardens were re-landscaped in the 19th century to create a pleasant park.

Zinzendorflaan 1. ⓒ 030/692-1704. www.slotzeist.nl. Admission 4€ ($5) adults, 2.50€ ($3.15) children. Mon–Fri 8am–5pm; Sat–Sun 1–5pm. Closed Jan 1, Easter Sunday, Dec 25 and 31. Bus: 50 or 54 from Utrecht Centraal station.

Where to Stay & Dine in Zeist
Golden Tulip Hotel Figi   Should you fall for the charms of Zeist, this modern, top-notch hotel ensures a pleasant stay. The guest rooms are decorated in a colorful, Mediterranean style. Four cinemas and the cozy brown Theatercafé are part of the hotel complex, accessible via the hotel and through their own street entrances.

Het Rond 3, 3701 HS Zeist. ⓒ 030/692-7543. Fax 030/692-74-68. www.figi.nl. 97 units. 182€–232€ ($228–$290) double; 282€–302€ ($353–$378) suite. AE, DC, MC, V. **Amenities:** 2 restaurants (Dutch/Continental). *In room:* TV, minibar.

Moments **A Painterly Place**

Visit the scene of a rich historical canvas, at Wijk bij Duurstede, on the bank of the Neder Rijn, 20km (12 miles) southeast of Utrecht. A windmill at the village was the star of Jacob van Ruysdael's painting *The Mill at Wijk bij Duurstede* (1670), now in Amsterdam's Rijksmuseum. An old windmill standing on the town's riverside ramparts might be the very one he painted.

2 Amersfoort

42km (26 miles) SE of Amsterdam; 20km (12 miles) NE of Utrecht

This lovely medieval town (pop. 115,000) on the Eem River has held onto its ancient character despite industrial development. Indeed, its medieval heart is guarded by a double ring of canals—the only city in Europe to have this feature. The De Stijl artist Piet Mondrian was born here in 1872.

ESSENTIALS

GETTING THERE   **Trains** arrive every hour from Amsterdam Centraal Station and from Utrecht. **Buses** arrive every half-hour on average from Utrecht. By **car,** take A1/E231 southeast from Amsterdam or A28/E34 northeast from Utrecht.

VISITOR INFORMATION   VVV **Amersfoort** is at Stationsplein 9–11, 3818 LE Amersfoort (© **0900/112-2364;** fax 033/465-0108; www.vvvamersfoort.nl). The office is open May to September, Monday to Friday from 9am to 5:30pm and Saturday from 9am to 5pm; October to April, Saturday from 10am to 2pm.

WHAT TO SEE & DO

Entering the town, you pass the oldest standing gateway, the **Kamperbinnenpoort,** constructed on the inner canal around 1260. The two other surviving gates are the **Koppelpoort,** a land and water gate from around 1400; and the **Monnikendam,** a water gate from 1430, both on the outer canal. Look for examples of 15th-century *muurhuizen* (wall houses) constructed into the ramparts and fortifications. If you visit Amersfoort on a summer Saturday, you may be lucky enough to encounter the colorful trumpeters who show up from time to time in the center city.

An impressive landmark is the tall, 15th-century **Onze-Lieve-Vrouwetoren (Our Lady's Tower),** in the west of the old town, which stands 100m (328 ft.) high, and is the third-tallest tower in the land; if you're here on a Friday, listen for its carillon concert between 10 and 11am. Other ancient religious buildings include the **Sint-Joriskerk,** started in 1243 and completed around 1534, and the beautifully restored 16th-century **Mariënhof Monastery.**

Housed in this monastery, the unusual **Culinair Museum Mariënhof,** Utrechtseweg 92 (© **033/463-1025**), at the northern end of the inner canal, offers a playful journey through the history of the culinary vices and virtues, from prehistoric times to the present day. A series of dioramas that include pieces of Meissen porcelain traces how the hunter-gatherer gradually transformed into the mass-production consumer. You can sample historical cooking in the restaurant. The museum is open Tuesday to Friday from 10am to 5pm; and Saturday, Sunday, and holidays from 2 to 5pm. Admission is 3€ ($3.75) for adults, 2€ ($2.50) for children.

For an illuminating look at Amersfoort's history, make a brief sojourn among the large collection of objects, models, and displays at the **Museum Flehite,** Westsingel 50 (© **033/461-9987;** www.museumflehite.nl). The museum is open Tuesday to Friday from 11am to 5pm; and Saturday, Sunday, and holidays from noon to 5pm (closed holidays). Admission is 5€ ($6.25) for adults, 2.50€ ($3.15) for students, and free for children under 18.

A NEARBY ATTRACTION FOR FAMILIES

Dolfinarium Harderwijk 🌟 *Kids*   Harderwijk, a lakeside town on the Veluwemeer, 26km (16 miles) northeast of Amersfoort, boasts one of Europe's largest sea wildlife centers. There's a dolphin research and rehabilitation station, as well as entertaining performances by the resident dolphins, sea lions, walruses, and seals. Additional highlights include a series of open-air pools, underwater viewing galleries, and a touch-tank filled with fish. A visit here is a thrilling and interesting day out, especially for families.

Strandboulevard Oost 1, Harderwijk. © **0341/467-467.** www.dolfinarium.nl. Admission 23€ ($29) adults, 20€ ($24) seniors and children 3–11, free for children under 3. Mid-Feb to June and Sept–Oct daily (except Mar Mon–Tues) 10am–5pm; July–Aug daily 10am–6pm. From Amersfoort you can get here by frequent trains, and by car on A28/E232; the Dolfinarium is beside the Veluwestrand leisure center and beach, and is clearly signposted all around town.

3 Apeldoorn

76km (47 miles) E of Amsterdam; 40km (25 miles) E of Amersfoort; 26km (16 miles) N of Arnhem

"Royal Apeldoorn" is a title often bestowed on this city (pop. 155,000), which has hosted the likes of Willem III in 1685, Louis Napoleon in 1809, Queen Wilhelmina from 1948 until her death in 1962, and Princess Margriet from 1962 to 1975. It's a city of many parks and gardens, and a good place in which to base yourself for a visit to Hoge Veluwe National Park (see below).

ESSENTIALS

GETTING THERE   There are **trains** every hour from Amsterdam Centraal Station and from Amersfoort and Arnhem. **Buses** leave every half-hour on average from the bus stations in Amersfoort and Arnhem. By **car,** take A1/E30 east from Amersfoort; A50 north from Arnhem.

VISITOR INFORMATION   VVV Apeldoorn is at Deventerstraat 18, 7311 LS Apeldoorn (© **055/526-0200;** fax 055/526-0209; www.vvvapeldoorn.nl). The office is open Monday to Friday from 9am to 5:30pm and Saturday from 9am to 5pm.

A ROYAL RETREAT

Rijksmuseum Paleis Het Loo 🌟🌟   The 1685 Het Loo palace and estate, outside Apeldoorn, has sheltered generations of Dutch royalty, being the favorite summer residence and hunting lodge of *Stadhouders* (Heads of State) and the royal house of Oranje-Nassau until 1975. Since 1984 it has served as the magnificent home of this museum, which celebrates the history of the House of Orange. After a complete renovation, in which it was stripped of its 19th-century trappings to reveal the original paneling and colorful damasks, this splendid palace is now an ideal setting for paintings, furniture, silver, glassware, and ceramics, and memorabilia of the royal family. Highlights include the lavish silk-and-damask–embellished private study (1690) and bedroom (1713) of *Stadhouder* William III, and the dining room (1686) decorated with tapestries illustrating themes of Ovid.

The fascinating vintage car and carriage collection in the stable block includes smooth models like a royal 1925 Bentley. But the jewel in the crown is the formal gardens. These were laid out during the renovation, using the original 17th-century plans and recreating an appropriately small-scale Dutch Versailles. They are in four sections: the King's Garden, Queen's Garden, Upper Garden, and Lower Garden—a harmonious mélange of plants, flowers, trees, pathways, statues, fountains, and pools.

Koninklijk Park 1, Oude Loo (on the northwest edge of Apeldoorn). ℂ 055/577-2400. www.paleishetloo.nl. Admission 5€ ($6.25) adults, 3€ ($3.75) children. Tues–Sun 10am–5pm. Closed Dec 25.

WHERE TO STAY

Bilderberghotel De Keizerskroon ☆ This attractive hotel on the edge of town is adjacent to Het Loo Palace. Each of the spacious rooms is furnished with a writing desk; some have balconies overlooking the landscaped grounds.

Koningstraat 7, 7315 HR Apeldoorn. ℂ 055/521-7744. Fax 055/521-4737. www.keizerskroon.nl. 94 units. 140€–190€ ($175–$238) double; 220€–290€ ($275–$363) suite. AE, DC, MC, V. **Amenities:** Restaurant (French); bar; indoor pool; health club and spa. *In room:* TV, minibar.

Hotel-Pension Berg en Bos In a quiet, peaceful setting near the Berg en Bos park and Het Loo Palace, you'll find comfortable, bright, and airy rooms here. Some overlook the garden.

Aquamarijnstraat 58, 7314 HZ Apeldoorn. ℂ 055/355-2352. Fax 055/355-4782. 17 units. 65€–85€ ($81–$106) double. Rates include continental breakfast. AE, DC, MC, V. **Amenities:** Restaurant (Dutch); bar; lounge. *In room:* TV.

WHERE TO DINE

De Echoput ☆ DUTCH/CONTINENTAL This widely acclaimed restaurant is named after the old well at which travelers once watered their horses (the "echoing well"). It's on the edge of the Royal Wood, about 10km (6 miles) west of Apeldoorn. From the outside, it has the look of a modern hunting lodge, but inside it's surprisingly modern and sophisticated. The lounge and dining room are decorated in shades of chocolate and pewter. Windows look out on pools and fountains and forest greenery. The specialty here is seasonal game (fall and winter), and summer specialties include lamb, beef, and poultry. No matter what the season, you can be sure your meal will be superb and memorable.

Amersfoortseweg 86, Hoog Soeren/Apeldoorn, just off the N344 Apeldoorn-Amersfoort Rd. ℂ 055/519-1463. www.echoput.nl. Fixed-price menus 45€–63€ ($56–$79). AE, DC, MC, V. Tues–Fri noon–2pm; Tues–Sat 6–9:30pm; Sun 1–9:30pm.

HOLLAND'S LARGEST NATIONAL PARK

A beautiful nature reserve between Apeldoorn and Arnhem, **Hoge Veluwe National Park** ☆☆ (ℂ **0900/464-3835;** www.hogeveluwe.nl) covers some 55 sq. km (21 sq. miles) of gently rolling heath, pine and birch woodland, fens, and sand dunes, populated by red and roe deer, wild boar, pine martens, badgers, polecats, and other wildlife, including non-native species like the long-haired mouflon Mediterranean wild mountain sheep, along with around 150 different bird species. You can observe the wildlife from various hides and observation posts.

The park has solved its transportation issues in a way that's both user-friendly and nature-friendly. Cars aren't permitted in the reserve proper, and a fleet of 800 free white bicycles, which you can pick up from one of several convenient spots next to the perimeter car parks, makes getting around both easy and pleasant—though some visitors have an unfortunate tendency to "borrow" other people's bikes as soon as the

Fun Fact **In the Saddle**

The average Hollander rides about 1,000km (620 miles) annually by bicycle.

original rider's back is turned. These bikes are the perfect way to explore the park, and you'll be able to see more than if you go on foot.

A leisurely ride takes you to the splendid **Jachtslot Sint-Hubertus** ⚜ (*(C)* **055/378-1237**), an extravagant hunting lodge on the park's northern edge, with a tower that soars high above it. The Art Deco lodge was designed in 1920 by architect Hendrik Petrus Berlage for the Kröller-Müller museum (see below). Inside, stained-glass windows tell the story of St. Hubert, the patron saint of hunters, and the house is full of symbolic references to his life. You can stroll through the rose garden or sit on the banks of the swan-shaped lake.

Entrances are at Otterloo, Rijzenburg (at Schaarsbergen), and Hoenderloo. The national park is open daily from 8 or 9am to between 6 and 10pm, depending on the time of year. The St. Hubert Hunting Lodge is open for guided tours April to October, daily every half-hour from 11am to 4:30pm (except 1pm); November to December and February to March, Monday to Friday at 2 and 3pm. Admission to the park alone is 6€ ($7.50) for adults, 3€ ($3.75) for children ages 6 to 12, and free for children under 6; a combination ticket including the St. Hubert Hunting Lodge and the Rijksmuseum Kröller-Möller is 12€ ($15) and 6€ ($7.50), respectively. Free white bicycles are available at several places, among them Hoenderloo, Otterlo, and Rijzenburg (near Schaarsbergen). Buses depart for the Hoge Veluwe every hour or so from outside both Apeldoorn and Arnhem rail stations.

The reserve offers camping facilities, bungalows, and other vacation accommodations, as well as picnic facilities.

Rijksmuseum Kröller-Müller ⚜⚜⚜   An unexpected treasure is embedded like a flower in the middle of Hoge Veluwe National Park. Perhaps a sunflower or iris would be the appropriate bloom, because the Kröller-Müller National Museum is home to 278 works by Vincent van Gogh, whose paintings of such fragile creations are valued by millions for their beauty, and at tens of millions as an investment. This major museum is where you find most of the van Gogh paintings that aren't in Amsterdam's Van Gogh Museum (see "Seeing the Sights," in chapter 12). Named after the art collector Helene Kröller-Müller, who gathered up some 120 works by van Gogh around the turn of the 20th century, the museum is a friendly rival to the Amsterdam museum.

However, the Kröller-Müller's pastoral setting and the light, airy structure of glass-walled pavilions add another dimension to a museum visit. It seems somehow surprising to find paintings like the *Café Terrace in Arles* (1881) by the great artist whose work inspires such passion—and prices—hanging on the wall of this isolated place. The collection includes paintings by Mondrian, Picasso, Braques, and Seurat, and Chinese porcelain and Delftware. An adjacent **sculpture garden** hosts pieces by equally renowned artists, like Rodin, Moore, Dubuffet, and Lipchitz, among others.

Houtkampweg 6, Otterloo. *(C)* **0318/591-241**. www.kmm.nl. Tues–Sun and holidays 10am–5pm. Admission included in Hoge Veluwe National Park's combination ticket (see above).

4 Arnhem ⊛

82km (51 miles) SE of Amsterdam; 55km (34 miles) E of Utrecht; 26km (16 miles) S of Apeldoorn

Gelderland's capital, founded in the 13th century and later a prosperous member of the Hanseatic League trading alliance, Arnhem became a household name during World War II, when its strategic road bridge over the Neder Rijn (Lower Rhine) became the target of a massive Allied airborne assault (see box "A Bridge Too Far," below). The center city was entirely destroyed during the fighting and reconstructed after the war.

ESSENTIALS

GETTING THERE   Direct **trains** to Arnhem Centraal station depart every hour from Amsterdam Centraal Station, going via Utrecht. By **car** from Amsterdam, take A2/E35 southeast to Utrecht and A12/E35 east to Arnhem; from Apeldoorn go south on A50.

VISITOR INFORMATION   VVV **Arnhem** is at Arnhem Tourist Info, Velper-buitensingel 25, 6828 CV Arnhem (© **0900/112-2344;** www.vvvarnhemnl), at the Musis Sacrum.

WHAT TO SEE & DO

One of the most emblematic yet most ordinary-looking sights in Arnhem is the road bridge over the Rhine in the center of town. A replica of the bridge destroyed during World War II, it is known as the **John Frost Bridge,** in honor of the commander and troops of the British 2nd Parachute Battalion. In September 1944, Lieutenant Colonel Frost's 600 valiant "Red Devils" took and for 4 days held the north end of the bridge against overwhelming German numbers and firepower, though the entire 10,000-man 1st Airborne Division had been expected to reach it and hold out for just 2 days against light opposition.

Contemporary and classic artworks, with an emphasis on modern Dutch painting and sculpture, can be found in the **Museum voor Moderne Kunst (Museum of Modern Art)** ⊛, Utrechtseweg 87 (© **026/351-2431;** www.mmkarnhem.nl). This is housed in a handsome 19th-century villa on the road to Oosterbeek (see below), and has a sculpture garden, a coffee room, and an open-air cafe overlooking the Neder Rijn. The **Historisch Museum Het Burgerweeshuis,** Bovenbeekstraat 21 (© **026/442-6900**), contains archaeological relics found in the province and an interesting topographical map of the Netherlands. Both museums are open Tuesday to Saturday from 10am to 5pm, and Sunday and holidays from 11am to 5pm (closed Jan 1,

---

⸨Moments Silent Running

Arnhemers do it on trolley buses. Since this is almost the only place in the Benelux lands where such an experience is possible (Ghent, in Belgium, has a trolley-bus line), be sure to join them. The blue, electrically powered trolley buses glide silently through the streets, justifying Arnhem's moniker of *trolley-busstad* (trolley-bus town). A ride on line 1 from Arnhem to Oosterbeek (see below) combines that environmentally friendly trolley-bus feeling with good views of Arnhem and an interesting destination.

A Bridge Too Far

On September 17, 1944, the Allies launched the greatest airborne assault in history: Operation Market Garden. In all, 35,000 paratroops and glider infantry were employed. The U.S. 101st Airborne Division landed near Eindhoven, and the 82nd Airborne Division parachuted onto the Nijmegen area. After hard and bloody fighting, the Americans captured both cities along with bridges over the Maas and Waal rivers. Meanwhile, the British 1st Airborne Division and the Polish 1st Parachute Brigade landed near Arnhem to capture the vital bridge over the Rhine.

The plan called for a ground force to break through the German front line along the Dutch-Belgian border; charge 100km (62 miles) north along a single road through Eindhoven, Nijmegen, and Arnhem; cross the bridges captured by the airborne; and get across Hitler's last big defensive barrier, the Rhine, before the Germans could react.

As one Allied commander feared, it turned out to be "a bridge too far." The British airborne troops landed close to the tanks and artillery of the German 2nd SS Panzer Corps and were plunged into a fight for survival. Bad weather prevented reinforcements and supplies being flown in on schedule. A single battalion of paratroops made it to the Rhine bridge and held it in 4 days of bitter fighting, but they were finally overwhelmed. The division's tenuous bridgehead across the Rhine at nearby Oosterbeek was lost when the relief column was held up along what was dubbed "Hell's Highway."

The British survivors withdrew across the Rhine on September 27, having suffered 13,000 casualties. American losses were around 3,500.

Apr 30, Dec 25). Admission is 5€ ($6.25) for adults, 4€ ($5) for seniors, and free for children under 18.

ORGANIZED TOURS

Boat trips from Arnhem by **Rederij Eureka** (© 0570/615-950; www.rederij-eureka. nl) depart from a quay below the John Frost Bridge and include daylong excursions on the Rhine and IJssel rivers. Some cruises cross the border into Germany, stopping at Emmerich; another visits the Dutch Hanseatic towns of Deventer, Doesburg, Zutphen, Zwolle, and Kampen (see "The Hanseatic Towns," below). Cruises start at 16€ ($20) for adults, 11€ ($13) for children ages 4 to 11, and free for children under 11.

PLACES OF INTEREST OUTSIDE ARNHEM

Northeast of town is **Veluwezoom National Park** ⋒, 46 sq. km (18 sq. miles) of pine and silver birch forest and heathland crisscrossed by riding, walking, and biking trails. The park is an extension of the larger Hoge Veluwe National Park to the west (see "Apeldoorn," above), the two being separated by about 5km (3 miles) and the A50 expressway. The **Visitor Center,** Heuvenseweg 5A, Rheden (© 026/417-9100; www. veluwezoom.nl), is open Tuesday to Sunday from 10am to 5pm. Admission is free.

TWO GREAT ESCAPES FOR KIDS

Burgers' Zoo 🌟 *Kids*   You can drive slowly through the grounds of this safari park covering .4 sq. km (⅕ sq. mile) on the northwestern edge of Arnhem and watch more than 300 animals roam freely behind protective fencing. Its chimpanzee and gorilla enclosures are internationally acclaimed. Tropical rainforest and subtropical desert habitats have been recreated in two enormous greenhouses, together with some of the fauna indigenous to these regions.

Antoon van Hoofplein 1 (near the Nederlands Openluchtmuseum). ℂ 026/442-4534. www.burgerszoo.nl. Admission 16€ ($20) adults, 15€ ($19) seniors, 14€ ($18) children 4–9, free for children under 4. Summer daily 9am–7pm; winter daily 9am–5pm.

Nederlands Openluchtmuseum 🌟 *Kids*   Don't miss this delightful open-air museum (the European Museum of the Year 2005), which brings to life Dutch history, customs, dress, and architecture from about 1800 to 1950. On its 44 hectares (109 acres), step-gabled town houses, farmhouses, windmills, antique means of transport, and colorful costumes of the past from around the country have been gathered together. It's a living museum, in the sense that frequent demonstrations of old arts and handicrafts are given.

Schelmseweg 89 (at Hoeferlaan). ℂ 026/357-6111. www.openluchtmuseum.nl. Admission 13€ ($16) adults, 12€ ($15) seniors, 9€ ($11) children 4–12, free for children under 4. Apr–Oct daily 10am–5pm. By car take A12/E35 and follow the signs to Arnhem-Noord/Openluchtmuseum; by bus take no. 3 from Arnhem Centraal station to Alteveer.

OOSTERBEEK

Adjoining Arnhem on the west, Oosterbeek (pronounced *Ohst*-uhr-bayk) traces its history back to the Roman era, and in the 19th century it was beloved by artists, who built handsome villas here. Stop by the old Catholic church to view Jan Toorop's *Fourteen Stations of the Cross.* The village was badly damaged during heavy fighting that accompanied the September 1944 Allied airborne offensive to capture the Rhine bridge at Arnhem during World War II, and was rebuilt after the war. In Oosterbeek is the Airborne Cemetery, where 1,748 of the Allied fallen rest. Local schoolchildren lay flowers on the graves for the annual day of remembrance, in a moving echo of the support Dutch civilians gave their liberators during the battle.

Airborne Museum Hartenstein 🌟   The former Hotel Hartenstein housed headquarters of the British 1st Airborne Division during the Battle of Arnhem. Most of that proud command was killed, wounded, or captured while trying to fight its way through strong German opposition to Arnhem and, after the failure of that assault, to maintain a bridgehead on the north bank of the Rhine at Oosterbeek until relief came from the south—relief that arrived too little and too late. The museum, surrounded by beautiful grounds and a park, is packed with exhibits that detail the savage fighting, when for a week the hotel and its surroundings were under constant attack.

You can walk the paratroop survivors' withdrawal route south through the park and suburban streets, to the Rhine at Westerbouwing. A passenger-and-bicycle ferry shuttles back and forth across this scenic stretch of the river, to dock near Driel on the south bank. In this village is a monument to Polish paratroops who landed here in the face of heavy German fire during Operation Market Garden.

Utrechtseweg 232 (on the western edge of the village). ℂ 026/333-7710. www.airbornemuseum.com. Admission 4.80€ ($5.65) adults; 3.80€ ($3.75) veterans, seniors, children 5–15; free for children under 5. Apr–Oct Mon–Sat 10am–5pm, Sun and holidays noon–5pm; Nov–Mar Mon–Sat 11am–5pm, Sun and holidays noon–5pm. Closed Jan 1, Dec 25.

5 Nijmegen

58km (36 miles) SE of Utrecht; 15km (9 miles) S of Arnhem

Nijmegen (pop. 160,000) has a long recorded history, and boasts dibs on being, officially, the oldest city in the Netherlands. In A.D. 104, the Roman Emperor Trajan granted city rights to the trading town of Ulpia Noviomagus Batavorum, which had grown up around a legionary fortress that protected this sector of the empire's Rhine frontier. The city lies in the orchard country of Gelderland's Betuwe (Fertile Wetlands) district, a peninsula squeezed between the Neder Rijn and Waal rivers, which in ancient times had been the heartland of the Batavians. An important Catholic center in the mainly Protestant north of Holland, the city is home to the prestigious Catholic University of Nijmegen.

GETTING THERE **Trains** depart every hour from Amsterdam Centraal Station and Arnhem to Nijmegen. **Buses** depart every half-hour on average from outside Arnhem rail station. By **car,** take A52 south from Arnhem.

VISITOR INFORMATION **Nijmeegs Uitburo/VVV** is at Keizer Karelplein 32H, 6511 NC Nijmegen (✆ **0900/112-2344;** www.vvvnijmegen.nl). The office is open Monday to Friday from 9:30am to 6pm, and Saturday from 10am to 5pm.

WHAT TO SEE & DO

Nijmegen's road bridge over the Waal was a key objective of Operation Market Garden during World War II. A combination of the destruction wrought by that battle, and an earlier raid by U.S. bombers that mistakenly struck the city instead of their intended target in Germany, devastated the old center. Postwar reconstruction was mostly along different lines. Around the handsome **Grote Markt,** look for the 1612 **Waag (Weigh House)** and the **Kerkboog** vaulted passageway from 1545 with a gable from 1605.

The city's strategic position is clearly visible from the **Valkhof (Falcon Court),** a park affording magnificent views. It's high on the south bank of the Waal—this is actually the main continuation of the Rhine, which splits in two after entering Holland—on the site of a 9th-century Frankish castle. Here, too, are the ruins of the 12th-century **Sint-Maartenskapel (St. Martin's Chapel),** and the octagonal **Sint-Niklaaskapel (St. Nicholas's Chapel)** from 1030, called the Carolingian Chapel because of the erroneous belief that Charlemagne ordered its construction. Equally good views are available from the nearby 15th-century **Belvedere,** a watchtower that now houses a restaurant.

Museum Het Valkhof The daring glass structure was designed by Ben van Berkel and opened in 1999 to accommodate Nijmegen's historical and art museum; it also integrates two older, smaller museums. The structure is worth viewing in its own right. Nijmegen's Roman period is a major emphasis of the museum, when the city was home base to the Tenth Legion and an important trade gateway between the Romanized Batavians and the "barbarians" to the north. The later Frankish era, when Nijmegen was a favorite residence of Charlemagne, is covered. In addition, there's an interesting array of fine-art objects and sculptures, and modern art.

Kelfkensbos 59. ✆ **024/360-8805.** www.museumhetvalkhof.nl. Admission 6€ ($7.50) adults, 4€ ($5) seniors, 3€ ($3.75) students and children 4–16, free for children under 4. Tues–Fri 10am–5pm; Sat–Sun and holidays noon–5pm. Closed Dec 25. Bus: 2, 3, 57, 58, 80, or 82.

Miniature Masters

Nijmegen was the birthplace of the brothers Herman, Paul, and Johan van Lim-burg, masters of the medieval art of manuscript illumination. From 1400 until their deaths in 1416 (all three seem to have been victims of the plague), while resident at the French court in Paris, they created incredibly detailed minia-tures, among them *Les Très Belles Heures du Duc de Berry* (ca. 1411–16), which is widely considered to be *the* masterpiece of the genre.

THE GROESBEEK HEIGHTS

The loftiest peak in this range of hills just off Nijmegen's southeastern flank, along the German border, soars to all of 99m (325 ft.). But for the Netherlands that's more than respectable. In any case, the wooded hills and open country make good strolling and cycling terrain, and host a cluster of surprising attractions.

Bijbels Openluchtmuseum (Biblical Open-Air Museum) ⍟⍟   Step back in time, into the world of the New Testament. Life-size period replicas of homes and street scenes from the biblical lands inhabit the 49-hectare (121-acre) museum, run by the Dutch Heilig Landstichting (Holy Land Foundation). The commitment to histor-ical verisimilitude in the dioramas—Jewish, Roman, Greek, and Egyptian homes; a synagogue; a Sea of Galilee fishing village; a stretch of Roman road—is impressive. During the Christmas period, there's a crib exhibit. In the visitor center are archaeo-logical finds and exhibits on Christian, Jewish, and Islamic scriptures. Due to the size of the place, you'll need a few hours to get much out of your visit, and a full morning or afternoon to do it any kind of justice.

Profetenlaan 2 (southeast of town on the Groesbeek road). © 024/382-3110. www.bijbelsopenluchtmuseum.nl. Admission 9.50€ ($12) adults, 8.50€ ($11) seniors, 5€ ($6.25) children 5–13, free for children under 5. Late Mar to early Nov and mid-Dec to 1st week Jan daily 10am–5pm (Jan 1 noon–5pm). Bus: 5 or 20 from Nijmegen Centraal station.

Nationaal Bevrijdingsmuseum (National Liberation Museum) 1944–1945 ⍟   During Operation Market Garden, the U.S. 82nd Airborne Division jumped onto drop zones around Groesbeek, to capture the bridges over the Maas River at Grave and the Waal at Nijmegen, and open the way for British armor to roll north toward Arnhem. A diorama depicts the scene when the paratroops converted themselves into "airborne Marines" and crossed the Waal in flimsy assault boats through a hail of fire to take the Nijmegen road bridge. It begins, however, with the rise of National Social-ism in Germany. Photographs, films, a slide show, and a model of the area evoke Hol-land's period of occupation during World War II, leading up to the story that began on September 17, when the skies above Groesbeek suddenly blossomed with thou-sands of parachutes. Guided tours of the battle zone are available from the museum.

Close to the museum, on Zevenheuvelenweg, is the **Groesbeek Canadian War Cemetery,** containing the graves of more than 2,300 soldiers who fell during the final offensive into Nazi Germany in 1945. Between the two, on Wylerbaan, lies the **Canada-Netherlands Memorial Park,** a grove of Canadian maple trees, dedicated on National Liberation Day (May 5), 1998.

Wylerbaan 4, Groesbeek, 9.5km (6 miles) from Nijmegen. © 024/397-4404. www.bevrijdingsmuseum.nl. Admis-sion 8€ ($10) adults, 7€ ($8.75) seniors, 4€ ($5) children 7–15, free for children under 7 and foreign veterans of World War II. Mon–Sat 10am–5pm; Sun and holidays noon–5pm. Closed Jan 1, Dec 25. Bus: 5 from Nijmegen.

6 The Hanseatic Towns ⟨★⟩

The Hanze Route (Hanseatic Route) runs along the IJssel River, which was the quick way from the Rhine to the Zuiderzee long before the sea was dammed in and became the freshwater IJsselmeer. Seven towns—Doesburg, Zutphen, Deventer, Hattem, Zwolle, Hasselt, and Kampen—along the 125km (78-mile) route through Gelderland and Overijssel played important roles in the international trade of yesteryear and profited handsomely from their membership in the medieval Hanseatic League, a Baltic-based association of more than 150 trading towns and cities in north and northwest Europe. You can tell this today by viewing the many old churches, public buildings, merchants' houses, and gateways that are still standing.

ZUTPHEN

26km (16 miles) NE of Arnhem; 18km (11 miles) SE of Apeldoorn

A handsome walled medieval town, Zutphen (pop. 32,000) stands on the east bank of the IJssel. From Arnhem, **trains** arrive every hour and **buses** every half-hour or so; by **car,** take N48. For tourist information, visit **VVV Zutphen,** Stationsplein 39, 7201 MH Zutphen (© **0900/269-2888;** fax 0575/517-928; www.achterhoektoerisme.nl).

Zutphen's magnificent Gothic **Sint-Walburgiskerk (St. Walburga's Church),** 's-Gravenhof (© **0575/514-178**), in the center of town, houses important works of art and the **Librije (Library)** from 1564. The medieval books and manuscripts here are still in use, chained to reading desks.

Zutphen is a gateway into Gelderland's **Achterhoek (Back Corner)** district, which stretches east from the IJssel to the German border. You can make a rewarding foray by bicycle or car into this tranquil landscape of farms, forests, and châteaux.

DEVENTER

14km (9 miles) N of Zutphen; 14km (9 miles) E of Apeldoorn

Just across the province line in Overijssel, Deventer (pop. 70,000) began in the 11th century and later became a fountain of religious and intellectual scholarship, with Thomas à Kempis, Erasmus, and Descartes among those who passed through its monastery school of the Brothers of the Common Life. You still see fine medieval and Renaissance buildings along its streets. The town is known for its spicy gingerbread, *Deventer koek.*

ESSENTIALS

GETTING THERE   **Trains** depart every hour from Arnhem via Zutphen. **Buses** leave every half-hour from Zutphen. By **car,** take N348 north from Zutphen.

VISITOR INFORMATION   **VVV Deventer** is at Keizerstraat 22, Deventer (© **0900/353-5355;** fax 0570/643-338; www.vvvdeventer.nl). The office is open Monday to Friday from 9am to 5:30pm, and Saturday from 9am to 4pm.

SEEING THE SIGHTS

The old center and the IJssel waterfront are dominated by the magnificent Gothic **Sint-Lebuïnuskerk (St. Lebuin's Church)** ★, Groote Poot (© **0570/612-548**), named after an 8th-century Saxon missionary. Its 17th-century Hemony carillon is among the finest in Holland. The church is open Monday to Saturday from 11am to 5pm; admission is free. In the neighboring 17th-century **Stadhuis (Town Hall),** Grote Kerkhof 4 (© **0570/649-959**), is a large library of medieval books and manuscripts that's well worth a look. It's open Monday to Friday from 10am to 4pm; admission is free.

Moments Ferry Tales

Following the course of the IJssel, you might want to cross back and forth from one bank to the other. A good place to do this is the scenic stretch north of Deventer, and a nice way to do it is by vehicle ferry rather than at a bridge in one of the towns. There are ferries at the villages of Olst and Wijhe. The trip takes just a few minutes.

Objects relating to the area and a marvelous collection of local costumes are exhibited in the **Historisch Museum Deventer,** Brink 56 (© **0570/693-780;** www.deventer musea.nl), in the extravagant 1528 **Waag (Weigh House)** on Deventer's main square. The museum is open Tuesday to Saturday from 10am to 5pm, and Sunday and holidays from 2 to 5pm (closed Jan 1, Easter weekend, Pentecost, Dec 25). Admission is 3€ ($3.75) for adults, 1€ ($1.25) for children ages 2 to 18, and free for children under 2.

Organized Tours

Rederij Eureka (© **0570/615-950;** www.rederij-eureka.nl) operates boat trips on the IJssel from Deventer, going north to Kampen and south to Arnhem.

Nearby Places of Interest

Just north of the pretty little village of **Holten,** 19km (12 miles) east of Deventer, are the ancient heathland and forests of the **Sallandse Heuvelrug (Salland Hills)** ✛. These rear up all of 76m (250 ft.) at the Holterberg, and mark the spot where the northern glaciers ground to a halt during the last Ice Age. Part of the area is a protected nature reserve, but you can hike and bike in the rest of it.

ZWOLLE ✛
28km (17 miles) N of Deventer; 34km (21 miles) N of Apeldoorn

The capital of Overijssel, Zwolle (pop. 100,000) was founded in the 9th century and flourished during the 14th and 15th. In that boom time, churches and civic buildings were enlarged or embellished, and Zwolle became an important religious and cultural center, and a hub of trade. Thomas à Kempis (1379–1471), who wrote the influential *Imitation of Christ,* was a monk at the Agnietenberg Augustinian monastery north of Zwolle and is buried in the town's Sint-Michaëlskerk. The fortified bastions and the distinctive star-shaped moat that makes an island of the old center date from the 17th century.

ESSENTIALS

GETTING THERE   There are **trains** every hour from Deventer and from Apeldoorn. **Buses** depart about every 30 minutes from Deventer and every hour from Apeldoorn. By **car,** take N337 north from Deventer; A50 north from Apeldoorn.

VISITOR INFORMATION   VVV Zwolle, Grote Kerkplein 14, 8011 PK Zwolle (© **0900/112-2375;** fax 038/421-4553; www.vvvzwolle.nl), is in the center of town. The office is open Monday from 1 to 5pm, Tuesday to Friday from 10am to 5pm, and Saturday from 10am to 4pm.

WHAT TO SEE & DO

Sint-Michaëlskerk (St. Michael's Church) ✛   Not to be confused with the small St. Michael's Church just outside the town center, where Thomas à Kempis is buried, this one dates from 1370 to 1446. Its dedication to the Archangel Michael, the winged guardian of Israel, is signified by a sculpture portraying him slaying the dragon, as told in *Revelations,* and by a relief on an earlier, Romanesque tympanum from around 1200 of Abraham with Michael and two other archangels. The interior is interesting for its octagonal vestry and the massive 4,000-pipe Schnitger organ from 1722, which is often used for concerts and recordings.

Grote Kerkplein. (C) **038/422-2299**. www.grotekerkzwolle.nl. Admission 5€ ($6.25) adults. May–Oct Tues–Fri 11am–4:30pm, Sat 1:30–4:30pm.

More Places of Interest

Most of the original city wall has been demolished. But you can follow the walkways along what's left and discover Zwolle's hidden charms. Particularly impressive is the red-brick **Sassenpoort (Saxon Gate),** Sassenstraat 53 ((C) **038/421-6626**), a fortified gateway from 1406 adorned with four octagonal towers. It holds an exhibit on the town's history. It's open Friday from 2 to 5pm, and weekends and holidays from noon to 5pm; admission is 1€ ($1.25) for adults.

Affectionately dubbed the *Peperbustoren* (Pepperpot Tower), the recently restored 1487 tower of the massive **Onze-Lieve-Vrouwbasiliek (Basilica of Our Lady),** Ossenmarkt ((C) **038/421-4894**; www.olvbasiliek-zwolle.org), west of the Grote Markt, is Zwolle's primary landmark. You can climb it and treat yourself to wide views over the town and the IJssel valley. Inside the 15th-century church are interesting medieval relics and statues. The church is open May to October, Monday from 1:30 to 4:30pm, and Tuesday to Saturday from 11:30 to 4:30; and November to April, Monday to Saturday from 1:30 to 3:30pm. Admission is 1€ ($1.25) for adults, and 0.50€ (65¢) for children under 12.

Especially for Kids

Ecodrome Zwolle ⚤ *(Kids)*   The different displays at this educational theme park allow you to get close to the earth's nature and environment. You start out in the Geology Pavilion, where you learn about the earth's past, and then head into the Biology Pavilion, to see how plant and animal life started—and how people began to interact and exercise influence over nature. Along the way you pass through the Piranha Tunnel, for a fish's-eye view of these needle-toothed little monsters, and visit the Rio Negro tropical rainforest and river. You come face-to-face with dinosaurs in the Dinorama, and can even dig up fossilized bones.

Willemsvaart 19 (10 min. on foot from the main rail station). (C) **038/423-7030**. www.ecodrome.nl. Admission 9.95€ ($12) adults, 8.50€ ($11) children 3–11, free for children under 3. Apr–Oct daily 10am–5pm; Nov–Mar Wed, Sat–Sun, and school vacations 10am–5pm. Closed Jan 1, Dec 25 and 31. By car, from A21 take the Zwolle-Zuid exit.

KAMPEN ⭐⭐
13km (8 miles) NW of Zwolle

With its handsome, bustling IJssel River waterfront and more than 500 historical monuments, including medieval merchants' houses, towers, and town gates, Kampen (pop. 33,000) still displays the signature of its boom period from 1330 to 1450, when it was an important member of the Hanseatic League. The Dutch Golden Age artist Hendrik Avercamp (1585–1663) lived, worked, and died in the town. Kampen is a good base from which to make bicycle and walking tours of the scenic riverside landscapes and nature reserves around the nearby mouth of the IJssel.

ESSENTIALS

GETTING THERE   From Zwolle, **trains** depart every hour and **buses** about every half-hour; by **car,** take N50 northwest.

VISITOR INFORMATION   **VVV Kampen,** Oudestraat 151, 8261 CL Kampen (© **0900/112-2375;** fax 038/332-8900; www.vvvkampen.nl), is in the town center. The office is open Monday to Friday from 9am to 5:30pm (to 5pm Nov–Apr), and Saturday from 10am to 4pm.

SEEING THE SIGHTS

The **Oude Raadhuis (Old Town Hall),** Oudestraat 133 (© **038/339-2999**), was reconstructed in 1543 after a fire that grievously damaged the original, from 1345 to 1350. Pass by for a look at the onion-shaped tower, and the oak-paneled 14th-century **Schepenzaal (Aldermen's Chamber)** with its carved-stone chimneypiece from 1545 and bust of Habsburg Emperor Charles V at its center. The Town Hall is open Monday to Friday from 10am to 4pm.

Across the way, the imposing Gothic **Sint-Nicolaaskerk (Church of St. Nicholas),** also known as the **Bovenkerk,** Koornmarkt 28 (© **038/331-6453**), achieved its final form around 1500. It has a massive organ with 3,200 pipes, and a tower that's 70m (230 ft.) high.

To get an idea of Kampen's illustrious history, visit the **Stedelijk (Municipal) Museum,** Oudestraat 158 (© **038/333-2294**), in the **Gotische Huis (Gothic House),** a late-15th-century merchant's store where herbs and spices were sold. In back is a working mill. The museum is open Tuesday to Saturday from 11am to 5pm; and Sunday in summer from 1 to 5pm. Admission is 3€ ($3.75) for adults, 2€ ($2.50) for seniors, and free for children under 13.

A few doors along, the **Nieuwe Toren (New Tower),** Oudestraat 146, dating from 1664, designed by Amsterdam architect Philips Vingboons, has a 47-bell Hemony carillon in its octagonal belfry. For a fine view over the town, climb the 152 interior steps. The tower is open May to August, Wednesday and Saturday from 2 to 5pm. Admission is 1€ ($1.25).

There's no better way to get close to the spirit of the Hanseatic League traders than by stepping aboard the *Kamper Kogge* ⚓, Havenweg 7 (© **038/331-0515;** www.kamper-kogge.nl), on the IJssel waterfront. Constructed of oak using original construction methods, this is a replica of the broad-beamed, deep-draft, single-masted merchant vessels, called cogs, that in the 13th and 14th centuries plied the Hanseatic League's Baltic and North Sea trade routes, connecting Lübeck, Bergen, London, Bruges, and other ports. Each could carry up to 200 tons of bulk cargo—salt, furs, wax, dried and salted fish, grain, cod-liver oil, beer, textiles. Without the sturdy Hanse cogs, the flourishing trade of medieval northern Europe would have been impossible. The ship's aftercastle was a kind of redoubt to defend against pirates and other enemies. The *Kamper Kogge* is open to visitors Monday to Friday from 10am to 5pm, unless it's being used for a special event.

Out of seven original fortified gates in the demolished town walls, three survive. The riverside **Koornmarktspoort,** IJsselkade 1, from the first half of the 14th century, is the oldest gate and for a long time was used as a prison and garrison quarters. West of the center, the **Broederpoort,** Tweede Ebbingestraat 50, dates from 1465 and was partly reconstructed in 1615 to 1617 in Renaissance style after losing its military role when the town defenses were pushed farther out. Like this gate, its near neighbor **Cellebroederpoort,** Tweede Ebbingestraat 1, with twin towers, was constructed in the second half of

Boat People

The Royal Huisman Shipyard at Vollenhove, 14km (9 miles) north of Kampen, builds luxury sailboats for the world's wealthy and world-class racing yachts that have won an occasional Admiral's Cup trophy and Round-the-World Race. Silicon Graphics and Netscape Communications founder Jim Clark is something of a regular customer. Huisman constructed his 89m (292-ft.) three-masted schooner *Athena,* and his 52m (170-ft.) sloop *Hyperion.*

the 14th century and, between 1615 and 1617, was partly reconstructed for the same reasons. On its town side are two sculptured lions bearing shields.

GIETHOORN 🎯
26km (16 miles) N of Zwolle

This picture-postcard village has no streets, only canals (and walking and biking paths). You can get here by hourly **bus** from Zwolle. By **car,** take N331 north along the Zwarte Water River to Zwartsluis, and N334 northeast across the beautiful Overijssel lakes. Then leave your car at a car park on the edge of Giethoorn and follow a signposted path to the main canal. Visitor information is available from **VVV Giethoorn,** Beulakerweg 114A, 8355 AM Giethoorn (📞 **0900/567-4637;** fax 0521/362-281; www.vvv giethoorn.nl), housed aboard a boat at the southern end of this canal.

A rented punt is a romantic way to glide under the village's humpback bridges, past farms, meadows, and enchanting old canal-side cottages with reed-thatched roofs and carefully tended gardens. Should punting seem too much like work, you can rent a launch with an electric motor and still enjoy the experience in tranquillity.

For an insight into the rural area's way of life, visit the **Museumboerderij (Farmhouse Museum) 't Olde Maat Uus,** Binnenpad 52 (📞 **0521/362-224;** www.olde maatuus.nl), in an 1826 house decked out with local craft and farming displays. The museum is open May to October, Monday to Saturday from 11am to 5pm, and Sunday from noon to 5pm; and November to April, Sunday from noon to 5pm, and during school vacations daily from noon to 5pm. North of Giethoorn stretches **De Weerribben National Park,** an extensive landscape of reed marshes and moorland crisscrossed by narrow water channels.

Just 8km (5 miles) to the west, the now inland village of **Blokzijl,** which lost its port to the IJsselmeer project, is a fair monument to past trading, fishing, and whaling wealth, from its days as a member of the Hanseatic League, to the 17th and 18th centuries, when ships of the United East India Company sheltered in its harbor while storms raged on the Zuiderzee. A maritime museum, **In De Coop'ren Duikhelm (In the Copper Diving Helmet),** Binnenpad 62 (📞 0521/362-211), takes as its theme the changing seascape of the Zuiderzee–IJsselmeer and, as its name suggests, has a section on diving. The museum is open March to October daily from 10am to 6pm; and November to February daily from 11am to 5pm.

WHERE TO STAY & DINE
Kaatje bij de Sluis 🎯🎯 CONTINENTAL   Weary travelers on the polders can settle in at this charming 17th-century mansion hotel in the heart of picturesque Blokzijl. Its name means "Kate's by the Sluice," which is appropriate enough, since it's located right beside a canal sluice and drawbridge. You see these, along with passing boats and

Moments **Step Back into Staphorst**

Staphorst, 16km (10 miles) north of Zwolle on the Meppel road, is the Dutch village of your imagination, with colorfully dressed residents living as their ancestors did. This is no tourist act—you seldom get an enthusiastic welcome from these devout and strict Calvinists, especially on Sunday, when the entire population observes a tradition that dates back centuries: With downcast eyes, separate lines of men and women form a silent procession to the churches. No automobiles are allowed into the village on the Sabbath—even bicycle riding is forbidden. Cameras are always frowned upon. Whenever you come to Staphorst—on Sunday or a weekday—be sure to respect the townspeople's conservative ways and keep cameras out of sight.

bicycles, when you look out of one of the big picture windows of the tastefully furnished, comfortable rooms. The finest views are from room nos. 12 and 14. Breakfast is served in a bright winter garden, and on a water-side terrace in the summer. Across the canal, the restaurant deserves its fine reputation. The menu is not extensive and changes seasonally according to what's special and available. You can expect a couple of fish dishes and three or four meat dishes, two of which are likely to be duck and beef tournedos.

Zuiderstraat 1, 8356 DZ Blokzijl. © 0527/291-833. Fax 0527/291836. www.kaatje.nl. 8 units. 150€ ($188) double. AE, DC, MC, V. Free parking. **Amenities:** Restaurant (Continental). *In room:* Minibar, coffeemaker, safe.

7 Lelystad & the Noordoostpolder

41km (25 miles) NE of Amsterdam; 30km (19 miles) W of Kampen

This ultramodern city (pop. 100,000) and capital of Holland's newest province, Flevoland, has little—nothing, really—in the way of traditional Dutch character to offer. Yet a number of standout attractions here justify an expedition across the flat, bare polders; indeed, a drive across those polders themselves, newly wrested from the IJsselmeer, has its own peculiar fascination. Should you visit Lelystad on a Saturday, be sure to go by the town square to see vendors clad in traditional dress hawking everything from smoked eels to crafts to cheese, in a delightful example of a people holding onto tradition in the middle of modern-day progress.

To complete the "Golden Circle" of the IJsselmeer, see "The Western IJsselmeer Shore," in chapter 13; and "The Eastern IJsselmeer Shore," in chapter 15.

ESSENTIALS
GETTING THERE **Trains** arrive in Lelystad every hour from Amsterdam Centraal Station. **Buses** arrive every half-hour on average from Amsterdam. By **car** from Amsterdam, take A6 northeast; from Kampen take N307 and N309 west.

VISITOR INFORMATION **VVV Lelystad** is at Het Ravelijn 1–11, 8233 BR Lelystad (© **0320/286-750;** fax 0320/258-080; www.vvvflevoland.nl). The office is open Monday to Friday from 9am to 5pm, and Saturday from 9am to 1pm.

WHAT TO SEE & DO
Nationaal Scheepshistorisch Centrum (Maritime History Center) ★★ *Kids*
Step aboard the moored, faithful reconstruction of the *Batavia,* a three-masted sailing

ship of the Vereenigde Oostindische Compagnie (United East India Company), and imagine yourself en route to the fabled Spice Islands. Launched in 1628 at the V.O.C.'s Amsterdam yard, the original *Batavia* sailed in 1629 on her maiden voyage to the East Indies, but struck a reef off Australia and broke up. The survivors' subsequent experience of mutiny, murder, rescue, and retribution electrified Dutch society.

This replica, 50m (160 ft.) long, cluttered with spars, sails, and rigging, was constructed at the Bataviawerf (Batavia Wharf) between 1985 and 1995 mostly by unemployed teens using 16th- and 17th-century tools and construction techniques. You can clamber over her and stand above the bowsprit, entertaining visions of the cruel sea and the romantic age of sail. You can visit the onshore workshops where the ship pieces were assembled.

Taking shape at the wharf, amid a clattering of hammers on wood, is a man-of-war, a replica of the 80-gun ship-of-the-line *De Zeven Provinciën (The Seven Provinces),* launched in Rotterdam in 1665 and later the flagship of Adm. Michiel de Ruyter. During a 30-year career, the original ship saw action in many a hard-fought sea battle in the wars against England and France. Construction of the replica began in 1995. (If you're fascinated by these replica sailing ships, be sure to visit the *Amsterdam,* at the Maritime Museum in Amsterdam; see "More Museums & Galleries," in chapter 12.)

The Batavia Wharf hosts in addition the **Netherlands Institute for Marine and Underwater Archaeology** (℃ **0320/269-700**). This unique museum exhibits ships and relics from ships that went to a watery grave in the Zuiderzee as far back as Roman times. Their remains were revealed as water was pumped out to make way for polders. The process of reconstructing old, sunken ships, after finding and recovering them, is made both visible and accessible to visitors.

Oostvaardersdijk 1–9 (just off the Markerwaard dike rd.). ℃ 0320/261-409. www.bataviawerf.nl. 9€ ($11) adults, 7€ ($8.75) seniors, 4.50€ ($5.65) children 6–12, free for children under 6. Daily 10am–5pm. Closed Jan 1, Dec 25.

Nieuwland Poldermuseum *(Kids*   The Dutch themselves have created a fair part of the solid ground their country stands on by taking new land from the sea, as polders. This fascinating museum affords an understanding of how they did it, in particular around the old Zuiderzee. You learn about the construction of dikes, the pumping process, the final drying-up operation, and making the new-won land habitable. Appropriately, the museum is housed in a building that represents a cross section of a polder dike. Children can get down and dirty with the "Play with Water" interactive exhibit, where they get to construct their own dikes.

Oostvaardersdijk 1–13 (just off the Markerwaard dike road). ℃ 0320/260-799. 4.30€ ($5.40) adults, 4€ ($5) seniors, 2.50€ ($3.15) children 5–16, free for children under 5. Mon–Fri 10am–5pm; Sat–Sun and holidays 11:30am–5pm. Closed Jan 1, Dec 25.

Moments Art of Earth & Sun

In 1977, American sculptor Robert Morris created a kind of modern Stonehenge, with his *Observatorium,* a little way northeast of Lelystad on N307. From inside twin concentric rings of embanked earth, 3m (10 ft.) high, you can look through openings that spot the sunrise on the first day of summer, the first day of winter, the vernal equinox (Mar 21), and the autumnal equinox (Sept 23).

NEARBY ATTRACTIONS

All kind of thrills and enjoyment for the whole family are on offer at **Walibi World,** Spijkweg 30 (© **0321/329-999;** www.walibiworld.nl), near Biddinghuizen, 22km (14 miles) east of Lelystad. Top billing goes to The Goliath, the highest, longest, fastest, and steepest roller coaster in the Benelux lands. There's plenty of other rides, a minitrain for young children, theme areas like Bugs Bunny World and Sherwood Forest, a Wild West show, and restaurants and snack bars. The park is open April to October, daily from 10am to 6pm (to 5pm weekdays Apr–May and Sept–Oct). Admission is 26€ ($33) for adults; 24€ ($29) for seniors, visitors with disabilities, and children ages 3 to 11; and free for children under 3. To get here from Lelystad, take N309 and N306.

Just outside Lelystad is Holland's largest wetlands nature reserve, the **Oostvaarder-splassen,** covering 60 sq. km (23 sq. miles). While this might not be wildly exciting to everybody, it should be for birders, since every year this area is visited by 100,000 nesting and migrating birds. The marshes lie west of town, on either side of the A6 Amsterdam expressway. There's a visitor center at Knardijk with information and several observation hides.

URK ⚐

19km (12 miles) N of Lelystad

This quaint fishing village was a Zuiderzee island for more than 700 years, its isolation undisturbed until the IJsselmeer reclamation project joined it to the mainland in 1942. Urk now lies on the west coast of the Noordoostpolder (Northeast Polder), a flat, reclaimed farm-landscape in the north of Flevoland province covering 480 sq. km (185 sq. miles).

ESSENTIALS

GETTING THERE **Buses** leave every hour on average from the bus station outside Lelystad rail station. By **car,** take A6 north from Lelystad, and then go west on N352. While you will certainly encounter cars on the narrow brick-paved streets, it's a good idea to park outside the village and take to your feet. In summer months, you can make a 90-minute trip by passenger-and-bicycle ferry, operated by **Rederij Duurstede** (© **0343/577-111;** www.urk-enkhuizen.nl), from Enkhuizen (see "The Western IJsselmeer Shore," in chapter 13), from where there are train connections with Amsterdam.

VISITOR INFORMATION VVV Urk is at Wijk 2/2, Urk (© **0527/684-040;** fax 0527/686-180). The office is open April to October, Monday to Friday from 10am to 5pm and Saturday from 10am to 1pm; November to March, it's open Monday to Friday from 10am to 2pm.

SEEING THE SIGHTS

As you walk past picturesque brick homes lining tiny streets, notice the decorated wooden doors and elaborate wrought ironwork. At the long piers in the busy harbor are moored sturdy fishing boats that sail in search of eels. Smoked eel is sold everywhere in Urk, and there's a busy fish market.

The small **Museum Het Oude Raadhuis,** Wijk 2/2 (© **0527/683-262;** www.museum.opurk.nl), in the old Town Hall, has exhibits about Urk's ancient and recent history, fishing traditions, and displays of local costumes and architecture. It's open

> **Tips Eel Selection**
>
> When buying smoked eels, demonstrate your expertise by selecting only the skinny ones (the fat ones aren't as tasty).

April to September, Monday to Friday from 10am to 5pm, and Saturday (Apr–May and Sept) from 10am to 1pm and (June–Aug) 10am to 5pm. Admission is 3€ ($3.75) for adults, 2.50€ ($3.15) for seniors, 1.50€ ($1.90) for children ages 6 to 12, and free for children under 6.

SCHOKLAND ✿
12km (7½ miles) E of Urk

Like Urk, this used to be an island, but it was uninhabited by the time the polders were created. Because of the threat of inundation, the island community was evacuated in 1859. Nowadays Schokland seems like a phantom island, outlined by trees emerging from the flat polder, with a lonely church, a cannon that was fired to warn of rising waters, and a few old anchors as witnesses to its past. It's special enough, though, to have been declared a UNESCO World Heritage Site.

If you make it here, don't miss the **Museum Schokland** (© **0527/251-396;** www.schokland.nl), in a 1834 church that stands on slightly raised ground. It holds Bronze Age tools, mammoth bones, and other prehistoric relics; and stone coffins from the 1100s and pottery dating as far back as 900. All were discovered on the sea bottom when the polder was drained. The museum is open April to October, Tuesday to Sunday (also Mon July–Aug) from 11am to 5pm; and November to March, Friday to Sunday from 11am to 5pm (closed Jan 1 and Dec 25). Admission is 3.50€ ($4.40) for adults, 2.75€ ($3.45) for seniors and children ages 6 to 12, and free for children under 6.

17

Zeeland, Noord-Brabant & Limburg

History, recreation, and attractive scenery are abundant here. The locals share a relaxed view of the world and place emphasis on life's pleasures, like eating well.

Zeeland's three-part harmony of sea, land, and sky is so smooth that it's sometimes hard to say where one begins and another ends. The province's islands have been stitched together by a succession of great dams and barriers that bring a measure of security to the inhabitants of this low-lying delta, where the Rhine, Waal, Maas, and Schelde rivers drain into the North Sea. Elegant harbor towns like Zierikzee and Veere, as well as tiny villages, retain the character of past centuries, when Zeeland's seafarers plied the world's oceans.

Scenic **Noord-Brabant (North Brabant)** has waterways and polders in the

north and west; sand drifts, moors, and fir and deciduous forests in the south and east; and tranquil villages and ancient towns.

Coming into **Limburg** from the north, you notice a gradual transformation taking place in the landscape. Gone are the flat fields interlaced with canals. Contours appear. The change becomes more pronounced the farther south you go, and culminates in steep hills. Truth be told, the hills aren't that high, yet in a country where you can get a view just by standing on a match, Limburg has hidden depths. Shaped like a leg stepping into the space between Germany and Belgium, the province combines a German capacity for organization with a Belgian embrace of the good life.

1 Zierikzee ★

48km (30 miles) SW of Rotterdam

This harbor town on the Oosterschelde (Eastern Schelde) shore of the former one-time islands, now joined together, of Schouwen and Duiveland, is reputedly the best-preserved town in the Netherlands. Just big enough (pop. 11,000) to escape the "sleepy" category, it's still guarded by the town walls constructed during the Middle Ages and has elegant whitewashed 16th- to 18th-century houses.

ESSENTIALS

GETTING THERE **Buses** arrive every hour from outside the rail station in nearby Goes. By **car** from Rotterdam, take A29 and N59 south and west. An alternative route, skirting the coast, is N57 south to the junction with N59, and then east on this road into town.

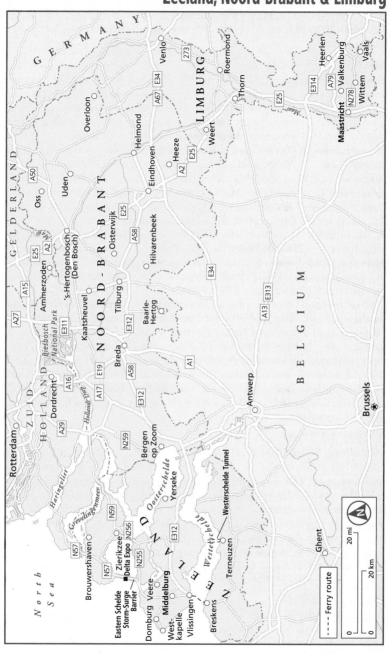

VISITOR INFORMATION   VVV Zierikzee, Nieuwe Haven 7, 4301 DG Zierikzee (© **0900/202-0233;** fax 0111/417-273; www.vvvschouwenduiveland.nl), is at the harbor.

WHAT TO SEE & DO

Strolling Zierikzee's narrow, cobblestone streets, you'll find it easy to imagine the everyday life of its citizens in earlier times, especially if you're here for a colorful Thursday market day. The entrance to the old harbor is guarded by two impressive fortified gates, the 14th- to 15th-century **Zuidhavenpoort** on the south side of the waterway, and the 15th- to 16th-century **Noordhavenpoort** on the north side.

In the center of the Old Town, the **Stadhuis (Town Hall)** began around 1550 as a covered market. Its carillon tinkles merrily at frequent intervals. The **Stadhuismuseum,** Meelstraat 6 (© **0111/454-454**) inside traces the town's history through archaeological finds and other relics. It's open May to November, Monday to Saturday from 10am to 5pm, and Sunday from noon to 5pm. Admission is 2€ ($2.50) for adults, 1€ ($1.25) for seniors and children ages 6 to 12, and free for children under 6.

On the corner of Poststraat, across from the Town Hall, is the oldest house in town, the 14th-century **Huis De Haene** (or Templiershuis). Look for the **Sint-Lievensmon-stertoren (Great Tower)** on the cathedral, west of the Town Hall. This 60m-tall (197-ft.) tower, begun in 1454, is actually incomplete, since townspeople lacked the funds to take it to its planned 204m (670-ft.) height.

Zierikzee's rich history as a maritime trading town is presented by way of antique model ships and other exhibits at the **Maritiem Museum,** Mol 25 (© **0111/454-464**), across from the Town Hall in the 16th-century 's-Gravensteen building. This was originally the town prison, and its upstairs cells still bear the marks of prisoners who carved their names and other graffiti on the oak walls. It's open April to October, Monday to Saturday from 10am to 5pm and Sunday from noon to 5pm; November to March, school vacations only from 10am to 5pm (closed Jan 1 and Dec 25). Admission is 2€ ($2.50) for adults, 1€ ($1.25) for seniors and children ages 6 to 12, and free for children under 6.

WHERE TO STAY

Hostellerie Schuddebeurs ⚸   Amid an area of villas in the wooded countryside outside the nearby village of Schuddebeurs, you'll find this bungalow-style, 3-centuries-old restored farmhouse. Its modern wings have some rooms on the ground floor with their own garden terraces. The hotel will make various gastronomic and golf arrangements at a nearby course. The top-notch, on-site restaurant locally sources many of its products—mussels, oysters, and Schouwen lamb, for instance—and in summer you can dine on the garden terraces.

Donkereweg 35, 4317 NL Schuddebeurs (3km/2 miles north of Zierikzee). © **0111/415-651.** Fax 0111/413-103. www.schuddebeurs.nl. 24 units. 122€–197€ ($153–$246) double. AE, DC, DISC, MC, V. **Amenities:** Restaurant (French/Dutch); bar; nearby golf course. *In room:* TV, minibar, coffeemaker, safe.

WHERE TO DINE

Auberge Maritime SEAFOOD   Overlooking the harbor and Zierikzee's fishing fleet, this informal bar-cafe-restaurant in the town center is a pleasant stop for a meal or for drinks and snacks. The atmosphere inside is reminiscent of high seas and sailors. Try the sea bass in a pastry crust with dill sauce, or the lamb cutlets with thyme and honey. Oysters and lobsters are kept fresh in a special aquarium. Outdoor seating is available in the summer.

Nieuwe Haven 21. ℂ **0111/412-156**. Main courses 15€–33€ ($18–$41); fixed-price menu 28€ ($34). AE, MC, V.
Sun–Thurs 11:45am–9pm; Fri–Sat 11:45am–10pm.

AROUND SCHOUWEN-DUIVELAND
On a wide Zeeland horizon from which an occasional church steeple rises amid a hazy
cluster of red-roofed houses, the former islands of Schouwen and Duiveland are great
places to explore by bicycle or car. The handsome little village of **Dreischor,** 7km
(4 miles) north of Zierikzee, is a good target for an excursion. It's ringed by a canal
and has a 14th- to 15th-century church with a leaning tower at its heart.

Approximately 17km (11 miles) west of Zierikzee is a great North Sea **beach**
backed by sea dunes, centered on the resort of Nieuw-Haamstede. It curves around
from Westenschouwen in the south to Renesse in the north. Many summer visitors'
activities in Zeeland stretch no farther than a stint on this beach. At Westenschouwen
is the northern access to the monumental Eastern Schelde Storm Surge Barrier (see
below).

The Oosterschelde estuary is an important feeding ground and stopover point for
migrating birds, and bird-watchers flock to these parts to admire them.

THE DELTA WORKS 🏃
For as long as people have lived in Zeeland and in the parts of neighboring provinces
that together form the delta of the rivers Rhine, Maas, Waal, and Schelde, their ten-
ancy depended on nature's consent. But on a cold, dark morning—February 1,
1953—that consent was withdrawn. A fierce hurricane sent the North Sea surging
across the land to a record depth of 4.6m (15 ft.), drowning more than 1,800 people.

Following the disaster, construction began on a massive system of dams, dikes,
sluice gates, and storm-surge barriers, known collectively as the **Deltawerken (Delta
Works)**. This colossal feat of engineering aimed to prevent a repeat performance. It
took 3 decades of dredging, dumping, towing, and building to create the network's
component parts. Dams on the seaward side close off the former Haringvliet and
Grevelingenmeer inlets, now lakes, and more dams protect the mainland coast.

The most impressive among the engineering marvels of the Delta Works is the
Eastern Schelde Storm Surge Barrier—a tongue-twisting ***Oosterscheldestormvloed-
kering*** in Dutch. This string of 65 gigantic sluice-gates across the tidal inlet between
Schouwen-Duiveland and Noord-Beveland can be opened and closed as storms and
tidal variations demand. The barrier's towers support a four-lane highway.

Waterland Neeltje Jans 🏃🏃   Even if you don't think you have any interest in
dams, engine rooms, and the like, a visit to the intriguing Delta Expo on a man-made
island called Neeltje Jans in the middle of the Oosterschelde is well worthwhile. To
give visitors an overall view of the massive undertaking of the Delta Works, a huge
scale model of the complex is accompanied by an easily understood explanation of
how everything works. You are treated to a film history and map demonstration, after
which you descend into the innards of one of the Eastern Schelde Storm Surge Barrier's 36 sluice-gate engine rooms. Other attractions include an exposition on whales
and a seal park. In addition, there's a seal basin, a 3-D film, and Holland's largest
exhibit on whales. Allow yourself no less than 2 hours, and additional time for a boat
tour that takes you around the barrier during the summer months.

Faelweg 5, Neeltje Jans island (15km/9 miles west of Zierikzee, off N57). ℂ **0111/655-655**. www.neeltjejans.nl.
Admission 16€ ($20) adults, 13€ ($16) seniors, free for children under 4. Apr–Oct daily 10am–5:30pm; Nov–Mar
Wed–Sun 10am–5pm.

Impressions

He who cannot master the sea is not worthy of the land.

—Dutch saying

2 Middelburg 🌀

74km (46 miles) SW of Rotterdam; 27km (17 miles) SW of Zierikzee

At the center of Zeeland is Walcheren (often still called Walcheren Island even though it has long been connected to the mainland), which holds the bustling provincial capital, Middelburg (pop. 40,000). A medieval town that has restored its 1,000 historical landmarks so successfully you'd think they've stood undisturbed through the centuries, it began as a 9th-century fortress, erected as a defense against Viking raiders. The fortifications expanded into a settlement around 1150, when an abbey was established.

On Middelburg's colorful **market day,** Thursday, you can mingle in the Markt square with locals, some of whom wear traditional dress.

ESSENTIALS

GETTING THERE   **Trains** arrive every hour from Amsterdam, Rotterdam, The Hague, and other points. By **car,** take A29 and N259 south from Rotterdam to Bergen op Zoom, and then go west on A58/E312.

VISITOR INFORMATION   **Tourist Shop Middelburg** is at Markt 65C, 4331 LK Middelburg (© **0118/674-300;** fax 0118/674-333; www.touristshop.nl), across from the Town Hall. The office is open Monday from 1 to 5pm, and Tuesday to Saturday from 9:30am to 5pm.

WHAT TO SEE & DO

Middelburg sights you shouldn't miss include the **picturesque streets** of Spanjaardstraat, crowned by the monumental **Oostkerk (East Church),** Kuiperspoort, and Bellinkstraat; the 1559 **Vismarkt (Fish Market),** with its Doric columns and little auctioneers' houses, where Thursdays in summer are **arts and crafts market** days; the **Blauwepoort (Blue Gate);** and the **Koepoort (Cow Gate).**

The side facing the market square of the elaborate **Stadhuis (Town Hall),** Markt (© **0118/675-450**), is Gothic and dates from the 15th century; the Noordstraat side, from the 17th and 18th centuries, is classic in style. Inside are Belgian tapestries from the 1600s, 17th-century Makkum tiles, and the Middelburg coat of arms. The banquet hall, originally the first cloth market in the Netherlands, is now used for official receptions and an occasional concert. The doors to the left of the main entrance open to the spacious vaulted Vleeshal (Meat Hall), which hosts contemporary art exhibits. The Town Hall is open for guided tours April to October, daily at 11:30am and 3:15pm. Admission is 3.95€ ($4.95) for adults; 3.50€ ($4.40) for seniors, visitors with disabilities, and children ages 6 to 12; and free for children under 6.

Abdij (Abbey) 🌀🌀   Middelburg's sprawling 13th-century abbey in the center of town had a life of traumatic ups and downs over the centuries, as it went from Catholic to Protestant to secular usages, all the while suffering from fires and careless alterations at the hands of whoever happened to be in charge. What you see today is a replica of the original, reconstructed following World War II bombings. Soaring

Middelburg

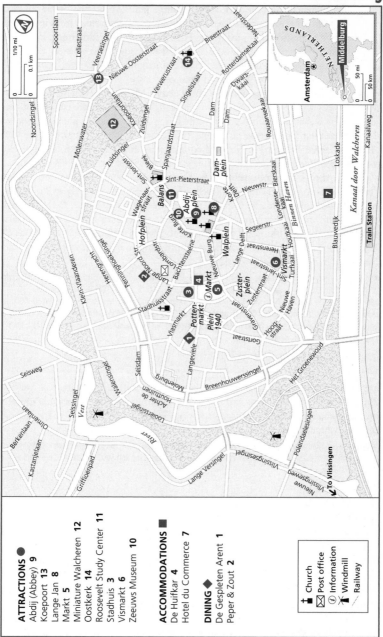

ATTRACTIONS ●
Abdij (Abbey) **9**
Koepoort **13**
Lange Jan **8**
Markt **5**
Miniature Walcheren **12**
Oostkerk **14**
Roosevelt Study Center **11**
Stadhuis **3**
Vismarkt **6**
Zeeuws Museum **10**

ACCOMMODATIONS ■
De Huifkar **4**
Hotel du Commerce **7**

DINING ◆
De Gespleten Arent **1**
Peper & Zout **2**

✝ ■ Church
⊠ Post office
ⓘ Information
✕ Windmill
╱ Railway

87m (289 ft.) into the sky, the 14th-century **Lange Jan (Long John) Tower** can be seen from any point on the island, and has magnificent panoramic views from its summit.

Part of the complex is occupied by the **Historama Abdij Middelburg,** in which the abbey's history is revealed during a fascinating walk through the cloisters, down to the cellars and the crypt, and back again. You'll be introduced to historical figures such as the Norbertine monks and William of Orange.

Another occupant of the abbey is the **Zeeuws Museum (Zeeland Museum)** ✿, which houses a collection of antiquities. Highlights include a Roman altar to pagan sea-goddess Nehallenia recovered from the beach after a storm, a medieval stone coffin that was used for watering cattle, and 16th-century tapestries depicting the victory of Zeeland over the Spanish. National costumes are displayed. The museum is closed for renovations until sometime in 2007.

Finally, there's the **Roosevelt Study Center,** established in honor of Theodore, Franklin Delano, and Eleanor Roosevelt, whose ancestors—the Belgian Protestant de la Noyes—emigrated to the New World in the 1640s from the Zeeland town of Tholen. The library here holds extensive research material, including audiovisual and slide presentations. The annual Four Freedoms Medals (based on FDR's famous 1941 "four freedoms" speech) are awarded in Middelburg in even-numbered years, and in New York in odd-numbered years.

Abdijplein (at Onder de Toren). Lange Jan: ℂ 0118/675-450. Admission 2€ ($2.50) adults, 1.20€ ($1.50) children. Easter–Oct Mon–Sat 10am–5pm. Historama Abdij Middelburg: Abdij 9. ℂ 0118/616-448. Admission 3€ ($3.75) adults, 1€ ($1.25) children. Mon–Sat 11am–5pm; Sun noon–5pm. Zeeuws Museum: ℂ 0118/653-000. www. zeeuwsmuseum.nl. Admission 2€ ($2.50) adults, 1€ ($1.25) children. Mon–Sat 11am–5pm; Sun noon–5pm. Roosevelt Study Center: ℂ 0118/631-590. www.roosevelt.nl. Free admission. Mon–Fri 10am–12:30pm and 1:30–4:30pm; other times by appointment.

Miniatuur Walcheren ✿ *Kids* You can play giant at this miniature version of Walcheren Island, where model villages and farms give a different perspective on the area. This marvelous one-twentieth-scale model is a faithful replication of more than 200 buildings, moving trains and ships, and windmills. A delight for both young and old, it's a good place to visit before exploring Walcheren, where you see the real structures on which these models are based.

Molenwater, at Nieuwe Haven (near the Abbey). ℂ 0118/612-525. www.miniatuurwalcheren.nl. Admission 8€ ($10) adults, 7€ ($8.75) seniors, and free for children under 3. Apr–June and Sept–Oct daily 10am–6pm; July–Sept daily 10am–7pm.

⟨*Moments* **Living Traditions**

As you explore Zeeland, keep an eye out for the local costume: a long, simple black dress with a blue pinafore, still worn on occasion in Walcheren and Zuid-Beveland. (In the latter, the women wearing bonnets shaped like conch shells are Protestant, while those wearing trapezoidal bonnets with a light-blue underbonnet are Catholic.) The gold-and-silver ornaments you see worn by both men and women with the national costume can be bought as souvenirs.

If you're lucky, you'll happen on the traditional game of *ringsteken*, in which contestants ride on bare horseback and try, as they gallop past, to thrust a pointed stick through a ring dangling from a line strung high between two poles.

WHERE TO STAY

De Huifkar   This pleasant little hotel overlooks the Market Square, right in the heart of the city. While not luxurious, the guest rooms are furnished in a modern style. Downstairs is a good restaurant with moderate prices, serving its own tourist menu. In the summer, you can dine on the lively sidewalk terrace on the Markt.

Markt 19, 4331 LJ Middelburg. ☏ 0118/612-998. Fax 0118/612-386. www.hoteldehuifkar.nl. 5 units. 77€–96€ ($96–$120) double. AE, DC, MC, V. **Amenities:** Restaurant (Dutch); bar. *In room:* TV.

Hotel du Commerce   Opposite the rail and bus terminal and an easy walk from the town center, this canal-side hotel is in one of the town's most convenient locations. The guest rooms are simply decorated. In the mornings, you can treat yourself to a varied breakfast buffet. For other meals, there's a good restaurant serving French and Spanish specialties at moderate prices.

Loskade 1, 4331 HV Middelburg. ☏ 0118/636-051. Fax 0118/626-400. www.hotelducommerce.nl. 46 units. 105€–125€ ($131–$156) double. Rates include continental breakfast. AE, MC, V. **Amenities:** Restaurant (Continental); bar; laundry room. *In room:* TV.

WHERE TO DINE

De Gespleten Arent ★★ FRENCH/CONTINENTAL   Meals here, though slightly more expensive than at most local restaurants, are exceptional. The friendly owner has created a warm and intimate atmosphere in this patrician-house setting. Food is prepared with an imaginative use of ingredients. For instance, specialties include lambs' tongue with fennel and pine nuts, and turkey stuffed with *pancetta* (Italian bacon).

Vlasmarkt 25–27 (near the Town Hall). ☏ 0118/636-122. www.degespletenarent.nl. Main courses 18€–24€ ($23–$30); fixed-price menus 30€–55€ ($38–$69). AE, DC, MC, V. Tues–Fri noon–2pm and 5:30–10pm, Sat–Sun 6–9:30pm.

Peper & Zout ★ CONTINENTAL   You'll find this cozy restaurant on a street next to the Gothic Town Hall. The place is full of small tables decked in yellow and brown. Besides serving almost any variety of fried and grilled fish, the restaurant's specialties include a succulent mussels au gratin Ste. Marie topped by a cream sauce, and *water-zooï,* a delicious Belgian fish stew.

Lange Noordstraat 8. ☏ 0118/627-058. www.peperenzout.com. Main courses 15€–20€ ($16–$25); fixed-price menus 20€–32€ ($25–$40). AE, DC, MC, V. Mon–Tues (not Tues Nov–Mar) and Thurs–Fri noon–2pm and 5:30–9:30pm; Sat–Sun 5:30–9:30pm.

AROUND WALCHEREN & ZUID-BEVELAND
VEERE ★
6km (4 miles) N of Middelburg

On the one-time island of Noord-Beveland, by the shore of a former sea inlet that is now a lake called the Veerse Meer, stands this charming village which was an important port for Scottish wool from the 14th to the 18th century. Those bygone trading links earned Scottish mariners the right to free hospitality—a right they surely took full advantage of. Veere's streets are lined with houses and buildings straight out of the past, and its original fortifications are still intact, the ancient harbor tower now housing an excellent hotel/restaurant (see below).

Buses go every hour from Middelburg. For visitor information, go to **VVV Veere,** Oudestraat 28, 4351 AV Veere (☏ **0900/202-0280;** fax 0118/583-455; www.zeeland. nl), in the village center.

The Zeeland Riviera

The western shore of Walcheren is a string of delightful small seaside villages, often called the **Zeeland Riviera** ⊛ because of its long stretches of wide, white-sand beaches. A few miles northwest of Vlissingen are **Koudekerke, West-kapelle,** and **Domburg**—all family-oriented resorts. Beaches are safe for swimming, and there are activities aplenty, including boating, golf, tennis, fishing, and walks in wooded areas near the beaches. This prime vacation country abounds with accommodations, including upscale hotels, bungalows, rustic cabins, and camping sites.

What to See & Do

The Gothic **Stadhuis (Town Hall),** Markt 5, dates in part from 1474—look outside for the *kaak,* an iron brace that locked around a wrongdoer's neck to hold him or her in place as townspeople threw refuse and insults. Over the *kaak* hang the "stones of the law," which an offender was forced to drag through the town in penance. Although today it's stripped to the bare bricks, the **Grote Kerk (Great Church),** Oud-estraat 26, constructed between 1405 and 1560, is awe-inspiring for its sheer size.

After a stroll through streets filled with venerable buildings, head for the handsome waterfront and the old harbor, which is now a haunt of leisure-time mariners busy with the comings and goings of sailboats. You'll pass the 16th- to 17th-century **Schotse Huizen (Scottish Houses)** at Kade 25–27, waterfront mansions that belonged to Scottish wool merchants, and arrive finally at the cannon-studded **Campveerse Toren (Campveer Tower),** dating from around 1500, which was the key to the harbor defenses.

Where to Stay & Dine

De Campveerse Toren ⊛ You couldn't ask for a more romantic location than the 16th-century waterfront fortress of which this delightful hotel, one of the oldest in the country, is a part. It offers simple but comfortable rooms with good light, wood floors, and antique furniture. The Veerse Meer is right below the windows. The proprietors run the expensive adjoining restaurant, perched in a 16th-century tower room overlooking the lake, so various gastronomic arrangements are available. The breakfast and dining room have been furnished in a 17th-century style, with wooden floors, wain-scoted walls, and a huge stone fireplace, creating an intimate atmosphere.

Kaai 2, 4351 AA Veere. ⓒ 0118/501-291. Fax 0118/501-695. www.campveersetoren.nl. 16 units. 75€–150€ ($94–$188) double. AE, DC, MC, V. **Amenities:** Restaurant (seafood); bar. *In room:* TV.

VLISSINGEN

6km (4 miles) S of Middelburg

The port town of Vlissingen (in English the name translates to Flushing) is a popular resort.

Essentials

GETTING THERE   There are trains every hour from Rotterdam and Amsterdam to Vlissingen, via Middelburg, and frequent buses from Middelburg. By car from Middelburg, drive south on N57. Passenger ferries cross the Westerschelde (Western Schelde) from Breskens on the coast of Zeeuws-Vlaanderen (Zeeland Flanders) to

Vlissingen, opening up easy travel options from the neighboring Belgian coast resorts, and from Bruges and Ghent (but when going by car from Zeeuws-Vlaanderen you need to take the tunnel under the Oosterschelde from Ternuizen).

VISITOR INFORMATION   **VVV Vlissingen,** Oude Markt 3, 4381 ER Vlissingen (© **0118/422-190;** fax 0118/422-191; www.zeeland.nl), is in the center of town.

What To See & Do

In the Old Town, the **Oude Markt** and the neighboring 14th-century **Sint-Jacobs-kerk (St. James's Church)** are well worth visiting. Also, don't miss a stroll down the **seafront promenade** that's named variously De Ruyter, Bankert, and Evertsen, in honor of those Dutch naval heroes.

Iguana Reptile Zoo *(Kids)*   This zoo is full of the animals that childhood nightmares are made of, but that kids seem to love just the same. It's a fascinating introduction to the lives of reptiles, amphibians, and insects from around the world. There are more than 500 specimens on display, from tiny, creepy scorpions to endless tiger pythons, but they're not all scary—you can watch frogs, turtles, and salamanders. In the baby room, you can even see eggs hatching and young animals crawling out of their shells.

Bellamypark 35 (south of Oude Markt). © **0118/417-219.** Admission 6€ ($7.50) adults and children; free for children under 4. June–Sept Sun–Mon 2–5:30pm, Tues–Sat 10am–12:30pm and 2–5:30pm; Oct–May daily 2–5:30pm. Closed Jan 1, Dec 25.

YERSEKE

30km (19 miles) E of Middelburg

This busy little fishing port in the eastern reaches of the Oosterschelde is noted for its extensive offshore mussel beds (see the box, "Mussel-Bound," below) and oyster farms, and for seafood restaurants that serve up these and other marine delights. Buses go to Yerseke every hour from the rail station at Goes.

Mussel-Bound

The waters of the Oosterschelde are ideal for building mussels. Whiplike branches sticking out of the shallow water off Yerseke mark the location of mussel merchants' "parcels"—stretches of water where mussels lie on the sandy bottom. In April and May, mussel boats are busy "planting" mussel-seed: young mussels that will form the next year's crop. By the time they've grown to 4 centimeters (1½ in.), they've joined together in dense mats for mutual support against tidal pull. These are scooped up and moved for 2 weeks to other parcels, called "wet warehouses," which are freer of sand, for the final growth to maturity. Once they reach 6 centimeters (2½ in.) or larger, they are ready for harvesting, destined for Belgium, Holland, and France. But as any skipper will tell you: "The biggest ones are for me."

From the start of mussel season in July until it ends the following April, fishing boats ply back and forth between port and parcels. On a good outing, a skipper can return to Yerseke with a thousand mussel-tonnes glistening in his hold—a mussel-tonne is 100 kilograms (220 lb.). In an average season, 100 million kilograms (2.2 million lb.) of mussels pass through here.

Where to Dine

Nolet/Het Reymerswale 😊😊 SEAFOOD   Fish can't get much fresher than at this special waterfront restaurant. A member of Holland's prestigious Alliance Gastronomique association of top restaurants, it sports a Michelin star. Most of what lands on your plate from master-chef Danny Nolet's kitchen comes right off the local fishing boats in the harbor below. Het Reymerswale is named after a coastal Zeeland village that vanished beneath the waves around 1500, and the interior is "decorated" with excavated items from the village. Try the decadent oysters and champagne, or a more restrained dish like grilled turbot with a béarnaise sauce.

Burgemeester Sinkelaan 5 (at the Yerseke yacht harbor). ✆ **0113/571-642.** Fixed-price menus 45€–65€ ($56–$81). AE, MC, V. Mon and Thurs–Sat (also Tues–Wed during holidays) noon–2:30pm and 6–9pm; Sun noon–9pm.

3 Bergen op Zoom

47km (29 miles) E of Middelburg

The center of this small town (Zoom is pronounced *zome,* as in "home"), close to Zeeland and the Belgian border, is alive with many cafes and restaurants.

ESSENTIALS

GETTING THERE   The town lies on the Amsterdam-Rotterdam-Vlissingen rail line, with **trains** every hour in both directions. By **car,** take A58/E312 east from Middelburg and west from Breda.

VISITOR INFORMATION   Contact **Toerisme Bergen op Zoom,** Grote Markt 1, 4611 NR Bergen op Zoom (✆ **0164/277-482;** fax 0164/240-176; www.bergsnet. com).

WHAT TO SEE & DO

Part of the monumental **Stadhuis (Town Hall),** on the Grote Markt, is a beautiful 14th-century castlelike structure (reconstructed after being destroyed by a fire). Three more buildings were attached to the complex in subsequent centuries.

Het Markiezenhof (The Marquis's Court)   Remnants of Bergen op Zoom's past as a small but powerful city-state can be found all over the center city, and this unique town palace is perhaps the most impressive example. It was constructed between 1485 and 1525, and was once home to the Marquis of Bergen op Zoom. Behind the striped facade of red brick and yellow sandstone, you'll find the town's history museum and a kids-oriented fairground museum.

Steenbergsestraat 8. ✆ 0164/277-077. www.markiezenhof.nl. Admission 5€ ($6.25) adults, 2.50€ ($3.15) children 3–12, free for children under 3. Daily 11am–5pm. Closed Jan 1.

WHERE TO STAY & DINE

Hotel de Draak 😊   Modern comfort awaits you in Holland's oldest hotel, founded in 1397, which now occupies three adjacent buildings—which themselves date from the beginning of the 17th century—overlooking the lively market square in the heart of town. The guest rooms are luxuriously decorated with antiques, flowery chintzes, and stylish wallpapers. Period furniture and a grand old fireplace lend the convivial lounge and bar a medieval character. The on-site restaurant **Hemingway Eten & Drinken** is furnished in a 17th-century style, and you can dine outdoors on a large sidewalk terrace when the weather's nice.

Grote Markt 30 and 36–38, 4611 NT, Bergen op Zoom. ☎ **0164/252-050.** Fax 0164/257-001. www.hoteldraak.com. 51 units. 143€–185€ ($179–$231) double; 250€ ($313) suite. AE, DC, MC, V. **Amenities:** Restaurant (French/Italian); lounge/bar. *In room:* TV, minibar.

4 Breda

36km (22 miles) NE of Bergen op Zoom; 38km (25 miles) SW of Den Bosch

Breda was granted its town charter in 1252. In 1625, it withstood a 9-month siege before surrendering to Spanish forces. In 1667, the Treaty of Breda (between England, France, the Dutch United Provinces, and Denmark) awarded the New World colonies of New Amsterdam and New Jersey to the English. Today, life in Breda centers around the rectangular Grote Markt and the town's many fine parks.

ESSENTIALS

GETTING THERE   Trains arrive at least every hour from Amsterdam, via Rotterdam and The Hague. By **car,** Breda lies just off the junction of A16/E19 from Rotterdam and Antwerp (in Belgium this expressway is designated A1/E19) and A27/E311 from Utrecht.

VISITOR INFORMATION   VVV Breda, Grote Markt 38, 4811 XS Breda (☎ **0900/522-2444;** fax 076/521-8530; www.vvvbreda.nl), is in the center of town. A second VVV office (same phone, fax numbers, and website) is at Willemstraat 17–19, across the street from the rail station.

WHAT TO SEE & DO

In the old center, **Kasteel Breda (Breda Castle),** dating from 1536, is now a military academy. The **Grote Kerk (Great Church),** dedicated to Our Lady, contains a striking tomb of Count Engelbert II and his wife.

The **Breda Museum,** Parade 12–14 (☎ **076/529-9300;** www.breda-museum.org), in the former Chassé Barracks (Kazerne), has an extensive collection focusing on the town's history and on products manufactured in the region. It has a collection of religious objects belonging to the Bishop of Tilburg. The museum is open Tuesday to Sunday and holidays from 10am to 5pm (closed Jan 1 and Dec 25). Admission is 3.50€ ($4.40) for adults, 2.30€ ($2.90) for seniors and children ages 4 to 13, and free for children under 4.

Parks that offer open-air relief from city sightseeing include Valkenburg, Brabant, Sonsbeek, and Trekpot. Breda is surrounded by beautiful **rural estates,** many of which open their grounds to the public, and by great **public forests** such as the **Mastbos** and **Liesbos,** whose ancient trees form peaceful retreats.

Fun Fact **Nobody's Town**

Baarle-Nassau/Baarle-Hertog, an oddity of a town 20km (12 miles) southeast of Breda, can't make up its mind whether to be in Belgium or in Holland—so it exists in both. Houses use colored number plates to identify their citizenship. If the figures are blue, the occupants are Dutch; if they're black on a white background with a black, yellow, and red vertical stripe, the occupants are Belgian. Must get confusing!

The Biesbosch National Park

The Nationaal Park De Biesbosch (Forest of Reeds), embedded in the Hollandse Diep south of Rotterdam, and shared between the provinces of Noord-Brabant and Zuid-Holland, bears the imprint of constant flooding by tidal surges and overflow from the rivers Maas and Waal. Once dry land, this area of marshland, meadows, and willow woods was formed during the St. Elisabeth floods of 1421, when 16 villages were submerged and the former polders became an inland sea. It has since been shaped by the interplay between the rivers and the tides. A unique culture developed on these isolated and partly drowned islands, where islanders harvested reeds that grew on the marshy land.

Since 1970, when the Haringvliet Dam, part of the Delta Works (see earlier in this chapter), was constructed at the seacoast, the Biesbosch has been a freshwater delta of creeks and inlets on and around the two rivers. Ecologically rich and one of the prized wetlands threatened worldwide by agriculture and urban sprawl, the Biesbosch is slowly being dried out by the flood-control measures that bring security to the coastal cities.

The marshes and islands are a habitat that supports a large and varied population of bird life. A boat trip into the Biesbosch is a journey into a different world from the nearby polders. Kingfishers dart along reed-clogged channels, while a discord of bleeps, twitters, and honks—music to any bird-watcher's ears—escapes from ponds and marshes where heron, storks, geese, spoonbills, ducks, and cormorants make their homes. Beavers, last seen in the wild here in 1826, have been successfully reintroduced in recent years.

Leisure activities in the Biesbosch include rowing and canoeing along its labyrinth of creeks, and hiking.

In Zuid-Holland, the visitor center, **Biesboschcentrum Dordrecht,** Baanhoekweg 53, Dordrecht (ⓒ **078/630-5353;** www.biesbosch.org), is open May to June, holidays, and school vacations, daily from 10am to 5pm; July to August, daily from 9am to 6pm; and September to April, Tuesday to Sunday from 10am to 5pm; admission is free. To get there from Rotterdam, on A15/E31 take Exit 23, pass through Papendrecht, and then follow the signs. From Breda, take A16 to Dordrecht and N3 toward Papendrecht; then follow the signs east across the Merwede River.

On the Noord-Brabant side, the visitor center, the **Biesbosch Bezoekerscentrum Drimmelen,** Biesboschweg 4, Drimmelen (ⓒ **0162/682-233;** www.biesbosch.org), 17km (11 miles) north of Breda, is open daily from 10am to 5pm; admission is free.

Art lovers will want to stop by the village of **Zundert,** which is 15km (9 miles) southwest of Breda, on N263. This is the birthplace of Vincent van Gogh. There's a touching statue (1963) here of the painter and his devoted brother, Theo, commissioned by the townspeople and sculpted by Ossip Zadkine.

5 Den Bosch

74km (51 miles) SE of Amsterdam; 64km (40 miles) SE of Rotterdam

The full name of the Noord-Brabant provincial capital is 's-Hertogenbosch, meaning The Duke's Wood, but the place is generally referred to simply as Den Bosch—maybe the locals, too, have given up on trying to pronounce the longer version! This cathedral town is more than 800 years old. Parts of the center have retained their medieval atmosphere, in particular around the crooked alleys leading up to the odd triangular market "square."

ESSENTIALS

GETTING THERE   **Trains** frequently run from Amsterdam via Utrecht, and from Rotterdam, The Hague, and Maastricht. By **car,** take A2/E35 and E25 southeast from Amsterdam.

VISITOR INFORMATION   **VVV 's-Hertogenbosch** is at Markt 77, 5211 JX 's-Hertogenbosch (© **0900/112-2334;** fax 073/612-8930; www.vvvs-hertogenbosch.nl). The office is open Monday from 1 to 6pm, Tuesday to Friday from 9:30am to 6pm, and Saturday from 9am to 5pm.

WHAT TO SEE & DO

Het Zwanenbroedershuis   The Brotherhood of Our Illustrious Lady, a charitable body founded in the 14th century that grew into an organization of considerable influence, is housed in this neo-Gothic building. Membership became a matter of prestige, attracting rich citizens and nobility, including Queen Beatrix and Crown Prince Willem-Alexander. Illuminated books of music especially commissioned for its choir are on display, along with gifts from its members and other memorabilia documenting the Brotherhood's history.

Hinthamerstraat 94. © **073/613-7383.** www.zwanenbroedershuis.nl. Admission 5€ ($6.25). Guided tours: Sept–July Tues and Thurs 1:30–4:30pm.

Noordbrabants Museum   A 17th-century neoclassical building, once the official residence of the Queen's Commissioner to Noord-Brabant from 1820 to 1983, now houses this stylish, provincial museum. Exhibits on local history focus on archaeological finds, such as Roman remains, religious objects, manuscripts, maps, weapons, and coins. The paintings on display emphasize the Dutch still life, with two rooms full of painted flowers from the 16th to 18th centuries. Contemporary sculptures decorate the gardens.

Verwersstraat 41. © **073/687-7800.** www.noordbrabantsmuseum.nl. Admission 7€ ($8.75) adults, 4.50€ ($5.65) seniors and students, free for children under 18. Tues–Fri 10am–5pm; Sat–Sun and holidays noon–5pm.

Sint-Janskathedraal (St. John's Cathedral) ⭐   Parts of this magnificent cathedral date back to the 1200s, though most of the present Gothic structure was finished in 1529. The cathedral suffered considerable damage during a fire in 1584, when the cupola and its tower collapsed. Some of the original 15th-century frescoes were revealed during restoration, among them those in the ambulatory depicting the *Joshua Tree* and *St. James.* Have a look at the 15th-century brass chandelier in the Chapel of the Holy Sacrament on the north side of the choir. The chapel (1497) is lavishly decorated and imbued with a soft light. Notice also the little stone figures on the flying buttresses and up the copings (miniature copies of these delightful figures are on sale in local gift stores). The 50-bell carillon in the rump of the 13th-century, late-Romanesque tower is played every Wednesday from 11:30am to 12:30pm.

Choorstraat 1. ✆ 073/613-0314. www.sint-jan.nl. Free admission. Daily 8am–5pm.

NEARBY ATTRACTIONS

De Efteling Family Leisure Park 🌟🌟 *(Kids)*   Most remarkable, in this 284-hectare (700-acre) recreational park, is the miniature city with towers, castles, and characters based on just about every fairy tale that ever stirred a child's imagination. Slightly weird and wacky figures, dreamed up by the park's creative team, exist here too. Many of the characters are animated or played by an actor in costume. Other attractions are exciting water rides and a boating lake, and there are cafeteria-type restaurants. Organization is good, so queuing is kept to a minimum even in busy school-vacation periods.

Outside Kaatsheuvel (a few kilometers/miles north of Tilburg). ✆ 041/628-8111. www.efteling.nl. Admission 26€ ($33) adults, 24€ ($30) seniors and visitors with disabilities, free for children under 4; add 10% July–Aug). Apr–Oct daily 10am–6pm (July–Aug to 9pm); Dec–Jan weekends and Dec 23–Jan 7 (except Jan 1) daily 11am–6, 8, or 10pm, depending on the day. From Den Bosch, take A59 westbound, Exit 37.

Kasteel Ammersoyen 🌟🌟   One of the best-preserved medieval castles in Holland, this place has had a colorful array of inhabitants over the centuries. It served as a nunnery and later as a depot for a manufacturer of washing machines. The foundation which now owns the castle has restored it and on the inside recreated the plain, austere atmosphere it would have had in the 14th century. Outside, a moat and four sturdy towers are connected to make a square, virtually impregnable building. You enter the castle through the cellar and go up staircases constructed inside the thick walls. Upstairs are a magnificent hall and some smaller tower rooms. In the attic is a small exhibit of objects found during restoration on the grounds and in the moat.

Kasteellaan 1, Ammersoyen, 11km (7 miles) northwest of Den Bosch. ✆ 073/594-9582. www.kasteel-ammersoyen. nl. Admission 4€ ($5) adults, 2€ ($2.50) children 5–12. Hourly guided tours only: Apr–Oct Tues–Fri 11am–4pm, Sat–Sun 1–4pm.

Safaripark Beekse Bergen 🌟 *(Kids)*   You can either stay in your own car or take a guided bus tour through this extensive open-air safari park. Some 125 different species live together here in a natural environment (even though it's not exactly native to many of the species that reside here).

Beekse Bergen 31, Hilvarenbeek. ✆ 0900/233-5732. www.beeksebergen.nl. Admission 15€ ($19) adults, 14€ ($17) seniors and children 3–11, free for children under 3. Dec–Jan daily 10am–4pm; Feb and Nov daily 10am–4:30pm; July–Aug daily 10am–6pm (Sat to 9 or 10pm); Mar–June and Sept–Oct daily 10am–5pm.

WHERE TO STAY

Eurohotel Den Bosch 🌟   The friendly owners of this small central hotel, 2 blocks east of the Markt, have made it a very convivial lodging. Reached by cream-colored marble stairs from the reception, the guest rooms are attractive and intimate, decorated in pastels and print fabrics, and furnished with stylish chairs and comfortable beds. The breakfast room overlooks a bustling pedestrian shopping street.

Kerkstraat 56 (at Torenstraat), 5211 KH Den Bosch. ✆ 073/613-7777. Fax 073/612-8795. www.eurohotel-denbosch. com. 42 units. 90€–145€ ($113–$181) double. Rates include breakfast. AE, DC, MC, V. Parking 7€ ($8.75). **Amenities:** Bar; laundry service. *In room:* TV, dataport.

Golden Tulip Hotel Central   You couldn't ask for a more romantic location than this, right on the city's medieval market square. The Central is large and modern, but somehow manages to be cozy. The guest rooms are nicely appointed. The restaurant **De Hoofdwacht** occupies a 14th-century cellar.

Burgemeester Loeffplein 98, 5211 RX Den Bosch. (✆ 073/692-6926. Fax 073/614-5699. www.hotel-central.nl. 132 units. 125€ ($156) double; 195€–295€ ($244–$369) suite. AE, DC, MC, V. **Amenities:** Restaurant (Dutch); bar; cafe; 24-hr. room service; laundry service. *In room:* A/C, TV w/pay movies, dataport, minibar, coffeemaker, hair dryer, safe.

WHERE TO DINE
De Raadskelder ★ REGIONAL   For an excellent meal at a moderate price, visit this huge, vaulted cellar restaurant under the Gothic Town Hall. The interior is medieval in theme: Lighting is provided by brass chandeliers and lanterns, and there are massive pillars and a grand stone fireplace. The imaginative menu includes fried pike perch with salsify, black olives, and beurre blanc, and veal stewed in a sauce of Kriek Lambic (Belgian cherry beer) and celeriac root.

Markt 1A. (✆ 073/613-6919. Main courses 16€–22€ ($20–$28); fixed-price menus 26€–45€ ($33–$56). AE, MC, V. Tues–Sat 10:30am–5pm and 5:30–10:30pm.

Pilkington's BRITISH/CONTINENTAL   As you enter this lovely cafe-restaurant that has the atmosphere of an English country home, you see a display of luscious cakes, sandwiches, quiches, and homemade pâtés. People sit at small tables along the wall on wicker chairs. At the back, overlooking a lovely garden with clipped hedgerows and rosebushes, is a roofed terrace where you can have a romantic dinner in summer. Seasonal specialties include wild boar, venison, and hare, all with delectable sauces. Try the tasty *speculaas* pudding—made with traditional Dutch spicy biscuits—for dessert.

Torenstraat 5 (across from Sint-Janskathedraal). (✆ 073/612-2923. www.pilkingtons.nl. Main courses 11€–16€ ($14–$20); fixed-price menu 22€ ($28). AE, DC, MC, V. Mon 11:30am–5pm; Tues–Sun 10am–10pm.

6 Eindhoven
32km (22 miles) SE of Den Bosch; 120km (82 miles) SE of Amsterdam

Its town charter dates from 1232, but Eindhoven limped along for centuries as not much more than a village. Today, it ranks as Holland's fifth-largest city (pop. 200,000)—thanks almost entirely to the Philips electronics corporation, which has been headquartered here for over 100 years. Despite its size, Eindhoven has only a few points of genuine interest for visitors.

ESSENTIALS
GETTING THERE   **Trains** go to Eindhoven every 30 minutes or so from Amsterdam, Rotterdam, and The Hague; and every hour from Maastricht. By **car,** Eindhoven lies on the main north-south A2/E35-E25 Amsterdam–Maastricht Expressway.

VISITOR INFORMATION   VVV **Eindhoven** is at Stationsplein 17, 5611 AC Eindhoven (✆ **0900/112-2363;** fax 040/243-3135).

WHAT TO SEE & DO
Museum Kempenland Eindhoven   Exhibits depicting the history of this city and region are housed here in an Italianate basilica that was constructed between 1917 and 1919. Note the stained-glass windows. There's a collection of 19th- and 20th-century art and sculpture by Dutch and Belgian artists.

Sint-Antoniusstraat 5–7. (✆ 040/252-9093. www.museumkempenland.nl. Admission 2.50€ ($2.50) adults, 1.25€ ($1.55) seniors and children 6–18, free for children under 6. Tues–Sun 1–5pm.

Zwemparadies (Swimming Paradise) De Tongelreep *(Kids)*   This park on the southern edge of Eindhoven is the perfect place for a time-out from sightseeing. The park contains a subtropical wave pool, chute-the-chute, bubble pools, a paddling pool, whirlpools, a 50m (165-ft.) indoor swimming pool, and an outdoor pool with a sunbathing area.

Antoon Coolenlaan. ℂ 040/238-1112. www.tongelreep.nl. Admission 5.90€ ($7.40) adults, 3.35€ ($4.20) seniors, 2.60€ ($3.25) children under 4. Wave pool: Mon–Fri 10am–10pm; Sat–Sun 10am–5:30pm. Outdoor pool: May–Aug Mon–Fri 10am–6pm, Sat–Sun 10am–5:30pm.

WHERE TO DINE

De Karpendonkse Hoeve 🍴 INTERNATIONAL   This first-class restaurant, a member of the prestigious Alliance Gastronomique Néderlandaise, specializes in game in season and always uses the best of local products. It's on the outskirts of town, in an 18th-century farmhouse surrounded by trees and overlooking a small lake. Tables are decked stylishly in green and pink. The menu offers delicacies like a "triple quail fantasy": mousse, sautéed breast and aspic of quail, or brill filet topped with steamed carrot and cucumber with a Noilly Prat sauce. In the summer, you can dine on a terrace overlooking the lake.

Sumatralaan 3. ℂ 040/281-3663. www.karpendonksehoeve.nl. Main course 20€–35€ ($25–$44); fixed-price lunch 34€–45€ ($43–$56); fixed-price dinner 65€–83€ ($81–$104). AE, MC, V. Mon–Fri noon–2:30pm and 6–9:30pm; Sat 6–9:30pm.

WHERE TO STAY & DINE NEARBY

Hostellerie Vangaelen 🍴   In the village of Heeze, a 20-minute drive from Eindhoven, this 18th-century coaching inn is directly across from a 17th-century château. The place has been redone with a curious Mediterranean touch that disavows its rustic heritage, and the guest rooms have opulent furnishings and tasteful decor. The restaurant, which belongs to the Alliance Gastronomique Néderlandaise, serves delicious food with a Mediterranean accent. Weather permitting, you can dine outdoors.

Kapelstraat 48, 5591 HE Heeze (8km/5 miles SE of Eindhoven). ℂ 040/226-3515. Fax 040/226-3876. www. hostellerie.nl. 14 units. 128€–185€ ($160–$231) double. AE, DC, MC, V. From Eindhoven take A67 east; then Exit 34 south to Heeze. **Amenities:** Restaurant (Mediterranean); wireless Internet. *In room:* A/C, TV.

A NEARBY BELL MUSEUM

The small town of Asten, 19km (12 miles) east of Eindhoven, is home to Royal Eijsbouts, the world's leading producer of large-scale carillon and swinging bells. Its bells grace church towers, town halls, university campuses, and memorials in Holland, Belgium, elsewhere in Europe, the United States, and beyond.

Nationaal Beiaardmuseum (National Carillon Museum) 🍴   The Eijsbouts bell-foundry's location in the town explains the existence of this fascinating museum, which embraces the centuries-old love in the Low Countries for bells clustered together as musical instruments. Here you can see the oldest surviving swinging bells in the Netherlands, from the 11th century, and carillon bells cast by the brothers François and Pieter Hemony in the 17th century.

Ostaderstraat 23, Asten. ℂ 0493/691-865. www.carillon-museum.nl. Admission 5.50€ ($6.90) adults, 4.70€ ($5.90) seniors, 2.70€ ($3.40) children 5–15, free for children under 5. Tues–Fri 9.30am–5pm; Sat–Mon and holidays 1–5pm. Closed Jan 1, Dec 25, and during Carnival.

7 Maastricht ★★★

215km (147 miles) SE of Amsterdam; 124km (85 miles) SE of Den Bosch

An exuberant center of history, culture, and hospitality, Maastricht (pop. 130,000) is a city of cafes and churches, and it's hard to tell which of these has the upper hand. Maastricht is generally reckoned to be Holland's most user-friendly city, blessed with a quality of life the northerners can't match. In between eating, drinking, church-going, stepping out for Carnival, and hanging onto their rich heritage, the citizens of Maastricht have created a modern, prosperous, and vibrant city. Discovering how they do it all can be quite an education.

The capital of Limburg province owes its name and existence to the Maas River and repays the debt with a handsome riverfront. The city traces its roots back to the Roman settlement of Mosae Trajectam, founded in 50 B.C. at a strategic bridge across the Maas at the foot of Sint-Pietersberg (Mt. St. Peter).

ESSENTIALS

GETTING THERE   You can **go by air** from Amsterdam to Maastricht–Aachen Airport, 10km (6 miles) north of the city, with **KLM Exel** (© 020/474-7747; www. klm.com), which has daily flights; flying time is 40 minutes. There are hourly **trains** from Amsterdam, Rotterdam, and The Hague. By **car,** take A2/E25.

VISITOR INFORMATION   VVV **Maastricht,** Kleine Staat 1, 6211 ED Maastricht (© **043/325-2121;** fax 043/321-3746; www.vvvmaastricht.nl), in a 1470 building, Het Dinghuis, formerly the local law courts, is both helpful and friendly. The office is open May to October, Monday to Saturday from 9am to 6pm, and Sunday from 11am to 3pm; November to April, Monday to Friday from 9am to 6pm, and Saturday from 9am to 5pm. A monthly magazine, *Uit in Maastricht,* tells you what's going on; it's in Dutch, but you can glean useful listings from it.

WHAT TO SEE & DO

Coming from the rail station to the center, you cross the Maas on the pedestrians-only **Sint-Servaasbrug (St. Servatius Bridge),** which dates from 1289 and is one of the oldest bridges in the Netherlands.

The **Vrijthof,** the city's most glorious square, is a vast open space bordered on three sides by restaurants and cafes with sidewalk terraces, and on the fourth by the Romanesque Sint-Servaas Church and the Gothic Sint-Jan's with its soaring red belfry. This is Maastricht's forum, especially in good weather, when the sidewalk terraces are filled with people soaking up the atmosphere and watching the world go by.

On the market square, the **Markt,** vendors, some from Belgium and Germany, gather on Wednesday and Friday mornings to open colorful stalls, watched over by

---

Fun Fact **The Lost Musketeer**

Maastricht was the last earthly place seen by the hero of Alexandre Dumas's *The Three Musketeers.* It was here that d'Artagnan lost his life during King Louis XIV's siege of the city in 1673. Dumas's musketeers are fictitious, but the siege actually happened, and d'Artagnan was based on captain of musketeers Charles de Batz-Castelmore, Comte d'Artagnan, who was indeed killed at Maastricht.

the cheerful little *'t Mooswief (Vegetable Woman)* statue. The sober-looking 17th-century **Stadhuis (Town Hall)**, in dignified gray stone, is surmounted by a tower containing a 43-bell carillon that breaks into song at every conceivable opportunity, and in a special concert on Saturday from 3:30 to 4:15pm.

Maastricht packs 1,590 protected historical monuments inside the city limits. This shows another side of Maastricht's character, its essential Dutchness, in the determination to hold what it has and display it to the best possible effect. The **Stokstraat Kwartier,** also known as the Roman district because this quarter was the ancient center city, is a case in point. It experienced a decades-long restoration that made of its 17th- and 18th-century buildings a baroque shopping and restaurant area. Between here and the medieval wall along the Jeker River lies the **Jeker Kwartier,** a haunt of the city's sizeable student population and location of some offbeat bars and boutiques. These narrow cobbled alleyways, where the past intersects the present, are an essential element of Maastricht's charm.

Keep your eye out for the little square called **Op de Thermen,** off Stokstraat, a couple of blocks inland from the Maas, where you can still see the outline of a Roman thermal bath on the cobblestones; and for the small, impish **Mestreechter Geis** statue (he embodies the *joie de vivre* of Maastrichters, and his name in local dialect means "Spirit of Maastricht") in a tiny square at nearby Kleine Stokstraat.

Walking along the remaining stretches of **fortifications,** in particular the triple line of bastions in the western suburbs and the south wall along the Jeker, it's easy to be impressed by their strength. The besieged could probably afford to poke fun at the besiegers, discounting the improbable chance of them getting in and having a good memory for faces.

MUSEUMS & OTHER ATTRACTIONS

Bonnefanten Museum ⚘   Designed by Italian architect Aldo Rossi and opened in 1995, the otherwise restrained riverside museum, amid the relentlessly modern architecture of the new Céramique district, is instantly recognizable with its striking, bullet-shaped dome. Works of art from the Maasland School include sculpture, silverwork, and woodcarvings from the Maas Valley in Limburg and Belgium (where the river is called the Meuse). This art dates as far back as the 13th century and had its apogee during the 15th and 16th centuries. Internationalism is illustrated in the museum's collection of Italian and Flemish Masters. These include works by Filippo Lippi and Bellini, and Pieter Brueghel the Younger's *Wedding In Front Of A Farm* and *Census At Bethlehem.* Archaeological finds dating from 250,000 years ago to the Middle Ages are displayed, with an emphasis on the Roman period. In the Wiebengahal next to the museum are changing exhibits by contemporary artists.

Av. Céramique 250 (next to the John F. Kennedy Bridge). ℂ 043/329-0190. www.bonnefanten.nl. Admission 7€ ($9.40) adults, 3.50€ ($7.50) children 13–18, free for children under 13. Tues–Sun 11am–5pm. Bus: 1, 5, 53, or 54.

Natuurhistorisch Museum (Natural History Museum)   Fossils from the marlstone walls of the Sint-Pietersberg Caves (see below), are displayed here. These include skeletons of Mosasaurier dinosaurs and giant turtles. In addition, there are rocks and minerals, and both rough and cut gemstones. The courtyard contains a botanical garden, with beautiful examples of the local flora.

De Bosquetplein 7 (near the Music Conservatory). ℂ 043/350-5490. www.nhmmaastricht.nl. Admission 3.50€ ($4.40) adults, 2.60€ ($3.25) seniors and children 4–11, free for children under 4. Mon–Fri 10am–5pm; Sat–Sun 2–5pm. Closed holidays.

Maastricht

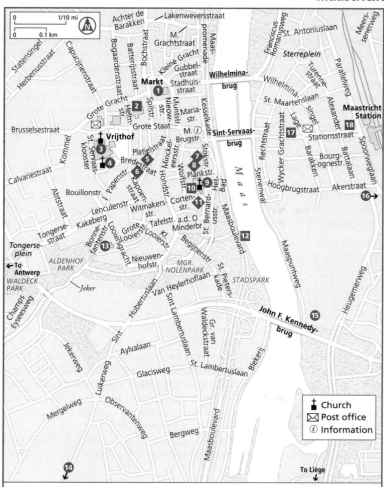

ATTRACTIONS ●
Bonnefanten Museum **15**
Margraten U.S. Military Cemetery **16**
Natuurhistorisch Museum **13**
Onze-Lieve-Vrouwbasiliek **9**
Sint-Janskerk **4**
Sint-Pietersberg Caves **14**
Sint-Servaasbasiliek **3**
Stadhuis **1**

ACCOMMODATIONS ■
Botel Maastricht **12**
Grand Hotel de l'Empereur **18**
Hotel du Casque **2**
Derlon **10**
Hotel Residence Beaumont **17**

DINING ◆
In de Moriaan **12**
India House **18**
Sagittarius Seafood & Grillades **2**
Toine Hemsen **10**
't Plenske **17**

Sint-Pietersberg Caves ✿✿ Don't miss these mysterious caverns that tunnel into the heart of high cliffs. The Romans and all who came after them took from Mount St. Peter great chunks of marlstone, a type of limestone that's as soft to carve as soap and hardens when exposed to air. Many Maastricht buildings are constructed of marlstone. As more and more marlstone was extracted over the centuries, the Sint-Pietersberg interior became honeycombed with 20,000 passages. From Roman times, to medieval sieges, to the 4 years of Nazi occupation during World War II, these chambers have served as a place of refuge. Many drawings and signatures have been left on the marlstone walls. During World War II, the caves sheltered from the Nazis Dutch masterpieces such as Rembrandt's *The Night Watch* and other treasures. You follow your guide's lantern through a labyrinth of 6- to 12m-high (20- to 40-ft.) tunnels. Stay close to that lantern—tales are told of those who entered the 200km (120 miles) of tunnels and were never seen again (ask about the four monks). The temperature underground is about 50°F (10°C), and it's damp, so bring a cardigan or a coat.

Entrance at Fort Sint-Pieter (southwestern edge of the city). ✆ 043/325-2121. www.pietersberg.nl. Guided tours 4€ ($5) adults, 2.75€ ($2.50) children under 13. Tours in English July–Sept daily 2:45pm. Bus: 4 from center city.

CHURCHES

Onze-Lieve-Vrouwbasiliek (Basilica of Our Lady) ✿ The west wing and crypts of this medieval Romanesque cruciform structure date from the 11th century, and there's evidence of an earlier church and even a pagan place of worship on the site. But the focus for most visitors is the side chapel containing the statue of Our Lady Star of the Sea. The richly robed statue, fronted by a blaze of candles, is credited with many miracles, even during long years when it was hidden away because of religious persecution. In the early 1600s, as many as 20,000 pilgrims came to worship at the shrine every Easter Monday. When the Calvinists took power in 1632, the statue went into hiding. Legend has it that in 1699 Our Lady herself established Maastricht's "prayer route" by stepping down from her pedestal and leading a devout parishioner through the muddy streets, and that the morning after the miraculous walk there was indeed mud on the hem of Our Lady's robe! The church treasury contains a rich collection of tapestries, reliquaries, church silver, and other religious objects.

Onze-Lieve-Vrouweplein. ✆ 043/325-1851. Basilica: free admission; Treasury: 1.60€ ($2.50) adults, 0.45€ (58¢) children. Basilica: daily 11am–5pm, except during services. Treasury: Easter to mid-Oct Mon–Sat 11am–5pm; Sun 1–5pm.

Sint-Janskerk (St. John's Church) The sober, whitewashed interior of the city's main Dutch Reformed (Protestant) church, dating from the 14th century and given to the Protestants in 1633, makes a study in contrast with the lavish Catholic decoration at St. Servatius's next door. But there are murals, sculpted corbels of the 12 Apostles, and grave monuments of local dignitaries and wealthy individuals. Most people come here, though, to climb the 218 narrow, winding steps to the 70m (230-ft.) belfry's windy viewing platform, 43m (141 ft.) above the streets, and for the fine views of the city it affords.

Henric van Veldekeplein (next to the Vrijthof). ✆ 043/325-2121. Church free admission; Tower 1.25€ ($1.25) adults, free for children under 13. Easter to mid-Oct Mon–Sat 11am–4pm.

Sint-Servaasbasiliek (Basilica of St. Servatius) ✿ The oldest parts of this majestic medieval cruciform church with its rich, glittering interior date from the year 1000. St. Servatius, Maastricht's first bishop, appointed around 380, is buried in the crypt. Over the centuries, worshipers have honored the saint with gifts, so the Treasury has a collection of incredible richness and beauty, including two superb 12th-century reliquaries fashioned by Maastricht goldsmiths. The basilica's interior is largely Romanesque, and restorations have given it a cool, restrained atmosphere, emphasizing the simple arches and vaults. A statue of Emperor Charlemagne stands in the church. The southern tower of the west wall holds *Grameer* (Grandmother), the largest bell in Holland and a beloved symbol of the city. In the summer, a daily concert is performed on the carillon from 8:30 to 9:30pm. The basilica was enlarged in the 14th and 15th centuries, when the south portal and the entrance to the cloister at Keizer Karelplein were added. These are adorned with statues and intricate stone carvings.

Keizer Karelplein (next to Vrijthof). ℂ 043/325-2121. Admission 2.50€ ($3.15) adults, 2€ ($2.50) seniors, 1€ ($1.25) children under 13. Treasury and basilica: Sept–June Mon–Sat 10am–5pm, Sun 1–5pm; July–Aug Mon–Sat 10am–6pm, Sun 1–5pm.

A NEARBY MILITARY CEMETERY
Margraten U.S. Military Cemetery   This cemetery is the final resting place for many American troops who died in Holland in World War II and whose remains were not repatriated. It's revered by the Dutch, who tend the graves and often leave wreaths and flowers behind as symbols of gratitude for the sacrifices that liberated them from Nazi oppressors.

5km (3 miles) east of Maastricht on N278. ℂ 043/458-1208. www.abmc.gov. Free admission. Daily 9am–5pm. Closed Jan 1, Dec 25.

ORGANIZED TOURS
One of the most pleasant ways to view Maastricht and the riverbanks upstream and down is to take a cruise provided by **Rederij Stiphout,** Maaspromenade 27 (ℂ **043/ 351-5300;** www.stiphout.nl). April to October, generally daily from noon to 4pm on the hour (some days start and/or finish later), and in November and December on Saturday and Sunday at 2 and 4pm, a riverboat leaves the landing stage on Maasboulevard at the Sint-Servaas bridge for a 50-minute cruise past Sint-Pietersberg (you can leave the boat, tour the caves, and catch the next boat to continue the cruise) and on to the sluices at the Belgian border. The fare without the caves tour is 6€ ($7.50) for adults, 3.75€ ($4.70) for children ages 4 to 12, and free for children under 4. In addition, there are brunch trips, day trips to Liège, and a romantic Candlelight Cruise that includes dancing and dinner; call for schedules and fares. *Note:* Reservations are required for all but the basic cruise.

Rederij Stiphout also organizes landlubber tours by **double-decker bus,** departing from the Vrijthof July to September on Tuesday, Wednesday, Friday, and Saturday.

At the VVV tourist office, you can pick up its **City Walk** and **Fortifications Walk** self-guided tour brochures. From March to November, the VVV conducts **guided walking tours** that depart from the VVV office and cost 3€ ($3.75) for adults, 2€ ($2.50) for children under 13. These include walks through the old city and among the fortifications.

WHERE TO STAY
EXPENSIVE
Hotel Derlon ✪   This jewel of a four-star hotel sits on one of the loveliest of the city's squares. In the summer, a sidewalk cafe opens under the trees. The hotel is constructed over the city's ancient Roman forum, and you can view excavated foundations

Maastricht Carnival Capers

The city seems to have gone mad. A tumult of garishly clad people with painted faces dance and sing through the elegant Vrijthof. Crowds flow and sway through the maze of narrow cobblestone alleyways beyond. Music from a hundred bands merges into a discordant medley of tunes and tempos, and blares out into the chill February air. The city's 500 bars and cafes, popular enough in ordinary times, burst their seams and spill revelers onto the streets, in a display of fervid celebration that contradicts the sober-sided character generally attributed to the Dutch.

Welcome to Maastricht Carnival, an event that dates back to the 15th century. On the Saturday before Ash Wednesday, the mayor of Maastricht hands over the keys of the city to Prince Carnival, who will reign over it and turn it completely upside-down over the next few days. The populace dress up and bring out colorful floats for the parades that take place each day. When the sun goes down, everyone disappears into the cafes and restaurants, continuing the party with wining and dining.

and objects in its cellar museum. The guest rooms are bright and airy, and nicely blend classic and modern decor. There's a brasserie on the premises.

Onze-Lieve-Vrouweplein 6, 6211 HD Maastricht. © **043/321-6770.** Fax 043/325-1933. www.derlon.nl. 42 units. 175€ ($219) double; from 430€ ($538) suite. AE, DC, MC, V. Limited paid parking. **Amenities:** Restaurant (brasserie); conference facilities; secretarial services; 24-hr. room service; babysitting; laundry service; dry cleaning; newspaper delivery; express checkout. *In room:* A/C, TV, minibar.

MODERATE

Grand Hotel de l'Empereur   This lovely old turreted hotel has comfortable, attractive guest rooms, and apartments that can sleep up to four people. Some rooms have trouser presses. A cozy lounge bar draws a local clientele, and there's a fine brasserie.

Stationsstraat 2 (across from the rail station), 6221 BP Maastricht. © **043/321-3838.** Fax 043/321-6819. www. hotel-empereur.nl. 80 units. 146€–164€ ($183–$205) double; 236€ ($295) suite. AE, DC, MC, V. Limited paid parking. **Amenities:** Restaurant (brasserie); bar; indoor swimming pool; sauna; solarium; whirlpool. *In room:* A/C, TV, minibar, hair dryer.

Hotel Beaumont ⚜   Halfway between the rail station and the river, this well-established hotel is just a short walk from the center city. The decor is warmly classical, and the guest rooms are comfortable and attractive. A 1999 extension added 40 rooms and a fitness room. The cozy but stylish in-house **Restaurant Alsacien** serves moderately priced meals with Alsatian specialties and wines.

Wijcker Brugstraat 2 (between the rail station and St. Servaas Bridge), 6221 EC Maastricht. © **043/325-4433.** Fax 043/325-3655. www.beaumont.nl. 117 units. 110€–160€ ($138–$200) double. AE, DC, MC, V. Limited paid parking. *In room:* TV.

Hotel Du Casque ⚜⚜   There's been an inn at this location since the 15th century. The present family-run hotel carries on the proud tradition, with modern facilities, comfortable rooms, and good old-fashioned friendliness. It faces the lively Vrijthof square; those rooms overlooking the Vrijthof have the finest view in town. If you're of a carnivorous nature, Gaucho's Grill steakhouse out front should please you.

Helmstraat 14 (at Vrijthof), 6211 TA Maastricht. © 043/321-4343. Fax 043/325-5155. www.hotelducasque.nl. 41 units. 124€–144€ ($155–$180) double. Rates include buffet breakfast. AE, DC, MC, V. Limited paid parking. *In room:* TV, minibar.

INEXPENSIVE

Botel Maastricht   Leggy guests aboard this converted river cruiser will appreciate Abraham Lincoln's rueful remark, after spending a night in a cramped U.S. Navy ship's bunk, that "You can't put a long blade into a short scabbard." The Botel's sparely furnished cabins have a compact form factor, but so do its rates, and the shipboard ambience and a nautically themed bar prove attractive to youthful travelers. If you can, get a cabin on the riverside, and then make due allowance for the fact that the Maas isn't the Seine—though, since we're reminiscing about U.S. presidents, the boat does have a view of the John F. Kennedy bridge.

Maasboulevard 95 (on the Maas, at Stadspark), 6211 JW Maastricht. © 043/321-9023. Fax 043/325-7998. www. botelmaastricht.nl. 28 units, 20 with bathroom. 42€ ($53) double without bathroom; 46€ ($58) double with bathroom. Rates include continental breakfast. No credit cards. Limited parking on nearby streets. *In room:* TV.

WHERE TO DINE

Maastricht is filled with good places to eat. Menus tend to be broadminded, drawing as they do on the culinary traditions of at least three nations—and that's just those that serve "local" cuisine. The VVV office provides the *Maastricht Culinair* brochure, for a taste of the best in town.

EXPENSIVE

Toine Hermsen ✿ REGIONAL/FRENCH   One of the city's top restaurants is the proud possessor of a Michelin star. You can expect good portions of impeccable food and superb but relaxed service. The chef cooks up classics of French cuisine and exploits regional seasonal ingredients such as Limburg's famous asparagus and chicory.

Sint Bernardusstraat 2–4 (corner of Onze-Lieve-Vrouweplein). © 043/325-8400. Reservations required. Fixed-price menus 25€–65€ ($31–$81). AE, DC, MC, V. Tues–Fri noon–2pm and 6–11pm; Sat 6–11pm.

MODERATE

India House TANDOORI INDIAN   For a change of pace from the city's general focus on regional and French cuisine, try this excellent Indian offering. It easily lives up to the local standard of elegance, in a tastefully reworked town house just off the main square. The line of *balti* menu dishes is superb, and these are backed up by *tandoori* and curry items. Fish and prawn dishes are at the high end of the price range, but opting for vegetarian takes you into "inexpensive" territory.

Bredestraat 45 (off Vrijthof). © 043/325-8186. www.theindiahouse.info. Main courses 13€–24€ ($16–$29); fixed-price menu 20€–30€ ($38). AE, DC, MC, V. Wed–Mon 5–11pm.

ⓘ *Tips* Eating the Proof

Pampering its collective stomach is a way of life in Maastricht. A culinary fair, the **Preuvenemint,** showcases this love affair with food annually during the last weekend of August (Fri–Mon). The Vrijthof is filled with stalls set up by top city restaurants, and visitors pile in. It's accompanied by a live-music program. The fair usually takes place during the last weekend in August.

't Plenkske ✸ REGIONAL/FRENCH   This fine restaurant, with its light, airy decor and outdoor patio overlooking the Thermen (site of the city's ancient Roman baths), is a great local favorite. Regional specialties from both Maastricht and Liège are prominent on the menu, with a number of French classics thrown in for good measure. Menu dishes include duck breast with lime sauce, and Limburg lamb with thyme and honey, garnished with garlic marmalade.

Plankstraat 6 (Stokstraat Quarter). ✆ 043/321-8456. www.hetplenkske.nl. Main courses 15€–24€ ($18–$29); fixed-price menu 20€–34€ ($25–$43). AE, DC, MC, V. Mon–Sat noon–2:30pm and 6–10:30pm.

INEXPENSIVE

In de Moriaan DUTCH/FRENCH   The Netherlands's smallest cafe (or so it claims), in a building dating from 1540, was the country's Wine Café of the Year 1997 and hasn't deteriorated one whit since that *annus mirabilis*. You can settle down in the cozy nook inside or, in fine weather, on an outside terrace on Op de Thermen, delineated by hedges and shaded by umbrellas. The menu is on the minimalist side, but the few items, such as bouillabaisse with big chunks of tuna and cod, and salade niçoise (for two) are excellent and the servings big.

Stokstraat 12. ✆ 043/321-1177. Main courses 8.50€–14€ ($11–$17). No credit cards. Tues–Sat 6–10pm.

Sagittarius Seafood & Grillades SEAFOOD   At this breezy restaurant in a long, glass-lit room, the chef prepares variations of local and French fish dishes and grilled meats in an open kitchen. The menu changes daily to employ the freshest ingredients. The *bouillabaisse et sa rouille,* a Provençal fish stew served with a spicy chile and garlic sauce, is excellent. In the summer months, there's pleasant garden dining.

Bredestraat 7 (off Vrijthof). ✆ 043/321-1492. Main courses 17€–24€ ($21–$30); fixed-price menu 29€ ($36). AE, MC, V. Tues–Sat 6–10pm.

WHERE TO STAY & DINE NEARBY

Château Neercanne ✸ FRENCH   Constructed in 1698, this gracious château (restaurant only) stands on a hill above the Jeker River. Its wide stone terrace, where you can dine or have drinks in fine weather, affords views of the scenic Jeker Valley. Inside, tasteful renovations have created a classic, romantic ambience, with baroque wallpaper, shades of beige and burgundy, and Venetian glass chandeliers. Marlstone caves in the hillside serve as wine cellars. Fresh herbs and vegetables from the château's own gardens and the best of local ingredients assure top quality. Try the signature rack of lamb in truffle gravy, or the cod in a tarragon butter sauce. An unusual dessert is the locally produced Valdieu cheese in a caramel beer sauce.

⌒Tips Southern Taste

Look out for locally produced **asparagus,** dubbed the "white gold of Limburg" (though most folks just call it asparagus), and for *vlaai,* a handcrafted pie into which goes a lip-smacking quantity of fruit. The province's seven breweries— Bavaria, Brand, Gulpen, Ridder, Leeuw, Alfa, and Lindeboom—make **beers** that are popular around the country. Last, but by no means least, is white wine, produced in modest quantities by the Apostelhoeve and Slavante vineyards near Maastricht, in the southernmost sliver of the Netherlands, close by the Belgian border.

Tips **Antique Virtue**

One of the world's premier art and antique shows, the annual **European Fine Art Fair**, is held at the Maastricht Exhibition and Congress Center (MECC); see "Holland Calendar of Events," in chapter 11.

Cannerweg 800, 5km (3 miles) southwest of Maastricht. ℂ **043/325-1359**. Main courses 20€–35€ ($25–$44); fixed-price menus 70€ ($88). AE, DC, MC, V. Tues–Fri and Sun noon–2:15pm; Tues–Sun 6–9:15pm. From N278 southwest, turn left on Bieslanderweg.

Kasteel Wittem ★★ For a taste of southern charm at its most alluring, stop by this romantic 15th-century castle where stately swans adorn the moat. If you're lucky, you'll draw one of the two tower rooms (one has panoramic windows in the bathroom). Castle guests over the centuries have included the Knights of Julemont, the duke of Burgundy, William the Silent, Emperor Charles V, any number of other noblemen, and even humble folk like traveling monks. The guest rooms have a cozy charm, with country-style decor and furnishings, and the hotel offers a variety of gastronomic arrangements. The expensive French restaurant (reservations required), paneled in French oak, has a warm, clubby atmosphere.

Wittemerallee 3, 6286 AA Wittem, 16km (10 miles) east of Maastricht. ℂ **043/450-1208**. Fax 043/450-1260. www.kasteelwittem.nl. 12 units. 170€–195€ ($213–$244) double; 240€ ($300) suite. AE, DC, MC, V. From Maastricht, take N278 east through Gulpen; then exit left to Wittem. **Amenities:** Restaurant (French); bar; lounge. *In room:* TV, minibar.

SHOPPING

One of the specialties of **Olivier Bonbons,** Kesselskade 55 (ℂ **043/321-5526**), is a porcelain reproduction of the city's much-loved *Grameer* bell filled with luscious chocolates. **Maison Florop,** Spilstraat 2 (ℂ **043/321-2155;** www.florop.com), is an excellent delicatessen. For a bakery that prides itself on its Limburg specialty, *vlaai* fruit tart, you need look no farther than **Sjef Duchateau,** Spilstraat 7–9 (ℂ **043/321-3079**).

A general **street market** takes place on Wednesday and Friday from 8am to 1pm at the Markt; a **food market** on Thursday from 2 to 8pm on Stationsstraat; and a **flea market** on Saturday from 10am to 4pm on Stationsstraat.

MAASTRICHT AFTER DARK

During winter months the city hosts performances of opera, classical music, dance, and theater (mostly in Dutch). Check with the VVV, and pick up a copy of *Uit in Maastricht,* for current happenings.

The city's main venue is the **Theater aan het Vrijthof,** Vrijthof 47 (ℂ **043/350-5555**); the box office is open Monday to Saturday from noon to 6pm (or until the evening performance begins), and Sunday for 1 hour before the evening performance begins. Among frequent performers here is the highly rated **Limburg Symphony Orchestra** (ℂ **043/350-7025**). The **Conservatoire,** Bonnefantenstraat 15 (ℂ **043/346-6680**), hosts regular musical performances by students from the Maastricht Conservatorium.

Maastricht is no place for a teetotaler. Much of the after-dark action takes place in the more than 500 bars and cafes around town. One of the best of these is **In den Ouden Vogelstruys** ★, Vrijthof 15 (ℂ **043/321-4888**). The traditional bar's rustic interior and faithful local clientele make it a great place to stop for a drink inside or, in fine weather, on a sidewalk terrace. A light-snacks menu is written in local dialect, so look out for items like *Mestreechter pâté* and *Ardenner sjink* (ham). Ask about the cannonball in its wall that lodged there in 1653.

NORTH ALONG THE MAAS

The Maas slides into the North Sea at Rotterdam, but above all it's the river of Limburg—a silver thread that runs the length of the province, an artery of commerce, and a glistening arena for watersports. The river has its share of day-trippers on tour boats departing from Maastricht. There are marinas filled to the gunwales with leisure boats, stretches for water-skiers and jet-skiers, and fishermen casting such quantities of hooks it seems miraculous if any fish can run the gauntlet. You can hop back and forth cheaply on an armada of little car ferries that link the opposite banks along most of the river's length. North of Maastricht, the stream has been diverted into worked-out gravel quarries, creating the Maasplassen miniature lakes.

Northern Limburg shelters vacation parks and villages in a landscape of wooded hills and broad heaths. At its hourglass waist, it almost feels like you should breathe in to squeeze through the narrow gap between Belgium and Germany.

THORN ⊛
48km (33 miles) N of Maastricht; 42km (29 miles) SE of Eindhoven

Early morning mist from the Maas sifting through cobblestone streets adds a ghostly air to the village's whitewashed buildings, which seem to float free from their foundations. Thorn (pronounced *torn*), dubbed the "White Village," looks almost too good to be true, as if it has been specially treated to preserve the graces of a bygone age. For centuries, the village was ruled by women, abbesses of a cloister founded in 992. The nobility of the Holy Roman Empire sent their daughters here to be educated in the ways of a Christian life.

Whether they succeeded or not is uncertain—there were back doors to each of the cottages where the girls lived—but Thorn itself has brought its own uplifting presence safely down the centuries. The old center seems like a page torn straight out of a history book, with its white walls, cobblestone courtyards, and wall-mounted lamps. It's reason enough to be diverted off the highway before the day gets fairly started, and stroll through the streets, sniffing the wood-smoke-scented air, freshly baked bread, and a timeless atmosphere that will struggle later to cope with tour-bus crowds.

The nearest rail station to Thorn is Weert (on the Amsterdam-Maastricht line), from where buses connect to Thorn. By car, leave A2/E25 southeast of Weert, and drive southwest. Visitor information is available from **VVV Thorn,** Wijngaard 14 (© **0475/562-761**).

Where to Stay & Dine

Hostellerie La Ville Blanche   In the village center, this small hotel offers nicely done-up guest rooms. Amenities include the Cellar Bar and **La Ville Blanche** restaurant, which serves excellent food.

Hoogstraat 2, 6017 AR Thorn. © 0475/562-341. Fax 0475/562-828. www.villeblanche.nl. 23 units. 105€ ($131) double. Rates include continental breakfast. AE, DC, MC, V. **Amenities:** Restaurant (Continental); lounge; bar. *In room:* TV, minibar.

8 Valkenburg ✪

13km (9 miles) E of Maastricht

Southern Limburg occupies the highest ground in the Netherlands. Nestled among gently sloping hills where lush forests alternate with pastures unfolding toward the Geul River, Valkenburg is best known for its spa, casino, and a ruined fortress up a steep hill that still seems to guard this bustling small town. Surrounded by parks and farms constructed in Limburg's characteristic half-timbered style, this is where the action is in summertime. Folks generally come to Limburg to unwind, but the pace is faster in Valkenburg. Even the Geul races through town, as though it's just gotten away with the casino takings. Out of season, Valkenburg is more like a ghost town of last summer's dreams.

GETTING THERE   From Maastricht, there's hourly **train** service, and two **buses** an hour from outside Maastricht rail station. By **car,** take A79 northeast.

VISITOR INFORMATION   VVV **Valkenburg** is at Theodoor Dorrenplein 5, 6301 Av. Valkenburg (✆ **0900/609-9798;** fax 043/609-8608; www.vvvzuidlimburg. nl). The office is open Monday to Friday from 9am to 5pm, and Saturday from 9am to 1pm.

WHAT TO SEE & DO

Some of Valkenburg's most intriguing sights are hidden. The rocks beneath Valkenburg are like Swiss cheese—for centuries (beginning with the Romans), people have excavated the soft marlstone for use as building material. Nowadays six caves are open to the public.

Gemeentegrot (Cauberg Cavern)   You can visit this cave on foot or aboard a little train. The interesting formations within include a subterranean lake that has formed over the centuries. A million years from now you might see some stalactites and stalagmites.

Cauberg 4 (the main hill in town). ✆ 043/601-2271. www.gemeentegrot.nl. Admission 4.50€ ($5.65) adults, 4€ ($5) seniors, 3.50€ children 4–11, free for children under 4. Guided tours daily every hour Apr–Oct 10:30am–4pm; July–Aug 9:30am–5pm; Nov–Mar Mon–Fri at 2pm, Sat–Sun 10:30am–4pm.

Holland Casino Valkenburg   This modern, hilltop casino offers French and American roulette, blackjack, and mini–punto banco. A separate area has slot machines of all shapes and sizes, plus two restaurants, two bars, and reception rooms. For an entire evening's entertainment, you can sit down to a dinner show. Note that a dress code is observed (jacket and tie, or turtleneck, for men; dress or dressy pantsuit for the ladies), and you need your passport to show you're over 18 years of age.

Kuurpark Cauberg 28 (across from Thermae 2000). ✆ 043/609-9600. www.hollandcasino.com. Admission 4€ ($5). Daily 1:30pm–3am.

Sprookjesbos (Fairy Tale Forest) ✪ *Kids*   Aimed mostly at younger kids, ages around 2 to 6 or 7, this sweet little theme park features children's fairy-tale favorites like Snow White and the Seven Dwarfs, Cinderella, Little Red Riding Hood, and Hansel and Gretel. Most of the "action" takes place in tiny houses and miniature castles dotted at intervals along a winding pathway through a "magical forest"; you stop to look in the doors and windows, behind which mechanical puppets act out scenes from fairy tales. There are a few low-intensity rides, including an artificial river with falls, and a puppet Western show. Some attractions are in need of refurbishment, and older kids will find the park's excitements limited. You need 2 hours to get around, longer if you plan on having a picnic or snack.

Sibbergrubbe 2A (off Gulpen Rd.). © **043/601-2985**. www.sprookjesbos.nl. Admission 7.95€ ($9.95) for all visitors. Mid-Apr to 1st week of Sept Mon–Sat 10am–5pm, Sun and holidays 10am–6pm; weekends in Sept after 1st week 10am–5pm. From Valkenburg center, take Gulpen Rd. to southern suburbs, where park is signposted to the right. Parking lot is on Gulpen Rd., about 180m (590 ft.) from park entrance.

Thermae 2000   The waters that simmer below Valkenburg's hills are the source of this futuristic health spa where you can relax completely in the soothing thermal baths, have a session in the sauna, and work out in the fitness center. Extra pampering possibilities include a massage and floating in a warm bath in an herbal bodywrap. There's an excellent hotel here (see below).

Kuurpark Cauberg 27. © **043/609-2000**. www.thermae2000.nl. Admission 28€ ($34) for a day (admission includes all services except massages, floats, and beautician and therapeutic treatments). Daily 9am–11pm.

WHERE TO STAY & DINE

Thermaetel ⭐   This is the place to overnight in Valkenburg. After checking in, you can put on your bathrobe and walk to the pool. The price of a room includes admission to the health spa for the length of your stay, including the day you arrive and the day you leave. The water in your hotel room comes from the spa's spring. Each room has a hillside garden terrace. The restaurant offers a tasty array of health-oriented dishes.

Kuurpark, Cauberg 27, 6300 AD Valkenburg. © **043/601-9445**. Fax 043/601-4777. www.thermae2000.nl. 69 units. 195€ ($244) double; 250€ ($313) suite. AE, DC, MC, V. **Amenities:** Restaurant (Dutch/French); bar; lounge; heated indoor pool; health club and spa; massage; babysitting. *In room:* TV, minibar.

NEARBY PLACES OF INTEREST

You can get legally high in Limburg. At the **Drielandenpunt (Three-Country Point),** near Vaals, in the province's southeast corner, the Netherlands, Belgium, and Germany share a common backyard in the "Land Without Frontiers." The elevation is the highest in Holland, a full 322m (1,056 ft.) above sea level—a veritable mountain!—and affords an excellent opportunity to look across miles of countryside in three different countries. From the timber King Baudouin Tower, surrounded by extensive forest, the German city of Aachen merges with the haze in one direction. In another, the green waves of Belgium's Ardennes Hills wash over the horizon. The "Dutch Alps" are behind you. Vaals is 30km (19 miles) east of Maastricht on N278; the Drielandenpunt is a farther .5km (⅓ mile) south.

Thermenmuseum (Roman Bath Museum) ⭐ *Kids*   Sixteen centuries have passed since anyone had a bath in Heerlen—at the city's Roman bath, that is. Ancient Coriovallum's 2nd-century-A.D. *thermae* are among Holland's most important classical sites. Heerlen, which back then was a major point on Roman roads, has preserved the remains of the sudatorium (sauna), natatio (swimming pool), and gymnasium. Aided by a sound-and-light show depicting "Lucius the Potter" on his first visit to the bath, you can recreate the intricate ritual of a Roman bath, which was such an important part of life in the Empire.

Coriovallumstraat 9, Heerlen; 24km (16 miles) northeast of Maastricht. © **045/560-5100**. www.thermenmuseum. nl. Admission 3.50€ ($4.40) adults, 3€ ($3.75) seniors, 2.50€ ($3.15) children 4–12, free for children under 4. Daily 10am–5pm. Closed Jan 1, Dec 24, 25, and 31. You get to Heerlen by hourly train from Maastricht; by car on A79.

Planning a Trip to Luxembourg

Good news: Traveling around Luxembourg is easy. Outside of Luxembourg City, most visitors are interested in two regions—the Luxembourg Ardennes in the north, and the wine country of the Moselle River valley in the southeast. This chapter provides the nuts-and-bolts information you'll need before setting off for the Grand Duchy.

For information that covers the Benelux countries in general, see chapter 2.

1 Visitor Information

VISITOR INFORMATION

International addresses for the Luxembourg National Tourist Office are given in "Visitor Information," in chapter 2. In Luxembourg, contact the **Luxembourg National Tourist Office,** Gare Centrale, BP 1001, 1010 Luxembourg-Ville (© **42-82-82-1;** fax 42-82-82-38; www.ont.lu).

There are local tourist offices in Luxembourg City and in towns and villages around the Grand Duchy. You'll find the addresses and other contact information for these offices in the "Visitor Information" sections in chapter 19.

2 When to Go

"In-season" in Luxembourg, as in the rest of the Benelux countries, means from about mid-April to mid-October. The peak of the tourist season is in July and August, when the weather is at its finest. The weather is never really extreme at any time of year, and if you favor shoulder- or off-season travel, you'll find the Grand Duchy every bit as attractive during those months. Not only are hotels and restaurants cheaper, less crowded, and more relaxed during this time, but some very appealing events are going on. Theater is most active during winter months in Luxembourg City.

CLIMATE

Luxembourg has a moderate climate, with less annual rainfall than either Belgium or the Netherlands, since North Sea winds have usually wept their tears before

they get this far inland. The vineyard-rich Moselle Valley in the southeast has the lowest rainfall, with between 30 and 41 centimeters (12–16 in.), and the western districts have the highest, with around 100 centimeters (40 in.). July and August temperatures in Luxembourg City average 63°F (17°C). Winter temperatures average 32°F (0°C). Snowfalls, which open up the cross-country and downhill skiing pistes in the Ardennes, are common but not guaranteed.

HOLIDAYS

National holidays in Luxembourg are New Year's Day (Jan 1), Shrove Monday (the Mon before Ash Wednesday), Easter Monday, Labor Day (May 1), Ascension Day (40 days after Easter), Pentecost Monday (Mon following the seventh Sun after Easter), Luxembourg National Holiday

The Euro

Luxembourg's currency is the euro (see "Currency," in chapter 2).

and the grand duke's official birthday (June 23), Assumption (Aug 15), All Saints' Day (Nov 1), and Christmas (Dec 25 and 26).

LUXEMBOURG CALENDAR OF EVENTS

March

Carnival Parade, Pétange. Mid-Lent Carnival. Contact **Pétange Tourist Office** (© **50-12-511**). Refreshment Sunday (3 weeks before Easter).

April

L'Emais'chen Folk Festival, Luxembourg City. Young lovers buy pottery items for each other. Contact **Luxembourg City Tourist Office** (© **22-28-09;** www.lcto.lu). Easter Monday.

Wine Fair, Grevenmacher. Contact **Grevenmacher Tourist Office** (© **75-82-75**). Thursday after Easter.

Musical Spring. Festival of music, including classical, jazz, and folk, at venues around Luxembourg City. Contact **Luxembourg City Tourist Office** (© . **22-28-09;** www.lcto.lu). April and May.

May

International Classical Music Festival, Echternach. National and visiting orchestras play in the Basilica and the Church of Saints Peter and Paul. Contact **Echternach Tourist Office** (© **72-02-30**). Mid-May to end of July.

Octave of Our Lady of Luxembourg, Luxembourg City and Diekirch. Grand religious processions in honor of the Virgin Mary. Contact **Luxembourg City Tourist Office** (© **22-28-09;** www.lcto.lu) and **Diekirch**

Tourist Office (© **80-30-23**). Fifth Sunday after Easter.

Féerie du Genêt Flower Parade, Wiltz. The festival includes a street market. Contact **Wiltz Tourist Office** (© **95-74-44**). Monday after Pentecost.

Dancing Procession, Echternach. Colorful and internationally renowned 1,200-year-old folk-dancing procession in honor of St. Willibrord. Contact **Echternach Tourist Office** (© **72-02-30**). Tuesday after Pentecost, beginning at 9am.

June

International Open-Air Theater Festival, Wiltz. Performances every Friday, Saturday, and Sunday. Incorporates a music program at the Château de Wiltz. Contact **Wiltz Tourist Office** (© **95-74-44**). June to July.

Luxembourg National Day, Luxembourg City. Gala celebration featuring festival activities, the grand duke reviewing his guards with all the pomp and ritual of centuries past, and fireworks. Contact **Luxembourg City Tourist Office** (© **22-28-09;** www.lcto.lu). June 23.

Wine Festival, Remich. Open-air celebrations and wine tasting. Contact **Remich Tourist Office** (© **23-69-84-88**). End of June to August.

July

Open-Air Concerts. Evening concerts on the place d'Armes, Luxembourg City. Contact **Luxembourg City Tourist Office** (© **22-28-09;** www.lcto.lu). Throughout July.

Remembrance Day, Ettelbruck. Celebration in honor of U.S. Gen. George

Luxembourg

S. Patton, whose troops liberated Luxembourg in World War II. Contact **Musée Patton,** rue du Dr. Klein 5 (℃ 81-03-22). Second weekend of July.

Old Diekirch Festival, Diekirch. Folklore events, music, and street market. Contact **Diekirch Tourist Office** (℃ 80-30-23). Second weekend of July.

Beer Festival, Diekirch. A popular event in this beer-brewing town. Contact **Diekirch Tourist Office** (℃ 80-30-23). Third Sunday in July.

August

Pottery Festival, Nospelt. The center of Luxembourg's pottery industry opens its workshops and hosts a street market for pottery and handicrafts. Contact **Musée de la Potterie** (℃ 30-01-99). First weekend in August.

Agricultural Fair, Ettelbruck. Contact **Ettelbruck Tourist Office** (℃ 81-20-68). First weekend in August.

Procession of the Holy Virgin, Girsterklaus. Pilgrimage dating back to 1328. Contact **Echternach Tourist Office** (℃ 72-02-30). Sunday after August 15.

Schobermesse, Luxembourg City. A big amusement fair and street market. Contact **Luxembourg City Tourist Office** (℃ 22-28-09; www.lcto.lu). Two weeks, beginning next-to-last Sunday in August.

September

Wine and Grape Festival, Grevenmacher. A splendid folklore procession celebrates the local grape harvest. Contact **Grevenmacher Tourist Office** (℃ 23-69-66-01). Second weekend in September.

Wine and Grape Festival, Greiveldange. Contact **Caves Coopératives des Vignerons** (℃ 69-83-14). Third weekend in September.

3 Special-Interest Vacations

FISHING

The rivers of the Grand Duchy are an anglers' paradise, but one that's strictly controlled by the authorities. Complex regulations govern fishing in private waters and some rivers. Licenses are issued by the district commissioners in Luxembourg City, Diekirch, and Grevenmacher, and by a few communal administrations, such as those in Ettelbruck, Vianden, and Wiltz. Check with the local tourist information office about the local regulations and licensing before going fishing.

GOLF

The Grand-Ducal Golf Club's course in Luxembourg City is known for its difficult, narrow fairways. Visitors can arrange to play the course by contacting **Golf Club Grand-Ducal,** route de Trèves 1, Senningerberg (℃ 34-00-90-1). The

Hotel Association of Clervaux offers attractive golf vacation packages at country hotels; contact the Clervaux Tourist Office (see "The Luxembourg Ardennes," in chapter 19 for the address).

HIKING

There are marked walking paths throughout the Grand Duchy. During the summer, organized walking tours of 10 to 40km (6–25 miles) are conducted from Luxembourg City. Contact the **Fédération Luxembourgeoise de Marche Populaire,** BP 1157, 1011 Luxembourg-Ville (℃ 021/50-06-77; www.flmp-ivv.lu), for more information.

HORSEBACK RIDING

Riding is a favorite sport in Luxembourg, with stables offering mounts at around 12€ ($15) per hour. For a list of stables and riding schools, contact the **Fédération**

Luxembourgeoise des Sports Equestres, av. de la Gare 14, 1610 Luxembourg-Ville (© **48-49-99;** www.hippoline.lu). The organization puts together horseback tours in Luxembourg City and around the Grand Duchy.

4 Getting Around

BY FOOT

Walking is a great way to travel through this beautiful land. You can do this on 21 separate signposted walking trails around the Grand Duchy. Known as Sentiers Nationaux (National Trails), these range in length from 13km (8 miles) to 84km (52 miles). Plus there's the Eifel-Ardennes Trail that crosses the border into Germany. Bookstores carry maps of these and other walking routes, and local tourist offices have brochures of walking tours in their area. The free Luxembourg Railways *Rail et Randonnée (Train and Tour)* brochure, available from stations, outlines 40 walking routes connecting stations; you can take the train to one station, follow the walking route to another, and return or go on by train from there. The **Luxembourg Youth Hostels Association,** rue du Fort Olisy 2, 2261 Luxembourg-Ville (© **26-27-66-40;** www.youthhostels.lu), issues detailed maps with walking paths marked in red. All youth hostels are on walking paths designated by white triangular signs. In total, these different kinds of trails and footpaths add up to some 5,000km (3,100 miles) of walks and hikes.

BY TRAIN & BUS

The **Chemins de Fer Luxembourgeois** (© **49-90-49-90;** www.cfl.lu) operates frequent trains throughout the Grand Duchy, with connecting bus service to those points the rails don't reach. Travelers over 65 are eligible for a 50% reduction except when traveling to or from a frontier point. In addition, special half-fare weekend and holiday round-trip tickets are offered throughout the system, again except to frontier points. A **1-day** *billet réseau* **(network ticket),** good for unlimited travel by train and bus, costs 5€ ($6.25). For a *carnet* (book) of five 1-day tickets, the cost is 20€ ($25).

BY CAR

Roads in the Grand Duchy are kept in good repair and are well signposted. But beware that some roadways are narrow, with many curves, especially in the Ardennes.

To park in the "blue zones" of Luxembourg City and some other towns, you may need a **parking disc.** These are cardboard or plastic discs with a revolving hour scale. When you park, you set your arrival time by turning the disc to the appropriate hour, displayed in a slot in the card, so that the parking inspectors know when you have overstayed your welcome. The discs are available from stores and banks, often at no charge. In many other places, there are parking meters or parking-ticket dispensers.

RENTALS If you plan to rent a car in the Grand Duchy, you need a driver's license valid in your own country. Car-rental rates begin at around 55€ ($69) a day and 65€ ($81) for a weekend. Leading car-rental firms in Luxembourg City are: **Avis,** place de la Gare 17 (© **48-95-95**) and Luxembourg Airport (© 43-51-71); **Budget,** rue de Longwy 300 (© **44-19-38**) and Luxembourg Airport (© 43-75-75); and **Hertz,** Luxembourg Airport (© **43-46-45**).

GASOLINE Fill up on gas *(benzine)* in Luxembourg! A low rate of tax on gas and diesel means you can save around 25% on gas prices in Luxembourg, compared to the prices in neighboring Germany, Belgium, and France.

DRIVING RULES   Speed limits are 50kmph (31 mph) in built-up areas, 90kmph (56 mph) on rural roads, and 120kmph (74 mph) on expressways. The use of seat belts is compulsory, and horn blowing is permitted only in case of imminent danger.

ROAD MAPS   An excellent road map of the Grand Duchy—which shows camping grounds, swimming pools, and tourist attractions in addition to main roads—is available at no cost from the Luxembourg National Tourist Office in Luxembourg City. Other good road maps include the Ordnance Survey maps (two sheets) and Michelin map no. 214, available from local bookstores and newsstands.

BREAKDOWNS/ASSISTANCE   A 24-hour emergency road service is offered

by the **Automobile Club du Grand Duché de Luxembourg** (✆ **45-00-45-1;** www.acl.lu).

BY BICYCLE

The Luxembourg countryside lends itself to biking. You're free to ramble down any road that strikes your fancy, but you should know that there are also biking trails leading through the most scenic areas. Local tourist offices can provide suggestions for tours on these trails and on less-traveled roadways. In addition, tourist offices in Luxembourg City, Diekirch, Echternach, Vianden, and other towns can arrange **bicycle rentals.** Bikes can be transported by train for a small fee, regardless of distance traveled, but this is subject to space availability (which is usually not a problem).

FAST FACTS: Luxembourg

American Express The nearest office is in Brussels (see "Fast Facts: Brussels," in chapter 5).

Area Codes See "Telephones," below.

Business Hours Banks are open Monday to Friday from 8:30am to noon and 1 to 4:30pm. Stores generally are open Monday to Saturday from 10am to 6pm, and many open on Sunday for shorter hours.

Car Rentals See "Getting Around," above.

Currency See "Money," in chapter 2.

Electricity Luxembourg runs on 220 volts electricity. You may need to take with you a small voltage transformer and a European-style adapter plug (available in drug and appliance stores and by mail order) that plugs into the round-holed European electrical outlet.

Embassies These are all in Luxembourg-Ville. **U.S.:** bd. Emmanuel-Servais 22 (✆ **46-01-23;** www.luxembourg.usembassy.gov). **U.K.:** bd. Joseph II 5 (✆ **22-98-64;** www.britishembassy.gov.uk). **Ireland:** route d'Arlon 28 (✆ **45-06-10**). Australia, Canada, and New Zealand do not have embassies in Luxembourg; the nearest embassies for these three countries are in Brussels (see "Fast Facts: Belgium," in chapter 4).

Emergencies For police assistance, call ✆ **113.** For an ambulance or the fire department, call ✆ **112.**

Holidays See "When to Go," earlier in this chapter.

Mail Postage for a postcard or letter to the U.S., Canada, Australia, New Zealand, and South Africa is 0.80€ ($1); to the U.K. and Ireland 0.75€ (95¢).

Pharmacies A pharmacy is called a *pharmacie* in French. Regular pharmacy hours are Monday to Saturday from 9am to 6pm (some close earlier on Sat). Each pharmacy has a list of after-hours pharmacies posted on its door.

Police For emergency police assistance, call ℂ **113**.

Post Office Most post offices are open Monday to Friday from 9am to 5pm.

Restrooms Restrooms often display an "H" or *Hommes* for men, and an "F" or *Femmes* for women (or a graphic that should leave no doubt either way). Be sure to pay the person who sits at the entrance to a *toilette*. He or she has a saucer where you put your money, usually around 0.40€ (50¢).

Safety You've got about as much chance of being a victim of crime here as you have of eating badly in a Luxembourg restaurant—which is to say, about none at all. But it can't hurt any to wear a money belt and keep an eye on your possessions, just in case.

Telephones The country code for Luxembourg is **352**. The entire country is in the same local dialing area, so no **area codes** are used. For example, if you're calling a Luxembourg City number from outside Luxembourg, you dial the international access code (which is **011** when calling from North America, and **00** from elsewhere in Europe) and then **352**, and then the local number.

When you're calling a Luxembourg number from anywhere in Luxembourg, you need only dial the local number. These numbers can be confusing enough, since you might need to dial a five-, six-, seven-, eight-, or even nine-digit subscriber number.

Almost all pay phones accept phone cards; these cost 5€ ($6.25), 10€ ($13), and 25€ ($31), and are sold at post offices and newsstands. Some phones accept 0.20€, 0.50€, and 1€ coins.

To charge a call to your calling card, phone: **AT&T** (ℂ 800/20-111); **MCI** (ℂ 800/20-112); **Sprint** (ℂ 800/20-115); **Canada Direct** (ℂ 800/20-119); **British Telecom** (ℂ 800/20-044); or **Telecom New Zealand** (ℂ 800/20-064).

Time Zone Luxembourg is on Western European Time (WET), which is Coordinated Universal Time (UTC) or Greenwich Mean Time (GMT) plus 1 hour. Clocks are advanced by 1 hour for Western European Summer Time (WEST) between the last Sunday in March and the last Sunday in October.

Tipping Restaurants and hotels will almost always include a 16% service charge on the bill. If you've had exceptional service, you may want to add a little more; it isn't necessary but it is common to do so.

Water You need have no concerns about Luxembourg's water—it's clear, pure, and safe.

Luxembourg

Two distinct regions comprise the tiny Grand Duchy of Luxembourg, creating a landscape of scenic beauty. The forested **Luxembourg Ardennes,** in the north, are part of a range of hills gouged by narrow rivers like the Our and the Sûre. South of the Ardennes are the rich farmlands of the **Bon Pays (Good Country),** a rolling plateau traversed by narrow valleys, and by Luxembourg's stretch of the Moselle River, with its celebrated riverside vineyards and wineries. Both regions are liberally sprinkled with pretty villages, castles, and vacation retreats.

Luxembourg City, in the center of the Bon Pays, was for centuries a thorn in Europe's side. The "Gibraltar of the North" occupies a natural fortress, and the immensely powerful fortifications constructed around it by a parade of rulers made it a tough proposition to assault. These were dismantled in 1867. Today, parks cover ground once occupied by forts, and the city is an attractive mixture of historical interest and contemporary charm.

1 Luxembourg City ★★

315km (195 miles) SE of Amsterdam; 189km (117 miles) SE of Brussels; 122km (76 miles) SE of Liège

Luxembourg-Ville, the Grand Duchy's diminutive capital, is a marvelously contrasting mix of the old and the new. The old part of town runs along a deep valley beneath brooding casemates that have lent themselves readily to defense in times of war, while the more modern part of town crowns steep cliffs overlooking the old. The city (pop. 120,000) is the headquarters of the European Court of Justice and of the European Investment Bank, and is one of the three seats of the European Parliament (along with Brussels and Strasbourg). Despite the many banks and the Euro-office towers, Luxembourg City has retained plenty of small-scale, provincial ambience.

ESSENTIALS

GETTING THERE   By Plane   For details on air travel to Luxembourg, see chapter 2. **Luxembourg Airport** (© **24-56-50-50;** www.aeroport.public.lu), a proud possessor of two shiny new terminals (2004 and 2007), is at Findel, 5km (3½ miles) northeast of Luxembourg City. Regular flights arrive from all major European capitals. City bus no. 16 to Gare Centrale, a 25-minute ride, costs 1.50€ ($1.90); one to four buses depart every hour. A taxi (© **43-43-43**) to the center city costs around 20€ ($25); add 10% from 10pm to 6am, and 25% to 35% (depending on the time) on Sunday and holidays.

By Train   Luxembourg City has rail connections from Belgium, France, and Germany. **Gare Centrale,** in the southern part of town, has a national tourist information office, currency-exchange office, and luggage-storage facilities inside, and a terminus for city

(Tips) Passport to Luxembourg

If you plan to do a lot of sightseeing and traveling on public transportation, both in Luxembourg City and around the Grand Duchy, a sound investment is the **LuxembourgCard.** This comes with a 32-page booklet listing more than 50 attractions offering cardholders free admission, and others offering discounted admission. In addition, the card lets you ride free on all public transportation buses and trains.

The LuxembourgCard, valid from Easter to October for 1, 2, or 3 days, is available from tourist offices. For a single person, it costs 9€ ($11), 16€ ($20), and 22€ ($28), respectively; a family card for two to five people is 18€ ($23), 32€ ($40), and 44€ ($55), respectively.

bus lines just outside. For train information (and bus service outside Luxembourg City), contact **Chemins de Fer Luxembourgeois** (© **49-90-49-90;** www.cfl.lu).

By Bus **Eurolines** (see "Getting There," in chapter 2) buses arrive in Luxembourg City from London, Brussels, Paris, and other European cities. The main bus station is outside the rail station (see above).

By Car Expressways A1/E44, A4/E25, and A31/E25, and highways N4 and N6 converge on Luxembourg City from Germany, France, and Belgium.

VISITOR INFORMATION The **Luxembourg City Tourist Office,** place Guillaume II 30, 1648 Luxembourg-Ville (© **22-28-09;** fax 46-70-70; www.lcto.lu), is in the center of town. The office is open April to September, Monday to Saturday from 9am to 7pm, Sunday and holidays from 10am to 6pm; October to March, Monday to Saturday from 9am to 6pm, Sunday and holidays from 10am to 6pm. It provides a free, detailed city map that lists the main attractions.

The Luxembourg National Tourist Office operates a **Bureau d'Acceuil (Welcome Desk)** at Gare Centrale (© **42-82-82-20;** fax 42-82-82-38; www.visitluxembourg.lu), open June to September, Monday to Saturday from 9am to 7pm, Sunday from 9am to 12:30pm and 1:45 to 6pm; October to May, daily from 9:15am to 12:30pm and 1:45 to 6pm.

Both the English-language weekly magazine *352 Luxembourg News* and its website **www.352.lu** have a "What's On" section. For information on cultural and tourist events and exhibits around the Grand Duchy, visit **www.agendalux.lu.**

CITY LAYOUT The heart of Luxembourg City revolves around two main squares in the Old Town. The small **place d'Armes** was once a parade ground, and this is where you find sidewalk cafes and band concerts during summer months. The larger **place Guillaume II** is the setting for the Town Hall, the city tourist office, and for statues of William II and Luxembourg poet Michel Rodange; it hosts morning markets on Wednesday and Saturday during the summer.

Main arteries bordering the Old Town are **boulevard Grande-Duchesse Charlotte** to the north, and **boulevard Franklin D. Roosevelt** to the south. The principal shopping street is **Grand Rue.** A pleasant walkway, the **promenade de la Corniche,** connects the Bock Casemates to the Citadelle du St-Esprit fortifications. There are steps, in addition to an elevator, from **place St-Esprit** down to the **Grund** neighborhood in the valley below.

Luxembourg City

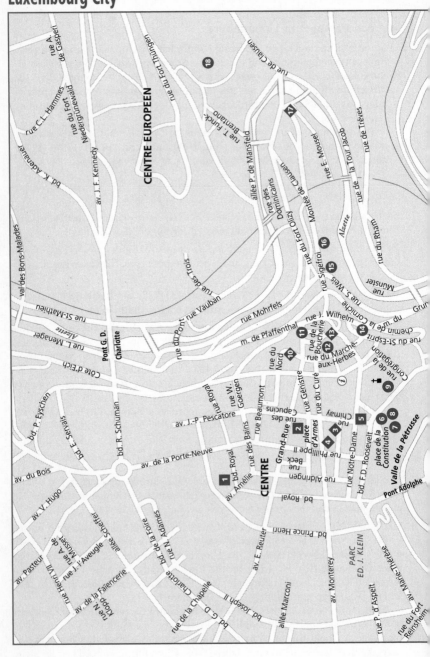

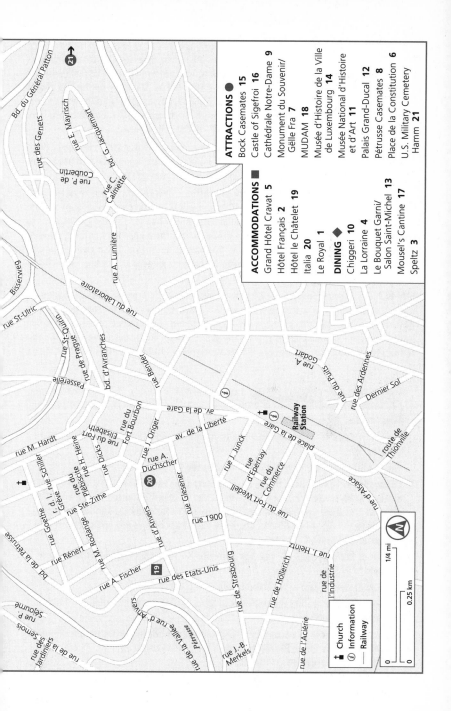

ATTRACTIONS
Bock Casemates **15**
Castle of Sigefroi **16**
Cathédrale Notre-Dame **9**
Monument du Souvenir/
  Gëlle Fra **7**
MUDAM **18**
Musée d'Histoire de la Ville
  de Luxembourg **14**
Musée National d'Histoire
  et d'Art **11**
Palais Grand-Ducal **12**
Pétrusse Casemates **8**
Place de la Constitution **6**
U.S. Military Cemetery
  Hamm **21**

ACCOMMODATIONS
Grand Hôtel Cravat **5**
Hôtel Français **2**
Hôtel le Châtelet **19**
Italia **20**
Le Royal **1**

DINING
Chiggeri **10**
La Lorraine **4**
Le Bouquet Garni/
  Salon Saint-Michel **13**
Mousel's Cantine **17**
Speltz **3**

Church
Information
Railway

1/4 mi
0.25 km

457

GETTING AROUND

BY BUS Because of the city's small size, you may have little need to use the bus network. Service is extensive and efficient but infrequent on some lines. The fare (valid for 1 hr.) is 1.50€ ($1.90); a 10-ticket pack costs 10€ ($13). A money-saving **day ticket** for 5€ ($6.25), and a 5-day pack for 20€ ($25), available from rail stations and the airport, can be used on buses and trains throughout the Grand Duchy. Luxembourg City bus information is available from **ADL** (✆ **47-96-29-75;** www.autobus.lu).

BY TAXI Taxis charge 2.05 € ($2.55) per kilometer, with a 10% surcharge from 10pm to 6am, and 25% on Sunday and holidays. Taxi service is available from **Benelux Taxis** (✆ **800/2-51-51** or 40-38-40; www.beneluxtaxi.lu).

BY CAR Driving in Luxembourg City isn't difficult, but most in-town attractions are within easy walking distance. My advice? Park your car and save it for day trips outside the city. For information on car rental and driving rules, see "Getting Around," in chapter 18. Street parking can present a problem, but there are many parking garages. The city map supplied by the tourist office (see above) has parking areas clearly marked. The three most centrally located underground parking garages are off boulevard Royal near the post office, off rue Notre-Dame, and at place du Théâtre.

ON FOOT Luxembourg City is made for walking—that's really the only way to do it justice. Most major attractions are within .5km (⅓ mile) of the center of town. Beyond that, though, the hilly nature of the city and the distance to other points of interest may start to take a toll. The many green spaces and parks invite either a soul-refreshing sit-down or a leisurely stroll to slow your sightseeing pace.

FAST FACTS: Luxembourg City

Airport See "Essentials," above.

American Express The nearest office is in Brussels (see "Fast Facts: Brussels," in chapter 5).

Car Rentals See "Getting Around," in chapter 18.

Currency Exchange One thing Luxembourg City isn't short of is banks, and around town there are branches with ATMs. To change money or use an ATM close to the Gare Centrale rail station, go to **Kredietbank Luxembourg,** place de la Gare 5–7 (✆ **47-97-60-01**). Currency-exchange offices are open daily at the airport and at Gare Centrale.

Doctor & Dentist Call ✆ **112** for referrals to English-speaking doctors and dentists.

Embassies See "Fast Facts: Luxembourg," in chapter 18.

Emergencies For police assistance, call ✆ **113.** For an ambulance or the fire department, call ✆ **112.**

Hospitals The most important city hospital is the modern **Centre Hospitalier de Luxembourg,** rue Emile Barblé 4 (✆ **44-11-11;** www.chl.lu; bus no. 7), off route d'Arlon in the northwest of the city.

Police In an emergency, call ✆ **113.** For routine matters, go to central police headquarters, rue Glesener 60 (✆ **40-94-04-400;** www.police.public.lu).

Post Office The main post office, rue Aldringen 25 (℡ **47-65-1;** www.ept.lu), is open Monday to Friday from 7am to 7pm, and Saturday from 7am to 5pm.

Safety Luxembourg City is a safe, low-crime city. There are no dangerous or unsafe areas. That's not to say being a victim of crime is impossible, just that it's extremely unlikely.

Taxis See "Getting Around," above.

Telephone See "Fast Facts: Luxembourg," in chapter 18.

Transit Info Public transportation information for Luxembourg City is available from **ADL** (℡ **47-98-29-57;** www.autobus.lu); and **Chemins de Fer Luxembour- geois** (℡ **49-90-49-90;** www.cfl.lu) for train and bus service around the Grand Duchy.

WHAT TO SEE & DO

Luxembourg City is a delight for the sightseer. Most attractions are in a compact area, and inexpensive coach tours can take you to places of interest farther afield. One of your greatest pleasures in Luxembourg may come on a balmy summer evening at a sidewalk cafe on tree-shaded **place d'Armes,** as a band plays on the square in front of you.

THE FORTIFICATIONS ★★

Luxembourg City grew up around Count Sigefroi's 10th-century castle at Montée de Clausen on the Bock promontory. The count's choice of location was astute—the 48m (156-ft.) cliffs overlooking the Alzette and Pétrusse river valleys were persuasive obstacles to invading forces. In time, there came to be three rings of battlements around the city, including the cliff bastions, 15 forts surrounding the bastions, and an exterior wall interspersed with nine more forts, three of them cut right into the rock.

Even more impressive than these aboveground fortifications were the 25km (16 miles) of underground tunnels that sheltered troops by the thousands, and their equipment, horses, workshops, artillery, arms, kitchens, bakeries, and slaughterhouses. Legend says that within these tremendous rocky walls of the fortress sits a beautiful maiden named Mélusine, whose knitting needles control the fate of Luxembourg (see "The Mysterious Maiden Mélusine," in appendix C).

Over the centuries, Burgundian, French, Spanish, Austrian, and German forces took control of these strategic fortifications, each in turn adding to the already formi- dable defenses. Europe's fears of the city's strength stood in the way of Luxembourg's very freedom and independence. Finally, in 1867, the Treaty of London ordered the dismantling of all these battlements, and what you see today represents only about 10% of the original works.

Fun Fact **Following the Money**

The Grand Duchy's neighbors take a dim view of the cash river their own citi- zens pour into the tax-evading vaults of Luxembourg City banks. There, pro- tected by bank secrecy laws, it rests undisturbed. "Who, us?" in a tone of injured innocence, is a rough paraphrase of Luxembourg's response.

You can visit the impressive **casemates** (𝄐 **22-28-09**)—granted World Heritage status in 1995—by entering from two points: The entrance on Montée de Clausen leads to the Bock Casemates, and the entrance on place de la Constitution leads to the Pétrusse Casemates. In the Bock Casemates, the **Crypte Archéologique (Archaeological Crypt)** features an audiovisual presentation that runs through the highlights of the Luxembourg fortress's history. The Bock Casemates are open March to October, daily from 10am to 5pm; the Pétrusse Casemates are open during school vacations daily from 11am to 4pm. Separate admission to both is 1.75€ ($2.20) for adults, and 1€ ($1.25) for children.

OTHER TOP SIGHTS

Cathédrale de Notre-Dame (Notre-Dame Cathedral) 𝄐𝄐 This magnificent

Gothic structure was constructed between 1613 and 1621. It holds the royal family vault and the huge sarcophagus of Count of Luxembourg John I of Bohemia ("John the Blind"; 1296–1346), in addition to a remarkable treasury (which can only be viewed on request, so ask the sacristan, whose office is on the right as you enter). The cathedral is the scene of the **Octave of Our Lady of Luxembourg,** an annual ceremony on the fifth Sunday following Easter, when thousands of pilgrims arrive to pray for protection to the miraculous statue of the Holy Virgin. They then form a procession to carry the statue from the cathedral through the streets to an altar covered with flowers on avenue de la Porte Neuve, north of place d'Armes.

Bd. Franklin D. Roosevelt (entrance on rue Notre-Dame). Free admission. Daily 10am–noon and 2–5:30pm (closed to non-worshipers during services).

Musée National d'Histoire et d'Art (National Museum of History and Art) 𝄐𝄐

In the oldest part of the city, this museum holds fascinating archaeological, geological, and historical exhibits, and decorative and popular art. The highlight of the collections is the Bentinek-Thyssen Collection of works of art by 15th- to 18th-century Low Countries artists, including Rubens, van Dyck, Brueghel, and Rembrandt.

Marché-aux-Poissons. 𝄐 **47-93-30-1**. www.mnha.lu. Admission 5€ ($6.25) adults, free for children under 18. Tues–Sun 2–4:45pm.

Palais Grand-Ducal (Palace of the Grand Dukes) 𝄐 This magnificent palace

evokes all the opulence of the Grand Duchy's medieval splendor. The oldest part of this interesting and recently renovated building dates back to 1572 (its "new" right wing dates from 1741). Next door is the Chamber of Deputies (Luxembourg's Parliament).

Rue du Marché-aux-Herbes 17. 𝄐 **47-96-27-09**. Admission only for guided tours 6€ ($7.50) adults, 3€ ($3.75) children. Tickets from Luxembourg City Tourist Office on place Guillaume II. Mid-July to early Sept Mon–Fri 2:30–5pm (in English 4:30pm only); Sat 10–11am (not in English).

THREE MORE FINE MUSEUMS

As its name suggests, the **Musée d'Histoire de la Ville de Luxembourg (Luxembourg City Historical Museum)** 𝄐, rue du St-Esprit 14 (𝄐 **47-96-45-00;** www.musee-hist.lu), takes you back along the corridors of the city's eventful history from the 10th century onward, by way of original objects and an interactive multimedia display. It's open Tuesday to Sunday from 10am to 6pm (Thurs 10am–8pm). Admission is 5€ ($6.25) for adults; 3.70€ ($4.65) for seniors, students, and children ages 12 to 18; and free for children under 12.

The **Musée National d'Histoire Naturelle (National Museum of Natural History),** rue Münster 24 (𝄐 **46-22-33-1;** www.mnhn.lu), should be of special interest

A Visit to the U.S. Military Cemetery

The serene **U.S. Military Cemetery** at Hamm (© **43-13-27;** www.abmc.gov), 5km (3 miles) east of Luxembourg City, is the final resting place of 5,076 of the 10,000 American troops who fell in Luxembourg during World War II, in the course of liberating the Grand Duchy and fighting the Battle of the Bulge (1944–45). There are 101 graves of unknown soldiers and airmen, and 22 sets of brothers buried side by side. The identical graves are arranged without regard to rank, religion, race, or place of origin, the only exception being the grave of Gen. George S. Patton (because of the many visitors to his gravesite).

To get to the cemetery, take bus no. 5 from Gare Centrale; by car, take boulevard Général Patton east, which becomes N2 outside of town. The cemetery is open daily from 9am to 5pm; admission is free.

to children, due to its permanent exhibit on people, cultures, and environment. It's open Tuesday to Sunday from 10am to 6pm. Admission is 4.50€ ($5.65) for adults, 3€ ($3.75) for students and children ages 6 to 18, and free for children under 6.

Opened in 2006 in a modernist building in the Quartier Européen (European district), designed by Chinese-American architect I. M. Pei, the **MUDAM (Musée d'Art Moderne Grand-Duc Jean/Grand-Duke Jean Museum of Modern Art),** parc Dräi Eechelen (© **45-37-85-1;** www.mudam.lu), presents both permanent and visiting collections of modern art from around the world. It's open Wednesday from 11am to 8pm, and Thursday to Monday from 11am to 6pm. Admission is 5€ ($6.25) for adults, 3€ ($4.65) for seniors and those ages 18 to 26, and free for children under 18.

MORE PLACES OF INTEREST

Place de la Constitution affords a marvelous view of the Pétrusse Valley and the impressive Adolphe Bridge that spans it. In the center of the square, the tall **Monument du Souvenir (Remembrance Monument),** a gold-plated female figure on a tall stone obelisk, is a memorial to those who have perished in Luxembourg's wars. Known affectionately as the **Gëlle Fra (Golden Lady),** the monument was erected in 1923, destroyed by the Nazis in 1940, partly reconstructed in 1958, and finally restored to its original form in 1985.

The suburban areas of **Clausen, Grund,** and **Pfaffenthal,** south of the Pétrusse Valley, are among Luxembourg City's oldest, most picturesque sections, and each merits at least an hour's visit, though be warned—you'll probably want to loiter at least half a day. Take a stroll alongside the Alzette River, and look up at the fortifications on the hills. There are many nightlife possibilities here, and cafes and restaurants, often with open-air terraces in good weather.

Belts of dense greenery ring the city, giving the visitor an easy, close-at-hand escape from city sightseeing. Take your pick: **Bambesch,** to the northwest, contains play areas for children, tennis courts, and footpaths through the **Grengewald** forest. **Kockelscheuer,** to the south, holds a campsite, ice rink, tennis courts, and a pond for fishing.

The ultramodern Euro-zone on the **Kirchberg** plateau, off avenue John F. Kennedy in the northeast of the city, is home to the European Court of Justice, the European

Investment Bank, and the European Parliament. It has all the charm intrinsic to any such modern-architecture desert-with-windows.

TOURS OF THE CITY

WALKING TOURS The Luxembourg City Tourist Office has an excellent brochure entitled **A Walk Through the Green Heart of Europe** to self-guide you through town. The tour can be covered in 1 to 2½ hours, depending on your route and how long you choose to tarry.

TRAIN TOUR One of the city's best tours is on the **Pétrusse Express** ✦ (© 26-65-11; www.sightseeing.lu), a *petit train touristique,* a brightly painted "little tourist train" on rubber wheels that takes the weight off your feet when you tour the city. Don't worry: You don't need to be a "little tourist" to step aboard. The train departs twice each hour from place de la Constitution and travels paved pathways through the Pétrusse and Alzette valleys, and on through some of the oldest sections of town to one of the original city gates. You can simply sit back and enjoy the passing scenery, or don earphones and listen to a historical commentary (in English, among other languages). The train runs from mid-March to October, daily every 30 minutes from 10am to 6pm. The 50-minute ride is 8€ ($10) for adults, 4€ ($5) for children ages 4 to 15, and free for children under 4.

BUS TOURS The **Hop On Hop Off** (© 26-65-11; www.sightseeing.lu) circular bus tour, onboard open-top double-deck buses, brings you to the cathedral, the grand duke's palace, the remains of the fortress, the European Center, and some of Luxembourg's most important avenues. The buses operate from the last week in March to October, daily, with departures every 30 minutes between 10am and 5pm, from place de la Constitution. The fare is 12€ ($15) for adults, 10€ ($13) for seniors and students, 6€ ($7.50) for children ages 4 to 15, and free for children under 4.

SPECIAL EVENTS

Wednesday and Saturday are the bustling and colorful **market days,** when place Guillaume II is awash with the color and exuberance of country folk tending stalls filled with brilliant blooms, fresh vegetables, and a vast assortment of other goods. It will have you pitting your bargain-acquisition skills against the moneymaking instincts of wily traders.

If you're in town during Lent, you'll find plenty of **street carnivals** and general festivity to keep you entertained. A solemn—but still colorful—seasonal celebration is the **Octave of Our Lady of Luxembourg** procession on the fifth Sunday after Easter (see the Notre-Dame Cathedral listing in "Other Top Sights," above).

On **National Day,** June 23, it's fun to watch as the grand duke reviews his troops. City streets continue to ring with festive sounds until well after dark, when the celebration concludes with spectacular fireworks over the Pétrusse Valley.

⌒ *Tips* Band Concerts

From June to October, place d'Armes hosts open-air concerts, performed by the Grand Ducal Big Band for Military Music, or bands from towns around Luxembourg. The program ranges from classical to light classics to show tunes. The concerts usually are on Sunday at 11am and 8:30pm.

WHERE TO STAY

VERY EXPENSIVE

Le Royal ⟨★⟩   The Royal fully deserves its recognized status as one of the Leading Hotels of the World. There isn't much that this hotel doesn't offer in the way of luxury service. It's on Luxembourg City's main financial street in the old center city, across from a park. The guest rooms are large and tastefully modern in style; some have balconies overlooking the park. There are two top-notch restaurants, the international **La Pomme Canelle,** and the Mediterranean-style **Le Jardin,** with terrace dining in summer. The Piano Bar features live music after 6pm.

Bd. Royal 12, 2449 Luxembourg-Ville. ⟨℃⟩ **241-61-67-56.** Fax 22-59-48. www.hotelroyal.lu. 210 units. 350€–480€ ($438–$600) double; from 575€ ($719) suite. AE, DC, MC, V. Parking 12€ ($15). **Amenities:** 2 restaurants (international/Mediterranean); bar; heated indoor pool; health club; Jacuzzi; sauna; bike rental; concierge; business center; salon; 24-hr. room service; massage; babysitting; laundry service; same-day dry cleaning; nonsmoking rooms. *In room:* A/C, TV, dataport, minibar, hair dryer, safe.

EXPENSIVE

Grand Hôtel Cravat ⟨★★⟩   The century-old hotel has retained much of its old-world charm, high standards, and friendly hospitality. It's a classy old place, but that hasn't stopped it from keeping up-to-date, albeit in a chintzy kind of a way. The guest rooms are cozily furnished. Some have balconies overlooking place de la Constitution and the Gëlle Fra monument. **Restaurant Le Normandy** serves fine French cuisine and seafood. In the gracious Le Trianon Bar, you often see Luxembourg's leading businesspeople gathered at the end of the day. Casual meals are served in the traditional Luxembourg brasserie **La Taverne.**

Bd. Roosevelt 29 (at the Gëlle Fra monument), 2450 Luxembourg-Ville. ⟨℃⟩ **22-19-75.** Fax 22-67-11. www.hotelcravat. lu. 60 units. 266€–275€ ($333–$344) double. Rates include buffet breakfast. AE, DC, MC, V. Limited street parking. **Amenities:** 2 restaurants (French/Luxembourgeois, Continental); bar; concierge; secretarial services; limited room service; babysitting; laundry service; dry cleaning; nonsmoking rooms. *In room:* TV w/pay movies, dataport, minibar, hair dryer.

MODERATE

Hôtel Français   The small, conveniently located Français is one of the nicest moderately priced hotels in town. The guest rooms are decorated in a bright, modern style; and though some are on the small side, they are all well laid out. The hotel is in a pedestrian-only zone, but cars and taxis are allowed to drop off and pick up people and baggage. On the ground floor is the popular French/Italian brasserie **Restaurant Français,** with a terrace on the square in summer. Four of the units are apartments.

Place d'Armes 14 (in the old center city), 1136 Luxembourg-Ville. ⟨℃⟩ **47-45-34.** Fax 46-42-74. www.hotelfrancais.lu. 25 units. 125€ ($156) double. Rates include continental breakfast. AE, DC, MC, V. No parking. **Amenities:** Restaurant (French/Italian). *In room:* TV.

Hôtel Le Châtelet ⟨★⟩   This small hotel, owned and operated by the friendly and gracious Mr. and Mrs. Ferd Lorang-Rieck, is a longtime favorite of visiting academics and businesspeople. Its rooms are divided between two lovely old Luxembourg homes; all have modern, comfortable, and attractive furnishings. The rustic restaurant, a local favorite, serves traditional Luxembourg specialties and a nice variety of fish and meat dishes at moderate prices.

Bd. de la Pétrusse 2 (near the Pétrusse Valley on the edge of the new center city), 2320 Luxembourg-Ville. ⟨℃⟩ **40-21-01.** Fax 40-36-66. www.chatelet.lu. 37 units. 88€–130€ ($110–$163) double. Rates include buffet breakfast. AE, DC, MC, V. Parking 8€ ($10). **Amenities:** Restaurant (Luxembourgeois); exercise room; Jacuzzi; sauna; nonsmoking rooms. *In room:* TV, hair dryer, iron, safe.

INEXPENSIVE

Italia   This friendly, small hotel (without an elevator) isn't far from the central rail station and is set in a generally quiet area, though rooms at the front can be affected by traffic noise. The comfortable but rather old-fashioned guest rooms are above a decent restaurant that serves Italian and other Continental dishes. There's a long a la carte menu, with outstanding specialties such as *scampi al ferri* and *entrecôte ala peperonata*.

Rue d'Anvers 15–17, 1130 Luxembourg-Ville. ℂ **48-66-261.** Fax 48-08-07. italia@euro.lu. 20 units. 80€ ($100) double. Rates include continental breakfast. AE, DC, MC, V. Limited street parking. **Amenities:** Restaurant (Italian/Continental); bar; limited room service. *In room:* TV.

WHERE TO DINE
VERY EXPENSIVE

La Lorraine ⭐ SEAFOOD/FRENCH   The popular, atmospheric La Lorraine excels in its preparation of seafood specialties. There are two dining sections here: Downstairs is a casual and airy brasserie-style room, with an oyster bar in the corner whose wood roof models the underside of a fishing boat's hull; upstairs, formal elegance reigns in the Art Deco–style main *salle*. Bouillabaisse is a standout, and there's a gigantic selection of Breton oysters, but the menu is not limited to fish; there's a deft French touch to the duck with honey-vinegar sauce and the succulent lamb. *Cuisine de nos grand-mères,* says the menu ("Just like grandma used to make").

Place d'Armes 7. ℂ **47-14-36.** www.lalorraine.lu. Main courses 17€–47€ ($21–$59); fixed-price menus 35€–50€ ($44–$63). AE, DC, MC, V. Mon–Fri 11:30am–2pm; daily 6–10:30pm.

EXPENSIVE

Le Bouquet Garni/Salon Saint-Michel ⭐⭐ FRENCH   Bare stone and wood beams mark this critically acclaimed, cozy place in the Old City, down a narrow side street near the Palace of the Grand Dukes. Flawless service and classic French cuisine from Michelin star chef Thierry Duhr and his wife Lysiane combine to make this family-run restaurant one of Luxembourg's most highly regarded. Seafood is the big deal here, but look too for meat dishes such as game poultry with truffles in season. The contents of the dessert trolley will make true believers of even the most waistline-conscious.

Rue de l'Eau 32. ℂ **26-20-06-20.** http://thierryduhr.com. Reservations required. Main courses 24€–36€ ($30–$45); fixed-price menus 32€–64€ ($40–$80). AE, DC, MC, V. Mon–Fri noon–2pm and 7–10pm; Sat 7–10pm.

Speltz ⭐ LUXEMBOURGEOIS/FRENCH   Set in a wood-paneled town house, refined and renowned Speltz serves traditional Luxembourg favorites such as game, in addition to superb fish and lobster dishes. The desserts are excellent, and there's a good wine list as well. Owners Carlo and Isabelle Speltz are food enthusiasts, and it shows in their delicious cuisine and friendly service. You can dine outdoors on a tree-shaded terrace in good weather.

Rue Chimay 8 (corner of rue Louvigny). ℂ **47-49-50.** www.restaurant-speltz.lu. Main courses 19€–29€ ($24–$36); fixed-price menus 25€–73€ ($31–$91). AE, MC, V. Tues–Sat 11:45am–2pm and 6:45–10pm; Sat 6:45–10pm.

MODERATE

Chiggeri ⭐⭐ *Finds* MEDITERRANEAN   The upstairs dining room in this rambling mansion on a quiet side street showcases African decorative motifs, like a ceiling-mounted dugout canoe, and elegant table settings. Its seasonal menu features inventive Mediterranean dishes with Asian influences. Reserve the bay-window table if you can, for fine views over the Alzette valley. When the weather's good, you'll likely want to dine on the outdoors terrace. Downstairs, a New Age–look cafe (and cybercafe) serves

30 different kinds of beer. In addition, a Saharan oasis–style *jardin d'hiver* (winter garden) patio-restaurant provides a light, airy space for raclettes, fondues, and other light meals. Different kinds of music, from rock to world music to classical, set an appropriate tone in each of the rooms.

Rue du Nord 15 (off Grand-Rue). ℂ **22-99-36.** www.chiggeri.lu. Main courses 9.50€–18€ ($12–$22); fixed-price menus 20€ ($25) lunch, 25€–50€ ($31–$63) dinner; 8€ ($10) Sun brunch. MC, V. Sun–Thurs 9am–1pm; Fri–Sat 9am–3am.

INEXPENSIVE
Mousel's Cantine   LUXEMBOURGEOIS   The Cantine is an excellent place to sample regional treats. Although much renovated, it's still rustic in decor, with plain wood tables and oil paintings in the back room. The front room overlooks the quaint street outside. A friendly staff serves up large portions of Luxembourg favorites such as sauerkraut with sausage, potatoes, and ham. To wash down this hearty fare, try a stein of the unfiltered local brew.

Montée de Clausen 46 (next to the Mousel Brewery, beside the Alzette River). ℂ **47-01-98.** Main courses 11€–23€ ($14–$29); *plat du jour* 11€ ($14). MC, V. Mon–Sat noon–2pm and 6–10pm.

SHOPPING
In the Old City, upmarket stores are clustered around **Grand-Rue** and adjacent streets and **rue de la Poste.** Many of Europe's leading designers are represented in boutiques in this area, and there are good art galleries as well. In the station area, **avenue de la Gare,** which joins the Passerelle (bridge) to the new city, is lined with stores, most in the moderate price range.

Souvenir stores abound, selling attractive **handcrafted items, clocks, pottery,** and miscellaneous objects. **Paintings** are featured at many fine galleries in the city. **Porcelain plates,** decorated with painted landscapes of the Grand Duchy, and **cast-iron wall plaques** produced by Fonderie de Mersch, depicting castles, coats of arms, and local scenes, are excellent mementos of a Luxembourg visit. The best place to find all these items is the streets leading off place d'Armes.

Two good sources of English-language books are **Chapter One,** rue Astrid 42 (ℂ **44-07-09**); and **Librairie Ernster,** rue du Fossé 27 (ℂ **22-50-77**).

LUXEMBOURG CITY AFTER DARK
Luxembourg City stays up late, and there are numerous nightspots, jazz clubs, theater performances, concerts, and other after-dark activities to choose from. Clubs come and go rather frequently, so it's a good idea to stop by the tourist office on place Guillaume II and pick up a copy of *La Semaine à Luxembourg (The Week in Luxembourg)* to see what's happening during your visit. In addition, get the *Luxembourg News,* an English-language newspaper published every Friday that highlights current events. *City Luxembourg Agenda* lists leading entertainment venues in addition to restaurants.

THE PERFORMING ARTS
CONCERTS, MUSIC & DANCE   From May to October, the **Grand Théâtre de la Ville de Luxembourg,** rond-point Robert Schuman (ℂ **47-96-39-00;** www.theater-vdl.lu), presents major concert artists from around the world, in addition to concerts by the **Grand Orchestre Philharmonique du Luxembourg** (ℂ **22-99-01-1;** www.opl.lu). There are dance (ballet and modern) performances and musical revues by visiting artists year-round. Admission varies according to what's on, but on average you

can expect to pay around 20€ ($25). Local **dance** and **jazz** school students have peri-odic performances at Théâtre des Capucins (see below).

THEATER The Round Tower Players present high-caliber productions (in English) at **Théâtre des Capucins,** place du Théâtre 9 (© **47-96-40-54;** www.theater-vdl.lu); admission is around 12€ ($15). For classic theater in French, there's the **Théâtre National du Luxembourg,** route de Longwy (© **26-44-12-70;** www.tnl.lu).

DANCE CLUBS

A popular among students is **Melusina,** rue de la Tour Jacob 145 (© **43-59-22;** www.melusina.lu), which alternates between rock and jazz groups; house spins in the separate Ultra Lounge. It's open on Friday and Saturday from 11pm to 3am; cover is 7.50€ ($9.40). There's also a restaurant, open Monday to Saturday.

For disco, dance, house, hip-hop, r'n'b, and salsa, head for **The Pulp Club,** bd. d'Avranches 36 (© **49-69-40;** www.pulp.lu), which spins tunes in three separate rooms; it's open Wednesday, Friday, and Saturday from 11pm to 3am. The attached **Humphrey's** restaurant (Mon–Sat) serves decent sushi.

If Latin is more your style, there's the hot-blooded **Cuba Libre,** place des Bains 5 (© **47-27-08**); it's open Monday to Thursday from 9pm to 1am, Friday and Satur-day from 9pm to 3am.

BARS

Two lively bars in the Old City are **Um Piquet,** rue de la Poste 30 (© **47-36-87**); and **Club 5,** rue Chimay 5 (© **46-17-63**), a trendy bar with a good upstairs eatery. Down in the valley, Grund is blessed with several good pubs: **Scott's,** Bisserwée 4 (© **22-64-74**), which serves Guinness and English ale to a mostly expatriate crowd; **Trader's Café,** Bisserwée 9 (© **26-20-04-15**), a popular watering hole across the street from Scott's, in an old building; and **Pygmalion,** rue de la Tour Jacob 19 (© **42-08-60**), a typical Irish pub.

A SIDE TRIP TO MONDORF-LES-BAINS ⋒
16km (10 miles) SE of Luxembourg City

Luxembourg's only casino and a widely recognized health club are in this spa town. Buses depart every hour from Luxembourg City. By car, take N3 south, and turn east at Frisange.

WHAT TO SEE & DO
Casino 2000 This is the place for gambling. Attached to the casino is a four-star hotel and multiple restaurants, ranging from buffet-style to serious French, and there are dinner/entertainment specials. A dress code requires jacket and tie (or turtleneck) for men and suitable dress for women, and you must have your passport to prove you're over 18.

Rue Th. Flammang. © **23-61-11-1.** www.casino2000.lu. Admission 2.50€ ($3.15) per day. Open year-round (except Dec 24) 7pm–3am (opens 4pm on Sun).

Domaine Thermal ⋒ This health resort is known for its idyllic location, with vine-yards and woods to the east and the Lorraine Hills to the west. Its thermal baths, health center, fitness center, and recreation facilities (tennis, golf, squash, fencing, archery, horseback riding, and an outdoor pool) are all excellent.

Av. des Bains. © **23-66-60.** www.mondorf.lu. Treatments and activities begin at 39€ ($49) per day. Mon 1:30–7pm; Tues–Fri 10am–7pm; Sat 9am–7pm; Sun and holidays 9am–6pm. Closed Dec 24–26, Jan 1.

Moments Touring the Valley of the Seven Castles

It's really just the valley of the Eisch River, but that doesn't have the same panache as "Valley of the Seven Castles," which is what the Luxembourg tourist literature calls it. This scenic little area holds one of Europe's finest concentrations of castles.

Steinfort, 16km (10 miles) northwest of Luxembourg City on N4, is the entry point to the valley. Thereafter your route is northeast to **Koerich,** and its ruined medieval castle. As you follow the course of the river (which is really no more than a stream), next up is **Septfontaines,** a high-sited village dominated by its ruined 13th-century castle. Below the castle are the seven springs *(sept fontaines)* that give the village its name.

From here the valley road turns east to **Ansembourg,** which has two castles, a 12th-century one with later modifications high on a hill, and a 17th-century one in the valley. A little way north is **Hollenfels,** with an 18th-century castle constructed around a 13th-century keep dramatically situated on a cliff top (it's now a youth hostel). From there you go northeast on a minor road to the castle at **Schoenfels.**

Go north now, to **Mersch,** the geographical center of the Grand Duchy. In addition to the early feudal Pettingen Castle, you find here the remains of a Roman villa that exhibits mosaics, sculpture, and wall paintings.

The crow's-flight distance from Steinfort to Marsch is just 16km (10 miles), but the winding nature of even the most direct roads will about triple that distance on the ground.

WHERE TO STAY & DINE

Hôtel du Grand Chef ⚝   Set in a private park facing the spa center, within walking distance of the casino, this gracious hotel occupies the 1852 home of a French nobleman. Although completely modernized, it has lost none of the charm and elegance of its beginnings. If it's peace and quiet you're after, take note that this hotel is a member of the Relais du Silence. Some rooms have heated terraces.

Av. des Bains 36, 5610 Mondorf-les-Bains. ✆ **23-66-80-12.** Fax 23-66-15-10. www.grandchef.lu. 40 units. 92€–147€ ($115–$184) double. Rates include buffet breakfast. AE, MC, V. Free parking. **Amenities:** Restaurant (French); bar. *In room:* TV, dataport, minibar, hair dryer, safe.

2 The Luxembourg Ardennes

This northern region, which spills over from the Belgian Ardennes, is a treat for the nature lover and a gift for those in search of a quiet vacation. Handsome castles are everywhere, with especially impressive examples at Clervaux and Esch-sur-Sûre. The area has its share of vacation resort towns, perhaps most notably in medieval Vianden, the proud site of a huge restored fortress surrounded by beautiful forests. In this area is Luxembourg's highest point, the Buurgplatz, 559m (1,835 ft.) high.

For Americans, the Ardennes area holds another fascination. In places like Berdorf, Clervaux, Ettelbruck, and Wiltz, U.S. forces engaged German troops in the Battle of the Bulge (winter 1944–45), and it bears more visible scars of World War II than any other part of Luxembourg. Memorials abound to the valiant GIs who fell in these fierce encounters (see also chapter 10).

While easily explored from a base in Luxembourg City, the Ardennes region deserves an extended visit. The region has excellent country inns and small hotels in all price ranges. Reserve accommodations as far in advance as possible because this is a popular summer vacation spot, and hotel rooms can be hard to come by. Restaurants in the hotels listed (indeed, in most hotels in the Ardennes) are excellent.

ETTELBRUCK
25km (16 miles) N of Luxembourg City

The first thing Americans may note about this crossroads of tourist routes (pop. 7,500) is **Patton Square,** on the edge of town in Patton Park. The square holds a 3m (9-ft.) statue of the general. Nearby is a Sherman tank similar to the ones that arrived to liberate Ettelbruck in September 1944. Patton's boys then had the job to do all over again at Christmas after the German army overran the town during the Battle of the Bulge.

ESSENTIALS
GETTING THERE   **Trains** and **buses** depart every hour or so from Luxembourg City. By **car,** take N7 north.

VISITOR INFORMATION   The **Syndicat d'Initiative et du Tourisme** is at place de la Gare 1, 9044 Ettelbruck (✆ **81-20-68;** fax 81-98-39; www.sit-e.lu). The office is open July to August, Monday to Friday from 9am to noon and 1:30 to 5pm, and Saturday from 10am to noon; September to June, Monday to Friday from 9am to noon and 1:30 to 5pm.

WHAT TO SEE & DO
Musée Général Patton ✪   This museum is dedicated to the flamboyant, hard-driving commander of the U.S. Third Army, whose troops liberated Ettelbruck and did so much to turn the tide in the Battle of the Bulge in World War II. More than 1,000 photographs and other documents portray the war years in Luxembourg. Displays of military equipment include excavations from the battlefield in recent years.

Rue Dr. Klein 5. ✆ **81-03-22.** www.patton.lu. Admission 2.50€ ($3.15) adults, 1.25€ ($1.50) children 14–17, free for children under 14. June to mid-Sept daily 10am–5pm; mid-Sept to May Sun 2–5pm.

DIEKRICH
4.5km (2¾ miles) E of Ettelbruck

Diekrich (pop. 6,000) was a Celtic stronghold in the days before recorded history. Ask the tourist office for directions to the prehistoric **dolmen,** dubbed the "Devil's Altar."

ESSENTIALS
GETTING THERE   **Trains** and **buses** arrive every hour or so from Luxembourg City, via Ettelbruck. By **car,** take N15 east from Ettelbruck.

VISITOR INFORMATION   The **Syndicat d'Initiative** is at place de la Libération 3, 9255 Diekrich (✆ **80-30-23;** fax 80-27-86; www.diekrich.lu). It's open July to August, Monday to Friday from 9am to 5pm, and weekends from 10am to 4pm; September to June, Monday to Friday from 9am to noon and 2 to 5pm, and Saturday from 2 to 4pm.

WHAT TO SEE & DO

Be sure to view the ancient **Eglise St-Laurent.** The church dates from the 7th and 9th centuries, and is open daily from 10am to noon and 2 to 6pm; admission is free. The **Musée Municipal (Town Museum),** on place Guillaume II, contains Roman mosaics from as far back as the 4th century. It's open Easter to October, daily from 10am to noon and 2 to 6pm; admission is free.

Musée National de l'Histoire Militaire (National Museum of Military History) 🏕🏕
The best Battle of the Bulge museum in Belgium and Luxembourg, better even than Bastogne's (see chapter 10), displays a series of superb life-size dioramas depicting U.S. and German military forces, and wartime civilians. Perhaps the finest of these portrays U.S. troops crossing the Sauer River near Diekirch in January 1945, a turning point in the battle. The dioramas all afford an eerie insight into what it might have been like to be there, struggling and fighting through the snow. Even Bulge veterans—who can see things among the hills and forests and hear sounds on the crisp Ardennes air that no other visitor ever will—are impressed by the museum. This incredibly realistic and moving display is augmented by military equipment, uniforms, weapons, maps, and large items such as a tank, artillery pieces, and tracked vehicles. In addition, the museum covers Luxembourg's occupation and liberation, and the history of its army.

Rue Bamertal 10. ⓒ **80-89-08.** www.nat-military-museum.lu. Admission 5€ ($6.25) adults; 3€ ($3.75) students and children 10–18; free for World War II veterans, visitors with disabilities, and children under 10. Jan–Mar and Nov–Dec daily 2–6pm; Apr–Oct daily 10am–6pm.

WHERE TO DINE

Hiertz REGIONAL   This small hotel in the town center has been widely recognized for the excellence of its kitchen, which has won it a coveted chef's toque in the Gault-Millau rating system. Local produce is featured in creative Luxembourg specialties. The hotel has seven guest rooms.

Rue Clairefontaine 1, 9220 Diekirch. ⓒ **80-35-62.** Fax 80-88-69. Fixed-price menu 38€–55€ ($48–$69). AE, DC, MC, V. Daily noon–2pm and 7–9:30pm.

WILTZ

40km (25 miles) NW of Luxembourg City; 18km (11 miles) NW of Ettelbruck

Wiltz is split right down the middle, with a 150m (500-ft.) difference in height between "uptown" and "downtown." This popular vacation town (pop. 4,600), which lies in a beautiful and heavily wooded setting and is a great place for hiking and other outdoor activities, witnessed fierce fighting in December 1944 during the Battle of the Bulge.

ESSENTIALS

GETTING THERE   **Trains** and **buses** depart every hour or so from Luxembourg City, via Ettelbruck. By **car,** take N15 northwest from Ettelbruck.

VISITOR INFORMATION   The **Syndicat d'Initiative** is at Château de Wiltz, 9516 Wiltz (ⓒ **95-74-44;** fax 95-75-56; www.wiltz.lu). The office is open July to August, daily from 10am to 6pm; September to June, Monday to Friday from 10am to noon and 2 to 5pm, and Saturday from 2 to 5pm.

WHAT TO SEE & DO

Just as the town itself is divided geographically, the town's attractions are divided historically between the medieval and the modern. Witness the 1502 **stone cross** at

Moments Luxembourg's Great Outdoors

On a bend of the Sûre River, 6km (4 miles) south of Wiltz, Esch-sur-Sûre has a ruined medieval castle. But it is the **Parc Naturel de la Haut-Sûre** ✿, on the village's doorstep, that brings visitors here in large numbers.

Though tiny by North American standards, the nature park occupies a significant chunk of Luxembourg's real estate, a protected scenic part of the Grand Duchy in the hills and forests around the waters of the Lac de Haut Sûre. This is the place for fishing, boating, hiking, horseback riding, and other outdoor activities, including cross-country skiing in winter. There's good bird-watching, too.

For the lowdown, stop by the visitor center in the **Maison du Parc,** route de Lultzhausen 15, Esch-sur-Sûre (ⓒ 89-93-31-1; www.naturpark-sure.lu). The center is open Monday to Friday from 10am to noon and 2 to 6pm, and weekends and holidays from 2 to 6pm (Nov–Mar closed Wed and at 5pm). Admission is 2€ ($2.50) for adults and 1.25€ ($1.55) for children. The park itself is open permanently and admission is free.

There are buses to Esch every hour or so from both Wiltz and Ettelbruck. By car, take N15 south from Wiltz and northwest from Ettelbruck.

whose feet the powerful lords of Wiltz once meted out justice; and the **1944 battle tank** that sits at the bend of the approach road. The 12th-century **Château (Castle),** "modernized" in the 1600s, perhaps best represents the town's dual traditions, since its ancient left wing houses a museum commemorating the fighting in 1944 and 1945. A memorial recalls those killed during and after a general strike protesting military conscription during the Nazi occupation.

The **Eglise Niederwiltz,** a Romanesque and Renaissance church, holds richly ornamented tombs of the counts of Wiltz. A 1743 Renaissance altar made by a local artist stands in the **Eglise Oberwiltz.**

A good side trip to make is southeast through the scenic wooded Wiltz Valley for 11km (7 miles) to the handsome village of **Kautenbach.**

CLERVAUX ✿
48km (30 miles) N of Luxembourg City; 13km (8 miles) NE of Wiltz

The handsome old town (pop. 1,800) occupies an incredibly scenic location in a steep valley of the Clerve River.

ESSENTIALS
GETTING THERE   **Trains** and **buses** depart every hour or so from Luxembourg City, via Ettelbruck. By **car,** take N7 north from Luxembourg City.

VISITOR INFORMATION   The **Syndicat d'Initiative** is at the Château de Clervaux, 9712 Clervaux (ⓒ **92-00-72;** fax 92-93-12; www.tourisme-clervaux.lu).

WHAT TO SEE & DO
Dominating this little town is its 12th-century **Château** (ⓒ **92-96-57;** www.can.lu), restored after suffering heavy damage during the Battle of the Bulge. Cut-off U.S.

troops held out in this Luxembourg "Alamo" until the Germans used a tank as a battering-ram to break through the timber gates. The castle houses scale models of other medieval fortresses, uniforms and arms from World War II, and Edward Steichen's moving *Family of Man* photographic essay. It's open March to December, Tuesday to Sunday from 10am to 6pm. Admission is 5€ ($6.25) for adults, 3€ ($3.75) for children ages 10 to 15, and free for children under 10.

WHERE TO STAY & DINE

Hôtel du Parc ✿   This lovely old manor house is on the outskirts of town, surrounded by a beautiful wooded park. Its interior has been completely modernized. The attractive and comfortable guest rooms eschew a determinedly modern look in favor of something more timeless. The restaurant and lounge have a refined old-world charm. Outside terraces overlook the picturesque little town. An excellent chef presides over the restaurant, which is graced with a good wine list.

Rue du Parc 2, 9708 Clervaux. ✆ **92-06-50.** Fax 92-10-68. www.hotelduparc.lu. 7 units. 75€–98€ ($94–$123) double. Rates include continental breakfast. MC, V. Free parking. **Amenities:** Restaurant (Luxembourgeois); sauna; solarium. *In room:* TV, hair dryer.

VIANDEN ✿
34km (21 miles) NE of Luxembourg City; 18km (11 miles) SE of Clervaux

In 1871, exiled French writer and Vianden resident Victor Hugo described the town (pop. 1,600) as a "jewel set amid splendid scenery, characterized by two both comforting and magnificent elements: the sinister ruins of its fortress and its cheerful breed of men."

ESSENTIALS
GETTING THERE   There are **trains** every hour or so from Luxembourg City to Diekirch, which connect with buses to Vianden. By **car,** take N7 north from Luxembourg City to Ettelbruck, and then go northeast on N19 and N17.

VISITOR INFORMATION   The **tourist office** is at rue du Vieux Marché 1A, 9419 Vianden (✆ **83-42-57;** fax 84-90-81; www.tourist-info-vianden.lu).

WHAT TO SEE & DO
For the best view of Vianden's narrow winding streets, castle, and the river valley, take the **chairlift** that operates Easter to mid-October Tuesday to Sunday (also Mon July–Aug) from 10am to 6pm. The round-trip fare is 4.25€ ($5.30) for adults and 3€ ($3.75) for children.

The **Maison Victor Hugo (Victor Hugo House),** rue de la Gare 37 (✆ **26-87-40-88;** www.victor-hugo.lu), is where the great French writer stayed during his sojourn in Vianden. Its museum is open Tuesday to Sunday from 11am to 5pm. Admission is 4€ ($5) for adults, 3.50€ ($4.40) for ages 13 to 25, 2.50€ ($3.15) for children ages 6 to 12, and free for children under 6.

Château de Vianden ✿   A mighty 9th-century fortress-castle perched on a hill above town draws most of Vianden's visitors. It has been restored to its original plans, so you can now see the 11th-, 12th-, and 15th-century additions that are even more impressive than the earlier sections.

Montée de Château. ✆ **84-92-91.** www.castle-vianden.lu. Admission 5.50€ ($6.90) adults; 4.50€ ($5.65) seniors, students; 2€ ($2.50) children 6–12; free for children under 6. Jan–Feb and Nov–Dec daily 10am–4pm; Mar and Oct daily 10am–5pm; Apr–Sept daily 10am–6pm. Closed Jan 1, Nov 2, Dec 25.

WHERE TO STAY & DINE

Hôtel-Restaurant Heintz ⭐   Even though the Heintz occupies one of the Grand Duchy's oldest buildings, a former Trinitarian monastery, you needn't worry about bare cells and being woken up for prayers at 3am. This lovely place has thoroughly modernized rooms, which manage to keep some old character and ambience. Twelve rooms face south and have large balconies. The restaurant serves local specialties, like the *truite de l'Our* (Our River trout).

Grand-Rue 55, 9410 Vianden. ℂ 83-41-55. Fax 83-45-59. www.hotel-heintz.lu. 30 units. 66€–80€ ($83–$100) double. Rates include continental breakfast. AE, DC, MC, V. Free parking. **Amenities:** Restaurant (Luxembourgeois); bar. *In room:* TV.

ECHTERNACH

30km (19 miles) NE of Luxembourg City

This enchanting little town (pop. 5,200) is a living open-air museum, from its patrician houses and picturesque market square to its medieval walls and towers.

ESSENTIALS

GETTING THERE   There are **buses** every hour or so from Luxembourg City. By **car,** take N7/E421 northeast from Luxembourg City.

VISITOR INFORMATION   The **Tourist Info office** is at parvis de la Basilique 9–10 (ℂ **72-02-30;** fax 72-75-24; www.echternach-tourist.lu), 6401 Echternach, at St. Willibrord Basilica.

WHAT TO SEE & DO

Be sure to take in the 1444 **Mairie (Town Hall)** and the 18th-century **Abbey** and **Basilica.** Echternach has been the repository of the ages since St. Willibrord arrived from England in 658 and established the abbey that made this one of the area's earliest centers of Christianity. Allow yourself enough time to soak up the medieval atmosphere that permeates the very air.

   If you arrive on Whit Tuesday—the sixth Tuesday after Easter—you encounter the spectacular and unique **Dancing Procession.** Pilgrims from all over Europe come to join this parade, during which they march, chant, sing, and dance to an ancient tune performed by bands. This event mixes religious solemnity with a liberal dose of native gaiety. The procession forms at 9am and ends at the basilica.

WHERE TO STAY & DINE

Hôtel Bel Air ⭐   This luxury hotel is a member of the Relais & Châteaux hotel chain, which is composed exclusively of converted manor houses and châteaux. It lies in its own park overlooking the Sûre Valley. The hotel features include lovely terraces and serene wooded walking paths just outside the door.

Route de Berdorf 1 (.8km/½ mile outside town), 6409 Echternach. ℂ 72-93-83. Fax 72-86-94. www.belair-hotel.lu. 39 units. 134€–179€ ($168–$224) double. Rates include buffet breakfast. AE, DC, MC, V. Free parking. **Amenities:** 2 restaurants (Luxembourgeois/French); lounge; tennis courts. *In room:* TV, hair dryer.

3 The Moselle Valley ⭐

Luxembourg's vineyard and winery region is set in a landscape that's quite different from that of the Ardennes. A tour of the area will take you along the flat banks of the broad Moselle River, with the gentle slope of low hills rising on both sides of the river. For miles, these slopes are covered with vineyards. The riverbanks themselves are alive with campers, boaters, and anglers. Several wineries open their doors to visitors: They take you on a guided tour, explain how their still or sparkling wine is made, and top off your visit with a glass of what comes out of their vats.

To explore the Moselle Valley, begin at Echternach, and follow the well-marked *Route du Vin* (Wine Route) south through Wasserbillig, Grevenmacher, Machtum, Wormeldange, Ehnen, Remich, and Wellenstein. You can do this as an easy day trip from Luxembourg City. Should you find yourself beguiled by this peaceful part of the country, there are plenty of accommodations along the route, and excellent small local restaurants.

GREVENMACHER
12km (7 miles) SE of Echternach

This scenic Moselle town, on the riverside road southeast of Wasserbillig, is noted both for its wine and its waters. There are regular buses from Echternach. The **tourist office** is at route du Vin 10, 6701 Grevenmacher (© **75-82-75;** fax 75-86-66; www.moselle-tourist.lu).

For tours of their wine cellars, visit the **Caves Coopératives des Vignerons (Cooperative Wine Cellars),** rue des Caves 12 (© **75-01-75**). They're open May to August, Monday to Saturday from 10am to 5pm (by appointment other months). The tour is 1.75€ ($2.20) for adults and 1€ ($1.25) for children.

Bernard-Massard, rue du Pont 8 (© **75-05-45-1;** www.bernard-massard.lu), has wine tours April to October, daily from 9:30am to 6pm; admission is 2.75€ ($3.45) for adults and 1.75€ ($2.20) for children.

The tourist cruise boat *Princesse Marie-Astrid* (© **75-82-75;** www.moselle-tourist.lu), which has an onboard restaurant, plows a furrow up and down the Moselle from Grevenmacher from Easter to the end of September. Cruises range from 4€ to 14€ ($5–$18), without meals; children ages 6 to 12 pay half fare, and children under 6 travel free.

A FINE NEARBY RESTAURANT
Chalet de la Moselle ✦ SEAFOOD   This charming chalet restaurant on the Wine Route between Grevenmacher and Ahn specializes in fish and other seafood dishes, and prides itself on its wine list. The best choices on the extensive seafood menu are *moules au Riesling* (mussels in a Riesling sauce), *sole meunière* (sole with lemon sauce), and the wonderful *cassolette de crustaces et de fruits de mer* (seafood casserole) for two. The Chalet offers two lovely upstairs guest rooms at modest rates.

Route du Vin 35, 6841 Machtum. © **75-91-91.** Main courses 12€–28€ ($15–$35). AE, DC, MC, V. Fri–Wed noon–3pm; Fri–Tues 6–11pm.

WORMELDANGE & EHNEN
8km (5 miles) SW of Grevenmacher

By bus and car, it's a quick trip on the riverside road from Grevenmacher to **Wormeldange,** where the **Caves des Crémants Poll Fabaire,** route du Vin 115 (© **76-82-11**), are open May to October, Monday to Friday from 7am to 8pm, Saturday from 10:30am to 8pm, and Sunday from 3 to 8pm (tastings are on a more restricted schedule). The tour is 2€ ($2.50) for adults and 1.25€ ($1.55) for children.

Less than 1km (½ mile) farther on is **Ehnen.** The pretty village's **Musée du Vin (Wine Museum)** ✦, route du Vin 115 (© **76-00-26**), is set in a beautiful old vintner's mansion that has been lovingly restored. It serves as an information center for the region's wineries. A comprehensive exhibit explaining viniculture processes now occupies what was once the fermenting cellar. The museum is open April to October, Tuesday to Sunday from 9:30 to 11:30am and 2 to 5pm. Admission is 3.50€ ($4.40) for adults (includes glass of wine), and 1.50€ ($1.90) for children.

WHERE TO STAY & DINE
Hôtel-Restaurant Bamberg's ⭐   This small, family-owned hotel occupies a renovated 19th-century town house overlooking the Moselle. Its guest rooms are furnished in a country style, and the public rooms have a homey feel. The restaurant, which draws locals in addition to visitors, and sources some of its fish from the river and accompanying wines from local wineries, has an old-world atmosphere, with a fireplace, dark wainscoting, and exposed rafters. This is a good place to stop for lunch or dinner, even if you're not staying in the hotel.

Route du Vin 131, 5416 Ehnen. © **76-00-22.** Fax 76-00-56. 12 units. 90€ ($113) double. Rates include buffet breakfast. MC, V. Free parking. **Amenities:** Restaurant (French/Luxembourgeois). *In room:* TV.

REMICH
6km (3½ miles) S of Ehnen

On the riverside road south from Grevenmacher, Remich (pop. 3,000) is an important wine center. **Remich tourist office,** Esplanade, 5533 Remich (© **23-69-84-88;** fax 23-69-72-95; www.moselle-tourist.lu), at the bus station, is open July to August, daily from 10am to 5pm.

The **Caves St-Martin (St-Martin Wine Cellars),** route de Stadtbredimus 53 (© **26-66-14-1**), offers an interesting and informative tour. They're open April to October, daily from 10am to noon and 1:30 to 6pm. Admission is 2.50€ ($3.15) for adults and 1.50€ ($1.90) for children.

WHERE TO STAY & DINE
Hôtel Saint-Nicolas ⭐   Overlooking the Moselle on a broad promenade beside the river, with a view across the water to Germany, this large terraced hotel has tastefully modern guest rooms. The French restaurant **Lohengrin** is excellent.

Esplanade 31, 5533 Remich. © **26-66-3.** Fax 26-66-36-66. www.saint-nicolas.lu. 40 units. 105€–130€ ($131–$163) double. Rates include buffet breakfast. AE, DC, MC, V. Limited street parking. **Amenities:** Restaurant (French); bar; lounge; health club; spa. *In room:* TV, dataport, minibar, hair dryer.

WELLENSTEIN
4km (2½ miles) SW of Remich

Wellenstein's **Caves Coopératives des Vignerons (Cooperative Wine Cellars),** rue des Caves 13 (© **26-66-14-1**), offers guided tours. It's open May to August, daily from 11am to 6pm. Admission is 1.75€ ($2.20) for adults, and 1€ ($1.25) for children.

Appendix A:
Getting to Know Belgium

Belgium is a small country. Not quite so small that if you blink you'll miss it, but small enough that a couple of hours of focused driving will get you from the capital, Brussels, to any corner of the realm. Yet the variety of culture, language, history, and cuisine crammed into this little space would do credit to a country many times its size. Belgium's diversity is a product of its location at the cultural crossroads of western Europe. The boundary between the Continent's Germanic north and Latin south—Europe's Mason-Dixon line—cuts clear across the country's middle, leaving Belgium divided into two major ethnic regions, Dutch-speaking Flanders and French-speaking Wallonia.

1 Belgium Today

After a long history of occupation by foreign powers, Belgium has emerged as a site for European nations to come together. Brussels—which hosts the headquarters of both NATO and the European Union—is now home to the world's largest concentration of international diplomats.

Modern Belgium is a parliamentary democracy under a constitutional monarch, Albert II. The legislature is composed of a senate and chamber of representatives, with members elected for 4-year terms. The government exists in a more-or-less permanent state of crisis due to the cultural and linguistic divide, with ambitious regional politicians, particularly in Flanders, often pushing the country to the brink of dissolution. Still, rumors of Belgium's demise have been heard before and have always proven greatly exaggerated, and it seems likely that the federation of autonomous regions will remain stable enough to see the country through.

The inhabitants of Flanders speak a derivation of German that evolved into Dutch and its Flemish variation (*Vlaams,* or just referred to as Dutch; or *Nederlands*). The inhabitants of Wallonia speak French (a minority still speak the old Walloon dialect). In Brussels, the two languages mingle, but French has the upper hand. So strong is the feeling for each language in its own region, that along the line where they meet it's not unusual for French to be the daily tongue on one side of a street and Flemish on the other. Throughout the country, road signs acknowledge both languages by giving multiple versions of the same place name—Brussel/Bruxelles or Brugge/Bruges, for example. There's a small area in eastern Belgium where German is spoken. Belgium, then, is left with not one, but three, official languages: Dutch, French, and German.

Impressions
Belgium suffers severely from linguistic indigestion.
—R. W. G. Penn, *Geographical Magazine* (Mar 1980)

Famous, That's All

Let there be no more "Name me one famous Belgian" jokes. Without even mentioning the great Flemish Old Masters, here is more than one from the modern era. Adolphe Sax (1814–94): invented the saxophone; Victor Horta (1861–1947): a founder of Art Nouveau; Belgian-American Leo Baekeland (1863–1944): invented Bakelite in 1909 and was called the "father of plastics"; Georges Simenon (1903–90): author of the Inspector Maigret books; Hergé, or Georges Rémi (1907–83): created Tintin.

Also Belgian: surrealist painter Renée Magritte (1898–1967); singer/songwriter Jacques Brel (1929–78); Agatha Christie's fictional detective Hercule Poirot (ageless). And the still very much alive "French" rocker Johnny Halliday; Hollywood star Jean-Claude "the Muscles from Brussels" Van Damme; schmaltzy singer Helmut Lotti; world champion Formula One driver Jacky Ickx; and multiple Tour de France winner Eddy "the Cannibal" Merckx? Belgian, or Belgian-born, every last one of them.

Tennis fans will also want to add women's-tour aces Kim Clijsters and Justine Hennene-Hardenne.

In short, far from being a homogeneous, harmonious people with one strong national identity, Belgians take considerable pride in their individualistic attributes.

The vast majority of Belgians are Catholic, though there's more than a smattering of Protestants, a small Jewish community, and a rising proportion of immigrant Muslims and their locally born children. Throughout the centuries, Belgians—nobles and peasants alike—have proclaimed their faith by way of impressive cathedrals, churches, paintings, and holy processions. The tradition continues today.

Folklore still plays a large part in Belgium's national daily life, with local myths giving rise to some of the country's most colorful pageants and festivals, such as Ypres's Festival of the Cats, Bruges's Pageant of the Golden Tree, and the stately Ommegang in Brussels. In Belgium's renowned puppet theaters, marionettes based on folkloric characters identify their native cities—Woltje (Little Walloon) belongs to Brussels, Schele to Antwerp, Pierke to Ghent, and Tchantchès to Liège.

Undoubtedly, Belgians have a finely tuned appreciation for the good things in life. Indeed, standards are high in every area of daily life, and woe betide the chef who tries to hoodwink patrons with less-than-fresh ingredients, the storekeeper who stocks shoddy merchandise, or any service person who is rude—their days are surely numbered. Belgians—Flemish or Walloon—are eminently practical, and none will spend hard-earned money for anything that doesn't measure up.

Ah, but when standards are met, watch Belgian eyes light up with enthusiasm. Appreciation then moves very close to reverence, whether inspired by a great artistic masterpiece, or a homemade mayonnaise of just the right lightness, or one of Belgium's more than 450 native beers. If you have shared that experience with a Belgian companion, chances are you find your own sense of appreciation taking on a finer edge.

2 History 101

EARLY HISTORY

Julius Caesar first marched his Roman legions against the ancient Belgae tribes in 58 B.C. For nearly 5 centuries thereafter, Belgium was shielded from the barbarians by the great Roman defense line on the Rhine, but subject to periodic incursions.

From the beginning of the 5th century, Roman rule gave way to the Franks. In 800, their great king Charlemagne was named emperor of the West. He instituted an era of agricultural reform, setting up underling local rulers known as counts, who rose up to seize more power after Charlemagne's death. In 843, Charlemagne's grandsons signed the Treaty of Verdun, which split French-allied (but Dutch-speaking) Flanders in the north from the southern (French-speaking) Walloon provinces.

Then came Viking invaders, who attacked the northern provinces. A Flemish defender known as Baldwin Iron-Arm became the first count of Flanders in 862;

his royal house eventually ruled over a domain that included the Low Countries and lands as far south as the Scheldt in France. Meanwhile, farther to the south, powerful prince-bishops controlled most of Wallonia from their seat in Liège.

FLANDERS RISING

As Flanders grew larger and stronger, its cities thrived, and its citizens wrested more and more self-governing powers. Bruges emerged as a leading center of European trade; its monopoly on English cloth attracted bankers and financiers from Germany and Lombardy. No one could have foreseen that Bruges's fine link to the sea, the Zwin inlet, would eventually choke with silt and leave the city high and dry, landlocked. Ghent and Ypres prospered in the wool trade. Powerful trade and manufacturing guilds emerged and erected splendid edifices as their headquarters. In Liège, great fortunes were made from iron foundries and the manufacture of arms.

Dateline

- **58 B.C.** Julius Caesar leads Roman legions against Belgae tribes.
- **4th–5th century A.D.** The Franks, a Germanic people, break into Belgium; the Romans allow them to settle permanently as "allies," and they later establish their first capital at Tournai.

- **814** Charlemagne, the great Frankish emperor of the West, dies.
- **843** Treaty of Verdun splits the empire of the Franks. Most of the Low Countries become part of the Middle Kingdom, squeezed between the German lands and France.
- **966** The first documented reference to Brussels calls it Bruocsella, meaning Settlement in the Marsh.

- **1302** At the "Battle of the Golden Spurs," near Kortrijk, an army of Flemish peasants defeats the French and kills many noble-born knights. But 3 years later France regains control.
- **1384** Duke Philip the Bold gains control of Flanders, beginning the acquisition of the Low Countries by the Burgundians.

continues

Fun Fact **Sales Talk**

In 1191, King Richard the Lionheart of England offered to swap Cyprus, which he had conquered while on his way to the Third Crusade, for half of Flanders. The Flemish count politely declined.

As towns took on city-state status, the mighty count of Flanders, with close ties to France, grew less and less mighty; in 1297, France's Philip the Fair attempted to annex Flanders. However, he had not reckoned on the stubborn resistance of Flemish common folk. Led by the likes of Jan Breydel, a lowly weaver, and Pieter de Coninck, a butcher, they rallied to face a heavily armored French military. The battle took place on July 11, 1302, in the fields surrounding Kortrijk. When it was over, victorious artisans and craftsmen scoured the bloody battlefield, triumphantly gathering hundreds of golden spurs from slain French knights. Their victory at the "Battle of the Golden Spurs" is celebrated by the Flemish to this day.

But this valiant resistance was crushed by 1328, and Flanders suffered under both the French and the English during the ensuing Hundred Years' War.

THE BURGUNDIAN ERA

Philip the Good, duke of Burgundy in the mid-1400s, gained control of virtually all the Low Countries. His progeny, through a series of advantageous marriages, consolidated their holdings into a single Burgundian "Netherlands," or Low Countries. Brussels, Antwerp, Mechelen, and Leuven attained new prominence as centers of trade, commerce, and the arts.

This era was one of immense wealth, much of which was poured into fine public buildings, impressive mansions, and soaring Gothic cathedrals that survive to this day. Wealthy patrons made possible the brilliant works of such Flemish artists as Jan van Eyck, Hieronymous Bosch, Rogier van der Weyden, and German-born Hans Memling. Flemish opulence became a byword around Europe—the merchant in Chaucer's *The Canterbury Tales* wears a fur hat imported from Flanders, a fact that emphasizes his wealth and love of ostentation.

By the end of the 1400s, however, Charles the Bold, last of the dukes of Burgundy, had lost the Duchy of Burgundy to the French king on the field of battle,

---

- 1400s Era of "Flemish Primitives"—artists Jan van Eyck, Hieronymous Bosch, Rogier van der Weyden, Hans Memling, and others.
- 1477 Beginning of the rule of the Austrian Habsburgs.
- 1500 The future Habsburg emperor and king of Spain Charles V is born in Ghent. He inherits the Low Countries in 1506.
- 1531 Brussels is the capital of the Spanish Low Countries.

- 1555 Philip II of Spain introduces Catholic Inquisition persecution against Protestants.
- 1566 Protestant rioters sack Catholic churches during the *Beeldenstorm* (Iconoclastic Fury).
- 1567 Philip II of Spain sends the duke of Alba to the Low Countries to confront the Protestant Reformation.
- 1568 Counts Egmont and Hoorn are beheaded on the Grand-Place in Brussels for

protesting the excesses of the Inquisition and Alba's reign of terror.
- 1576 Spanish troops sack Antwerp, an event recalled as the "Spanish Fury." The Pacification of Ghent, a treaty establishing freedom of worship in the Low Countries, is signed, but is soon proven worthless.
- 1608 Peter Paul Rubens is appointed court painter to the Spanish governor in Antwerp.

and once more French royalty turned a covetous eye on the Low Countries. Marriage to Mary of Burgundy, the duke's heir, appeared a sure route to bringing the Low Countries under French rule, and a proposal (in reality an ultimatum) was issued to Mary to accept the hand of the French king's eldest son. To the French prince's consternation, Mary promptly wrote a proposal of marriage to Maximilian of Austria. The Austrian's acceptance meant that the provinces became part of the extensive Austrian Habsburg Empire.

A grandson of that union, Charles V, born in Ghent and reared in Mechelen, presided for 40 years over most of Europe, including Spain and its New World possessions. He was beset by the Protestant Reformation, which created dissension among the once solidly Catholic populace. It all proved too much for the great monarch, and he abdicated in favor of his son, Philip II of Spain.

THE SPANISH INVASION

Philip ascended to power in an impressive ceremony at Coudenberg Palace in Brussels in 1555. An ardent Catholic who spoke neither Dutch nor French, he brought the infamous instruments of the Inquisition to bear on an increasingly Protestant—and increasingly rebellious—Low Countries population. The response from his Protestant subjects was violent:

For a month in 1566 they went on a rampage of destruction that saw churches pillaged, religious statues smashed, and other religious works of art burned.

An angry Philip commissioned the zealous duke of Alba to lead some 10,000 Spanish troops in a wave of retaliatory strikes. The atrocities committed by order of Alba and his "Council of Blood" as he swept through the "Spanish Netherlands" are legendary. He was merciless—when the Catholic counts of Egmont and Hornes tried to intercede with Philip, he put them under arrest for 6 months, and then had them publicly beheaded on the Grand-Place in Brussels.

Instead of submission, however, this sort of intimidation gave rise to a brutal conflict that lasted from 1568 to 1648. Led by William the Silent and other nobles who raised private armies, the Protestants fought on doggedly until finally independence was achieved for the seven undefeated provinces to the north, which became the fledgling country of the Netherlands. Those in the south remained under the thumb of Spain and gradually returned to the Catholic Church. As an act of revenge, Holland closed the Scheldt River to shipping, and Antwerp, along with other Flemish cities, withered away to a shadow of its former prosperity.

- **1695** Bombardment and destruction of Brussels's Grand-Place by the French.
- **1713** Belgium comes under rule of Habsburgs of Austria.
- **1795** French rule of Belgium begins.
- **1815** Napoleon defeated at Waterloo. Belgium becomes part of the Netherlands.
- **1830** Belgian War of Independence breaks out.
- **1831** Belgium becomes a constitutional monarchy headed by King Leopold I.
- **1835** The Continent's first railway, between Brussels and Mechelen, opens.
- **1914–18** German forces invade and occupy most of the country during World War I.
- **1940** World War II: Nazi Germany invades, May 10. King Leopold III surrenders 3 weeks later.
- **1944** Brussels liberated September 3 by British troops. Battle of the Bulge, in the Ardennes, begins December 16.
- **1945** World War II ends.
- **1948** Benelux Customs union with the Netherlands and Luxembourg.
- **1949** Belgium joins NATO.

continues

> **Fun Fact**   **Vive New York!**
>
> *Quel shock!* The first European inhabitants of New York spoke French—kind of. In 1624, the Dutch West India Company established a fur-trading post at the tip of Manhattan Island, manning it with a handful of poor Protestant Walloon refugees from what is now Belgium.

WARS OF SUCCESSION

At the beginning of the 18th century, the grandson of Louis XIV ascended to the Spanish throne, thereby bringing French domination to Spain's possessions in the Low Countries. That domination was short-lived, however; in 1713, the Spanish Netherlands was returned to the Habsburgs of Austria. A series of revolts against reforms instituted by Joseph II, emperor of Austria, helped to consolidate a sense of nationalism among the Low Country natives, who—for the first time—began to call themselves Belgians. Austrian-Belgian conflicts raged fiercely until 1789, when all of Europe was caught up in the French Revolution.

In 1795, Belgium wound up once more under the rule of France. It was not until Napoleon Bonaparte's crushing defeat at Waterloo—just miles from Brussels—that Belgians began to think of national independence as a real possibility. Its time had not yet come, however; under the Congress of Vienna, Belgium was once more united with the provinces of Holland. But the Dutch soon learned that governing the unruly Belgians was more than they had bargained for, and the 1830 rioting in Brussels was the last straw. A provisional Belgian government was formed with an elected National Congress. On July 21, 1831, Belgium officially became a constitutional monarchy when a relative of Queen Victoria, Prince Leopold of Saxe-Coburg-Gotha, became king, swearing allegiance to the constitution.

AN INDEPENDENT NATION

The new nation soon set about developing its coal and iron natural resources, and rebuilding its textile, manufacturing, and shipbuilding industries. The country was hardly unified by this process, however, for most of the natural resources were to be found in the French-speaking Walloon regions in the south, where prosperity returned much more rapidly than in Flanders.

- **1951** King Leopold III abdicates in favor of his eldest son, Baudouin.
- **1958** Belgium joins the European Economic Community, the forerunner of today's European Union (EU).
- **1971** Constitutional reforms grant some regional autonomy.
- **1993** King Baudouin dies and is succeeded by his brother, Albert II (b. 1934). Constitution is amended to create a federal state composed of the autonomous regions of Flanders and Wallonia, and Brussels-Capital, with the German-speaking district a largely self-governing part of Wallonia.
- **1996** The nation reacts with horror to the deaths of four girls (two children and two teens) kidnapped by a pedophile ring. Mass street demonstrations take place, amid allegations of police and official incompetence and cover-ups.
- **1999** Prince Philippe, son of King Albert II and heir to the throne, marries Mathilde d'Udekem d'Acoz.
- **2001** October 21: Princess Elisabeth, a daughter to Prince Philippe and Princess Mathilde, is born. Should she succeed to the throne, she will be the first queen of the Belgians since the dynasty was founded in 1831. Demise

Impressions

Say something positive to a Belgian about their country and they say, yes, but have you seen how much better they do it in France? Or the Netherlands?
—Harry Pearson, *A Tall Man in a Low Land* (1999)

The Flemish, while happy to be freed from the rule of their Dutch neighbors, resented the greater influence of their French-speaking compatriots. It took yet another invasion to bring a semblance of unity. When German forces swept over the country in 1914, the Belgians mounted a defense that made them heroes of World War I—even though parts of the Flemish population openly collaborated with the enemy, hailing them as "liberators" from Walloon domination. Still, tattered remnants of the Belgian national army—led by their "soldier-king," Albert I—held a tiny strip of land between De Panne and France for the entire 4 years of the war.

With the coming of peace, Belgium found its southern coal, iron, and manufacturing industries reeling, while the northern Flemish regions were moving steadily ahead by developing light industry, especially around Antwerp. Advanced agricultural methods yielded greater productivity and higher profits for Flemish farmers. By the end of the 1930s, the

Flemish population outnumbered the Walloons by a large enough majority to install their beloved language as the official voice of education, justice, and civil administration in Flanders.

With the outbreak of World War II, Belgium was once more overrun by German forces. In the face of overwhelming military superiority, King Leopold III decided to surrender to the invaders, remain in Belgium, and try to soften the harsh effects of occupation. The Belgian Resistance was among the most determined and successful of the underground organizations that fought against Nazi occupation in Europe. On the other side, Flemish and Walloon quislings formed separate Waffen-SS formations that fought for the Nazis in Russia. By the war's end, the king was imprisoned in Germany and a regent was appointed as head of state. His controversial decision to surrender led to bitter debate when he returned to the throne in 1950, and in 1951 he stepped down in favor of his son, Baudouin.

of the country's flag carrier Sabena; the new SN Brussels Airlines takes over many of its European routes.

■ **2002** Euro banknotes and coins replace the Belgian franc.

■ **2003** The nation's highest court upholds "universal jurisdiction" and rules that war crimes, crimes against humanity, and genocide can be prosecuted in the country, even if the accused isn't

Belgian, and the alleged offences took place in another country. The first indictee is Ariel Sharon, followed closely by George W. Bush, Tony Blair, Colin Powell, Donald Rumsfeld, Gen. Tommy Franks, and Belgian foreign minister Louis Michel. The law is later amended to prevent politically motivated lawsuits.

■ **2004** A Supreme Court ruling that it is racist forces the

nationalist Vlaams Blok (Flemish Block) political party—the most popular in Flanders, say opinion polls—to disband. It is refounded as the Vlaams Belang (Flemish Interest).

■ **2007** Belgium marks the 100th anniversary of the birth of Tintin creator Hergé (Georges Rémi; 1907–83). A fresco of Tintin greeting visitors is unveiled at Brussels's Gare du Midi railway station.

Impressions

Our country has the unique advantage of lying at the crossroads of the great cultures of Europe.

—The late King Baudouin (1990)

UNITY & DISUNITY

During King Baudouin's 42 years on the throne, much progress was made in achieving harmony among Belgium's linguistically and culturally diverse population. In the 1970s, efforts were made to grant increasing autonomy to the Flemish and Walloons in the areas where each was predominant, and to apportion power to each group within the national government and the political parties. Finally, in 1993, the constitution was amended to create a federal state, made up of the autonomous regions of Flanders and Wallonia, together with the bilingual city of Brussels and its semi-autonomous German-speaking community.

Baudouin died in 1993, removing one of the pillars of unity. His successor, his brother Albert II, while winning respect for conscientious effort in what is a difficult job, has not made the same personal connection with the people.

The downside of all the constitutional tinkering aimed at keeping the country intact was that it brought the country perilously close to splitting up, as each regional government went its own way, leaving the increasingly marginalized federal government walking a tightrope between them. With so many layers of government—federal, regional, provincial, city, and communal—all of which needed an impressively outfitted administration, taxation and bureaucracy were coming dangerously close to choking the life out of the economy.

The center-left coalition government of prime minister Guy Verhostadt has made some improvements at home in the areas of governmental competence and financial prudence, and has at least trimmed a little the overweening bureaucracy. Internationally, its vocal opposition to the Iraq war and its refusal to join George Bush's coalition "of the willing" has cooled relations with the U.S.

3 Great Belgian Artists

Despite its small geographic size, Belgium has exerted a significant influence on Western art. The works of Bosch, Brueghel, Rubens, van Dyck, the brothers van Eyck, and Magritte represent only a fraction of the treasures you see gracing the walls of the notable art museums in Brussels, Bruges, Ghent, and Antwerp.

The golden age of Flemish painting occurred in the 1400s, a century dominated by the so-called Flemish Primitives—so-dubbed because they were "first," not because they were unsophisticated—whose work was almost always religious in theme, usually commissioned

for churches and chapels, and largely lacking in perspective. As the medieval cities of Flanders flourished, more and more princes, wealthy merchants, and prosperous guilds became patrons of the arts.

Art's function was still to praise God and illustrate religious allegory, but **Jan van Eyck** (ca. 1390–1441), one of the earliest Flemish Masters, brought a sharp new perspective to bear on traditional subject matter. His *Adoration of the Mystic Lamb,* created with his brother Hubert for St. Bavo's Cathedral in Ghent, incorporates a realistic landscape into its biblical theme. The Primitives sought to mirror reality, to portray both people and nature exactly as they appeared to the human eye, down to the tiniest detail, without classical distortions or embellishments. These artists would work meticulously for months—even years—on a single commission, often painting with a single-haired paintbrush to achieve a painstakingly lifelike quality.

The greatest Flemish artist of the 16th century lived and worked for many years in Antwerp. From 1520 to 1580 the city was one of the world's busiest ports and banking centers, and it eclipsed Bruges as a center for the arts. Many of the artists working here looked to the Italian Renaissance Masters for their models of perfection. **Pieter Brueghel the Elder** (ca. 1520–69), who had studied in Italy, integrated Renaissance influences with the traditional style of his native land. He frequently painted rural and peasant life, as in his *Wedding Procession,* on view at the Musée de la Ville in Brussels.

Brueghel painted fewer than 50 oils (although he finished another 250-plus drawings and etchings), but he is still considered one of the greatest 16th-century artists. His works are filled with allusions and allegorical references to the politics and culture of the period, and with many plausible and explicit period details. Much of Brueghel's symbolism is obscure to us today, but it would have been clear to the contemporary Flemish audience full of hatred for their Spanish masters. The artist had a fabulous, grotesque side, clearly influenced by the artist Hieronymus Bosch; see *The Fall of the Rebel Angels* in the Musées Royaux des Beaux-Arts, Brussels.

In 1563, Brueghel moved to Brussels, where he lived at rue Haute 132. Here his two sons, also artists, were born. **Pieter Brueghel the Younger** (ca. 1564–1637) became known for copying his father's paintings; **Jan Brueghel the Elder** (1568–1625) specialized in decorative paintings of flowers and fruits.

Peter Paul Rubens (1577–1640) was the most influential baroque painter of the early 17th century. The drama in his works, such as *The Raising of the Cross,* housed in the Antwerp cathedral, comes from the dynamic, writhing figures in his canvases. His renditions of the female form gave rise to the term "Rubenesque," which describes the voluptuous women who appear in his paintings.

Portraitist **Anthony van Dyck** (1599–1641), one of the most important talents to emerge from Rubens's studio, served as court painter to Charles I of England, though some of his best religious work remains in Belgium. Look for the *Lamentation* in the Museum voor Schone Kunsten in Antwerp, and the *Crucifixion* in Mechelen Cathedral.

Belgium's influence on the art world is by no means limited to the Old Masters. **James Ensor** (1860–1949) was a late-19th-century pioneer of modern art. One of his most famous works is the *Entry of Christ into Brussels.* Ensor developed a broadly expressionistic technique, liberating his use of color from the demands of realism. He took as his subject disturbing, fantastic visions and images.

Surrealism flourished in Belgium, perhaps because of the earlier Flemish artists

---

(Fun Fact **Surfer in Spirit**

Betcha didn't know that a Belgian invented the Internet. Well . . . kind of. In 1934, Paul Otlet wrote a paper titled *Traité de Documentation* in which he foresaw a Universal Network for Information and Documentation. Access would be through multimedia workstations. These didn't exist yet—an inconvenient fact that, since he was a lawyer, Otlet was perfectly able to disregard.

with a penchant for the bizarre and grotesque. **Paul Delvaux** (1897–1989) became famous, but the best known of the Belgian surrealists was unquestionably **René Magritte** (1898–1967). His neatly dressed man in the bowler hat, whose face is always hidden from view, became one of the most famous images of the surrealist movement. Many of these modern works can be seen in the Musées Royaux des Beaux-Arts in Brussels and the Konikljke Museum voor Schone Kunsten in Antwerp. The fine-arts museums in Ghent, Tournai, and Liège, and the modern art museums in Antwerp and Ostend, are also major sources.

4 A Taste of Belgium

Belgian chefs may be influenced by the French, but they add their own special touches. Native specialties in Wallonia include *jambon d'Ardenne* (ham from the hills and valleys of the Ardennes) and savory *boudin de Liège* (a succulent sausage mixed with herbs). Almost every menu lists *tomates aux crevettes* (tomatoes stuffed with tiny, delicately sweet North Sea shrimps and light, homemade mayonnaise), which is filling enough for a light lunch and delicious as an appetizer. A special treat awaits visitors in May and June in the form of Belgian asparagus, and from October to March there's endive, which is known in Belgium as *witloof* (white leaf).

Belgian cuisine is based on the country's own regional traditions and produce, such as asparagus, chicory (endive), and the humble Brussels sprout. A tradition in Brussels is to cook with local beers like *gueuze* and *faro*. In addition, look for great steaming pots of Zeeland mussels, which have a fanatical local following. Most places serve both a *plat du jour/dagschotel* (plate of the day) and a value-for-money, two- or three-course menu.

Flanders has added its own ingredients to the mix of Belgian cuisine. The Flemish share the Dutch fondness for raw herring, generally eaten with equally raw onions, while *sole à l'Ostendaise* (sole in a white-wine sauce) and the small, gray North Sea shrimps are firm favorites. River fish used to be the main ingredient of the Flemish souplike stew called *waterzooï*, but today's rivers being polluted, chicken is now a more familiar ingredient.

If you're basically a potatoes person, you're in good company, for Belgians dote on their *steak-frites*, available at virtually every restaurant—even when not listed on the menu. Lest you think that *frites* in Belgium are the same as American "french fries," let me enlighten you. These are twice-fried potatoes, as light as the proverbial feather. They're sold in paper cones on many street corners and (in my opinion) are best when topped with homemade mayonnaise, though you may prefer curry or even your usual ketchup. *Frites* will accompany almost anything you order in a restaurant.

Seafood anywhere in Belgium is fresh and delicious. *Moules* (mussels) are a specialty in Brussels, where you find a concentration of restaurants along Petite rue des Bouchers that feature them in just about every guise you can imagine. (Ironically, Belgian mussels actually come from Zeeland in Holland and may, in fact, be

---

(Tips) False Friend

Watch out for *steak américain*, which might sound like a nice, big, mouthwateringly juicy American-style steak, but is in fact raw chopped beef!

Fun Fact Belgian Fries

Let's get this straight: "French fries" are really Belgian fries. U.S. and British soldiers serving in Belgium during World War I were served fries by folks who
spoke French and, *voila!*, a popular misconception was born. The modest Belgians didn't think to tell the troops they'd been eating Belgian fries for more
than 300 years, ever since a very cold winter around 1600.

the only Dutch products Belgians will
admit to being any good.) *Homard* (lobster) comes in a range of dishes. Don't
miss the heavenly Belgian creation called
écrevisses à la liègeoise (crayfish in a rich
butter, cream, and white-wine sauce).
Eel, often "swimming" in a grass-green
sauce, is popular in both Flanders (where
it's called *paling in 't groen*) and Wallonia
(anguilles au vert).

No matter where you eat, you should
know that **service** will be professional but
not necessarily speedy. Belgians don't just
dine; they savor each course—if you're in
a hurry, you're better off heading for a
street vendor or an imported fast-food
establishment.

Finally, a word on **Belgian chocolate.**
Whatever the Swiss or anyone else might
say to the contrary, Belgian chocolates are
the world champs; they're so lethally
addictive they ought to be sold with a
government health warning. They can be
wonderful gifts for friends back home.
Those made by Chocolatier Mary, Wittamer, Nihoul, Neuhaus, and Leonidas
ought to do the trick. Buy them loose, in
bags weighing from 100 grams to boxes
of 2 kilograms or more. Take a prepared
box, or simply point to those you want,
or ask the assistant for a mixture. Made
with real cream, they do not keep well—
but you weren't planning on keeping
them for long anyway, were you?

BEER & GIN

What to drink with all those tasty dishes?
Why, beer, of course! Belgium is justly

famous for its brewing tradition, and this
tiny country has more than 100 breweries
producing around 450 different brews.
Some are pilsners, like Stella Artois,
Jupiler, Maes, Primus, and Eupener. The
majority, however, are local beers, specialties of a region, city, town, or village; some
are made by monks. Each beer has a distinct, and often beautiful, glass, which is
why you can instantly tell what everyone
is drinking in a Belgian bar. Needless to
say, with so many choices it may take
quite a bit of sampling to find a favorite.
Among names to look for are Duvel, Chimay, Hoegaarden, De Koninck, and
Kwak; and Faro, Krieklambiek, and Lam-
biek from the area around Brussels.

The most unusual Belgian style is lambic, a light, effervescent brew often infused
with fruit flavors, which is made only in a
small region near Brussels. Unlike the
modern steel-tanks-and-gauges approach
to brewing, lambics are left to ferment naturally in shallow open containers.

Then there are the heavenly tasting
beers brewed by Trappist monks. There
are six Trappist breweries in the land: Chimay, Orval, Rochefort, Sint-Benedictus of
Achel, Westmalle, and Westvleteren. The
Trappist ales from the Abbaye de Notre
Dame de Scourmont at Chimay in the
south of Belgium are produced using a
special yeast isolated by one of the monks
after World War II. An extra helping of
this yeast is added to the beer when it's
being bottled to enhance its flavor.

For a *digestif,* you might try a gin, in
Flanders known as *jenever* (or, colloquially,

as *witteke*), and in Wallonia known as *genièvre* (colloquially as *pèkèt*). This stiff grain-spirit is often served in glasses little bigger than a thimble. Belgium's 70 *jenever* distilleries produce some 270 varieties, some flavored with juniper, coriander, or other herbs and spices. Among notable brands are Filliers Oude Graanjenever, De Poldenaar Oude Antwerpsche, Heinrich Pèkèt de la Piconette, Sint-Pol, and van Damme. *Jenever* in a stone bottle makes an ideal gift.

Appendix B:
Getting to Know Holland

Like an Atlantis in reverse, Holland emerged, dripping, from the sea. The country was once mainly a pattern of islands, precariously separated from the North Sea by dunes. As the centuries rolled past, these islands were patiently stitched together with characteristic Dutch ingenuity and hard work. The outcome is a canvas-flat, green-and-silver Mondrian of a country, with nearly half its territory and two-thirds of its 16 million inhabitants below sea level. Perhaps no other country has so intimate a relationship with the sea, after 2,000 years of raising dikes against its permanent threat. Holland without water is as unimaginable as Arabia without sand.

1 Holland Today

The Netherlands is a tiny country, barely half the size of the state of Maine. A burst of vigorous driving will get you from one corner of the realm to the other in a morning, and you can travel by train from Amsterdam to the farthest point of the rail network in an afternoon. The nation's 41,865 sq. km (16,325 sq. miles) are among the most densely populated in the world, holding 16 million people, or approximately 1,000 per square mile. The crowding is most noticeable in the *Randstad* (Rim City), the heavily populated area that includes the cities of Amsterdam, Rotterdam, The Hague, Leiden, Haarlem, Utrecht, and Delft. Elsewhere, the land is much more sparsely populated. For the visitor, Holland today presents much the same face it has over the centuries—a serene landscape and an industrious population who treasure their age-old tradition of tolerance and who welcome people of all political, religious,

and ideological persuasions. In recent years there have been indications that, faced with threats from radical Islamists, the welcome mat is wearing thin.

Holland is a constitutional monarchy headed by the ever-popular Queen Beatrix of the House of Orange (opinion surveys regularly give her an 80% approval rating). The heir-apparent is their oldest son, Willem-Alexander (b. 1967). Parliament consists of two houses—an Upper Chamber and a Lower Chamber.

The Dutch can be both the most infuriating and the most endearing people in the world. One minute they treat you like a naughty child (surely you've heard the expression about someone talking to you like a Dutch uncle) and the next they're ready for a laugh and a beer. They can be rude or cordial (it may depend on the weather), domineering or ever ready to please (it may depend on you). In a store, they may get annoyed with you if you don't

---

Thin Red Line

Prostitution is legal in Holland, and prostitutes work in clean premises, pay taxes, receive regular medical checks, are eligible for welfare, and have their own trade union. The streetwalker "heroin whores" need to be excluded from this ostensibly idyllic picture of the world's oldest profession.

accept what they have, or get mad at themselves if they don't have what you want.

Dutch people have a passion for detail that would boggle the mind of a statistician—and a sense of order and propriety that sends them into a tailspin if you mess things up. They organize everything (people, land, flower beds), and they love to make schedules and stick to them. They may allow you to indulge an occasional whim, though they haven't a clue what it means to "play it by ear." They do love to quote homilies ("While the cat's away, the mice will play"; "Everybody talks about my drinking, but no one knows about my thirst"; "In the concert of life, no one gets a program"), including a number that suffer in translation ("Try to find it out with a wet thumb"; "It fits like a hand shoe").

They aren't particularly emotional or hotheaded, but they aren't shy about speaking their minds either. They are fiercely independent and yet are (or have been) so tolerant of other people's problems and attitudes that their country nearly equals the United States as a traditional haven for the world's exiles and émigrés. (You find in the telephone book Italian, Spanish, and French names that belong to centuries-old Dutch families as respectable as the van Dijks and van Delfts.)

"The Dutch Disease," a conservative U.S. columnist called Holland's social liberalism. But not many of the hookers in Amsterdam's Red Light District are Dutch, and relatively few denizens of the smoking coffeeshops are Dutch. If Amsterdam's a latter-day Sodom and Gomorrah, it's one mainly for visitors. The Dutch themselves are a moderate, conservative lot, whose stable history in a small, densely populated land has led them to seek social consensus rather than confrontation whenever possible.

The uniquely Dutch combination of tolerance and individualism impacts on areas of personal and social morality that in other countries are still red-button issues. In 2001, the world's first same-sex marriage, with a legal status identical to that of heterosexual matrimony, took place in Amsterdam. The Dutch parliament legalized regulated euthanasia ("mercy killing"); making the Netherlands the first country in the world to do so. And then, there's prostitution and drug use.

Authorities are not duty-bound to prosecute criminal acts, leaving a loophole for social experimentation in areas that technically are illegal. It has been wryly said that the Netherlands has one of the lowest crime rates in Europe because whenever something becomes a criminal problem the Dutch make it legal, thereby reducing crime with a stroke. Don't laugh—at least not in Holland. The Dutch will take aim at anyone, on any issue, outside their borders. Just so long as it's understood that everything *inside* has arrived at that hallowed state of perfection.

Run through any list you care to write of America's international misdemeanors and the Dutch will nod sagely and open-mindedly in agreement. Laugh to your heart's content about the soap-opera antics of Britain's House of Windsor, and they will laugh right along with you. But refer, however obliquely, to negative aspects of the Dutch Way, and watch the air turn cool. Go so far as to openly criticize the country, or to joke about Queen Beatrix, and you'll find that you've touched the natives where they're tender.

Popular opinion notwithstanding, narcotic drugs are illegal in the Netherlands. But the Dutch treat drug use mainly as a medical problem rather than purely as a crime. The authorities distinguish between soft drugs like cannabis, which are considered unlikely to cause addiction and pose a minor health risk, and hard drugs like heroin and cocaine, which are highly addictive and pose significant risks to users' health. Both types are illegal, but the law is tougher on hard drugs. Dealers who import and export drugs face 4 years in jail for soft drugs and 12 years for hard drugs.

In recent years, the Netherlands has bowed to pressure from surrounding countries regarding its drug policy and has tightened the rules for "coffeeshops"—establishments in which cannabis is sold. You used to be allowed to buy and retain 30 grams of soft drugs for personal use; now you can buy only 5 grams at a time for personal use, though you're still allowed to be in possession of 30 grams of soft drugs for personal use. Coffeeshops are not allowed to sell hard drugs or to advertise and cannot sell to minors. If they create a public nuisance, the local *burgemeester* (mayor) can shut them down.

Supplying free heroin to addicts, with medical support, has helped combat AIDS in Holland and has slashed the drug's street price so that addicts commit fewer crimes to feed their habit. Both healthcare and law-enforcement costs have gone down. The Netherlands has significantly lower rates of heroin addiction, drug use and addiction in general, and of drug-related deaths than Britain, France, Germany, and other European countries that criticize Holland so fiercely on this issue.

2 History 101

If your knowledge of Dutch history is confined to Peter Minuit buying Manhattan Island and Peter Stuyvesant as governor of New Amsterdam, read on. A working knowledge of the history of this fascinating country will add interesting dimensions to your visit.

EARLY HISTORY
In view of Holland's preference for peaceful international relations, it's ironic that the Dutch first made their appearance on history's stage amid a welter of violence and blood, defending their homeland against those iron-fisted conquerors, the Romans. The earliest inhabitants of what is now the Netherlands were three tribal groups who settled the marshy deltas of the "Low Countries" in the dawn of recorded history. They were the Belgae of the southern regions; the Batavii, who settled in the area of the Great Rivers; and the fiercely independent Frisii, who had taken up residence along the northern coast. Each tribe posed a challenge to Julius Caesar when he came calling in the mid–1st century B.C., but the Romans managed, after prolonged and effective objections from the locals, to get both the Belgae and the Batavii to knuckle under.

By Caesar's own account, the Batavians made a fair job of defending their "fertile wetlands." They were, he wrote, the fiercest

Dateline
- **1st century** B.C. The area's first inhabitants—Frisians, Batavians, and other tribes—settle the coastal territory along the Rhine River. The Batavians become allies of Rome.
- **4th–5th century** A.D. Barbarian invasions. Saxons settle in the east and Franks in the south.
- **843** Treaty of Verdun splits the empire of the Franks.

Most of the Low Countries become part of the Middle Kingdom, squeezed between the German lands and France.
- **10th century** The counts of Holland and Zeeland and the bishopric of Utrecht begin to gain greater control of their own affairs.
- **1275** Count Floris V of Holland grants "Aemstelledamme" freedom from

tolls on travel and trade. The year is regarded as Amsterdam's official foundation date.
- **1384** Duke Philip the Bold begins to gain control of the Low Countries for Burgundy.
- **1421** A storm on St. Elizabeth's Day breaks dikes along the Maas and Waal rivers, causing a flood that drowns 10,000 people.

continues

Double Dutch, Anyone?

If foreign languages interest you, Dutch should prove a fascinating study. It's a Germanic tongue that at first sounds like a close cousin to German because of the guttural, rolled "s" and "sch" sounds, and the abundance of the letters *k*, *v*, and *b*; but after a couple of days, English speakers may begin to hear words that sound familiar. In fact, Dutch is a bridge language between German and English. In the northern province of Friesland, you can hear a Dutch regional language that's supposedly the closest cousin to Old English.

fighters his legions had ever encountered. In their swampy, tide-washed homeland, between the Roman devil and the deep gray sea, the Batavians struggled mightily to avoid going under. They later became allies of Rome, and the dashing Batavian cavalry took on a romantic aura not unlike that of Jeb Stuart.

Roman legionary bases, one of which grew into the city of Nijmegen, were used as jumping-off points for invasions of Friesland to the north and Germany to the east. But Rome never did have its way with the Frisians, those hardy *terpen* dwellers in the north. In A.D. 47, Emperor Claudius gave up the costly attempt to acquire the marshy northlands, settling for the Rhine as the northern frontier of the Roman Empire.

Having seen off the Romans, the Frisians in the 5th century repelled the next wave of would-be conquerors, hordes of Saxons and Franks, who had overrun the Romano-Batavians. Although the Franks in the late 5th century embraced Christianity, not until the late 8th century did the Frisians abandon their pagan gods, and then only when the mighty Charlemagne, king of the Franks and emperor of the West, compelled them to. Yet even he was obliged to promise that the Frisians would remain free "so long as the wind blows out of the clouds and the world stands."

GOOD FOR BUSINESS

By the 13th and 14th centuries, the nobility were busy building most of the castles and fortified manor houses throughout Holland that now attract tourists. Meanwhile, the Catholic hierarchy grew both powerful and wealthy; the bishops of Maastricht and Utrecht played key roles in politics, and preserved their legacy by erecting splendid cathedrals, abbeys, and monasteries.

- **1477** Beginning of the rule of the Austrian Habsburgs.
- **1506** Holland is inherited by the future Habsburg Emperor and King of Spain Charles V.
- **1555** Philip II of Spain introduces Catholic Inquisition persecution against Protestants.
- **1567** Philip II of Spain sends the duke of Alba to the Low Countries to confront the Protestant Reformation.

- **1568** Dutch rally against Spain in the beginning of the Eighty Years' War.
- **1574** William of Orange's relief of besieged Leiden turns the tide of the war against Spain.
- **1578** Amsterdam abandons the Spanish, and Catholic, cause; Calvinists take over the city in what is called the *Alteratie*.

- **1579** The Union of Utrecht unites the seven provinces of the northern Low Countries.
- **1581** The United Provinces declare their independence from Spain.
- **1602** The United East India Company (V.O.C.), destined to become a powerful force in Holland's "Golden Age" of discovery, exploration, and trade, is founded.

> **_Fun Fact_ Beer Days**
>
> Dutch researchers believe that from 1300 to 1650 average annual beer consumption in the Low Countries was between 400 and 450 liters (880–990 pints) per person.

During the 14th and 15th centuries, Holland's position at the mouths of the great west European rivers made it a focal point in power struggles. The House of Burgundy became the first major feudal power in the Low Countries, consolidating its hold on the region by acquiring fiefdoms one by one through the various means of marriage, inheritance, and military force. Its day soon passed, however, and the Austrian Habsburg emperor Maximilian acquired the Low Countries from the Burgundians by much the same means.

Amsterdam began its rise to commercial prosperity in 1323, when Count Floris VI established the city as one of two toll points for the import of beer. The city's skillful merchants established guilds of craftsmen and put ships to sea to catch North Sea herring (an industry that took a big leap forward in 1385, when Willem Beukelszoon discovered a way to cure herring at sea). They expanded into trade in salted Baltic herring, Norwegian salted or dried cod and cod-liver oil, German beer and salt, bales of linen and woolen cloth from the Low Countries and England, Russian furs and candle wax, Polish grain and flour, and Swedish timber and iron. They opened up lucrative trade by both doing business with, and competing against, the powerful Baltic-based Hanseatic League.

RELIGIOUS CONFLICT, REBELLION & WAR

Dutch citizens began to embrace the Protestant church at the same time that the Low Countries came under the rule of Charles V, the Catholic Habsburg emperor and king of Spain. Holland became a pressure point and fulcrum for the shifting political scene that the Reformation occasioned everywhere in Europe. The rigorous doctrines of John Calvin and his firm belief in the separation of church and state began to take root.

When Charles relinquished the Spanish throne to his son Philip II in 1555, things took a nasty turn for the Dutch. An ardent Catholic, Philip was determined to defeat the Reformation and set

- **1609** Beginning of the 12-year truce with Spain. The English navigator Henry Hudson, under contract to the United East India Company, sails from Amsterdam and "discovers" Manhattan Island and the future site of New York.
- **1621** Dutch West India Company chartered to control trade with the Americas.
- **1634** "Tulip mania" begins; the price of tulip bulbs soars to crazy heights.
- **1637** Great Tulip Crash.
- **1642** Rembrandt paints _The Night Watch_.
- **1648** End of Eighty Years' War with Spain.
- **1689** Stadhouder William III and his wife, Mary, become king and queen of England.
- **1782** Dutch become first to officially recognize nationhood of the United States.
- **1795** Velvet Revolution. French troops occupy Holland
- with the aid of Dutch revolutionaries and establish the Batavian Republic. William V flees to England.
- **1799** The United East India Company is liquidated.
- **1806–10** Louis Bonaparte, Napoleon's brother, reigns as king of Holland.
- **1813–14** The Netherlands regains independence from the French and becomes a

continues

out to hunt heretics throughout his empire. He dispatched the infamous duke of Alba to the Low Countries to carry out the Inquisition's "death to heretics" edict. The Dutch resented Philip's intrusion into their affairs and began a resistance movement, led by William of Orange, count of Holland, known as William the Silent, who loudly declared: "I cannot approve of princes attempting to control the conscience of their subjects and wanting to rob them of the liberty of faith."

Rallying behind William and the League of Protestant Nobles, the Dutch mounted a fierce resistance, though they had no army, no money to raise one, and little support from the Dutch cities, including Catholic Amsterdam, which were interested mostly in maintaining their prosperous trade. William and his brother John of Nassau waged war on Spain despite all this, their only ally a ragtag "navy" of Protestant pirates called the Sea Beggars. They were helped when Spain levied a new tax on its Dutch "colony," an action so unpopular as to rally the majority of Dutch people—Protestant and Catholic alike—to the anti-Spanish cause.

Those towns that declined to join the fight were spared destruction when the Spanish invaded. Spanish armies marched inexorably through Holland, besting the defenses of each city to which they laid siege, with few exceptions. In an ingenious if desperate move in 1574, William saved Leiden by flooding the province, allowing the Sea Beggars to sail their galleons right up to the city's walls. The attack surprised the Spaniards in the middle of dinner, and they were routed. A stew pot left behind by the fleeing enemy became a cherished national symbol of the triumph of freedom, and its contents inspired the traditional Dutch dish called *hutspot*.

This victory galvanized the Dutch in fighting for their independence. The Calvinist merchants of Amsterdam turned out their Catholic city council in 1578 in a revolution called the *Alteratie* (Changeover), and the city abandoned the Spanish cause. As the Protestant Reformation took hold, the city's many Catholics were forbidden to hold public office or to worship openly, a situation that continued for more than a century.

In 1579, the Dutch nobles formed the Union of Utrecht, in which they agreed to fight together in a united front. Although the union was devised solely to prosecute the battle against Spain, consolidation inevitably occurred, and by the turn of the 17th century the seven northern provinces of what had been the Spanish Netherlands became the United Provinces—Holland, Zeeland, Utrecht, Friesland, Groningen, Gelderland, and Overijssel.

constitutional monarchy headed by Willem I, of the House of Oranje-Nassau.

■ **1830** Belgium breaks free from Dutch rule.

■ **1890** Death by suicide of Vincent van Gogh.

■ **1917** Despite Dutch neutrality in World War I (1914–18), the Netherlands suffers from severe food shortages, triggering street riots.

■ **1920** Dutch airline KLM launches the world's first

scheduled air service, between Amsterdam and London.

■ **1928** Amsterdam Olympics.

■ **1932** Afsluitdijk (Enclosure Dike) at the head of the Zuiderzee is completed, transforming the sea into the freshwater IJsselmeer Lake.

■ **1934** The Great Depression leads to shortages and riots; the government calls out the army to maintain public order.

■ **1940**: World War II: Nazi Germany invades, May 10. The Netherlands surrenders 4 days later after the aerial bombardment of Rotterdam. Queen Wilhelmina goes into exile in London.

■ **1941** Dockworkers and other workers in Amsterdam launch the "February Strike" against persecution and deportation of the city's Jewish community.

■ **1942** Anne Frank and her family, along with other Jewish

What's in a Name?

Let's clear up some matters of nomenclature. *Dutch* is the result of a 15th-century misunderstanding on the part of the English, who couldn't distinguish too clearly between the people of the northern Low Countries and the various German peoples. So, to describe the former, they simply corrupted the German "Deutsch" to Dutch.

The term *Holland* is a bit of a misnomer since, strictly speaking, it refers only to the provinces of Noord-Holland and Zuid-Holland and not to the whole country. The Dutch themselves call their country *Nederland* (the Netherlands) and themselves *Nederlanders*. But they recognize that *Dutch* and *Holland* are popular internationally and are here to stay so, being a practical people, they make use of them.

The struggle with Spain continued until 1648, and became known as the Eighty Years' War. By the early 1600s, William's son, the brilliant general and notorious philanderer Prince Maurice, was *Stadhouder* (Head of State) of the United Provinces, initiating a new era. The States-General, a parliament under the chairmanship of a Grand Pensionary, was the governing body. Holland's strength was growing and a new, prosperous era was about to begin.

THE DUTCH GOLDEN AGE

Over the first 50 to 75 years of the 17th century, the legendary Dutch entrepreneurial gift would come into its own. These years have since become known as the Golden Age. It seemed every business venture the Dutch initiated during this time turned a profit and that each of their many expeditions to the unknown places of the world resulted in a new jewel in the Dutch trading empire. Colonies and brisk trade were established to provide the luxury-hungry merchants at home with new delights, such as fresh ginger from Java, foxtails from America, fine porcelain from China, and flower bulbs from Turkey that produced big, bright, waxy flowers and grew quite readily in Holland's sandy soil—tulips. Holland was getting rich.

Amsterdam grew into one of the world's great cities. In 1602, traders from each of the major cities in the Republic of the Seven Provinces set up the Vereenigde

---

friends, go into hiding in Amsterdam. Dutch East Indies occupied by Japan.

- **1944** The Frank family refuge is betrayed and its occupants are transported. Anne dies the following year at Bergen-Belsen concentration camp.
- **1944–45** Thousands die during the "Hunger Winter," when Nazi occupation forces blockade western Holland.
- **1945** May 5: German forces in the Netherlands capitulate.

- **1947** *The Diary of Anne Frank* is published.
- **1948** Benelux Customs union with Belgium and Luxembourg takes effect.
- **1949** Holland joins NATO. The Dutch East Indies wins independence as Indonesia, after a bitterly fought liberation struggle.
- **1953** Devastating North Sea storms produce significant coastal flooding. Dutch embark on long-range Delta

Project to seal off river estuaries in the southwest.
- **1958** Holland joins the European Economic Community, the forerunner of today's European Union (EU).
- **1966** Street protests in Amsterdam mar Princess Beatrix's marriage to German Claus von Amsberg, a former soldier in the World War II German army.

continues

Impressions

The energetic and practical Hollanders . . . were after trade, not empire or conversion, and were highly adept at avoiding bloodshed. When they realized that the time had come to bow gracefully from the scene, they did so without any death-or-glory nonsense.

—Arthur C. Clarke, "A Clear Run to the South Pole,"
in *Greetings Carbon-Based Bipeds!* (1999)

Oostindische Compagnie (V.O.C.), the United East India Company, which was granted a monopoly on trade in the East. The company's purpose was to mount safe, cost-effective, exploratory voyages and trading ventures to the East Indies. It was wildly successful and established the Dutch presence in the Spice Islands (Indonesia), Goa, South Africa, and China. The big Dutch East India Company merchant vessels could hold twice as much cargo as their English rivals.

Dutch explorers were establishing the infant Nieuw Amsterdam (later to be called New York City); Abel Tasman was sailing around the South Pacific, discovering New Zealand, the Fiji Islands, Tonga, and Tasmania; and the Dutch Indonesian colonies were established. At home, the merchants who financed all those voyages grew richer, built gabled houses, dug canal after canal, and applauded as the young William III married into the English royal family and shared the English throne with his wife.

Holland was becoming a refuge for persecuted groups. The Pilgrims stopped in Leiden for a dozen years before embarking for America, Jews fled the oppressive Spanish and welcomed the tolerance of the Dutch, and refugees straggled in from France and Portugal. William the Silent had helped create a climate of tolerance in Holland, which attracted talented newcomers who contributed to the expanding economic, social, artistic, and intellectual climate of the country.

Golden Age Holland can be compared to Renaissance Italy and Classical Greece for the great flowering that transformed society. "There is perhaps no other example of a complete and highly original civilization springing up in so short a time in so small a territory," wrote the historian Simon Schama in *The Embarrassment of Riches* (1987).

- **1975** Amsterdam's 700th anniversary. Cannabis use is decriminalized.
- **1980** Queen Beatrix takes the throne.
- **1987** The *Homomonument,* the world's first public memorial to persecuted gays and lesbians, is unveiled in Amsterdam.
- **2001** The world's first real same-sex marriage, husband and husband, with a legal status identical to that of heterosexual matrimony, takes place in Amsterdam.
- **2002** Euro banknotes and coins replace the guilder. Crown Prince Willem-Alexander marries Argentine Máxima Zorreguieta. Dutch parliament legalizes regulated euthanasia ("mercy killing"), making the Netherlands the first country in the world to do so. Pim Fortuyn, a flamboyant, gay, populist right-wing politician, is shot to death in Holland's first political assassination of the modern era.
- **2003** The permanent International Criminal Court, for prosecuting large-scale crimes against humanity, is inaugurated in The Hague, despite opposition to the court from countries that include the U.S. In a project to test the medical efficacy of cannabis, the drug is made legal under controlled conditions and when

> (Fun Fact **Beating the Dutch**
>
> The 17th-century Dutch got up the noses of the English by competing against them aggressively and successfully for maritime trade and, in 1667, by sailing boldly up the Medway near London and trashing the English fleet. So the English added verbal abuse to their counterattack arsenal. That's why we have "Dutch courage" (alcohol-induced courage), "Dutch treat" (you pay for yourself), "going Dutch" (everybody pays their share), and "double Dutch" (gibberish). Americans were kinder to their Revolutionary War supporters, speaking of "beating the Dutch" (doing something remarkable).

When the war with Spain finally ended in 1648, Holland had a fleet of 2,700 trading ships. Though the Nieuw Amsterdam colony was lost to the English in 1664, the Dutch continued to grow wealthy from their Spice Islands holdings. The ascension of William III and his wife, Mary, to the English throne in 1688 may have been the beginning of the end for the Dutch Republic, however. Wars, commercial failures, misguided political decisions, and low morale were the hallmarks of the next century of Dutch history, which ended with the House of Orange in exile.

The Dutch call 1672 the *Rampjaar* (Year of Disaster). France, under Louis XIV, invaded the United Provinces by land and the English attacked by sea. This war (1672–78) and the later War of the Spanish Succession (1701–13) drained the country's wealth and morale. The buccaneering, can-do, go-anywhere spirit of traders, artists, and writers began to ebb, replaced by conservatism and closed horizons.

Still, in the 1680s the Dutch merchant fleet was larger than those of England, Spain, Portugal, and France combined, and in Amsterdam the illumination from more than 2,000 whale oil–burning lamps made the nighttime streets among the safest in the world.

DECLINE & FALL

Conflict arose between Holland and England—in part because of their lively competition on the seas. Needless to say, Dutch support for the new United States of America (Holland was the first to recognize the fledgling country's nationhood and extended three substantial loans to

prescribed by a physician for patients suffering from a range of terminal and chronic illnesses, including cancer and AIDS.

■ **2004** Controversial film director Theo van Gogh, 47, is stabbed and shot to death on the streets of Amsterdam; he had received death threats after making a film critical of Muslims. Police arrest and charge a suspect holding joint Dutch and Moroccan citizenship. The killing ignites a wave of anti-Islamic violence across Holland, and national soul-searching about the country's famed tolerance.

■ **2006** Work begins on a 5-year redevelopment of Amsterdam's Centraal Station, preparing the way for a new Metro line, an integrated bus station, and new harbor-ferry docks.

the new government) did little to heal the breach with the British. By the time William V—with his mixed Dutch-Anglo background—ascended the Dutch throne, anti-British sentiment was so strong that in 1795 he was exiled to England.

Revolutionary France invaded Holland in 1794, capturing Amsterdam and establishing the Batavian Republic in 1795, headed by the pro-French Dutch Patriots. Napoleon brought the short-lived republic to an end in 1806 by setting up his brother, Louis Napoleon, as king of the Netherlands, and installed him in a palace that had been Amsterdam's Town Hall. What Napoleon the emperor wanted, of course, was a fraternal puppet on the Dutch throne to do his bidding. Far from being a puppet, Louis did a such a good job of representing the interests of his new subjects—for instance, permitting them to trade surreptitiously with Britain, which was at war with Napoleon and under French blockade—that in 1810 Napoleon deposed him and brought the Netherlands formally into the empire.

The French reign was short-lived, but the taste of royalty proved sweet. When the Dutch recalled the House of Orange in 1814, it was to fill the role of king in a constitutional monarchy. The monarch was yet another William of Orange; however, because his reign was to be a fresh start for the republic, the Dutch started numbering their Williams all over again (which makes for a very confusing history). Then came Waterloo in 1815 and Napoleon's final defeat.

MODERN TIMES

The Netherlands escaped the worst ravages of World War I by maintaining a strict neutrality, but the war still had an impact. In 1917, food riots were suppressed by the army, and the authorities responded with soup kitchens and rationing. In the 1920s, Holland shared in the wealth as Europe's condition improved, but conditions were very bad during the 1930s, when the widespread unemployment brought on by the Great Depression caused the government to use the army in 1934 to control the unruly masses.

In World War II, Nazi troops invaded the country in 1940. A brutish Austrian Nazi, Arthur Seyss-Inquart, was put in charge of the occupied Netherlands. The occupation was complete and devastating: An estimated 104,000 of Holland's 140,000 Jews were murdered, Rotterdam sustained heavy bombings, and the rest of the country suffered terribly at the hands of its invaders. During the war the Dutch operated one of the most effective underground movements in Europe, which became an important factor in the liberation in 1945.

Among those murdered in the Nazi terror was a teenage girl who came to symbolize many other victims of the Holocaust—Anne Frank (1929–45). Anne and her diary, a profoundly moving record of a Jewish teenager's struggle to cope with the horrific realities of war and the Nazi occupation, are famous all over the world. When the Germans began deporting the Jews, Anne and her family went into hiding in an Amsterdam canal house, now the Anne Frankhuis. Cut off from other outlets for her energies, she began to keep a journal telling of her thoughts, feelings, and experiences. The last entry was on August 1, 1944, shortly before she and her family

---

(**Fun Fact** **Prohibition? No Thanks**

In April 1933, 100 gallons of beer from the Heineken brewery in Rotterdam arrived in Hoboken, New Jersey. This was the first legal shipment of beer to the United States in 13 years.

were discovered and deported to concentration camps. Anne and her sister Margot were sent to Bergen-Belsen, where they died of typhus a few days before Allied troops liberated the camp. Otto Frank, Anne's father, was the only survivor of the Frank family, and it was he who first had Anne's diary published.

Holland's liberation began with the largest airborne assault in military history, Operation Market Garden, in September 1944. Amid grim fighting, the operation was a partial success, but the critical bridge over the Rhine River at Arnhem remained in German hands. The unliberated parts of Holland were plunged into the terrible Hunger Winter, as Allied troops fought their way slowly forward through mud and flooded polder. The west and north of the country experienced liberation only after Germany's unconditional surrender in May 1945.

3 The (Un)Natural Environment

For all that the Bible says otherwise, the Dutch insist the Creation took 8 days, not 7—on the eighth day they reclaimed their country from the sea with their own hands. The all-important dikes, which hold back the sea, began to evolve as far back as the 1st century A.D., when the country's earliest inhabitants settled on unprotected coastal wetlands in the northern regions of Friesland and Groningen. These settlers first attempted to defend their land by building huge earthen mounds *(terpen)* on which they constructed their homes during recurring floods. Around the 8th and 9th centuries, they were building proper dikes and by the end of the 13th century, entire coastal regions were enclosed by dikes that held back unruly rivers and the sea.

Holland is the great river delta of northwest Europe, tucked into a corner between Germany and Belgium. It's an embroidery of canals, rivers, lakes, and drainage channels—there are 7,925 sq. km (3,090 sq. miles) of water within Holland's borders—with a dense, sandy, and peatlike soil that tends to settle over time. The country sinks an average of 1m, or 39 inches, every 1,000 years. As a result, approximately 25% of Holland, an area that holds about two-thirds of its people, now lies *below* sea level, protected from flooding only by sand dunes, dikes, and Dutch engineering ingenuity. The fact that the solid, timeless buildings of Amsterdam and the city's 740,000 inhabitants stand where waves should by all rights be lapping is a difficult concept for foreigners to grasp.

In 1953, devastating North Sea storms broke through the dikes in many places along Holland's southwest coast, flooding significant areas. There was a substantial loss of life and property. In order to assure greater protection along its coastal areas, Holland embarked upon a long-range Delta Project to seal off the river estuaries in the southwest of the country.

While visiting Holland in 1859, Matthew Arnold was so amazed at what he saw that he wrote home, "The country has no business to be there at all." Maybe so, but the Dutch have a ready answer: "God made the earth," they tell you, "and the Dutch made Holland." Around half of the country's land area has been

Dutch Dikes

If you think a dike is a high wall, you'll be surprised to see that actually many of them are great mounds of earth and stone that extend for miles. Indeed, many of the roads you travel on are built along the tops of dikes.

Impressions

Here a wretched race is found, inhabiting either the more elevated spots or artificial mounds.

—Roman geographer Pliny the Elder (1st c. A.D.)

reclaimed, from the sea, lakes, and marshes. Some 2,600 sq. km (1,000 sq. miles) of the country was under water just 100 years ago.

Natural regions are formed by the low hills of the southeast; the forest in the center of the country (the provinces of Utrecht and Gelderland); the islands and former islands along the coast of the North Sea (the province of Zeeland in the southwest and a string of sandbar islands off the coast of the province of Friesland in the north); the polders of the former Zuiderzee; and the flat farmland of the rest of the country (some of which is actually old and well-established polder).

The "Great Rivers"—the Rhine, the Waal, and the Maas (or Meuse, as it is known in Belgium, and in France where its headwaters lie)—divide the country along geographic and spiritual lines. The Dutch living in the lower land "above," or north of, the rivers have long been predominantly Calvinist, whereas the population of the higher lands "below," or south of, the rivers has been traditionally Catholic. (Interestingly, the southerners, whose spiritual capital is Maastricht, lump Amsterdammers together with the other "cold-blooded" northerners as people too straitlaced to know how to enjoy themselves.)

In flat Holland, wind is ever present, so it is not surprising that the Dutch have made use of windmills to do their hard labor, from pumping water off the land to drain polders, to milling grain and sawing timber. Nowadays, you're as likely to see the whirling blades of wind-turbines, generating a growing proportion of the nation's electrical power.

4 Great Dutch Artists

The 17th century was the undisputed Golden Age of Dutch art. During this busy time, artists were blessed with wealthy patrons whose support allowed them to give free reign to their talents. Art held a cherished place in the hearts of average Dutch citizens, too, as Peter Mundy, who traveled to Amsterdam in 1640, observed: "Many times blacksmiths and cobblers will have some picture or other by their forge and in their stall. Such is the general notion, inclination, and delight that these country natives have to paintings." The Dutch were particularly fond of pictures that depicted their world: landscapes, seascapes, domestic scenes, portraits, and still lifes. The art of this period remains some of the greatest ever created.

One of the finest landscape painters of all time was **Jacob van Ruysdael** (1628–82), who depicted cornfields, windmills, and forest scenes, along with his famous views of Haarlem. In some of his works the human figure is very small, and in others it does not appear at all; instead the artist typically devoted two-thirds of the canvas to the vast skies filled with the moody clouds that float over the flat Dutch terrain.

Frans Hals (1581–1666), the undisputed leader of the Haarlem school, specialized in portraiture. The relaxed relationship between the artist and his subject in his paintings was a great departure from the formal masks of Renaissance portraits. With the lightness of his brushstrokes, Hals was able to convey an immediacy and intimacy. He not only produced perceptive psychological portraits, but had a genius for comic characters—he showed men and women as they are and as a little less than they are in such works as *Malle Babbe* (1650). Hals excelled in producing group portraits, such as *The Archers of St. Aidan*. He carefully planned and balanced the directions of pose, gesture, and glance, but his *alla prima* brushwork (direct laying-down of a pigment) makes these public images appear as spontaneous reportage. It's worth visiting the Frans Hals Museum in Haarlem to study his techniques.

One of the geniuses of Western art was **Rembrandt Harmenszoon van Rijn** (1606–69). This highly prolific and influential artist had a dramatic life filled with success and personal tragedy. Rembrandt was a master at showing the soul and inner life of humankind, in both his portraits and illustrations of biblical stories. His most famous work, the group portrait known as *The Night Watch* (1642), is on view in the Rijksmuseum in Amsterdam.

Rembrandt's use of lights and darks was influenced by Caravaggio, like Hals and Van Honthorst before him, but was much more refined. For him, the values of light and dark gradually and softly blended together; although his paintings probably lose some of the drama of chiaroscuro, they achieve a more truthful appearance. The light that falls upon a face in a Rembrandt portrait is mysterious yet revealing of character. His series of religious paintings and prints are highly personal and human in spirit. The overall stillness of his religious work reflects an inner contemplation. He depicted Christ as a humble and gentle Nazarene, with a loving and melancholy expression. Rembrandt's religious prints (etchings) were a major source of income during his lifetime.

A spirituality reigns over his self-portraits as well; Rembrandt did about 60 of these during his lifetime. The *Self-Portrait with Saskia* shows the artist with his wife during prosperous times, when he was often commissioned by wealthy merchants to do portraits. But later self-portraits show his transition from an optimist to an old man worn down by care and anxiety. At the Rembrandt House in Amsterdam—which has been restored to much the way it was when the artist lived and worked there—you can see the above self-portrait along with some 250 etchings.

In his later years, while at the height of his artistic powers, Rembrandt's work was judged too personal and eccentric by his contemporaries. Many considered him to be a tasteless painter obsessed with the ugly and ignorant of color; this was the prevailing opinion until the 19th century, when Rembrandt's genius was reevaluated.

Perhaps the best known of the "Little Dutch Masters," who restricted themselves to one type of painting, such as portraiture, is **Jan Vermeer** (1632–75) of Delft. The main subjects of Vermeer's work are the activities and pleasures of simple home life. Vermeer placed the figure(s) at the center of his paintings, and typically used the background space to convey a feeling of stability and serenity. Vermeer excelled at reproducing the lighting of his interior scenes. Art historians know that Vermeer made use of mirrors and the *camera obscura*, an early camera, as compositional aids. His paintings give a wonderful illusion of three-dimensionality: As light—usually afternoon sunshine pouring in through an open window—moves across the picture plane, it caresses and modifies all the colors.

If **Vincent van Gogh** (1853–90) had not failed as a missionary in the Borinage mining region of Belgium, he might not have turned to painting and become the greatest Dutch artist of the 19th century. *The Potato Eaters* (1885) was van Gogh's first masterpiece. This rough, crudely painted work shows a group of peasants gathered around the table for their evening meal after a long day of manual labor. Gone are the traditional beauty and serenity of earlier Dutch genre painting.

After the death of his father, Vincent traveled first to Antwerp and then to Paris to join his brother, Theo. In Paris he discovered and adopted the rich, brilliant color palette of the Impressionists. Through Theo, an art dealer, Vincent met Paul Gauguin, and the two had many conversations on the expressive power of pure color. Van Gogh developed a thick brushwork—with a textilelike texture—that complemented his intense color schemes.

In 1888, Vincent traveled to Arles in Provence, where he was dazzled by the Mediterranean sun. His favorite color, yellow, which signified love to him, dominated landscapes such as *Wheatfield with a Reaper* (1889). For the next 2 years, he remained in the south of France, painting at a frenetic pace in between bouts of madness. In *The Night Café* (1888), the red walls and green ceiling combine with a sickly yellow lamplight to give an oppressive air to this billiard-hall scene. (With red and green, Vincent wrote, he tried to represent "those terrible things, men's passions.") We see the halos around the lights swirl as if we, like some of the patrons slumped over at their tables, have had too much to drink. Perhaps his best-known nightscape is *The Starry Night* (1889); with its whirling starlight, Vincent's turbulent universe is filled with personal anxiety and fear.

The Van Gogh Museum in Amsterdam has more than 200 of his paintings—including all those named above—presented to Holland by Theo's wife and son with the provision that they not leave Vincent's native land. Vincent sold only one painting in his lifetime (Theo sold it), but he did "sell" others, to pay for food, drink, and lodgings—and maybe some went for a song.

Before **Piet Mondrian** (1872–1944) became an originator of De Stijl (or neoplasticism), he painted windmills, cows, and meadows. His Impressionistic masterpiece, *The Red Tree* (1909)—which looks as though it's bursting into flame against a background of blue—marked a turning point in his career. He had always said that when he discovered his true personality, he would drop one of the two *a*'s in his surname (originally Mondriaan), and this was the first canvas he signed as Mondrian.

With Theo van Doesburg, Mondrian began a magazine in 1917 entitled *De Stijl* (The Style) in which he expounded the principles of neoplasticism: a simplification of forms or, in other words, a purified abstraction; an art that would be derived "not from exterior vision but from interior life." In part, this movement was an outgrowth of and reaction against the cubist work of Picasso and Braque, which Mondrian had seen while he lived in Paris from 1912 to 1914.

The geometric painters of the De Stijl school attempted a "controllable precision." Their basic form was the rectangle—with horizontal and vertical accents at right angles. Their basic colors were the primaries—red, blue, and yellow—along with black and white. In works like his 1936 *Composition in Blue, Yellow, and Black* (Gemeentemuseum Den Haag), no part of the picture plane is more important than any other; with its design, Mondrian achieves an equilibrium but does not succumb to a mechanical uniformity.

Mondrian suppressed the use of curves and the color green in his later work because, he said, these reminded him of nature. But it's ironic to note that to support himself Mondrian had to paint flowers on porcelain for much of his life. In 1940, Mondrian moved to New York, which he loved, to escape the war in Europe. In the evenings he would take walks around the Art Deco Rockefeller Center; the geometry of the lighted windows reminded him of his paintings. Mondrian's last paintings were lively abstract representations of New York, like *Broadway Boogie Woogie* (1942–43) (MoMA, New York) and *Victory Boogie Woogie* (1944, Gemeentemuseum Den Haag).

5 A Taste of Holland

Dutch national dishes tend to be of the ungarnished, hearty, wholesome variety—solid, stick-to-your-ribs stuff. A perfect example is *erwtensoep,* a thick pea soup cooked with ham or sausage that provides inner warmth against cold Dutch winters and is filling enough to be a meal by itself. Similarly, *hutspot,* a potato-based "hotchpotch," or stew, is no-nonsense nourishment to which *klapstuk* (lean beef) is sometimes added. *Hutspot* has an interesting intangible ingredient—see "History 101," earlier, for the story of its origin.

Seafood, as you might imagine in this traditionally seafaring country, is always fresh and well prepared. Fried sole, oysters, and mussels from Zeeland, and herring (fresh in early June—great excitement surrounds the first catch of the season, part of which goes to the queen and the rest to restaurateurs amid spirited competition—pickled other months) are most common. In fact, if you happen to be in Holland for the beginning of the herring season, it's an absolute obligation—at least once—to interrupt your sidewalk strolls to buy a "green" herring from a pushcart. The Dutch are uncommonly fond of oily freshwater eel *(paling)* and Zeeland oysters and mussels (*Zeeuwse oesters* and *Zeeuwse mosselen*), from September to March.

At **lunchtime,** you're likely to find yourself munching on *broodjes,* small buttered rolls usually filled with ham and cheese or beef, although a *broodje gezond* (healthy sandwich) with cheese and vegetables is a good choice for vegetarians. Not to be missed are the delicious, filling pancakes called *pannekoeken,* often eaten as a savory dish with bacon and cheese. *Poffertjes* are a sweet, lighter, penny-size version that are especially good topped with apples, jam, or syrup. **Desserts** at any meal lean toward dairy products, fruit with lots of fresh cream, ice cream, or *appelgebak,* a lovely and light apple pastry. Dutch *gebak* (pastries) are fresh, varied, and inexpensive; and you will notice the Dutch sitting down for a *koffee* and one of these delicious *hapjes* (small snacks, or literally, "bites") throughout the day—why not join them?

That, briefly, is the Dutch cuisine—which is not to say that it's the only cuisine available in Holland. Far from it! The popular Indonesian **rijsttafel** (rice table), a feast of 15 to 30 small portions of different dishes eaten with plain rice, has been a national favorite ever since it arrived in the 17th century. If you've never experienced this minifeast, it should definitely be on your "must-eat" list for Holland—the basic idea behind the rijsttafel is to sample a wide variety of complementary flavors, textures, and temperatures: savory and sweet, spicy and mild. In addition, you'll find the cuisines of France, China, Italy, Greece, Turkey, Yugoslavia, and many other nations.

THE RESTAURANTS

At the top of the restaurant scale are those posh dining rooms affiliated with the prestigious Alliance Gastronomique Néerlandaise or the Relais du Centre. They're likely to be elegant and sophisticated or atmospherically Old World and quaint. They will certainly be expensive. Some restaurants are not open for lunch. Although more and more restaurants are staying open later, the Dutch in general dine early; in many cases last orders are taken no later than 10pm.

Unless you eat especially early or late, reservations are generally recommended at expensive restaurants and, at least on weekends, at those on the high end of the moderate price range. Restaurants are often small and may be crowded with neighborhood devotees. Outside terraces are always in big demand on pleasant summer evenings. Smokers are everywhere, but nonsmoking rooms in restaurants and cafes are rare. So be warned, and try to sit outside in good weather.

For authentic Dutch dishes, look for the **Neerlands Dis** sign, which identifies restaurants specializing in the native cuisine. Then there are the numerous moderately priced restaurants and the brown cafes, which are cozy social centers with simple but tasty food, sometimes served outside on sidewalk tables in good weather. Sidewalk vendors, with fresh herring and the ubiquitous *broodjes* (sandwiches) or other light specialties, are popular as well.

Though there's no such thing as a free lunch, there is the next best thing—a *dagschotel* (plate of the day) and *dagmenu* (menu of the day). Another way to combat escalating dinner tabs is to take advantage of the tourist menu offered by many restaurants. Dutch menus list appetizers, *not main courses,* under "entree"; and 15% service plus value-added tax (BTW) is almost always included in the prices.

BEER, GIN & WINE

What to drink? **Beer,** for one thing. As you make the rounds of the brown cafes (the traditional Dutch watering holes), you can get the regular brands such as Heineken, Grolsch, or Amstel, or you could try something different. I happen to like the *witte* (white) beer, like Wiekse Witte, which is sweeter than *pils,* the regular beer. Or, on the opposite end of the spectrum, you can have a Belgian dark beer, like De Koninck or Duvel. (Belgian beers are popular in Holland and are, in general, better made, more artisanal, than the local brews.)

Then there is the potent native gin known as **jenever** (the name comes from the Dutch word for "juniper"), a fiery, colorless spirit distilled from grain or malt, served ice-cold and drunk neat—without any mixer, or even ice. It was once the drink of the masses in Holland, where it originated as a kind of medicine. Juniper oil was added to the distillate for its diuretic properties. *Jonge* (young) *jenever* is less sweet and creamy than the *oude* (old) variety—*jenever* grows smooth and soft with age—but both are known for their delayed-action effectiveness. There are very good Dutch liqueurs, such as Curaçao and Triple Sec. Wines from all over the world are available as well.

There are even Dutch wines. Respectable white wine is produced in modest quantities by the Apostelhoeve and Slavante vineyards near Maastricht, in the southernmost sliver of the Netherlands, close by the Belgian border.

Appendix C:
Getting to Know Luxembourg

The Grand Duchy of Luxembourg—covering an area of just 2,600 sq. km (1,000 sq. miles), is tiny. Smaller than Rhode Island, the smallest state in the United States, the country's borders seem unlikely to embrace so many worthy travel delights. Yet within this country are the remnants of a rich history and a landscape with scenery that varies from wild highlands to peaceful river valleys to plains dotted with picturesque villages and farmlands. Outside of the capital, Luxembourg City, the classic Luxembourg settlement is a village or small town of whitewashed houses clustered around a medieval castle and church.

1 Luxembourg Today

The Grand Duchy of Luxembourg is a constitutional monarchy headed by Grand Duke Henri of the House of Nassau. A one-house legislature, the Chamber of Deputies, is made up of 64 members who are elected for 5-year terms. Economically, the strength of its banking and financial institutions has attracted more than 200 foreign banks, including the headquarters of the European Investment Bank. The 440,000 residents have among the highest income levels per capita of any country in the world.

Agriculture is still important. Around half of the total land area is farmed, though less than 5% of Luxembourgers now live and work on farms, and that percentage continues to fall. Despite problems caused by overproduction of European wines in general, the vineyards of Luxembourg's Moselle Valley are still competitive. And the enchanting Luxembourg countryside, particularly its northern reaches in the Ardennes, is a popular vacation destination for Luxembourgers and visitors from neighboring countries.

Having played a key role in establishing the institutions that evolved into the European Union, Luxembourg today hosts the secretariat of the European Parliament, the European Court of Justice, and the European Investment Bank.

THE LUXEMBOURGERS

In such a small country, with bigger neighbors on its doorstep, Luxembourgers have a distinctive individuality that even extends to the national language, which is vaguely related to both French and German, yet quite different from both. They have a personality that's hard to capture in words. *Mir welle bleiwe wat mir sin* ("We want to remain what we are"), they say, and evidently feel no need to spell out "what we are" in detail. You'll see that national motto inscribed over old door frames, hear it echoed in songs, and recognize its essence in everyone you meet in the Grand Duchy.

Impressions
We are very much a combination of what surrounds us.
—Prince Jean de Luxembourg

Try a Little *Lëtzebuergesch*

The national language, *Lëtzebuergesch,* has a vaguely German base with overtones of French, yet is distinct from both of those languages. For anyone who isn't a native, forget it—it's a tongue twister. Not to worry; while the language is widely used among Luxembourgers, and although French is most often used in official and cultural activities, and German is heard frequently, virtually everyone speaks English. In other words, you'll encounter few, if any, language difficulties in the Grand Duchy.

Some of their character traits are easy to pin down. They're definitely hard-working. One look at the country's well-tended farms or shops will reveal the industriousness of their owners. Go into a Luxembourg home and the cleanliness and order will speak more loudly than the proud homemaker ever could.

The people of Luxembourg are cosmopolitan. From their cuisine (a combination of the best from surrounding countries) to their culture and dress, they're at home in the world, eager to travel, and secure enough in their uniqueness to appreciate the special qualities of others. But in addition to this openness, they're essentially proud and patriotic. Centuries of domination by foreign rulers could not kill their independent spirit.

They do have a reputation for smugness that's not entirely undeserved. If you are a citizen of one of the world's wealthiest countries per capita, it may be no more than human nature to assume that this pleasing fact is due to your own native industry or superiority, rather than to, for instance, enabling the citizens of less-blessed countries—like Germany and France, to name but two of many—to engage in fiscal fiddling and stash the illicit proceeds in your banks.

Some 95% of Luxembourgers are Roman Catholic, although a significant percentage of those hasten to make it clear that they're non-practicing. It's rare to meet someone who doesn't observe some of the customs, traditions, and mores of the church. But, despite their Catholicism, Luxembourgers follow a policy of religious freedom. Along with Catholic priests, the state supports the chief rabbi and the official Protestant pastor. There are small clusters of other Christian and non-Christian faiths, the most important being Islam. While religious instruction is a part of the school curriculum, upper levels can choose instead an ethics-and-morality course.

Finally, to say that Luxembourgers are fond of eating is an understatement. If there's an important matter to discuss, decision to be made, or social crisis to resolve, Luxembourgers repair to the nearest cafe or pastry store. It goes without saying, then, that they're fond of cooking—don't go away without indulging in their luscious pastries. And forget the calories!

2 History 101

THE EARLY YEARS

Long before recorded history, the territory of today's Grand Duchy was home to Magdalenian and Celtic tribes. The Treviri, a fierce Celtic people who resisted invaders to the death, finally fell in the 1st century A.D. to Roman legions. Thereafter, one Roman emperor after another put down numerous uprisings of the independent-minded inhabitants, who stubbornly refused to give up their worship of Druidism for the paganism of Rome.

As Rome suffered military defeats and Christianity became more widespread, the Roman hold on the region weakened. By the 5th century the only reminders of the Romans left in Luxembourg were the bits and pieces of their urban civilization, a network of bridges, and place names like Ettelbruck (Attila's Bridge), named for the Hun warlord who dealt the knockout blow to the Western Roman Empire. Luxembourg was by then firmly in the camp of the Franks.

Along with monasteries that sprang up and flourished came educational and cultural influences that helped form the foundation of today's Luxembourg. The great Frankish leader Charlemagne brought in Saxons to settle the Ardennes, thus adding another ethnic imprint to the face of the region.

In the 10th century, Siegfried, the youngest of the counts of the Ardennes, obtained a large land grant from the Abbey of St. Maximin (the deed, dated Apr 12, 963, is kept in the Pescatore Museum in Luxembourg). He built his castle on the ruins of Castellum Lucilinburhuc, an ancient Roman fort that had guarded the crossroads of the important roads from Paris to Trier and from Metz to Aix-la-Chapelle (Aachen). On that strategic spot grew a town and eventually a country by the name of Luxembourg.

ENLIGHTENED FEMALE RULE

By the 12th century, the counts of Luxembourg were at the helm. They enlarged their territory by wars with other noblemen, astute marriages, and diplomatic shenanigans. But soon they began to absent themselves for long periods; some of the nobility joined the forces of Godfrey of Bouillon to travel to the Holy City during the Crusades. Some never returned, and those who did found that much of their land had been confiscated by other overlords during their absence.

When Henry the Blind's daughter, Countess Ermesinda, reached adulthood in the early 1200s, things were in disarray. But Ermesinda was able to restore some of Luxembourg's lost territory through a few marriages, as she inherited lands previously held by her ailing spouses. When her last husband died in 1225, she boldly took charge of the affairs of state. By bringing noblemen who had always been at each other's throats together in a central governing body, she achieved such revolutionary reforms as the establishment of a court of justice and limited judicial rights for ordinary citizens. The tight rein of feudal lords was somewhat loosened. Countess Ermesinda

Dateline

- **963** Siegfried, count of the Ardennes and founder of the House of Luxembourg, acquires an old Roman fortress called Lucilinburhuc and builds a small castle on a rocky outcrop called the Bock, laying the foundation for the future city of Luxembourg.
- **1244** Countess Ermesinda, who is credited with being the founder of Luxembourg,

grants rights and freedoms to the citizens of the town of Luxembourg and autonomy to its administration.
- **1288** Luxembourg suffers a crushing defeat in the Battle of Worringen, putting an end to its acquisition of land in Limburg and Brabant.
- **1308** Henry VII, count of Luxembourg, is elected king of Germany, and in 1312 is crowned Holy Roman Emperor Henry IV.

- **1354** Holy Roman Emperor Charles IV, the grandson of Henry IV, raises Luxembourg's status from a county to a duchy.
- **1418** First documented reference to the Town Hall of Luxembourg City, on the site where now stands the Palace of the grand dukes.
- **1443** Duke Philip the Good of Burgundy captures the

continues

began to establish convents and monasteries to provide education and culture for her people. Her legacy was a united nation with enlightened social standards.

IMPERIAL GLORY

In 1308, Henry VII of the House of Luxembourg became emperor of the Holy Roman Empire. He spent the rest of his life trying to unite all of Europe under his rule. His son, John the Blind, was a valiant warrior who perished at Crécy fighting the forces of Edward III of England, after ordering his men to lead him into the thickest part of battle. Today he is revered as Luxembourg's national hero. John's son, Charles IV, favored extending his domain through treaty and marriage; by the time his son, Wenceslas, gained the throne, the House of Luxembourg ruled a territory some 500 times the size of today's Luxembourg.

The glory days did not last long, however. King Wenceslas's son, Sigismund, was far less capable than his ancestors. By the mid-1400s Luxembourg itself was a province ruled by the dukes of Burgundy. During the next 400 years that rule shifted among Spain, France, and Austria.

QUARRELS OVER A TINY NATION

To quell the locals' growing unrest, each successive ruler found it necessary to further strengthen a capital city that was already one of Europe's best defended. Luxembourg, then, became a problem for the rest of Europe: Its position was too strategic and its fortifications too strong to allow it to be self-governing—or even to be controlled by any one nation. The answer seemed to be to divide Luxembourg among several nations; therefore, the Congress of Vienna in 1815 handed over most of the country to Holland's William of Orange-Nassau, and the remainder to Prussia. Then, with the Treaty of London in 1839, more than half of Holland's piece of Luxembourg was given to Belgium (the resulting Belgian province still bears the name Luxembourg).

Since its boundaries were becoming smaller and smaller, the Grand Duchy posed no real threat to anyone. Still, its many fortifications made it all but impregnable, so in 1867 the European powers convened in London and decided that freedom would be granted the Grand Duchy on condition that its fortifications be dismantled. Luxembourgers were overjoyed. In October 1868, they affirmed a constitution that boldly proclaimed "The Grand Duchy of Luxembourg forms a free state, independent and indivisible." Today, there are green parks throughout the capital city to mark the sites of mighty fortifications, now vanished.

---

fortress of Luxembourg and establishes Burgundian rule.

- **1506** Luxembourg is inherited by the future Habsburg Emperor and King of Spain Charles V.
- **1573** Following the 1554 destruction of the Town Hall by a gunpowder explosion, construction is completed on the original wing of the ducal palace.
- **1684** France captures the fortress, ends the rule of the

Spanish Habsburgs, and brings the country under French rule.

- **1697** A second period of Spanish rule begins, when France returns the duchy to Spain.
- **1713** Beginning of Luxembourg's Golden Age, when it comes under rule of Habsburgs of Austria.
- **1794–95** The Revolutionary French besiege Luxembourg City. Starvation forces the

fortress's Austrian garrison to surrender.

- **1814** The French garrison withdraws from the fortress.
- **1815** Treaty of Vienna partitions Luxembourg; lands east of the Moselle, Sûre, and Our are ceded to Prussia, and the remainder go to Holland's King William of Orange as the Grand Duchy of Luxembourg.
- **1839** Luxembourg's Walloon districts are ceded to Belgium.

The Mysterious Maiden Mélusine

Luxembourg has a rich folklore tradition, and the tale of Mélusine the mermaid is perhaps the nation's most famous myth. Legend says that imprisoned within the rock that helped form Luxembourg City's tremendous defenses is a beautiful maiden named Mélusine. She passes the time by knitting, but she manages only one stitch each year—and it's a very good thing she's so slow. You see, should she finish her knitting before she's released, all of Luxembourg and its people will vanish into the rock with her!

Mélusine was imprisoned after Siegfried married her without knowing that she was really a mermaid. At first, she kept her secret by reverting to her natural state only on Saturday, a day she told her husband that was reserved for her personal privacy. But when his curiosity got the better of him and he peeked, she vanished into the rock.

Once every 7 years, Mélusine returns, either as a serpent with a golden key in its mouth or as a beautiful woman. All it will take to win her freedom is for some brave soul to kiss the womanly vision or take the key from the serpent's mouth. That brave soul has yet to appear, and in the meantime all of Luxembourg (or at least that part of Luxembourg that believes in the legend) prays for her to drop a stitch or two so that whatever she's knitting will take a very long time to complete!

WAR & PEACE

Since that momentous announcement of independence, Luxembourg has seen periods of prosperity (largely due to its steel industry) and periods of decline that have prompted thousands to emigrate in search of work. Twice—in World War I and World War II—it suffered military occupation. The heroism of the Luxembourg underground resistance movement during World War II is legendary. Many of the younger men made their way to Allied countries to fight in their ranks, while those at home actually went out on strike when the Nazis imposed compulsory service in the Wehrmacht—a move that brought swift retribution from the Nazis.

- **1867** Luxembourg's neutrality is guaranteed under the protection of the great powers. Luxembourg City fortifications are razed.
- **1890** Luxembourg cuts its ties to Holland's House of Orange. Adolf of Nassau serves as the first "indigenous" grand duke.
- **1912** Marie Adelaide of Nassau becomes the first grand duchess.

- **1914–18** German troops invade and occupy the country during World War I.
- **1922** Agreement on economic union with Belgium.
- **1940** World War II: Nazi Germany invades, May 10. The country is quickly occupied and the royal family and government go into exile.
- **1944** September: U.S. troops begin liberation of Luxembourg.

- **1944–45** Battle of the Bulge. Hitler's last great offensive brings destruction to parts of the Grand Duchy. The German army is thrown back again by American troops.
- **1948** Benelux Customs union with Belgium and the Netherlands.
- **1949** Luxembourg joins NATO.

continues

Luxembourg's Windtalkers

During World War II, when French was banned by the Nazis, *Lëtzebuergesch*, which was not understood by the Germans, served as a kind of secret code for the Resistance.

In the winter of 1944 and 1945, part of the Battle of the Bulge was fought in the Ardennes region of northern Luxembourg. General George S. Patton's Third Army turned the tide of that battle, with an assault from Martelange that relieved the besieged U.S. 101st Airborne Division at Bastogne in Belgium. Thousands of Americans killed in the heavy fighting of Hitler's last great offensive are buried in a U.S. military cemetery just outside Luxembourg City.

The little country didn't just work to rebuild itself in those postwar years. In 1945, Luxembourg joined the United Nations. In 1948, it formed a Customs union called Benelux with Belgium and the Netherlands that later became an economic union, and in 1949 was a founding member of NATO.

3 A Taste of Luxembourg

Among the national favorites are some of the best pastries you're ever likely to eat; delicious Luxembourg cheese; trout, crayfish, and pike from local rivers; Ardennes ham smoked in saltpeter; hare, wild boar, and other game during the hunting season; and in September lovely small plum tarts called *quetsch*. Other tasty treats include the national dish of smoked neck of pork with broad beans *(judd mat gaardebounen)*; a *friture* of fried small river fish such as bream, chub, gudgeon, roach, and rudd; calves' liver dumplings *(quenelles)* with sauerkraut and boiled potatoes; black pudding *(treipen)* and sausages with mashed potatoes and horseradish; and a green-bean soup *(bouneschlupp)*. French cuisine majors on restaurant menus, and German and Belgian influences make their presence felt.

Luxembourg City, because of its large number of international diplomatic and business visitors, has many fine restaurants offering international cuisine. It has just as many small cafes and bistros featuring traditional dishes. In smaller towns and villages, hotel restaurants are often quite good, as are the small local cafes.

- **1952** As a founding member of the European Coal and Steel Community, Luxembourg is chosen as the seat of important European institutions.
- **1958** Luxembourg joins the European Economic Community, the forerunner of today's European Union (EU).
- **1964** Grand Duchess Charlotte abdicates in favor of her son, Grand Duke Jean.
- **1966** Opening of the European Center on the Kirchberg.
- **1993** Luxembourg opposes efforts of other EU members to impose withholding tax on savings and investments in the Grand Duchy.
- **2000** Grand Duke Jean abdicates and is succeeded by his son Henri.
- **2002** Euro banknotes and coins replace the Luxembourg franc.
- **2003** Luxembourg joins Germany, Belgium, and France in opposing the invasion of Iraq, prompting sour comment from pro-war countries about the Grand Duchy throwing its "weight" around on the international stage.
- **2007** Another new terminal opens at Luxembourg Airport (the first was in 2004), greatly improving service for passengers arriving in the Grand Duchy.

Winemaking along the Moselle has a history that dates back to the Romans. And, of course, the Moselle wines (mostly white) will top any list. Look for Riesling, Pinot Gris, Pinot Noir, Pinot Blanc, Auxerrois, Rivaner, Elbling, Gewürztraminer, and Crémant de Luxembourg, and for the National Mark, which certifies that they're true Luxembourg wines. In beers, look for such brand names as unfiltered Mousel (pronounced "*mooz*-ell"), Bofferding, and Henri Funck.

Index

See also Accommodations and Restaurant indexes, below.

ACCOMMODATIONS— BELGIUM

THE NEW TRAVELOCITY GUARANTEE

EVERYTHING YOU BOOK WILL BE RIGHT, OR WE'LL WORK WITH OUR TRAVEL PARTNERS TO MAKE IT RIGHT, RIGHT AWAY.

*To drive home the point,
we're going to use the word "right" in every single sentence.*

Let's get right to it. Right to the meat! Only Travelocity guarantees everything about your booking will be right, or we'll work with our travel partners to make it right, right away. Right on!

Here's a picture taken smack dab right in the middle of Antigua, where the guarantee also covers you.

The guarantee covers all but one of the items pictured to the right.

For example, what if the ocean view you booked actually looks out at a downright ugly parking lot? You'd be right to call – we're there for you. And no one in their right mind would be pleased to learn the rental car place has closed and left them stranded. Call Travelocity and we'll help get you back on the right track.

Now, you may be thinking, "Yeah, right, I'm so sure." That's OK; you have the right to remain skeptical. That is until we mention help is always right around the corner. Call us right off the bat, knowing that our customer service reps are there for you 24/7. Righting wrongs. Left and right.

Now if you're guessing there are some things we can't control, like the weather, well you're right. But we can help you with most things – to get all the details in righting,* visit **travelocity.com/guarantee**.

*Sorry, spelling things right is one of the few things not covered under the guarantee.

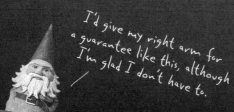

I'd give my right arm for a guarantee like this, although I'm glad I don't have to.

travelocity
You'll never roam alone.